T0399160

Ancient and Medieval Thought
on Greek Enclitics

Ancient and Medieval Thought on Greek Enclitics

STEPHANIE ROUSSOU
PHILOMEN PROBERT

OXFORD
UNIVERSITY PRESS

OXFORD
UNIVERSITY PRESS

Great Clarendon Street, Oxford, OX2 6DP,
United Kingdom

Oxford University Press is a department of the University of Oxford.
It furthers the University's objective of excellence in research, scholarship,
and education by publishing worldwide. Oxford is a registered trade mark of
Oxford University Press in the UK and in certain other countries

First Edition published in 2023

Published in the United States of America by Oxford University Press
198 Madison Avenue, New York, NY 10016, United States of America

British Library Cataloguing in Publication Data
Data available

Library of Congress Control Number: 2022944289

ISBN 978–0–19–287167–1

DOI: 10.1093/oso/9780192871671.001.0001

Printed and bound by
CPI Group (UK) Ltd, Croydon, CR0 4YY

For our teachers

Preface

This book has its origins in a discussion between the two authors about a passage of Greek, which took us on a remarkable journey through ancient and medieval texts on Greek enclitics via accent marks on papyri and in medieval manuscripts. The textual problem we originally set out to solve turned out to have an answer known already to Aldus Manutius, but in the meantime apparently disparate sources of information on enclitic accents had started coming together in a surprising way. We found further exploration irresistible, and this book is the result.

A compelling intellectual quest does not write a book by itself, however, and we have numerous individuals and institutions to thank for much help, encouragement, and support. Stephanie Roussou was able to work intensively on her side of this project in 2017, thanks to funding from the John Fell OUP Research Fund, the Lorne Thyssen Research Fund for Ancient World Topics at Wolfson College, and the A. G. Leventis Foundation, as well as a three-week Research Scholarship from the Fondation Hardt. Philomen Probert was able to work intensively on her side during two periods of sabbatical leave, generously granted by the Faculties of Classics and Linguistics at the University of Oxford in 2015 and 2019. She was fortunate in being able to spend both periods of leave at the University of Leiden, as an academic visitor in 2015 and as a Spinoza Visiting Scholar in 2019. She would like to thank Ineke Sluiter, everyone in the Classics Department, and the University Library for providing ideal conditions and wonderful discussions. Both authors have benefitted from a Fellowship granted to Stephanie by Harvard University's Center for Hellenic Studies, which enabled us both to spend two productive weeks at the Center in 2017.

We have benefitted from numerous opportunities to present and discuss aspects of our work on enclitics. In this connection Philomen gave talks to the panel on Greek and Latin Linguistics at the Annual Meeting of the Society for Classical Studies (San Francisco, 2016), the Workshop on Ancient Grammar held at the University of Cologne (2017), and the Philological Society (2019). Stephanie spoke at the event 'From Homer to Modern Greek: diachronic approaches to Greek language' hosted by the Society for the Promotion of Education and Learning and the Center for Hellenic Studies (Athens, 2017). We gave joint talks in Oxford to the Comparative Philology Seminar and to the Ancient World Cluster at Wolfson College (2017). We would like to thank the organizers and participants in all these events for their insights and useful discussion.

The new editions of the texts presented in Chapter 2, prepared primarily by Stephanie, could not have been produced without digital images supplied to us by the Biblioteca Apostolica Vaticana, the Biblioteca Casanatense, the Biblioteca

Comunale Augusta, the Biblioteca Comunale di Palermo, the Biblioteca Medicea Laurenziana, the Biblioteca Nacional de España, the Bibliothèque Nationale de France, the Biblioteca Nazionale Marciana, the Biblioteca Nazionale di Napoli, the Biblioteca Nazionale Universitaria di Torino, the Biblioteca Riccardiana di Firenze, the Biblioteca Statale di Cremona, Cambridge University Library, the Kongelige Bibliotek København, the Real Biblioteca del Monasterio de San Lorenzo de El Escorial, the State Historical Museum of Russia, the Vědecká knihovna v Olomouci, and the Veneranda Biblioteca Ambrosiana. We are further grateful to several of these and more libraries for digital images which we did not need to request, because the libraries had already made them available to everybody. And we are grateful for permission for Philomen to examine manuscripts in person at the Biblioteca Medicea Laurenziana and the Σπουδαστήριον Βυζαντινῆς καὶ Νεοελληνικῆς Φιλολογίας, and for Stephanie to examine manuscripts in person at the Bibliothèque Nationale de France. The librarians of the Σπουδαστήριον Βυζαντινῆς καὶ Νεοελληνικῆς Φιλολογίας were kind enough also to put us in touch with Gina Zavakou, whom we would like to thank for informative discussion of codex Atheniensis 25. At a workshop on Herodian, held in Oxford in June 2010, Nigel Wilson drew our attention to the text on enclitics in codex Laurentianus Plut. 58.24 and generously suggested that Stephanie might work on it further; this significant discovery (subsequently made independently by Chiara Telesca: see section 2.1.1) provides a particularly early witness to the treatise that we present in section 2.1. On top of this, Nigel has read the critical editions and given us the benefit of expert advice. Stephanie would further like to thank her co-author for inspiring her to persevere in the face of a seemingly impossible web of textual traditions.

   Chapter 3 of this book, on the accent of ἐστί(ν) or ἔστι(ν), originated as an independent project of Philomen's; it was inspired by those scholars who had written to her asking where they should print the accent on particular instances of ᾽ΕΣΤΙ(N), and not least by Graham Shipley. Lesley Brown provided further inspiration for work on this topic, by initiating valuable discussion of the semantics of verbs 'to be' at an ideal moment. Also in this connection, Sandra Paoli responded with characteristic kindness and helpfulness to questions on the typology of extra-clausal elements, as did Paul Elbourne and Marta Abrusán to questions on the semantics of existential sentences; Nigel Wilson pointed Philomen in the direction of Serbian; and Ana Kotarcic gave her generous help with Serbian questions. The participants in the 2010 workshop on Herodian provided valuable feedback on a talk resulting from an early stage of this work. But the questions attached to the accent of ᾽ΕΣΤΙ(N) behaved like the heads of the Hydra, and by the time we started to collaborate Philomen had all but despaired of answering them. She would like to thank her co-author for providing renewed inspiration and the perfect context to grapple with all this again, and for improving the textual foundations for this work.

Chapter 4, on sequences of enclitics, is the result of extensive brainstorming between both authors. In its final form the chapter is due mainly to Philomen, but Stephanie collected most of the papyrological data discussed in section 4.3.

Eleanor Dickey, Maria Giovanna Sandri, Jesse Lundquist, Dieter Gunkel, Jan Kwapisz, Helena Teleżyńska, and two anonymous readers have read the whole book and been generous with encouragement and advice. We owe special thanks to Eleanor for lengthy discussions and keen observations on the manuscript traditions of texts on enclitics, at an early stage of our work, and to Maria Giovanna for keen observations at a later stage and for alerting us to at least eleven manuscripts that we would otherwise have missed. Maria Giovanna has also been kind enough to share work of hers with us in advance of publication.

It was hardly to be taken for granted that a publisher would share our enthusiasm for ancient and medieval thought on Greek enclitics. We would like to thank Charlotte Loveridge, Vicki Sunter, Clare Jones, and the Delegates of Oxford University Press for their warm encouragement and support of this project, Louise Larchbourne for her meticulous copy-editing of such a complex manuscript, and Tim Beck for expert proof-reading.

We would like to thank our families, friends, and colleagues for their friendship and support. This book is dedicated to all our teachers, with gratitude and in hopes that some of what follows might meet with their approval. For the rest, the responsibility lies with us alone.

S.R.
P.P.

Thessaloniki and Oxford
May 2022

Contents

Machine-readable versions of Tables 4.2, Ap.1, Ap.2, and Ap.3 are available at https://dx.doi.org/10.5281/zenodo.7534838, https://dx.doi.org/10.5281/zenodo.7535149, https://dx.3doi.org/10.5281/zenodo.7535718, and https://dx.doi.org/10.5281/zenodo.7535843 respectively.

General abbreviations

For abbreviations of ancient authors' names, collections of texts, and titles of series of texts, see *Ancient authors and works, with editions used* (p. xviii).

LSJ	H. G. Liddell, R. Scott, H. S. Jones, R. McKenzie, P. G. W. Glare, and A. A. Thompson, *A Greek-English Lexicon*, 9th edn with revised supplement (Oxford 1996).
Martini-Bassi	E. Martini and D. Bassi, *Catalogus codicum graecorum Bibliothecae Ambrosianae* (Milan 1906).
Patrologia Graeca	J.-P. Migne (ed.), *Patrologiae cursus completus, series graeca* (Paris 1857–66).
P.Flor.	G. Vitelli and D. Comparetti, *Papiri greco-egizii pubblicati dalla R. Accademia dei Lincei*, i: *Papiri Fiorentini* (Milan 1906–15).
P.Giss. i	O. Eger, E. Kornemann, and P. M. Meyer, *Griechische Papyri im Museum des oberhessischen Geschichtsvereins zu Giessen* (Leipzig 1910–12).
P.Lond.Lit.	H. J. M. Milne, *Catalogue of the Literary Papyri in the British Museum* (London 1927).
P.Oxy.	B. P. Grenfell, A. S. Hunt, et al., *The Oxyrhynchus Papyri* (London 1898–).
P.Paris	A.-J. Letronne, W. Brunet de Presle, and E. Egger, *Notices et textes des papyrus du Musée du Louvre et de la Bibliothèque Impériale* (Notices et Extraits de manuscrits de la Bibliothèque Impériale et autres bibliothèques, 18.2) (Paris 1865).
P.Schub.	W. Schubart (ed.), *Griechische literarische Papyri* (Berlin 1950).
Rev. Ég.	*Revue d'Égyptologie* (Paris 1933–).
TLG	*Thesaurus Linguae Graecae* <www.tlg.uci.edu>.
UPZ	U. Wilcken, *Urkunden der Ptolemäerzeit (ältere Funde)* (Berlin 1927–57).

Abbreviations used in the critical apparatus

add.	*addidit*	(has added)
coll.	*collato, collatis*	(by comparison with)
fr.	*fragmentum*	(fragment)
i.l.	*in linea*	(on the line)
i.m.	*in margine*	(in the margin)
i.t.	*in textu*	(in the text)
n.l.	*non liquet*	(it is not clear)
om.	*omisit, omiserunt*	(has/have omitted)
s.l.	*supra lineam*	(above the line)

Symbols used in presenting Greek texts and translations

{ }   Used in presenting Greek texts, to indicate portions of text considered spurious.

⟨ ⟩   Used in presenting Greek texts, to indicate editorial additions.

( )   Used in presenting Greek texts, and in translations of those texts, to indicate a parenthetical remark belonging to the text itself.

[ ]   Used in translations of texts, to indicate clarifications not present in the original. On the rarer occasions where square brackets are used in the quotation of a text preserved on papyrus, they indicate lost letters.

ΤΙΣ   Upper-case letters are used to quote Greek words and phrases in a way that is neutral as regards their accentuation.

Ancient authors and works, with editions used

Series are indicated as follows: B = Collection des universités de France publiée sous la patronage de l'Association Guillaume Budé; CCSG = Corpus Christianorum, Series Graeca; GG = Grammatici Graeci; L = Loeb Classical Library; OCT = Scriptorum Classicorum Bibliotheca Oxoniensis; T = Bibliotheca Scriptorum Graecorum et Romanorum Teubneriana. Spurious works and works of uncertain authorship are alphabetized under the name of the author to whom they are traditionally attributed. Well-known authors and works are not generally listed here if they are mentioned in the book only to identify a quotation in a grammatical text, or an example from a cited papyrus or printed edition.

Ap. Dysc., *Adv.*	*L. Dumarty, Apollonius Dyscole: Traité des Adverbes.* Paris 2021.
Ap. Dysc., *Conj.*	C. Dalimier, *Apollonius Dyscole: Traité des conjonctions.* Paris 2001.
Ap. Dysc., *Constr.*	J. Lallot, *Apollonius Dyscole, De la construction (syntaxe).* Paris 1997.
Ap. Dysc., *Pron.*	P. Brandenburg, *Apollonios Dyskolos: Über das Pronomen.* Munich 2005.
Pseudo-Arcadius	S. Roussou, *Pseudo-Arcadius' Epitome of Herodian's De prosodia catholica.* Oxford 2018.
Aristarchus, fr. . . . Schironi	F. Schironi, *I frammenti di Aristarco di Samotracia negli etimologici bizantini.* Göttingen 2004.
Aristophanes	N. G. Wilson (OCT) 2007.
Bacchylides	H. Maehler, *Bacchylides: carmina cum fragmentis,* 11th edn. Munich 2003.
Callimachus, *Aetia*	A. Harder, *Callimachus: Aetia.* Oxford 2012.
Callimachus, fr. . . . Pfeiffer	R. Pfeiffer, *Callimachus.* Oxford 1949–53.
Choeroboscus, *Th.*	A. Hilgard, *Theodosii Alexandrini canones : Georgi Choerobosci scholia : Sophronii Patriarchae Alexandrini excerpta* (GG IV.i–ii). Leipzig 1889–94, vol. i, p. 103–vol. ii, p. 371.
Demosthenes	M. R. Dilts (OCT) 2002–9.
Dio Chrysostom	J. von Arnim, *Dionis Prusaensis quem vocant Chrysostomum quae exstant omnia.* Berlin 1893–6.
Dionysius of Halicarnassus, *De compositione uerborum*	G. Aujac and M. Lebel (B) 1981.
(Ps.)-Dionysius Thrax, Supplement *Περὶ προσῳδιῶν*	G. Uhlig, *Dionysii Thracis Ars Grammatica* (GG I.i). Leipzig 1883, pp. 105–14.
Et. Gud. . . . Sturz	F. W. Sturz, *Etymologicum Graecae linguae Gudianum.* Leipzig 1818.

Et. Gud.... de Stefani	E. L. de Stefani, *Etymologicum Gudianum quod vocatur*. Leipzig 1909–20.
Ep. Hom. alph.	A. R. Dyck, *Epimerismi Homerici qui ordine alphabetico traditi sunt*, in A. R. Dyck, *Epimerismi Homerici*, ii, pp. 1–822. Berlin 1995.
Etymologicum Magnum	T. Gaisford, *Etymologicum Magnum*. Oxford 1848.
Etymologicum Parvum	R. Pintaudi, *Etymologicum Parvum quod vocatur*. Milan 1973.
Etymologicum Symeonis	For lemmata beginning with *Γ-E*:
	D. Baldi, *Etymologicum Symeonis (Γ-E)* (CCSG, 79). Turnhout 2013.
Eustathius, *In Iliadem*	M. van der Valk, *Eustathii archiepiscopi thessalonicensis commentarii ad Homeri Iliadem pertinentes*. Leiden 1971–87.
Eustathius, *In Odysseam*	G. Stallbaum, *Eustathii archiepiscopi thessalonicensis commentarii ad Homeri Odysseam, ad fidem exempli Romani editi*. Leipzig 1825–6.
Gregory of Corinth, *Περὶ συντάξεως λόγου*	D. Donnet, *Le traité Περὶ συντάξεως λόγου de Grégoire de Corinthe*. Brussels 1967.
Gregory Nazianzen, *Carmina*	A. Tuilier, G. Bady, and J. Bernardi (B) 2004–.
Hermas, *Pastor*	See *Pastor Hermae*
Hesiod	F. Solmsen, R. Merkelbach, and M. L. West (OCT) 1990.
Hesychius	K. Latte, P. A. Hansen, and I. C. Cunningham, *Hesychii Alexandrini Lexicon*, volumes i (2nd edn), ii (2nd edn), iii, iv. Berlin 2005–20.
Homer	See *Il.* and *Od.*
Il.	*Iliad*, M. L. West (T) 1998–2000.
John Philoponus, *Praecepta Tonica*	G. A. Xenis, *Iohannes Alexandrinus: Praecepta Tonica*. Berlin 2015.
Lexicon Αἱμωδεῖν	A. R. Dyck, *Lexicon ΑΙΜΩΔΕΙΝ quod vocatur seu verius ΕΤΥΜΟΛΟΓΙΑΙ ΔΙΑΦΟΡΟΙ*, in A. R. Dyck, *Epimerismi Homerici*, ii, pp. 825–1034. Berlin 1995.
[Longinus], *De sublimitate*	D. A. Russell (OCT) 1968.
Menander	F. H. Sandbach (OCT) 1990.
New Testament	E. Nestle, E. Nestle, B. Aland, K. Aland, J. Karavidopoulos, C. M. Martini, and B. M. Metzger, *Novum Testamentum Graece*, 28th revised edn, 5th corrected printing. Stuttgart 2016.
Od.	*Odyssey*, M. L. West (T) 2017.
Pastor Hermae	M. Whittaker, *Die apostolischen Väter*, i: *Der Hirt des Hermas*, 2nd edn. Berlin 1967.
Photius, *Lexicon*	C. Theodoridis, *Photii Patriarchae Lexicon*. Berlin 1982–.
Plato, *Phaedo*	E. A. Duke et al. (OCT), vol. i, 1995.
Plato, *Republic*	S. R. Slings (OCT) 2003.
Quintilian, *Inst.*	For *Inst.* 1.4–8 (the only portion cited in this book):
	W. Ax, *Quintilians Grammatik (*Inst. orat. *1,4–8)*. Berlin 2011.
Sch. D. Thr.	A. Hilgard, *Scholia in Dionysii Thracis Artem grammaticam* (GG I.iii). Leipzig 1901.
Sch. *Il.*	H. Erbse, *Scholia graeca in Homeri Iliadem (Scholia Vetera)*. Berlin 1969–88.

Sch. *Od.*	For Books 1–10: F. Pontani, *Scholia graeca in Odysseam*. Rome 2007–. For Books 11–24: W. Dindorf, *Scholia graeca in Homeri Odysseam*. Oxford 1855.
Scholia vetera in Eur.	E. Schwartz, *Scholia in Euripidem*. Berlin 1887–91.
Sophocles, fr. . . . Radt	S. Radt, *Tragicorum Graecorum fragmenta*, iv, corrected and expanded edn. Göttingen 1999.
Sophronius, *Excerpta e Charace*	A. Hilgard, *Theodosii Alexandrini canones : Georgi Choerobosci scholia : Sophronii Patriarchae Alexandrini excerpta*, ii (GG IV.ii), pp. 373–434. Leipzig 1894.
Thucydides	H. S. Jones (OCT) 1942.
Vergil	R. A. B. Mynors (OCT) 1969.
Συναγωγὴ λέξεων χρησίμων	I. C. Cunningham, *Synagoge: Συναγωγὴ λέξεων χρησίμων*. Berlin 2003.

1

Introduction

Generations of classicists have learned that an enclitic is a special word with no accent of its own, or alternatively a special word with a propensity to throw its accent back onto the preceding word. Either way, there is a list of enclitics to learn, and a set of principles governing the ways in which an enclitic affects the accent of the preceding word. A basic lesson on enclitics might look something like this:[1]

A basic lesson on enclitics

1. The following words are enclitics:
   - The indefinite τις, with its inflected forms τινά, τι, τινός/του, τινί/τῳ; τινέ, τινοῖν; τινές, τινάς, τινά, τινῶν, τισί.
   - The indefinite adverbs πω 'up to this time', πη 'somehow', που 'somewhere', ποι 'to somewhere', πως 'somehow', ποτέ 'at some time', ποθέν 'from somewhere', and ποθί 'somewhere'.
   - The unemphatic oblique personal pronoun forms με, μου, μοι; σε, σου, σοι; ἑ, οὑ, οἱ; μιν, νιν, σφε/σφεάς/σφας/σφᾶς, σφεά, σφεων, σφι(ν), σφισί(ν), σφωέ, and σφωῖν.
   - The present indicative forms of εἰμί 'I am' and φημί 'I say', except for the second persons singular εἶ and φής.
   - The particles γε, τε, νυν, νυ, κε(ν), τοι, ῥα, περ, ταρ, θην.
2. How to accent an ordinary word followed by an enclitic:
   - If the ordinary word is oxytone (i.e. has an acute on its final syllable), it keeps the acute on its final syllable. The enclitic has no accent: πατήρ τις, πατήρ που, πατρί τινι, πατήρ φησιν.
   - If the ordinary word is perispomenon (i.e. has a circumflex on its final syllable), it keeps the circumflex on its final syllable. The enclitic again has no accent: πῦρ τι, φιλῶ σε, καλῶς πως, καλοῦ τινος, καλῶς ἐστιν, καλῶν τινων.

---

[1] Our basic lesson is a slightly adapted version of the textbook presentation in Probert (2003: 142–3, 147–8).

Ancient and Medieval Thought on Greek Enclitics. Stephanie Roussou & Philomen Probert, Oxford University Press. © Stephanie Roussou and Philomen Probert 2023.
DOI: 10.1093/oso/9780192871671.003.0001

- If the ordinary word is proparoxytone (i.e. has an acute on its ante-penultimate syllable) or properispomenon (i.e. has a circumflex on its penultimate syllable), it keeps its usual accent and acquires an additional acute accent on its final syllable. The enclitic again has no accent: ἔλαβέ τις, ἄνθρωπός τις, ἄνθρωποί τινες, οἶκός τις, οἶκοί τινων.
- If the ordinary word is paroxytone (i.e. has an acute on its penultimate syllable), it simply keeps its usual accent before the enclitic. If the enclitic is monosyllabic, it again has no accent. If the enclitic is disyllabic, it will have an acute on its final syllable (which may turn into a grave in connected speech), or a circumflex in the case of τινῶν or τινοῖν: λέγε τι, λέγω τι, σῴζω πως, μεγάλοι τινές, μεγάλα τινά, μεγάλοι εἰσί, παίδοιν τινοῖν.

So far so good, but it becomes clear sooner or later that our lesson does not cover all the finer points. For example, what happens if an enclitic is elided, or if the word before the enclitic is elided? Or if more than one enclitic occurs in a sequence? Some words are enclitic only some of the time, like σε (or σέ), σου (or σοῦ), and ἐστί (or ἔστι): when was the enclitic form used, and when was it the non-enclitic or 'orthotonic' form? Some editors print ἔνθά τε rather than ἔνθα τε,[2] or ἄρά σφιν rather than ἄρα σφιν,[3] or κῆρύξ τις rather than κῆρυξ τις:[4] what's all that about?

To see where all these modern practices come from, we need to delve into the surviving ancient and medieval discussions of Greek enclitics. This book is a study of those discussions, and has two complementary aims. The first is to improve our grasp of the ideas that ancient and medieval scholars pass down to us on Greek enclitics. The second is to show how a close look at these ancient and medieval sources yields new answers to two questions concerning the facts of the ancient Greek language itself: (i) When is the enclitic ἐστί used and when do we have non-enclitic ἔστι? (ii) What accentuation rule applied when two or more enclitics followed one another?

Chapter 2 firstly provides new editions and translations of the most extensive ancient and medieval texts on Greek enclitics that survive. Secondly, this chapter draws out the main doctrines and the conceptual apparatus and metaphors which were used to think and talk about enclitic accents, and considers the antiquity of these ideas within the Greek grammatical tradition. Chapter 3 turns to the

---

[2] So West (1998–2000) at *Il.* 2.594, 4.247, and 5.305, while Monro and Allen (1920) print ἔνθα τε.
[3] So West (1998–2000) at *Il.* 5.592, while Monro and Allen (1920) print ἄρα σφιν.
[4] So Smyth (1922) and Bowen (2013) at Aeschylus, *Suppl.* 727, while Page (1972) prints κῆρύξ τις. Yet another option, κῆρυξ τις, is taken by West (1990), but what is at stake here is the quantity of the υ in *ΚΗΡΥΞ* rather than the principles governing the accentuation of words followed by enclitics; on this question, see Chapter 4, n. 96.

question of ἐστί(ν) versus ἔστι(ν), and Chapter 4 to sequences of consecutive enclitics. A brief concluding chapter draws together the most important themes to emerge from the book.

Before we proceed, a word about the scope of the term 'enclitic' is in order. Recent linguistic work on ancient Greek enclitics tends to explore their syntactic behaviour at least as much as their accentual effects, and some scholars extend the term 'enclitic' (or with fewer implications 'clitic') to items whose syntactic behaviour resembles that of the items traditionally considered enclitics, regardless of whether they exhibit the accentual behaviour that makes them enclitics from an ancient or medieval point of view.[5] But this book centres on ancient and medieval thought. For our purposes, therefore, Greek 'enclitics' will be the items that our ancient and medieval sources recognize as enclitics, on the basis of shared accentual effects: the items that classicists traditionally call 'enclitics'.

In keeping with its focus on ancient and medieval thought, this book will also have much more to say about the accentual effects associated with enclitics than about their syntactic behaviour: accentuation was what most interested ancient and medieval scholars about enclitics as a category.[6] Syntax will enter the discussion in Chapter 3, in connection with the distribution of enclitic ἐστί(ν) and non-enclitic ἔστι(ν)—but for reasons to be explained there, the available evidence allows us to advance our understanding of the syntactic facts in at best a modest and partial way. Chapter 4, on sequences of enclitics, will have nothing to say about the syntactic principles prompting enclitics to occur consecutively in the first place, and in certain orders but not others. What this chapter does is to put forward a new proposal as to how exactly sequences of two or more enclitics were accented.

---

[5] For a clear account of the similarities and differences between (a) the Greek enclitics that ancient sources recognize and (b) other items displaying similar syntactic behaviour, see Goldstein (2016: 10, 49–60).

[6] For discussion of the famously limited role of syntax in the Greek grammatical tradition, see Swiggers and Wouters (2003), and other contributions to the same volume.

2

Ancient and medieval sources

When we want to know what ancient scholars thought on questions of accentuation, we normally start by asking ourselves what Herodian said. Living in Rome in the second century AD, Herodian was the son of Apollonius Dyscolus and an enormously prolific and influential writer on Greek prosody. Unfortunately, almost none of his works survive in anything like their original state,[1] and the difficulties are especially severe when it comes to his thought on enclitics. At this point, readers may object that two accounts of enclitic accents appear in Pseudo-Arcadius' epitome of Herodian's Περὶ καθολικῆς προσῳδίας 'On prosody in general', one of our most important sources for the content of this massive lost work. We will indeed be considering (and re-editing) these accounts of enclitic accents, but they cannot be considered an original part of Pseudo-Arcadius' epitome of Herodian; we shall return to this topic further on (section 2.1).

The most complete surviving accounts of the accentual effects of enclitics comprise a series of short treatises whose history is difficult to unravel, including the two (or three, depending how one counts them: see section 2.1) that find their way into the text of Pseudo-Arcadius. All these treatises circulated in the Renaissance, sometimes under the names of well-known grammarians (Herodian, John Charax, Choeroboscus, John Tzetzes) and sometimes without ascription to any particular author, and for the most part they are preserved in manuscripts dating to the fifteenth century and later. However, important witnesses to medieval stages of the tradition comprise a tenth-century manuscript of the treatise we call *About* ’ΕΣΤΙΝ (see section 2.5.1, on manuscript S_a); a quotation from *About* ’ΕΣΤΙΝ in the twelfth-century author Eustathius (see section 2.5.1, on passage (2.1)); and a twelfth-century copy of the treatise we call *On enclitics 1*, recently discovered by Nigel Wilson and independently by Chiara Telesca (see section 2.1.1, on manuscript M).

In this chapter we first provide new editions and translations of the treatises in question (sections 2.1–2.6). Section 2.7 then draws out the main doctrines to emerge from these texts, and section 2.8 considers how far we can trace these doctrines back in time. For this purpose, scattered comments on enclitics in the surviving works of Apollonius Dyscolus will be particularly helpful, together with Homeric scholia likely to derive from the work of Herodian.

---

[1] An exception is the Περὶ μονήρους λέξεως 'On lexical singularity', on which see Sluiter (2011), to whom we owe the English version of the title 'On lexical singularity'. But this work does not help us with enclitics.

Ancient and Medieval Thought on Greek Enclitics. Stephanie Roussou & Philomen Probert,
Oxford University Press. © Stephanie Roussou and Philomen Probert 2023.
DOI: 10.1093/oso/9780192871671.003.0002

Our editions of short treatises on enclitics comprise the first full critical editions of these texts,[2] and take into account all the witnesses that we have been able to discover. A first challenge has been to locate these witnesses: in catalogues of manuscript collections, copies of what have traditionally been considered unremarkable grammatical texts often lurk under uninformative headings such as 'grammatica varia'. Despite our best efforts, there will inevitably be witnesses we have missed.

A second challenge has been quite how many distinct treatises on enclitics to recognize. On the one hand, if we consider our treatises in relation to one another, all of them contain abundant echoes of one another and/or of a shared stock of material, so that none can be said to exist in isolation from the others. On the other hand, there is significant variation internal to the tradition of each treatise too: these texts were deliberately revised in transmission, as scholars and teachers inserted their own favourite examples, provided additional explanations, removed material they considered redundant, and so on. We consider there to be six recognizably different treatises whose text can sensibly be reconstructed (for precedents for this decision, see 2.1.2, 2.2.2, 2.3.2, 2.4.2, 2.5.2, and 2.6.2): no two of these stand in a clear stemmatic relationship to one another, such that they could be derived from a common archetype as a single treatise. On the other hand, decisions to print more than one recension of a treatise could have been made in some instances. For example, the text of *About 'ΕΣΤΙΝ* is significantly revised by the archetype of one family of manuscripts (our **m**), and the decision not to print **m**'s version as a separate recension is a purely practical one: the alterations made by **m** are visible in the critical apparatus, and this is likely to be sufficient for most purposes (see also section 2.5.1.1, Table 2.37). For each treatise we aim to reconstruct a text close to the archetype of the copies that survive, but lightly cleaned up where we or other scholars—including copyists of manuscripts—can offer corrections or emendations with a clear basis in the transmitted text.

To avoid unhelpfully overloading our apparatus, where a sub-family of manuscripts descends from a hyparchetype whose reading can be confidently reconstructed, we generally report the reconstructed reading of the hyparchetype (using our siglum for that hyparchetype) rather than the readings of the individual manuscripts within it. In such cases the siglum for the hyparchetype should not be taken to represent the unanimous reading of all the manuscripts in the sub-family; we ignore individual variations that clearly do not go back to the

---

[2] A partial exception concerns the treatises on enclitics that find their way into the text of Pseudo-Arcadius' epitome of Herodian's *Περὶ καθολικῆς προσῳδίας* (those that we present in sections 2.1, 2.3, and 2.5), since these have been edited as part of the text of Pseudo-Arcadius. Unlike the editions of Pseudo-Arcadius (Barker 1820, Schmidt 1860, Roussou 2018a), our editions take into account not only the manuscripts of Pseudo-Arcadius but also the manuscripts in which these texts are transmitted independently. On a smaller scale, specific manuscripts outside the Pseudo-Arcadius tradition have been taken into account in the editions of *On enclitics 1* by Donnet (1967) and Telesca (2021): for details see section 2.1.2.

hyparchetype. Sigla are presented in the order in which they appear on our stemma for the relevant text, from left to right.

We do not record minor differences in accents, breathings, iota subscript, elision, οὐ/οὐκ/οὐχ and the like, and the use of movable ν; we make an exception for accents that are actually under discussion, but only where there is room for doubt about what accent was actually intended. We have not standardized post-classical syntax when this is supported by the manuscript tradition. Where first-person singular verb forms such as *scripsi* appear in the apparatus, the understood subject is Stephanie Roussou.

The third volume of Bekker's *Anecdota Graeca* (Bekker 1821: 1142–58) includes an edition of the texts that we present in sections 2.1, 2.2, 2.4, 2.5, and 2.6, and does not always clarify whether readings come from manuscripts or are conjectures. We have not systematically reported all of these, especially where they resemble readings that we find in manuscripts.

Where our treatises provide literary or invented examples to illustrate a point, in our translations we use underlining to draw attention to the words most pertinent to the point in question. In some instances these comprise the whole example, but in others they comprise a small portion of a longer example. At *On enclitics 1*, §f, for instance, we underline the words δέ σφισιν in the example δίχα δέ σφισιν ἥνδανε βουλή: for the point that ΣΦΙΣΙΝ can be enclitic, these are the crucial words.

2.1 On enclitics 1

The treatise we call *On enclitics 1* provides a systematic treatment of enclitic accents, organized around two main topics: which word forms are enclitic, and under what circumstances do enclitics 'throw back' their accents? The work is best known as a section on enclitics appearing in Pseudo-Arcadius' epitome of Herodian's Περὶ καθολικῆς προσῳδίας (most recently printed by Roussou 2018a: 302–8), where it is preceded by a version of the text we call *On enclitics 3* (Roussou 2018a: 299–302; see section 2.3) and followed by a version of the text we call *About ἘΣΤΙΝ* (Roussou 2018a: 308; see section 2.5). In the manuscripts of Pseudo-Arcadius the transition between *On enclitics 1* and *About ἘΣΤΙΝ* is made seamlessly, so that we appear to have two treatises altogether rather than three. But it is unclear why an epitome of Herodian's work should contain two sections on enclitics, especially as they overlap substantially in content: like all our treatises on enclitics, they belong to a complex tradition drawing on a common stock of material (cf. section 2.8). Moreover, in Pseudo-Arcadius all this material on enclitics is appended to a book (Book 15) which is otherwise about the accents of oblique cases and of dual and plural forms. The table of contents which we are lucky enough to have for Pseudo-Arcadius' work (Roussou 2018a:

113–14) announces that Book 15 will deal with oblique cases and grammatical numbers, and says nothing about a treatment of enclitics at this point in the work. On all these grounds, the material on enclitics appears to be an intrusion into Book 15 of Pseudo-Arcadius.[3] In addition to all this, all the treatises on enclitics found in Pseudo-Arcadius are well-attested outside the manuscript tradition of Pseudo-Arcadius: they were evidently pre-existing treatises that somebody thought it worthwhile to insert into the text of Pseudo-Arcadius.

Donnet (1967) recognized that one manuscript—our **C**—that does not transmit a text of Pseudo-Arcadius has a version of our enclitics treatise attributed to John Tzetzes, as do two further manuscripts whose copies of the text are derived from the one in **C** (see section 2.1.1, on family δ). Donnet saw that **C**'s copy belongs to a different branch of the tradition from the one in Pseudo-Arcadius and is closer to an Aldine version that we call **Ald.₂**, which attributes the text to Αἴλιος (i.e. Aelius Herodian). Since Donnet took the version that appears in Pseudo-Arcadius to derive from Herodian's Περὶ καθολικῆς προσῳδίας, like Pseudo-Arcadius' epitome as a whole, he suggested that the different and in some respects fuller text in **C** and **Ald.₂** derives from Herodian's work independently of Pseudo-Arcadius' epitome (Donnet 1967: 21–2). Given the evidence that the sections on enclitics in Pseudo-Arcadius comprise an intrusion into that text, we reserve judgement on the relationship between our text (or any version thereof) and any work of Herodian's. We also reserve judgement on any involvement that John Tzetzes might have had at any stage of the tradition: like Herodian, John Tzetzes was a famous scholar to whom a grammatical work might come to be attributed.

The edition we present is based on all the witnesses known to us, including but not limited to the manuscripts of Pseudo-Arcadius and those witnesses discussed by Donnet.

2.1.1 Sources and stemma

On enclitics 1 is transmitted in the following manuscripts and early printed books, listed here according to the main families and sub-families that we posit:[4]

Family j
M (12th cent.): Florence, Biblioteca Medicea Laurenziana, Laurentianus Plut. 58.24, folios 4v–6v. As mentioned by Roussou (2018a: 28), this copy was recently discovered by Nigel Wilson. It has since been discovered independently by Telesca (2021), and is a significantly early witness to the text.

---

[3] For further discussion, see Roussou (2018a: 27–30).
[4] Here and throughout the book, information on copyists and places of copying is from <https://pinakes.irht.cnrs.fr>, unless otherwise stated.

The text is incomplete owing to the loss of one or more leaves after folio 6: it breaks off just before ἡ λέξις in §q. On the basis of the handwriting, Nigel Wilson has identified the scribe as an extremely active copyist of the twelfth century called Ioannikios.[5]

Π (15th cent.): Florence, Biblioteca Medicea Laurenziana, Laurentianus Plut. 57.24, folio 150v. This manuscript has a version of the text which is both abbreviated and truncated; it breaks off at the end of §j.

Family δ

C (14th cent.):[6] Florence, Biblioteca Medicea Laurenziana, Laurentianus Plut. 55.7, folios 307v–308v,[7] copied by a scribe named Νικόλαος.

Ald.₂ (1496): The Aldine *Thesaurus: Cornu copiae et Horti Adonidis* (for further details, see the bibliography under Aldus 1496), folios 232r–234v. (In addition to this copy of the treatise we call *On enclitics 1*, this early printed book contains a copy of another version of the text, for which see under Ald.₁ later in this list. We call the two versions Ald.₁ and Ald.₂, after the order of their appearance in the book.)

Cremona, Biblioteca Governativa, Cremonensis Graecus 160 (15th cent.), folio 103r, copied by Isidorus of Kiev. This is a copy of C.[8]

Vatican City, Biblioteca Apostolica Vaticana, Vaticanus Ottobonianus Graecus 384 (16th cent.), folios 306v–309v, copied by Konstantinos Mesobotes. This too is a copy of C.[9]

Rome, Biblioteca Casanatense, Casanatensis 1710 (16th cent.), folios 81r–86v, copied by Petros Hypsilas. This is a copy of Ald.₂. (The same manuscript contains a copy of Ald.₁, for which see later in this list).

Manuscript Q

Q (late 13th cent.): Venice, Biblioteca Nazionale Marciana, Marcianus Gr. Z. 512 = coll. 678, folios 53r–53v. This manuscript contains a highly abbreviated version of the text.

Family ψ, sub-family σ

G_v (15th cent.): Vatican City, Biblioteca Apostolica Vaticana, Vaticanus Graecus 1405, folios 227r–228r, copied by Scipione Forteguerri.

G_w (15th cent.): Wolfenbüttel, Herzog August Bibliothek, Guelferbytanus Gud. Gr. 20, folios 122v–123r.

---

[5] Nigel Wilson, personal communication. On Ioannikios, cf. Vuillemin-Diem and Rashed (1997, especially 175–80).

[6] For the date of this manuscript see Turyn (1972: 120).

[7] The manuscript has two sets of folio numbers, one at the top right of most rectos and the other at the bottom right. Like Bandini (1768: 263) we use the numbers at the top right.

[8] So already Donnet (1967: 16–18).   [9] So already Donnet (1967: 16–18).

G (15th–16th cent.): Cambridge, University Library, Cantabrigiensis Dd XI 70 = 696, folios 11r–12v, copied by Demetrius Moschus.

G$_r$ (15th cent.): Vatican City, Biblioteca Apostolica Vaticana, Vaticanus Graecus 1356, folios 85r–87v.

G$_m$ (16th cent.): Bergamo, Biblioteca Civica Angelo Mai, Bergomensis 339, folios 163r–164r.

G$_p$ (15th cent.): Paris, Bibliothèque Nationale de France, Parisinus Graecus 2594, folios 152v–154r, copied by Michael Souliardos.

G$_b$ (16th cent.): Oxford, Bodleian Library, Bodleianus Canonicianus Graecus 13, folios 39r–40r.

Ald.$_1$ (1496): The Aldine *Thesaurus: Cornu copiae et Horti Adonidis* (for further details, see the bibliography under Aldus 1496), folios 231r–232r. In addition to this version of the treatise *On enclitics 1*, this early printed book contains a second version which we take to belong to family χ (our **Ald.$_2$**). Copies of the text derived from **Ald.$_1$** appear in further early printed books[10] including the work listed in the bibliography as Curio (1522) (at quire Θ, folio vi r–v), and the following works whose copies derive from Curio (1522): de Gourmont (1523) (at folios 9r–9v, in the fourth of five sequences of folio numbers this book contains); Froben (1524) (at quire V, folios 6v–7r); Aldus (1524) (at quire M, folios vii verso–viii recto, i.e. folios 95v–96r in the second of two series of folio numbers this book contains); Sessa and de Ravanis (1525) (at quire G, folio iii recto). The two sixteenth-century manuscripts listed next contain further copies derived from printed books.

Rome, Biblioteca Casanatense, Casanatensis 1710 (16th cent.), folios 79r–81r, copied by Petros Hypsilás. This is a copy of **Ald.$_1$**. (The same manuscript contains a copy of **Ald.$_2$**, for which see the entry earlier in this list.)

Turin, Biblioteca Nazionale Universitaria, Taurinensis B VI 8 = Zuretti 10 (16th cent.), folios 6b–8a. This is a copy of the text in Aldus (1524).

Family ψ, sub-family ϕ

A$_1$ (15th cent.): Milan, Biblioteca Ambrosiana, Ambrosianus D 30 sup. = Martini-Bassi 225, folios 63r–66r. (This manuscript contains two versions of the treatise: see **A$_2$** later in this list.)

T$_2$ (15th cent.): Madrid, Biblioteca Nacional de España, Matritensis 4635 = de Andrés 92 (previously N 114), folios 125v–127v. (This manuscript contains two versions of the treatise: see **T$_1$** later in this list.)

A$_2$ (15th cent.): Milan, Biblioteca Ambrosiana, Ambrosianus D 30 sup. = Martini-Bassi 225, folios 66v–67v. This copy of the treatise breaks off in §l,

---

[10] For more information on these early printed books see Botley (2010).

just before αἱ δὲ λοιπαί. (This manuscript contains two versions of the treatise: see **A₁**, earlier in this list.)

T₁ (15th cent.): Madrid, Biblioteca Nacional de España, Matritensis 4635 = de Andrés 92 (previously N 114), folio 123r–v. This copy of the treatise breaks off in §l, just before αἱ δὲ λοιπαί. (This manuscript contains two versions of the treatise: see **T₂**, earlier in this list.)

Rₐ (1488): Madrid, Biblioteca Nacional de España, Matritensis 4689 = de Andrés 139 (previously N 56), folio 198r–v, copied by Konstantinos Laskaris. This copy of the treatise breaks off part-way through §j.

Family ψ, sub-family ξ: manuscripts of Pseudo-Arcadius

R (15th cent.): Madrid, Biblioteca Nacional de España, Matritensis 4575 = de Andrés 32 (previously N 38), folios 42r–44r, copied by Konstantinos Laskaris in Messina (see Roussou 2018*a*: 83–4).

F (1495): Oxford, Bodleian Library, Baroccianus 179, folios 47r–49r, copied by Leon Chalkiopoulos in Messina (see Roussou 2018*a*: 84–5).

K (15th cent.): Copenhagen, Det Kongelige Bibliotek, Hauniensis regius GKS 1965 4°, pp. 148–54, copied by Urbano Bolzanio (also known as Urbano Dalle Fosse or Urbano da Belluno). This copy of the text is derived from the copy in **R** (cf. Roussou 2018*a*: 85). Roussou (2018*a*: 99) suggests that the scribe of manuscript **K** consulted the source of our **R**, and not only **R** itself—but the doubts of Pontani (2019) are well taken, and none of the instances of potential contamination concern the treatises on enclitics transmitted as part of Pseudo-Arcadius. For these reasons, we exclude **K** from our apparatus.

Δ (16th cent.): Paris, Bibliothèque Nationale de France, Parisinus Graecus 2603, folios 52r–54r (see Roussou 2018*a*: 85). This copy of the text is derived from the copy in **R** (cf. Roussou 2018*a*: 91–8 and just below under **Z**).

Z (16th cent.): Paris, Bibliothèque Nationale de France, Parisinus Graecus 2102, folios 194v–200r, copied by Jacob Diassorinus (see Roussou 2018*a*: 86). Up until now this copy of the text was thought to share a common hyparchetype with **Δ** (see Roussou 2018*a*: 87–8, 100 with further bibliography). In an article in preparation, however, Maria Giovanna Sandri argues convincingly that it is derived from the copy in **Δ**. We mention **Z** in our apparatus for two good conjectures.

We reconstruct the stemma for *On enclitics 1* as shown in Figure 2.1.

The subsections that follow explain the reasoning behind the most important points of this stemma (but not the reasoning behind the hyparchetypes π, **p**, **z**, γ, **f**, ν, or λ, which are of little significance for the reconstruction of the text).

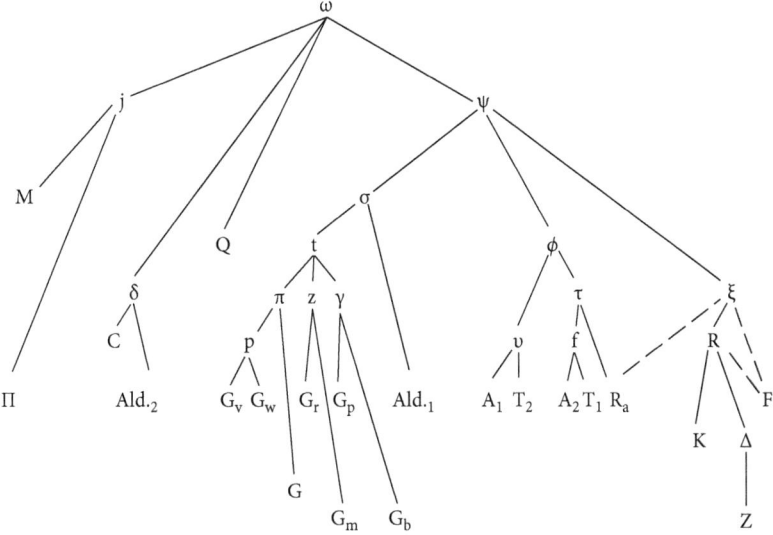

Fig. 2.1 Stemma for *On enclitics 1*

2.1.1.1 Evidence for family ψ

We consider many of the witnesses to *On enclitics 1* to share the hyparchetype we call ψ. In essence (but see what follows), the evidence for this hyparchetype consists of a series of readings which cannot be classified as clear errors, but which are unique to the sub-families we place under ψ. These readings are shown in Table 2.1.

Table 2.1 Evidence for family ψ

Reading(s) of the sub-families we place under ψ (or those that transmit the relevant passage)	Reading(s) of family j (comprising M and where relevant *Π*), family δ (comprising C and Ald.₂), and the highly abbreviated text of Q where this is available
§a, note h: σφξ omit the phrase found in jδ	τῶν δὲ λοιπῶν τριῶν — οὔτε μετοχή (μετοχαὶ **C**: μετοχ^x *Π*) οὔτε ἄρθρον (ἄρθ^ρ *Π*: ἄρθρα δ) οὔτε πρόθεσις (προθέσεις δ) jδ
§b, note e: στξ omit the word found in jδ (υ omits the whole paragraph.)	μόνου (μόνον *Π* **Ald.₂**) jδ
§c, note e: ἄνθρωπός (οἷον ἄνθρωπός σT₁) τις ἤκουσά τινος συT₁ξ (A₂ lacks examples at this point.)	οἶκός (οἷον οἶκός **Ald.₂**) τις ἔμαθόν τινος (τινες δ) Mδ (*Π* lacks examples at this point.)
§c, note r: τὸν δὲ κατὰ φύσιν τόνον ἔχοντα σξ	τὸν κατὰ φύσιν δὲ τόνον ἔχοντα **M Ald.₂**: τὰ κατὰ φύσιν **C** (*Π* reworks the whole sentence, with a result that does not include this phrase.)

Continued

Table 2.1 *Continued*

Reading(s) of the sub-families we place under ψ (or those that transmit the relevant passage)	Reading(s) of family j (comprising M and where relevant Π), family δ (comprising C and Ald.₂), and the highly abbreviated text of Q where this is available
§d, note e: τούτου (οὗ τ) τὸ δεύτερον φῇς ἀνέγκλιτον **τξ** (*v* omits this sentence entirely, as does *σ*, the latter as part of a larger omission.)	τούτου (τοῦτο **Ald.₂**) δὲ (δὲ om. **δ**) τὸ δεύτερον ἀνέγκλιτόν ἐστι λέγω δὲ (δὴ **C**) τὸ φῇς **Μδ**: πλὴν τοῦ δευτέρου τοῦ φῇς **Π**: οὗ τὸ δεύτερον ἀνέγκλιτον **Q** (These readings diverge from one another, but none has the sequence φῇς ἀνέγκλιτον found in **τξ**.)
§f, note m: καὶ τὰ πληθυντικὰ **συξ** (*τ* has an innovation of its own: καὶ ἐπὶ τῶν πληθυντικῶν ὁμοίως.)	καὶ αἱ πληθυντικαὶ **Μ**: καὶ αἱ πληθυντικαὶ δὲ **δ** (**Π** omits this phrase as part of a large omission.)
§g, note i: παράλογος **νξ** (*σ* and *τ* omit the relevant sentence as part of larger omissions.)	παραλόγως **Μδ** (**Π** omits this word as part of a large omission.)
§h, note y: **νξ** omit the phrase found in **Μδ** (*σ* and *τ* have larger omissions at this point.)	ταῦτα καὶ (καὶ deest in **Ald.₂**) περὶ ἀντωνυμιῶν **Μδ** (**Π** omits this phrase as part of a large omission.)
§i, note v: ἦλθέ ποθι **νξ** (*σ* omits this and the following examples, and *τ* has a larger omission at this point.)	ἦλθέν ποθεν **Μδ** (**Π** omits this phrase as part of a larger omission.)
§l, note l: βαρύνεται **νξ** (*σ* omits this word as part of a larger omission, and the text of *τ* breaks off before this point.)	βαρύτονος **ΜδQ** (The text of **Π** breaks off before this point.)
§m, note f: ὁμοίως **νξ** (*σ* omits the relevant phrase, and the text of *τ* breaks off before this point.)	ὁμοίων **Μδ** (The text of **Π** breaks off before this point.)

Since none of the ψ-family readings shown here can be classified as a clear error, one might ask whether these readings could go back to the archetype rather than to our hyparchetype ψ. Before we tackle this question, it is worth observing that there is also a series of readings unique to the witnesses we place outside ψ. Once again none of these amounts to a clear error, but we ought to consider whether these shared readings could point to a hyparchetype common to the 'non-ψ' portions of the tradition: family **j**, consisting of **M** and (where relevant) **Π**; family **δ**, consisting of C and **Ald.₂**; and on the rare occasions when it provides us with a reading, the highly abbreviated text in **Q**. Table 2.2 gives a selection of these readings.

Attentive readers will have noticed that some of the entries in Table 2.2 also appeared in Table 2.1. Each of these entries speaks either for our family ψ or for a

Table 2.2 Selection of readings unique to **j**, δ, and occasionally **Q**

Reading of j (comprising M, and *Π* where available), δ (comprising C and Ald.₂) and occasionally Q	Reading(s) of the rest of the tradition (or those parts of the tradition which transmit the relevant passage)
§a, note e: ὀκτὼ δὲ ὄντων τῶν τοῦ λόγου μερῶν τὰ ἐν οἷς ἐστιν ἐγκλινόμενα εἰσὶ (εἰσὶ om. j) πέντε **jδ** (Q has a unique phrasing of its own: ἰστέον ὅτι πέντε μέρη λόγου ἐγκλίνονται)	πέντε γάρ εἰσιν ἀπὸ τῶν τοῦ λόγου μερῶν τὰ ἐγκλινόμενα **σ**: ὀκτὼ δὲ ὄντων τῶν μερῶν τοῦ λόγου τὰ (τὰ deest in **τ**) πέντε ἐγκλίνονται **τξ**: πέντε ὄντων μερῶν τῶν ἐγκλινομένων **υ**
§a, note h: τῶν δὲ λοιπῶν τριῶν — οὔτε μετοχή (μετοχˣ *Π*: μετοχαὶ C) οὔτε ἄρθρον (ἄρθᵖ *Π*: ἄρθρα δ) οὔτε πρόθεσις (προθέσεις δ) **jδ**	**σφξ** omit this phrase
§b, note e: μόνου (μόνον *Π* **Ald.₂**) **jδ**	**στξ** omit this word (**υ** omits the whole paragraph.)
§c, note e: οἶκός (οἷον οἶκός **Ald.₂**) τις ἔμαθόν τινος (τινες δ) **Mδ** (*Π* lacks examples at this point.)	ἄνθρωπος (οἷον ἄνθρωπός **σT₁**) τις ἤκουσά τινος **συT₁ξ** (**A₂** lacks examples at this point.)
§c, note n: ταῦτα δὲ πάντα **Mδ** *Π* has ἅπαντα δὲ ταῦτα as part of a reworking of the whole sentence: thus all and only the witnesses under **jδ** have πάντα or ἅπαντα.	ταῦτα δὲ G **Ald.₁** **ξ**: ταῦτα δὲ τὰ **pz**: ταῦτα τὰ **Gₚ**: ταῦτα γὰρ τὰ **Gᵦ** (**φ** omits the whole sentence.)
§e, note h: αἱ (οἱ C) δὲ τῶν πρωτοτύπων πτώσεις **jδ**: ἀλλ᾽ αἱ πρωτότυποι Q Only **jδQ** have a form of the word πρωτότυπος.	αἱ δὲ τῶν παραγώγων πλάγιαι **υ**: αἱ ἄλλαι δὲ πτώσεις **τ**: αἱ δὲ τῶν παραγώγων πτώσεις **ξ** (**σ** rewords the text at this point, with a result that does not include this phrase.)
§g, note i: παραλόγως **Mδ** (*Π* omits this word as part of a large omission.)	παράλογος **υξ** (**σ** and **τ** omit the relevant sentence as part of larger omissions.)
§h, note y: ταῦτα καὶ (καὶ deest in **Ald.₂**) περὶ ἀντωνυμιῶν **Mδ** (*Π* omits this phrase as part of a large omission.)	**υξ** omit this phrase (**σ** and **τ** have larger omissions at this point.)

Continued

Table 2.2 *Continued*

Reading of j (comprising M, and *Π* where available), δ (comprising C and Ald.₂) and occasionally Q	Reading(s) of the rest of the tradition (or those parts of the tradition which transmit the relevant passage)
§l, note h: ἐγείρεται (οὐκ ἐγείρεται **Q**) **MδQ** (The text of *Π* breaks off before this point.)	ἐγείρετο *v*: ἐγείρει *ξ* (σ omits this word as part of a larger omission, and the text of *τ* breaks off before this point.)
§l, note l: βαρύτονος **MδQ** (The text of *Π* breaks off before this point.)	βαρύνεται *vξ* (σ omits this word as part of a larger omission, and the text of *τ* breaks off before this point.)
§m, note f: ὁμοίων **Mδ** (The text of *Π* breaks off before this point.)	ὁμοίως *vξ* (σ omits the relevant phrase, and the text of *τ* breaks off before this point.)

hyparchetype linking **jδQ**, but not necessarily for both: the question is which readings are innovations and which go back to the archetype. Moreover, in all cases where σφξ (our family ψ) share a reading not found in **jδQ**, and in all cases where **jδQ** (in practice usually represented by **jδ** or **Mδ**) share a reading not found in σφξ, the textual evidence taken by itself leaves it uncertain whether we are dealing with an innovation in σφξ (and thus evidence for our family ψ) or in **jδQ** (and thus evidence for a hyparchetype linking these branches of the tradition).

At §c, note r (shown in Table 2.1), for example, we think it likely that the 'postponed δέ' of **M** and **Ald.₂** derives from the archetype and has been re-positioned in ψ (represented for this passage by sub-families σ and ξ) and independently eliminated in a different way in **C**, but in principle the archetype could have had τὸν δὲ κατὰ φύσιν τόνον ἔχοντα, with a hyparchetype of **jδQ** introducing 'postponed δέ', and **C** eliminating this again via the rephrasing τὰ κατὰ φύσιν. At §a, note h (shown in Tables 2.1 and 2.2), the phrase τῶν δὲ λοιπῶν τριῶν—οὔτε πρόθεσις could be a clarificatory addition in **jδ**, but it could also have been present in the archetype and removed in σφξ. At §e, note h (shown in Table 2.2), a form of the word πρωτότυπος 'underived' makes good sense of the passage, but it is found only in **jδQ**; has this word been inherited from the archetype or has it been introduced by conjecture in one branch of the tradition?

Fortunately, an additional element of evidence can be brought to bear in favour of our family ψ, whether or not **jδQ** also comprise a family (a question to which we shall return shortly). In all the σ- and ξ-family manuscripts, the text of *On enclitics 1* is preceded immediately by a text of *On enclitics 3*. Manuscripts **M**, *Π*, **C**, and **Q**, on the other hand, transmit *On enclitics 1* without *On enclitics 3*; and while the Aldine *Thesaurus* (Aldus 1496) contains two versions of *On enclitics 1*, only the one we place under sub-family σ (our **Ald.₁**) is preceded by a copy of *On enclitics 3*. (Altogether, the *Thesaurus* contains one version of *On enclitics 3* and two versions of *On enclitics 1*, in the order *On enclitics 3*; *On enclitics 1* version **Ald.₁**; *On enclitics 1* version **Ald.₂**.)

In the φ-family manuscripts, the position is different again, and varies from one φ-family manuscript to another. The manuscript that gives us versions **A₁** and **A₂** of *On enclitics 1* also has a copy of *On enclitics 3*, in the order *On enclitics 1* version **A₁**; *On enclitics 1* version **A₂**; *On enclitics 3*. The manuscript that gives us versions **T₁** and **T₂** of *On enclitics 1* also has a copy of *On enclitics 3*, but this time the order is *On enclitics 1* version **T₁**; *On enclitics 3*; *On enclitics 1* version **T₂**. The manuscript that gives us *On enclitics 1* version **Rₐ**, does not have a copy of *On enclitics 3*.

The consistent common arrangement of material in the manuscripts under σ and ξ suggests that these manuscripts derive *On enclitics 1* from a common source in which *On enclitics 1* was preceded immediately by *On enclitics 3*, while the copies of *On enclitics 1* in **jδQ** and φ either stand outside this family or have changed the arrangement of material. When all this is taken together with the tendency for σ, φ, and ξ to agree against **jδQ**, the most straightforward inference is that sub-family φ goes back to the same family as σ and ξ but has changed the arrangement of material, while **jδQ** stand outside the family comprising σφξ. In section 2.3.1, we shall see that as far as our evidence allows us to tell, the copies of *On enclitics 3* preserved in two φ-family manuscripts stand in a different relationship to those in ξ- and σ-family manuscripts, compared to the copies of *On enclitics 1* in the same manuscripts. This point helps to explain how the material has come to be arranged differently in the manuscripts under φ, and will be discussed further under *On enclitics 3* (section 2.3.1).

For these reasons, then, we posit the hyparchetype ψ. Doing so considerably weakens the case for also positing a hyparchetype linking **j**, δ, and **Q**. Shared readings such as those shown in Table 2.2 can in all cases derive from the archetype, and if σφξ form a family (our ψ) then we do not require a hyparchetype linking **j**, δ, and **Q** in order to explain any of the instances where **jδQ** share one reading and σφξ another (see e.g. Table 2.2 under §a, note h).

Since stemmatic relationships are ideally established on the basis of clear errors, we note that there is one clear error shared by **M** and **Ald.₂** only, against the rest of the tradition including **C** and **Q**: see Table 2.3. If this error was

Table 2.3 Common error found in **M** and **Ald.₂** only

Reading of M and Ald.₂	Readings of the rest of the tradition
§p, note a: κἂν προπαροξύνοιτο **M Ald.₂**	κἂν παροξύνοιτο **Cσυξ**: καὶ εἰ παροξύνοιτο **Q** (The text of *Π* and that of *τ* break off before this point.)

inherited from a hyparchetype linking j, δ, and **Q**, we would have to assume that it was corrected independently in **Q** and **C**. While this would certainly be an easy enough correction, the error could as easily be independent in **M** and **Ald.₂**, or it could be an error in the archetype that was corrected independently in **Q**, **C**, and ψ.

All in all, then, we consider there to be sufficient evidence to support a hyparchetype ψ, but not to support a hyparchetype linking j, δ, and **Q**. On this basis we tentatively consider j, δ, and **Q** to derive from the archetype independently of one another. The position of **Q** in the tradition must remain especially tentative, however, given that this manuscript has a highly abbreviated text.

We now turn to the evidence for the equally tentative reconstruction of a hyparchetype (our j) linking **M** with the highly abbreviated and truncated text in *Π*, followed by the evidence for a hyparchetype (our δ) linking **C** and **Ald.₂**, and finally to the evidence for the main sub-families we posit under family ψ.

2.1.1.2 Evidence for family j

We tentatively consider **j** to form a sub-family on the basis of the point shown in Table 2.4, where the agreement of **δσξ** suggests that the archetype had πάλιν τῶν ἐγκλινομένων, and hence that **M*Π***'s reading is an innovation.

Table 2.4 Evidence for family j

Reading of M and *Π*	Readings of the rest of the tradition
§b, note b: τὰ δὲ ἐγκλινόμενα **M*Π***	πάλιν τῶν ἐγκλινομένων **δσξ**: τούτων δὲ τῶν ἐγκλινομένων τ

2.1.1.3 Evidence for family δ

We reconstruct the hyparchetype δ linking manuscript **C** and the Aldine edition **Ald.₂**, on the basis of a series of readings on which **C** and **Ald.₂** agree against the rest of the tradition. While none of these can be classified as a clear error, they are likely to be innovations in cases where a different reading can be reconstructed for the archetype on the basis of representatives of family ψ and at least one witness falling outside family ψ (in practice this most often means **M**). The most significant instances of this kind are shown in Table 2.5.

2.1.1.4 Evidence for sub-family σ (with further subgroup t)

Sub-family σ comprises the manuscripts we place under hyparchetype **t**, plus the Aldine version **Ald.₁** (and its derivatives). Table 2.6 gives a selection of the common errors and other innovations specific to sub-family σ.

Table 2.5 Evidence for family δ

Reading of C and Ald.₂	Reading(s) of the rest of the tradition
§a, note g: ὀνόματα, ῥήματα, ἀντωνυμίαι, ἐπιρρήματα, σύνδεσμοι **C Ald.₂**	ὄνομα, ῥῆμα, ἀντωνυμία, ἐπίρρημα, σύνδεσμος (καὶ σύνδεσμος **τ**) **jστξ** (**v** omits this list.)
§c, notes m, s: πευστικὰ **C Ald.₂**	πυσματικὰ **jσξ** (**φ** omits this word as part of a larger omission.)
§d, note k: τοῦτό φησιν **C Ald.₂**	ἄνθρωπός φησιν **Mστ**: τί φησιν οὗτος **ξ**: ἐστί καί φησι **v** (**Π** omits this material as part of a larger omission.)
§f, note v: καὶ αἱ τοῦ τρίτου πληθυντικαὶ ἐγκλίνονται **C Ald.₂**	καὶ αἱ τοῦ τρίτου πληθυντικαὶ ὀξύνονται **Mσ**: καὶ αἱ τοῦ τρίτου προσώπου πληθυντικαὶ ὀξυνόμεναι ἐγκλίνονται **ξ**: καὶ τὰ πληθυντικὰ τοῦ γ **v** (**Π** and **τ** omit this material as part of separate larger omissions.)
§f, note y: κἂν διαιρεθῶ· καί σφεας φωνήσας· τῶ σφεων πόλεσι καὶ ἡ ΣΦΙΣΙΝ ἐπεκτανθεῖσα, δίχα δέ φησιν ἥνδανε βουλή· καὶ εὔλογόν **C**: κἂν διαιρεθῶσι· καί σφεας φωνήσας· τῶ σφεων πολέεσκε· ἧς φησιν ἐπεκταθεῖσα, δίχα δέ σφιν ἥνδανε βουλή· καὶ εὔλογόν **Ald.₂**	καὶ εὔλογόν **Mσξ** (**Π**, **v**, and **τ** omit this phrase as part of separate larger omissions.)

Given the agreement of **M** with **σξ**, the additional material found in C and **Ald.₂** is likely to reflect a conjecture on the part of **δ**. It is a good conjecture that improves the sense, and for this reason we adopt it into our text, reconstructing its original form as follows:

κἂν διαιρεθῶσι· ʽκαί σφεας φωνήσαςʼ· τῶ σφεων πολέες κακόνʼ· ἡ ΣΦΙΣΙΝ ἐπεκταθεῖσα, ʽδίχα δέ σφισιν ἥνδανε βουλήʼ· καὶ εὔλογόν

§g, note e: κόψε (κόψαι **Ald.₂**) γάρ αὐτον ἔχοντα **C Ald.₂**	ἔλαβέν αὐτον **Mξ** (**Π**, **σ**, **v**, and **τ** each omit this phrase as part of separate larger omissions.)
§h, note f: ὑμῖν μὲν θεοὶ δοῖεν ὀλύμπια δώματ' (δώματα **C**) ἔχοντες ἐκπέρσαι (ἐκπέρσεν **C**) πριάμοιο πόλιν· ἀντὶ διαστέλλεται γάρ· παῖδα δέ μοι λύσατε φίλην **C Ald.₂** This material is likely to be an addition in **δ**.	The material found in **δ** does not appear anywhere else in the tradition. In particular, **Mφξ** have versions of the wider context in which this material appears in **δ**, but not this material itself.

Continued

Table 2.5 *Continued*

Reading of C and Ald.₂	Reading(s) of the rest of the tradition
§i, note o: πῇ ἔβη Ἀνδρομάχη **C Ald.₂**	πῇ ἦλθεν, ἦλθέν πη **Mφ**: πῇ ἦλθες· ἦλθές πη **σξ**
	(**Π** omits this phrase as part of a larger omission.)
§l, note k: οὐκ ὀξύνομεν γάρ, οὔτε τὴν τω συλλαβὴν τῆς οὕτω· οὔτε τὴν δη τῆς ἤδη **C Ald.₂**	καὶ οὔτε τὴν τω συλλαβὴν ὀξύνομεν τοῦ οὕτω οὔτε τὴν δη τοῦ ἤδη **M**: καὶ οὔτε τὴν τω συλλαβὴν τοῦ οὕτω ὀξύνομεν, οὔτε τὴν δη τοῦ ἤδη **ξ**: καὶ οὔτε τὴν τω τοῦ οὕτω ὀξύνομεν, οὔτε τὴν δη τοῦ ἤδη **v**: οὐδὲ γὰρ λέγει οὕτώ που οὐδὲ ἤδή τις **Q**
	(In the archetype, this point is likely to have been phrased so as to start with καὶ οὔτε τὴν τω, as in **Mvξ**. The text of **Π** breaks off before this point, and **Q** has a rephrasing of its own.)

Table 2.6 Evidence for sub-family σ

Reading of t and Ald.₁	Reading(s) of the rest of the tradition (or the portions that transmit the relevant passage)
§d, note b: omission in **t Ald.₁**	πεζὸς — τρίτον ἐγκλίνεται τὸ *ΦΗΣΙ*
§e, note a: omission in **t Ald.₁**	τῶν δὲ ἀντωνυμιῶν — εὐθεῖαι τῶν πρωτοτύπων
§e, note g: αἱ ἀντωνυμίαι τοῦ πρώτου προσώπου ἐγκλίνονται **t Ald.₁**	αἱ δὲ τῶν πρωτοτύπων πτώσεις — τοῦ πρώτου προσώπου ἐγκλινόμεναι
§e, note t: phrase omitted in **t Ald.₁**	μονοσύλλαβοι (μονοσύλλαβαι **Ald.₂**) οὖσαι **δξ**: μονοσύλλαβοι **M**
	(The manuscripts belonging to **φ** omit this phrase as part of larger omissions.)
§e, note w: ὕβρισά σε καί οἱ ἐπευχόμενοι θωρῆξαι ἐκέλευε **t Ald.₁**	καὶ οἱ ἐπευχόμενος **δξ**: ἔτι καί οἱ ἐπευχόμενος **τ**: καὶ οἱ ἐπευχόμενοι **M**
	(**v** omits this example as part of a larger omission.)
§f, note bb: phrase omitted in **t Ald.₁**	ἵνα μὴ βαρύτονοι οὖσαι ἐγκλίνωνται (ἐγκλίνονται **F**) **δξ**: ἵνα βαρύτονοι οὖσαι ἐγκλίνονται **M**
	(**v** omits this clause as part of a larger omission.)
§i, note f: omission found only in **t Ald.₁**	εἰ μὲν ὀρθοτονοῖντο — ἐγκλίνοιντο ἀόριστα

Reading of t and Ald.₁	Reading(s) of the rest of the tradition (or the portions that transmit the relevant passage)
§i, notes v–w: **t Ald.₁** give no examples here	ἦλθέν ποθεν **M**: ἦλθέν ποθεν· αἴ κέ ποθι Ζεύς· καί ποτέ τις εἴπῃσιν **δ**: ἦλθέ ποθι· αἴ κέ ποθι Ζεύς· καί ποτέ τις εἴπῃσιν **υξ** (τ lacks examples here as part of a larger omission.)
§j, note p: omission only in **t Ald.₁**	τὸν οὖν παραπληρωματικὸν — καταλαμβάνεται ἡ ἔγκλισις
§m, note f: phrase omitted in **t Ald.₁**	καὶ ἐπὶ τῶν ὁμοίων ὡσαύτως (ὡσαύτως om. **C**) **Mδ**: καὶ ἐπὶ τῶν ὁμοίως ὡσαύτως **υξ** (The text of τ breaks off before this point.)
§n, note e: omission in **t Ald.₁**	ἐν γὰρ τῇ *AN* συλλαβῇ καὶ τῇ *ΠΟΣ* — 'οἰκός τις', 'Σκῶλόν τε', 'Κνῆμόν τε'
§r, note b: καὶ αἱ ὀξεῖαι **t Ald.₁**	καὶ (αἱ **ξ**) παράλληλοι (ἐπάλληλοι **Ald.₂**) αἱ (αἱ om. **FZ**) ὀξεῖαι **δυξ** (The text of **M** is lost by this point, and that of τ breaks off before this.)
§r, note c: phrase omitted in **t Ald.₁**	ὡς παρ' Ὁμήρῳ **δυξ** (The text of **M** is lost by this point, and that of τ breaks off before this.)
§r, note f: τρεῖς εἰσιν ἐφεξῆς αἱ ὀξεῖαι **t Ald.₁**	τρεῖς γάρ εἰσιν ἐφεξῆς αἱ ὀξεῖαι **υξ**: τρεῖς γὰρ ἐφεξῆς ὀξεῖαι **δ** (The text of **M** is lost by this point, and that of τ breaks off before this.)
§r, note m: εἰ καὶ σπάνιον **t Ald.₁**	εἰ καὶ σπάνιον τὸ τοιοῦτον (τοιοῦτο **Ald.₂**) **δυξ** (The text of **M** is lost by this point, that of τ breaks off before this.)
§r, note n: διὰ τὴν τοῦ πνεύματος συνέχειαν **t Ald.₁**	διὰ τὴν τοῦ πνεύματος συνέχειαν δεομένην ἀναπαύσεως **υξ**: διὰ τὴν τοῦ πνεύματος συνέχειαν δεομένην (δεόμενον **Ald.₂**) ἀναπνεύσεως **δ** (The text of **M** is lost by this point, and that of τ breaks off before this.)
§s, note a: omission in **t Ald.₁**	εἰ δέ, παραλλήλων ὄντων — καὶ τῇ *NA* ἡ ὀξεῖα (i.e. a whole paragraph present in **δυξ**) (The text of **M** is lost by this point, and that of τ breaks off before this.)

Continued

Table 2.6 *Continued*

Reading of t and Ald.₁	Reading(s) of the rest of the tradition (or the portions that transmit the relevant passage)
§t, note h: omission in **t Ald.₁**	οὕτω που — δισύλλαβον εἴη τὸ ἐγκλιτικὸν μόριον (i.e. substantial material present in **δυξ**)
	(The text of **M** is lost by this point, and that of τ breaks off before this.)
§u, note f: omission in **t Ald.₁**	οὕτω ποτέ — ἡ ὀξεῖα πίπτει (i.e. substantial material present in **δυξ**)
	(The text of **M** is lost by this point, and that of τ breaks off before this.)

Table 2.7 Errors potentially attributable to **t** (for clearer evidence for **t**, see section 2.3.1.3)

Common innovations unique to the manuscripts under t	Reading(s) of the rest of the tradition, including Ald.₁
§c, note g: ἐδίδαξά τινι **GwGₚG**ᵦ (Gᵥ G, Gᵣ and **Gₘ** have ἐδίδαξά τινα, presumably a correction)	ἐδίδαξά τινα **MCτξ Ald.₁**: ἐδίδαξάν τινα **Ald.₂**: ἔτυψά τινα **υ**
§n, note b: παροξύνοιτο **GᵥGwGGᵣGₘGₚG**ᵦ	προπαροξύνοιτο
§u, note e: τὸ φησίν ὀξύνομεν (ὀξυνόμενον **GᵥGw**) **GᵥGwGGᵣGₘGₚG**ᵦ	τὸ εἰσίν ὀξύνομεν **δ Ald.₁ ξ**: τὸ εἰσίν ὀξύνεται **υ**

Within sub-family σ we tentatively posit the further subgroup **t**, comprising all the representatives of sub-family σ other than **Ald.₁**. As far as *On enclitics 1* is concerned, the only errors that might be attributable to **t** (shown in Table 2.7) could also be errors in σ that were corrected by **Ald.₁**. All of these would have been easy to correct, and the first was indeed corrected by some of the manuscripts we place under **t**. As noted already (section 2.1.1.1), however, these manuscripts transmit *On enclitics 1* along with the text we call *On enclitics 3*, and *On enclitics 3* provides us with three somewhat clearer pieces of evidence favouring the reconstruction of hyparchetype **t** (see section 2.3.1.3, Table 2.21). Since the two texts were transmitted together in all the witnesses deriving from σ, this evidence is also relevant for *On enclitics 1*, and on this basis we posit the subgroup **t**.

2.1.1.5 Evidence for sub-family ϕ (with further subgroups v and τ)

Sub-family ϕ comprises the manuscripts we place under the hyparchetypes v and τ. Table 2.8 shows the innovations (most of them omissions) shared by v and τ against the rest of the tradition, Table 2.9 gives a selection of innovations specific to the manuscripts under v, and Table 2.10 shows the innovations specific to those under τ.

Table 2.8 Evidence for sub-family ϕ

Reading of v and τ	Reading(s) of the rest of the tradition
§c, note m: omission in $v\tau$	ταῦτα δὲ πάντα — ταὐτὸν δὲ καὶ τὰ πληθυντικὰ
§d, note n: phrase omitted in $v\tau$	ἔτι (ἔστι C) καὶ τὸ ʼΕΙΜΙ **Μδσξ**
§d, note t: καὶ μετὰ τοῦ οὖ $v\tau$	καὶ μετὰ τῆς ʼΟΥ ἀποφάσεως **Μδξ** (σ omits this phrase as part of a larger omission.)
§f, note d: omission in $v\tau$	διὰ τὴν βαρεῖαν τάσιν· νῶϊ, νῶϊν, σφῶϊ, σφῶϊν· προπερισπῶνται γάρ
§f, note k: word/phrase omitted in $v\tau$	ἐγκλίνονται **Μtξ**: ἀεὶ ἐγκλίνονται **Ald.₂**: ἐκλίνονται **Ald.₁**: σφῶε καὶ σφῶϊν ἀεὶ ἐγκλίνονται **C**

Table 2.9 Evidence for v

Common innovations unique to the manuscripts under v (A₁ and T₂)	Reading(s) of the rest of the tradition
§a, note g: list omitted in **A₁T₂**	ὄνομα, ῥῆμα, ἀντωνυμία, ἐπίρρημα, σύνδεσμος (καὶ σύνδεσμος τ) **jστξ**: ὀνόματα, ῥήματα, ἀντωνυμίαι, ἐπιρρήματα, σύνδεσμοι **δ**
§b, note a: omission in **A₁T₂**	πάλιν τῶν ἐγκλινομένων — ὡς τὰ λοιπά
§d, note i: word/phrase omitted in **A₁T₂**	ἐγκλίνεται τὸ φησί **M**: φησὶν ἐγκλίνεται **δ**: ἐγκλίνεται **τξ**
§d, note k: ἐστί καί φησι **A₁T₂**	ἄνθρωπός φησιν **Mστ**: τοῦτό φησιν **δ**: τί φησιν οὗτος **ξ**
§d, note o: example omitted in **A₁T₂**	ἄνθρωπός εἰμι **Mσ**: ἔτι ἄνθρωπός εἰμι **τ**: ἄνθρωπός εἰμι Διὸς δέ τοι ἄγγελός εἰμι **C**: Διὸς δέ τοι ἄγγελός εἰμι **ξ**: καλός εἰμι **Ald.₂**
§d, note aa: omission in **A₁T₂**	οἴ μοι σκυζομένῳ — ἄνθρωποί ἐσμεν ἄνθρωποί ἐστε ἄνθρωποί εἰσιν (τ has an overlapping omission, which both begins and finishes earlier: see §d, note y.)

Table 2.10   Evidence for τ

Common innovations unique to the manuscripts under τ (A$_2$, T$_1$, and R$_a$)	Reading(s) of the rest of the tradition
§d, note gg: σχέτλιός ἐσσι φίλος A$_2$T$_1$R$_a$	σχέτλιός ἐσσι γεραιέ **Ald.**$_2$ **ξ**: σχέτλιός ἐσσι **υ**: deest in **MCσ**
§d, note p: αἵματός ἐστιν ἀγαθοῦ A$_2$T$_1$R$_a$	αἵματός εἰς ἀγαθοῖο (ἀγαθοῖς C), ἄνθρωπός ἐστιν **δ**: καὶ τὸ (τὸ deest in t) ἔστιν ἄνθρωπός ἐστιν **Mσ**: ἄνθρωπός ἐστι αἵματός ἐστιν (αἵματός ἐστιν deest in **A**$_1$) **υ**: τὸ δὲ εἶ ἀνέγκλιτον· τὸ δὲ ἔστιν ἐγκλίνεται αἵματός ἐστιν ἀγαθοῦ **ξ**
§c, note l: ἔλεξά τῳ εἰπόντι A$_2$T$_1$R$_a$	ἔλεξά τῳ φράσοντι **M**: ἔδωκά τῳ (τινι s.l. **υ**) φίλῳ **υ**: ἀντέλεξά τῳ φράσαντι **σ**: ἤκουσά τω καὶ τὸ φράσας **C**: ἔδωκά τῳ (τω **Rλ**) **ξ**: deest in **Π Ald.**$_2$
§d, note y: omission in A$_2$T$_1$R$_a$ (R$_a$ in fact omits up to ἄνθρωποί εἰσί, but this could be a further individual innovation.)	καὶ τὸ ΈΣΤΟΝ δυϊκὸν ἐγκλίνεται — καὶ τὰ πληθυντικὰ (**υ** has an overlapping omission, which both begins and finishes later: see §d, note aa.)
§i, note q: omission in A$_2$T$_1$R$_a$	ταῦτα πυσματικὰ — καί ποτέ τις εἴπῃσιν
§l, note b: the text of A$_2$ and T$_1$ breaks off after αἱ δὲ λοιπαί. (R$_a$ further truncates the text by breaking off part-way through §j.)	αἱ δὲ λοιπαί — end of the treatise (§u)

2.1.1.6 Evidence for sub-family ξ

Sub-family ξ comprises the manuscripts of Pseudo-Arcadius, where *On enclitics 1* appears under the heading ἔτι περὶ τῶν ἐγκλινομένων (see further section 2.1). Table 2.11 shows a selection of common errors and other innovations specific to sub-family ξ.

2.1.1.7 Possible evidence that R$_a$ is contaminated with sub-family ξ

Manuscript R$_a$ shares two common innovations with sub-family ξ (for which see section 2.1.1.6); these are shown in Table 2.12. Either of these could have taken place independently (and indeed the example Διὸς δέ τοι ἄγγελός εἰμι also appears in C), but they may suggest a degree of contamination when taken together with external evidence for the feasibility of contamination between R$_a$ and sub-family ξ. Both R$_a$ and R (the latter in sub-family ξ) were copied by Konstantinos Laskaris, who could have recalled readings from R or from his source for R when copying R$_a$. On this basis, our stemma tentatively links R$_a$ with sub-family ξ via a dotted line.

Table 2.11 Evidence for sub-family *ξ*

Common innovations unique to sub-family *ξ*	Readings of the rest of the tradition (or the portions that transmit the relevant passage)
§c, note u: **RF** omit the phrase found elsewhere	ταὐτὸν δὲ καὶ τὰ πληθυντικὰ **M**: καὶ τὰ τούτων πληθυντικὰ ὁμοίως **δ**: καὶ τὰ πληθυντικὰ τούτων **t**: καὶ τὰ πληθυντικὰ τούτων τίνες τίνων τίσι τίνας **Ald.₁** (*φ* omits this phrase as part of a larger omission.)
§d, note m: **RF** provide no examples here	ἐκεῖνό φαμεν ἢ φατε ἢ φασιν **M Ald.₂ σ**: ἐκεῖνό φαμεν· ἐκεῖνό φατε· ἐκεῖνό φασι **Cτ**: ἐγώ εἰμι ἐγώ φημι *υ*
§d, notes dd–ee: **RF** provide no examples here	ἄνθρωποί ἐσμεν (ἄνθρωποίδαμεν **C**), ἄνθρωποί ἐστε, ἄνθρωποί εἰσιν **MC**: ἄνθρωποί ἐσμεν, ἄνθρωποί ἐστε, οὗτοί εἰσὶ **Ald.₂**: ἄνθρωποί ἐσμεν ἐστε εἰσι (αἴτιοί εἰσι *T₁*) *τ*: ἄνθρωποί ἐστε, ἄνθρωποί εἰσιν *σ* (*υ* omits this material as part of a larger omission.)
§d, note p: τὸ δὲ εἶ ἀνέγκλιτον· τὸ δὲ ἔστιν ἐγκλίνεται αἵματός ἐστιν ἀγαθοῦ **RF**	αἵματός εἰς ἀγαθοῖο (ἀγαθοῖς **C**), ἄνθρωπός ἐστιν **δ**: καὶ τὸ (τὸ deest in **t**) ἔστιν ἄνθρωπός ἐστιν **Mσ**: ἄνθρωπός ἐστι αἵματός ἐστιν (αἵματός ἐστιν deest in **A₁**) *υ*: αἵματός ἐστιν ἀγαθοῦ *τ*
§e, note h: αἱ δὲ τῶν παραγώγων πτώσεις **RF**	αἱ (οἱ **C**) δὲ τῶν πρωτοτύπων πτώσεις **jδ**: ἀλλ' αἱ πρωτότυποι **Q**: αἱ δὲ τῶν παραγώγων πλάγιαι *υ*: αἱ ἄλλαι δὲ πτώσεις *τ* (*σ* omits this phrase as part of a larger omission.)
§f, note e: βραχεῖαν **RF**	βαρεῖαν **Mδσ** (*φ* omits this word as part of a larger omission.)
§f, note i: περισπῶνται **RF**	προπερισπῶνται **Mδσ** (*φ* omits this word as part of a larger omission.)

Table 2.12 Evidence for contamination between manuscript **Rₐ** and sub-family *ξ*

Innovations common to sub-family *ξ* and manuscript Rₐ	Readings of the rest of the tradition
§d, note o: Διὸς δέ τοι (τι **F**) ἄγγελός εἰμι **Rₐ ξ**	ἄνθρωπός εἰμι **Mσ**: ἔτι ἄνθρωπός εἰμι *τ*: ἄνθρωπός εἰμι Διὸς δέ τοι ἄγγελός εἰμι **C**: καλός εἰμι **Ald.₂**: deest in *υ*
§f, note x: καί σφων· καί σφιν· καί σφας **Rₐ ξ**	*ΣΦΩΝ, ΣΦΙΝ* (σφίν **MGυ**: σφῖν **Ald.₂ Ald.₁**: σφεῖσι sic **G̲ᵣγ̲**: σφίσι **p**), *ΣΦΑΣ*, καί σφων, καί σφιν, καί σφας (καί σφας καί σφας κακοὺς κάκιστα **C**) **Mδσυ**

2.1.2 Previous editions

The first text of *On enclitics 1* to appear in relatively modern times was that of Barker (1820: 141–7), as part of his edition of Pseudo-Arcadius' epitome of Περὶ καθολικῆς προσῳδίας (see section 2.1). This was based almost entirely on a transcript of the Pseudo-Arcadius manuscript we call **Z** (see Roussou 2018*a*: 101).

Soon afterwards, Bekker printed a self-standing text of *On enclitics 1* in the third volume of his *Anecdota Graeca* (Bekker 1821), as two sections entitled Καὶ ἄλλως περὶ ἐγκλινομένων (on pp. 1156–7) and then Αἰλίου περὶ ἐγκλινομένων λέξεων (on pp. 1157–8). For reasons we have not been able to uncover, the order in which Bekker presents these two sections is the reverse of that in which the corresponding portions of text appear in manuscripts of *On enclitics 1*, and Bekker's second section breaks off abruptly with the comment 'Reliqua v. apud Arcadium p. 142' (i.e. for the rest see Barker 1820: 142).

Bekker's text lacks a critical apparatus, but he notes on p. 1142 that for treatises on enclitics he consulted the Aldine *Thesaurus: Cornu copiae et Horti Adonidis* (Aldus 1496), a second Aldine edition likely to be the work listed in our bibliography as Aldus (1524),[11] and five Paris manuscripts, of which only Parisinus Graecus 2594 (our **G$_p$**) is relevant for *On enclitics 1*. Three of the others will become relevant when we consider *On enclitics 2*, *Charax*, and *About ἘΣΤΙΝ* (see sections 2.2.2, 2.4.2, 2.5.2) while the fifth is Parisinus Graecus 2542, which contains our treatise *On enclitics 3* (see section 2.3.1, manuscript **E$_p$**) but none of the texts on enclitics that Bekker himself prints.

Since Bekker, further texts of *On enclitics 1* have appeared in further editions of Pseudo-Arcadius: that of Schmidt (1860: 162–9), which was based on the Pseudo-Arcadius manuscripts we call **Δ**, **K**, and **Z** (see Roussou 2018*a*: 101–3), and that of Roussou (2018*a*: 302–8), which is based on all the manuscripts we list under sub-family **ξ** (see section 2.1.1).

Drawing attention to a different branch of the tradition from the one represented in manuscripts of Pseudo-Arcadius, Donnet (1967: 22–9) provides a text based on the manuscript we call **C**, and drawing also on the closely related Aldine edition we call **Ald.$_2$**. Drawing attention to a different branch again, Telesca (2021) provides an edition based on the text of manuscript **M**, with corrections informed by a comparison with the manuscripts of Pseudo-Arcadius and with the manuscripts used by Bekker (on which see the beginning of this section). We learned of Telesca's work at a late stage in the preparation of our book, after we had collated manuscript **M** by autopsy, but on the publication of her work we compared our readings with hers. Where these differ, we stand by our readings. On

---

[11] Bekker calls this work an Aldine edition, refers to it as 'Dictionar.', and notes that the texts on enclitics which he prints begin on f. 93r. All this would be consistent with Aldus (1524), which contains two sequences of folio numbers, with texts on enclitics beginning on f. 93r of the second sequence. The texts of these treatises in Aldus (1524) are ultimately derived from Aldus (1496).

the other hand, Telesca records a particular feature of manuscript **M** in considerably more detail than we do: at numerous points letters have been wholly or partly obscured in this manuscript by what we take to be small white patches of paper stuck onto the pages. We do not note these points unless there is room for doubt about the reading, but we refer interested readers to Telesca's apparatus.

Lentz's collected edition of Herodian's works does not provide a text of *On enclitics 1* as such, but material from *On enclitics 1*, *On enclitics 2*, and *About 'ΕΣΤΙΝ* is combined into one text entitled Ἐκ τῶν Ἡρωδιανοῦ περὶ ἐγκλινομένων (Lentz 1867–70: i. 551–64).[12]

As mentioned above (section 2.1), the version of *On enclitics 1* that we find in Pseudo-Arcadius ends with a version of the treatise we call *About 'ΕΣΤΙΝ*. We present *About 'ΕΣΤΙΝ* as a separate text (section 2.5), since it is often transmitted as such, but our edition of *About 'ΕΣΤΙΝ* takes into account the manuscripts of Pseudo-Arcadius along with witnesses that present *About 'ΕΣΤΙΝ* as a self-standing text.

---

[12] For discussion of the compilatory nature of Lentz's edition of Herodian, see Roussou (2018*a*: 80–2), with further bibliography.

2.1.3 *On enclitics 1*: text and translation

§a *Περὶ[a] ἐγκλιτικῶν*

Πᾶν[b] [c] ἐγκλινόμενον μόριον ἢ ὀξύνεται ἢ περισπᾶται, οὐδὲν[d] δὲ βαρύνεται. ὀκτὼ[e] δὲ ὄντων τῶν τοῦ λόγου μερῶν τὰ ἐν οἷς ἐστιν ἐγκλινόμενα εἰσὶ πέντε· ὄνομα,[f] [g] ῥῆμα, ἀντωνυμία, ἐπίρρημα, σύνδεσμος. τῶν[h] δὲ λοιπῶν τριῶν οὐδὲν ἐγκλίνεται, οὔτε μετοχή, οὔτε ἄρθρον, οὔτε πρόθεσις.

§b πάλιν[a] [b] τῶν ἐγκλινομένων τὰ μὲν κόσμου[c] ἕνεκεν ἐγκλίνονται[d] μόνου[e], ὡς τὰ ῥήματα καὶ οἱ σύνδεσμοι, τὰ[f] δὲ σημασίας, ὡς τὰ λοιπά.

§a

[a]   *Περὶ ἐγκλιτικῶν* (ἐγκλιτιτῶν **M**) **M**: περὶ τῶν ἐγκλινομένων μορίων **f**: περὶ τῶν ἐγκλινομένων *v***R**ₐ: ἔτι περὶ τῶν ἐγκλινομένων **ξ**: καὶ ἄλλως αἰλίου περὶ ἐγκλινομένων λέξεων **Ald.**₂: περὶ ἐγκλινομένων τινῶν **Q**: ερὶ (sic) ἐγκλινομένων **Π**: Ἰωάννου γραμματικοῦ τοῦ Τζέτζου περὶ ἐγκλιτικῶν μορίων **C**: sine titulo σ

[b]   *Πᾶν ἐγκλινόμενον μόριον* — *οὐδὲν δὲ βαρύνεται* deest in **Q***v*

[c]   *Πᾶν ἐγκλινόμενον μόριον ἢ* (ἢ om. **τ**) *ὀξύνεται ἢ περισπᾶται* **jστξ**: πᾶν ἐγκλινόμενον ὑποτάσσεται πάντως ἐκείνῳ, ᾧ καὶ τὸν ἑαυτοῦ τόνον ἐγκλίνει, ἦλθέ τις, ἔδωκάς (ὅδωκάς **Ald.**₂) μοι, ἤκουσά σου **Ald.**₂: ἀναγκαῖον δὲ καὶ περὶ τῶν ἐγκλινομένων λέξεων διαλαβεῖν· πᾶν ἐγκλινόμενον ὑποτάσσεται πάντως ἐκείνῳ, ᾧ καὶ τὸν ἑαυτοῦ τόνον ἐγκλίνει ἦλθέ τις, ἔδωκάς μοι, ἤκουσά σου **C**

[d]   *οὐδὲν δὲ βαρύνεται* **jτξ**: οὐδέποτε δὲ βαρύνεται σ: deest in δ

[e]   *ὀκτὼ δὲ ὄντων τῶν τοῦ λόγου μερῶν τὰ ἐν οἷς ἐστιν ἐγκλινόμενα εἰσὶ* (εἰσὶ om. **j**) *πέντε* **jδ**: ὀκτὼ δὲ ὄντων τῶν μερῶν τοῦ λόγου τὰ (τὰ deest in **τ**) πέντε ἐγκλίνονται **τξ**: πέντε ὄντων μερῶν τῶν ἐγκλινομένων *v*: ἰστέον ὅτι πέντε μέρη λόγου ἐγκλίνονται **Q**: πέντε γάρ εἰσιν ἀπὸ τῶν τοῦ λόγου μερῶν τὰ ἐγκλινόμενα σ

[f]   *ὄνομα* — *ὡς τὰ λοιπὰ* deest in **Q**

[g]   *ὄνομα, ῥῆμα, ἀντωνυμία, ἐπίρρημα, σύνδεσμος* (καὶ σύνδεσμος **τ**) **jστξ**: ὀνόματα, ῥήματα, ἀντωνυμίαι, ἐπιρρήματα, σύνδεσμοι δ: deest in *v*

[h]   *τῶν δὲ λοιπῶν τριῶν* — *οὔτε μετοχὴ* (μετοχαὶ **C**: μετοχ[χ] **Π**) *οὔτε ἄρθρον* (ἄρθρα δ: ἄρθ[ρ] **Π**) *οὔτε πρόθεσις* (προθέσεις δ) **jδ**: deest in σφξ

§b

[a]   *πάλιν τῶν ἐγκλινομένων* — *ὡς τὰ λοιπά* deest in *v*

[b]   *πάλιν τῶν ἐγκλινομένων* **δσξ**: τὰ δὲ ἐγκλινόμενα **j**: τούτων δὲ τῶν ἐγκλινομένων **τ**

[c]   *κόσμου ἕνεκεν* **Mδτ**: ἕνεκεν κόσμου σ: χάριν κόσμου **ξ**: κόσμου χάριν **Π**

[d]   *ἐγκλίνονται* **jCτξ**: ἐκλίνονται (sic) **Ald.**₂: ἐγκλίνεται **Ald.**₁: deest in **τ**

[e]   *μόνου* **MC**: μόνον **Π** **Ald.**₂: deest in στξ

[f]   *τὰ δὲ σημασίας* (σημασία **MC**t) *ὡς τὰ λοιπὰ* **jδσξ**: τὰ δὲ λοιπὰ σημασίας χάριν **τ**

§a On enclitics

Every enclitic item[13] is either oxytone or perispomenon; none is barytone. While the parts of speech are eight in number,[14] those among which there are enclitics are five: nominal,[15] verb, pronoun, adverb, conjunction. Among the other three none behaves as an enclitic: neither participle, nor article, nor preposition.

§b Returning to the enclitics, some throw back their accents for the sake of seemliness alone, like the verbs and conjunctions, while some of them do so because of their meaning, like the others.

---

[13] The term μόριον is often translatable as 'word', but it can be used for items whose classification as words (or as specific parts of speech) is being left open: see Dalimier (2001: 391–2).

[14] On this system of eight parts of speech, deriving from Alexandrian scholarship, see Matthaios (1999); Wouters and Swiggers (2014).

[15] The term ὄνομα covers what we would today call adjectives as well as nouns, and some words that we would call pronouns. The closest equivalent in modern linguistic terminology is the word 'nominal', and we adopt this word to translate ὄνομα.

§c ἔν^a μὲν οὖν ὀνόμασι^b τὸ *ΤΙΣ* μόνον ἐγκλίνεται καὶ αἱ τούτου πτώσεις καὶ οἱ ἀριθμοὶ καὶ τὸ οὐδέτερον· 'οἶκός^{c d e} τις', 'ἔμαθόν τινος', 'ἔδωκά^f τινι', 'ἐδίδαξά^g τινα', 'ἔμαθόν^h τι' καὶⁱ τὰ ἰσοδυναμοῦντα τούτοις, τὸ^j *ΤΟΥ* καὶ *ΤΩΙ*· 'ἤκουσά^k του λέγοντος', 'ἔλεξά^l τῳ φράσοντι'. ταῦτα^{m n} δὲ πάντα ἐγκλινόμενα μὲν^o ὥς^p πρόκειται ἀόριστά^q ἐστι, τὸν^r κατὰ φύσιν δὲ τόνον ἔχοντα πυσματικὰ^s γίνεται· τίς,^t ⟨...⟩, τίνος, τίνι, τίνα, τί, ταὐτὸν^u δὲ καὶ τὰ πληθυντικά.

§c
^a ἐν μὲν οὖν **j Ald.**₂ **ξ**: ἐν μὲν **Cσφ**: deest in **Q**
^b ὀνόμασι τὸ *ΤΙΣ* μόνον ἐγκλίνεται καὶ αἱ τούτου (αὐτοῦ σ. τούτων **C**) πτώσεις καὶ οἱ (οἱ om. **Ald.**₂) ἀριθμοὶ καὶ τὸ (τὸ τί **C**) οὐδέτερον (post οὐδέτερον add. αὐτὸ τὸ τι **Ald.**₂) **Μδσξ**: ὀνόμασιν ἐγκλίνεται τὸ τίς καὶ τὸ τί μόνον καὶ αἱ πτώσεις τούτων **υ**: τοῖς ὀνόμασιν ἐγκλίνεται τὸ τῖς ἐν παντὶ ἀριθμῷ καὶ πτώσει **τ**: ὀνόμασι τὸ τίς μόνον ἐγκλίνεται καὶ αἱ τούτου πτώσεις **Π**: ὄνομα· τίς **Q**
^c οἶκός τις — ταὐτὸν δὲ καὶ τὰ πληθυντικὰ deest in **Q**
^d οἶκός τις — ἔμαθόν τι deest in **Π**
^e οἶκός (οἷον οἶκός **Ald.**₂) τις ἔμαθόν τινος (τινες **δ**) **Μδ**: ἄνθρωπός (οἷον ἄνθρωπός **σΤ**₁) τις ἤκουσά τινος **συΤ**₁**ξ**
^f ἔδωκά τινι **ΜΣσφξ**: ἔδωκάν τινι **Ald.**₂
^g ἐδίδαξά τινα **ΜCG**ᵥ**Gz Ald.**₁ **τξ**: ἐδίδαξάν τινα **Ald.**₂: ἐδίδαξά τινι **G**ᵥ**γ**: ἔτυψά τινα **υ**
^h ἔμαθόν τι **Μ**: ἔλαβόν τι **Ald.**₂: καὶ ἐπὶ τῶν λοιπῶν ὡσαύτως **Ald.**₁ **ξ**: καὶ τὰ ἑξῆς **υ**: ἦλθόν (**Τ**₁: ἤκόν **R**ₐ) τινες ἤκουσά τινων ἐπέστειλά τισιν ἐδίδαξά τινας **τ**: ἤκουσά τινων ἀπέστειλά τισιν **C**: deest in **t**
ⁱ καὶ τὰ ἰσοδυναμοῦντα **jCτυξ**: καὶ ἰσοδυναμοῦντα **Ald.**₁: ἀορίστως πάντα καὶ τὰ ἰσοδυναμοῦντα **τ**: deest in **Ald.**₂
^j τὸ *ΤΟΥ* καὶ *ΤΩΙ* (τω **ΜΑ**₁) **Μυ**: τὸ του καὶ τὸ τω **Cσ**: τὸ του τὸ τω **Π**: του καὶ τω **τξ**: deest in **Ald.**₂
^k ἤκουσά του (τινος s.l. **υ**) λέγοντος **Μσφ**: ἤκουσά του **ξ**: ἤκουσά τινων ἐπέστειλά τισι **C**: deest in **Π Ald.**₂
^l ἔλεξά τῳ φράσοντι **Μ**: ἔδωκά τῳ (τινι s.l. **υ**) φίλῳ **υ**: ἔλεξά τῳ εἰπόντι **τ**: ἀντέλεξά τῳ φράσαντι σ: ἤκουσά τω καὶ τὸ φράσας **C**: ἔδωκά τῳ (τω **R**) **ξ**: deest in **Π Ald.**₂
^m ταῦτα δὲ πάντα — ταὐτὸν δὲ καὶ τὰ πληθυντικὰ] ἅπαντα δὲ ταῦτα ἀόριστα ὄντα ἐγκλίνονται πυσματικὰ δὲ οὔ **Π**: deest in **φ**
ⁿ ταῦτα δὲ πάντα **Μδ**: ταῦτα δὲ **G Ald.**₁ **ξ**: ταῦτα δὲ τὰ **pz**: ταῦτα τὰ **G**ₚ: ταῦτα γὰρ τὰ **G**ᵦ
^o μὲν **MC**: deest in **Ald.**₂ **σξ**
^p ὡς πρόκειται **MCξ**: deest in **Ald.**₂ **σ**
^q ἀόριστά (ἀόριστα) ἐστι **Μδσ**: ἀόριστά εἰσι **ξ**
^r τὸν κατὰ φύσιν δὲ τόνον ἔχοντα **Μ Ald.**₂: τὸν δὲ κατὰ φύσιν τόνον ἔχοντα **σξ**: τὰ κατὰ φύσιν **C**
^s πυσματικὰ γίνεται **Μσ**: πυσματικὰ γίνονται **ξ**: πευστικὰ γίνονται **δ**
^t τίς, ⟨...⟩ (fortasse verba οἷον τίς πόθεν vel οἷον τίς πόθεν εἰς ἀνδρῶν exciderunt), τίνος, τίνι, τίνα, τί scripsi: πόθεν τίς τίνος τίνι τίνα τί **Μ**: πόθεν τίς τίνος τίνι τίνα **Ald.**₁: πόθεν τίς τίνος ἵνα (sic) τί **t**: τίς τίνος τίνι τίνα **ξ**: τίς πόθεν εἰς ἀνδρῶν· τίνος ἡ πόλις; τίνος ἐστὶ τὸ δῶ **Ald.**₂: τίς· πόθεν εἰς ἀνδρῶν· τίνος μὲν ἔκατι γῆς ἀποστελεῖς κρέον· τίνι μόρῳ θνήσκεις· τίνα καὶ πείθειν δοκεῖς· τοῦ γάρ ἐστι τὸ δῶ **C**
^u ταὐτὸν (litteris αὐ obfuscatis) δὲ καὶ τὰ πληθυντικὰ **Μ**: καὶ τὰ τούτων πληθυντικὰ ὁμοίως **δ**: καὶ τὰ πληθυντικὰ τούτων **t**: καὶ τὰ πληθυντικὰ τούτων τίνες τίνων τίσι τίνας **Ald.**₁: deest in **ξ**

§c Among the nominals, then, only *TIΣ* is enclitic, along with its cases and numbers and the neuter, as in οἶκός τις, ἔμαθόν τινος, ἔδωκά τινι, ἐδίδαξά τινα, ἔμαθόν τι,[16] and their equivalents *TOY* and *TΩI*, as in ἤκουσά του λέγοντος, ἔλεξά τῳ φράσοντι.[17] And when all these are enclitic, as in the examples, they are indefinite, but when they have their natural accents they become interrogative: τίς…τίνος, τίνι, τίνα, τί, and similarly for the plurals.

---

[16] 'A certain house'; 'I learned from someone'; 'I gave to someone'; 'I taught someone'; 'I learned something'.
[17] 'I heard someone saying'; 'I said to someone who would tell'.

§d ἐν^a δὲ ῥήμασιν ἐγκλίνεται τὸ *ΦΗΜΙ* καὶ *ΕΙΜΙ*· 'πεζὸς^{b c} δ' ἕνδεκά φημι', 'τόσσον^d ἐγώ φημι'. τούτου^e δὲ τὸ δεύτερον ἀνέγκλιτόν ἐστι, λέγω δὲ τὸ *ΦΗΣ*. τὸ^{f g h} δὲ τρίτον ἐγκλίνεταιⁱ τὸ *ΦΗΣΙ*· {'ἐγώ^j φημι', 'ἐγώ εἰμι',} 'ἄνθρωπός^k φησιν', ἔσθ'^l ὅτε δὲ καὶ τὰ πληθυντικά· 'ἐκεῖνό^m φαμεν' ἢ 'φατέ' ἢ 'φασιν'. ἔτιⁿ καὶ τὸ *ΕΙΜΙ*· 'ἄνθρωπός^o εἰμι', 'αἵματός^p εἰς ἀγαθοῖο', 'ἄνθρωπός ἐστιν'. τοῦτο^q δὲ τὸ *ΕΣΤΙΝ* ἐν ταῖς ἀρχαῖς τῶν λόγων βαρύνεται· 'ἔστι^r πόλις Ἐφύρη'· καὶ^{s t} μετὰ τῆς *ΟΥ* ἀποφάσεως· 'οὐκ^u ἔστιν πόλις'· καὶ^v μετὰ τοῦ *ΚΑΙ* συνδέσμου· 'καὶ^w ἔστιν πόλις'· καὶ^x μετὰ τοῦ *ΩΣ* ἐπιρρήματος· ὡς ἔστιν εἰπεῖν. καὶ^{y z} τὸ

§d
a ἐν δὲ ῥήμασιν ἐγκλίνεται τὸ φημί καὶ εἰμί **Μτξ**: ἐν δὲ ῥήμασιν ἐγκλίνεται τὸ εἰμί καὶ φημί **σΤ₂**: ἐν δὲ ῥήμασιν τὸ εἰμί καὶ φημί **Α₁**: ἐν δὲ ῥήμασι ἐγκλίνεται τὸ φημί **Ald.₂**: ἐν ῥήμασιν ἐγκλίνονται φημί **C**: ἐν δὲ τοῖς ῥήμασι τὸ φημὶ καὶ εἰμί καὶ τὰ πρὸ (πρὸ i.l.: ἀπὸ s.l.) ἅπαντα τούτων ἐνικὰ δυϊκὰ πληθυντικὰ **Π**: ῥῆμα· φημί **Q**
b πεζὸς — τρίτον ἐγκλίνεται τὸ *ΦΗΣΙ* deest in σ
c πεζὸς (οἷον πεζὸς **Τ₁**) δ' ἕνδεκά (ἕνδεκα **R**: ἕνεκά sic **Ald.₂**) φημι **Ald.₂ Τ₁ξ**: deest in jCQvΑ₂Rₐ
d τόσσον (τόσσον scripsi: τόσον **τξ**) ἐγώ φημι **τξ**: τόσσον ἐγὼ φημι πλέας (πλέεις **C**) ἔμμεναι **δ**: deest in jQv
e τούτου (τοῦτο **Ald.₂**) δὲ (δὲ om. **δ**) τὸ δεύτερον ἀνέγκλιτόν ἐστι λέγω δὲ (δὴ **C**) τὸ φῆς **Μδ**: οὗ τὸ δεύτερον ἀνέγκλιτον **Q**: οὗ (τούτου **ξ**) τὸ δεύτερον φῆς ἀνέγκλιτον **τξ**: πλὴν τοῦ δευτέρου τοῦ φής **Π**: deest in v
f τὸ δὲ τρίτον ἐγκλίνεται — σχέτλιός ἐσσι γεραιέ deest in **Π**
g τὸ δὲ τρίτον ἐγκλίνεται — ἄνθρωποί εἰσιν deest in **Q**
h τὸ δὲ τρίτον **δτξ**: τὸ τρίτον **Μ**: deest in v
i ἐγκλίνεται τὸ φησί **Μ**: φησὶν ἐγκλίνεται **δ**: ἐγκλίνεται **τξ**: deest in v
j 'ἐγώ φημι', 'ἐγώ εἰμι' **Μ**, delevi: ἐγώ φημι· ἐγώ φημι **σ**: deest in **δφξ**
k ἄνθρωπός φησιν **Μστ**: τοῦτό φησιν **δ**: τί φησιν οὗτος **ξ**: ἐστί καί φησι v
l ἔσθ' ὅτε δὲ καὶ τὰ πληθυντικὰ **Μ**: ἔσθ' ὅτε δὲ καὶ τὰ πληθυντικὰ ἐγκλίνονται **δ**: ἔσθ' ὅτε καὶ τὰ πληθυντικὰ **τ**: καὶ τὰ πληθυντικὰ ἔσθ' ὅτε v: ἔσθ' ὅτε καὶ πληθυντικά **σ**: ἔσθ' ὅτε καὶ τὰ πληθυντικὰ ἐγκλίνεται **ξ**
m 'ἐκεῖνό φαμεν' ἢ (ἤ **G**: ἢ **Ald.₁**) 'φατέ' ἢ (ἤ **G**: ἢ **Ald.₁**) 'φασιν' **Μ Ald.₂ σ**: ἐκεῖνό φαμεν· ἐκεῖνό φατε· ἐκεῖνό φασι **Cτ**: ἐγώ εἰμι ἐγώ φημι v: deest in **ξ**
n ἔτι (ἔστι **C**) καὶ τὸ *ΕΙΜΙ* **Μδσξ**: deest in φ
o ἄνθρωπός εἰμι **Μσ**: ἔτι ἄνθρωπός εἰμι **τ**: ἄνθρωπός εἰμι Διὸς δέ τοι ἄγγελός εἰμι **C**: Διὸς δέ τοι ἄγγελός εἰμι **ξ**: καλός εἰμι **Ald.₂**: deest in v
p αἵματός εἰς ἀγαθοῖο (ἀγαθοῖς **C**), ἄνθρωπός ἐστιν **δ**: καὶ τὸ (τὸ deest in **t**) ἔστιν ἄνθρωπός ἐστιν **Μσ**: ἄνθρωπός ἐστι αἵματός ἐστιν (αἵματός ἐστιν deest in **Α₁**) v: αἵματός ἐστιν ἀγαθοῦ **τ**: τὸ δὲ εἶ ἀνέγκλιτον· τὸ δὲ ἔστιν ἐγκλίνεται αἵματός ἐστιν ἀγαθοῦ **ξ**
q τοῦτο δὲ τὸ ἔστιν ἐν ταῖς ἀρχαῖς τῶν λόγων βαρύνεται **Μδσξ**: ἐν ἀρχῇ δὲ τὸ ἔστι βαρύνεται μόνον v: τοῦτο δὲ τὸ ἔστιν ἐν ἀρχῇ βαρύνεται **τ**
r ἔστι πόλις Ἐφύρη **Ald.₂ στξ**: καὶ ἔστι πόλις Ἐφύρη **C**: ἔστιν πόλις **Μ**: deest in v
s καὶ μετὰ τῆς *ΟΥ* ἀποφάσεως — καὶ ἔστιν πόλις deest in σ
t καὶ μετὰ τῆς *ΟΥ* ἀποφάσεως **Μδξ**: καὶ μετὰ τοῦ ο͞υ φ
u οὐκ ἔστιν πόλις (πόλις deest in **Α₂**) **Μτ**: οὐκ ἔστιν οὐδὲν δεινὸν ὧδ' (ὥδ' **C**: ὥς δ' **Ald.₂**) εἰπεῖν ἔπος οὐδὲ πάθος οὐδὲ ξυμφορά (οὐδὲ πάθος οὐδὲ ξυμφορὰ deest in **Ald.₂**) **δ**: οὐκ ἔστιν ἀγαθὸν **ξ**: deest in v
v καὶ μετὰ τοῦ *ΚΑΙ* συνδέσμου **Μδ**: καὶ μετὰ τοῦ κ͞αι **τξ**: καὶ κ͞αι v
w καὶ ἔστιν πόλις· **Μ**: deest in **δφξ**
x καὶ μετὰ τοῦ ὡ͞ς ἐπιρρήματος· ὡς ἔστιν εἰπεῖν **Μt**: καὶ μετὰ τοῦ ὡ͞ς ἐπιρρήματος πάλιν παροξύνεται· 'καὶ ἔστιν εἰπεῖν' 'ὡς ἔστιν εἰπεῖν' **δ**: καὶ (deest in **Δ**) ὡ͞ς παροξύνεται (παροξύνεται deest in **Α₂**)· καὶ ἔστιν ἰδεῖν· ὡς ἔστιν εἰπεῖν **τξ**: καὶ μετὰ τοῦ ως ἐπιρρήματος· ὡς ἔστιν εἰπεῖν· καὶ μετὰ τοῦ ἀλλά· ἀλλ' ἔστι· καὶ μετὰ τοῦ τοῦτο τοῦτ' ἔστι· καὶ μετάγεται εἰς ἐπίρρημα τουτέστι· καὶ μετὰ τοῦ κ͞αι· καὶ ἔστι· καὶ μετὰ τοῦ οὐκ· οὐκ ἔστι **Ald.₁**: καὶ ὡ͞ς· ὡς ἔστιν εἰπεῖν v
y καὶ τὸ *ΕΣΤΟΝ* δυϊκὸν ἐγκλίνεται — καὶ τὰ πληθυντικὰ deest in τ
z καὶ τὸ ἐστόν δυϊκὸν ἐγκλίνεται **Μ**: καὶ τὸ δυϊκὸν δὲ ἐστόν ἐγκλίνεται **Ald.₂**: καὶ τὸ ἐστὸν ἐγκλίνεται **C**: καὶ τὸ ἐστὸν ἐγκλίνεται v: καὶ ἐστόν δυϊκὸν ἐγκλίνεται **σ**: ὁμοίως καὶ τὰ δυϊκὰ **ξ**

§d And among the verbs, *ΦHMI* and *'EIMI* are enclitics, as in πεζὸς δ' ἔνδεκά
φημι,[18] τόσσον ἐγώ φημι.[19] But the second person [singular] of this one [i.e.
ΦHMI], I mean *ΦHIΣ*, is not enclitic. The third person, *ΦHΣI*, is enclitic, as in
ἄνθρωπός φησιν,[20] and their plurals sometimes throw their accent back too, as in
ἐκεῖνό φαμεν or [ἐκεῖνό] φατε or [ἐκεῖνό] φασιν.[21] And likewise *'EIMI*, as in
ἄνθρωπός εἰμι,[22] αἵματός εἰς ἀγαθοῖο,[23] ἄνθρωπός ἐστιν.[24] And this word, *'EΣTIN*,
is barytone at the beginnings of clauses,[25] as in ἔστι πόλις 'Εφύρη,[26] and with the
negation *'OY*, as in οὐκ ἔστιν πόλις,[27] and with the conjunction *KAI*, as in καὶ
ἔστιν πόλις,[28] and with the adverb *'ΩΣ*, as in ὡς ἔστιν εἰπεῖν.[29] And the dual

[18] *Il.* 9.329 'and on foot I say [I have sacked] eleven [cities].'
[19] *Il.* 2.129: 'by so much I say'.
[20] 'A person says'.
[21] 'We say that'; 'you [pl.] say [that]'; 'they say [that]'.
[22] 'I am a person'.
[23] *Od.* 4.611: 'You are of good lineage'.
[24] 'He/she is a person'.
[25] Here and in similar contexts, we take λόγος to mean roughly 'clause'; see also section 3.1.
[26] *Il.* 6.152: 'There is a city, Ephurē'.
[27] 'There is no city'.
[28] 'And there is a city'.
[29] 'As it is possible to say'.

ΈΣΤΟΝ δυϊκὸν ἐγκλίνεται· 'οἴ^{aa bb} μοι σκυζομένῳ περ Ἀχαιῶν φίλτατοί ἐστον' καὶ^{cc} τὰ πληθυντικά· 'ἄνθρωποί^{dd} ἐσμεν', 'ἄνθρωποί ἐστε', 'ἄνθρωποί^{ee} εἰσιν' καὶ^{ff} τὸ ΈΣΣΙ δεύτερον ἐγκλίνεται· 'σχέτλιός^{gg} ἐσσι γεραιέ'.^{hh}

---

^{aa} οἴ μοι σκυζομένῳ — ἄνθρωποί ἐσμεν ἄνθρωποί ἐστε ἄνθρωποί εἰσιν deest in υ

^{bb} οἴ μοι (scripsi: οἴμοι **Ald.₂**) σκυζομένῳ περ (παρ' **C**) Ἀχαιῶν φίλτατοί ἐστον **δ**: καλώ ἐστον **Ald.₁**: ἀνθρώπω ἐστόν **t**: deest in **Μξ**

^{cc} καὶ τὰ πληθυντικὰ **Μδσ**: καὶ τὰ πληθυντικὰ ἐγκλίνονται **ξ**

^{dd} ἄνθρωποί ἐσμεν (ἄνθρωποίδαμεν **C**), ἄνθρωποί ἐστε **Μδ**: ἄνθρωποί ἐσμεν ἐστε **τ**: ἄνθρωποί ἐστε σ: deest in **ξ**

^{ee} ἄνθρωποί εἰσιν **ΜCσ**: οὗτοί εἰσὶ (sic) **Ald.₂**: εἰσι αἴτιοί εἰσι **Τ₁**: εἰσι **Α₂**: deest in **ξ**

^{ff} καὶ τὸ (τὸ deest in **Ald.₂**) ΈΣΣΙ (ἐσσὲ **C**) δεύτερον ἐγκλίνεται (post ἐγκλίνεται verba καθότι τῶν εἰς μι ἐστιν habet **C**) **δφ**: καὶ τὸ ἐσσὶ δεύτερον ἐνικὸν ἐγκλίνεται **ξ**: deest in **Μσ**

^{gg} σχέτλιός ἐσσι γεραιέ **Ald.₂ ξ**: σχέτλιός ἐσσι φίλος **τ**. σχέτλιός ἐσσι υ: deest in **ΜCσ**

^{hh} post γεραιέ verba τὸ γὰρ εἶ ἄνθρωπος εἶ· ἀγαθός εἶ οὐκ ἐγκλίνεται καθότι οὐ τῶν εἰς μι ἐστί habent **Ald.₂**

᾿ΕΣΤΟΝ is enclitic: οἵ μοι σκυζομένῳ περ Ἀχαιῶν <u>φίλτατοί ἐστον</u>.[30] And like-wise the plurals, as in <u>ἄνθρωποί ἐσμεν, ἄνθρωποί ἐστε, ἄνθρωποί εἰσιν</u>.[31] And the second person ᾿ΕΣΣΙ is enclitic: <u>σχέτλιός ἐσσι γεραιέ</u>.[32]

---

[30] *Il.* 9.198: 'Who are the dearest of the Acheans to me, angry though I am'.
[31] 'We are people'; 'you [pl.] are people'; 'they are people'.
[32] *Il.* 10.164: 'you're unstoppable, old man'.

§e τῶν[a] [b] δὲ ἀντωνυμιῶν αἱ[c] μὲν κτητικαὶ οὐδέποτε ἐγκλίνονται, ἀλλ᾿[d] οὐδὲ αἱ[e] εὐθεῖαι τῶν[f] πρωτοτύπων. αἱ[g] [h] δὲ τῶν πρωτοτύπων πτώσεις, χωρὶς[i] τῆς κλητικῆς ἐγκλίνονται·[j] γενική,[k] [l] δοτική, αἰτιατική. ἀλλ᾿[m] αἱ μὲν τοῦ πρώτου[n] προσώπου ἐγκλινόμεναι καὶ τὸ[o] κατ᾿ ἀρχὴν Ε ἀποβάλλουσιν· ‘ἤκουσάς[p] μου’, ‘ἔδωκάς μοι’, ‘ὕβρισάς με’. αἱ[q] [r] [s] δὲ τοῦ δευτέρου καὶ τρίτου προσώπου μονοσύλλαβοι[t] οὖσαι οὐδεμίαν στοιχείου ποιοῦνται[u] ἀποβολήν· ‘ἤκουσά σου’, ‘ἔδωκά σοι’, ‘ἐδίδαξά σε’,[v] ‘καί[w] οἱ ἐπευχόμενος’, ‘καί[x] ἑ νέον πολέεσσιν’, ‘καί μιν[y] φωνήσας’.

§e
[a] τῶν δὲ ἀντωνυμιῶν — εὐθεῖαι τῶν πρωτοτύπων deest in σ
[b] τῶν δὲ ἀντωνυμιῶν **jfξ**: τῶν ἀντωνυμιῶν **Ald.₂**: αἱ τῶν ἀντωνυμιῶν **C**: ἐν δὲ ἀντωνυμίαις **υRₐ**: ἀντωνυμίαι **Q**
[c] αἱ μὲν κτητικαὶ **Πδfξ**: αἱ μὲν κλητικαὶ (κλητικαὶ manu secunda, κλιτικαὶ manu prima) **M**: αἱ κτητικαὶ **QυRₐ**
[d] ἀλλ᾿ οὐδὲ **MCφξ**: ἀλλ᾿ οὐδέποτε **Ald.₂**: οὔτε **Π**: deest in **Q**
[e] αἱ εὐθεῖαι **jδυA₂ξ**: εὐθεῖαι **τ**: deest in **Q**
[f] τῶν πρωτοτύπων **jδυξ**: τῶν πρωτοτύπων καὶ κλητικαὶ **τ**: deest in **Q**
[g] αἱ δὲ τῶν πρωτοτύπων πτώσεις — τοῦ πρώτου προσώπου ἐγκλινόμεναι] αἱ ἀντωνυμίαι τοῦ πρώτου προσώπου ἐγκλινόμεναι σ
[h] αἱ (οἱ **C**) δὲ τῶν πρωτοτύπων πτώσεις **jδ**: ἀλλ᾿ αἱ πρωτότυποι **Q**: αἱ δὲ τῶν παραγώγων πλάγιαι **υ**: αἱ ἄλλαι δὲ πτώσεις **τ**: αἱ δὲ τῶν παραγώγων πτώσεις **ξ**: de σ vide §e, notam g
[i] χωρὶς τῆς κλητικῆς (κλιτικῆς **M**) **jδξ**: deest in **Qφ**
[j] ἐγκλίνονται **jδυξ**: deest in **Qτ**
[k] γενική — usque ad finem §h deest in **Π**
[l] γενική, δοτική, αἰτιατική **MC**: γενικαὶ δοτικαὶ αἰτιατικαὶ **Ald.₂**: ἡ γενικὴ καὶ δοτικὴ καὶ αἰτιατικὴ **ξ**: deest in **Qφ**
[m] ἀλλ᾿ αἱ μὲν τοῦ πρώτου προσώπου ἐγκλινόμεναι deest in **Qφ**
[n] πρώτου **MC**: πρωτοτύπου **ξ**: προτοτύπου **Ald.₂**
[o] καὶ τὸ κατ᾿ ἀρχὴν (ἀρχὰς **C**) Ε ἀποβάλλουσιν **Mδσξ**: καὶ αἱ ἔχουσαι τὸ ε ἀποβάλλουσιν **υ**: χωρὶς τοῦ ε **τ**: deest in **Q**
[p] ἤκουσάς μου, ἔδωκάς μοι, ὕβρισάς με **Mσ**: ἔδωκάς μοι· ἤκουσάς μου· ὕβρισάς με (ἤκουσάς μου· ὕβρισάς με **C**: ὕβρισάς με· ἤκουσάς μου **Ald.₂**) **δ**: ἤκουσάς μου· ἔδωκάς μοι· ἐδίδαξέ με **ξ**: ἤκουσάς μου· ἔδωκάς μοι· ἔτυψάς με· ἤκουσά σου· ἔδωκά σοι· ἔτυψά (ὕβρισά **T₂**) σε **υ**: ἤκουσάς μου· ἔδωκάς μοι· ἐδίδαξάς με· ἤκουσά (ἤκουσά deest in **A₂**) σου· ἔδωκά (ἔδωκά deest in **A₂**) σοι· ἐδίδαξά (ἐδίδαξά **Rₐ**: ὕβρισά **T₁**: deest in **A₂**) σε (**T₁ᵖ·ᶜ·**: με **T₁ᵃ·ᶜ·**) **τ**: οἷον ἤκουσάς μου· ἄνθρωπός μου· ταῦτα δὲ οὐκ ἔχουσιν ἐν συνεχείᾳ δύο ὀξείας, ὡς ἐλέγομεν ἄνω· μέσον γὰρ βαρεῖα κεῖται εἰς τὸ κου· καὶ εἰς τὸ θρω· τοῦ ἄνθρωπος κατὰ τοὺς παλαιοὺς **Q**
[q] αἱ δὲ τοῦ δευτέρου — καί σφῶιν δὸς ἄγειν (§f) deest in **Q**
[r] αἱ δὲ τοῦ δευτέρου — καί μιν φωνήσας deest in **υRₐ**
[s] αἱ δὲ τοῦ δευτέρου — ἐδίδαξά σε deest in **f**
[t] μονοσύλλαβοι οὖσαι **Cξ**: μονοσύλλαβαι (sic) οὖσαι **Ald.₂**: μονοσύλλαβοι **M**: deest in σ
[u] ποιοῦνται ἀποβολὴν **Mδσ**: ἀποβολὴν ποιοῦσιν **ξ**: ἀποβολήν ποιοῦνται **z**
[v] σε **M Ald.₂ ξ**: σοι **t**
[w] καί οἱ ἐπευχόμενος **δξ**: ἔτι καὶ οἱ ἐπευχόμενος **τ**: καὶ οἱ ἐπευχόμενοι **M**: ὕβρισά σε καί οἱ ἐπευχόμενοι θωρῆξαι ἐκέλευε σ
[x] καί ἑ νέον πολέεσσιν scripsi cum Apollonio Rhodio: καὶ ἑ νέον ἐν (ἐν om. λ) πόλεσι **ξ**: καὶ νεοπόλεσσι (νεοπόλεσι a.c.) **M**: καί ἑ νέον πόλεσσι **C**: καί ἑ νέον **τ**: deest in **Ald.₂ σ**
[y] μιν **δστξ**: μην (sic) **M**

§e Among the pronouns, the possessive ones are never enclitic, nor are the nominatives of underived pronouns [i.e. personal pronouns]. But the [oblique] case forms of the underived pronouns, with the exception of the vocative, are enclitic, that is the genitive, dative, and accusative. But when the pronouns of the first person are enclitic, they also drop their initial *E*, as in ἤκουσάς μου, ἔδωκάς μοι, ὕβρισάς με.[33] But the pronouns of the second and third person being monosyllabic, do not drop any letter: ἤκουσά σου, ἔδωκά σοι, ἐδίδαξά σε,[34] καί οἱ ἐπευχόμενος,[35] καί ἑ νέον πολέεσσιν,[36] καί μιν φωνήσας.[37]

---

[33] 'You heard me'; 'you gave to me'; 'you mistreated me'.
[34] 'I heard you'; 'I gave to you'; 'I taught you'.
[35] *Il.* 16.829 and *Il.* 21.121: 'And gloating over him'.
[36] Apollonius Rhodius, *Argonautica* 1.273: 'and [she continuously maltreats] her afresh with many [insults]'.
[37] E.g. *Il.* 1.201: 'and speaking [he addressed winged words to] her'.

§f αἱᵃ δυϊκαὶ τοῦᵇ πρώτου καὶ δευτέρου προσώπου οὐδέποτεᶜ ἐγκλίνονται διὰᵈ τὴν βαρεῖανᵉ τάσιν·ᶠ 'νῶϊ,ᵍ 'νῶϊν', 'σφῶϊ,ʰ 'σφῶϊν'· προπερισπῶνταιⁱ γάρ. αὖ δὲ τοῦ τρίτου ὀξυνόμεναι ἐγκλίνονται·ᵏ 'τίςˡ τάρ σφωε θεῶν', 'καί σφωῖν δὸς ἄγειν'. καὶᵐ αἱ πληθυντικαὶ τοῦⁿ τε πρώτου καὶ δευτέρου, 'ἡμῶν', 'ὑμῶν', 'ἡμῖν', 'ὑμῖν', 'ἡμᾶς', 'ὑμᾶς', τετράχρονοι οὖσαι, ἐπειδὰν ἐγκλίνωνται τὴν πρώτην συλλαβὴν ὀξύνουσιν· 'ἤκουσενᵒ ἥμων λαλούντων', 'ἔδωκενᵖ ἥμιν' καὶᑫ ʳ ἐπὶ τῶν λοιπῶν ὁμοίως. ἀδύνατονˢ γὰρ ὑπερβῆναι τοὺς τέσσαρας χρόνους τὴν ὀξεῖαν. καὶᵗ ᵘ ᵛ αἱ τοῦ τρίτου πληθυντικαὶ ὀξύνονται ⟨ἢ περισπῶνται⟩,ʷ ΣΦΩΝ,ˣ ΣΦΙΝ, ΣΦΑΣ, 'καί σφων', 'καί σφιν', 'καί σφας'· κἂνʸ διαιρεθῶσι· 'καί σφεας φωνήσας'· 'τῶ σφεων πολέες κακόν'· ἡ ΣΦΙΣΙΝ ἐπεκταθεῖσα, 'δίχα δέ σφισιν ἤνδανε βουλή'· καὶᶻ εὔλογόν γεᵃᵃ οἶμαι λέγειν, ὅτι μετὰ τὴν ἔγκλισιν τὸ πάθος ἐπηκολούθησεν, ἵναᵇᵇ μὴ βαρύτονοι οὖσαι ἐγκλίνωνται.

§f
ᵃ αἱ δυϊκαὶ **M Ald.₂ σξ**: αἱ δὲ δυϊκαὶ **Cτ**: τὰ δυϊκὰ **υ**
ᵇ τοῦ πρώτου καὶ δευτέρου προσώπου **Mδσυ**: τοῦ α΄ καὶ β΄ **τ**: τοῦ πρωτοτύπου τοῦ πρώτου καὶ δευτέρου προσώπου **ξ**
ᶜ οὐδέποτε **Mδξ**: οὐκ **σφ**
ᵈ διὰ τὴν βαρεῖαν τάσιν· νῶϊ, νῶϊν, σφῶϊ, σφῶϊν· προπερισπῶνται γάρ deest in **φ**
ᵉ βαρεῖαν **Mδσ**: βραχεῖαν **ξ**
ᶠ τάσιν] στάσιν **z**
ᵍ νῶϊ νῶῖν **σ**: νῶϊν **ξ**: νῶῖ **M**: νῶῖ σφῶῖ **Ald.₂**: σφῶϊ **C**
ʰ σφῶῖ σφῶῖν **Mσ**: νῶῖν σφῶῖν **δ**: σφῶῖν **ξ**
ⁱ προπερισπῶνται **Mδσ**: περισπῶνται **ξ**
ʲ αἱ δὲ τοῦ τρίτου ὀξυνόμεναι **M Ald.₂ σξ**: αἱ δὲ τοῦ τρίτου ὀξύνονται **C**: τὰ τοῦ τρίτου δὲ **υRₐ**: τοῦ δὲ τρίτου **f**
ᵏ ἐγκλίνονται **Mtξ**: ἀεὶ ἐγκλίνονται **Ald.₂**: ἐκλίνονται **Ald.₁**: σφῶε καὶ σφῶϊν ἀεὶ ἐγκλίνονται **C**: deest in **φ**
ˡ τίς τάρ **Ald.₂**: τίς τ΄ ἄρ **σξ**: τίς τάρ **φ**: τίς γάρ **MC**
ᵐ καὶ αἱ πληθυντικαὶ **M**: καὶ αἱ πληθυντικαὶ δὲ **δ**: καὶ τὰ πληθυντικὰ **συξ**: καὶ ἐπὶ τῶν πληθυντικῶν ὁμοίως **τ**: deest in **Q**
ⁿ τοῦ τε πρώτου (πρώτου **M Ald.₂**: πρώτου προσώπου **ξ**) καὶ δευτέρου· ἡμῶν, ὑμῶν, ἡμῖν, ὑμῖν, ἡμᾶς (ὑμᾶς **Ald.₂**), ὑμᾶς τετράχρονοι (post τετράχρονοι add. δὲ **Ald.₂**) οὖσαι, ἐπειδὰν (ἐπείδ΄ ἂν **Ald.₂**) ἐγκλίνωνται (ἐγκλίνονται **C**: ἐγκλίν.νται littera obfuscata **M**) τὴν πρώτην συλλαβὴν ὀξύνουσιν **Mδξ**: τοῦ α΄ καὶ β΄ προσώπου ἐγκλίνονται **υ**: ἐπεὶ ἐγκλίνονται τὴν πρώτην συλλαβὴν ὀξύνουσιν **σ**: τὸ δὲ ἡμῶν· ὑμῶν· ἡμῖν ὑμῖν· ἡμᾶς· ὑμᾶς, ἐπειδὰν ἐγκλίνωνται, τὴν πρώτην συλλαβὴν ὀξύνουσιν **Q**: deest in **τ**
ᵒ ἤκουσεν ἥμων λαλούντων **MQ**: ἤκουσας ἥμων λαλούντων **σ**: ἤκουσεν ἥμων (ἡμῶν **C**) **δυξ**: ἤκουσας ἥμων· ἀπήλαυσεν (ἀπήλαυσα **T₁**) ὕμων **τ**
ᵖ ἔδωκεν ἥμιν **Mδ Quξ**: ἔδωκας ἥμιν ὕμιν ἔτυψας ἥμας ὕμας **τ**: ἔδωκας ἥμιν **σ**
ᑫ καὶ ἐπὶ τῶν λοιπῶν ὁμοίως — τέσσαρας χρόνους τὴν ὀξεῖαν deest in **συ**
ʳ καὶ ἐπὶ τῶν λοιπῶν ὁμοίως **Mδ**: καὶ ἐπὶ τῶν λοιπῶν οὕτως **ξ**: deest in **Qτ**
ˢ ἀδύνατον γὰρ ὑπερβῆναι τοὺς τέσσαρας χρόνους τὴν ὀξεῖαν **Mδξ**: ἐπὶ τῆς παραληγούσης οὐ προπαραληγούσης· ἀδύνατον γὰρ ὑπερβῆναι τὴν ὀξεῖαν τοὺς δ χρόνους **τ**: οὐ δύνανται γὰρ ὑπερβῆναι τοὺς δίχρονᵒ τὴν ὀξεῖαν **Q**
ᵗ καὶ αἱ τοῦ τρίτου πληθυντικαὶ — ταῦτα καὶ περὶ ἀντωνυμιῶν (§h) deest in **Q**
ᵘ καὶ αἱ τοῦ τρίτου πληθυντικαὶ — ἐγκλίνεται δὲ ἀεὶ καὶ ἡ ΜΙΝ (§g) deest in **τ**
ᵛ καὶ αἱ τοῦ τρίτου πληθυντικαὶ ὀξύνονται **Mσ**: καὶ αἱ τοῦ τρίτου πληθυντικαὶ ἐγκλίνονται **δ**: καὶ αἱ τοῦ τρίτου προσώπου πληθυντικαὶ ὀξυνόμεναι ἐγκλίνονται **ξ**: καὶ τὰ πληθυντικὰ τοῦ γ **υ**
ʷ ⟨ἢ περισπῶνται⟩ scripsimus
ˣ ΣΦΩΝ, ΣΦΙΝ (σφίν **MGυ**: σφῖν **Ald.₂ Ald.₁**: σφέϊσι sic **G.ᵧ**: σφῖσι **p**), ΣΦΑΣ, καί σφων, καί σφιν, καί σφας (καί σφας καί σφας κακοὺς κάκιστα **C**) **Mδσυ**: καί σφων· καί σφιν· καί σφας **ξ**
ʸ κἂν διαιρεθῶσι (διαιρεθῶ **C**)· καί σφεας φωνήσας· τῶ σφεων πολέες κακόν (πολέες κακόν scripsi e Od. 3.134: πόλεσι καὶ **C**: πολέεσκε **Ald.₂**) ἡ ΣΦΙΣΙΝ (ἡ ΣΦΙΣΙΝ **C**: ἧς φησιν **Ald.₂**) ἐπεκταθεῖσα (ἐπεκτανθεῖσα **C**), δίχα δέ σφισιν (σφίσιν ο Il. 18.510 et Od. 3.150 scripsi: σφίν **Ald.₂**: φησιν **C**) ἤνδανε βουλή· καὶ εὔλογόν (per coniecturam) **δ**: καὶ εὔλογόν **Μσξ**
ᶻ καὶ εὔλογόν γε οἶμαι λέγειν — ἔλαβέν αὐτον (§g) deest in **υ**
ᵃᵃ γε **MR**: τε **δF**: deest in **σ**
ᵇᵇ ἵνα μὴ βαρύτονοι οὖσαι ἐγκλίνωνται (ἐγκλίνονται **F**) **δξ**: ἵνα βαρύτονοι οὖσαι ἐγκλίνωνται **M**: deest in **σ**

§f The duals of the first and second person, νῶϊ, νῶϊν, σφῶϊ, and σφῶϊν, are never enclitic because of their barytone accentuation, for they are properispomenon. But those of the third person, which are oxytone, are enclitic, as in τίς τάρ σφωε θεῶν[38] and καί σφωϊν δὸς ἄγειν.[39] And the plural pronouns of the first and second [person], ἡμῶν, ὑμῶν, ἡμῖν, ὑμῖν, ἡμᾶς, ὑμᾶς, since they contain four units of time, give their first syllables an acute accent when they throw back their accents, as in ἤκουσεν ἥμων λαλούντων, ἔδωκεν ἥμιν,[40] and similarly for the others. For it is impossible for the acute accent to go further back than four units of time. And those of the third person plural, ΣΦΩΝ, ΣΦΙΝ, ΣΦΑΣ, are oxytone or perispomenon [i.e. they have an acute or circumflex as their natural accent, and so can be enclitic], as in καί σφων, καί σφιν, καί σφας.[41] And with diaeresis as in καί σφεας φωνήσας[42] and τῶ σφεων πολέες κακόν,[43] and the extended form ΣΦΙΣΙΝ as in δίχα δέ σφισιν ἥνδανε βουλή.[44] And I think it is reasonable to say that the modification took place after the throwing back of the accent, so that they do not throw their accent back while they are barytone.[45]

---

[38] *Il.* 1.8: 'Who of the gods, then, [threw] the two of them [together to quarrel with strife]?'.
[39] *Il.* 1.338: 'and give her to them to take away'.
[40] 'He/she heard us talking'; 'he/she gave to us'.
[41] 'And of them'; 'and to them'; 'and them'.
[42] E.g. *Il.* 4.284 'and speaking [he addressed winged words] to them'.
[43] *Od.* 3.134: 'For that reason many of them [met] an awful [fate]'.
[44] *Il.* 18.510, *Od.* 3.150: 'and opposing plans met with approval among them'.
[45] The idea here is that the disyllabic forms ΣΦΕΑΣ, ΣΦΕΩΝ, and ΣΦΙΣΙΝ (which are accented on the first syllable when not enclitic) are only apparent exceptions to the principle that only 'naturally' oxytone and perispomenon words can be enclitic. The basic forms with their 'natural accents' are considered to be monosyllabic σφᾶς, σφῶν, and σφίν, and these can give rise to σφεας, σφεων, and σφισιν via two ordered rules: (i) the throwing back of the accent (giving σφᾶς, σφων, σφιν), and (ii) the division of one syllable into two (giving σφεας, σφεων, σφισιν). For the meaning, see *Et. Gud.* 292.25–35 Sturz.

§g τῶνᵃ ᵇ καλουμένων μονοπροσώπων μόνηꟲ ἡ αἰτιατικὴ *ΑΥΤΟΝ*ᵈ ἐγκλίνεται, 'ἔλαβένᵉ αὐτον'. ἐγκλίνεταιᶠ δὲ ἀεὶ καὶ ἡ *ΜΙΝ·* 'καᵍ μιν φωνήσας'· καὶʰ ἡ *ΕΘΕΝ* παραλόγωςⁱ διότιʲ παράγωγος καὶ βαρύτονος.ᵏ

§g
ᵃ τῶν καλουμένων μονοπροσώπων — ταῦτα καὶ περὶ ἀντωνυμιῶν (§h) deest in σ
ᵇ τῶν **MCξ**: τῶν δὲ **Ald.₂**
ꟲ μόνη **δξ**: deest in **M**
ᵈ *ΑΥΤΟΝ* ἐγκλίνεται **Ald.₂**: τῆς αὐτὸς ἐγκλίνεται **C**: deest in **Mξ**
ᵉ ἔλαβέν αὐτον **Mξ**: κόψε (κόψαι **Ald.₂**) γάρ αὐτον ἔχοντα **δ**
ᶠ ἐγκλίνεται δὲ ἀεὶ (δὲ ἀεὶ deest in **C**) καὶ ἡ μίν (μῆν **M**) **MCξ**: ἔτι καὶ ἡ μίν υ: ἐγκλίνεται δὲ ἡμῖν (sic) ἀεί **Ald.₂**
ᵍ καί μιν φωνήσας **Cυξ**: καί μην φωνήσας **M**: καί μιν φονήσας (sic) **Ald.₂**: ἔτι καί μιν φωνήσας· ἔτι ἀλλά οἱ αὐτῷ (αὐτῶ **T₁**) ζεὺς (ζεύς **A₂**) δοίη τ
ʰ καὶ ἡ *ΕΘΕΝ* παραλόγως — ταῦτα καὶ περὶ ἀντωνυμιῶν (§h) deest in τ, sed verba αἱ μὲν ἐγκλινόμεναι ἀντωνυμίαι ὀρθοτονούμεναι μὲν ἀντιδιαστολήν ἔχουσιν ἑτέρου προσώπου· ἐμοὶ ἔδωκας οὐκ ἄλλῳ δηλονότι· ἐμοῦ ἤκουσας οὐκ ἄλλου· ἐμὲ ὕβρισας οὐκ ἄλλον· ἐγκλινόμεναι δὲ ἀπόλυτα πρόσωπα δηλοῦσι· ἤκουσά σου· ἔδωκά σοι· ἔτυψά σε in fine tractatus leguntur in **T₁**
ⁱ παραλόγως **Μδ**: παράλογος **υξ**
ʲ διότι παράγωγος καὶ βαρύτονος **δξ**: δι' ὅτι παράγωγον καὶ βαρύτονον **M**: deest in υ
ᵏ post βαρύτονος verba ἐπεὶ (ἐπειδὴ **C**) οὗ ἔθεν ἐστὶ χερείων praebet **δ**

§g And among the pronouns called μονοπρόσωποι [i.e. referring to one person only, without corresponding forms for other persons], only the accusative *ΑΥΤΟΝ* is an enclitic, as in ἔλαβέν αὐτον.[46] And *MIN* too is always an enclitic, as in καί μιν φωνήσας.[47] And *ΕΘΕΝ* is an enclitic irregularly, because it is a derivative and barytone.

---

[46] 'He/she grasped him'.
[47] E.g. *Il.* 1.201: 'and speaking [he addressed winged words to] her'.

§h αἷ[a] μὲν οὖν ἐγκλινόμεναι τῶν ἀντωνυμιῶν εἰσὶν[b] αὗται, αἵτινες[c] ὀρθοτονούμεναι
μὲν ἀντιδιαστολὴν ἔχουσιν ἑτέρου προσώπου· 'ἐμοί[d] ἔδωκας οὐκ ἄλλῳ', 'ἐμοῦ
ἤκουσας οὐκ ἄλλου', 'ἐμὲ[e] ὕβρισας οὐκ ἄλλον'·[f] ἐγκλινόμεναι δὲ ἀπόλυτα[g] δηλοῦσιν
πρόσωπα· 'ἔδωκά[h] σοι', 'ἤκουσά σου'. καὶ ἡ μὲν γενικωτάτη αἰτία τῆς ὀρθῆς τάσεως
ἡ ἀντιδιαστολὴ τοῦ προσώπου, αὕτη[i] δὲ διαιρεῖται εἰς πλείονα εἴδη. αἵ[j] τε γὰρ
συμπεπλεγμέναι ἢ διεζευγμέναι ὀρθοτονοῦνται· 'καὶ[k] ἐμοὶ καὶ Ἀπολλωνίῳ', 'ἢ ἐμοὶ
ἢ Ἀπολλωνίῳ'· καὶ[l] αἱ μετὰ τοῦ ΕΝΕΚΑ συνδέσμου· 'ἕνεκα σοῦ', 'ἕνεκα ἐμοῦ. καὶ
αἱ μετὰ προθέσεως δὲ ὀρθοτονοῦνται, 'διὰ σέ', 'περὶ σοῦ', 'κατ' ἐμέ', 'ἐπὶ σοί'. αἱ[m] μετὰ
τῆς ἐπιταγματικῆς ἀντωνυμίας τῆς[n] ΑΥΤΟΣ ἀεὶ ὀρθοτονοῦνται· 'αὐτὸν[o] ἐμέ',
'ἐμοὶ αὐτῷ'. ὑπεξαιρείσθωσαν[p] νῦν[q] αἵ[r] παρὰ τοῖς ποιηταῖς μετὰ τῆς ἐπιταγματικῆς
παραλόγως ἐγκλινόμεναι· 'ἀλλά[s] οἱ αὐτῷ Ζεὺς ὀλέσειε βίην' καὶ[t] 'Εὐρύαλος δέ ἑ
αὐτόν'. καὶ[u] τινες ἄλλαι μετὰ προθέσεων[v] ἢ συνδέσμων ἐνεκλίθησαν[w] παραλόγως.
αἱ κατ' ἀρχὴν τιθέμεναι κἂν μὴ ἔχωσιν ἀντιδιαστολὴν διὰ[x] τὸν ἀρκτικὸν τόπον
ὀρθοτονοῦνται· 'ἐμὲ δ' ἔγνω καὶ προσέειπε'. ταῦτα[y] καὶ περὶ ἀντωνυμιῶν.

§h
[a] αἱ μὲν οὖν ἐγκλινόμεναι τῶν ἀντωνυμιῶν **Μδυξ**: αἱ (ἔτι αἱ **R**ₐ) μὲν ἐγκλινόμεναι ἀντωνυμίαι τ (de
T₁ vide etiam §g, notam h)
[b] εἰσὶν αὗται **Μδυ**: αὗταί εἰσιν **ξ**
[c] αἵτινες ὀρθοτονούμεναι **Μδυξ**: ὀρθοτονούμεναι τ (de **T**₁ vide etiam §g, notam h)
[d] ἐμοὶ ἔδωκας οὐκ ἄλλῳ, ἐμοῦ ἤκουσας οὐκ ἄλλου **Μδ**: ἐμοί ἤκουσας οὐκ ἄλλου, ἐμοί ἔδωκας οὐκ
ἄλλῳ **ξ**: ἐμοί ἔδωκας καὶ οὐκ ἄλλῳ ἐμοί ἤκουσας καὶ οὐκ ἄλλου **υ**: ἐμοὶ ἔδωκας οὐκ ἄλλῳ δηλονότι
ἐμοῦ ἤκουσας οὐκ ἄλλου **T**₁ (de **T**₁ vide etiam §g, notam h): ἐμοῦ ἤκουσας καὶ οὐκ ἄλλου δηλαδή **R**ₐ
[e] ἐμὲ ὕβρισας οὐκ ἄλλον **ΜδT**₁ (de **T**₁ vide etiam §g, notam h): ἐμὲ ἐδίδαξας οὐκ ἄλλον **ξ**: deest in **υR**ₐ
[f] post ἄλλον habet ὑμῖν μὲν θεοὶ δοῖεν Ὀλύμπια δώματ' ἔχοντες ἐκπέρσαι (ἐκπέρσεν **C**) πριάμοιο
πόλιν· ἀντὶ διαστέλλεται γάρ· παῖδα δέ μοι λύσατε φίλην δ
[g] ἀπόλυτα δηλοῦσιν πρόσωπα **Μδ**: ἀπόλυτα πρόσωπα δηλοῦσιν **φξ** (de **T**₁ vide etiam §g, notam h)
[h] ἔδωκά σοι, ἤκουσά σου **Μδυ**: ἤκουσά σου, ἔδωκά σοι **ξ**: ἤκουσά σου· ἔδωκά σοι· ἔτυψά σε **T**₁ (de
T₁ vide etiam §g, notam h): ἔδωκά σοι **R**ₐ
[i] αὕτη δὲ **MC**υ**ξ**: καὶ **Ald.**₂
[j] αἵ τε γὰρ συμπεπλεγμέναι ἢ διεζευγμέναι ὀρθοτονοῦνται scripsi: αἵ τε γὰρ διεζευγμέναι
(διεζευγμένον **T**₂) ὀρθοτονοῦνται **Μυξ**: αἱ γὰρ συμπεπλεγμέναι ἢ διεζευγνύμεναι δ
[k] καὶ ἐμοὶ καὶ (καὶ deest in **T**₂) Ἀπολλωνίῳ· ἢ ἐμοὶ ἢ Ἀπολλωνίῳ υ**ξ**: καὶ ἐμοὶ καὶ Ἀπολλωνίῳ **MC**:
deest in **Ald.**₂
[l] καὶ αἱ (αἱ deest in υ**ξ**) μετὰ τοῦ ἕνεκα συνδέσμου· ἕνεκα σοῦ, ἕνεκα ἐμοῦ. καὶ αἱ μετὰ προθέσεως
δὲ (δὲ **M**: δὲ ἀεὶ **T**₂**R**: δὲ ἀεὶ **A**₁**F**) ὀρθοτονοῦνται, διὰ σέ, περὶ σοῦ, κατ' ἐμέ, ἐπὶ σοί **Μυξ**: ὁμοίως
καὶ μετὰ τοῦ ἕνεκα συνδέσμου ἀεὶ ὀρθοτονοῦνται διὰ σέ· περὶ σοῦ· κατ' ἐμέ **C**: διὰ σέ· περὶ σοῦ·
κατὰ μέ, ὀρθοτονοῦνται· αἱ μετὰ προθέσεως· ἕνεκα σοῦ· ἕνεκα ἐμοῦ ἀεὶ ὀρθοτονοῦνται **Ald.**₂
[m] αἱ μετὰ τῆς ἐπιταγματικῆς ἀντωνυμίας **Ald.**₂ υ**ξ**: αἱ μετὰ τῆς ταγματικῆς (sic) ἀντωνυμίας **M**:
καὶ μετὰ τῆς ἐπιταγματικῆς ἀντωνυμίας **C**
[n] τῆς αὐτὸς **Μδξ**: deest in υ
[o] αὐτὸν ἐμέ, ἐμοὶ αὐτῷ **M**: αὐτὸν ἐμέ· αὐτῷ ἐμοί **Ald.**₂ υ: αὐτὸν ἐμοί ἐμὲ αὐτῷ **C**: ἐμοί αὐτῷ· αὐτὸν ἐμέ υ
[p] ὑπεξαιρείσθωσαν δυ**ξ**: ὑπεξαιρήσθωσαν **Ald.**₂: ὑφαιξηρείσθωσαν **M**
[q] νῦν **Μδ**: δὲ υ**ξ**
[r] αἱ παρὰ τοῖς ποιηταῖς μετὰ τῆς ἐπιταγματικῆς παραλόγως ἐγκλινόμεναι **Μυξ**: αἱ παρὰ τοῖς
ποιηταῖς παραλόγως μετὰ τῆς ἐπιταγματικῆς ἐγκλινόμεναι **Ald.**₂: αἱ παρὰ τοῖς ποιηταῖς
παραλόγως μετὰ τοῦ ἐπιταγματικοῦ ἐγκλινομένου **C**
[s] ἀλλά οἱ αὐτῷ Ζεὺς ὀλέσειε βίην υ**ξ**: καί οἱ αὐτῷ Ζεὺς ὀλέσειε βίην **C**: καί οἱ αὐτὸν Ζεὺς ὀλέσειε
βίον (sic) **Ald.**₂: deest in **M**
[t] καὶ Εὐρύαλος δέ ἑ αὐτόν Schmidt (1860: 165) ex Homero: καὶ Εὐρύαλος δὲ αὐτόν **ξ**: καὶ Εὐρύαλος
δὲ (δὲ **T**₂: σε **A**₁) αὐτόν υ: Εὐρύαλος δέ ἑαυτόν **C**: deest in **M Ald.**₂
[u] καί τινες ἄλλαι υ**ξ**: εἰ καί τινες ἄλλαι δ: deest in **M**
[v] προθέσεων **ξ**: προθέσεως δυ: deest in **M**
[w] ἐνεκλίθησαν παραλόγως **Ald.**₂ υ: ἐνεγκλίθησαν παραλόγως **Cξ**: deest in **M**
[x] διὰ τὸν ἀρκτικὸν τόπον (τόπον **Ald.**₂: τὸ πᾶν **C**) ὀρθοτονοῦνται δ: διὰ τῶν ἀρκτικῶν τόπων
ὀρθοτονοῦνται υ**ξ**: διὰ τῶν ἀρκτικῶν τόνων ὀρθοτονοῦνται **M**
[y] ταῦτα καὶ (καὶ deest in **Ald.**₂) περὶ ἀντωνυμιῶν **Μδ**: deest in υ**ξ**

§h And those pronouns that are enclitic are those that convey a contrast with another person when orthotonic, as in ἐμοὶ ἔδωκας οὐκ ἄλλῳ, ἐμοῦ ἤκουσας οὐκ ἄλλου, ἐμὲ ὕβρισας οὐκ ἄλλον,[48] and when they are enclitic they convey persons in the absolute [i.e. non-contrastively], as in ἔδωκά σοι, ἤκουσά σου.[49] And the most general cause of orthotonic accentuation is the contrast of persons, but this is divided into several types. For pronouns that are conjoined or disjoined are orthotonic, as in καὶ ἐμοὶ καὶ Ἀπολλωνίῳ, ἢ ἐμοὶ ἢ Ἀπολλωνίῳ,[50] as are those with the conjunction *ENEKA*, as in ἕνεκα σοῦ, ἕνεκα ἐμοῦ.[51] And those with a preposition are orthotonic, e.g. διὰ σέ, περὶ σοῦ, κατ᾽ ἐμέ, ἐπὶ σοί.[52] And those with the subsidiary pronoun *ΑΥΤΟΣ* are always orthotonic, e.g. αὐτὸν ἐμέ, ἐμοὶ αὐτῷ.[53] One must make an exception for those that have a subsidiary pronoun and are irregularly enclitic in the poets: ἀλλά οἱ αὐτῷ | Ζεὺς ὀλέσειε βίην,[54] and Εὐρύαλος δέ ἑ αὐτόν.[55] And some others are irregularly enclitic with prepositions or conjunctions. Pronouns placed in initial position are orthotonic on account of the initial position, even if they do not convey a contrast, as in ἐμὲ δ᾽ ἔγνω καὶ προσέειπε.[56] So much for the pronouns.

---

[48] 'You gave to me, not to anyone else'; 'you heard me, not anyone else'; 'you mistreated me, not anyone else'.

[49] 'I gave to you, I heard you'.

[50] 'Both to me and to Apollonius'; 'either to me or to Apollonius'.

[51] 'On account of you'; 'on account of me'.

[52] 'Because of you'; 'concerning you'; 'after me [in pursuit]'; 'against you'.

[53] 'Me myself'; 'to me myself'.

[54] *Od.* 4.667–8: 'But may Zeus destroy his vigour'.

[55] *Od.* 8.396 (with the reading αὐτόν, rather than Bentley's conjecture αὐτός): 'and [let] Euryalus [appease] him'.

[56] *Od.* 11.91: 'and he recognized and addressed me'.

§i ἔν[a] δὲ ἐπιρρήμασιν ἐγκλίνεται τὰ ὑποκείμενα *ΠΩΣ*,[b] *ΠΗ*, *ΠΟΥ*,[c] [d] *ΠΟΤΕ, ΠΟΘΕΝ*,[e] *ΠΟΘΙ*· εἰ[f] [g] μὲν ὀρθοτονοῖντο βαρυνόμενα[h] πυσματικά[i] ἐστιν, εἰ[j] δὲ ἐγκλίνοιντο ἀόριστα. καὶ[k] [l] τὰ ὑποδείγματα δῆλα· 'πῶς[m] ἦλθεν', 'ἦλθέν[n] πως', 'πῆ[o] ἦλθεν', 'ἦλθέν πη', 'πόθεν[p] ἦλθες', 'ἦλθές ποθεν'. ταῦτα[q] [r] πυσματικὰ ὄντα[s] βαρύνεται, ἀόριστα[t] δὲ ὀξύνεται, καὶ[u] ἐν τῇ συντάξει ὑποτασσόμενα ἐγκλίνεται· 'ἦλθέν[v] ποθεν', 'αἴ[w] κέ ποθι Ζεύς', 'καί ποτέ τις εἴπῃσιν'.

§i
[a] ἐν δὲ (δὲ deest in *Π*) ἐπιρρήμασιν (τοῖς ἐπιρρήμασιν **συξ**) ἐγκλίνεται (ἐγκλίνονται *ΠC*) τὰ ὑποκείμενα **jδσυξ**: ἐγκλίνονται (γκλίνονται sic **T₁**) δὲ τὰ ἐπιρρήματα ταῦτα *τ*: ἐν δὲ τοῖς ἐπιρρήμασι **Q**
[b] *ΠΩΣ ΠΗ* **jδφξ**: πῶς (πώς sic **G**) *σ*: τὸ πῶς, τὸ πῆ **Q**
[c] *ΠΟΥ ΠΟΤΕ* — ἦλθέν ποθεν deest in **Q**
[d] *ΠΟΥ ΠΟΤΕ* **Cφξ**: ποῦ πόσε πότε *Π*: π̄ότ̄ε **M**: ποῦ **Ald.₂**: ποτέ *σ*
[e] *ΠΟΘΕΝ ΠΟΘΙ* **jδστξ**: πόθι· πόθεν **υ**
[f] εἰ μὲν ὀρθοτονοῖντο — ἐγκλίνοιντο ἀόριστα deest in *σ*
[g] εἰ μὲν ὀρθοτονοῖντο **M**: ἄπερ εἰ μὲν ὀρθοτονοῖτο **Ald.₂**: σπέρει μὲν ὀρθοτονοῖτο **C**: εἰ μὲν ὀρθοτονοῦνται *Πυξ*: ὀρθοτονούμενα (supra lineam **T₁**) *τ*
[h] βαρυνόμενα *Πδξ*: τὰ βαρυνόμενα **M**: βαρυνόμεναι **υ**: deest in *τ*
[i] πυσματικά ἐστιν *Πδξ*: πτυσματικά (sic) ἐστιν **M**: πυσματικαί εἰσιν **υ**: πυσματικὰ λέγονται (supra lineam **T₁**) *τ*
[j] εἰ δὲ ἐγκλίνοιντο ἀόριστα **jξ**: εἰ δὲ ἐγκλίνοιτο ἀόριστα **δ**: εἰ δὲ ἐγκλίνοιντο, ἀόρισται **υ**: ἐγκλινόμενα δὲ ἀόριστα (supra lineam **T₁**) *τ*
[k] καὶ τὰ ὑποδείγματα — usque ad finem §i deest in *Π*
[l] καὶ τὰ ὑποδείγματα δῆλα (δήλα **G**) **Mδσυξ**: deest in *τ*
[m] πῶς ἦλθεν **Mξ**: πῶς ἦλθες **δ Ald.₁ φ**: πῶς **t**
[n] ἦλθέν πως **Muξ**: ἦλθές πως *στ*: deest in **δ**
[o] πῆ ἦλθεν, ἦλθέν πη **Mφ**: πῆ ἔβη Ἀνδρομάχη **δ**: πῆ ἦλθες· ἦλθές πη *σξ*
[p] πόθεν ἦλθες, ἦλθές ποθεν **Mt**: πόθεν ἦλθες· ἦλθές ποθεν· πόθι ἦλθες· ἦλθές ποθι **Ald.₁**: πόθεν ἦλθες; πόθι τοι (τοι deest in **C**) πτόλις; πότε γράφεις; **δ**: πότε γράφεις γράφεις ποτέ πόθεν ἦλθες ἦλθές ποθεν πόθι τοι πτόλις (πόλις **A₁**) **υξ**: καὶ τἆλλα ἀορίστως· τὰ ἀνταποδοτικὰ τῶν πευστικῶν πότε· ποτέ· ἐάν ποτε· πόθεν ποθέν· ἐάν ποθεν· πόθι, ποθί (τὰ ἀνταποδοτικὰ τῶν πευστικῶν πότε· ποτε· ἐάν ποτε· πόθεν ποθέν· ἐάν ποθεν· πόθι, ποθί supra lineam **T₁**)· ἐάν ποθι (ἐάν ποθι **A₂**: αἴ κέν ποθι supra lineam **T₁**) *τ*
[q] ταῦτα πυσματικὰ — καί ποτέ τις εἴπῃσιν deest in *τ*
[r] ταῦτα πυσματικὰ **δσυξ**: ταῦτα τὰ πυσματικὰ **Gᵇ**: ταῦτα πτυσματικὰ (sic) **M**
[s] ὄντα βαρύνεται **Mδσ**: ὄντα βαρύνονται **υξ**
[t] ἀόριστα δὲ ὀξύνεται **Mδξ**: ἀόριστα δὲ ὀξύνονται **συ**
[u] καὶ ἐν τῇ συντάξει ὑποτασσόμενα ἐγκλίνεται **MC**: καὶ ἐν τῇ συντάξει ὑποτασσόμενα ἐγκλίνονται **συξ**: καὶ ἐγκλίνεται **Ald.₂**
[v] ἦλθέν ποθεν **Mδ**: ἦλθέ ποθι **υξ**: deest in *σ*
[w] αἴ κέ ποθι Ζεύς· καί ποτέ τις εἴπῃσιν **δυξ**: deest in **Mσ**

§i Among the adverbs, the following are enclitic: *ΠΩΣ, ΠΗ, ΠΟΥ, ΠΟΤΕ, ΠΟΘΕΝ, ΠΟΘΙ.* If they are orthotonic and barytone they are interrogative, while if they are enclitic they are indefinite. And the examples are clear: πῶς ἦλθεν, ἦλθέν πως, πῆ ἦλθεν, ἦλθέν πη, πόθεν ἦλθες, ἦλθές ποθεν.[57] When these are interrogative they are recessive, but when they are indefinite they are oxytone and throw their accents back when postposed in connected speech: ἦλθέν ποθεν,[58] αἴ κέ ποθι Ζεύς,[59] καί ποτέ τις εἴπῃσιν.[60]

---

[57] 'How did he/she come?'; 'he/she somehow came'; 'how did he/she come?'; 'he/she somehow came'; 'from where did you come?'; 'you came from somewhere'.
[58] 'He/she came from somewhere'.
[59] E.g. *Il.* 1.128: 'if ever Zeus'.
[60] E.g. *Il.* 6.459: 'and one day someone will say'.

§j ἔν[a] δὲ συνδέσμοις ἐγκλινόμενοί εἰσιν οἵδε· *ΤΕ*·[b] 'καί[c] τε χαλιφρονέοντα', *ΠΕΡ*·[d] 'ἀγαθός[e] περ ἐών', *ΤΟΙ*·[f] 'καί τοι', *ΓΕ*·[g] 'τοῦτό[h] γε',[i][j] *'ΡΑ*·[k] 'ὅς[l] ῥα νόθος', *ΘΗΝ*·[m] 'οὐ μέν θην κείνης γε χερείων εὔχομαι εἶναι', *ΚΕΝ*·[n] 'καί[o] κεν δή'. τόν[p][q][r][s][t] *'ΟΥΝ* παραπληρωματικὸν μετὰ τῆς *'ΟΥΚ*[u] ἀρνήσεως, ὅτε[v] ἀποφαντικῶς παραλαμβάνεται, ἐγκλίνουσιν· 'οὔκουν'.[w] περισπώμενος[x] γὰρ κατάφασιν σημαίνει συλλογιστικὸς ὢν ἢ ἐπιφορικός· 'οὐκοῦν'.[y] καί[z] τὸ *ΠΩΣ* δὲ καὶ τὸ *ΝΥΝ* ἐγκλινόμενα συνδέσμους εἶναί φασι.[aa]

---

§j

[a] ἐν δὲ συνδέσμοις ἐγκλινόμενοί εἰσιν jσ· ἐν δὲ συνδέσμοις οἱ ἐγκλινόμενοί εἰσιν **δυξ**· ἐγκλίνονται δὲ καὶ σύνδεσμοι τ· ἐν δὲ συνδέσμοις **Q**

[b] *ΤΕ* **jδσφξ**· ὁ τε **Q**

[c] καί τε χαλιφρονέοντα **Cυ** (post περ· τοι· γε in **υ**)· καί τε καλιφρονέοντα (sic) **Ald.₂**· καί τε χαλίνου (post *ΘΗΝ*) **T₁**· deest in jQσA₂R₄**ξ**

[d] *ΠΕΡ* **ΠCtυ**· περ νυ τ· ὁ περ **Q**· περ...καίπερ (post *ΘΗΝ*) **G Ald.₁**· καὶ περ **Mξ**· deest in **Ald.₂**

[e] ἀγαθός περ ἐών (post καί τε χαλιφρονέοντα in **Cυ**, post *ΘΗΝ* in **T₁**) **CυT₁**· deest in **j Ald.₂ QσA₂R₄ξ**

[f] *ΤΟΙ* καί τοι **δ**· καὶ τοι **M**· καίτοι et postea ὑπέρ τοι (ante τοῦτό γε) **T₁**· τοι...καίτοι (post γε θην καίπερ) **Ald.₁ G**· τοι (post νυ **A₂**· post γε **ξ**) **τυA₂ξ**· τοι (post κεν) *Π*· deest in **Q**

[g] *ΓΕ* **Mδσυξ**· ποι· γε **A₂**· ποι· καί γε **T₁**· γε (post τοι) *Π*· deest in **Q**

[h] τοῦτό γε (τοῦτό γε post καίτοι· καίγε σ· τοῦτό γε post ἀγαθός περ ἐών· ὑπέρ τοι **T₁**· τοῦτό γε post ἀγαθός περ ἐών **υ**· post τοι καίτοι **δ**· τοῦτό γε (τε **γ**) post θην **t**) **MδτυT₁**· deest in **QA₂ξ**

[i] post τοῦτό γε verba νυ μή νύ τοι οὐ χραίσμῃ leguntur in **δ**

[j] post τοῦτό γε verba οὔ θην οὔ νυ τοι· στέον (sic) ὅτε ἡ λέξις ἐστὶ τετράχρονος οὐ γίνεται ὁ τόνος ἐπὶ τῆς τελευταίας τῆς προηγουμένης λέξεως, ἀλλ' ἐπὶ τῇ ἀρχῇ τῆς ἐπομένης (sic)· οἷον ἤκουσας ἥμων (sic) et postea verba αἱ μὲν ἐγκλινόμεναι ἀντωνυμίαι ὀρθοτονούμεναι μὲν ἀντιδιαστολὴν ἔχουσιν ἑτέρου προσώπου· ἐμοὶ ἔδωκας οὐκ ἄλλῳ δηλονότι· ἐμοῦ ἤκουσας οὐκ ἄλλου· ἐμὲ ὕβρισας οὐκ ἄλλον· ἐγκλινόμεναι δὲ ἀπόλυτα πρόσωπα δηλοῦσι· ἤκουσά σου· ἔδωκά σοι· ἔτυψά σε. ἐν συνδέσμοις ἐγκλίνεται ὅ τε καί τε· ὁ περ καὶ περ· νυ (ο νυ s.l.) καί νυ· τοι· καί τοι· ποι καὶ ποι· γε τοῦτο γε· θήν οὔ θην ex verbis anterioribus iteravit **T₁**

[k] *'ΡΑ* **δ**· deest in **jQσφξ**

[l] ὅς ῥα νόθος (νόθος μὲν ἔην **C**) **δ**· deest in **jQσφξ**

[m] *ΘΗΝ*· οὐ μέν θην κείνης γε χερείων εὔχομαι εἶναι **Ald.₂**· υμηνοσθηνκε sic **M**· θην...ἡμῖν οὔ θην (haec verba post τοῦτό γε) **G Ald.₁**· θην...ὑμῖν ἔν θήκε (haec verba post τοῦτό γε) **G_p**· θην...ὑμῖν ὤθηνκε (haec verba post τοῦτό γε) **pG_r**· haec verba post τοῦτό τε **G_b**· **pG_rG_b**· θην (post γε **A₂**) τ· θην ὥς θην καὶ σὸν ἐγὼ λυσόμενος οὐ μέθην κείνης γε χερείων εὔχομαι εἶναι **C**· ὥς θην **υ**· θην ἢ **ξ**· θην (post περ) *Π*· deest in **Q**

[n] *ΚΕΝ* **Πδξ**· deest in **MQσφ**

[o] καί κεν δή **Ald.₂**· καί κεν δή πάλαι ἤσθασο **C**· ὥς κεν **υ**· αἴ κε· σκῶλόν τε **Ald.₁**· σκῶλόν τε μνήμων τε **t**· deest in **MΠQτξ**

[p] τὸν οὖν παραπληρωματικὸν — καταλαμβάνεται ἡ ἔγκλισις (§l) deest in **σ**

[q] τὸν οὖν παραπληρωματικὸν — παρατήρησιν τῆς πρὸ αὐτῶν λέξεως (§k) deest in **Qτ**

[r] τὸν οὖν παραπληρωματικὸν — ἀποφαντικῶς παραλαβάνεται ἐγκλίνουσιν deest in **M**

[s] τὸν οὖν παραπληρωματικὸν — συνδέσμους εἶναι φασίν] οὖν πω. ὁ τε προηγουμένου σπονδείου ἢ πυρριχ(ίου) ἢ ἰάμβου οὐκ ἐγκλίνεται. ὁ πῶς καὶ τὸ νυ ἐγκλινόμενα συνδέσμους φασί. (τ)ὸ ποῦ ἐγκλινόμενον οὐ συνεγκλίνει ἄνθρωπόν τινά που φησί *Π*· deest in **ξ**

[t] τὸν οὖν παραπληρωματικὸν **υ**· τὸ οὖν περιπληρωματικὸν (sic) **Ald.₂**

[u] οὐκ **Ald.₂**· οὐ **υ**· om. **C**

[v] ὅτε...παραλαμβάνεται **υ**· ὅτε...περιλαμβάνονται **Ald.₂**· ὅταν...παραλαμβάνωσιν **C**

[w] οὔκουν **Mυ**· οὔκουν (οὔκουν οὔκουν **C**) ἐάσω (γε ἄσω **Ald.₂**) τήνδε γῆν οἰκεῖν ἔτι **δ**

[x] περισπώμενος γὰρ κατάφασιν σημαίνει συλλογιστικὸς ὢν ἢ (ἢ om. **Ald.₂**) ἐπιφορικός **δ** (per coniecturam)· deest in **Mυ**

[y] οὐκοῦν **Mυ**· οὐκ οὖν ἂν ἤδη τῶν θεατῶν τις λέγοι **δ**

[z] καὶ τὸ (τὸν **C**) *ΠΩΣ* (**Mυ**· *ΠΩ* **δ**) δὲ καὶ τὸ (τὸν **C**) *ΝΥΝ* ἐγκλινόμενα (ἐγκλινομένους **C**) συνδέσμους εἶναί (εἶναι deest in **M**) φασι **Mδυ**

[aa] post φασι verba δευρό νυν ἢ τρίποδος (τρίποδος περιδώμεθα **C**)· τὸ δὲ (δὲ **C**· deest in **Ald.₂**) νῦν χρονικὸν ἐπίρρημα, ὀρθοτονεῖται (καὶ ὀρθοτονεῖται **C**) καὶ μακρὸν ἔχει τὸ υ, μήπω (μήπω deest in **C**) praebet **δ**

§j And among the conjunctions the following are enclitic: *TE*, as in <u>καί τε</u> χαλιφρονέοντα,[61] *ΠΕΡ*, as in <u>ἀγαθός περ ἐών</u>,[62] *ΤΟΙ*, as in <u>καί τοι</u>,[63] *ΓΕ*, as in <u>τοῦτό γε</u>,[64] *'ΡΑ*, as in <u>ὅς ῥα νόθος</u>,[65] *ΘΗΝ*, as in <u>οὐ μέν θην κείνης γε χερείων εὔχομαι εἶναι</u>,[66] *ΚΕΝ*, as in <u>καί κεν δή</u>. They make the filler *'ΟΥΝ* with the negative *'ΟΥΚ* enclitic, when it is used negatively: οὔκουν.[67] For when it is perispomenon it conveys an affirmation, being inferential or deductive: οὐκοῦν.[68] And they say that the enclitic *ΠΩΣ* and *ΝΥΝ* are conjunctions.

---

[61] *Od.* 23.13: 'and [they bring] a foolish person [to sense]'.
[62] E.g. *Il.* 1.131: 'Great though you are' / *Il.* 15.185: 'Great though he is'.
[63] 'And, you see'.
[64] 'This at any rate'.
[65] *Il.* 5.70: 'who [was] an illegitimate child'.
[66] *Od.* 5.211: 'I claim to be no worse than her'.
[67] 'Therefore not'.
[68] 'Therefore'.

§k τὰ[a] [b] μὲν οὖν ἐγκλιτικὰ μόριά ἐστι ταῦτα· οὐχ ὡς ἔτυχε δὲ ἐγκλίνονται,[c] ἀλλὰ κατά τινα παρατήρησιν τῆς πρὸ αὐτῶν λέξεως.

§k
[a] τὰ μὲν οὖν — usque ad finem (§u) deest in *Π*
[b] τὰ μὲν οὖν ἐγκλιτικὰ μόριά ἐστι ταῦτα **M**: τὰ μὲν οὖν ἐγκλινόμενα μόρια ταῦτά ἐστιν **Cυξ**: τὰ μὲν οὖν ἐγκλινόμενα μόρια, τοιαῦτά ἐστιν **Ald.₂**
[c] ἐγκλίνονται **Mυξ**: ἐγκλίνεται **δ**

§k These are the enclitic items, then. And they do not throw their accents back at random, but on the basis of a certain observation of the preceding word.

§1 αἱ^a μὲν οὖν τετράχρονοι τῶν ἐγκλιτικῶν ἐπὶ τὴν πρώτην συλλαβὴν ἑαυτῶν τὴν ἔγκλισιν ἀναπέμπουσιν ὡς μηδεμιᾶς δεόμεναι παρατηρήσεως τῆς πρὸ αὐτῶν λέξεως· 'ἤκουσεν ἥμων,' 'ἔδωκεν ἥμιν'. αἱ^{b c d} δὲ λοιπαὶ τὴν πρὸ αὐτῶν ἐγείρουσαι βαρεῖαν οὐκ ἐπὶ πάσης συλλαβῆς ταύτην ἐγείρειν δύνανται· οὐ^e γὰρ εἰ σπονδειακὴ^f τυγχάνοι^g ἡ προκειμένη λέξις καὶ βαρύνοιτο, ἡ βαρεῖα ταύτης ἥ^h ἐπὶ τέλει ἐγείρεται· 'οὕτωⁱ που Διὶ μέλλει ὑπερμενέϊ φίλον εἶναι,' 'ἤδη^j τις εἶπεν,' καὶ^k οὔτε τὴν ΤΩ συλλαβὴν ὀξύνομεν τοῦ οὕτω οὔτε τὴν ΔΗ τοῦ ἤδη· ἀλλ'^l οὔτε, εἰ ἰαμβικὴ τύχοι βαρύτονος· οἷον^m 'λέβηςⁿ τις,' 'ὅπως γε,' οὔτε, εἰ^o πυρριχαϊκὴ τύχοι^p καὶ βαρύνεται· 'φίλος^q τις,' 'ξένος τις·' ἐπὶ γὰρ^r τούτων τῷ νοῖ μόνῳ καταλαμβάνεται ἡ ἔγκλισις· δι'^{s t} ὃ σημειοῦται τὸ^u 'ἔνθ' ἔσάν οἱ πέπλοι παμποίκιλοι ἔργα γυναικῶν'. παραλόγως^v γὰρ^w ἐνεκλίθη ἡ ΟΙ ἀντωνυμία πυρριχίου προκειμένου.

§1

^a αἱ μὲν οὖν τετράχρονοι τῶν ἐγκλιτικῶν (ἀντωνυμιῶν C) ἐπὶ τὴν πρώτην συλλαβὴν ἑαυτῶν τὴν ἔγκλισιν ἀναπέμπουσιν (ἀναπέμπουσαι C) ὡς (ὡς deest in C) μηδεμιᾶς (οὐδεμιᾶς C) δεόμεναι (δεόμενα M: δεόμεα υξ: δύνανται C) παρατηρήσεως τῆς (καὶ τῆς M) πρὸ αὐτῶν λέξεως· ἤκουσεν ἥμων (ἡμῶν C), ἔδωκεν (φέρε C) ἥμιν (ἡμῖν C) MCυξ: ἰστέον (sic A₂: στέον sic T₁), ὅτε ἡ λέξις ἐστί τετράχρονος οὐ γίνεται ὁ τόνος ἐπὶ τῆς τελευταίας τῆς προηγουμένης λέξεως· ἀλλ' ἐπὶ τῇ ἀρχῇ τῆς ἑπομένης (sic)· οἷον ἤκουσας ἥμων τ: ἤκουσεν ἥμων· φέρετε ἥμιν Ald.₂: οἱ μὲν οὖν τετράχρονοι τῶν ἐγκλιτικῶν ἐπὶ τὴν πρώτην συλλαβὴν ἑαυτῶν τὴν ἔγκλισιν ἀναφέρουσι· ἤκουσεν (sic) ἥμων· ἡ δὲ αἰτία ἔρρε^θ ἄνω Q

^b αἱ δὲ λοιπαὶ — usque ad finem (§u) deest in τ

^c αἱ δὲ λοιπαὶ — ταύτην ἐγείρειν δύνανται deest in Q

^d αἱ δὲ λοιπαὶ τὴν πρὸ αὐτῶν (αὐτῶν scripsimus: αὐτῶν Mυ) ἐγείρουσαι βαρεῖαν Mυ: αἱ δὲ λοιπαὶ τὴν πρὸ αὐτῶν ἐγείρουσι βαρεῖαν ξ Ald.₂

^e οὐ γὰρ εἰ Mυξ: οὔτε γὰρ εἰ δ: εἰ δὲ Q

^f σπονδειακὴ] σπονδιακὴ M

^g τυγχάνοι (F^{p.c.}: τυγχάνει F^{a.c.}) ἡ προκειμένη λέξις καὶ βαρύνοιτο M Ald.₂ υξ: τυγχάνει ἡ προκειμένη λέξις καὶ ταῦτα μηκύνοιτο C: τυγχάνει ἡ πρώτη λέξις καὶ βαρύνοιτο Q: ἡ προκειμένη λέξις καὶ βαρύνοιτο λ

^h ἡ ἐπὶ τέλει ἐγείρεται M: ἡ ἐπὶ τέλει οὐκ ἐγείρεται Q: ἡ ἐπὶ τέλους ἐγείρεται Ald.₂: ἡ βαρεῖα ταύτης ἐπὶ τέλους ἐγείρεται C: ἡ ἐπὶ τέλει ἐγείρει ξ: ἡ ἐπὶ τέλει ἐγείρετο T₂: ἐπὶ τέλει ἐγείρετο A₁

ⁱ οὕτω (οἷον οὕτω δ) που Διὶ μέλλει ὑπερμενέϊ φίλον εἶναι δυξ: οὕτω που MQ

^j ἤδη τις εἶπεν (εἶπεν Cυξ: εἰπεῖν Ald.₂) δυξ: ἤδη τις MQ

^k καὶ οὔτε τὴν ΤΩ συλλαβὴν ὀξύνομεν τοῦ οὕτω οὔτε τὴν ΔΗ τοῦ ἤδη M: καὶ οὔτε τὴν τω συλλαβὴν τοῦ οὕτω ὀξύνομεν, οὔτε τὴν δη τοῦ ἤδη ξ: οὐκ ὀξύνομεν γάρ, οὔτε (ἄτε C) τὴν τω συλλαβὴν τῆς οὕτω· οὔτε τὴν δη τῆς ἤδη δ: καὶ οὔτε τὴν τω τοῦ οὕτω ὀξύνομεν, οὔτε τὴν δη τοῦ ἤδη υ: οὐδὲ γὰρ λέγει αὐτώ που οὐδὲ ἤδη τις Q

^l ἀλλ' οὔτε, εἰ (εἰ om. C) ἰαμβικὴ τύχοι (τύχη Q: τυγχάνει C) βαρύτονος MδQ: ἀλλ' οὔτε εἰ (εἰ om. λ) ἰαμβικὴ τύχοι βαρύνεται υξ

^m οἷον δQυξ: deest in M

ⁿ λέβης (λέβη sic Ald.₂) τις, ὅπως γε MδυR: λέβης τις Q

^o εἰ πυρριχαϊκὴ QυR: εἰ πυρριχαικὴ (litteris ια obfuscatis) M: εἰ πυρριχιακὴ C: ἡ πυρριχιακὴ Ald.₂

^p τύχοι καὶ βαρύνεται M: βαρύνεται δ: τύχοι, βαρύνεται υR: deest in Q

^q φίλος τις, ξένος τις M: οἷον φίλος τις, ξένος τις υR: οἷον φίλος τις (τις Ald.₂: τε C) ξένος τε δ: λόγος τις Q

^r γὰρ τούτων τῷ νοῖ (νῷ A₁) μόνῳ καταλαμβάνεται ἡ ἔγκλισις Mυ: γὰρ τούτων τῷ νῷ μόνῳ παραλαμβάνεται ἡ ἔγκλισις C: γὰρ τούτῳ τῷ νῦν περιλαμβάνεται ἡ ἔγκλισις Ald.₂: περὶ γὰρ ταῦτα, τῶ (sic) νοῖ μόνῳ (sic) καταλαμβάνεται ἡ ἔγκλισις Q

^s δι' ὃ σημειοῦται — ἐν δὲ τοῖς λοιποῖς οὐκέτι (§n) deest in Q

^t δι' ὃ σημειοῦται M: δι' ὃ σημειοῦνται συξ: σημειοῦνται Ald.₂: καὶ ἰσοδυναμοῦνται C

^u τὸ ἔνθ' ἔσάν (ἔσάν συξ) οἱ πέπλοι παμποίκιλοι ἔργα γυναικῶν υξ: τὸ ἐνθὲς ἀσάν (sic) οἱ πέπλοι πανποίκιλοι (sic) ἔργα γυναικῶν M: τὸ ἔνθ' ἔσάν οἱ πέπλοι παμποίκιλοι σ: τὸ ἔθεν ἔσαν· ἔσαν οἱ πέπλοι παντίκοιλοι (sic) Ald.₂: τὸ ἔνθ' ἔσαν οἱ δέκα πέπλοι παμποίκιλοι C

^v παραλόγως MCσυξ: παραλόγων (sic) Ald.₂

^w γὰρ Mδσ: δ' (δὲ T₂R) υξ

§1 Those of the enclitics containing four units of time throw back their accents [literally 'their enclisis'] onto their own first syllable, needing no observation of the preceding word: ἤκουσεν ἥμων, ἔδωκεν ἥμιν.[69] And the others, which wake up the grave accent before themselves, cannot wake this up on every syllable. For if the preceding word happens to be spondaic and barytone, the grave on its final syllable is not woken up: οὕτω που Διὶ μέλλει ὑπερμενέϊ φίλον εἶναι[70] and ἤδη τις εἶπεν,[71] and we neither put an acute on the syllable *TΩ* of οὕτω, nor on the syllable *ΔH* of ἤδη. And [the grave on the final syllable is] also not [woken up] if the word happens to be iambic and barytone, as in λέβης τις, ὅπως γε,[72] nor if the word happens to be pyrrhic and barytone, as in φίλος τις, ξένος τις.[73] For in the case of these words the enclisis is grasped only by the mind. For this reason ἔνθ' ἔσάν οἱ πέπλοι παμποίκιλοι ἔργα γυναικῶν[74] is an exception. For the pronoun *ΟΙ* has thrown back its accent irregularly, with a pyrrhic word preceding.

[69] 'He/she heard us'; 'he/she gave to us'.
[70] E.g. *Il.* 2.116: 'So, I suppose, it probably seems good to exceedingly mighty Zeus'.
[71] Aristophanes, *Acharnians* 45: 'Has someone already spoken?'.
[72] 'A certain basin'; 'so that at any rate'.
[73] 'A certain friend'; 'a certain stranger'.
[74] *Il.* 6.289: 'where she had intricate robes, the creations of women'.

§m σημειοῦνται[a] καὶ[b] τὰς διὰ τοῦ ΣΦ ἀντωνυμίας· καὶ[c] αὗται γὰρ πυρριχίου προκειμένου ἐγκλίνονται· ἱνά[d] σφ' ἀγορή τε θέμις τε, ‹ὅτίς›[e] σφεας εἰσαφίκηται’, καὶ[f] ἐπὶ τῶν ὁμοίων ὡσαύτως.

§n εἰ μέντοι[a] προπαροξύνοιτο[b] ἡ προκειμένη λέξις τῶν ἐγκλιτικῶν μορίων, ἐγείρει τὴν ἐν τῷ τέλει αὐτῆς[c] βαρεῖαν, οἷον[d] ‘ἄνθρωπός τις’ (ἐν[e] γὰρ τῇ ΑΝ συλλαβῇ καὶ ΠΟΣ ὀξεία τίθεται), ‘ἤκουσέ[f] μου’, ‘ἄνθρωποί εἰσιν’, ‘κάκιστοί εἰσιν’. εἴπομεν γάρ, ὡς ἐν ἐπιρρήμασι μόνοις καὶ[g] ἐν εὐκτικοῖς ἥ[h] ΑΙ καὶ ἡ ΟΙ μακραί εἰσιν· ἐν[i] δὲ τοῖς λοιποῖς οὐκέτι.

§o ὁμοίως[a] καὶ εἰ προπερισπῷτο ἡ[b] προκειμένη λέξις, ἐγκλιτικοῦ ἐπιφερομένου ἐγείρει[c] τὴν μετὰ τὴν περισπωμένην βαρεῖαν, οἷον·[d] ‘οἰκός τις’, ‘Σκῶλόν[e] τε’, ‘Κνημόν τε’.

§p κἂν[a] παροξύνοιτο τροχαϊκὴ[b] οὖσα· ‘ἄλλός τις’, ‘ἔστί τις’, ‘ἐνθά ποτε’.

---

§m
[a] σημειοῦνται — πυρριχίου προκειμένου deest in **M**
[b] καὶ τὰς διὰ τοῦ σφ ἀντωνυμίας **υξ**: καὶ τὰς διὰ τοῦ σφι ἀντωνυμίας **G Ald.₁**: καὶ διὰ τοῦ σφι ἀντωνυμίας **G,γ**: καὶ διὰ τοῦ σφὶν ἀντωνυμίας **p**: καὶ γὰρ τοῦ σφ ἀντωνυμίας **C**: καὶ τὰς τοῦ σφῶν ἀντωνυμίας **Ald.₂**: δὲ καὶ διὰ τῆς σφι ἀντωνυμίας **G_m**
[c] καὶ αὗται γὰρ πυρριχίου προκειμένου ἐγκλίνονται **υξ**: καὶ αὗται γὰρ πυρριχίου προηγουμένου ἐγκλίνονται **δ**: καὶ αὗται πυρριχίου ὄντος ἐγκλίνονται **σ**: ἐγκλίνονται **M**
[d] ἱνά σφ' ἀγορή τε θέμις τε **Ald.₂ συ**: ἱνα σφ' ἀγορή τε θέμιστές τε **ξ**: ἱνα σφαγορῆται θεμιστυοῖ (sic) **M**: ἱνά σφ' ἄγητε θέμις **C**
[e] ὅτίς scripsi: ὅτί **σ**: οἵ τε **υF**: οἵ γε **R**: ὅτέ **δ**: τε **M**
[f] καὶ ἐπὶ τῶν ὁμοίων ὡσαύτως **M Ald.₂**: καὶ ἐπὶ τῶν ὁμοίως ὡσαύτως **υξ**: καὶ ἐπὶ τῶν ὁμοίων **C**: deest in **σ**

§n
[a] μέντοι **Μσυξ**: μὲν **δ**
[b] προπαροξύνοιτο] παροξύνοιτο **t**
[c] αὐτῆς **T₂**: αὐτῆς **M Ald.₁ A₁ξ**: αὐτοῦ **t**: deest in **C**
[d] οἷον ἄνθρωπός τις ἐν γὰρ τῇ αν συλλαβῇ (συλλαβῇ om. **υ**) καὶ πος (πῶς **M**: τῇ πος **ξ**) ὀξεία τίθεται (τίθετο **M**) **Μυξ**: ἄνθρωπός τις ἐν γὰρ τῇ αν καὶ τῇ πος, ὀξείαν τίθεμεν (τίθησιν **C**) **δ**: ἄνθρωπός τις **σ**
[e] ἐν γὰρ τῇ ΑΝ συλλαβῇ καὶ τῇ ΠΟΣ — ‘οἰκός τις’, ‘Σκῶλόν τε’, ‘Κνημόν τε’ (§o) deest in **σ**
[f] ἤκουσέ μου, ἄνθρωποί εἰσι, κάκιστοί (κάκισταί **δ**) εἰσιν **δυξ**: ἤκουσέν μου, ἄνθρωποί εἰσιν **M**
[g] καὶ ἐν εὐκτικοῖς **Μξ**: καὶ εὐκτικοῖς (εὐτικοῖς sic **A₁**) **Cυ**: καὶ ἐν τοῖς εὐκτικοῖς ῥήμασι **Ald.₂**
[h] ἡ αι καὶ ἡ οι **δξ**: ἡ αι καὶ οι **υ**: ἡ αι καὶ ἡ οι καὶ **M**
[i] ἐν δὲ τοῖς λοιποῖς οὐκέτι **δυ**: ἐν δὲ τοῖς λοιποῖς οὐκέτι μακραί εἰσιν **ξ**: ἐν δὲ τοῖς λοιποῖς οὐκέτι κάκιστά εἰσιν **M**

§o
[a] ὁμοίως καὶ εἰ scripsi: ὁμοίως καὶ ἡ **M**: ὁμοίως εἰ **υξ**: ὁμοίως κἂν **δ**: εἰ δὲ **Q**
[b] ἡ προκειμένη λέξις ἐγκλιτικοῦ (ἐγκτιτικοῦ sic **M**) ἐπιφερομένου **Μυξ**: ἡ προκειμένη λέξις ἐγκλιτικοῦ (ἐγκλιτ **C**) ἐπιφερομένη **δ**: ἡ προκειμένη λέξις **Q**
[c] ἐγείρει τὴν μετὰ τὴν περισπωμένην βαρεῖαν **Μδυξ**: ἐγείρει τὴν βαρεῖαν **Q**
[d] οἷον (deest in **Ald.₂**) οἰκός τις, σκῶλόν (σκῶλον **Ald.₂**) τε, κνημόν τε **Μδυξ**: οἷον οἰκός (sic) τις· δῆμός τις **Q**
[e] Σκῶλόν τε Κνημόν τε] fortasse Σχοῖνόν τε Σκῶλόν τε πολύκνημόν τ' (Il. 2.497)

§p
[a] κἂν παροξύνοιτο **Cσυξ**: κἂν προπαροξύνοιτο **M Ald.₂**: καὶ εἰ παροξύνοιτο **Q**
[b] τροχαϊκὴ οὖσα· ἄλλός τις· ἔστί τις· ἐνθά ποτε **Μδσυξ**: τροχαϊκὴ οὖσα, ἐγείρει τὴν βαρεῖαν· μόνη γὰρ αὕτη οἷον ἄλλός τις· ἔστί τις **Q**

§m And they also note the pronouns beginning with $\Sigma\Phi$ as exceptions; for these too throw their accent back when a pyrrhic precedes, as in <u>ἵνά σφ᾽ ἀγορή τε θέμις τε</u>[75] and <u>ὅτίς σφεας εἰσαφίκηται</u>,[76] and likewise in similar instances.

§n But if the word preceding the enclitic items is proparoxytone, it wakes up the grave on its final syllable, as in <u>ἄνθρωπός τις</u>[77] (for an acute accent is placed on the syllable AN and on $\Pi O\Sigma$), <u>ἤκουσέ μου, ἄνθρωποί εἰσιν, κάκιστοί εἰσιν</u>.[78] For we have said that AI and OI are long only in adverbs and optatives; in other forms they are not [long].

§o And similarly if the preceding word is properispomenon, if an enclitic follows it wakes up the grave after the circumflex, as in <u>οἶκός τις</u>,[79] <u>Σκῶλόν τε</u>,[80] <u>Κνῆμόν τε</u>.[81]

§p And [likewise] if the preceding word is paroxytone and trochaic, as in <u>ἄλλός τις, ἔστί τις, ἔνθά ποτε</u>.[82]

---

[75] *Il.* 11.807: 'where their meeting-place and place of justice [were]'.
[76] *Od.* 12.40, *Od.* 16.228, and *Od.* 20.188: 'whoever comes to them'.
[77] 'A certain person'.
[78] 'He/she heard me'; 'they are people'; 'they are very bad'.
[79] 'A certain house'.
[80] *Il.* 2.497: 'and Skōlos'.
[81] 'And Knēmos'.
[82] 'Someone else'; 'there is someone'; 'where once'.

§q ἔτι[a] [b] καὶ αἱ[c] ὀξυνόμεναι λέξεις, βαρυνόμεναι[d] δὲ διὰ τὴν συνέπειαν, ἐγκλιτικοῦ ἐπιφερομένου τὴν βαρεῖαν ἐγείρουσιν· ʼαὐτόν[e] με, ʼαὐτός μοι. εἰ[f] δὲ περισπῷτο ἡ[g] λέξις, φυλάττεται[h] ἡ περισπωμένη· ʼπῶ[i] ποτε, ʼπῇ με φέρεις, ʼκαλῶς με βεβωλοκόπηκεν.

§r ἐὰν[a] οὖν συμβῇ πλείονα ἐφεξῆς ἐγκλιτικὰ εἶναι, πολλαὶ ἔσονται καὶ[b] παράλληλοι αἱ ὀξεῖαι, ὥς[c] παρ᾽ Ὁμήρῳ· ʼἤ νύ σέ που[d] δέος ἴσχει[e] ἀκήριον. τρεῖς[f] γάρ εἰσιν ἐφεξῆς αἱ ὀξεῖαι. δυνατὸν δὲ καὶ πλείονας ἐπινοῆσαι, οἷον·[g] ʼεἴ πέρ τίς σέ[h] μοί φησίν[i] ποτε. τὸ[j] μὲν γὰρ ΕΙ ὀξύνεται διὰ τὴν ἐπιφορὰν τοῦ ΠΕΡ ἐγκλιτικοῦ· τὸ[k] δὲ ΠΕΡ διὰ τὸ ΤΙΣ, τὸ δὲ ΤΙΣ διὰ τὸ ΣΕ, τὸ δὲ ΣΕ διὰ τὸ ΜΟΙ, τὸ δὲ ΜΟΙ διὰ τὸ ΦΗΣΙΝ, τὸ δὲ ΦΗΣΙΝ διὰ τὸ ΠΟΤΕ. ὥστε[l] ἐφεξῆς εἶναι ὀξείας ἕξ, εἰ[m] καὶ σπάνιον τὸ τοιοῦτον διὰ[n] τὴν τοῦ πνεύματος συνέχειαν δεομένην ἀναπαύσεως.

§q
[a] ἔτι καὶ αἱ ὀξυνόμεναι λέξεις — usque ad finem (§u) deest in **Q**
[b] ἔτι καὶ **MCυξ**: ἔτι δὲ καὶ **Ald.₂**: ἔτι σ
[c] αἱ ὀξυνόμεναι λέξεις **υξ**: ὀξυνόμεναι λέξεις **Mσ**: αἱ ὀξύτονοι λέξεις **Ald.₂**: ὀξύνοιντο **C**
[d] βαρυνόμεναι δὲ (δὲ deest in δ) διὰ τὴν συνέπειαν **Mδσξ**: βαρυνόμεναι δὲ διὰ τῆς συνεπείας υ
[e] αὐτόν με, αὐτός μοι scripsi: αὐτό με, αὐτός μοι **M**: αὐτόν με πρώτιστα, Ζεύς τε καταχθόνιος (τε καταχθόνιος om. **Ald.₂**)
[f] εἰ δὲ περισπῷτο **υξ**: εἰ δὲ περισπᾶται σ. οἱ (sic) δὲ περισπᾶται **Ald.₂**: εἰ δὲ περισπᾶτο **MC**
[g] ἡ λέξις — usque ad finem (§u) deest in **M**
[h] φυλάττεται ἡ περισπωμένη **δυξ**: φυλάττεται πάλιν ἡ περισπωμένη σ
[i] πῶ (πῶς **C**) ποτε, πῇ με φέρεις, καλῶς με βεβωλοκόπηκεν (βεβελοκόπηκεν **C**) δ: πῶς ποτε, πῇ με φέρεις, καλῶς με βεβίακεν σ: πῶ ποτε πώποτε πῇ με φέρεις **ξ**: πῶ, πότε, πώποτε υ

§r
[a] ἐὰν οὖν συμβῇ πλείονα ἐφεξῆς **υξ**: ἐὰν οὖν πλείονα συμβῇ ἐφεξῆς σ: ἐὰν οὖν συμβαίνῃ (συμβαίη **C**) πλείονα ἐφεξῆς δ
[b] καὶ παράλληλοι αἱ ὀξεῖαι **Cυ**: αἱ παράλληλοι ὀξεῖαι **F**: αἱ παράλληλοι αἱ ὀξεῖαι **R**: καὶ ἐπάλληλοι αἱ ὀξεῖαι **Ald.₂**: καὶ αἱ ὀξεῖαι σ
[c] ὡς παρ᾽ Ὁμήρῳ **δυξ**: deest in σ
[d] που **δσυ**: πού **ξ**
[e] ἴσχει ἀκήριον **δG Ald.₁**: ἰσχία κηρίων **T₂ξ**: ἴσχεια κήριον **G_wG_r**: ἴσχια κήριον **G_v**: deest in **γΑ₁**
[f] τρεῖς γάρ εἰσιν ἐφεξῆς αἱ ὀξεῖαι **υξ**: τρεῖς γὰρ ἐφεξῆς ὀξεῖαι δ: τρεῖς εἰσιν ἐφεξῆς αἱ ὀξεῖαι σ
[g] οἷον **δυξ**: deest in σ
[h] σέ μοί **συR**: σέ μέ δ: σ᾽ ἐμοί **F**
[i] φησίν ποτε scripsi, ut partem trimetri iambici faciat: φησί ποτε **δσυξ**
[j] τὸ μὲν γὰρ ει ὀξύνεται διὰ τὴν ἐπιφορὰν τοῦ περ ἐγκλιτικοῦ υ: τὸ γὰρ ʼειʼ ὀξύνεται διὰ τὴν ἐπιφορὰν τοῦ ʼπερʼ ἐγκλιτικοῦ **ξ**: τὸ μέντοι ει ὀξύνεται διὰ τὴν ἐπιφορὰν τοῦ ἐγκλιτικοῦ περ σ: τὸ μὲν ει ὀξύνεται διὰ τὴν ἐπιφορὰν τοῦ πέρ δ
[k] τὸ δὲ περ διὰ τὸ τίς· τὸ δὲ τίς, διὰ τὸ σέ· τὸ δὲ σέ διὰ τὸ μοί· τὸ δὲ μοί, διὰ τὸ φησί **συξ**: τὸ δὲ (δὲ deest in **C**) περ (πέρ) διὰ τὸ τίς· τὸ δὲ τίς, διὰ τὸ σέ· τὸ δὲ σὲ διὰ τὸ μέ· τὸ δὲ μὲ διὰ τὸ φησι δ
[l] ὥστε ἐφεξῆς εἶναι ὀξείας ἕξ scripsi: ὥστε ἐφεξῆς εἶναι ὀξεῖαι **υξ**: ὥστε ἐφεξῆς ὀξεῖαι ἕξ **Ald.₁**: ὥστε ἕξ εἶναι ἐφεξῆς ὀξείας δ: ὥστε ἐφεξῆς ὀξεῖαι **Gz**: ὅθεν ἐφεξῆς ὀξεῖαι γ: ἔστε ἐφεξῆς ὀξεῖαι **p**
[m] εἰ καὶ σπάνιον τὸ τοιοῦτον (τοιοῦτο **Ald.₂**) **δυξ**: εἰ καὶ σπάνιον σ
[n] διὰ τὴν τοῦ πνεύματος συνέχειαν δεομένην ἀναπαύσεως **υξ**: διὰ τὴν τοῦ πνεύματος συνέχειαν δεομένην (δεομένη **C**: δεόμενον **Ald.₂**) ἀναπνεύσεως δ: διὰ τὴν τοῦ πνεύματος συνέχειαν σ

§q And words that are oxytone but receive a grave because of the connectedness of discourse also wake up the grave if an enclitic follows, as in αὐτόν με, αὐτός μοι.[83] But should the word be perispomenon, the circumflex is kept, as in πῶ ποτε, πῇ με φέρεις, καλῶς με βεβωλοκόπηκεν.[84]

§r If several enclitics happen to occur in a row, the acute accents will be many and consecutive, as in Homer's ἤ νύ σέ που δέος ἴσχει ἀκήριον.[85] For the acutes are three in a row. And it is possible to think of more, as in εἴ πέρ τίς σέ μοί φησίν ποτε.[86] For the ’ΕΙ has an acute because of the addition of the enclitic ΠΕΡ, and the ΠΕΡ because of the ΤΙΣ, and the ΤΙΣ because of the ΣΕ, and the ΣΕ because of the ΜΟΙ, and the ΜΟΙ because of the ΦΗΣΙΝ, and the ΦΗΣΙΝ because of the ΠΟΤΕ, with the result that there are six acutes in a row—even if this happens rarely, because of the fact that the continuity of the breath needs a break.

[83] ‘Me myself’ (e.g. Callimachus, fr. 813 Pfeiffer, hence δ’s expansion to αὐτόν με πρώτιστα); ‘himself…to me’.

[84] ‘When…ever?’; *Homeric Hymn to Hermes* 307 ‘Where are you taking me?’; Menander, *Dyscolus* 514–15 ‘he harrowed me finely’ (the direct tradition has καλῶς γέ με | βεβωλοκόπηκεν).

[85] *Il.* 5.812: ‘or perhaps spiritless fear has got hold of you’.

[86] ‘If ever anyone says to me that you’.

§s εἰ[a] δέ, παραλλήλων ὄντων ἐγκλιτικῶν, ἐν[b] τῷ μεταξὺ περισπώμενον[c] εἴη, ὡς[d] ἐπὶ τοῦ ΠΟΥ, ΠΗ, ΠΩΣ, καὶ[e] μετὰ τοῦτο ἐπιφέροιτο ἕτερον ἐγκλιτικόν, τοῦτο[f] τὸ περισπώμενον οὔτε περισπᾶται διὰ[g] τὸ ἐγκλῖναι τὸν ἴδιον τόνον, οὔτε[h] ὀξύνεται, ἐπεὶ μὴ πέφυκεν ἡ περισπωμένη κατὰ τὸ κοινὸν ἔθος συστολῆς μὴ παρακολουθούσης[i] εἰς ὀξεῖαν μετατίθεσθαι, οἷον· 'οὔ[j] πως ἐστ',[k] Ἀγέλαε' (ἐν[l] γὰρ τῇ ΟΥ διφθόγγῳ μόνον[m] ἡ ὀξεῖα), 'ἤ[n] που τίς σφιν εἶπεν' (ἐν[o] τῷ Ἠ καὶ ἐν τῷ ΤΙΣ ἡ ὀξεῖα), 'ἄνθρωπόν[p] τινά που φησὶ μελῳδεῖν'[q] (πάλιν[r] ἐν τῇ ΠΟΝ συλλαβῇ καὶ[s] τῇ ΝΑ ἡ ὀξεῖα).[t]

§s
[a] εἰ δέ, παραλλήλων ὄντων — καὶ τῇ ΝΑ ἡ ὀξεῖα deest in σ
[b] ἐν τῷ μεταξὺ vξ: τὸ μεταξὺ δ
[c] περισπώμενον εἴη δ: περισπωμένων vξ
[d] ὡς ἐπὶ τοῦ ΠΟΥ, ΠΗ, ΠΩΣ vξ: ὡς ὁ ποῦ, πῆ, πῶς Ald.₂: ὡς τοῦ ποῦ πῆ πῶς C
[e] καὶ μετὰ τοῦτο ἐπιφέροιτο ἕτερον ἐγκλιτικὸν Ald.₂ RF: καὶ μετὰ τοῦτο ἕτερον ἐπιφέροιτο ἐγκλιτικὸν C: καὶ μετὰ τοῦτο ἐπιφέροιτο ὕστερον ἐγκλιτικὸν v
[f] τοῦτο τὸ (τὸ deest in C) περισπώμενον οὔτε περισπᾶται δ: τοῦτο τὸ περισπώμενον ὅτε vξ
[g] διὰ τὸ ἐγκλῖναι τὸν ἴδιον τόνον vξ: διὰ τὸ ἐγκλῖναι τὸν ἴδιον τόνον (τὸν ἴδιον τόνον C: τὸ ἴδιον Ald.₂) τῷ (τῷ C: τῶν Ald.₂) πρὸ αὐτοῦ δ
[h] οὔτε ὀξύνεται δ: deest in vξ
[i] παρακολουθούσης Cvξ: περικολουθείσης Ald.₂
[j] οὔ πως δ: οὔπω vξ
[k] ἔστ' ἀγέλαε vξ: ἔσταγελαέ C: ἔστ' ἀγεσίλαε Ald.₂
[l] ἐν γὰρ τῇ ου διφθόγγῳ δ: ἐν τῇ γὰρ ου διφθόγγῳ vRF
[m] μόνον Ald.₂ v: μόνη Cξ
[n] ἤ που τίς σφιν εἶπεν R: ἤ που τίς φιν εἶπεν v: οὔπω τίς σφιν εἶπεν F: ἤ που τίς φησιν ἔνισπεν C: εἴ που τίς φησὶ Ald.₂
[o] ἐν τῷ η καὶ ἐν τῷ τις ἡ ὀξεῖα vξ: ἐνίοτεν (sic) ἐν τῇ οι καὶ ἐν τῷ τίς ὀξοῖα (sic) Ald.₂: ἐν τῷ ταυτῶ καὶ ἐν τῷ τις ἡ ὀξεῖα C
[p] ἄνθρωπόν τινά — ἡ ὀξεῖα deest in v
[q] μελῳδεῖν Z (per coniecturam): μελοιδορεῖν δ: μελυδρεῖν ξ
[r] πάλιν ἐν τῇ πον συλλαβῇ Z (per coniecturam): πάλιν εἰς μὲν τὴν πον συλλαβὴν Ald.₂ R: πάλιν εἰς μὲν τὴν που συλλαβὴν F: πάλιν εἰς μὲν τὴν πον C
[s] καὶ τῇ ΝΑ ἡ ὀξεῖα scripsi: καὶ εἰς τὴν να ἡ ὀξεῖα Ald.₂: καὶ τὴν να συλλαβὴν ὀξεῖα C: καὶ τὴν (τῇ Z) α ἡ ὀξεῖα τίθεται ξ
[t] post ὀξεῖα verba καὶ εἰς τὸ (τὴν C) φησιν οὐκ ἔτι μέντοι εἰς τὸ (τὴν C) πού, οὔτε περισπωμένη οὔτε ὀξεῖα τίθεται habent δ

§s But if there are enclitics next to one another, and one in the middle is ['natur-ally'] perispomenon, like [indefinite] *ΠΟΥ*, *ΠΗ*, and *ΠΩΣ*, and after this there is another enclitic, the perispomenon one neither gets a circumflex (because it has thrown its own ['natural'] accent off) nor gets an acute (because a circumflex is not normally exchanged for an acute unless a vowel is shortened). For example: οὔ πως ἐστ᾽, Ἀγέλαε[87] (with an acute only on the diphthong ᾿ΟΥ); ἤ που τίς σφιν εἶπεν[88] (with an acute on ᾿Η and *ΤΙΣ*); ἄνθρωπόν τινά που φησὶ μελῳδεῖν[89] (again the acute goes on the syllable -*ΠΟΝ* and on -*ΝΑ*).

---

[87] *Od.* 22.136: 'I suppose it's not possible, Agelaos'. The treatise assumes that ἐστ᾽ is an enclitic here.
[88] 'Either I suppose somebody said to them' (cf. *Il.* 6.438).
[89] 'I suppose he says that some person sings'.

§t κἀκεῖνο[a] δὲ παραφυλακτέον ὅτι[b] τῶν ἐγκλινομένων εἰ[c] σπονδειακὴ προηγεῖται λέξις ἢ[d] πυρριχαϊκή, εἰ[e] μὲν μονοσύλλαβον εἴη τὸ ἐπιφερόμενον ἐγκλιτικόν,[f] ὡς[g] παρεθέμην, ἐγκλίνεται· 'οὕτω[h] [i] που', 'ἤδη τις'. οὔτε τὸ ἐγκλιτικόν δέχεται τὸν ἴδιον τόνον, οὔτε[j] ἡ βαρεῖα τῆς δευτέρας συλλαβῆς τῆς[k] προηγουμένης ἐγείρεται λέξεως, ἀλλὰ νοῒ[l] μόνῳ νοεῖται τὰ τῆς ἐγκλίσεως, ὡς ἔφθημεν εἰπόντες.

§u εἰ μέντοι δισύλλαβον[a] εἴη τὸ ἐγκλιτικὸν μόριον, τότε τὸν ἴδιον δέχεται τόνον, οὔτε δυνάμει, οὔτε ἐνεργείᾳ ἐγκλινόμενον· οἷον[b] 'ἤδη φαμέν' (ὀξύνομεν[c] γὰρ τὸ ΦΑΜΕΝ)· 'φίλοι εἰσίν' (ὁμοίως καὶ[d] τὸ[e] ΕΙΣΙΝ ὀξύνομεν)· 'οὕτω[f] ποτέ' (πάλιν[g] καὶ[h] τὸ ΠΟΤΕ ὀξύνομεν). καὶ τοῦτο εἰκότως· οὔτε γὰρ[i] τῆς προηγουμένης λέξεως τὴν ἐπὶ τέλει βαρεῖαν[j] ἐγεῖραι δυνατόν, οὔτε τὴν ἔγκλισιν νοεῖσθαι κατὰ τὴν πρώτην συλλαβὴν τῶν σπονδείων ἢ τῶν πυρριχίων. οὐδέποτε γὰρ τετάρτη ἀπὸ τέλους ἡ ὀξεῖα πίπτει.

§t
[a] κἀκεῖνο δὲ παραφυλακτέον **συξ**: κἀκεῖνο δὲ φυλακτέον **δ**
[b] ὅτι τῶν ἐγκλινομένων **συξ**: ὅτι ὅτε τῶν ἐγκλινομένων **δ**
[c] εἰ σπονδειακὴ **υ**: ἢ σπονδειακὴ **ξ**: ἢ σπονδιακὴ (sic) **σ**. σπονδιακὴ (sic) **δ**
[d] ἢ πυρριχαϊκὴ **συ**: ἢ πυρριχιακὴ **δ**: ἢ τροχαϊκὴ **ξ**
[e] εἰ μὲν μονοσύλλαβον εἴη **δτυξ**: εἰ μὲν μὴ μονοσύλλαβον εἴη **Ald.₁**
[f] ἐγκλιτικόν **Cυξ**: ἐγκλίνεται **Ald.₂**: ἐγκλιτικὸν μόριον **t**: μόριον **Ald.₁**
[g] ὡς παρεθέμην, ἐγκλίνεται scripsi: ὥσπερ ἐθέμην, ἐγκλίνεται **υξ**: ὡς ἐφ᾽ ὧν (ὧν **C**: ὃν **Ald.₂**) παρεθέμην πρότερον **δ**: deest in **σ**
[h] οὕτω που — δισύλλαβον εἴη τὸ ἐγκλιτικὸν μόριον (§u) deest in **σ**
[i] οὕτω που, ἤδη τις **C**: οὕτω που ἴδη τις **ξ**: οὕτω που οὔδη τις **Ald.₂**: οὕτω πω, ἤδη τις **A₁**: οὕτω (οὕτω sic **T₂**) πω ἴδη τις **T₂**
[j] οὔτε **δ**: οὐδὲ **υξ**
[k] τῆς προηγουμένης **δ**: προηγουμένης **υξ**
[l] νοῒ **υξ**: νῷ **δ**

§u
[a] δισύλλαβον **δT₂ξ**: δυσύλλαβον (sic) **A₁**
[b] οἷον **δυξ**: deest in **σ**
[c] ὀξύνομεν (ὀξυνόμενον **C**) γὰρ τὸ φαμέν **Cσυξ**: deest in **Ald.₂**
[d] καὶ **Ctυξ**: δὲ καὶ **Ald.₁**: deest in **Ald.₂**
[e] τὸ εἰσίν ὀξύνομεν **δ Ald.₁ ξ**: τὸ εἰσίν ὀξύνεται **υ**: τὸ φησίν ὀξύνομεν (ὀξυνόμενον **p**) **t**
[f] οὕτω ποτέ — ἡ ὀξεῖα πίπτει deest in **σ**
[g] πάλιν **Ald.₂ υ**: deest in **ξ**
[h] καὶ **υξ**: deest in **δ**
[i] γὰρ **υξ**: deest in **δ**
[j] βαρεῖαν] ἂν βαρεῖαν **Ald.₂**

§t And one must be aware that if a spondaic or pyrrhic word precedes enclitics, if the following enclitic is monosyllabic, as I have laid out, it throws its accent back, as in οὕτω που,⁹⁰ ἤδη τις.⁹¹ The enclitic does not receive its own accent, nor is the grave of the second syllable of the preceding word woken up, but the facts of enclisis are understood only in the mind, as we have already said.

§u But if the enclitic word is disyllabic, then it receives its own accent, since it does not throw its accent back, either in principle or in practice, as in ἤδη φαμέν⁹² (for we give an acute to the final syllable of *ΦΑΜΕΝ*), φίλοι εἰσίν⁹³ (and similarly we give an acute to the final syllable of *ΕΙΣΙΝ*), οὕτω ποτέ⁹⁴ (and again we give an acute to the final syllable of *ΠΟΤΕ*). And this happens quite reasonably. For it is not possible to wake up the grave on the final syllable of the preceding word, nor to understand the throwing back of the accent in association with the first syllable of spondaic or pyrrhic words. For the acute never falls on the fourth unit of time from the end.

---

⁹⁰ E.g. *Il.* 2.116: 'So, I suppose'.
⁹¹ 'Someone already' (cf. Aristophanes, *Acharnians* 45, quoted in §l).
⁹² 'We already say'.
⁹³ 'They are friends'.
⁹⁴ 'Thus at some time'.

2.2 *On enclitics 2*

Less widely known today than those texts on enclitics which found their way into Pseudo-Arcadius' epitome of Herodian's Περὶ καθολικῆς προσῳδίας (see section 2.1), the text we call *On enclitics 2* is transmitted under the title Ἡρωδιανοῦ Περὶ ἐγκλινομένων καὶ ἐγκλιτικῶν καὶ συνεγκλιτικῶν μορίων 'Herodian's *On oxytone words in the sentence, on enclitics, and on enclitic items in succession*', or variations thereof. This title is evidently derived from the opening of the treatise itself, which reveals a concern with definitions and categories. The author—if author is the right word for a text of this kind—begins with definitions of ἐγκλινόμενον (here in the sense 'oxytone word that turns its acute into a grave in connected speech'), ἐγκλιτικόν, and συνεγκλιτικόν, expands on the distinction between ἐγκλινόμενον and ἐγκλιτικόν, categorizes enclitics into monosyllabic and disyllabic ones, and then proceeds to categorize disyllabic enclitics into those with two morae and those with three.

This obsession with definitions and categories gives this treatise a somewhat distinct character compared to our other treatises on enclitics, but there is also abundant evidence of the shared tradition in which all our treatises stand. The two overarching topics of *On enclitics 1* appear again, albeit in the opposite order: what principles govern the accentual effects of enclitics, and which word forms are enclitic? Further parallels between the two works are pervasive, from large-scale structural devices such as the part-of-speech by part-of-speech treatment of which word forms are enclitic, to small-scale verbal parallels such as ἐν μὲν οὖν ὀνόμασι τὸ ΤΙΣ μόνον ἐγκλίνεται καὶ αἱ τούτου πτώσεις καὶ οἱ ἀριθμοὶ καὶ τὸ οὐδέτερον . . . καὶ τὰ ἰσοδυναμοῦντα τούτοις (*On enclitics 1*, §c) and ἐκ μὲν ὀνομάτων ἐγείρει τὴν ὀξεῖαν τὸ ΤΙΣ καὶ αἱ τούτου πτώσεις καὶ τὰ ἰσοδυναμοῦντα τούτῳ (*On enclitics 2*, §g).

2.2.1 Sources and stemma

On enclitics 2 is transmitted in the following manuscripts and early printed books, listed here according to (where relevant) the main families and sub-families we posit:

Manuscript Φ
Φ (13th–14th cent.): Vatican City, Biblioteca Apostolica Vaticana, Vaticanus Graecus 2226, folios 168v–169v.

Family μ, sub-family η
O (1469): London, British Library, Londiniensis Add. 10064, folios 155v–158v, copied by Iohannes Rhosos in Venice.

Ω (15th cent.): Vatican City, Biblioteca Apostolica Vaticana, Vaticanus Reginensis Graecus 104, folios 124r–127v.

Family *μ*, sub-family *ϵ*

A (15th cent.): Milan, Biblioteca Ambrosiana, Ambrosianus D 30 sup. = Martini-Bassi 225, folios 69r–72r.

J (16th cent.): El Escorial, Real Biblioteca del Monasterio de San Lorenzo, Escorialensis *Ψ*.IV.23 = de Andrés 497, folios 147r–150r.

Σ (15th–16th cent.): Vatican City, Biblioteca Apostolica Vaticana, Vaticanus Graecus 1751, folios 299r–301v, copied by a scribe named *Μανουήλ*.

Family q

K (15th cent.): Copenhagen, Det Kongelige Bibliotek, Hauniensis regius GKS 1965 4°, pp. 251–255bis,[95] copied by Urbano Bolzanio (see Roussou 2018*a*: 85).

Y (1493): Paris, Bibliothèque Nationale de France, Parisinus Graecus 1773, folios 17v–19v, copied by Bartolomeo Comparini da Prato at Padua.

Ald. (1496): *Thesaurus: Cornu copiae et Horti Adonidis*, printed by the Aldine Press in Venice (for further details, see the bibliography under Aldus 1496), folios 223v–225v. Copies of the text derived from **Ald.** appear in further early printed books including the work listed in the bibliography as Curio (1522) (at quire *Θ*, folios iiir–iiiir), and the following whose copies derive from Curio (1522): de Gourmont (1523) (at folios 6r–6v, in the fourth of five sequences of folio numbers this book contains), Froben (1524) (at quire V, folio 4r–v), Aldus (1524) (at quire M, folios v recto–vi recto, i.e. folios 93r–94r in the second of two series of folio numbers this book contains), and Sessa and de Ravanis (1525) (at quire F, folio viii verso–quire G, folio i recto). The remaining items in this list comprise further copies derived ultimately from **Ald.**

Rome, Biblioteca Casanatense, Casanatensis 1710 (16th cent.), folios 66r–69v, copied by Petros Hypsilas. This is a copy of **Ald.**

Ald.1512 (1512): Ἐρωτήματα τοῦ Χρυσολωρᾶ, printed by the Aldine Press in Venice (for further details, see the bibliography under Aldus 1512), pp. 265–72. There are some good and some interesting readings in **Ald.1512** that do not come from **Ald.**; these may be conjectures due to Marcus Musurus (acknowledged at Aldus 1512: 2 for having encouraged Aldus to edit Chrysoloras' *Erotemata*) or due to a now lost source. We mention **Ald.1512** in our apparatus for these readings. Copies of the text derived from **Ald.1512** appear in further early printed books, including those listed in the bibliography as de Brocar (1514) (at quire T, folios vi verso–viii

---

[95] There is a problem of page numbering in this part of this manuscript. After p. 255, the next visible number is 261, but there are seven intervening pages rather than the expected five. *On enclitics 2* ends on the page after 255, which we call 255bis.

verso),[96] Junta (1515) (at pp. 240–5), and Aldus (1517) (at pp. 265–72). The three sixteenth-century manuscripts listed next contain further copies derived ultimately from **Ald.1512**.

P (16th cent.): Venice, Biblioteca Nazionale Marciana, Marcianus Gr. XI. 26 = coll. 1322, folios 87v–89v. This is ultimately derived from **Ald.1512**, via an intermediate source shared with the manuscript listed next. We mention **P** in our apparatus for occasional conjectures and corrections.

Athens, *Σπουδαστήριον Βυζαντινῆς καὶ Νεοελληνικῆς Φιλολογίας,* **Atheniensis 25** (16th cent.), folios 203r–206v, copied by Pachomios Rousanos.[97] This is ultimately derived from **Ald.1512**, via an intermediate source shared with **P**.

Cambridge, University Library, Cantabrigiensis Nn III 14 = 2625 (beginning of 16th cent.),[98] folios 208r–209r. This is a copy of **Ald.1512**.

We reconstruct the stemma for *On enclitics 2* as shown in Figure 2.2. For the possibility that **Ald.1512** has an additional source besides **Ald.**, see the list of manuscripts just above, under **Ald.1512**.

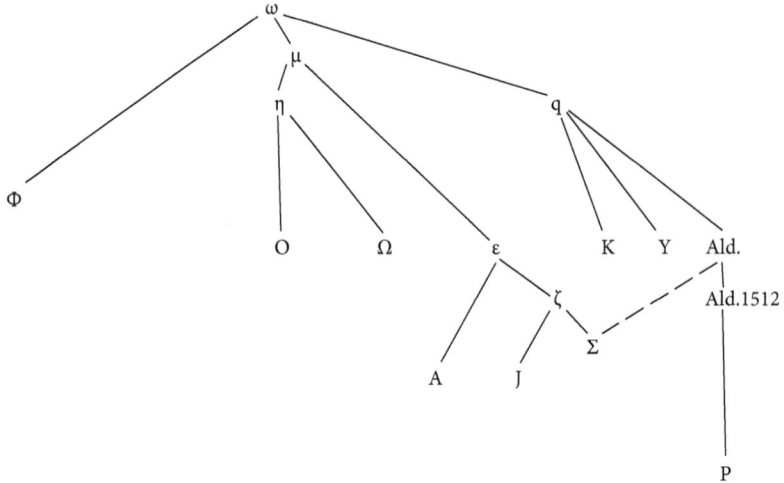

Fig. 2.2 Stemma for *On enclitics 2*

[96] Cf. Botley (2010: 133), who suggests that this edition of Chrysoloras was probably based on a copy of Aldus (1512) brought to Spain by Demetrius Ducas.

[97] Zoras and Mpoumpoulidis (1963–4: 234) date this manuscript to the fifteenth century, but Demetrakopoulos (1979: 204) argues that the handwriting is that of the monk Pachomios Rousanos (and that Rousanos was not simply the owner of the manuscript, as had been thought, but its scribe), and thus that the manuscript dates to the sixteenth century; he further points out that evidence from watermarks confirms this dating. See further Demetrakopoulos (2005); Zavakou (2017: 35).

[98] This manuscript consists of two manuscripts bound together. In a forthcoming catalogue entry, Matteo di Franco dates the second part, to which our treatise belongs, to the beginning of the sixteenth century; we are indebted to him for sharing this information. Luard et al. (1861: 482) dated the second part of this manuscript to the late fifteenth or early sixteenth century.

In the subsections that follow, we explain the reasoning behind the most import-ant points of this stemma (but not the reasoning behind the hyparchetype ζ, which is of little significance for the reconstruction of the text).

2.2.1.1 Evidence for families μ and q

We consider all the witnesses to the text apart from Φ to fall into two families, μ and q. Table 2.13 shows the points on which family μ innovates against Φ KY Ald. While three of these innovations could have been made independently, the second item is significant. The sentence ἀλλ' οὔτε ἐν ἰάμβῳ, πάρος γε μὲν οὔ τι θαμίζεις is found in Φ and the witnesses we place under q, but not in those we place under μ—except that it appears in the margin of Σ, which is contaminated with Ald. (see section 2.2.1.3). The sentence cannot be an independent addition in Φ and q, because it is too unusual a sentence, with the quotation πάρος γε μὲν οὔ τι θαμίζεις failing to illustrate the point being made (see n. 113). Nor do we have any other indications of a close connection between Φ and q, such as could raise the possibility of an addition in a single branch of the tradition (*vel sim.*). We infer that the sentence was present in the archetype and was inherited by Φ and q, but removed by μ because it was problematic. It is unlikely that this solution was adopted more than once independently, since it is not the only or even the most obvious solution to the problem. We ourselves suppress πάρος γε μὲν οὔ τι θαμίζεις and keep ἀλλ' οὐδὲ ἐν ἰάμβῳ in the text (with Ald.'s emendation of οὔτε to οὐδὲ), since ἀλλ' οὐδὲ ἐν ἰάμβῳ makes a point that we expect here: a paroxy-tone word ending in an iambic sequence fails to receive an additional accent before an enclitic. The other three points in Table 2.13 carry little weight, but for what they are worth, they point in the same direction.

Table 2.13 Evidence for family μ

Reading of μ (comprising sub-families η and ϵ)	Reading(s) of the rest of the tradition
§e, note f: παροξυτόνων η ϵ	τῶν παροξυτόνων Φq
§e, note j: omission in η ϵ (For the appearance of the sentence in the margin of Σ, see section 2.2.1.3.)	ἀλλ' οὔτε (οὐδὲ Ald. Σ [i.m.]) — θαμίζεις Φq Σ [i.m.]
§e, note s: γὰρ is simply omitted in η, while the manuscripts under ϵ have δὲ instead. (We surmise that γὰρ was present in the archetype and inherited by Φ and q but removed by μ. ϵ then repaired the lack of connective by adding δὲ.)	γὰρ Φq
§h, note c: ἢ η ϵ	ἐπεὶ ἢ (ἐπειὴ K) Φq

Table 2.14 shows the points on which we take family **q** to innovate against Φ and μ. The strongest evidence for hyparchetype **q** is the error ἐνοίσης for ἐν οἷς at §g, note d, further corrupted to ἐν ἴσης in **Ald.**

We now turn to the evidence for the two main sub-families we posit under family μ.

Table 2.14 Evidence for family **q**

Reading(s) of K, Y, and Ald.	Reading(s) of the rest of the tradition
§g, note d: ἐνοίσης **KY**: ἐν ἴσης **Ald.**: ἐνίσης Σ i.m.	ἐν οἷς $\Phi\mu$
(We take ἐνοίσης to be the reading of **q**, reproduced by **K** and **Y** but turned into ἐν ἴσης in **Ald.**, and taken over into the margin of Σ by contamination with **Ald.**: see section 2.2.1.3.)	
§k, note a: πρὸς **KY Ald.**	πρὸ $\Phi\mu$
§j, note d: ἐγκλιματικαὶ **KY Ald.**	ἐγκλιτικαὶ $\Phi\mu$
§n, note i: καγκαλόωσι **KY**: παγκαλόωσι **Ald.**	καγχαλόωσι $\Phi\mu$
(We take καγκαλόωσι to be the reading of **q**, with an individual further change to παγκαλόωσι in **Ald.**)	
§n, note g: **KY Ald.** continue the quotation to the end of the line, i.e. μή νύ τοι οὐ χραίσμῃ σκῆπτρον καὶ στέμμα θεοῖο	$\Phi\mu$ end the quotation after μή νύ τοι οὐ χραίσμῃ

2.2.1.2 Evidence for sub-families η and ε

We consider the manuscripts of family μ to fall into two sub-families, η (comprising manuscripts OΩ) and ε (comprising manuscripts AJΣ). Table 2.15 shows the shared errors specific to sub-family η, and Table 2.16 a selection of shared errors and other innovations specific to sub-family ε.

Table 2.15 Evidence for sub-family η

Error in O and Ω	Reading(s) of the rest of the tradition, including sub-family ε
§e, note p: οὐδέν OΩ	οὐδὲ (οὐδ' $\Phi\epsilon$) $\Phi\epsilon$q
§i, note e: προστακτικῶν OΩ	προτακτικῶν $\Phi\epsilon$K **Ald.** (Y omits the word)
§i, note i: παρακειμένην OΩ	προκειμένην $\Phi\epsilon$q
§j, note b: ἐγείρουσι OΩ	ἐγείρουσαι $\Phi\epsilon$q

Table 2.16 Evidence for sub-family ϵ

Reading of sub-family ϵ (manuscripts AJΣ)	Reading(s) of the rest of the tradition, including sub-family η
§e, note i: *ἐπακολουθεῖ* **AJΣ**	*παρακολουθεῖ* **$\Phi\eta$q**
§e, note u: *κυδωνίων* **AJΣ**	*κυδωνίω* **$\Phi\eta$q**
§g, note b: *ὅσα* **AJΣ**	*ὅτε* **$\Phi\eta$q**
§h, note d: *σκυζομένων* **AJΣ**	*σκυζομένῳ* **$\Phi\eta$q**
§j, note i: *ταῦτα γὰρ* **AJΣ**	*τούτων* (*τούτω* O) *γὰρ* **η**: *τούτων* **Φq**
§k, note e: *ἀντιδιαστέλλον* **AJΣ**	*ἀντιδιαστέλλονται* **$\Phi\eta$q**
§l, note h: word omitted in **AJΣ**	*ὀξεῖαν* **$\Phi\eta$q**
§l, note k: *ἐπεὶ ἐκήδετο* **AJΣ**	*ἐκήδετο* **$\Phi\eta$q**
§l, note p: word omitted in **AJΣ**	*Ζεὺς* (*ὁ Ζεὺς* Ω) **$\Phi\eta$q**
§l, note r: word omitted in **AJΣ**	*ψιλῶς* **$\Phi\eta$q**

2.2.1.3 Evidence that Σ is contaminated with **Ald.**

We infer that Σ was influenced by **Ald.**, or a closely related witness to the text, on the basis of the readings shown in Table 2.17, which Σ shares with **Ald.** against the other manuscripts of sub-family ϵ (**A** and **J**). For three of the five items, the reading shared with **Ald.** appears in the margin of Σ—an additional indication that a secondary source has been consulted (on palaeographical grounds it is possible but not certain that the marginal notes are by the same hand as the main text). For four of the items, the precise reading that passed into Σ is otherwise found *only* in **Ald.**, and not also in other representatives of the **q** family, or anywhere else. The exception is §g, note a, where *τὴν ὀξεῖαν* is found in all witnesses to the text except those under ϵ (aside from the margin of Σ), but given the other evidence that Σ consulted specifically the printed book **Ald.**, or a closely related source, the instance of *τὴν ὀξεῖαν* in the margin is overwhelmingly likely to come from the same source.

Table 2.17 Evidence that Σ was influenced by **Ald.**

Readings which Σ did not inherit from ϵ but shares with Ald.	Reading(s) of the rest of the tradition, including the other manuscripts of sub-family ϵ (A and J)
§e, note d: Ἀρκεσίλαόν **Ald.** Σ	Ἀρκεσίλαός (Ἀρχεσίλαός **A**) **Φ** O**Ω** **AJ KY** (i.e. all witnesses apart from **Ald.** Σ)
§e, note j: ἀλλ' οὔτε — θαμίζεις (οὐδὲ **Ald.** $\Sigma^{\text{i.m.}}$) **Φq** $\Sigma^{\text{i.m.}}$ We take ἀλλ' οὔτε — θαμίζεις to be the reading of the archetype, inherited by **Φ** and **q** and removed by μ: see section 2.2.1.1. In **Ald.**, οὔτε was emended to οὐδὲ, and in this form the sentence passed into Σ.	ἀλλ' οὔτε — θαμίζεις is absent from all witnesses under μ (O**Ω**AJ$\Sigma^{\text{i.t.}}$), apart from its appearance in the margin of Σ.
§g, note a: τὴν ὀξεῖαν **Φ** **η** **q** $\Sigma^{\text{i.m.}}$	τὴν ὀξεῖαν is absent from all witnesses under ϵ (AJΣ), apart from its appearance in the margin of Σ.
§g, note d: ἐν ἴσης **Ald.**: ἐνίσης $\Sigma^{\text{i.m.}}$ Σ inherited the reading ἐν οἷς from the archetype, via μ and ϵ, but wrote ἐνίσης in the margin after consulting **Ald.**	**KY** have ἐνοίσης, while **Φ** and all manuscripts under μ (including **AJ** and $\Sigma^{\text{i.t.}}$) have the good reading ἐν οἷς.
§m, note f: τὸ μὲν γὰρ που ἐγκλιτικόν ἐστιν **Ald.** Σ We infer that που was omitted in the archetype, **Ald.** repaired the error by conjecture, and Σ introduced που under the influence of **Ald.**	τὸ μὲν γὰρ ἐγκλιτικόν ἐστιν **Φ** **η** **J** (**A** omits this phrase as part of a longer omission; που is missing in all other witnesses apart from **Ald.** Σ.)

2.2.2 Previous editions

Bekker printed this text in the third volume of his *Anecdota Graeca* (Bekker 1821: 1142–8), on the basis of **Ald.**, a further Aldine edition likely to be Aldus (1524), and the manuscript Parisinus Graecus 1773 (our **Y**) (see also section 2.1.2).

Lentz (1867–70: i. 551–64) does not provide a text of *On enclitics 2* as such, but combines material from *On enclitics 1*, *On enclitics 2*, and *About* ’Ε*ΣΤΙΝ* into one text entitled Ἐκ τῶν Ἡρωδιανοῦ περὶ ἐγκλινομένων.

2.2.3 *On enclitics 2*: text and translation

§a Ἡρωδιανοῦ[a] Περὶ ἐγκλινομένων καὶ ἐγκλιτικῶν καὶ συνεγκλιτικῶν μορίων

Ἐγκλινόμενόν ἐστι μόριον λέξις κατὰ τὸ τέλος ὀξυνομένη,[b] τρέπουσα[c] δὲ[d] εἰς βαρεῖαν κατὰ τὴν τοῦ λόγου σύνταξιν, καθάπερ ἔχει 'εἴ[e] μὴ μητρυιὴ περικαλλὴς[f] Ἠερίβοια.'[g]

§b ἐγκλιτικόν ἐστι μόριον, ὃ τὴν ἰδίαν ὀξεῖαν κοιμίζον τὴν προκειμένην βαρεῖαν εἰς ὀξεῖαν μεθίστησιν, ᾧ ἢ δυνάμει ἢ φύσει ἑτέρα βαρεῖα ὑπέρκειται, δυνάμει μὲν ὡς τὸ[a] 'δῶμά[b] τε', φύσει δὲ καθάπερ Ἀρκεσίλαός τε'·

§c συνεγκλιτικὸν δέ ἐστι σύνταξις δυοῖν[a] ἢ πλειόνων μορίων ἐγκλιτικῶν ἐπαλλήλων ὀξυνομένων, ὡς ἔχει τὰ τοιαῦτα· 'ἤ νύ σέ που δέος ἴσχει'. ὁ μὲν γὰρ Η ὀξύνεται διὰ τὸ[b] ΝΥ ἐγκλιτικόν, τὸ δὲ ΝΥ διὰ τὴν ἀντωνυμίαν τὴν ΣΕ, ἡ δὲ ΣΕ ἀντωνυμία διὰ τὸν[c] ΠΟΥ παραπληρωματικὸν σύνδεσμον. εἴρηται δὲ 'συνεγκλιτικόν' διὰ τὸ σὺν ἐγκλιτικῷ παραλαμβανόμενον διεγείρειν[d] τὴν ὑπερκειμένην ἐν τῷ τέλει τῆς λέξεως ὀξεῖαν.

---

§a
[a] Ἡρωδιανοῦ — συνεγκλιτικῶν μορίων **ηΚ Ald.**: Ἡρωδιανοῦ περὶ ἐγκλινομένων καὶ ἐγκλιτικῶν καὶ συνεγκλιτικῶν **ΑΥ**: Περὶ ἐγκλινομένων καὶ ἐγκλιτικοῦ καὶ συγκλιτικοῦ **J**: Ἡρωδιανοῦ περὶ ἐγκλινομένων καὶ ἐγκλητικοῦ και συνεγκλιτικοῦ **Σ**: τοῦ αὐτοῦ περὶ ἐγκλινομένων **Φ**
[b] ὀξυνομένη **μq**: ἐγκλινομένη **Φ**
[c] τρέπουσα **μq**: τρέπουσαν **Φ**
[d] δὲ **ω**: δὲ τὴν ὀξεῖαν **P**
[e] εἰ **P**: ἡ **eq**: ἢ **Φ**: ἦ **O**: ἤ **Ω**
[f] περικαλλὴς **Φηq**: περικαλὴς **ε**
[g] Ἠερίβοια **P**[p.c.]: ἐρίβοια **μq**: περίβοια (sic) **Φ**

§b
[a] τὸ **ηq**: τὰ **ε**
[b] δῶμά τε scripsimus: δώματά μοι **ω**: δῶμά μοι Thierfelder (1935: 24 n. 2)

§c
[a] δυοῖν **μq**: δι' ἢν **Φ**
[b] τὸ **μq**: τοῦ **Φ**
[c] τὸν **μq**: τὸ **Φ**
[d] διεγείρειν **μq**: διεγείρει **Φ**

§a Herodian's *On oxytone words in the sentence, on enclitics, and on enclitic items*[99] *in succession*

An *enclinomenon* item is a word that has an acute accent on its final syllable but turns this into a grave in connected speech, as in εἲ μὴ μητρυιὴ περικαλλὴς Ἠερίβοια.[100]

§b An enclitic item is one that lulls its own acute accent and changes a preceding grave into an acute if another grave lies before this, either in effect or in actual fact:[101] in effect as in δῶμά τε,[102] and in actual fact as in Ἀρκεσίλαός τε.[103]

§c *Synenclitic* is the putting together of two or more enclitic items that are oxytone in succession, as in the following sort of example: ἦ νύ σέ που δέος ἴσχει.[104] For the Ἦ is oxytone because of the enclitic ΝΥ, and the ΝΥ because of the pronoun ΣΕ, and the pronoun ΣΕ because of the filler conjunction ΠΟΥ. And it is called a *synenclitic* because of the fact that when used together with an enclitic it wakes up the acute that lies before it on the final syllable of the word.

---

[99] On the meaning of μόριον, see n. 13.

[100] *Il.* 5.389: 'had not their stepmother, very beautiful Eeriboia, [told Hermes]'. From an ancient point of view, the word εἲ (as well as μὴ, μητρυιὴ, and περικαλλὴς) would have been considered to have a contextual grave accent here: see section 2.7.1.

[101] The syllables considered to contain a grave 'in effect' are those with a circumflex, because the circumflex is considered a sequence of acute and grave in a single syllable. For clear explanations of this point see Choeroboscus, *Th.* i. 117.32–7; Sophronius, *Excerpta e Charace* 417.28–30.

[102] 'And a house'.

[103] *Il.* 2.495: 'And Arkesilaos'.

[104] *Il.* 5.812: 'or perhaps fear has got hold of you'.

§d διαφέρει δὲ ἐγκλινόμενον ἐγκλιτικοῦ, ᾗ τὸ μὲν ἐγκλινόμενον κοινὸν ὄνομα πάσης λέξεώς ἐστι κατὰ τὸ τέλος ὀξυνομένης τρεπούσης τε εἰς βαρεῖαν,[a] τὸ δὲ ἐν ἰδίοις[b] θέμασι καταλειπόμενον[c] ἀριθμῷ ἰδίῳ· καὶ ὅτι τὸ μὲν[d] αὐτὸ[e] μόνον τὴν ἐπὶ[f] τέλους ὀξεῖαν ἀμείβει εἰς βαρεῖαν, τὸ δὲ καὶ μετατίθησιν εἰς τὴν ὑπερκειμένην συλλαβήν, εἰ[g] τὰ τοῦ λόγου ἐπιδέχοιτο.[h]

§d
[a] βαρεῖαν **Φηq**: βαρεῖαν τὴν ὀξεῖαν **ε**
[b] ἰδίοις **μq**: ἰδίας **Φ**
[c] καταλειπόμενον **Φηq**: καταλοιπόμενον **A**: καταλιπόμενον **ζ**
[d] μὲν **μq**: μὴν **Φ**
[e] αὐτὸ μόνον Bekker: αὐτὴν μόνην **μq**: αὐτὴν μόνον **Φ**
[f] ἐπὶ τέλους **Φηq**: ἐπὶ τοῦ τέλους **ε**
[g] εἰ Ald.1512: καὶ ω
[h] ἐπιδέχοιτο **Φηq**: ἐπιδέχεται **ε**

§d And an *enclinomenon* differs from an *enclitic* in that 'enclinomenon' is the common noun for every word that has its accent on the final syllable and turns it into a grave, whereas the other [i.e. the enclitic] is restricted to its own stems in its own number;[105] and in that the first [i.e. the *enclinomenon*] just changes the acute on its final syllable into a grave, whereas the second also changes its place to the preceding syllable, if the facts of the syntax allow.

---

[105] The point here appears to be that only words built on specific stems are enclitics, and even then singular forms (for example) may be enclitic while dual and plural forms are not.

§e πᾶν τοίνυν ἐγκλιτικὸν μόριον ἢ μονοσύλλαβόν ἐστιν ἢ δισύλλαβον. καὶ πᾶν
ἐγκλιτικὸν ὑπὲρ μίαν συλλαβὴν ⟨ἢ δίχρονον ἢ⟩ᵃ τρίχρονόνᵇ ἐστιν, ἀναπέμπει
τε τὴν ὀξεῖαν ἐπὶ τὴν ὑπερκειμένην βαρεῖαν ἐν τῇ συντάξει καθόλου ἐπὶ μόνων
τῶν προπαροξυτόνων καὶᶜ προπερισπωμένων, οἷον ‘Ἀρκεσίλαόςᵈ τε’, ‘Σχοῖνόν
τε Σκῶλόν τε’· οὐδέποτε δέᵉ· ἐπὶ τῶν περισπωμένων, διὰ τὸ τὴν περισπωμένη
μηδὲν πάσχειν ἐν τῇ συντάξει. ἐπὶ δὲ τῶνᶠ παροξυτόνων μόνων τῶνᵍ τροχαίων,
‘Λάμπέ τε’, ‘φύλλά τε καὶ φλοιόν’. οὐδέποτε δὲ τοῦτο ἐνʰ σπονδείῳ
παρακολουθεῖ,ⁱ ὡς δὴ ἐπὶ τοῦ ‘Ἀτρείδης τε ἄναξ ἀνδρῶν’, ‘Φοίβῳ θ’ ἱερὴν
ἑκατόμβην’. ἀλλ’ʲ οὐδὲᵏ ἐν ἰάμβῳ, {‘πάροςˡ γεᵐ μὲν οὔ τιⁿ θαμίζεις’}.ᵒ ἀλλ’ οὐδέᵖ
ἐν πυρριχίῳ,ᑫ ‘ὅτι οἱ συμφράσσατοʳ βουλάς’. ἐὰν δέ ποτε τροχαῖος γένηται
διπλασιασθέντος τοῦ Τ, ἔσονται ἐπάλληλοι ὀξεῖαι, οἷον ‘ὅττί μιν ὡς ὑπέδεκτο’.
πλὴν εἰ μὴ τὸ ἐπιφερόμενον μόριον δισύλλαβον εἴη ἀπὸ τοῦ ΣΦ ἀρχόμενον·
ἀκολουθήσει γάρˢ καὶ τοῖς παροξυνομένοις οὐκ ἐν μόνῳ τροχαίῳ, ἀλλὰ καὶ ἐν
ἄλλοις ποσίν, οἷον ‘ἵνά σφισι δῶκ’ Ἐνοσίχθων’, ‘ἔνθά σφεας ἐκίχανεν υἱὸς
Δολίοιο Μελανθεύς’, ‘τόξούᵗ σφεών τις ἄριστα Κυδωνίου’.ᵘ

§f τάξει δὲ χρῆται τῇ ὑποτακτικῇ, τοῦ τοιούτου εὐλόγως πάνυ γινομένου· εἰ
γὰρ διὰ τὸ ἀναπέμπειν τὴν ὀξεῖαν εἰς τὰ ὑπερκείμεναᵃ ἐγκλιτικὰ καλεῖται,
σαφὲς ὅτι ἀποδέξεται τὸ ὑποτάσσεσθαι, ἵνα καὶ τὸ ἰδίωμα ἐνδείξηται.

§e
ᵃ ἢ δίχρονον ἢ inseruit Lentz (1867–70: i. 552)
ᵇ τρίχρονόν **μq**: τριχρόνου **Φ**
ᶜ καὶ deest in **Φ**
ᵈ Ἀρκεσίλαός **ΦηJKY**: Ἀρκεσίλαόν **Σ Ald.**: Ἀρχεσίλαός **A**
ᵉ δὲ deest in **Φ**
ᶠ τῶν παροξυτόνων **Φq**: παροξυτόνων **μ**
ᵍ τῶν τροχαίων **Φηq**: τροχαίων **ε**
ʰ ἐν σπονδείῳ deest in **Φ**
ⁱ παρακολουθεῖ **Φηq**: ἐπακολουθεῖ **ε**
ʲ ἀλλ’ οὐδὲ — θαμίζεις deest in **μ** (verba in margine leguntur in **Σ**)
ᵏ οὐδὲ **Σⁱ·ᵐ· Ald.**: οὔτε **ΦΚΥ**
ˡ πάρος — θαμίζεις delevi
ᵐ γε μὲν Bekker (cf. γέ μεν **Ald.1512**): γέ μιν **ΦΣq**
ⁿ οὔ τι **Σⁱ·ᵐ·q**: οὔτε **Φ**
ᵒ θαμίζεις **Ald.1512**: θαμίζειν **ΦΣⁱ·ᵐ·q**
ᵖ οὐδὲ **Φεq**: οὐδὲν **η**
ᑫ πυρριχίῳ (πυριχίῳ **ΦΟΥ**) **ΦμΥ**: τῷ πυρριχίῳ **K Ald.**
ʳ συμφράσσατο apud Homerum: συμφράσατο **ω**
ˢ γὰρ **Φq**: δὲ **ε**: deest in **η**
ᵗ τόξού apud Callimachum (vide n. 118): τόξά **ω**
ᵘ Κυδωνίου scripsimus (cf. *Charax* §t et Pfeiffer 1949–53: i 397, fr. 560): κυδωνίῳ **Φηq**: κυδωνίων **ε**

§f
ᵃ ὑπερκείμενα **μq**: ὑποκείμενα **Φ**

§e Every enclitic item, then, is either monosyllabic or disyllabic. And every enclitic that has more than one syllable has two or three units of time,[106] and in connected speech an enclitic generally only throws its acute accent back onto the preceding grave in the case of proparoxytone and properispomenon words, as in Ἀρκεσίλαός τε[107] and Σχοῖνόν τε Σκῶλόν τε,[108] and never in the case of perispomenon words, because of the fact that the circumflex undergoes no change in connected speech. And in the case of paroxytone words [an enclitic throws its accent back] only when they [i.e. their last two syllables] are trochaic, as in Λάμπέ τε[109] and φύλλά τε καὶ φλοιόν.[110] And this never occurs in the case of a spondaic word, as in Ἀτρείδης τε ἄναξ ἀνδρῶν[111] or Φοίβῳ θ᾽ ἱερὴν ἑκατόμβην.[112] Nor does it occur in the case of an iambic word,[113] nor in the case of a pyrrhic word, as in ὅτι οἱ συμφράσσατο βουλάς.[114] But if ὅτι becomes trochaic with a doubling of the Τ, there will be acute accents in succession, as in ὅττί μιν ὣς ὑπέδεκτο.[115] Unless the following item is disyllabic and begins with ΣΦ; for [the throwing back of the accent] will occur even for paroxytone words, not only in the case of a trochee but also in the case of other feet, as in ἵνά σφισι δῶκ᾽ Ἐνοσίχθων,[116] ἔνθά σφεας ἐκίχανεν υἱὸς Δολίοιο Μελανθεύς,[117] τόξού σφεών τις ἄριστα Κυδωνίου.[118]

§f And [enclitic words] use postpositive order, and this sort of thing very much stands to reason. For if they are called 'enclitics' because of the fact that they throw their acute back onto what precedes, it is clear that they will admit of being postposed, so that their characteristic will actually be displayed.

[106] The idea is that every enclitic with more than one syllable consists either of two short syllables or of one long and one short (in either order).
[107] Il. 2.495: 'and Arkesilaos'.
[108] Il. 2.497: 'and Skhoinos and Skōlos'.
[109] Il. 8.185: 'and Lampos'.
[110] Il. 1.237: 'leaves and bark'.
[111] Il. 1.7: 'Atreus' son, lord of men, and …'.
[112] Il. 1.443: 'and [to sacrifice] a sacred hecatomb to Phoebus'.
[113] Here we have deleted the example πάρος γε μὲν οὔ τι θαμίζεις (Il. 18.386 = 18.425) 'up to now you haven't been coming often'. The word πάρος is iambic in this phrase only because of the effect of the initial γ- of γε, but other attestations of the doctrine we find here suggest that the following word should have been left out of account. See section 4.1 with n. 9.
[114] Il. 1.537: 'that [silver-footed Thetis] had thought up plans with him'.
[115] Od. 14.52: 'that he welcomed him like this'.
[116] Od. 7.35: 'where the Earth-shaker has granted it to them'. The direct tradition of Homer has ἐπεί σφισι δῶκ᾽ Ἐνοσίχθων 'since the Earth-shaker has granted it to them'.
[117] Od. 17.212: 'There Dolios' son Melantheus came upon them'.
[118] Callimachus, fr. 560 Pfeiffer: 'someone … of them … excellently … of the Cydonian bow'. The manuscripts (followed by Bekker 1821: 1143, line 26) read τόξά, but other witnesses to the fragment have τόξού and suggest that the word makes a spondee: see Charax, §t and Pfeiffer (1949–53: i. 397). The logic of our passage also works better with a spondaic word here, so that the three examples illustrate enclitics beginning with ΣΦ after three different metrical sequences: pyrrhic (ἵνα), trochaic (ἔνθα), and spondaic (τόξου).

§g ἐκ μὲν ὀνομάτων ἐγείρει τὴν[a] ὀξεῖαν τὸ *ΤΙΣ* καὶ αἱ τούτου πτώσεις καὶ τὰ ἰσοδυναμοῦντα τούτῳ, ὅτε[b] ἀοριστωδῶς[c] ἐκφέρεται, οἷον 'ἦλθέ τις', 'ἐλάλησέ τις', ἐν[d] οἷς καὶ πάντοτε ὑποτακτικόν ἐστι. τὸ μὲν οὖν *ΤΙΣ* ἐγείρει ἐν τῷ 'εἰ μέν τις τὸν ὄνειρον'· *ΤΙΝΟΣ*, 'μή τινος'· *ΤΙΝΙ*, 'οὖ τινι[e] κοιμηθεῖσα'· *ΤΙΝΑ*, 'καί τινα Τρωϊάδων'· *ΤΙΝΕΣ*, 'οἵ τινες ἀνέρες[f] εἰσίν'· *ΤΙΝΑΣ*, 'οὖς[g] τινας μεθιέντας ἴδοι'. ἰσοδυναμεῖ δὲ τῷ μὲν *ΤΙΝΟΣ* τὸ *ΤΕΥ*, 'ἀλλ' οὔ τευ οἶδα', τῷ δὲ *ΤΙΝΙ* τὸ *ΤΩΙ*, οἷον 'οὔτε σοὶ οὔτέ τῳ ἄλλῳ'.

§h ἐκ δὲ ῥημάτων[a] τὸ *ΕΙΜΙ* καὶ *ΦΗΜΙ* μόνα ἐγκλιτικά εἰσιν, οἷον 'ὅσον σέο φέρτερός εἰμι'. καὶ ἀπὸ τούτου ἐγκλιτικά εἰσιν *ΕΙΣ*, οἷον 'αἵματός εἰς[b] ἀγαθοῖο', *ΕΣΣΙ*, 'ἐπεὶ[c] ἦ πολὺ φέρτερός ἐσσι', *ΕΣΤΟΝ*, 'οἵ μοι σκυζομένῳ[d] περ Ἀχαιῶν[e] φέρτεροί ἐστον', *ΕΣΜΕΝ*, 'αὐτοὶ γάρ ἐσμεν', *ΕΙΣΙΝ*, 'οἵ μευ[f] φέρτεροί εἰσι νοῆσαί τε κρῖναί[g] τε', καὶ[h] τὸ *ΦΗΜΙ*, 'πεζὸς[i] δ' ἔνδεκά φημι κατὰ Τροίην[j] ἐρίβωλον'.

§g
[a] τὴν ὀξεῖαν **Φηq**: deest in **ε** (in margine legitur in **Σ**)
[b] ὅτε **Φηq**: ὅσα **ε**
[c] ἀοριστωδῶς **ΦηAq**: ἀοριστοδῶς **ζ**
[d] ἐν οἷς **Φμ**: ἐνοίσης **ΚΥ**: ἐνίσης **Σ**[i.m.] **Ald.**
[e] τινι **μq**: τι **Φ**
[f] ἀνέρες εἰσίν **Ald.1512**: ἀναίρεσιν **ω**
[g] οὖς τινας **μq**: οὔ τινας **Φ**

§h
[a] ῥημάτων **μq**: ῥήματος **Φ**
[b] εἰς ἀγαθοῖο **ΦηAq**: ἀγαθοῖο **ζ**
[c] ἐπεὶ deest in **μ**
[d] σκυζομένῳ **Φηq**: σκυζομένων **ε**
[e] Ἀχαιῶν **μq**: Ἀχαιοὶ **Φ**
[f] μευ **Φ**: με **μq**
[g] κρῖναί **ΦΩεΚ**: κρῖνή **ΟΥ Ald.**
[h] καὶ τὸ *ΦΗΜΙ* — ἐρίβωλον deest in **A**
[i] πεζὸς **Φηq**: πεζόν **ζ**
[j] Τροίην **μq**: τὴν Τοίην **Φ**

§g Among the nominals[119] *ΤΙΣ* wakes up the acute accent, as do its cases and the forms which are equivalent to it, when they are produced as indefinites, as in ἦλθέ τις, ἐλάλησέ τις,[120] in which [types of examples] *ΤΙΣ* is always postpositive. So *ΤΙΣ* wakes up [the acute] in εἰ μέν τις τὸν ὄνειρον,[121] *ΤΙΝΟΣ* [does so] in μή τινος,[122] *ΤΙΝΙ* in οὔ τινι κοιμηθεῖσα,[123] *ΤΙΝΑ* in καί τινα Τρωϊάδων,[124] *ΤΙΝΕΣ* in οἵ τινες ἀνέρες εἰσίν,[125] *ΤΙΝΑΣ* in οὕς τινας μεθιέντας ἴδοι.[126] And *ΤΕΥ* is equivalent to *ΤΙΝΟΣ*, as in ἀλλ' οὔ τευ οἶδα,[127] and *ΤΩΙ* to *ΤΙΝΙ*, as in οὔτε σοὶ οὔτέ τῳ ἄλλῳ.[128]

§h Among the verbs, *ἘΙΜΙ* and *ΦΗΜΙ* alone are enclitic, as in ὅσον σέο φέρτερός εἰμι.[129] And from this verb [i.e. *ἘΙΜΙ*] the following are enclitic: *ἘΙΣ*, as in αἵματός εἰς ἀγαθοῖο,[130] *ἘΣΣΙ*, as in ἐπεὶ ἦ πολὺ φέρτερός ἐσσι,[131] *ἘΣΤΟΝ*, as in οἵ μοι σκυζομένῳ περ Ἀχαιῶν φέρτεροί ἐστον,[132] *ἘΣΜΕΝ*, as in αὐτοὶ γάρ ἐσμεν,[133] and *ἘΙΣΙΝ*, as in οἵ μευ φέρτεροί εἰσι νοῆσαί τε κρῆναί τε.[134] And *ΦΗΜΙ*, as in πεζὸς δ' ἕνδεκά φημι κατὰ Τροίην ἐρίβωλον.[135]

---

[119] On the meaning of ὄνομα, see n. 15.

[120] 'Someone came'; 'Someone spoke'.

[121] *Il.* 2.80: 'If anybody [else among the Achaeans had related] the dream'.

[122] 'Lest...of someone'.

[123] Hesiod, *Theogony* 213: 'Not having slept with anyone'.

[124] *Il.* 18.122: 'and [let me cause] someone among the Trojan women [to weep]'.

[125] *Od.* 16.236: 'what sort of men they are'.

[126] 'Those whom he saw slacking off': an approximate quotation of *Il.* 4.240 (οὕς τινας αὖ μεθιέντας ἴδοι).

[127] 'But I do not know anyone': an approximate quotation of *Il.* 18.192 (ἄλλου δ' οὔ τευ οἶδα; for textual variants see West 1998–2000, apparatus *ad loc.*).

[128] *Il.* 1.299: 'neither with you nor with anybody else'.

[129] 'As much as I am mightier than you': an approximate quotation of *Il.* 16.722 (τόσον σέο φέρτερος εἴην).

[130] *Od.* 4.611: 'You are of good lineage'.

[131] *Il.* 4.56: 'since you are truly much mightier'.

[132] As transmitted, this is an inaccurate quotation of *Il.* 9.198, οἵ μοι σκυζομένῳ περ Ἀχαιῶν φίλτατοί ἐστον: 'who are the dearest of the Achaeans to me, angry though I am'.

[133] Aristophanes, *Acharnians* 504: 'For we are by ourselves'.

[134] *Od.* 5.170 (with the variant reading κρῖναί for κρῆναί): 'who are mightier than I at planning and deciding'.

[135] *Il.* 9.329: 'and by land I say [that I have sacked] eleven [cities] around the fertile Troad'.

§i ἐκ δὲ μετοχῶν οὐχ οἷόν[a] τέ ἐστιν ἐγκλιτικὸν μόριον· ἀεὶ γὰρ ταῦτα ἐκ θέματος ἀνάγεται, αἱ[b] δὲ μεταλήψεις ῥημάτων εἰσίν. ἀλλ' οὐδὲ ἐξ ἄρθρου. τῇ γὰρ συντάξει ἡ παράθεσις τῶν ἄρθρων μάχεται· ἅπαντα γὰρ ταῦτα προτακτικά[c] ἐστιν οὐχ[d] ἥκιστα δὲ τὰ ὑποτακτικά, ἀρκτικώτερα ὄντα τῶν καλουμένων προτακτικῶν,[e] ᾗ κατάρχει ὅλου λόγου, 'ἢ μυρί' Ἀχαιοῖς ἄλγε' ἔθηκεν' καὶ 'ὃς μάλα πολλὰ | πλάγχθη'. διὰ τοῦτο καὶ ἰδίῳ ῥήματι κατακλείεται,[f] πρὸ αὐτοῦ τε πίπτουσιν αἱ στιγμαί. καὶ ἐξ ἁπάντων τῶν ὄντων ⟨οὐ⟩[g] πολλὰ ἔστι[h] μόρια εὑρεῖν, ἃ εἰς τὴν προκειμένην[i] σύνταξιν ὑπάγεται.[j]

§j ἐκ δὲ ἀντωνυμιῶν[a] αἱ μὲν ἐγείρουσαι[b] τὴν ὀξεῖαν τὴν πρὸ αὐτῶν[c] ἐγκλιτικαὶ[d] καλοῦνται, αἱ δὲ μὴ ἐγείρουσαι[e] ὀρθοτονούμεναι. αἱ μὲν οὖν ἀεὶ ἐγείρουσαι τὴν πρὸ αὐτῶν[f] ὀξεῖάν εἰσιν[g] αἵδε, ΜΕΥ, ΜΟΥ,[h] ΜΟΙ, ΤΟΙ, ΜΕ, ΜΙΝ, ΣΦΙΝ, ΣΦΕ, ΣΦΩΕ. τούτων[i] παραδείγματα, τῆς μὲν ΜΕΥ 'κλῦθί μευ ἀργυρότοξε'· ΜΟΙ, 'οὐ γάρ μοι βωμός'· ΤΟΙ,[j] 'καί τοι ἐγὼ συνέριθος'·[k] ΜΕ, 'καί με[l] φίλησ', ὥς[m] εἴ τε πατήρ'· ΜΙΝ, 'καί μιν φωνήσας ἔπεα πτερόεντα προσηύδα'· ΣΦΙΝ, 'καί σφιν ἅμ'[n] ἐστὶ Μέδων'· ΣΦΕ, 'γίνωσκε γάρ σφε πάρος'· ΣΦΩΕ,[o] 'τίς[p] τάρ[q] σφωε θεῶν'.[r]

§i
[a] οἷόν **μq**: οἱ οἱ **Φ**
[b] αἱ δὲ **Ald.1512**: καὶ **A**: αἱ μετοχαὶ **Φ**: deest in **ηζq**
[c] προτακτικά **εq**: προστακτικά **Φη**
[d] οὐχ ἥκιστα δὲ τὰ ὑποτακτικὰ **Ald.1512**: deest in **ω**
[e] προτακτικῶν **ΦεΚ Ald.**: προστακτικῶν **η**: deest in **Y**
[f] κατακλείεται **Ald.1512**: κατακλείσεται **Φ**: κατακλίσεται **ηq**: κατακλίνεται **ε**
[g] οὐ add. Bekker: deest in **ω**
[h] ἔστι Bekker: ἐστι **Φηq**: εἰσι **ε**
[i] προκειμένην **Φεq**: παρακειμένην **η**
[j] ὑπάγεται **ΦηAq**: ἐπάγεται **ζ**

§j
[a] ἀντωνυμιῶν **ηAq**: τῶν ἀντωνυμιῶν **Φζ**
[b] ἐγείρουσαι **Φεq**: ἐγείρουσι **η**
[c] αὐτῶν Bekker: αὐτῶν **μq**: αὐτοῦ **Φ**
[d] ἐγκλιτικαὶ **Φμ**: ἐγκλιματικαὶ **q**
[e] ἐγείρουσαι — αἱ μὲν οὖν ἀεὶ in margine leguntur in **Φ**
[f] αὐτῶν Bekker: αὐτῶν **ω**
[g] εἰσιν **μq**: εἰσὶν δὲ **Φ**
[h] ΜΟΥ **μq**: ἐμοῦ **Φ**
[i] τούτων **Φq**: ταῦτα γὰρ **ε**: τούτων (τούτω **Ο**) γὰρ **η**
[j] ΤΟΙ — σφωε θεῶν **Φηζq**: καὶ τἄλλα **A**
[k] συνέριθος **Φq**: ἀωέριθος (sic) **Ο**: ἔριθος **Ω**: deest in **ζ**
[l] με φίλησ' **Ald.1512**: με φίλησεν **ΦηΣq**: μ' ἐφίλησε **J**
[m] ὡς εἴ τε πατήρ deest in **K**
[n] ἅμ' **Ald.1512**: ἅμα **ω**
[o] ΣΦΩΕ **μq**: σφω **Φ**
[p] τίς **μq**: τε **Φ**
[q] τάρ **J**: τ' ἄρ **ΦηΣq**
[r] θεῶν **Φηq**: θεῶν ἔριδι **ζ**

§i But among participles, an enclitic item is not possible. For the latter [i.e. enclitic items] always come straight from the stem, whereas the former [i.e. participles] are transformations of verbs. Nor [is it possible to have an enclitic item] among the articles.[136] For the juxtaposition of articles in connected speech prevents it. For all of these [i.e. 'articles'] are prepositive and not least the postposed ones; these have an even stronger tendency to go at the beginning than those called 'preposed', in that they begin a whole clause: ἦ μυρί' Ἀχαιοῖς ἄλγε' ἔθηκεν[137] and ὅς μάλα πολλὰ | πλάγχθη.[138] And because of this they are completed by their own verb, and the punctuation marks fall before them. And of all items that exist it is not possible to find many that come under the syntax at hand.

§j Among the pronouns, those that wake up the acute accent before themselves are called *enclitic*, while those that do not wake it up [are called] *orthotonic*. And those that always wake up the acute accent before themselves are the following: *MEY, MOY, MOI, TOI, ME, MIN, ΣΦIN, ΣΦE,* and *ΣΦΩE*. Examples of these are: of *MEY*, κλῦθί μευ ἀργυρότοξε,[139] of *MOI*, οὐ γάρ μοι βωμός,[140] of *TOI*, καί τοι ἐγὼ συνέριθος,[141] of *ME*, καί με φίλησ', ὡς εἴ τε πατήρ,[142] of *MIN*, καί μιν φωνήσας ἔπεα πτερόεντα προσηύδα,[143] of *ΣΦIN*, καί σφιν ἅμ' ἐστὶ Μέδων,[144] of *ΣΦE*, γίνωσκε γάρ σφε πάρος,[145] of *ΣΦΩE*, τίς τάρ σφωε θεῶν.[146]

---

[136] The ancient Greek category of 'articles' includes what we would call forms of the relative pronoun, as well as forms of the definite article. The former are the so-called 'postposed articles' (see e.g. Matthaios 1999: 432–4, 508–9).

[137] *Il.* 1.2: 'which gave countless griefs to the Achaeans'.

[138] *Od.* 1.1–2: 'who wandered far and wide'.

[139] *Il.* 1.37 = 1.451: 'Hear me, lord of the silver bow'.

[140] 'For my altar did not': an approximate quotation of *Il.* 4.48 and *Il.* 24.69 (οὐ γάρ μοι ποτὲ βωμός...).

[141] *Od.* 6.32: 'and I [shall come with] you as a helper'.

[142] *Il.* 9.481: 'And he treated me kindly, like a father...'.

[143] E.g. *Il.* 1.201: 'and speaking he addressed winged words to her'.

[144] *Od.* 16.252: 'and with them is Medōn'.

[145] 'For he knew them previously': an approximate quotation of *Il.* 11.111 (γινώσκων· καὶ γάρ σφε πάρος...).

[146] *Il.* 1.8: 'Who of the gods, then, [threw] the two of them [together to quarrel with strife]?'

§k αἱ δὲ ποτὲ μὲν ἐγείρουσαι τὴν πρὸ[a] αὐτῶν[b] ποτὲ δὲ μή, *ΣΕΥ, ΣΕΟ,*
ΣΟΥ, ΣΟΙ, ΣΕ, ΕΥ,[c] *ΟΙ, ΕΘΕΝ, ΣΦΙ, ΣΦΩ, ΣΦΙΣΙ, ΣΦΕΑΣ.* ὅτε μὲν οὖν[d]
ἀπολελυμένως λέγονται καὶ οὐχὶ πρὸς ἕτερον πρόσωπον ἀντιδιαστέλλονται,[e]
ἐγείρουσι τὴν πρὸ αὐτῶν[f] ὀξεῖαν· ὅτε δὲ κατὰ τὴν πρός τι ἕτερον διαστολὴν
ἐκφέρονται, ὀρθοτονοῦνται. οἷον[g] ἀπολελυμένως, *ΣΕΥ,* 'ἀλλά σευ ἀκάματος',
ὀρθοτονουμένως δέ, 'σεῦ δ' ἐπεὶ ἐξέλετο ψυχήν'· *ΣΕΟ,* ἀπολελυμένως, 'ὥς σεο
νῦν ἔραμαι' ⟨ἐπὶ[h] τοῦ Πάριδος. ἐπὶ δὲ τοῦ Διὸς ὀρθοτονουμένως 'ὡς σέο νῦν
ἔραμαι'. *ΣΕ,* ἀπολελυμένως⟩ 'καί σε πρῶτον[i] ἔθηκα', ὀρθοτονουμένως δέ, 'μή[j]
σέ γ' ἐν ἀμφιάλῳ Ἰθάκῃ'.

§k
[a] πρὸ **Φμ**: πρὸς **q**
[b] αὐτῶν Bekker: αὑτῶν **μq**: αὐτοῦ **Φ**
[c] εὐ **q**: εὐ ἕο **Φμ**
[d] οὖν **Φηq**: deest in **ε**
[e] ἀντιδιαστέλλονται **Φηq**: ἀντιδιαστέλλον **ε**
[f] αὐτῶν Bekker: αὑτῶν **ω**
[g] οἷον **μq**: οἷσε **Φ**
[h] ἐπὶ τοῦ Πάριδος — ΣΕ, ἀπολελυμένως addidimus
[i] πρῶτον **μq**: πρῶτα **Φ**
[j] μή σέ γ' Lentz (1867–70: i. 555) ex Homero: μήτε (μὴ τα **O**) σέο **Φηq**: μετά σέο **ε**

§k And those which sometimes wake up the acute before themselves but some-times not are *ΣΕΥ, ΣΕΟ, ΣΟΥ, ΣΟΙ, ΣΕ, ἙΥ, ὉΙ, ἙΘΕΝ, ΣΦΙ, ΣΦΩ, ΣΦΙΣΙ*, and *ΣΦΕΑΣ*. When these are produced in the absolute [i.e. non-contrastively] and are not contrasted with another person, they wake up the acute accent before themselves; but when they are produced in contrast to something else, they are orthotonic. For example, *ΣΕΥ* is non-contrastive in ἀλλά σευ ἀκάματος,[147] but orthotonic in σεῦ δ' ἐπεὶ ἐξέλετο ψυχήν.[148] *ΣΕΟ* is non-contras-tive in ὥς σεο νῦν ἔραμαι[149] as spoken by Paris. But as spoken by Zeus the word is orthotonic: ὥς σέο νῦν ἔραμαι. *ΣΕ* is non-contrastive in[150] καί σε πρῶτον ἔθηκα,[151] but orthotonic in μὴ σέ γ' ἐν ἀμφιάλῳ Ἰθάκῃ.[152]

---

[147] 'But...of you...immortal'.

[148] *Il.* 24.754: 'but when he had taken away *your* life'. (Hektor is here contrasted with others whom Achilles has killed.)

[149] *Il.* 3.446 = *Il.* 14.328 (but see also n. 150): 'as I love you now'.

[150] Our supplement here ('as spoken by Paris'—'non-contrastive in') is along lines suggested by Lentz (1867–70: i. 555, lines 16–18) and supported by the parallel passage *Charax*, §p. The idea is that the phrase *ΩΣ ΣΕΟ ΝΥΝ ἘΡΑΜΑΙ* occurs twice in the *Iliad*, and that *ΣΕΟ* is non-contrastive in the first passage and contrastive in the second. At *Il.* 3.446 the speaker is Paris, *ΣΕΟ* refers to Helen, and no contrast is drawn between Helen and other women. At *Il.* 14.328 the speaker is Zeus, *ΣΕΟ* refers to Hera, and Hera is contrasted with other women. (Monro and Allen (1920) print ὥς σεο νῦν ἔραμαι at *Il.* 3.446 and ὥς σέο νῦν ἔραμαι at *Il.* 14.328, in accordance with this ancient view. From a modern point of view one might prefer to see *ΣΕΟ* as enclitic in both passages, since the immediately preceding words make νῦν rather than *ΣΕΟ* contrastive in both. West (1998–2000) accordingly prints ὥς σεο νῦν ἔραμαι in both places.)

[151] 'And I first made you...': an approximate quotation of *Il.* 9.485 (καί σὲ τοσοῦτον ἔθηκα).

[152] *Od.* 1.386: 'May not [the son of Kronos make] you [king] in Ithaka surrounded by the sea'.

§1 ⟨ἡ⟩[a] *ΣΦΩ* ὅτε μὲν ἐπὶ τοῦ[b] τρίτου προσώπου λέγεται, ἐγείρει τὴν πρὸ αὐτῆς[c]
ὀξεῖαν.[d] αἱ δὲ τοῦ τρίτου προσώπου ἑνικαί τε καὶ πληθυντικαί,[e] ὅτε μὲν τό[f] ἐξ αὐτῶν
μεταφραζόμενόν ⟨ἐστιν αὐτός⟩, ὃ καὶ ἐπίταγμα λέγεται, ἐγείρουσι τὴν πρὸ αὐτῶν[g]
ὀξεῖαν.[h] ἡ μὲν *ΕΟ* 'ἐπεί ἑο κήδετο λίην'· ἔστι γάρ, 'ἐπεὶ[i] αὐτοῦ (τοῦ Ὀδυσσέως)[j]
ἐκήδετο[k] λίαν ὁ Εὔμηλος'. ὅτε δὲ μεταφραζομένη μετὰ τοῦ *Ε* λέγεται ἡ χώρα, τοῦ *Ε*[l]
ἐκφερομένου δασυνομένου, οὐκ ἐγείρουσιν, οἷον '*Δηΐφοβος δὲ* | *ἀσπίδα ταυρείην*
σχέθ᾽ ἀπὸ ἕο'· ἔστι γὰρ 'ἀφ᾽ ἑαυτοῦ'. εἰσὶ δὲ *ΕΟ, ΕΥ, ΕΘΕΝ, ΟΙ, Ε, ΣΦΕΩΝ,*
ΣΦΙΣΙ, ΣΦΕΑΣ. αὗται δὲ καὶ σὺν τοῖς ἐπιτάγμασι λέγονται,[m] ὅτε δή[n] καὶ[o]
ὀρθοτονοῦνται πάντως, οἷον '*πὰρ δὲ οἷ αὐτῷ*'. ἐὰν δὲ ἐκ περισσοῦ τὸ ἐπίταγμα
λαμβάνηται, ἐγκλίνονται, '*ἀλλά οἱ αὐτῷ* | *Ζεὺς*[p] *ὀλέσειε βίην*'· ἔστι γὰρ[q] 'ἀλλ᾽ αὐτῷ'
ψιλῶς.[r] ὑποδείγματα[s] τῶν ἐγκλινομένων, *ΕΟ,* 'ἐπεί ἑο κήδετο λίην', *ΕΥ,* 'ἐπεί εὖ
φημι βίῃ πολὺ φέρτερος', *ΕΘΕΝ,* 'ἐπεὶ οὗ ἕθέν ἐστι χερείων',[u] *ΟΙ,* 'καί οἱ εὐχόμενοι',[v]
Ε, 'καί ἑ κακὴ βούβρωστις', *ΣΦΕΩΝ,* 'τῶ καί σφεων πολέες κακὸν οἶτον ἐπέσπον',
ΣΦΙΣΙΝ, 'ἀπό τέ σφισιν[w] ὕπνος ὀλώλει', *ΣΦΕΑΣ,* 'καί σφεας φωνήσας'· τῶν δὲ
ὀρθοτονουμένων, *ΕΟ,* '*Δηΐφοβος δὲ*[x] | *ἀσπίδα ταυρείην σχέθ᾽ ἀπὸ ἕο*', *ΕΥ,* '*φρίξας δ᾽*
εὖ λοφίην', *ΕΘΕΝ,*[y] '*Αἰνείας δ᾽*[z] *ἐάλη καὶ ἀπό*[aa] *ἕθεν ἀσπίδ᾽ ἀνέσχε*', *ΟΙ,* 'ἐπεί οὗ τινά
φησιν ὁμοῖον | *οἷ ἔμεναι*[bb] *Δαναῶν*', *Ε,* '*κάλεόν*[cc] *τέ μιν εἰς ἓ*[dd] *ἕκαστος*',

§1
[a] ἡ add. Bekker
[b] τοῦ deest in ε
[c] αὐτῆς Bekker: αὐτοῦ ω
[d] post ὀξεῖαν verba ὅτε δὲ ἐπὶ δευτέρου ὀρθοτονεῖται· σφὼ δὲ μάλλ᾽ ἠθέλετον habet **Ald.1512**
[e] πληθυντικαὶ **μq**: πληθυντικαὶ πτώσεις πλαγίας σημαντικαί **Φ**
[f] τὸ ἐξ αὐτῶν μεταφραζόμενόν ⟨ἐστιν⟩ ⟨ἐστιν add. Bekker⟩ ⟨αὐτός⟩ ⟨αὐτός add. Lentz 1867–70: i.
557⟩ ω (post μεταφραζόμενον **AJ Ald.** spatium vacuum habent): τὸ ἐκ τῆς αὐτὸς μεταφραζόμεναι
δηλοῦσιν **Ald.1512**: τὸ αὐτὸς μεταφραζόμεναι δηλοῦσιν **P**
[g] αὐτῶν Bekker: αὐτῶν ω
[h] ὀξεῖαν deest in ε
[i] ἐπεὶ **Ω**: ἐπ᾽ **Oεq**: deest in **Φ**
[j] Ὀδυσσέως **ΑΣ**: ὀδυσσέος **ΦηJq**
[k] ἐκήδετο **Φηq**: ἐπεί ἐκήδετο ε
[l] ε **ΦΩJ**: ι **ΟΣq**: deest in **A**
[m] λέγονται **ΦΩA**[p.c.] **Ald.**: λέγεται **OA**[a.c.]**JΣΚΥ**
[n] δὴ **ηq**: δὲ **Φε**
[o] καὶ deest in **Φ**
[p] Ζεὺς **ΦOq**: ὁ Ζεὺς **Ω**: deest in ε
[q] γὰρ deest in **Φ**
[r] ψιλῶς **Φηq**: deest in ε
[s] ὑποδείγματα **Φε**: ὑποδείγματι **ηq**
[t] λίην **Σ**: λίαν **ΦηAJq**
[u] χερείων **ΦηAq**: χειρίων ζ
[v] εὐχόμενοι **μq**: εὐχόμενος **Φ**
[w] σφισιν **Oεq**: σφιν **ΦΩ**
[x] δὲ apud Homerum: δ᾽ **μq**: deest in **Φ**
[y] ΕΘΕΝ **Ωεq**: ὅθεν **ΦΟ**
[z] δ᾽ ἐάλη apud Homerum: δὲ ω
[aa] ἀπὸ ε: ὑπὸ **Φηq**
[bb] ἔμεναι **Ald.1512**: ἔμμεναι ω
[cc] κάλεόν τε apud Homerum: καλέονταί **ΦηAq**: καλόν τέ **J**: καλόν ται **Σ**
[dd] ἓ deest in **Φ**

§1 When [the pronoun] *ΣΦΩ* is said in relation to the third person, it wakes up the acute accent before itself. And the singular and plural [pronouns] of the third person wake up the acute accent before themselves when the paraphrase of them is *αὐτός*; this [type of usage] is also called a 'subsidiary item'. The [pronoun] *῾ΕΟ* [does this in] *ἐπεί ἑο κήδετο λίην*.[153] For this means *ἐπεὶ αὐτοῦ* (i.e. *τοῦ ᾿Οδυσσέως*) *ἐκήδετο λίαν ὁ Εὔμηλος*.[154] And when the location [of some action] is paraphrased with the use of (a pronoun beginning with the letter) Ε, and the Ε is produced with a rough breathing, they do not wake up [the acute]; thus *Δηίφοβος δὲ | ἀσπίδα ταυρείην σχέθ᾽ ἀπὸ ἕο*.[155] For it means *ἀφ᾽ ἑαυτοῦ*.[156] And there is *῾ΕΟ, ῾ΕΥ, ῾ΕΘΕΝ, ῾ΟΙ, ῾Ε, ΣΦΕΩΝ, ΣΦΙΣΙ*, and *ΣΦΕΑΣ*. And these are also produced together with subsidiary items, when they are at all events orthotonic, as in *πὰρ δὲ οἷ αὐτῷ*.[157] But if the subsidiary item is understood as superfluous, they are enclitic, as in *ἀλλά οἱ αὐτῷ | Ζεὺς ὀλέσειε βίην*.[158] For it means simply *ἀλλ᾽ αὐτῷ*.[159] Examples of the enclitics are *῾ΕΟ*, as in *ἐπεί ἑο κήδετο λίην*,[160] *῾ΕΥ*, as in *ἐπεί εὖ φημι βίη πολὺ φέρτερος*,[161] *῾ΕΘΕΝ*, as in *ἐπεὶ οὔ ἑθέν ἐστι χερείων*,[162] *῾ΟΙ*, as in *καί οἱ εὐχόμενοι*,[163] *῾Ε*, as in *καί ἑ κακὴ βούβρωστις*,[164] *ΣΦΕΩΝ*, as in *τῶ καί σφεων πολέες κακὸν οἶτον ἐπέσπον*,[165] *ΣΦΙΣΙΝ*, as in *ἀπό τέ σφισιν ὕπνος ὀλώλει*,[166] and *ΣΦΕΑΣ*, as in *καί σφεας φωνήσας*.[167] And [examples] of the orthotonic [counterparts] are *῾ΕΟ*, as in *Δηίφοβος δὲ | ἀσπίδα ταυρείην σχέθ᾽ ἀπὸ ἕο*,[168] *῾ΕΥ*, as in *φρίξας δ᾽ εὖ λοφίην*,[169] *῾ΕΘΕΝ*, as in *Αἰνείας δ᾽ ἐάλη καὶ ἀπὸ ἕθεν ἀσπίδ᾽ ἀνέσχε*,[170] *῾ΟΙ*, as in *ἐπεὶ οὔ τινά φησιν ὁμοῖον | οἷ ἔμεναι Δαναῶν*,[171] *῾Ε*, as in *κάλεόν τέ μιν εἰς ἓ ἕκαστος*,[172]

---

[153] *Od.* 14.461: 'since he cared about him very much'.
[154] 'Since Eumēlos cared very much about him (i.e. Odysseus)'.
[155] *Il.* 13.162–3: 'And Dēiphobos held his ox-hide shield away from himself'.
[156] 'Away from himself'.
[157] *Od.* 15.285: 'and he [seated Theoklumenos] next to himself'.
[158] *Od.* 4.667–8: 'But may Zeus destroy his vigour'.
[159] In context this means 'but…his' (rather than 'but…his own').
[160] *Od.* 14.461: 'since he cared about him very much'.
[161] *Il.* 15.165: 'since I say [that I am] far superior to him in might'.
[162] *Il.* 1.114: 'since she is not inferior to her'.
[163] 'And praying to him'. Cf. *καί οἱ ἐπευχόμενος* at *Il.* 16.829 and *Il.* 21.121 'and gloating over him'.
[164] *Il.* 24.532: 'and terrible poverty [drives] him'.
[165] 'For that reason too many of them met an awful fate': an approximate quotation of *Od.* 3.134 (*πάντες ἔσαν· τῶ σφεων πολέες κακὸν οἶτον ἐπέσπον*), possibly stemming from an alternative reading of the line (e.g. *πάντες· τῶ καί σφεων πολέες κακὸν οἶτον ἐπέσπον*).
[166] 'And sleep had perished for them': an approximate quotation of *Il.* 10.186 (*ἀπό τέ σφισιν ὕπνος ὀλώλεν*).
[167] E.g. *Il.* 4.284: 'and speaking [he addressed winged words to] them'.
[168] *Il.* 13.162–3: 'And Dēiphobos held his ox-hide shield away from himself'.
[169] 'And having made its own back bristle', an alternative reading of *Od.* 19.446 (for *φρίξας εὖ λοφιήν*) known to Apollonius Dyscolus (*Pron.* 76.14–16).
[170] *Il.* 20.278: 'And Aineias drew himself together and held his shield away from himself'.
[171] *Il.* 9.305–6: 'since he thinks that none of the Danaans is a match for himself'.
[172] *Il.* 23.203: 'and each of them called her to himself'.

ΣΦΩΝ, 'σφῶν τ'[ee] αὐτῶν καὶ κλισιάων', ΣΦΙΣΙ, 'καὶ τὰ μὲν εὖ δάσσαντο[ff] μετὰ σφίσι', ΣΦΕΑΣ, 'ἐρχομένων δὲ κατὰ ἄστυ διὰ σφέας'.

§m ἐξ ἐπιρρημάτων δὲ[a] ἐγερτικά[b] ἐστι τὰ ἐκ πεύσεως ἀοριστούμενα, ἔχοντα τὴν αὐτὴν ἀκολουθίαν[c] τῶν φωνῶν[d] τήν τε ποσότητα τῶν συλλαβῶν. τὸ[e] μὲν γὰρ ΠΟΥ[f] ἐγκλιτικόν ἐστιν, ὡς ἐν τῷ 'εἴ που ἐσαθρήσειεν',[g] τῶν πευστικῶν ἑκάστοτε ὀρθοτονουμένων. ἐκ πεύσεως δὲ ἀοριστούμενα, ΠΟΤΕ, 'καί ποτέ τοι[h] τρὶς τόσσα', ΠΟΘΙ, 'αἴ κέ ποθι Ζεύς', ΠΗΙ, 'ἀλλά πη ἄλλη', ΠΟΘΕΝ, 'καί ποθεν ἐλθών', ΠΩΣ, 'ἀλλ'[i] οὔ πως ἄμα πάντα', καὶ[j] χωρὶς τοῦ Σ, 'μὴ[k] δή πω ὑπ' ὄχεσφι'.[l]

§n ἐκ δὲ συνδέσμων ἐγείρουσι τὴν πρὸ αὐτῶν[a] οἴδε, ἐκ μὲν συμπλεκτικῶν ΤΕ, 'καί[b] τε θεοὶ ξείνοισι', ΚΕΝ, 'καί κεν ἐλαφρότερος', ΚΕ, 'καί[c] κε τὸ βουλοίμην', ἐκ δὲ παραπληρωματικῶν ΓΕ, 'εἴ[d] γε μὴν ἤδεις', ΤΑΡ, 'εἴ ταρ ὅ γ'[e] εὐχωλῆς',[f] ΝΥ, 'μή[g] νύ τοι οὐ χραίσμη', ΝΥΝ, 'δεῦρό νυν, ἢ τρίποδος', ΠΟΥ, 'ᾗ[h] που καγχαλόωσι',[i] ΠΕΡ, 'μὴ δ' οὕτως ἀγαθός περ ἐών', ΘΗΝ, 'οὔ θην Ἕκτορι πάντα', ΡΑ, 'ἄλλοι μέν ρα θεοί τε'.[j] ὁ δὲ ΑΡΑ οὐ παραλαμβάνεται, ἐπεὶ ἀπὸ φωνήεντος ἄρχεται. ὥσπερ γὰρ αἱ ἀντωνυμίαι τὸ κατ' ἀρχὰς Ε ἀποβάλλουσαι ἐγκλιτικαὶ ἐγίνοντο,[k] ΕΜΟΥ ΜΟΥ, ΕΜΟΙ ΜΟΙ, ΕΜΕ ΜΕ, οὕτως[l] τὸ ΑΡΑ ἀπέβαλε τὸ Α καὶ ἐγένετο ΡΑ καὶ ἐνεκλίθη. καὶ ταῦτα μὲν οὕτως.

[ee] τ' apud Homerum: τε **ω**
[ff] δάσσαντο apud Homerum: δάσαντο **ω**

§m
[a] δὲ deest in **Φ**
[b] ἐγερτικά ἐστι **ΦΥ** Ald.: ἐγερτικά εἰσι **K**: ἐγερτικά **Σ**[i.m.]: ἐγκλιτικά **ε**: ἐγκλιτικά ἐστι **Ω**: ἐγ(spatium vacuum)τικά ἐστι **O**
[c] ἀκολουθίαν **ΦΩΣΚ** Ald.: ἀκόλου[θ] **J**: ἀκόλουθιν **A**: ἀκολουθείαν **ΟΥ**
[d] φωνῶν scripsimus: τόνων **ω**
[e] τὸ μὲν γὰρ — ὑπ' ὄχεσφι deest in **A**
[f] ΠΟΥ Σ Ald.: deest in **ΦηJΚΥ**
[g] ἐσαθρήσειεν **Φζ**: ἐσαθρησείων **ηq**
[h] τοι **μq**: τις **Φ**
[i] ἀλλ' οὔ apud Homerum: ἀλλά **ω**
[j] καὶ deest in **Φ**
[k] μὴ δή πω apud Homerum: μηδέπω (μὴ δέ πω **ΩΚ**) **ω**
[l] ὄχεσφι **J**: ὄχεσφιν **Ωq**: ὄσχεσφιν **ΟΣ**: ὄχεθι **Φ**

§n
[a] αὐτῶν Bekker: αὑτῶν **μq**: αὐτοῦ **Φ**
[b] dehinc usque ad finem (ταῦτα μὲν οὕτως) desunt exempla in **A**
[c] καί κε τὸ βουλοίμην **ζ**: καί κε τὸ βουλοίμεθα **Φηq**
[d] εἴ γε μὴν **Φηq**: εἴ γε μὴ **ζ**
[e] γ' **Φηq**: δ' **ζ**
[f] εὐχωλῆς **ΦΩζ**: εὐχολῆς **Οq**
[g] μή νύ τοι οὐ χραίσμη **Φμ**: μή νύ τοι οὐ χραίσμη σκῆπτρον καὶ στέμμα θεοῖο **q**
[h] ᾗ (ἤ **J**; sic fortasse voluit grammaticus propter ἐγείρουσι) που **J**: εἴ που **ΦηΣq**
[i] καγχαλόωσι **Φμ**: καγκαλόωσι **ΚΥ**: παγκαλόωσι Ald.
[j] post τε verba καὶ ἀνέρες add. **Σ**
[k] ἐγίνοντο deest in **ε**
[l] οὕτως **Φηq**: οὕτω (οὕτω καὶ **J**) **ε**

ΣΦΩΝ, as in σφῶν τ' αὐτῶν καὶ κλισιάων,[173] ΣΦΙΣΙ, as in <u>καὶ τὰ μὲν εὖ δάσσαντο</u>
<u>μετὰ σφίσι,</u>[174] and ΣΦΕΑΣ, as in <u>ἐρχομένων δὲ κατὰ ἄστυ διὰ σφέας.</u>[175]

§m And among the adverbs, the ones that wake up [acute accents] are the indefinites that come from interrogatives and have the same sequence of sounds and
syllable quantities. For example, ΠΟΥ is enclitic as in <u>εἴ που ἐσαθρήσειεν,</u>[176]
while the interrogatives are always orthotonic. And indefinites coming from
interrogatives are ΠΟΤΕ, as in <u>καί ποτέ τοι τρὶς τόσσα,</u>[177] ΠΟΘΙ, as in <u>αἴ κέ</u>
<u>ποθι Ζεύς,</u>[178] ΠΗΙ, as in <u>ἀλλά πῃ ἄλλῃ,</u>[179] ΠΟΘΕΝ, as in <u>καί ποθεν ἐλθών,</u>[180]
ΠΩΣ, as in <u>ἀλλ' οὔ πως ἅμα πάντα,</u>[181] and without Σ <u>μὴ δή πω ὑπ' ὄχεσφι.</u>[182]

§n And among the conjunctions, the following wake up [the acute accent] before
themselves: among the copulative conjunctions ΤΕ, as in <u>καί τε θεοὶ ξείνοισι,</u>[183]
ΚΕΝ, as in <u>καί κεν ἐλαφρότερος,</u>[184] ΚΕ, as in <u>καί κε τὸ βουλοίμην,</u>[185] and among
the filler conjunctions ΓΕ, as in <u>εἴ γε μὴν ᾔδεις,</u>[186] ΤΑΡ, as in <u>εἴ ταρ ὅ γ'</u>
<u>εὐχωλῆς,</u>[187] ΝΥ, as in <u>μή νύ τοι οὐ χραίσμῃ,</u>[188] ΝΥΝ, as in <u>δεῦρό νυν, ἢ</u>
<u>τρίποδος,</u>[189] ΠΟΥ, as in <u>ἦ που καγχαλόωσι,</u>[190] ΠΕΡ, as in <u>μὴ δ' οὕτως ἀγαθός</u>
<u>περ ἐών,</u>[191] ΘΗΝ, as in <u>οὔ θην Ἕκτορι πάντα,</u>[192] and ῬΑ, as in <u>ἄλλοι μέν ῥα θεοί</u>
<u>τε.</u>[193] And ἄρα is not included, because it begins with a vowel. For just as the
pronouns that drop Ε at the beginning become enclitic (ἘΜΟΥ ~ ΜΟΥ, ἘΜΟΙ
~ ΜΟΙ, ἘΜΕ ~ ΜΕ), in this way ἌΡΑ dropped the Α, and became ῬΑ and
enclitic. And so much for these things.

---

[173] *Il.* 12.155: '[defending] themselves and the huts'.
[174] *Il.* 1.368: 'And [the sons of the Achaeans] divided those things up well amongst themselves'.
[175] 'And coming through the city among them': an approximate quotation of *Od.* 7.40 (ἐρχόμενον κατὰ ἄστυ διὰ σφέας).
[176] *Il.* 3.450: 'to see if by chance he could see'.
[177] *Il.* 1.213: 'one day [there will be] three times as many [splendid gifts] for you'.
[178] E.g. *Il.* 1.128: 'if ever Zeus'.
[179] *Od.* 3.251: 'but somewhere else'.
[180] 'And coming from somewhere': an approximate quotation of *Od.* 1.115 or *Od.* 20.224 (εἴ ποθεν ἐλθών).
[181] *Il.* 4.320: 'but I suppose [the gods have] not [granted] everything [to humans] at once', or *Il.* 13.729: 'but I suppose [you will] not [be able to have] everything [for yourself] all at once'.
[182] *Il.* 23.7: '[Let us] not yet [release our single-hoofed horses] from under the chariots'.
[183] *Od.* 17.485: 'And gods, [looking like] strangers…'.
[184] *Il.* 22.287: 'and [the war would become] lighter'.
[185] *Il.* 3.41 = *Od.* 11.358 = *Od.* 20.316: 'I would want even that…'.
[186] 'If you knew'.
[187] *Il.* 1.65: 'whether [he is resentful] about a prayer'.
[188] *Il.* 1.28: 'lest [the staff and wreath of the god] don't help you'.
[189] *Il.* 23.485: 'Come then, [let us bet] either a tripod [or a cauldron]'.
[190] *Il.* 3.43: 'I suppose [the long-haired Achaeans] are rejoicing'.
[191] *Il.* 1.131 = *Il.* 19.155: 'Great though you are, do not thus…'.
[192] *Il.* 10.104: 'Truly [all-wise Zeus will] not [bring] all [plans to fulfilment] for Hektor'.
[193] *Il.* 2.1 = *Il.* 24.677: 'The other gods and…'.

2.3 *On enclitics 3*

On enclitics 3 provides a briefer introduction to enclitic accents than *On enclitics 1* or *On enclitics 2*, but it is organized around the two main topics already familiar from those treatises (in the order in which they appear in *On enclitics 1*): which word forms are enclitic, and what are the principles governing their accentual behaviour? Like *On enclitics 1*, the treatise is best known as one of two sections on enclitics appearing in Pseudo-Arcadius' epitome of Herodian's Περὶ καθολικῆς προσῳδίας (Roussou 2018a: 299–302), but it is well attested independently of the Pseudo-Arcadius tradition and shows every sign of being an intrusion into that text (see section 2.1).

2.3.1 Sources and stemma

On enclitics 3 is transmitted in the following manuscripts and early printed books, listed here according to the main families and sub-families that we posit.[194]

Family d (treatise breaks off after κανόνος λέγοντος at §d, line 3)
E (15th cent.) = Oxford, Bodleian Library, Baroccianus 116, folio 51r.

E$_m$ (15th cent.) = Venice, Biblioteca Nazionale Marciana, Marcianus Graecus XI. 4 (coll. 1008), folios 172v–173r.

E$_b$ (16th cent.) = London, British Library, Royal 16 D XIV, folios 64v–65r.

E$_p$ (16th cent.) = Paris, Bibliothèque Nationale de France, Parisinus Graecus 2542, folio 2r–v, copied by Konstantinos Palaeokappa.

Family b, sub-family σ
G$_v$ (15th cent.): Vatican City, Biblioteca Apostolica Vaticana, Vaticanus Graecus 1405, folios 226r–227r, copied by Scipione Forteguerri.

G$_w$ (15th cent.): Wolfenbüttel, Herzog August Bibliothek, Guelferbytanus Gud. Gr. 20, folio 122r–v.

G (15th–16th cent.): Cambridge, University Library, Cantabrigiensis Dd XI 70 = 696, folios 9v–11r, copied by Demetrius Moschus.

G$_r$ (15th cent.): Vatican City, Biblioteca Apostolica Vaticana, Vaticanus Graecus 1356, folios 83r–85r.

G$_m$ (16th cent.): Bergamo, Biblioteca Civica Angelo Mai, Bergomensis 339, folios 161v–163r.

---

[194] In addition, the first sentence of *On enclitics 3*, and the beginning of the second sentence, are transmitted in manuscripts Baroccianus 57 (14th–15th cent., Oxford: Bodleian Library, folio 192v) and in ΜΠΤ (Μετόχιον του Παναγίου Τάφου) 509 (15th–16th cent., Athens: National Library of Greece/Εθνική Βιβλιοθήκη της Ελλάδος, folio 197v).

G_p (15th cent.): Paris, Bibliothèque Nationale de France, Parisinus Graecus 2594, folios 151v–152v, copied by Michael Souliardos.

G_b (16th cent.): Oxford, Bodleian Library, Bodleianus Canonicianus Graecus 13, folios 38v–39r.

Ald. (1496): *Thesaurus: Cornu copiae et Horti Adonidis*, printed by the Aldine Press in Venice (for further details, see the bibliography under Aldus 1496), folios 229v–230v. Copies of the text derived from **Ald.** appear in further early printed books, including the work listed in the bibliography as Curio (1522) (at quire Θ, folios v verso–vi recto), and the following works whose copies derive from Curio (1522): de Gourmont (1523) (at folios 8v–9r, in the fourth of five sequences of folio numbers this book contains); Froben (1524) (at quire V, folio 6v); Aldus (1524) (at quire M, folio vii verso, i.e. folio 95v in the second of two series of folio numbers this book contains); Sessa and de Ravanis (1525) (at quire G, folios ii verso–iii recto). The two sixteenth-century manuscripts listed next contain further copies derived from printed books.

Rome, Biblioteca Casanatense, Casanatensis 1710 (16th cent.), folios 77r–79r, copied by Petros Hypsilas. This is a copy of **Ald.**

Turin, Biblioteca Nazionale Universitaria, Taurinensis B VI 8 = Zuretti 10 (16th cent.), folios 5b–6b. This is a copy of the text in Aldus (1524).

Family b, sub-family ϕ

A (15th cent.): Milan, Biblioteca Ambrosiana, Ambrosianus D 30 sup. = Martini-Bassi 225, folios 67v–68v.

T (15th cent.): Madrid, Biblioteca Nacional de España, Matritensis 4635 = de Andrés 92 (previously N 114), folios 124r–125r.

Family ξ: manuscripts of Pseudo-Arcadius

R (15th cent.): Madrid, Biblioteca Nacional de España, Matritensis 4575 = de Andrés 32 (previously N 38), folios 41r–42r, copied by Konstantinos Laskaris in Messina (see Roussou 2018*a*: 83–4).

F (1495): Oxford, Bodleian Library, Baroccianus 179, folios 46r–47r, copied by Leon Chalkiopoulos in Messina (see Roussou 2018*a*: 84–5).

K (15th cent.): Copenhagen, Det Kongelige Bibliotek, Hauniensis regius GKS 1965 4°, pp. 144–8, copied by Urbano Bolzanio. This copy of the text is derived from the copy in **R** (see section 2.1.1).

Δ (16th cent.): Paris, Bibliothèque Nationale de France, Parisinus Graecus 2603, folios 51v–52r (see Roussou 2018*a*: 85). This copy of the text is derived from the copy in **R** (cf. Roussou 2018*a*: 91–8 and section 2.1.1).

Z (16th cent.): Paris, Bibliothèque Nationale de France, Parisinus Graecus 2102, folios 192v–194v, copied by Jacob Diassorinus (see Roussou 2018*a*: 86). Following work in progress by Maria Giovanna Sandri, we take this copy of the text to be derived from the one in Δ (see section 2.1.1).

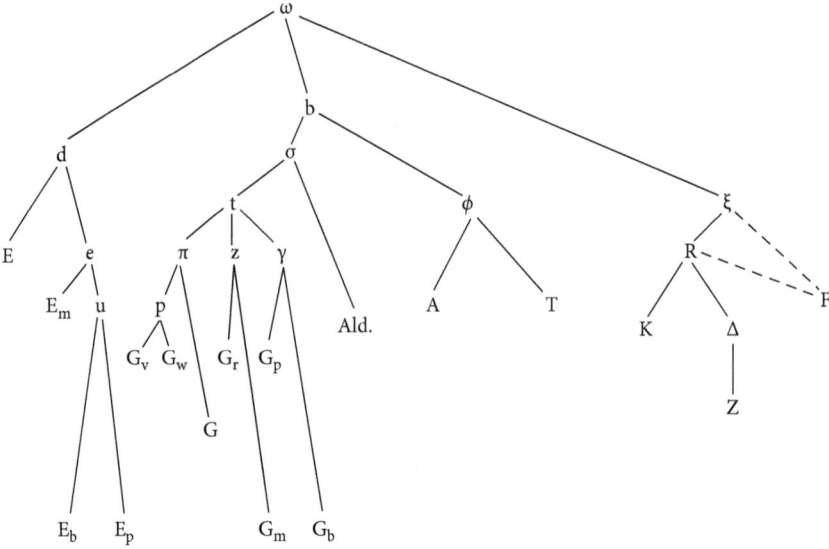

Fig. 2.3 Stemma for *On enclitics 3*

We reconstruct the stemma for *On enclitics 3* as shown in Figure 2.3.[195]

On enclitics 3 is often transmitted alongside *On enclitics 1*, and for the most part this stemma resembles that of *On enclitics 1* (see section 2.1.1). There are four differences, however. Firstly, we lack copies of *On enclitics 3* corresponding to those of *On enclitics 1* found in manuscripts **M**, **Q**, *Π*, and family **δ**, that is to say outside the *ψ*-family of witnesses to *On enclitics 1*. Secondly, *On enclitics 3* has an additional group of witnesses in the form of family **d**. Thirdly, although the witnesses we place under family *φ* come from two of the three manuscripts that also transmit *On enclitics 1*, these manuscripts (**A** and **T**) each preserve two versions of *On enclitics 1* but only one version of *On enclitics 3*. Lastly, the *σ*- and *φ*-sub-family witnesses to *On enclitics 3* appear to stand in a different relationship to one another, in comparison with the *σ*- and *φ*-family witnesses to *On enclitics 1*: for *On enclitics 3* only, the textual evidence speaks in favour of a hyparchetype (our **b**) linking *σ* with *φ*.

We have already seen (section 2.1.1.1) that in all the *ξ*- and *σ*-manuscripts, the text of *On enclitics 3* immediately precedes that of *On enclitics 1*, whereas in the *φ*-manuscripts that preserve both treatises (**A** and **T**) the situation is different. In addition to having two versions each of *On enclitics 1* but only one of *On enclitics 3*, these two manuscripts arrange the material in two different ways: in **A**, *On*

---

[195] For the reasons given in section 2.1.1 , our stemma for this treatise differs slightly from that of Roussou (2018*a*: 100) with respect to the witnesses belonging to family *ξ* (the Pseudo-Arcadius manuscripts).

enclitics 3 follows the two versions of *On enclitics 1*, whereas **T** has *On enclitics 3* sandwiched between the two versions of *On enclitics 1*.

The apparently different relationship between σ and φ for *On enclitics 3*, in comparison to *On enclitics 1*, and the different arrangement of the material in the φ-manuscripts compared to that of the ξ- and σ-manuscripts, would be consistent with a history in which all surviving copies of *On enclitics 3*, and all ψ-family copies of *On enclitics 1*, were ultimately derived from a manuscript in which *On enclitics 3* was followed immediately by *On enclitics 1*. This manuscript would correspond to ω in the stemma for *On enclitics 3*, and to ψ in the stemma for *On enclitics 1* (section 2.1.1; let us for the moment call this manuscript 'ω/ψ'). But whereas the pair of treatises *On enclitics 3* + *On enclitics 1* passed down to ξ and σ en bloc (and *On enclitics 3* also passed down to **d**, without *On enclitics 1*), φ got its text of *On enclitics 3* from a manuscript closely related—and ancestral—to σ (called **b** in the stemma in Figure 2.3) and got two versions of *On enclitics 1* from other sources. These other sources also derived from ω/ψ, but as far as the textual evidence for *On enclitics 1* allows us to tell, they did not do so via **b**. One wonders whether the acquisition of these two versions of *On enclitics 1* was responsible for φ's decision not to copy **b**'s version of *On enclitics 1* as well: two versions of this treatise (even if conceptualized as distinct texts) perhaps seemed sufficient.

The subsections that follow explain the reasoning behind the most important points of this stemma (but not the reasoning behind the hyparchetypes **e**, **u**, π, **p**, z, γ, ν, or λ, which are of little significance for the reconstruction of the text).

2.3.1.1 Evidence for family d
Table 2.18 shows a selection of common errors and innovations specific to family **d**.

Table 2.18 Evidence for family **d**

Common errors and innovations unique to sub-family d (comprising $EE_mE_bE_p$)	Reading(s) of the rest of the tradition
§a, note c: word or phrase omitted in $EE_mE_bE_p$	Ἰστέον σT: δεῖ εἰδέναι ξ (**p** and **A** omit the whole of §a, perhaps via a *saut du même au même*, since §b also begins with ἰστέον.)
§a, note t: omission in $EE_mE_bE_p$	ἐάν ποτε — ποθέν
§a, note w: word omitted in $EE_mE_bE_p$	αἴ σTR[p.c.]F[p.c.]: ἐάν F[a.c.] (and perhaps R[a.c.])
§c, note b: οὐκ ἀναπέμπει $EE_mE_bE_p$	τότε ἀναπέμπει **b**ξ
§c, note e: προπαροξύτονος ἢ $EE_mE_bE_p$	προπαροξύτονος ἢ παροξύτονος (παροξύτονος s.l. **T**) φξ: σ omits the words.
§d, note h: In $EE_mE_bE_p$, the text breaks off after κανόνος λέγοντος.	Text of **b**ξ continues to the end of §f.

2.3.1.2 Evidence for family **b** (with sub-families σ and φ)

We posit the hyparchetype **b**, linking sub-families σ and φ, as the most economical hypothesis to explain the two points shown in Table 2.19. Taken individually, neither point makes a straightforward case: the first item could in principle suggest a hyparchetype linking **dξ** as easily as one linking **σφ**, and the second item occurs in the part of the text that **d** lacks, so one might ask if we could have an insertion in **ξ** rather than an omission in σφ. However, at §d, note l, the words οἷον Ζεύς—χωρὶς τοῦ ΤΙΣ improve the sense of what follows, and their omission would involve a straightforward *saut du même au même*, from one instance of χωρὶς τοῦ ΤΙΣ to another. A hypothesis that can explain both the points in Table 2.19 is that σ and φ share a hyparchetype (our **b**), which changed the wording at §d, note g and omitted οἷον 'Ζεύς'—'χωρὶς τοῦ ΤΙΣ' at §d, note l.

Table 2.19 Evidence for family **b** (comprising sub-families σ and φ)

Reading of sub-families σ and φ	Reading(s) of the rest of the tradition
§d, note g: κανών ἐστιν ὁ λέγων **σφ**	τοῦ κανόνος λέγοντος **d**: κανόνος λέγοντος **ξ**
§d, note l: omitted in **σφ**	οἷον 'Ζεύς'—'χωρὶς τοῦ ΤΙΣ' **ξ**

A possible further innovation on the part of **b** occurs at §f, note o, again in the part of the text that is missing in **d**. Here σφ have a sentence that is lacking in ξ, and which we tentatively exclude from our text as a likely insertion by **b**. In this instance, however, there are no strong grounds for preferring this possibility to the removal of the sentence by **ξ**.

Family **b** comprises two sub-families, σ and φ. Within sub-family σ, all witnesses except **Ald.** share the hyparchetype we call **t**. Table 2.20 shows a selection of innovations specific to sub-family σ, while Table 2.21 shows the most significant errors specific to **t**.

Table 2.20 Evidence for sub-family σ (comprising **t** and **Ald.**)

Reading of t and Ald.	Reading(s) of the rest of the tradition
§c, note e: omission in **t Ald.**	προπαροξύτονος ἢ παροξύτονος (παροξύτονος s.l. T) **φξ**: προπαροξύτονος ἢ **d**
§d, note s: omission in **t Ald.**	ὠκύς **φ**: οἷον· 'ὠκὺς Ἀχιλλεύς'· ἐπιφερομένη στιγμὴ οὐ κοιμίζει τὴν ὀξεῖαν εἰς βαρεῖαν τοῦ ἐγκλιτικοῦ ἐπιφερομένου **ξ** (For our view of this passage, see Table 2.23 under §d, note s.)
§f, notes q and r: τὰ ὀξυνόμενα ῥήματα ἐγκλίνονται **t Ald.**	τὰ μὴ ὀξυνόμενα ῥήματα οὐκ ἐγκλίνονται **φξ**

As noted in connection with *On enclitics 1* (section 2.1.1.4), all the σ-family witnesses to that treatise except **Ald.**₁ are also likely to go back to hyparchetype **t**, but
the errors shown in Table 2.21 provide somewhat clearer evidence for **t** than is
available for *On enclitics 1*. That is to say, it is fairly unlikely that **Ald.** would have
corrected all three errors in ways that amounted to a precise reversal.

Table 2.21 Evidence for **t**

Common errors unique to t (comprising manuscripts $G_vG_wGG_rG_mG_pG_b$)	Reading(s) of the rest of the tradition, including Ald.
§d, note a: περισπώμενος προηγουμένου $G_vG_wGG_rG_mG_pG_b$	περισπωμένη προηγουμένη (προηγουμένου A^{a.c.}T^{a.c.}) **d Ald. φξ**
§e, note a: omission in $G_vG_wGG_rG_mG_pG_b$	λέξις πυρριχαϊκή **Ald. φξ**
§f, note h: ὅτι $G_vG_wGG_rG_mG_pG_b$	οὐδὲ **Ald. φξ**

Returning to the second of the two main sub-families we posit under family **b**,
Table 2.22 shows a selection of common errors and innovations specific to sub-
family **φ**.

Table 2.22 Evidence for sub-family **φ**

Common errors and innovations unique to sub-family φ (comprising AT)	Reading(s) of the rest of the tradition
§b, note e: συμπίπτει **AT**	πίπτει **dσξ**
§c, note j: περισπωμένην **AT**	προπερισπωμένη **Gz Ald.**: προπερισπωμένην **dpγξ**
§c, note l: θέσιν **AT**	θέσει **dσξ**
§d, note d: καλῶς μοι **AT**	καλῶς, καλῶς μοι **dσξ**
§d, note q: φέροιτο **AT**	ἐπιφέρηται **σξ**

2.3.1.3 Evidence for family ξ

Sub-family **ξ** comprises the manuscripts of Pseudo-Arcadius' epitome of
Herodian's Περὶ καθολικῆς προσῳδίας, where *On enclitics 3* appears under
the heading περὶ τῶν ἐγκλινομένων μορίων (see section 2.1). Not surprisingly, the copies of *On enclitics 3* transmitted within the text of Pseudo-
Arcadius derive from a common hyparchetype, as do those of *On enclitics 1*
transmitted in the same way (see section 2.1.1.6). Table 2.23 shows the most
significant errors and other innovations specific to family **ξ**, for the text of *On
enclitics 3*.

Table 2.23 Evidence for family ξ

Common errors and other innovations unique to family ξ	Reading(s) of the rest of the tradition
§a, note c: δεῖ (δεῖ δὲ F) εἰδέναι **RF**	Ἰστέον **Σt**: **d** omits the word/phrase.
§a, note g: καὶ αἱ (om. **F**[i.t.]) ἑξῆς πτώσεις καὶ ἀριθμοί **RF**	καὶ αἱ ἑξῆς πτώσεις **d**: καὶ ἐξ πτώσεις **t**: ἐν πάσαις ταῖς πτώσεσιν **Ald.**: ἐγκλίνεται ἐν ταῖς ἐξ πτώσεσιν **T**
§a, note i: ἄνθρωπός τις ἀνθρώπῳ τινε **RF**	ἄνθρωπός τις **dσT**
§a, note v: πόθι ποτί **RF**	πόθι ποθί **d**: ποθί πόθι **Σt**
§d, note s: οἷον· ᾿ὠκὺς Ἀχιλλεύς᾿· ἐπιφερομένη στιγμὴ οὐ κοιμίζει τὴν ὀξεῖαν εἰς βαρεῖαν τοῦ ἐγκλιτικοῦ ἐπιφερομένου **RF**	ὠκύς **φ**: omitted in **σ**
We print Stephanie Roussou's conjecture ὠκὺς Ἀχιλλεύς, ὠκύς· (intended to convey the idea that ᾿ΩΚΥΣ has a grave accent before Ἀχιλλεύς but an acute before punctuation). We suspect that **φ**'s reading derives from this via a *saut du même au même*, and **ξ**'s reading via omission of the second ὠκύς and then a clarificatory addition. **Σ**'s omission of the whole example looks like an attempt to get rid of some words that were easily corrupted, and difficult to understand even without corruption.	

2.3.2 Previous editions

Like *On enclitics 1*, *On enclitics 3* is printed by Barker (1820: 139–41), Schmidt (1860: 159–62), and Roussou (2018a: 299–302) as part of the text of Pseudo-Arcadius, on the basis of manuscripts belonging to family ξ (the Pseudo-Arcadius manuscripts). The sources on which these editions are based are as laid out for *On enclitics 1* (section 2.1.2).

Unlike our other treatises on enclitics, Bekker (1821) did not print a text of *On enclitics 3* treatise in his *Anecdota graeca*—presumably because it provides much of the same information as *On enclitics 1* and *On enclitics 2*, but in less detail.

2.3.3 *On enclitics 3*: text and translation

§a *Περὶ*[a] *ἐγκλινομένων*

Ἰστέον[b] [c] ὅτι[d] ἐν ὀνόμασι καὶ ἀντωνυμίαις καὶ ῥήμασι καὶ ἐπιρρήμασι καὶ
συνδέσμοις εὑρίσκεται ἐγκλινόμενα. καὶ ἐν[e] ὀνόμασι μὲν[f] τὸ *ΤΙΣ* καὶ[g] αἱ ἑξῆς
πτώσεις· ‘ἄνθρωπός[h] τις’,[i] ‘ἄνθρωποί τινες’. ἐν ἀντωνυμίαις[j] δὲ τὰ[k] σημαίνοντα
ἀπόλυτα πρόσωπα· ‘ἤκουσάς μου’, ‘ἔδωκάς μοι’, ‘ἔτυψάς[l] με’. ἐν[m] δὲ ῥήμασι τὸ
ΦΗΜΙ[n] [o] καὶ *ΕΙΜΙ* καὶ *ΕΣΤΙ* καὶ τὰ ὅμοια.[p] οἷον[q] ‘Ἀρκεσίλαόν φημι’,
‘ἄνθρωποί εἰσιν’, ‘Ὅμηρός ἐστιν’. ἐν δὲ τοῖς ἐπιρρήμασι τὰ ἀνταποδοτικὰ τῶν
πευστικῶν, οἷον· ‘πότε[r] [s] ποτέ’ ‘ἐάν[t] ποτε’, ‘πόθεν[u] ποθέν’ ‘ἐάν ποθεν’, ‘πόθι[v]
ποθί’ ‘αἴ[w] κέ ποθί’. ἐν δὲ τοῖς συνδέσμοις ἐγκλίνονται ὁ *ΤΕ* καὶ[x] ὁ[y]

§a
[a] *Περὶ ἐγκλινομένων* **dt**: *Περὶ τῶν ἐγκλινομένων* **φ**: *Περὶ τῶν ἐγκλινομένων μορίων* **ξ**: *καὶ ἄλλως*
περὶ ἐγκλινομένων **Ald.**
[b] Ἰστέον — ἀγαθός περ ἐών deest in **pA**
[c] Ἰστέον σ**T**: δεῖ εἰδέναι **ξ**: deest in **d**
[d] ὅτι ἐν ὀνόμασι καὶ ἀντωνυμίαις καὶ ῥήμασι (ἐν ἀντωνυμίαις καὶ ἐν ῥήμασι **d**: ῥήμασι καὶ
ἀντωνυμίαις **R**ᵃ·ᶜ·) καὶ (καὶ deest in **RF**) ἐπιρρήμασι (ἐν ἐπιρρήμασι **dRF**) καὶ συνδέσμοις (ἐν
συνδέσμοις **d**) εὑρίσκεται ἐγκλινόμενα **dξ**: ὅτι τὰ ἐγκλινόμενα εὑρίσκεται ἐν ὀνόμασι καὶ ἐν
ἀντωνυμίαις καὶ ἐν ῥήμασι καὶ ἐν ἐπιρρήμασι καὶ ἐν συνδέσμοις (**t**: ἀντωνυμίαις καὶ ῥήμασι καὶ
ἐπιρρήμασι καὶ συνδέσμοις **Ald.**: ἐν ῥήμασιν ἐν ἀντωνυμίαις ἐν ἐπιρρήμασι καὶ ἐν τοῖς
συνδέσμοις **T**) σ**T**
[e] καὶ ἐν **dtξ**: ἐν **Ald. T**
[f] μὲν σ**ξ**: deest in **dT**
[g] καὶ αἱ ἑξῆς πτώσεις **d**: καὶ αἱ ἑξῆς πτώσεις καὶ ἀριθμοί **ξ**: καὶ ἐξ πτώσεις **t**: ἐν πάσαις ταῖς
πτώσεσιν **Ald.**: ἐγκλίνεται ἐν ταῖς ἐξ πτώσεσιν **T**
[h] ἄνθρωπός σ**Tξ**: οἷον ἄνθρωπός **d**
[i] τις **dσT**: τις ἀνθρώπω τινε **ξ**
[j] ἀντωνυμίαις δὲ **Tξ**: δὲ ἀντωνυμίαις **Ald.**: ἀντωνυμίαις **dt**
[k] τὰ σημαίνοντα ἀπόλυτα πρόσωπα **dσξ**: εἰς τὰ ἀπόλυτα ῥήματα **T**
[l] ἔτυψάς με **dξ**: deest in σ**T**
[m] ἐν δὲ ῥήμασι **dσξ**: ἐν ῥήμασι **T**
[n] *ΦΗΜΙ καὶ ΕΙΜΙ* **dξ**: εἰμὶ καὶ φημὶ σ**T**
[o] *ΦΗΜΙ καὶ ΕΙΜΙ* — Ἀρκεσίλαόν φημι] εἰμὶ καί φημι καὶ ἐστὶ καὶ τὰ ὅμοια τούτων· οἷον ἐγὼ
εἰμι· ἀρκεσίλαόν φημι post ἐν ὀνόμασι — ἄνθρωποί τινες praebet **T**
[p] ὅμοια **dξ**: ὅμοια τούτων σ**T**
[q] οἷον Ἀρκεσίλαόν (Ἀρκεσίλαόν scripsi: Ἀρκεσίλαός **E**ᵦᵖ·ᶜ·: Ἀρεσίλαός **E**ᵦᵃ·ᶜ·**E**ₚ: Ἀκεσίλαός **EE**ₘ)
φημι, ἄνθρωποί εἰσιν, Ὅμηρός ἐστιν **d**: ‘ἄνθρωπός εἰμι’, ‘ἄνθρωποί εἰσιν’, ‘Ἀρκεσίλαόν (**K**ᵖ·ᶜ·:
Ἀκεσίλαόν **RFK**ᵃ·ᶜ·) φημι’ **ξ**: οἷον Ἀρκεσίλαόν φημι, φίλός εἰμι, Ὅμηρος ἐστὶν **t**: οἷον Ἀρκεσίλαόν
φημι· Ὅμηρός ἐστιν **Ald.**: ἐγὼ εἰμι· Ἀρκεσίλαόν φημι **T**
[r] πότε — αἴ κέ ποθι] ποτέ πότε ποθέν πόθεν ποθί πόθι ἐάν ποτε ἐάν ποθεν αἴ κέ ποθι μή ποτε (ποθε
Gᵦ: ποθε εν **G**ₚ)· μή ποθεν σ**T**
[s] πότε ποτέ **ξ**: ποτέ πότε **dσT** (vide etiam §a, notam o)
[t] ἐάν ποτε — ποθέν deest in **d**
[u] πόθεν ποθέν **ξ**: ποθέν πόθεν σ**T** (vide etiam §a, notam o)
[v] πόθι ποθί **d**: ποθί πόθι σ**T** (vide etiam §a, notam o): πόθι ποτί **RF**
[w] αἴ σ**TR**ᵖ·ᶜ·**F**ᵖ·ᶜ·: ἐάν **F**ᵃ·ᶜ·, fortasse **R**ᵃ·ᶜ·: deest in **d**
[x] καὶ **dξ**: deest in σ**T**
[y] ὁ deest in **T**

§a On enclitics

One should know that enclitics are found among the nominals,[196] pronouns, verbs, adverbs, and conjunctions. And among the nominals, $TI\Sigma$ and the subsequent cases [are enclitic]: ἄνθρωπός τις, ἄνθρωποί τινες.[197] And among the pronouns, those that convey persons in the absolute [i.e. non-contrastively]: ἤκουσάς μου, ἔδωκάς μοι, ἔτυψάς με.[198] And among the verbs, *ΦΗΜΙ, ʾΕΙΜΙ, ʾΕΣΤΙ*, and so on, as in Ἀρκεσίλαόν φημι, ἄνθρωποί εἰσιν, Ὅμηρός ἐστιν.[199] And among the adverbs, those that correspond to interrogatives: so ποτέ [corresponding to] πότε, as in ἐάν ποτε,[200] and ποθέν [corresponding to] πόθεν, as in ἐάν ποθεν,[201] and ποθί [corresponding to] πόθι, as in αἴ κέ ποθι.[202] And among the conjunctions *ΤΕ*,

---

[196] On the meaning of ὄνομα, see n. 15.
[197] ʻA certain personʼ; ʻcertain peopleʼ.
[198] ʻYou heard meʼ; ʻyou gave to meʼ; ʻyou hit meʼ.
[199] ʻI say [that] Arkesilaosʼ; ʻthey are peopleʼ; ʻHomer isʼ.
[200] ʻIf everʼ.
[201] ʻIf from somewhereʼ.
[202] E.g. *Il.* 1.128: ʻif everʼ.

ΝΥ καὶ[z] ὁ ΠΟΥ καὶ[aa] ὅ[bb] ΘΗΝ, ὁ ΓΕ, ὁ ΤΟΙ καὶ ὁ ΠΕΡ· οἷον 'καί τε πολέας ἐσάωσε' καὶ 'οἱ δέ νυ λαοί' καὶ 'οὕτω που Διὶ μέλλει' καὶ 'οὔ θην Ἕκτορι' καὶ 'μὴ γὰρ ἐμοί γε | σήμαινε' καὶ 'οὔ τοι ἀπόβλητ' ἐστί' καὶ 'ἀγαθός περ ἐών'.

§b *ἰστέον δέ, ὅτι, ἡνίκα ἐστὶ λέξις τετράχρονος, οὐκ ἀναπέμπει τῇ προηγουμένῃ λέξει[a] τὸν[b] τόνον, ἀλλὰ τῇ προηγουμένῃ συλλαβῇ· 'ἄνθρωπος[c] ἤμων', 'ἔτυψας[d] ἤμας'· ἐπειδὴ οὐδέποτε πρὸ τεσσάρων χρόνων τόνος πίπτει.[e]*

§c *ἐὰν δὲ εὑρεθῇ λέξις τρίχρονος, ἢ[a] δίχρονος, ἢ μονόχρονος, τότε[b] ἀναπέμπει τῇ προηγουμένῃ λέξει[c] τὸν τόνον κατὰ τὴν[d] διαίρεσιν. ἡνίκα εὑρεθῇ ἡ προηγουμένη λέξις ἢ προπαροξύτονος[e] ἢ παροξύτονος τροχαϊκὴ ἀπὸ τόνου, ὡς ἐπὶ[f] τοῦ τυφθέντα (ἀπὸ γὰρ τοῦ[g] τόνου ἐπὶ[h] τὴν λήγουσαν ἀναποδίζων τροχαῖον εὑρίσκω[i]) ἢ προπερισπωμένῃ[j] μὴ ἔχουσα[k] τὴν τελευταίαν θέσει[l] μακράν,[m] τότε ἀναπέμπουσι[n] τῇ προηγουμένῃ λέξει, οἷον·*

---

[z] *καὶ ὁ ΠΟΥ* **d**: *ὁ π͞ου* **σ**· *καὶ ὁ ποι* **ξ**: *που* **T**

[aa] *καὶ* **dξ**: deest in *σT*

[bb] *ὁ θην, ὁ γε, ὁ τοι καὶ ὁ περ* (*σ*: *θην· γε· τοι· περ* **T**)· *οἷον καί τε πολέας* (*πολέας* apud Homerum: *πόλιν* **Ald. T**: *πόλις* **t**) *ἐσάωσε* (*ἐσάωσε* **tT**: *ἐσάοσε* **Ald.**) *καὶ οἱ δέ νυ λαοί καὶ οὕτω που Διὶ μέλλει* (*μέλλει* **tT**: *μέλει* **Ald.**) *καὶ οὔ θην Ἕκτορι καὶ μὴ γὰρ ἐμοί γε* (*ἐμοί γε* scripsi: *ἔμοιγε* **σT**) *σήμαινε καὶ οὔ τοι ἀπόβλητ' ἐστί καὶ ἀγαθός περ ἐών* **σT**: *ὁ θήν οἷον οὔ θην καί τε κατέξανα φρονέοντα καί νυ καί που καί γε τοῦτό τοι καὶ ὁ περ ἀγαθός περ ἐόν* **E**: *ὁ θήν οἷον οὔ θην καί τε καί νυ καί που καί γε τοῦτό τοι καὶ ὁ περ ἀγαθός περ ἐὼν* **e**: *τοι καὶ θην περ* (*καὶ περ* **K**) *γε* (*καὶ γε* **K**) **ξ**

§b
[a] *λέξει* **dtφξ**: deest in **Ald.**
[b] *τὸν* deest in **ξ**
[c] *ἄνθρωπος* **d Ald. φξ**: *οἷον ἄνθρωπος* **t**
[d] *ἔτυψας ἤμας* deest in **A**
[e] *πίπτει* **dσξ**: *συμπίπτει* **φ**

§c
[a] *ἢ δίχρονος* deest in **eA**
[b] *τότε ἀναπέμπει* **bξ**: *οὐκ ἀναπέμπει* **d**
[c] post *λέξει* ~~ἀρκεσίλαός~~ *τε* habet **T**
[d] *τὴν* deest in **Ald.** **φ**
[e] *προπαροξύτονος ἢ παροξύτονος* (*παροξύτονος* s.l. **T**) **φξ**: *προπαροξύτονος ἢ* **d**: deest in *σ*
[f] *ἐπὶ* **eσφξ**: *ἐπεὶ* **E**
[g] *τοῦ* **dtφξ**: deest in **Ald.**
[h] *ἐπὶ τὴν λήγουσαν ἀναποδίζων* **dξ**: *ἀναποδίζων τὴν λήγουσαν* **Ald.**: *τὴν λήγουσαν ἀναποδίζων* **tφ**
[i] *εὑρίσκω* **dtφR**[a.c.]: *εὑρίσκει* **Ald.** **R**[p.c.]**F**
[j] *προπερισπωμένη* **Gz Ald.**: *προπερισπωμένην* **dργξ**: *περισπωμένην* **φ**
[k] *ἔχουσα* **Ald.**: *ἔχουσαν* **etφξ**: *σχοῦσαν* **E**
[l] *θέσει* **dσξ**: *θέσιν* **φ**
[m] *μακράν* **dtφξ**: *μακράν· ἢ περισπωμένη ἢ προπαροξύτονος ἢ παροξύτονος* **Ald.**
[n] *ἀναπέμπουσι* **dtφξ**: *ἀναπέμπει* **Ald.**

NY, ΠΟΥ, ΘΗΝ, ΓΕ, ΤΟΙ, and *ΠΕΡ* are enclitics, as in καί τε πολέας ἐσάωσε,[203] and οἱ δέ νυ λαοί,[204] and οὕτω που Διὶ μέλλει,[205] and οὔ θην Ἕκτορι,[206] and μὴ γὰρ ἐμοί γε | σήμαινε,[207] and οὔ τοι ἀπόβλητ᾿ ἐστί,[208] and ἀγαθός περ ἐών.[209]

§b And one should know that when a word has four units of time, it does not send its accent back onto the preceding word but onto the preceding syllable: ἄνθρωπος ἥμων, ἔτυψας ἥμας,[210] since the accent never falls more than four units of time from the end.

§c But if the enclitic consists of three units of time, or two, or one, then it throws its accent back onto the previous word as dictated by the classification [of the shape of the previous word]. If the preceding word is proparoxytone, or is paroxytone and trochaic from the accent to the end, as in τυφθέντα (for on going back from the accent to the final syllable I find a trochee), or is properispomenon and does not have its final syllable long by position, then they send it back onto the preceding word, as in Ἀρκεσίλαός τε,[211] Ὅμηρός ἐστι,[212] γυναῖκές εἰσι,[213] and τυφθέντά τε.[214]

[203] *Il.* 13.734 (with the reading πολέας): 'And he saves many people'.
[204] *Il.* 1.382: 'And the people…'.
[205] *Il.* 2.116: 'So, I suppose, it probably [seems good] to Zeus'.
[206] *Il.* 10.104: 'Truly [all-wise Zeus will] not [bring all plans to fulfilment] for Hektor'.
[207] *Il.* 1.295–6: 'do not give orders to me'.
[208] *Il.* 3.65: '[the splendid gifts of the gods] are not to be thrown away'.
[209] E.g. *Il.* 1.131: 'Great though you are' / *Il.* 15.185: 'Great though he is'.
[210] 'Our person'; 'you hit us'.
[211] *Il.* 2.495: 'And Arkesilaos'.
[212] 'Homer is'.
[213] 'Women are'.
[214] 'And beaten'.

'Ἀρκεσίλαός[o] *τε', '"Ομηρός ἐστι', 'γυναῖκές εἰσί', 'τυφθέντά τε'. πρόσκειται*[p] *δὲ 'μὴ ἔχουσα*[q] *τὴν τελευταίαν θέσει*[r] *μακράν' διὰ τὸ φοῖνιξ*[s] *καὶ κῆρυξ·*[t] *τούτων γὰρ προηγουμένων οὐ γίνεται ἔγκλισις· οἷον*[u] *'φοῖνιξ ἐστί', 'κῆρυξ*[v] *ἐστίν'.*

§d *ἐὰν δὲ εὑρεθῇ λέξις ὀξύτονος ἢ περισπωμένη*[a] *προηγουμένη τοῦ ἐγκλιτικοῦ, φυλάττεται ἡ*[b] *ὀξεῖα καὶ ἡ περισπωμένη, οἷον·*[c] *'Ζεύς' 'Ζεύς τε', 'καλῶς'*[d] *'καλῶς μοι', 'σαφῶς'*[e] *'σαφῶς γε', τοῦ*[f] [g] *κανόνος λέγοντος, ὅτι*[h] *πᾶσα λέξις*[i] *ὀξύτονος πολλάκις ἐν*[j] *τῇ συνεπείᾳ*[k] *κοιμίζει τὴν ὀξεῖαν εἰς βαρεῖαν, χωρὶς τοῦ ΤΙΣ, οἷον·*[l] *'Ζεύς' 'Ζεὺς δέ'· 'καλός' 'καλὸς ἄνθρωπος'· 'σοφός' 'σοφὸς ἀνήρ'. πρόσκειται 'χωρὶς τοῦ ΤΙΣ', ἐπεὶ τοῦτο φυλάττει*[m] *τὴν ὀξεῖαν, οἷον·*[n] *'τίς πόθεν εἰς*[o] *ἀνδρῶν'. δεῖ δὲ προσθεῖναι*[p] *τῷ κανόνι 'χωρὶς εἰ μὴ ἐπιφέρηται*[q] *στιγμὴ ἢ ἐγκλιτικόν'. τότε*[r] *γὰρ οὐ κοιμίζεται ἡ ὀξεῖα εἰς βαρεῖαν, 'ὠκὺς*[s] *Ἀχιλλεύς', 'ὠκύς·'.*

o *Ἀρκεσίλαός τε "Ομηρός ἐστι γυναῖκές εἰσι τυφθέντά τε* **dtφξ**: *τυφθέντά τε γυναῖκές εἰσι πῶς τε Ἀρκεσίλαός τε "Ομηρός ἐστι* **Ald.**
p *πρόσκειται δὲ* **dσ**: *πρόσκειται* **ξ**: *πρόκειται δὲ* **φ**
q *ἔχουσα* **d Ald.**: *ἔχουσαν* **tφξ**
r *θέσει* **dσξ**: *θέσιν* **φ**
s *φοῖνιξ* $\mathbf{E}_{p}$**zγ Ald.**: *φοίνιξ* **E**$\mathbf{E}_{m}\mathbf{E}_{b}\mathbf{G}_{w}$**Gφξ**: *φοί̂νιξ* duobus accentibus $\mathbf{G}_{v}$
t *κῆρυξ* $\mathbf{E}_{p}$**Gz Ald. F**$^{a.c.}$: *κήρυξ* **dpφRF**$^{p.c.}$: *κύριξ* (*κῦριξ* $\mathbf{G}_{b}$) sic **γ**
u *οἷον φοῖνιξ* (*φοίνιξ* **π**) *ἐστί* **E**$\mathbf{E}_{m}\mathbf{E}_{p}$**σ**: *φοίνιξ ἐστί* $\mathbf{E}_{b}$**ξ**: deest in **φ**
v *κῆρυξ ἐστίν* **ez Ald.**: *κήρυξ ἐστίν* **Eπγξ**: deest in **φ**

§d
a *περισπωμένη προηγουμένη* (*προηγουμένου* **A**$^{a.c.}$**T**$^{a.c.}$) **d Ald. φξ**: *περισπώμενος προηγουμένου* **t**
b *ἡ ὀξεῖα καὶ ἡ περισπωμένη* **Ald. φξ**: deest in **dt**
c *οἷον 'Ζεύς'* **d Ald. ξ**: *Ζεύς* **t**: deest in **φ**
d *'καλῶς'* **dσξ**: deest in **φ**
e *'σαφῶς' 'σαφῶς γε'* **dσξ**: *σαφῶς γε* (*γε* **T**$^{p.c.}$: *μοι* **T**$^{a.c.}$) **T**: deest in **A**
f *τοῦ κανόνος λέγοντος* — usque ad finem (§f) deest in $\mathbf{E}_{p}$
g *τοῦ κανόνος λέγοντος* **d**: *κανόνος λέγοντος* **ξ**: *κανών ἐστιν ὁ λέγων* **b**
h verba *ὅτι πᾶσα* — usque ad finem (§f) deest in **d**
i *λέξις* **σTξ**: deest in **A**
j *ἐν* deest in **tφ**
k *συνεπείᾳ* **Ald. ξ**: *συνθέσει* **tφR**$^{s.l.}$: *συνθέσει συνεπείᾳ* **F**
l *οἷον 'Ζεύς' — 'χωρὶς τοῦ ΤΙΣ'* **ξ**: deest in **b**
m *φυλάττει* **φξ**: *φυλάσσει* **σ**
n *οἷον* **σξ**: deest in **φ**
o *εἰς* scripsi: *εἷς* **Ald. A**: *εἶς* **tTξ**
p *προσθεῖναι* **Ald. φξ**: *προσθῆναι* sic **t**
q *ἐπιφέρηται* **σξ**: *φέροιτο* **φ**
r *τότε γὰρ* **Ald. ξ**: deest in **tφ**
s *'ὠκὺς Ἀχιλλεύς', 'ὠκύς·'* scripsi: *ὠκύς* **φ**: *οἷον· 'ὠκὺς Ἀχιλλεύς'· ἐπιφερομένη στιγμὴ οὐ κοιμίζει τὴν ὀξεῖαν εἰς βαρεῖαν τοῦ ἐγκλιτικοῦ ἐπιφερομένου* **ξ**: deest in **σ**

The words 'and does not have its final syllable long by position' are included because of the words φοῖνιξ and κῆρυξ. For when these precede there is no throwing back of the accent: φοῖνιξ ἐστί,[215] κῆρυξ ἐστίν.[216]

§d But if one finds an oxytone or perispomenon word preceding the enclitic, the acute or the circumflex is kept, as in Ζεύς and Ζεύς τε,[217] καλῶς and καλῶς μοι,[218] σαφῶς and σαφῶς γε.[219] The rule says that every oxytone word often lulls its acute to a grave in connected speech, apart from [interrogative] ΤΙΣ, as in Ζεύς but Ζεὺς δέ,[220] καλός but καλὸς ἄνθρωπος,[221] σοφός but σοφὸς ἀνήρ.[222] The words 'apart from ΤΙΣ' are included because this word keeps its acute, as in τίς πόθεν εἰς ἀνδρῶν.[223] And one needs to add to the rule 'unless punctuation or an enclitic follows'. For then the acute is not lulled to a grave, as in ὠκὺς Ἀχιλλεύς, but ὠκύς.[224]

---

[215] 'A Phoenician is'.
[216] 'A herald is'.
[217] 'And Zeus'. The phrase is possibly intended as a quotation, e.g. of *Il.* 9.457.
[218] 'Well to me'.
[219] 'Clearly at any rate'.
[220] 'But Zeus'. The phrase is possibly intended as a quotation, e.g. of *Il.* 1.533.
[221] 'Beautiful person'.
[222] 'Wise man'.
[223] E.g. *Il.* 21.150: 'Who are you, and from where among men?'
[224] E.g. *Il.* 1.58: 'swift Achilles'; 'swift'.

§e εἰ δὲ πρὸ τοῦ ἐγκλιτικοῦ εὑρεθῇ λέξις[a] πυρριχαϊκὴ ἀπὸ τόνου, δηλονότι ἐπὶ τὴν λήγουσαν, ὡς ἐπὶ τοῦ 'πολλάκις', ἢ ἰαμβικὴ ἀπὸ τόνου, ὡς ἐπὶ τοῦ 'μεταμέλει', ἢ σπονδειακὴ[b] ἀπὸ τόνου, ὡς ἐπὶ[c] τοῦ 'Ἀτρείδης', καὶ ἐπιφέρονται δισύλλαβα ἐγκλιτικά, φυλακτικὰ γίνονται τῶν ἰδίων τόνων, ὡς[d] 'Ἀτρείδης ἐστί', 'μεταμέλει[e] ἡμῖν', 'πολλάκις εἰσί'. δεῖ δὲ προσθεῖναι[f] 'χωρὶς τῶν ἀπὸ τοῦ[g] ΣΦ[h] ἀρχομένων ἀντωνυμιῶν'. αὗται γὰρ ἀναπέμπουσι τὸν τόνον τῇ προηγουμένῃ λέξει, οἷον·[i] 'Ἀτρείδής[j] σφισι', 'πολλάκίς[k] σφεας'. εἰ δὲ μὴ ὦσι δισύλλαβα, ἀλλὰ μονοσύλλαβα, τῷ νῷ μόνῳ γίνεται ἡ[l] ἔγκλισις· 'μεταμέλει[m] μοι', 'πολλάκις τις', 'Ἀτρείδης τε'. ταῦτα γὰρ οὔτε τὸν ἴδιον τόνον δύνανται[n] φυλάττειν, οὔτε ἀναπέμπουσιν αὐτὸν[o] [p] τῇ προηγουμένῃ λέξει.

§e

[a] λέξις πυρριχαϊκὴ deest in **t**
[b] σπονδειακὴ **Ald.** ξ: σπονδιακὴ **t**: σπονδαϊκὴ φ
[c] ἐπὶ τοῦ σξ: deest in φ
[d] ὡς **Ald.** ξ: deest in **t**φ
[e] μεταμέλει σξ: καὶ μεταμέλει φ
[f] προσθεῖναι **Ald.** φξ: προσθῆναι **t**
[g] τοῦ **b**: om. ξ
[h] ΣΦ **A**ξ: σφι σ**T**
[i] οἷον **Ald.** ξ: deest in **t**φ
[j] Ἀτρείδής σφισι π**G**ₘ **Ald.** φ(**T**ᵖ·ᶜ·): Ἀτρείδή φησι **G**ₚ**T**ᵃ·ᶜ·ξ: Ἀτρειδή φησι **G**ᵦ: Ἀτρείδής φισὶ **G**ᵣ
[k] πολλάκίς σφεας **Ald.** ξ: πολλάκίς σφεων (πολλακίσφεων **G**ᵥγ: πολλάκίσφεων **G**ᵣ) **t**φ
[l] ἡ σ**T**ξ: deest in **A**
[m] μεταμέλει **G**ᵥ**G**z **Ald.** φξ: μεταμέλλει **G**ᵥ**G**ₚ: μεταμμέλει **G**ᵦ
[n] δύνανται **b**F: δύναται **R**
[o] αὐτὸν τῇ προηγουμένῃ λέξει — παραπέμψουσι (§f) deest in π
[p] αὐτὸν deest in **Ald.**

§e But if one finds before the enclitic a word that is pyrrhic starting from the accent—that is [from there] up to the final syllable—, as in πολλάκις, or iambic starting from the accent, as in μεταμέλει, or spondaic starting from the accent, as in Ἀτρείδης, and disyllabic enclitics follow, they preserve their own accents, as in Ἀτρείδης ἐστί, μεταμέλει ἡμῖν, πολλάκις εἰσί.[225] And one must add 'apart from the pronouns beginning with ΣΦ'. For these send their accents back onto the preceding word, as in Ἀτρείδής σφισι, πολλάκίς σφεας.[226] And if they are not disyllabic but monosyllabic, the throwing back of the accent happens only in the mind, as in μεταμέλει μοι, πολλάκις τις, Ἀτρείδης τε.[227] For these enclitics can neither keep their own accent, nor do they throw it back onto the preceding word.

[225] 'The son of Atreus is', 'we are sorry', 'they are often'.
[226] 'The son of Atreus…to them', 'often…them'.
[227] 'I am sorry', 'often someone', 'and the son of Atreus'.

§f γίνωσκε[a] δέ, ὅτι οὐδὲν προτακτικὸν[b] ἐγκλίνεσθαι δύναται· τίνι γὰρ παραπέμψουσι[c] τὸν ἴδιον τόνον; ἀλλ᾽ οὐδὲ[d] τὰ ἔχοντα προηγουμένην στιγμήν· πῶς γὰρ διαζεύξεως προηγουμένης ἔγκλισις γένηται;[e] καί[f] τούτου χάριν τὰ ἄρθρα οὐκ ἐγκλίνονται.[g] οὐδὲ[h] τὰ βαρυνόμενα αὐτὰ καθ᾽ αὑτὰ[i] ἐν[j] τῇ συντάξει δύνανται[k] ἐγκλίνεσθαι· τὰ[l] γὰρ ἐγκλινόμενα αὐτὰ καθ᾽ ἑαυτὰ[m] θέλουσιν ἔχειν ἐπὶ τέλους τὸν τόνον. ὅτι[n] τὰ ἐγκλινόμενα κατὰ τὴν εὐθεῖαν καὶ κατὰ τὰς ἄλλας πτώσεις ἐγκλίνεσθαι[o] δύνανται. ὅτι[p] τὰ μὴ[q] ὀξυνόμενα ῥήματα οὐκ[r] ἐγκλίνονται, καὶ ὅτι[s] τὰ ἐγκλινόμενα κατὰ τὸν ἐνεστῶτα οὐ πάντως κατὰ[t] τὰ λοιπὰ ἐγκλίνονται.[u]

§f
[a] γίνωσκε δὲ deest in **zγ**
[b] προτακτικὸν **Gₘ Ald. Aξ**: προστακτικὸν **GᵣγT**
[c] παραπέμψουσι (παραπέμψωσι **Ald. ξ**) **Ald. ξ**: ἀποπέμψουσι **Tᵖ·ᶜ·**: ἀποπέμπουσι **zφ**: ἀναπέμπουσι **γ**
[d] οὐδὲ **Ald. Tξ**: οὐ **tA**
[e] γένηται **σAξ**: γίνεται **T**
[f] καὶ **σξ**: deletum legitur in **T**: deest in **A**
[g] ἐγκλίνονται **Ald. φξ**: ἐγκλίνεται **t**
[h] οὐδὲ **Ald. φξ**: ὅτι **t**
[i] αὐτὰ **φξ**: ἑαυτὰ **σ**
[j] ἐν τῇ συντάξει — αὐτὰ καθ᾽ ἑαυτὰ deest in **t**
[k] δύνανται **Ald. Tξ**: δύναται **A**
[l] τὰ γὰρ ἐγκλινόμενα — ἐπὶ τέλους τὸν τόνον deest in **Ald.**
[m] ἑαυτὰ **Tξ**: αὐτὰ **A**
[n] ὅτι **tφξ**: ἔτι **Ald.**
[o] ἐγκλίνεσθαι δύνανται **ξ**: ἐγκλίνεσθαι δύνανται (δύνανται **Ald.**: θέλουσι **tφ**)· διὸ οὔτε αἱ προθέσεις οὔτε αἱ μετοχαὶ ἐγκλίνεσθαι δύνανται (ἐγκλίνεσθαι δύνανται **φ**: ἐγκλίνεσθαι δύνασθαι **Tᵃ·ᶜ·**: ἐγκλίνεσθαι θέλουσιν **σ**) **b**
[p] ὅτι **tφξ**: ἔτι **Ald.**
[q] μὴ **φξ**: deest in **σ**
[r] οὐκ **φξ**: deest in **σ**
[s] ὅτι **tφξ**: deest in **Ald.**
[t] κατὰ **Ald. φξ**: καὶ κατὰ **t**
[u] post ἐγκλίνονται verba ἐν γὰρ τοῖς ῥήμασι τάδε μόνον ἐγκλίνονται· εἰμί· εἶς· εἶ δὲ ἀνέγκλιτον· ἐστί· ἐστόν· ἐσμέν· ἐστέ· εἰσέν (sic)· φημί· φῆς δέ, ἀνέγκλιτον· φησί· φαμέν· φατέ· φασί praebet **Ald.**

§f And know that no prepositive word can be enclitic. For onto what will they throw their own accent back? Nor those with a preceding punctuation mark. For if there is a discontinuity, how will the throwing back of the accent happen? And this is why articles [i.e. the definite article and the relative pronoun] are not enclitic. Nor can words that are barytone [i.e. accented on a non-final syllable] when by themselves be enclitic in connected speech. For enclitics are normally accented on the final syllable when by themselves. Enclitics can throw their accents back in the nominative and in the other cases. Verbs that are not oxytone are not enclitic, and those that are enclitic in the present are not always enclitic in the other tenses.

2.4 *Charax*

The treatise attributed to John Charax shares many features of form and content with our other treatises on enclitics. Like *On enclitics 1*, for instance, this treatise begins by telling us that while there are eight parts of speech, five of them contain enclitics. Further on (§§l–w) there is an account of which word forms are enclitic, in the familiar part-of-speech by part-of-speech arrangement. And yet a distinctive, and combative, authorial voice emerges too: the author alludes to disagreements between different grammarians, assertively states his own positions, and names individuals he disagrees with (see §§g, i, j, m, n, q, v, w). The attribution to Charax may or may not be reliable, and Charax is in any case a figure about whom not much is known (see Kaster 1988: 391–2, who dates him between the sixth and the ninth centuries), but for convenience we shall call the author Charax and the treatise *Charax*. In sections 2.7.4–2.7.5 we shall return to some of the debates Charax engages in, to consider what was at stake.

A curious feature of the textual tradition of *Charax* is that in eight of the manuscripts (out of twenty non-derivative witnesses altogether) the text breaks off before the end. With two exceptions (the closely related copies in manuscripts **ΦH**, and those in **UX**), all the breaking-off points occur at different places in the text and must be at least partly independent of one another. Some of the hyparchetypes may have become difficult to read beyond a certain point, and this would explain why manuscripts in family **w₁**—with the notable exception of **B**—and those in family **s**, sub-family **a** tend to break off at points close to one another. It remains curious, however, that this should have happened at several different points in the tradition (the hyparchetypes of family **w₁** and family **s**, and a source of manuscript **Γ**). Alternatively, or in addition, one might wonder if Charax's combative style—which gives us such a valuable window onto late antique or medieval debates and controversies—made some medieval and Renaissance scholars tire of his work more quickly than they did of our other treatises, which lay out rules more straightforwardly and in a shorter compass.

2.4.1 Sources and stemma

Charax is transmitted in the following manuscripts and early printed books, listed here according to (where relevant) the main families and sub-families we posit:

Family w₁

Φ (13th–14th cent.): Vatican City, Biblioteca Apostolica Vaticana, Vaticanus Gr. 2226, folios 190v–191v. The text breaks off after πυσματικά at §o, line 5.

H (14th–15th cent.): London, British Library, Harleianus 5624, folios 73v–77r, copied by Iohannes Chionopoulos. The text breaks off after πυσματικὰ at §o, line 5.

G (15th cent.): Modena, Biblioteca Estense Universitaria, Mutinensis α.Q.5.20 (87 Puntoni), folios 83v–85r, copied by Andronikos Kallistos. The text breaks off after πρώτης ἐγένετο at §n, line 8.

Cambridge, University Library, Cantabrigiensis Dd XI 70 = 696 (15th–16th cent.), folios 124r–125v / 148r–149v (there are two sets of folio numbers), copied by Michael Souliardos. This is a copy of the text in **G**. (For practical reasons, this is the codex we call **G** for *On Enclitics 1* and *3*.)

B (14th cent.): Milan, Biblioteca Ambrosiana, Ambrosianus G 27 sup. = Martini-Bassi 389, folios 76r–84v.

Λ (14th–16th cent.): Florence, Biblioteca Riccardiana, Riccardianus 62, folios 149v–150v. The text breaks off after σχέτλιός at §m, line 8.

Manuscript *Γ*

Γ (15th cent.): Paris, Bibliothèque Nationale de France, Parisinus Graecus 2558, folio 39r–v. The text breaks off after ὦσιν ὡς at §i, line 13.

Family w₂

Θ (15th cent.): Perugia, Biblioteca Comunale Augusta, Perugiensis G 11, folios 73r–78v.

Y (15th cent.): Paris, Bibliothèque Nationale de France, Parisinus Graecus 1773, folios 284v–288r.

L (14th cent.): Florence, Biblioteca Medicea Laurenziana, Laurentianus Plut. 57.26, folios 51r–57v.

Lᵥ (16th cent.): Vatican City, Biblioteca Apostolica Vaticana, Vaticanus Ottobonianus Graecus 384, folios 325r–330r, copied by Konstantinos Mesobotes.

V (15th cent.): Olomouc, Státní Vědecká Knihovna, Olomoucensis M 79, folios 138v–141r, copied by Demetrius Tribolis.

Manuscript N

N (late 13th cent.): Florence, Biblioteca Medicea Laurenziana, Laurentianus Plut. 58.25, folios 7r–10r; copied by Cyriacus Prasianus (?), in southern Italy (see Crostini 2019: 147–8).

Family s, sub-family a

Q (late 13th cent.): Venice, Biblioteca Nazionale Marciana, Marcianus Graecus Z. 512 = coll. 678, folios 52v–53r. This manuscript contains a highly abbreviated version of the text, which breaks off after ποιήσω at §g, line 9.

U (15th–16th cent.): Naples, Biblioteca Nazionale di Napoli, Neapolitanus II D 3, folios 30v–31v. The text breaks off after διδάξομεν at §k, line 2.

X (15th–16th cent.): Paris, Bibliothèque Nationale de France, Parisinus Coislinianus 176, folios 38r–38v, copied by Konstantinos Mesobotes. The text in this manuscript too breaks off after διδάξομεν at §k, line 2.

Family s, sub-family ρ

J (16th cent.): El Escorial, Real Biblioteca del Monasterio de San Lorenzo, Escorialensis Ψ.IV.23 = de Andrés 497, folios 151r–156v.

Σ (15th–16th cent.): Vatican City, Biblioteca Apostolica Vaticana, Vaticanus Graecus 1751, folios 302r–306r, copied by a scribe named Μανουήλ.

S (c.1485): Madrid, Biblioteca Nacional de España, Matritensis 4615 = de Andrés 72 (previously N 83), folios 75r–78r.

T (15th cent.): Madrid, Biblioteca Nacional de España, Matritensis 4635 = de Andrés 92 (previously N 114), folios 128r–132v. Due to our oversight this is not included in the stemma or apparatus, but the text would be unaffected.

K (15th cent.): Copenhagen, Det Kongelige Bibliotek, Hauniensis regius GKS 1965 4°, pp. 255/2–64,[228] copied by Urbano Bolzanio.

Ald. (1496): *Thesaurus: Cornu copiae et Horti Adonidis*, printed by the Aldine Press in Venice (see the bibliography under Aldus 1496), folios 226r–229v. Copies of the text derived from **Ald.** appear in further early printed books including Curio (1522) (at quire Θ, folios iiii recto–v verso), and the following whose copies derive from Curio (1522): de Gourmont (1523) (at folios 7r–8v, in the fourth of five sequences of folio numbers); Froben (1524) (at quire V, folios 4v–6r); Aldus (1524) (at quire M, folios vi recto – vii recto, i.e. folios 94r–95r in the second of two series of folio numbers), and Sessa and de Ravanis (1525) (at quire G, folios i verso – ii verso). Three further copies derived ultimately from **Ald.** are listed next.

Rome, Biblioteca Casanatense, Casanatensis 1710 (16th cent.), folios 70v–76v, copied by Petros Hypsilas. This is a copy of **Ald.**

Turin, Biblioteca Nazionale Universitaria, Taurinensis B VI 8 = Zuretti 10 (16th cent.), folios 2a–5a. This is a copy of the text in Aldus (1524).

W (17th cent.): Palermo, Biblioteca Comunale di Palermo, Palermo 2 Qq A 77 (17th cent.), folios 133r–134v. This is a copy of the text in Aldus (1524). We mention **W** in our apparatus for one nice correction.

Latin translation

Vatican City, Biblioteca Apostolica Vaticana, Vaticanus Barberinianus Graecus 108 (15th–16th cent.), folios 20r–23v. This Latin text is primarily a translation of *Charax*; we suspect it is based at least in part on the Aldine version of the Greek text we call **Ald.** The Latin text also includes some material reminiscent of *On enclitics 2*, §c (folio 20v) and §j (folio 22v).

---

[228] On the page numbering problem in this part of this manuscript, see n. 95. *Charax* begins two pages after p. 255, and we call the relevant page 255/2.

At folio 21v there is some material reminiscent of *On enclitics 1*, §d, in the Aldine version we call **Ald.₁** (see section 3.2, passage (3.9)), and more distantly reminiscent of *About ΈΣΤΙΝ*, §a, in the Aldine version **Ald.** The Latin translation has not provided us with any useful readings not found in other sources.

We reconstruct the stemma for *Charax* as shown in Figure 2.4.

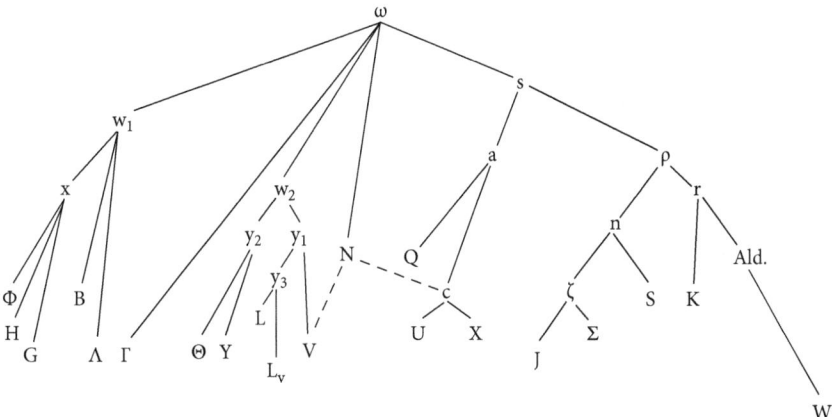

Fig. 2.4 Stemma for *Charax*

We consider all witnesses to the text except for manuscripts *Γ* and **N** to fall into three families, which we call **w₁**, **w₂**, and **s**. As mentioned already, however, in numerous witnesses the text breaks off before the end, and in some considerably earlier: **Q** breaks off towards the end of §g, *Γ* towards the end of §i, **UX** towards the end of §k, *Λ* part way through §m, **G** part way through §n, and **ΦH** part way through §o (for more detail, see the list of manuscripts earlier in this section). Once we are missing **Q**, *Γ*, and **UX**, we thus have four branches of the tradition (**w₁**, **w₂**, **N**, and **s**) rather than five (**w₁**, *Γ*, **w₂**, **N**, and **s**), and in addition **s** is represented only by its sub-family *ρ*. In effect, after διδάξομεν at §k, line 2, the tradition has the shape shown in Figure 2.5.

Once we are also missing *Λ*, **G**, *Φ*, and **H** (after πυσματικὰ at §o, line 5), the tradition is further reduced with branch **w₁** represented by only the single manuscript **B** (see Figure 2.6).

The subsections that follow explain the reasoning behind the most important points of the more detailed stemma shown in Figure 2.4 (but not the reasoning behind the hyparchetypes **y₃** and **ζ**, which are of little significance for the reconstruction of the text). The progressively reduced state of the evidence as we proceed through the text will be kept in view.

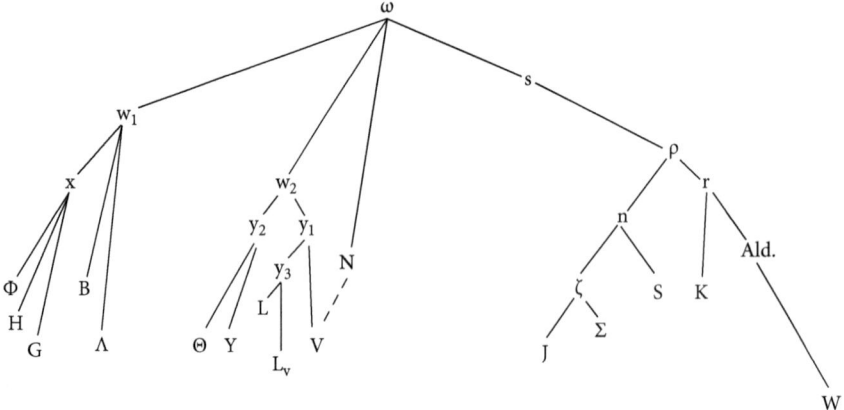

Fig. 2.5 Reduced stemma for Charax, showing only those representatives preserving the text beyond διδάξομεν at §k, line 2.

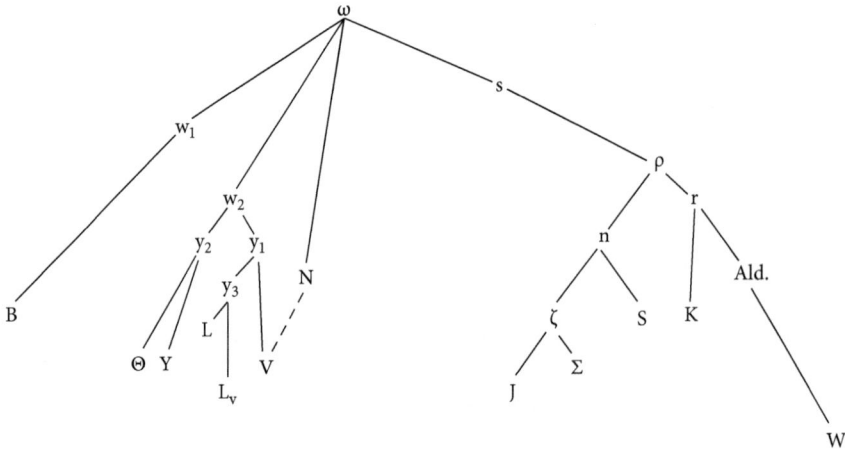

Fig. 2.6 Further reduced stemma for Charax, showing only those witnesses preserving the text beyond πυσματικὰ at §o, line 5.

2.4.1.1 Evidence for family w₁ (with sub-family x)

Clear evidence for family **w₁** can come only from the part of the text up to σχέτλιός at §m, line 8, after which the text starts to break off in representatives of this family. The clearest item of evidence is the one shown in Table 2.24: a series of four examples is omitted in all witnesses to **w₁**, but found in the rest of the tradition—where in practice the 'rest of the tradition' means **w₂Nρ**, because by this point the text has already broken off in *Γ* and in the manuscripts under **a**.

Within family **w₁**, manuscripts *Φ*, **H**, and **G** form a sub-family which we call **x**. Evidence can only come from the part of the text up to πρώτης ἐγένετο at §n, line 8, which is preserved in all three manuscripts *Φ*, **H**, and **G**. Table 2.25 shows the most significant common errors and other innovations specific to sub-family **x**.

Table 2.24 Evidence for family w_1

Reading of family w_1 (comprising $\mathbf{\Phi}$HGBΛ)	Reading of the rest of the tradition (minus the portions which do not transmit §l)
§l, note u: omission in $\mathbf{\Phi}$HGBΛ	ἄνθρωποί τινες, ἤκουσά τινων, δέδωκά τισιν, ὕβρισέ (ὕβρισά ρ) τινας w_2Nρ

Table 2.25 Evidence for sub-family x

Common errors and innovations unique to sub-family x (manuscripts $\mathbf{\Phi}$HG)	Reading(s) of the rest of the tradition, including the other representatives of family w_1 (B and Λ)
§b, note d: αὐτῆς $\mathbf{\Phi}$HG	αὐτοῦ BΛ Γ w_2 N ρ: αὐτῶν UX
§d, note b: προεγείρειν $\mathbf{\Phi}$HG	ἐγείρειν BΛ Γ w_2 N UX (ρ omits §§c–d: see §c note a.)
§g, note v: προπαροξυτόνως $\mathbf{\Phi}$HG	προπαροξυτόνου (προπαροξυτόνος Y) BΛ Γ w_2 s: ὀξυτόνου προπαροξυτόνου N (V has προπαροξυτόνου ὀξυτόνου, probably by contamination with N: see section 2.4.1.4.)
§h, note d: ὕβρισά τινος $\mathbf{\Phi}$HG	ἤκουσά τινος BΛ Γ w_2 N ρ (The only representatives of **a** to have the sentence in which this example occurs—manuscripts **UX**—rephrase the sentence, but their version of the text also uses the example ἤκουσά τινος: see §h, note c.)
§h, note s: phrase omitted in $\mathbf{\Phi}$HG We take the reading of the archetype to be οὕτως ἔμεινεν ἐγκλινόμενα. This was omitted by x, expanded by Θ to οὕτως ἔμεινεν ἐγκλινόμενα οἷον δέδωκεν ἡμῖν, and corrected by Λ, Γ, y_1, N, and s to οὕτως ἔμεινεν ἐγκλινόμενον (and then rearranged to οὕτως ἐγκλινόμενον ἔμεινεν in **a**).	οὕτως ἔμεινεν ἐγκλινόμενα **BY**: οὕτως ἔμεινεν ἐγκλινόμενα οἷον δέδωκεν ἡμῖν Θ: οὕτως ἔμεινεν ἐγκλινόμενον Λ Γ y_1 N ρ: οὕτως ἐγκλινόμενον ἔμεινεν UX
§i, notes m–o: μέλει (μέλλει $\mathbf{\Phi}$H) μοι ἔδει εἶναι μέλει (μέλλει $\mathbf{\Phi}$H) ἐμοί $\mathbf{\Phi}$HG We take the reading of the archetype to be μέλει μοι ἔδει ὀρθοτονηθῆναι ἐμοί: '[the μοι in] μέλει μοι should have been orthotonic, [i.e.] ἐμοί'. x rephrases this, and **a** rephrases it in a similar but not identical way. In addition, N and (we suggest) s change ὀρθοτονηθῆναι to ὀρθοτονεῖσθαι, which is corrupted to εἶναι τὸ ἀρνεῖσθαι in **a**.	μέλει μοι ἔδει ὀρθοτονηθῆναι (ὀρθοτονεῖσθαι Nρ) ἐμοί BΛ Γ w_2 N ρ: μέλλει μοι ἔδει εἶναι τὸ ἀρνεῖσθαι, μέλλει (μέλλεις U) ἐμοί UX
§j, note m: omission in $\mathbf{\Phi}$HG	οἷον — ἐγκλινόμεναι καλοῦνται BΛ w_2 N s (The text of Γ has broken off by this point.)

Manuscript **G** often rephrases the text significantly, and our apparatus does not generally record these divergences on the part of **G** alone. We make an exception at §i, note t, which concerns a passage whose textual history we delve into in section 2.7.4.

2.4.1.2 Evidence for family w_2 (with sub-families y_2 and y_1)

Table 2.26 shows two clear errors specific to family w_2, of which the first constitutes the clearest piece of evidence for the family.

Table 2.26 Evidence for family w_2

Error specific to family w_2 (manuscripts ΘYLL$_v$V, or those of them that transmit the relevant passage)	Reading(s) of the rest of the tradition (or the portions that transmit the relevant passage)
§m, note cc: ταῦτά περ τοῦτέστιν w_2 (represented for this passage by ΘYLL$_v$) We take ταῦτα περὶ τοῦ ἐστιν to be the reading of the archetype, which was inherited by **N** and w_1 (the latter represented for this passage by ΦGB, of which **G** omits the sentence and **B** makes a minor change to ταῦτα δὲ περὶ τοῦ ἐστιν). In w_2, the sentence was corrupted to ταῦτά περ τοῦτέστιν. For further discussion, see section 3.2.	ταῦτα περὶ τοῦ ἐστιν ΦHN: ταῦτα δὲ περὶ τοῦ ἐστιν **B** (**G** omits the whole sentence) (At this point in the text, family **s** is represented by sub-family ρ, which has a larger omission at this point: see §m, note y.)
§n, note f: τοῦ δὲ φῆς τὸ δεύτερον ΘYLL$_v$: τὸ δὲ β^{ov} τὸ φης **V** We take τὸ δὲ φῆς τὸ δεύτερον to be the reading of the archetype, inherited by **N** and w_1 (the latter represented for this passage by x**B**, of which **B** makes an individual change to τοῦ δὲ φημὶ τὸ δεύτερον). **s** is represented at this point by ρ, which makes a change to τὸ δὲ φῆς δεύτερον, while w_2 makes a different change to τὸ δὲ φῆς τὸ δεύτερον. This is reproduced by ΘYLL$_v$, while **V** makes an individual change to τὸ δὲ β^{ov} τὸ φης.	τὸ δὲ φῆς τὸ δεύτερον x**N**: τοῦ δὲ φημὶ τὸ δεύτερον **B**: τὸ δὲ φῆς δεύτερον ρ

Within family w_2 we reconstruct two sub-families, y_2 (comprising manuscripts ΘY) and y_1 (comprising manuscripts LL$_v$V). Table 2.27 gives a selection of common errors and other innovations specific to y_2 (concentrating mostly on the earlier part of the text, for which more of the tradition is present) and Table 2.28 gives the common errors and other innovations specific to y_1.

2.4.1.3 Evidence for family s (with sub-families a and ρ)

Evidence for family **s** (comprising sub-families **a** and ρ) can only come from the part of the text up to §k, line 2 (διδάξομεν), since no representatives of sub-family

Table 2.27 Evidence for sub-family y₂

Common errors and other innovations unique to sub-family y₂ (manuscripts *ΘY*)	Reading(s) of the rest of the tradition, including sub-family y₁
§a, note i: *εὐβαρίθμητοι* *ΘY*	*εὐαρίθμητοι* **w₁** *Γ* **y₁ N s**
§c, note e: *ἤκουσαν* *ΘY*	*ἤκουσας* **w₁** *Γ* **y₁ NUX** (*ρ* omits §§c–d: see §c note a.)
§d, note c: *ἐγκλιματικὰ* *ΘY*	*ἐγκλιτικὰ* **w₁** *Γ* **y₁ NUX** (*ρ* omits §§c–d: see §c note a.)
§h, note i: *αὐτῶν συλλαβῇ* *ΘY*	*συλλαβῇ αὐτῶν* **w₁** *Γ* **y₁ N s**
§i, note r: *ἀναβιβάζουσιν* *ΘY*	*ἀνεβίβασαν* **w₁** *Γ* **y₁ NUX**: *ἀνεβίβασεν* **n**: *ἀνεβίβασεν* **r**
§i, note cc: *λίαν* *ΘY*	*ἐστιν* (*ἐσὶν Λ*) **B** *Λ* *Γ* **y₁ N s** (*ΦH* omit this word as part of a larger omission: see §i, note bb. **G** rewrites this part of the paragraph: see §i, note t.)
§j, note r: negative omitted in *ΘY*	*οὐχὶ* **w₁ y₁ N s** (The text of *Γ* has broken off by this point.)
§n, note s: *αὐχεῖς τὸ δεύτερον* *ΘY*	*αὐχεῖς* **w₁** (represented at this point by *ΦHB*) **y₁ N** (The text of *Γ* has broken off by this point, and *ρ* omits this material as part of a larger omission: see §n, note g.)
§o, note q: *ἔχουσαι* *ΘY*	*ἔχουσι* (*ἔχουσι* **y₃N**: *ἔχουσαι* **BV**) *καὶ ὁ τόπος οὐκ ἀπαιτεῖ αὐτὰς ἐγκλίνεσθαι ὡς ἐν ἀρχῇ καὶ αἱ βαρύτονοι* (*αἱ βαρύτονοι* **y₁B**: *βαρύτονος* **N**)· *πολλάκις γὰρ καὶ ἀπόλυτον σημασίαν ἔχουσαι* **B y₁ N** (Only **B, w₂, N**, and *ρ* continue the text up to this point, and *ρ* omits this material as part of a larger omission: see §o, note d.)
§o, note t: *κλητικὴ* *ΘY*	*κτητικὴ* **B y₁ N** (Again only **B, w₂, N**, and *ρ* continue the text up to this point, and *ρ* omits this material as part of a larger omission: see §o, note d.)

a continue the text beyond this point (see section 2.4.1). The clearest piece of evidence consists of the third and (relatedly) the fourth item in Table 2.29, where the reading of family **s** is a clear error. The first two items are less probative, but they too can readily be understood as innovations in **s**. The first item involves an expansion of elliptical *μέρεσι* 'parts [of speech]' to *μέρεσι τοῦ λόγου*, and the

Table 2.28 Evidence for sub-family y_1

Common errors and other innovations unique to sub-family y_1 (manuscripts LL_vV)	Reading(s) of the rest of the tradition, including sub-family y_2
§g, note x: προηγουμένων **LV** (προηγουμένου in L_v is plausibly a correction.)	προηγουμένου w_1 Γ y_2 L_v **N** s
§n, note n: πρώτη LL_vV	πρώτης w_1 (represented at this point by **xB**) y_2: α **N** (Only w_1, w_2, **N**, and ρ continue the text up to this point, and ρ has an omission that includes this word: see §n, note g.)
§o, note i: ἀορίστω ... σημασίαν LL_vV	ἀορίστω ... σημασίᾳ **B**: ἀορίστων ... σημασίαν y_2: ἀοριστ ... σημασίαν **N** (Only **B**, w_2, **N**, and ρ continue the text up to this point, and ρ has an omission that includes this phrase: see §o, note d.)
§v, note p: ἐκ πλάτει LL_vV	ἐν πλάτει **B** y_2 **N** ρ (Only **B**, w_2, **N**, and ρ continue the text up to this point.)
§w, note z: ὀρφῇοιμνησόμεθα LL_vV	ὀρφῇϊ μνησόμεθα **B**: ὀρφῆος μνησόμεθα y_2: ὀρφῆ ὑμνησώμεθα **N**: Ὀρφῆος μνησώμεθα ρ (Again only **B**, w_2, **N**, and ρ continue the text up to this point.)
§w, note ff: τὸν γε LL_vV	τὸ γε **B** y_2 **N** ρ (Again only **B**, w_2, **N**, and ρ continue the text up to this point.)

Table 2.29 Evidence for family **s** (comprising sub-families **a**, ρ)

Reading of sub-families a and ρ	Reading(s) of the rest of the tradition (or the portions that transmit the relevant passage)
§a, note f: ὀκτὼ μέρεσι τοῦ λόγου **UX** (representing **a**) and **JΣSK Ald.** (= ρ)	ὀκτὼ μέρεσι w_1 w_2 **N** Γ
§f, note a: omission in **UX** (representing **a**) and **JΣSK Ald.** (= ρ)	ὅτε ἐγκλίνονται (ἐγκλίνεται **H**) w_1 Γ w_2 **N**
§h, note r: συστεῖλαι **UX** (representing **a**) and **JΣSK Ald.** (= ρ)	συστεῖλαν w_1 w_2 **N**: συστεῖλας Γ
§h, note v: συστεῖλαι **UX** (representing **a**) and **JΣSK Ald.** (= ρ)	συστεῖλαν w_1 Γ w_2 **N**

Reading of sub-families a and ρ	Reading(s) of the rest of the tradition (or the portions that transmit the relevant passage)
Independently of the variation συστεῖλαι ~ συστεῖλαν, **ΦΗΛΓ**w₂ ρ have οὐ before συστεῖλαι/συστεῖλαν, while **GBNc** have συστεῖλαι/συστεῖλαν without οὐ. We suspect that οὐ was present in the archetype but was removed by conjecture in **G**, **B**, and **N** independently, and in **c** independently or by contamination with **N** (we tentatively adopt this conjecture into our text: see §h, note v).	

Table 2.30 Evidence for sub-family **a**

Reading of sub-family a (comprising QUX)	Reading(s) of the rest of the tradition (including sub-family ρ)
§g, note d: ἐν μιᾷ **QUX**	μιᾷ **w₁** *Γ* **w₂ N** ρ
§g, note e: ἐτίθουν **QUX**	ἐζήτουν δοῦναι **ΦH** y₂L₊V ρ: ἐ (spatium vacuum) ζήτουν δοῦναι **B**: ἐκζήτουν δοῦναι *ΛΓ***L**: ἤθελον δοῦναι **G**: ἐζήτουν **N**
§g, note t: ποιήσεως **QUX**	τῆς ποιήσεως **w₁** *Γ* **w₂ N** ρ

second an omission of two words (ὅτε ἐγκλίνονται) whose presence improves the sense.

Family **s** has two sub-families, **a** and **ρ**. Table 2.30 shows the clearest evidence for sub-family **a**, consisting of innovations found in all three of **QUX**. Not surprisingly, these are not plentiful, given the highly abbreviated nature of the text in **Q**, and given that no representative of sub-family **a** continues the text beyond §k, line 2 (διδάξομεν). There is a larger number of innovations shared between **UX** alone, in places where **Q** provides no reading that can be compared (see for instance §b, note g; §f, note h; §h, note e; §h, note h). In principle these could all be further innovations on the part of **a**, or some (or many) of them could be due to a hyparchetype shared by **UX** alone. In the absence of the necessary evidence from **Q**, the existence of such a hyparchetype cannot be established for certain—but for reasons to be discussed in section 2.4.1.4 we tentatively take **UX** to share a hyparchetype which we call **c**.

Table 2.31 shows the common errors and other innovations specific to sub-family **ρ**. In order to provide evidence for **ρ** as a sub-family of **s**, these too can only come from the portion of the text for which we also have representatives of sub-family **a**: again up to διδάξομεν at §k, line 2. (The siglum **ρ** appears in our apparatus beyond this point, for readings shared by the witnesses we place under **ρ**—but

Table 2.31 Evidence for sub-family ρ

Reading of sub-family ρ, comprising further subgroups n (manuscripts JΣS) and r (manuscript K and Ald.)	Reading(s) of the rest of the tradition (including sub-family a, represented in all relevant places by manuscripts UX only)
§a, note c: ἐγκλιτικὰ μόρια **n r**	ἐγκλιτικὰ **ΦΗΛΓ**VNUX: ἐγκλιματικὰ **w₂**B: ἐγκλητικὰ **G**
§b, note e: word omitted in **n r**	ὡς **w₁** **Γ** **w₂** NUX
§c, note a: omission in **n r**	καὶ ἰστέον ὅτι — πάντα ἐγκλιτικὰ καλοῦνται **w₁** **Γ** **w₂** NUX
§e, note a: ἔχει δὲ τὰ τοιαῦτα ὀξεῖαν ἢ περισπωμένην **n r**	πάντα δὲ τὰ ἐγκλιτικὰ (ἐγκλινόμενα UX) θέλει πρῶτον ὀρθοτονούμενα ἔχειν ὀξεῖαν ἢ περισπωμένην **w₁** **Γ** **w₂** NUX
§e, note e: ῥηθησόμενα **n r**	περὶ ὧν διαληψόμεθα **w₁** **Γ** **w₂** NUX
§f, note b: λέξις προπαροξύτονος **n r**	προπαροξύτονος λέξις **w₁** **Γ** **w₂** NUX
§f, note d: example omitted in **n r**	'ἄνθρωπος' ἄνθρωπός μου' **w₁** **Γ** **w₂** N: ἄνθρωπός μου **GUX**
§g, note k: σοφός τις μία ἐστίν **n r**	σοφός τις· μία ἐστὶ γὰρ **ΦΗΛΓw₂**N: σοφός τις μία ἐστὶν ὀξεῖα UX
	(**GB** repair the problematic text at this point by omitting material that includes this phrase: see §g, note j.)
§i, note s: ἐφύλαξεν **n r**	ἐφύλαξαν **w₁** **Γ** **w₂** NUX
§i, note z: παρέχει **n r**	παρέχουσι **w₁** **Γ** **w₂** NUX
§j, note f: ἐγκλινόμενόν ἐστιν ἢ θέμις ἐγκλιτικὸν καὶ ἐγκλινόμενον **n r**	ἐγκλινόμενόν ἐστιν (ἐστιν deest in **N**)· ἦλθέ τις, ἐγκλιτικὸν καὶ ἐγκλινόμενον **ΦΗ** **w₂** N: ἐγκλινόμενον ἐστίν· τὸ γὰρ ἔφησε τις· ἐγκλιτικὸν καὶ ἐγκλινόμενον **G**: ἐγκλινόμενον ἐστὶν **B**: ἐγκλινόμενον ἐγκλιᵗ καὶ ἐγκλινόμενον **Λ**: ἐγκλινόμενον ἦλθέ τις UX
	(The text of **Γ** has broken off by this point.)
§k, note a: περὶ ἑκάστου δὲ μέρους **n r**	διαλαμβάνοντες δὲ περὶ ἑκάστου μέρους B**Λ** **w₂** N: διαλαμβάνοντες περὶ ἑκάστου μέρους UX: διαλαμβάνονται δὲ περὶ ἑκάστου μέρους **ΦΗ**
	(**G** has an omission that includes this phrase, and the text of **Γ** has broken off by this point.)

once the text has broken off in all representatives of **a**, any reading of **ρ** could potentially have been present already in **s**.)

2.4.1.4 Evidence that V and c are contaminated with N

In the four places shown in Table 2.32, **V** has a reading similar or identical to that of **N**, against the rest of family **w₂**. All four innovations look like attempts to

Table 2.32 Evidence that **V** is contaminated with **N**

Readings of VN	Reading(s) of the rest of the tradition (including the rest of family w₂)
§g, note v: προπαροξυτόνου ὀξυτόνου **V**: ὀξυτόνου προπαροξυτόνου **N** We take the προπαροξυτόνου to be the reading of the archetype, corrected by **N** to ὀξυτόνου προπαροξυτόνου, which was taken over with a change of word order into **V**, under the influence of **N**.	προπαροξυτόνου (προπαροξυτόνος **Y**) **BΛ Γw₂ s**: προπαροξυτόνως **x**
§i, note i: ἐγκλινόμεναι προηγουμένων τῶν προειρημένων λέξεων· ἄλλων δὲ λέξεων προηγουμένων μὴ δεχομένων **VN**	ἐγκλινόμεναι προηγουμένων μὴ δεχομένων **ΛΓw₂ρ**: ἐγκλινόμενον προηγουμένων μὴ δεχομένων **ΦH**: ἐγκλινόμεναι· τῶν δὲ προηγουμένων μὴ δεχομένων **G**: ἐγκλινομένων προηγουμένων μὴ δεχομένων **B**: ἐγκλινόμεναι προηγουμένων τῶν προειρημένων λέξεων· ἄλλων δὲ λέξεων προηγουμένων **UX** (On the reading of **UX**, which is close to that of **VN**, see immediately below this table.)
§i, note aa: the words αὐτῇ καλοῦ μου (οἷον καλοῦ μου **UX**)· εἰ δὲ ἄλλος τόνος εἴη παρέχουσι τὸν τόνον are added by **VNUX** (On the agreement of **UX** with **VN**, see immediately below this table.)	words not present in **w₁ Γw₂ρ**
§o, note s: οὐδεμία **VN**	οὐδὲ **B w₂** (**ρ** has an omission which includes this word: see §o, note d.)

emend the text, made by **N** and taken into **V** by contamination with **N**; we ourselves take the first, second, and fourth of these innovations to be on the right lines (see our text of the relevant passages). The third innovation (discussed further in section 2.7.4) is particularly unlikely to have been made independently more than once.

In the three places shown in Table 2.33, manuscripts **UX** have a reading similar to that of **N**, against the rest of family s—where the remainder of family s is represented in all three instances by sub-family **ρ**, in the absence of **Q**. The first two items also featured in Table 2.32: they appear to be significant attempts to emend corrupt passages, which passed from **N** not only into **V** but also into manuscripts **UX**. The third innovation, a mere loss of δέ, may not be significant, but it occurs in the vicinity of the others and may be stylistically motivated in its context ('stylistic' or 'expressive' asyndeton, for which see [Longinus], *De sublimitate* 19–21; Denniston 1950: xlv–xlvi; Humbert 1960: 371; Sicking 1993: 43–4).

Table 2.33 Evidence that **c** is contaminated with **N**

Readings of c (comprising UX) and N (and where applicable also V)	Reading(s) of the rest of the tradition (including the rest of family s, represented in these instances by ρ)
§i, note i: ἐγκλινόμεναι προηγουμένων τῶν προειρημένων λέξεων· ἄλλων δὲ λέξεων προηγουμένων μὴ δεχομένων **VN**: ἐγκλινόμεναι προηγουμένων τῶν προειρημένων λέξεων· ἄλλων δὲ λέξεων προηγουμένων **UX**	ἐγκλινόμεναι προηγουμένων μὴ δεχομένων **ΛΓw₂ρ**: ἐγκλινόμενον προηγουμένων μὴ δεχομένων **ΦΗ**: ἐγκλινόμεναι· τῶν δὲ προηγουμένων μὴ δεχομένων **G**: ἐγκλινομένων προηγουμένων μὴ δεχομένων **B**
§i, note aa: the words αὐτῇ καλοῦ μου (οἷον καλοῦ μου **UX**)· εἰ δὲ ἄλλος τόνος εἴη παρέχουσι τὸν τόνον are added by **VNUX**	words not present in **w₁ Γw₂ρ**
§i, note cc: ψευδές ἐστιν **NUX**	ψευδές δέ ἐστιν (ἐσὶν **Λ**) **ΒΛΓy₃**: ψευδὴς γάρ ἐστιν **Vρ**: ψευδές δὲ λίαν **y₂**: ψευδές γάρ ἐστιν **Σ**
	(**x** has an omission which includes this phrase: see §i, note bb.)

In the absence of **Q** for the relevant passages, we cannot establish whether hyparchetype **a** was already influenced by **N**, or whether **UX** share a hyparchetype which was influenced by **N**. On balance we slightly favour the latter possibility. **Q** is a late thirteenth-century manuscript, and hyparchetype **a** must be at least slightly earlier than **Q**—but it cannot be too much earlier if it was influenced by **N**, which is also a late thirteenth-century manuscript. This chronological diffi-culty disappears if **a** was influenced by a source of **N** rather than by **N** itself, but it also disappears if **N** influenced a later hyparchetype shared only by the fifteenth- or sixteenth-century manuscripts **UX**. Since the text of **U** is very close to that of **X**, it is on balance likely that they share a common source more recent than the thirteenth century. For this reason, and also because contamination is generally more prevalent in the Renaissance than in earlier centuries, we tentatively con-sider **UX** to derive from the hyparchetype we call **c**, which was influenced by **N** or a closely related source.

2.4.2 Previous editions

Bekker printed this treatise in the third volume of his *Anecdota Graeca* (Bekker 1821: 1149–55), on the basis of the text in the Aldine *Thesaurus* (Aldus 1496, our **Ald.**), Parisinus Graecus 2558 (our *Γ*; the manuscript shelfmark is misprinted as 2258 at Bekker 1821: 1142), Parisinus Graecus 1773 (our **Y**), Parisinus

Coislinianus 176 (our **X**), and a second Aldine edition likely to be Aldus (1524) (see also section 2.1.2).

Thomas Gaisford printed part of *Charax* in the first volume of his *Georgii Choerobosci Dictata in Theodosii Canones, nec non Epimerismi in Psalmos* (Gaisford 1842: 19–21). In essence, Gaisford's edition appears to be based on Parisinus Coislinianus 176 (our **X**); in places Gaisford prints an error found in this manuscript, with his own correction in parentheses. Gaisford also consulted Bekker's edition, and in a couple of places he draws on it to supply part of the text that is omitted in **X**.

2.4.3 *Charax*: text and translation

§a Ἰωάννου[a] γραμματικοῦ τοῦ Χάρακος περὶ ἐγκλινομένων

Ἰστέον ὅτι τὰ[b] ἐγκλιτικὰ[c] οὐκ[d] εἰσὶν ἐν τοῖς[e] ὀκτὼ[f] μέρεσι, ἀλλ᾽ ἐν πέντε·[g] ὀνόμασι, ῥήμασιν, ἀντωνυμίαις, ἐπιρρήμασι καὶ[h] συνδέσμοις. καὶ οὐ πᾶσα λέξις ἐν τούτοις ἐγκλίνεται, ἀλλ᾽ εὐαρίθμητοί[i] καὶ ἐν ἑκάστῳ μέρει ὀνομαζόμεναι. εἰσὶ δὲ ἐν[j] ταῖς ἐγκλινομέναις τινὲς διάφορον σημαινόμενον ἀναφαίνουσαι[k] ἐν τῷ ὀρθοτονεῖσθαι καὶ[l] ἐγκλίνεσθαι.

§b ὀρθοτονεῖσθαι δέ[a] φαμεν, ὅτε τὸν ἀνάλογον καὶ[b] κατὰ φύσιν τόνον φυλάττει, ἐγκλίνεσθαι[c] δέ, ὅτε τὸν τόνον ἀναβιβάζει τῇ πρὸ αὐτοῦ[d] λέξει, ὡς[e] ἀπὸ μεταφορᾶς τῶν ἐγκλινόντων[f] ἐπὶ[g] τὰ ὀπίσω τὰ σώματα αὐτῶν.

§a
a Ἰωάννου γραμματικοῦ τοῦ Χάρακος περὶ ἐγκλινομένων **ΒΛΓΥy₁N**: Περὶ ἐγκλιτικῶν **G**: Περὶ ἐγκλιτικῶν ἕτερον **J**: Περὶ ἐγκλινομένων τινῶν **Q**: Ἰωάννου γραμματικοῦ τοῦ Χάρακος **c**: Ἰωάννου γραμματικοῦ Χάρακος περὶ τῶν ἐγκλινομένων **Σ Ald.**: Ἰωάννου γραμματικοῦ τοῦ Χάρακος περὶ τῶν ἐγκλινομένων **K**: Ἰωάννου γραμματικοῦ τοῦ Χάρακος περὶ τῶν ἐγκλινομένων μορίων **S**: sine titulo **ΦΗΘ**
b τὰ ἐγκλιτικὰ — δεῖ εἰπεῖν τὴν αἰτίαν (§g) deest in **Q**
c ἐγκλιτικὰ **xΛΓVNc**: ἐγκλιματικὰ **Bw₂**: ἐγκλιτικὰ μόρια **ρ**
d οὐκ om. **y₃**
e τοῖς **w₁Γw₂N**: ταῖς (sic) **Ald.**
f ὀκτὼ μέρεσι **w₁Γw₂N**: ὀκτὼ μέρεσι τοῦ λόγου **s**
g πέντε **s**: πέντε μέρεσιν **ΦΗΛΓw₂N**: πέντε μόνοις **B**: πέντε μόνον **G**
h καὶ deest in **c**
i εὐαρίθμητοι καὶ (post καὶ verbum αἱ habet **N**[s.l.]) ἐν (ἐν deest in N) ἑκάστῳ μέρει ὀνομαζόμεναι **ΓΝ**[s.l.]: εὐαρίθμητοι καὶ τὰς ἐν (ἐν deest in N) ἑκάστῳ μέρει ὀνομαζομένας **ΦΗΛy₃Ν**[i.t.]: εὐαρίθμητα καὶ τὰς ἑκάστω μέρει ὀνομαζομένας **B**: εὐαρίθμητοι· λέγει δὲ καὶ τοῖς ἐν ἑκάστω μέρει ὀνομαζομένοις **V**: εὐαρίθμητοί εἰσιν καὶ τῶν ἐν ἑκάστοις μέρεσιν ὀνομαζομένων **c**: εὐβαρίθμητοι (sic) καὶ τὰς ἐν ἑκάστω μέρει ὀνομαζομένας **y₂**: εὐαρίθμητοι **nK**: εὐαρίθμητοι τινές **G**: ἐναρίθμητοι (sic) **Ald.**
j ἐν ταῖς ἐγκλινομέναις τινὲς **ΒΛΓw₂N**: ἐν τοῖς ἐγκλινομένοις τινὰ **c**: τινες ἐν ταῖς ἐγκλινομέναις **Gρ**: ἐν ταῖς συγκλινομέναις τινες **ΦΗ**
k ἀναφαίνουσαι Bekker: ἀναφέρουσαι **w₁Γw₂Νρ**: ἀναφαίνοντα **U**: ἀναφαίνονται **X**
l καὶ **w₁Γw₂Νs**: τε καὶ **B**

§b
a δέ φαμεν **w₁Γw₂Νρ**: μέν φαμεν **Bc**
b καὶ κατὰ φύσιν **ΒΛΓw₂N**: κατὰ φύσιν **xU**: κατὰ φύσιν κατὰ φύσιν (sic) **X**: καὶ φυσικὸν **nK**: φυσικὸν **Ald.**
c ἐγκλίνεσθαι **GBcΣ**: ἐγκλινόμενον **ΦΗΛΓw₂Νρ**
d αὑτοῦ Bekker: αὐτοῦ **ΒΛΓw₂Νρ**: αὐτῆς **x**: αὐτῶν **c**
e ὡς **w₁Γw₂Νc**: deest in **ρ**
f ἐγκλινόντων **xΛΓw₂ΝSr**: ἐγκλινομένων **Βζ**
g ἐπὶ τὰ ὀπίσω τὰ (τὰ deest in y₂) σώματα αὐτῶν (αὐτῶν Bekker: αὑτῶν **w₁Γw₂Νρ**) **w₁Γw₂Νρ**: ἑαυτῶν τὰ σώματα ἐπὶ τὰ ὀπίσω **c**

§a The *On enclitics of* John Charax the grammarian

One should know that the enclitics do not occur in the eight parts [of speech] but in five: in nominals,[229] verbs, pronouns, adverbs, and conjunctions. And not every word in these categories is enclitic, but the enclitics are easy to count and they are named under each part of speech. And among the enclitics there are some that display a different meaning depending on whether they are orthotonic or enclitic.

§b And we say that a word is *orthotonic* when it keeps its regular and natural accent, and that it is *enclitic* when it throws the accent back onto the word before itself, as from the metaphor of those who lean their bodies backwards.

---

[229] On the meaning of ὄνομα, see n. 15.

§c καὶ[a] ἰστέον ὅτι τὰ ἕνεκεν[b] διαφόρου σημαινομένου ⟨ἐγκλινόμενα⟩[c] κυρίως[d] 'ἐγκλιτικά' καλοῦσιν, οἷον 'ἐμοῦ ἤκουσας'[e] ἀντιδιαστολή· 'ἤκουσάς μου' ἀπόλυτος[f] σημασία.

§d τὰ δὲ τὴν αὐτὴν σημασίαν φυλάττοντα οἱ[a] πολλοὶ 'ἐγερτικά' καλοῦσι διὰ τὸ ἐγείρειν[b] τὴν πρὸ αὐτῶν ὀξεῖαν καὶ μηδὲν ἄλλο δηλοῦν. ὅμως δὲ κοινῶς πάντα 'ἐγκλιτικά'[c] καλοῦνται.

§e πάντα[a] δὲ τὰ ἐγκλιτικὰ θέλει πρῶτον ὀρθοτονούμενα ἔχειν ὀξεῖαν ἢ περισπωμένην· βαρύτονος γὰρ[b] λέξις οὐκ[c] ἐγκλίνεται, εἰ μὴ κατὰ πάθος εἴη ἡ βαρεῖα, ὡς τὸ 'σφέας'[d] καί τινα ἄλλα, περὶ[e] ὧν διαληψόμεθα.

§f προηγεῖται δὲ τούτων τῶν ἐγκλινομένων, ὅτε[a] ἐγκλίνονται, ἢ[b] προπαροξύτονος λέξις,[c] 'ἄνθρωπος'[d] 'ἄνθρωπός μου', καὶ[e] 'ἄνθρωπός τις', ἢ ὀξύτονος, ὡς[f] 'μαθητής μου' καὶ[g] 'σοφός τις', ἢ τροχαϊκή,[h] ὡς 'δοῦλός μου', 'ἄλλός[i] μοι', 'ἔνθά μοι'.

§c
[a] καὶ ἰστέον ὅτι — πάντα ἐγκλιτικὰ καλοῦνται (§d) deest in ρ
[b] ἕνεκεν w₁Γγ₁N: ἕνεκα y₂c
[c] ἐγκλινόμενα scripsimus
[d] κυρίως w₁Γw₂N: deest in c
[e] ἤκουσας w₁Γγ₁Nc: ἤκουσαν y₂
[f] ἀπόλυτος σημασία w₁Γw₂N: deest in c

§d
[a] οἱ πολλοὶ ἐγερτικὰ w₁Γw₂N: ἐνεργητικὰ οἱ πολλοὶ X: ἐνεργετητικὰ (sic) οἱ πολλοὶ U
[b] ἐγείρειν ΒΛΓw₂Nc: προεγείρειν x
[c] ἐγκλιτικὰ w₁Γγ₁Nc: ἐγκλιματικὰ y₂

§e
[a] πάντα δὲ τὰ ἐγκλιτικὰ ⟨ἐγκλινόμενα c⟩ θέλει πρῶτον ὀρθοτονούμενα ἔχειν ὀξεῖαν ἢ περισπωμένην w₁Γw₂Nc: ἔχει δὲ τὰ τοιαῦτα ὀξεῖαν ἢ περισπωμένην ρ
[b] γὰρ w₁Γw₂NcSr: δὲ ζ
[c] οὐκ w₁Γw₂Nρ: οὐδέποτε c
[d] σφέας w₁Γw₂Nρ: σφᾶς X: σφᾶς φέας (sic) U
[e] περὶ ὧν διαληψόμεθα w₁Γw₂Nc: ῥηθησόμενα ρ

§f
[a] ὅτε ἐγκλίνονται GBΛΓw₂N: ὅτε ἐγκλίνεται ΦΗ: deest in s
[b] ἢ προπαροξύτονος λέξις w₁Γw₂Nc: λέξις προπαροξύτονος ρ
[c] λέξις w₁Γw₂N: λέξις ὡς ρ: λέξις οἷον Bc
[d] 'ἄνθρωπος' 'ἄνθρωπός μου' w₁Γw₂N: ἄνθρωπός μου Gc: deest in ρ
[e] καὶ ἄνθρωπός τις xBΓw₂c: ἄνθρωπός τις ΛNρ
[f] ὡς ΒΓw₂NcΣ Ald.: ὡς τὸ x: ὁ Λ: deest in nK
[g] καὶ σοφός τις w₁Γw₂c: σοφός τις Nρ
[h] τροχαϊκή w₁Γw₂Nρ: τροχαϊκὴ ἀπὸ τόνου c
[i] ἄλλός μοι xΓw₂Ns: ἄλλος μου ΒΛ

§c And one must know that they call words that throw back their accent on account of a different meaning *enclitic* properly speaking. For example, ἐμοῦ ἤκουσας[230] [is an instance of] a contrast; ἤκουσάς μου[231] [is an instance of] a non-contrastive meaning.

§d And most people call those that keep the same meaning *egertic* because they wake up the acute accent before themselves and do not indicate anything else. But they are nevertheless all called *enclitic* as a cover term.

§e All enclitics tend to have an acute or a circumflex [on the final syllable] in the first instance when they are orthotonic. For a barytone word does not behave as an enclitic unless the grave accent [on the final syllable] is due to a modification, as in σφέας and some others, which we will deal with separately.

§f And when these enclitics throw back their accent, they are preceded by a pro-paroxytone word, as in ἄνθρωπος but ἄνθρωπός μου and ἄνθρωπός τις,[232] or an oxytone word, as in μαθητής μου and σοφός τις,[233] or one that is trochaic, as in δοῦλός μου, ἄλλός μοι, ἔνθά μοι.[234]

---

[230] 'You heard *me*' [as opposed to someone else].
[231] 'You heard me'.
[232] 'My person'; 'a certain person'.
[233] 'My pupil'; 'a certain wise man'.
[234] 'My slave'; 'someone else to me'; 'where to me' (e.g. *Od.* 4.635).

§g ἄλλων[a] δὲ προηγουμένων οὐκ ἐγκλίνονται,[b] 'ἀνθρώπου[c] τινός', 'ἄλλου τινός', 'ἄλλῳ τινί'. καὶ δεῖ εἰπεῖν τὴν αἰτίαν. μιᾷ[d] λέξει κατὰ συνέχειαν δύο ὀξείας οἱ παλαιοὶ οὐκ ἐζήτουν[e] δοῦναι· κακοφωνίαν γὰρ ποιοῦσι. τὸ οὖν 'ἄνθρωπός τις' οὐκ ἔστι κατὰ συνέχειαν, ἀλλὰ[f] μεσοσυλλαβεῖ βαρεῖα[g] ἡ[h] ἐν τῷ[i] ΘΡΩ. 'σοφός[j] [k] τις'· μία ἐστὶ γὰρ ἡ[l] εἰς τὸ ΟΣ· ⟨...⟩·[m] ἔστι[n] περισπωμένη καὶ ὀξεῖα, ὅθεν[o] μέμφονται οἱ ἀκριβεῖς τὸν θέσει τροχαϊκὸν ἔχοντα δύο ὀξείας[p] ἐφεξῆς, 'ἄλλός τις'· καὶ εὐλόγως εἰς τὴν ἀρχὴν τῆς Ὀδυσσείας ὁ Ἀρίσταρχος οὐκ ἠβουλήθη[q] δοῦναι εἰς τὸ[r] 'ἄνδρα μοι'[s] δύο ὀξείας, ἀλλὰ μίαν εἰς τὸ ΑΝ, φάσκων, 'ἐν ἀρχῇ τῆς[t] ποιήσεως παράλογον οὐ μὴ ποιήσω'. ἁπλῶς[u] οὖν προπαροξυτόνου[v] ⟨ἢ[w] ὀξυτόνου ἢ προπερισπωμένου⟩ τροχαϊκοῦ προηγουμένου[x] αἱ[y] ἐγκλίσεις γίνονται.

§g

[a] ἄλλων δὲ προηγουμένων **y₂cr**: ἄλλως δὲ προηγουμένως **xΛΓy₁N**: ἄλλως δὲ προηγουμένων **n**: ἄλλης δὲ προηγουμένης **BLᵥ**

[b] ἐγκλίνονται **xΛΓw₂ρ**: ἐγκλίνεται **BNc**

[c] ἀνθρώπου **w₁Γw₂Nρ**: οἷον ἀνθρώπου **c**

[d] μιᾷ **w₁Γw₂Nρ**: ἐν μιᾷ **a**

[e] ἐζήτουν δοῦναι **ΦHy₂LᵥVρ**: ἐ (spatium vacuum) ζήτουν δοῦναι **B**: ἐκζήτουν δοῦναι **ΛΓL**: ἤθελον δοῦναι **G**: ἐζήτουν **N**: ἐτίθουν **a**

[f] ἀλλὰ deest in **c**

[g] βαρεῖα **w₁Γw₂Nρ**: γὰρ ἡ βαρεῖα **c**

[h] ἡ **w₁w₂NXr**: deest in **ΓLUn**

[i] τῷ ΘΡΩ **GBΛΓw₂Nρ**: τῇ θρω συλλαβῇ **c**: τῷ ΠΟΣ **ΦΗ**

[j] 'σοφός τις' — ἔστι περισπωμένη καὶ ὀξεῖα om. (in spatio vacuo **B**) **GB**

[k] 'σοφός τις'· μία ἐστὶ γὰρ **ΦΗΛΓw₂N**: σοφός τις μία ἐστὶν **ρ**: σοφός τις μία ἐστὶν ὀξεῖα **c**

[l] ἡ εἰς τὸ ΟΣ **ρ**: ἡ πος **ΦΗΛΓw₂**: ἡ φος **N**: deest in **c**

[m] lacunam statuimus; unum exemplum nominis properispomeni cum pronomine probabiliter excidit, velut δοῦλός μου

[n] ἔστι περισπωμένη καὶ ὀξεῖα **ΦΗΛΓw₂NnK**: deest in **a Ald.**

[o] ὅθεν μέμφονται (καὶ μέμφονται **ΦΗ**) οἱ ἀκριβεῖς τὸν θέσει τροχαϊκὸν ἔχοντα δύο ὀξείας **w₁Γw₂Nρ**: οἱ ἀκριβεῖς ὅθεν μέμφονται τὸν θέσει τροχαϊκὸν ἔχοντα δύο ὀξείας **c**: ὅθεν οὐδὲ ἐγκλίνουσιν οὕτως οἱ ἀκριβεῖς **Q**

[p] ὀξείας **w₁Γw₂Ns**: ὀξεῖα **y₂**

[q] ἠβουλήθη **w₁Γw₂Nc**: ἐβουλήθη **Qρ**

[r] τὸ **w₁Γw₂Naζ**: τὸν **Sr**

[s] μοι **w₁Γw₂Ns**: μοι ἔννεπε μοῦσα **VQ**

[t] τῆς ποιήσεως **w₁Γw₂Nρ**: ποιήσεως **a**

[u] ἁπλῶς οὖν προπαροξυτόνου — usque ad finem (§w) deest in **Q**

[v] προπαροξυτόνου **BΛΓΘy₃s**: ὀξυτόνου προπαροξυτόνου **N**: προπαροξυτόνου ὀξυτόνου **V**: προπαροξυτόνως **x**: προπαροξυτόνος (sic) **Y**

[w] addidimus

[x] προηγουμένου **w₁Γy₂LᵥNs**: προηγουμένων **y₁**

[y] αἱ deest in **c**

§g But when other words precede, they do not throw their accent back, as in ἀνθρώπου τινός, ἄλλου τινός, ἄλλῳ τινί.[235] And it is necessary to give the reason. The ancients did not seek to give two acute accents in succession to a single word, for they produce an unpleasant sound. Thus in ἄνθρωπός τις the two acute accents are not in succession, but the grave accent on the syllable ΘΡΩ intervenes. In σοφός τις there is a single one [i.e. acute accent], on the ΟΣ...there is a circumflex and an acute accent, whence those who are precise find fault with words that are trochaic by position having two acute accents in succession, as in ἄλλός τις.[236] And at the beginning of the *Odyssey* Aristarchus reasonably did not want to give ἄνδρα μοι[237] two acute accents, but just one on the *AN*, saying 'at the beginning of the poem I will not create an irregularity'.[238] So throwings back of the accent only occur when a proparoxytone word, an oxytone one, or a properispomenon trochaic one precedes.

---

[235] 'Of some person'; 'of someone else'; 'to someone else'.
[236] 'Someone else'.
[237] *Od.* 1.1: '[Tell] for me [of] the man'.
[238] Cf. Sch. *Od.* 1.1a Pontani (MᵃO), with sections 2.7.5 and 2.8.3.

§h καὶ πρὸς σαφήνειαν δὲ^a δεῖ εἰπεῖν^b ὅτι τὰ ἐγκλινόμενα ἢ μονοχρονοῦσιν, 'ὕβρισέ^c με', ἢ διχρονοῦσιν, 'ἤκουσά^d τινος', ἢ^e τριχρονοῦσιν, 'ἤκουσά τινων'.^f καὶ τότε^g τῇ πρώτῃ λέξει ἀναβιβάζουσι τὸν τόνον, ὡς ἐλαφρὰ ὄντα. ὅτε^h δὲ τετραχρονοῦσι, τῇ πρώτῃ συλλαβῇⁱ αὐτῶν, 'ἡμῶν^j ἤμων', 'ὑμᾶς ὕμας', 'ὑμῖν ὕμιν'. ἰστέον δὲ ὡς ταῦτα^k τὰ τετράχρονα, καὶ εἰ^l συστέλλουσι τὸ τέλος καὶ γίνονται τρίχρονα, οὐκ^m ἀναβιβάζουσινⁿ τῇ πρώτῃ λέξει, ἀλλὰ^o φυλάττουσι τὸν τόνον, ὡς ἦσαν^p ἀπ' ἀρχῆς ἐγκλινόμενα. οἷον 'δέδωκεν ἡμῖν'^q συστεῖλαν^r τὸ Ι παρὰ τοῖς Ἴωσιν οὕτως^s ἔμεινεν^t ἐγκλινόμενον. 'ὕβρισεν ὕμας'^u συστεῖλαν^v τὸ Α κατὰ διάλεκτον ἐφύλαξεν^w ἐν^x τῇ αὐτῇ συλλαβῇ τὸν αὐτὸν τόνον.

§h
^a δὲ deest in **xN**
^b εἰπεῖν **w₁Γw₂NcSr**: ποιεῖν **ζ**
^c ὕβρισέ με — ἤκουσά τινος] ἢ διχρονοῦσιν· οἷον ὕβρισέ με· ἤκουσά τινος **c**
^d ἤκουσά τινος **BΛΓw₂Nρ**: ὕβρισά τινος **x**
^e ἢ τριχρονοῦσιν 'ἤκουσά τινων' deest in **c**
^f τινων **w₁Γw₂NnK**: τινος **Ald.**
^g τότε **ΦΗΛw₂Ns**: τότε δὴ **G**: ποτὲ μὲν **B**: πότε **Γ**
^h ὅτε δὲ τετραχρονοῦσι **w₁Γw₂Nρ**: ἢ τετράχρονα· καὶ τότε **c**
ⁱ συλλαβῇ αὐτῶν **w₁Γy₁Ns**: αὐτῶν συλλαβῇ **y₂**
^j ἡμῶν ἤμων ὑμᾶς ὕμας ὑμῖν ὕμιν **ΦΗΓw₂N**: ὑμῶν ὕμων ὑμᾶς ὕμας ὑμῖν ὕμιν **B**: ἡμῶν ὑμᾶς ὕμας ὑμῖν ὕμιν **nK**: ἡμῶν ἤμων ἡμᾶς ἤμας ἡμῖν ἤμιν **G Ald.**: οἷον (οἷον deest in **X**) 'ἡμῶν ἤμων', 'ἡμῖν ἤμιν', 'ἡμᾶς ἤμας' **c**: alii aliter
^k ταῦτα τὰ τετράχρονα **w₁Γw₂Nρ**: τὰ τετράχρονα ταῦτα **c**
^l εἰ συστέλλουσι **w₂Nρ**: εἰ συστέλουσι **Γ**: εἰ καὶ συστέλλουσι **ΦΗ**: εἰ σοστέλουσι (sic) **Λ**: ἰσοστέλλουσι **B**: συστέλλουσι **c**: ἀλλὰ καὶ συστείλαντα **G**
^m οὐκ deest in **c**
ⁿ ἀναβιβάζουσι **w₁Γw₂Nρ**: ἀναβιβάζουσι τὸν τόνον **c**
^o ἀλλὰ φυλάττουσι τὸν τόνον **w₁Γw₂Nρ**: ἀλλὰ φυλάττουσιν αὐτὸν **G**: καὶ οὐ φυλάττουσιν αὐτὸν **c**
^p ἦσαν **w₁Γw₂NcnK**: ὄντα **Ald.**
^q ἡμῖν Bekker: ἤμιν **Gn Ald.**: alii ἡμῖν vel ὑμῖν variis accentibus
^r συστεῖλαν **w₁w₂N**: συστεῖλαι **s**: συστείλας **Γ**
^s οὕτως ἔμεινεν ἐγκλινόμενον deest in **x**
^t ἔμεινεν ἐγκλινόμενον **ΛΓy₁Nρ**: ἔμεινεν ἐγκλινόμενα **By₂**: ἐγκλινόμενον ἔμεινεν **c**
^u ὕμας scripsimus: ὕμας **ΛΓV**: alii ὑμᾶς vel ἡμᾶς variis accentibus
^v συστεῖλαν **GBN**: συστεῖλαι **c**: οὐ συστεῖλαν **ΦΗΛΓw₂**: οὐ συστεῖλαι **ρ**
^w ἐφύλαξεν **ΦΗBΓw₂NXnK**: ἐφύλαξαν **GΛU**: ἐφύλασσαν **Ald.**
^x ἐν τῇ αὐτῇ συλλαβῇ τὸν αὐτὸν τόνον **x**: ἐν αὐτῇ τῇ συλλαβῇ τὸν αὐτὸν τόνον **BΛΓw₂Nρ**: οὕτως ἐγκλινόμενον **c**

§h And for clarity one should say that enclitics have either a single unit of time, as in ὕβρισέ με,[239] or two units of time, as in ἤκουσά τινος,[240] or three units of time, as in ἤκουσά τινων.[241] And under these circumstances they throw their accent back onto the first word, because they are light. But when they have four units of time [they throw their accent back onto] their own first syllable, as in ἡμῶν ~ ἥμων, ὑμᾶς ~ ὕμας, ὑμῖν ~ ὕμιν. And one should know that these enclitics with four units of time do not throw their accent back onto the first word even if they shorten their final syllable and come to have three units of time, but they keep their accent, since they threw the accent back to begin with.[242] For example, δέδωκεν ἥμιν,[243] having shortened the I in the Ionic dialect, has remained like this with the accent thrown back. ὕβρισεν ὕμας,[244] having shortened the A dialectally, has kept the same accent on the same syllable.[245]

---

[239] 'He/she mistreated me'.

[240] 'I heard someone'.

[241] 'I heard some people'.

[242] The idea is that forms such as ἥμιν (with short ι) can be considered enclitics that have thrown their accent back onto their own first syllable, even though they have only three units of time, on the basis that the basic form is ἡμῖν, and that two ordered rules may apply: (i) if the form is treated as an enclitic, the accent is thrown back onto the first syllable (giving ἥμῖν); and (ii) the vowel of the second syllable may then be shortened (giving ἥμιν). At the second step, the accent is considered unchanged (φυλάττουσι τὸν τόνον), as the change of an acute to a circumflex can be taken for granted. For parallels, see Roussou (2018b: 267 with n. 5).

[243] 'He/she has given to us'.

[244] 'He/she has mistreated you'.

[245] The text is problematic here. As we read it, the form ὕμας provides a further illustration of the point just made: the basic form is ὑμᾶς, and ὕμας comes about via two ordered rules: (i) the throwing back of the accent (giving ὕμᾶς), and (ii) the shortening of the α (giving ὕμας). At the second step, the 'same accent' is said to remain on the same syllable. If this is the correct text, the accent of ὕμᾶς is said to be 'the same' as that of ὕμας, despite the change of an acute to a circumflex. Alternatively, one might consider reading e.g. ἐφύλαξεν ἐν τῇ αὐτῇ συλλαβῇ τὸν τόνον, ⟨οὐ μὴν⟩ τὸν αὐτόν 'it has kept the accent on the same syllable, but not the same accent' (for parallels, see Roussou 2018b: 268–70).

§i δεῖ δὲ νοῆσαι[a] ὅτι αἱ[b] δισύλλαβοι ἀναμφιβόλως[c] καὶ[d] ἀναβιβάζουσιν ἐγκλινόμεναι[e] καὶ φυλάττουσιν ὀρθοτονούμεναι, οἷον[f] 'ἤκουσά τινος', 'ἀνθρώπου[g] τινός', 'ἀφ' οὗ τινος'. αἱ δὲ μονοσύλλαβοι[h] ἀναβιβάζουσι μὲν ἐγκλινόμεναι[i] προηγουμένων τῶν προειρημένων λέξεων· ἄλλων δὲ λέξεων προηγουμένων ⟨τῶν⟩ μὴ δεχομένων τὴν[j] ἔγκλισιν τὴν ἐπιφερομένην ἄφατον σύγχυσιν[k] ἐποίησαν.[l] οἷον 'ἀνθρώπου μου' ἔδει εἶναι 'ἀνθρώπου ἐμοῦ'. 'μέλει[m] μοι' ἔδει ὀρθοτονηθῆναι,[n] 'ἐμοί'.[o] ὅμως μονοσυλλαβοῦντα[p] οὔτε[q] ἀνεβίβασαν[r] οὔτε ἐφύλαξαν,[s] ἀλλ' ὡς μιᾶς λέξεως οὔσης ὁ τόνος ἐτέθη, 'ἀνθρώπου μου'. καὶ οὕτως ἡμεῖς δοξάζομεν. ἄλλοι[t] δέ τινες συγχέουσιν,[u] ὡς καὶ ὁ[v] Ῥωμανὸς λέγων, εἰ[w] περισπωμένη προηγεῖται,[x] ⟨παρέχουσι[y] τὸν τόνον, 'καλοῦ μου',

§i

[a] νοῆσαι **w₁Γw₂Nρ**: γιγνώσκειν **U**: γινώσκειν **X**

[b] αἱ] οἱ **ζ**

[c] ἀναμφιβόλως **GBΛΓy₁Ncn**: ἀναμφιβολῶς (sic) **r**: ἀμφιβόλως (sic) **ΦHy₂**

[d] καὶ deest in **Gc**

[e] ἐγκλινόμεναι **GΛYy₁NcnK**: ἐγκλινόμενα **BΘ**: ἐγκλινόμενον **Φ Ald.**: αἰγκλινόμεναι (sic) **Γ**

[f] οἷον deest in **BΛ**

[g] ἀνθρώπου τινός ἀφ' (ἐφ' **H**) οὗ τινος (τίνος **H**) **w₁w₂N**: καὶ ἀνθρώπου (ΣSK: ἀνθρώπου **J**) τινος· ἀφ' οὗ τινος **nK**: ἀφ' οὗ τινος **Ald.**: ἀνθρώπου τινὸς **GΓc**

[h] μονοσύλλαβοι **w₁Γw₂Ncn**: μονοσύλλαβαι **r**

[i] ἐγκλινόμεναι προηγουμένων τῶν προειρημένων λέξεων· ἄλλων δὲ λέξεων προηγουμένων ⟨τῶν⟩ (add. Bekker) μὴ δεχομένων **VN**: ἐγκλινόμεναι προηγουμένων τῶν προειρημένων λέξεων· ἄλλων δὲ λέξεων προηγουμένων **c**: ἐγκλινόμεναι προηγουμένων μὴ δεχομένων **ΛΓw₂ρ**: ἐγκλινόμενων προηγουμένων μὴ δεχομένων **B**: ἐγκλινόμεναι· τῶν δὲ προηγουμένων μὴ δεχομένων **G**: ἐγκλινόμενον προηγουμένων μὴ δεχομένων **ΦH**: ἐγκλινόμεναι τῶν προειρημένων λέξεων προηγουμένων· ἄλλων δὲ λέξεων προηγουμένων τῶν μὴ δεχομένων Bekker

[j] τὴν ἔγκλισιν τὴν ἐπιφερομένην deest in **c**

[k] σύγχυσιν **xBΓy₁Ns**: σύγχησιν (sic) **Λy₂ζ**

[l] ἐποίησαν **xΛΓy₁Ns**: ἐποίησεν **By₂**

[m] μέλει **GBΛΓw₂Nρ**: μέλλει **ΦHc**

[n] ὀρθοτονηθῆναι **BΛΓw₂**: ὀρθοτονεῖσθαι **Nρ**: εἶναι **x**: εἶναι τὸ ἀρνεῖσθαι **c**

[o] ἐμοί] μέλλεις ἐμοί **U**: μέλλει ἐμοί **ΦHX**: μέλει μοι **G**

[p] μονοσυλλαβοῦντα **c**: μεσοσυλλαβοῦντα **ρ**: μεσοσυλλαβοῦντες **xBYy₃**: οὐ μεσοσυλλαβοῦνται **N**: μεσοσυλλαβοῦντος **V**: οὐ μεσοσυλλάβου **Γ**: μεσοσυλλαβεῖοῦντες sic **Θ**: μεσοσυλλαβοῦν[τ] **Λ**

[q] οὔτε...οὔτε Bekker: οὐδὲ...οὐδὲ **w₁Γw₂Ns**

[r] ἀνεβίβασαν **w₁Γy₁Nc**: ἀνεβίβασεν **n**: ἀναβίβασεν (sic) **r**: ἀναβιβάζουσιν **y₂**

[s] ἐφύλαξαν **w₁Γw₂Nc**: ἐφύλαξεν **ρ**

[t] ἄλλοι δέ τινες συγχέουσιν — ἢ ὀξύτονος ἢ τροχαϊκή] Ῥωμανὸς μὲν οὖν καὶ ἄλλοι (sine accentu) τινὲς τὸ περὶ τούτου συγχέουσιν· ἡμεῖς δέ φαμεν ὡς ἢν παροξύτονος ἢ περισπώμενος προηγεῖται οὐ παρέχουσι τὸν τόνον ταῖς προηγουμέναις· ἀλλὰ δεῖ προηγεῖσθαι ὡς εἴπομεν προπαροξύτονον ἢ ὀξύτονον ἢ τροχαϊκὴν **G**

[u] συγχέουσιν **ΦHΓVNcρ**: συγχύουσιν **BΛw₂**

[v] ὁ ῥωμανὸς λέγων **ΛΓYy₁Nρ**: Ῥωμανὸς λέγων **Θ^{p.c.}**: ὁ ῥωμανὸς λέγει **ΦHB**: ῥωμανὸς λέγει **c**: Ῥωμανὸς λέγεται **Θ^{a.c.}**

[w] εἰ] οἷον πόθεν τις· καὶ ὅθεν με· δέον πόθεν τις λέγειν· καὶ ὅθεν με, εἰ **c**

[x] προηγεῖται] προηγεῖτο **c**

[y] lacunam statuimus et verba παρέχουσι — προηγεῖται addidimus (exemplum καλοῦ μου exempli gratia scripsimus, cf. codices **VNc** infra)

§i And one must notice that the disyllabic enclitics unambiguously both throw
their accent back when they are enclitic and keep it when they are orthotonic, as
in ἤκουσά τινος, ἀνθρώπου τινός, ἀφ᾽ οὗ τινος.²⁴⁶ And the monosyllabic ones
throw back the accent when enclitic, when the aforementioned words precede;
and when other words precede that do not admit the throwing back of the following accent, people have caused an unutterable confusion. For example,
ἀνθρώπου μου²⁴⁷ should have been ἀνθρώπου ἐμοῦ, and [the μοι in] μέλει μοι²⁴⁸
should have been orthotonic, [i.e.] ἐμοί. When they are nevertheless monosyllabic they neither throw their back nor maintain it, but the accent is
placed as if the word were one, as in ἀνθρώπου μου. And this is what we believe.
But some others cause confusion, including Romanus,²⁴⁹ who says that if a perispomenon word precedes, enclitics pass their accent on to it, as in καλοῦ μου,²⁵⁰

²⁴⁶ 'I heard someone'; 'of some person'; 'from whoever/whatever'.
²⁴⁷ 'Of my person'.
²⁴⁸ 'It concerns me'.
²⁴⁹ On the little evidence we have for this grammarian named Romanus, see Kaster (1988: 350–1).
Choeroboscus (Th. i. 106.3–4; i. 309.28–9) refers to him as a teacher of John Philoponus—but as
Kaster notes, such claims are difficult to evaluate and may be meant more or less literally.
²⁵⁰ 'Of my beautiful…'.

εἰ δὲ παροξύτονος προηγεῖται⟩ οὐ παρέχουσι[z] τὸν τόνον,[aa] 'πόθεν[bb] τις', 'ὅθεν
με'. ψευδὲς[cc] δέ ἐστιν· εἰς γὰρ ὁ[dd] τόνος τίθεται,[ee] καὶ οὐ παρέχουσι τὸν τόνον
ταῖς[ff] προηγουμέναις, εἰ μὴ ὦσιν, ὡς εἴπομεν,[gg] προπαροξύτονος[hh] ἢ ὀξύτονος
ἢ τροχαϊκή.

§j ἰστέον[a] δὲ ὅτι διαφέρει ἐγκλιτικὸν ἐγκλινομένου,[b] οὐχ ὡς λέγει ὁ Φιλόπονος[c]
ἐν τῇ ἀντωνυμίᾳ, ὃν ἐλέγχομεν ἐκεῖ, ἀλλὰ τῷ[d] καθόλου καὶ τῷ μερικῷ. πᾶν
γὰρ[e] ἐγκλιτικὸν καὶ ἐγκλινόμενόν[f] ἐστιν· ἦλθέ τις, ἐγκλιτικὸν καὶ ἐγκλινόμενον·
οὐ[g] πᾶν δὲ ἐγκλινόμενον καὶ ἐγκλιτικόν ἐστιν. αἱ[h] γὰρ[i] λέξεις αἱ ὀξύτονοι[j] ἐν τῇ
συνεχείᾳ[k] κοιμίζουσαι[l] τοὺς τόνους ἐγκλινόμεναι καλοῦνται, οἷον[m] 'εἴ[n] μὴ
μητρυιὴ περικαλλὴς'.[o] ἰδοὺ αὗται κοιμίζουσαι[p] ἐν[q] τῇ συνεχείᾳ ἐγκλινόμεναι
καλοῦνται καὶ οὐχὶ[r] ἐγκλιτικαί. ἀλλὰ πᾶν ἐγκλιτικὸν ἐγκλινόμενον.[s]

[z] παρέχουσι w₁Γw₂Nc: παρέχει ρ
[aa] verba αὐτῇ καλοῦ μου (οἷον καλοῦ μου c)· εἰ δὲ ἄλλος τόνος εἴη παρέχουσι τὸν τόνον inseru-
erunt VNc
[bb] πόθεν — καὶ οὐ παρέχουσι τὸν τόνον deest in x
[cc] ψευδὲς δέ ἐστιν BΓy₃: ψευδὴς γάρ ἐστιν Vρ: ψευδὲς ἐστιν Nc: ψευδὲς δὲ λίαν y₂: ψευδές γάρ ἐστιν
Σ: ψευδὲς δὲ ἐσὶν (sic) Λ: ψευδὲς δὲ λίαν ἐστίν Bekker
[dd] ὁ deest in c
[ee] τίθεται BΛΓw₂Nρ: ἐστὶ καὶ τίθεται c
[ff] ταῖς προηγουμέναις, εἰ (εἰ w₁y₂y₃N: κεὶ ρ) μὴ ὦσιν, ὡς εἴπομεν w₁y₂y₃Nρ: ὡς εἴπομεν ταῖς
προηγουμέναις εἰ μὴ εἴη ὡς εἴπομεν c: ταῖς προειρημέναις εἰ μὴ ὦσιν ὡς εἴπομεν V: ταῖς
προσηγουμέναις (sic), εἰ μὴ ὦσιν ὡς Γ: ὡς εἴπομεν, ταῖς προηγουμέναις, εἰ μὴ εἴη Bekker
[gg] εἴπομεν — usque ad finem (§w) deest in Γ
[hh] προπαροξύτονος — τροχαϊκή (τροχαϊκὸς N) w₁w₂Nρ: προπαροξύτονος ἢ τροχαϊκή c

§j
[a] ἰστέον δὲ ὅτι w₁w₂Ncr: ἰστέον ὅτι ζ
[b] ἐγκλινομένου] καὶ ἐγκλινόμενον c
[c] Φιλόπονος] fortasse legendum Ἀπολλώνιος (cf. Ap. Dysc., *Pron.* 35.22–36.5, etiamsi hic locus
Apollonii interpolatus esse possit, ut Maas 1907 putavit; cf. n. 406)
[d] τῷ καθόλου...τῷ μερικῷ xBy₂NnK: τὸ καθόλου...τῷ μικρῷ Ald.: τὸ καθόλου...τῷ μερικῷ
Λy₃S: τῷ μερικῷ...τῷ καθόλου c: τῷ καθόλου...μερικῷ V
[e] γὰρ w₁w₂Nρ: μὲν γάρ c
[f] ἐγκλινόμενόν ἐστιν (ἐστιν deest in N)· ἦλθέ τις, ἐγκλιτικὸν καὶ ἐγκλινόμενον ΦΗw₂N:
ἐγκλινόμενον ἐστίν· τὸ γὰρ ἔφησε τις· ἐγκλιτικὸν καὶ ἐγκλινόμενον G: ἐγκλινόμενόν ἐστιν ἢ
θέμις ἐγκλιτικὸν καὶ ἐγκλινόμενον ρ: ἐγκλινόμενον ἦλθέ τις c: ἐγκλινόμενον ἐγκλιτ[τ] καὶ
ἐγκλινόμενον Β: ἐγκλινόμενον ἐστιν Λ
[g] οὐ πᾶν δὲ ἐγκλινόμενον καὶ w₁w₂NcnK: οὐ πᾶν γε ἐγκλινόμενον καὶ Ald.
[h] αἱ w₁w₂Nρ: αἱ μὲν c
[i] γὰρ deest in Ald.
[j] ὀξύτονοι ἐν τῇ συνεπείᾳ deest in c
[k] συνεχείᾳ w₁w₂ρ: συνεπείᾳ N
[l] κοιμίζουσαι w₁w₂Ns: κοιμίζουσι ΦΗζ
[m] οἷον — ἐγκλινόμεναι καλοῦνται deest in x
[n] εἰ μὴ BΛw₂NSK: ἢ μὴ Uζ: ἡ Ald.: ἡ ἐμῇ X
[o] περικαλλὴς BΛVNS Ald.: περικαλλῆς y₃: περικαλῆς J: περικαλλῆ (sic) y₂K: περικαλλὴς
Ἡερίβοια U: περικαλῆς ἢ ἐροίβια X: περικαλῆς ἐρίβοια Σ
[p] κοιμίζουσαι Bw₂NXSr: κοιμίζουσιν Uζ
[q] ἐν τῇ συνεχείᾳ w₂cnK: ἐν τῇ συνεπείᾳ N: ἐν τῇ συνεχείᾳ τὸν τόνον Ald.: τοὺς τόνους ἐν τῇ
συνεχείᾳ B: de Λ n.l.
[r] οὐχὶ deest in y₂
[s] ἐγκλινόμενον] ἐγκλινόμενον· οὐ πᾶν δὲ ἐγκλινόμενον ἐγκλιτικὸν c

but if a paroxytone word precedes, they do not pass on their accent, as in πόθεν τις, ὅθεν με.[251] But this is wrong. For the accent that is placed is one; and enclitics do not pass their accent on to preceding words unless, as we have said, the preceding word is proparoxytone or oxytone or trochaic.

§j And one must know that an *enclitic* differs from an *enclinomenon* not in the way that Philoponus[252] says in his work on the pronoun—and we refuted him in our discussion of that topic—but by a relationship of whole and part. For every enclitic is also an enclinomenon: [thus the τις in] ἦλθέ τις is both an enclitic and an enclinomenon; but not every enclinomenon is also an enclitic. For oxytone words that put their accents to sleep in connected speech are called *enclinomena*, as in εἰ μὴ μητρυιὴ περικαλλὴς.[253] There you are: these words, which put [their accents] to sleep in connected speech, are called *enclinomena* but not *enclitics*. But every *enclitic* is an *enclinomenon*.

---

[251] 'From where does someone…?'; 'from where…me'.

[252] On the sixth-century grammarian and philosopher John Philoponus, see Kaster (1988: 334–8). But we suspect that Apollonius Dyscolus may be intended here: see the critical apparatus.

[253] *Il.* 5.389: 'had not their stepmother, very beautiful [Eeriboia, told Hermes]'. On the contextual grave accent of εἰ, see n. 100. The word περικαλλὴς would have been considered to have a contextual grave accent in this example too, because the word Ἠερίβοια follows in the line of Homer with no intervening punctuation.

§k διαλαμβάνοντες[a] δὲ περὶ ἑκάστου μέρους δείξομεν[b] ὀλίγα ἐναντιούμενα τοῖς προειρημένοις, περὶ ὧν ἐν εὐκαίρῳ διδάξομεν. διαλάβωμεν[c] [d] μέντοι περὶ[e] ὀνομάτων.

§l καθόλου[a] ἐν τοῖς ὀνόμασιν οὐδὲν ἐγκλίνεται, εἰ μὴ τὸ ΤΙΣ ἐν ὅλαις ταῖς πτώσεσι καὶ τοῖς[b] ἀριθμοῖς καὶ ἐν[c] τοῖς γένεσι. καὶ[d] ἐν ταῖς εὐθείαις ἀντωνυμίας μὴ ἐγκλινομένης, τὸ ΟΥΤΙΣ[e] πανταχοῦ ἐγκλίνεται, καὶ τὸ ΤΟΥ καὶ τὸ[f] ΤΩΙ τὰ ἰσοδυναμοῦντα τῷ ΤΙΝΟΣ καὶ[g] ΤΙΝΙ ἐν[h] μόνῃ γενικῇ[i] καὶ δοτικῇ ἑνικῇ. ταῦτα δὲ καὶ τὸ ΤΙΣ πρὸς διάφορον σημαινόμενον ⟨ἐγκλίνεται⟩[j] {καὶ[k] τὰ κινήματα ταῦτα}. πυσματικὰ γὰρ ὄντα βαρύνονται ὀρθοτονούμενα·[l] ‘τίνος’, ‘τίνι’, ‘τίνα’, ‘τίνε’,[m] ‘τίνοιν’,[n] ‘τίνες’, ‘τίνων’, ‘τίσι’, ‘τίνας’. καὶ τὸ ΤΙΣ τῷ λόγῳ τῆς ἀρχούσης ἔχει τὴν ὀξεῖαν, ὅθεν οὐ κοιμίζεται ἐν τῇ[o] συνεχείᾳ, ‘τίς ἦλθε;’ καὶ τὸ ΤΟΥ περισπᾶται καὶ τὸ ΤΩΙ.[p] ἅτε[q] οὖν πυσματικὰ ὄντα ὀρθοτονοῦνται,[r] ἀόριστα δὲ ἀποφαντικὰ ἐγκλίνονται, ‘ἄνθρωπός τις’, ‘ἤκουσά τινος’, ‘δέδωκά τινι’, ‘ὕβρισέ[s] [t] τινα’, ‘ἄνθρωποί[u] [v] τινες’, ‘ἤκουσά τινων’, ‘δέδωκά τισιν’, ‘ὕβρισέ[w] τινας’, ‘ἤκουσά[x] του λέγοντος’, ‘δέδωκά τῳ’. ταῦτα[y] περὶ τοῦ ὀνόματος· ἔλθωμεν[z] δὲ εἰς τὸ ῥῆμα.

§k

[a] διαλαμβάνοντες δὲ περὶ ἑκάστου μέρους B**Λ**w₂N: διαλαμβάνοντες περὶ ἑκάστου μέρους **c**: διαλαμβάνονται δὲ περὶ ἑκάστου μέρους **ΦH**: περὶ ἑκάστου δὲ μέρους **ρ**

[b] δείξομεν w₁w₂Ns; an διέξιμεν?

[c] διαλάβωμεν μέντοι — usque ad finem (§w) deest in **c**

[d] διαλάβωμεν μέντοι B: διαλάβωμεν μέντοι **Λ**w₂: νῦν δὲ διαλάβωμεν **ρ**: διαλάβωμεν τοι N: διαλαμβάνομέν τοι V: διαλάβωμεν δὲ τὰ **Φ**: διαλάβοιμεν δὲ H: νῦν μέντοι διαλάβωμεν Bekker

[e] περὶ ὀνομάτων w₁w₂N: περὶ τοῦ ὀνόματος **ρ**

§l

[a] ante καθόλου titulum ἐγκλιτικὰ ἐν τοῖς ὀνόμασιν praebet **Ald.**

[b] τοῖς w₁w₂N: deest in **ρ**

[c] ἐν τοῖς B**Λ**w₂N: τοῖς G: ἐν ταῖς **ΦH**: deest in **ρ**

[d] καὶ ἐν ταῖς εὐθείαις ἀντωνυμίας B **Ald.**: καὶ ἐν ταῖς εὐθείαις εὐθείας ἀντωνυμίας **ΦH**w₂NnK: καὶ ταῦτα τῆς εὐθείας τῆς ἀντωνυμίας G: de **Λ** n.l.

[e] ΟΥΤΙΣ **ΦHΛ**w₂ρ: οὐ B: γοῦν τίς G: τις N

[f] τὸ w₁w₂N: deest in L**ρ**

[g] καὶ xBy₂y₃N: deest in **ΛV**ρ

[h] ἐν w₁N **Ald.**: καὶ τοῦ τίνος καὶ τίνι ἐν nK: τοῦ τίνος τῷ τίνι ἐν w₂

[i] γενικῇ καὶ δοτικῇ ἑνικῇ nK: γενικῇ ἑνικῇ καὶ δοτικῇ N: γενικῇ καὶ δοτικῇ **Ald.**: γενικῇ ἑνικῇ xBy₂y₃

[j] ἐγκλίνεται addidimus

[k] καὶ τὰ κινήματα ταῦτα delevimus: deest in B

[l] ὀρθοτονούμενα w₁w₂Nn: ὀρθοτονούμεναι K **Ald.**

[m] τίνε **ΦBΛ**w₂NnK: καὶ τίνε **Ald.**: deest in HG

[n] τίνοιν **Φ**JK **Ald.**: deest in HGB**Λ**w₂N**Σ**S

[o] τῇ συνεχείᾳ w₁w₂ρ: τῇ συνεπείᾳ N

[p] ΤΩΙ Gρ: τῷ τουτέστι τὸ δῶ (fortasse corruptio verborum τοῦτ᾽ ἔστι τὸ δοτικόν) **ΦHΛ**w₂N: τῷ τουτέστιν τῷ B

[q] ἅτε οὖν πυσματικὰ ὄντα scripsimus: οὔτε οὖν πυσματικὰ ὄντα **Λ**w₂N: ὅτε οὖν πυσματικὰ ὄντα B: ὅτε γὰρ πυσματικὰ ὄντα ρ: ὅτε πυσματικὰ ὄντα **Φ**: ὅτι πυσματικὰ ὄντα H: πυσματικὰ μὲν οὖν G

[r] ὀρθοτονοῦνται **ΦH**By₃y₃Nρ: ὀρθοτονεῖται G**ΛV**

[s] ὕβρισέ τινα — δέδωκά τισιν deest in **Ald.**

[t] ὕβρισέ τινα B**Λ**w₂N: ὕβρισά τινα xnK

[u] ἄνθρωποί τινες — ὕβρισέ τινας deest in w₁

[v] ἄνθρωποί τινες nK: Αἴαντέ τινε ἄνθρωποί τινες w₂N

[w] ὕβρισέ τινας w₂N: ὕβρισά τινας ρ

[x] ἤκουσά του λέγοντος B**Λ**y₁Nρ: ἤκουσά τινος λέγοντος **ΦH**y₂: ἤκουσά του G

[y] ταῦτα w₁w₂N: καὶ ταῦτα μὲν ρ

[z] ἔλθωμεν δὲ (δὲ καὶ **ΦHN**) εἰς τὸ ῥῆμα **ΦHB**y₂Nρ: ἔλθωμεν δὲ εἰς τὸ ῥῆμα **ΛL**ᵥ: ἔλθον δὲ εἰς τὸ ῥῆμα L: deest in GV

§k Dealing separately with each part of speech, we will show a few things that contradict what has been said above, and we will provide instruction about them at the right moment. But now let us deal with nominals.[254]

§l In general there is no enclitic among the nominals, with the exception of *TIΣ* in all its cases and numbers and genders. And among the nominatives of a pronoun that is not an enclitic, [the *TIΣ* of] *ΟΥΤΙΣ* is always an enclitic; also [enclitic are] *TOY* and *TΩI*, which are the equivalent of *TINOΣ* and *TINI* in the genitive and dative singular alone. And these and *TIΣ* are enclitic to express a different meaning. For when they are interrogative they are barytone and orthotonic: τίνος, τίνι, τίνα, τίνε, τίνοιν, τίνες, τίνων, τίσι, τίνας. And [interrogative] *TIΣ* has the acute accent by the principle of the first [syllable],[255] whence it is not put to sleep in connected speech, as in τίς ἦλθε;.[256] And [interrogative] *TOY* and *TΩI* are perispomenon. When these are interrogative, then, they are orthotonic, but when they are indefinite and declarative [i.e. non-interrogative] they are enclitic, as in ἄνθρωπός τις, ἤκουσά τινος, δέδωκά τινι, ὕβρισέ τινα, ἄνθρωποί τινες, ἤκουσά τινων, δέδωκά τισιν, ὕβρισέ τινας, ἤκουσά του λέγοντος, δέδωκά τῳ.[257] So much for the nominal; let us come to the verb.

---

[254] On the meaning of ὄνομα, see n. 15.
[255] For the idea being expressed here, see section 2.8.1.
[256] 'Who has come?'
[257] 'A certain person'; 'I heard someone'; 'I have given to someone'; 'he/she mistreated someone'; 'certain people'; 'I heard some people'; 'I have given to some people'; 'he/she mistreated some people' 'I heard someone saying'; 'I have given to someone'.

§m ἐν τοῖς ῥήμασιν οὐδὲν ἐγκλίνεται εἰ μὴ δύο[a] μόνα εἰς -μι, *ΦΗΜΙ*[b] καὶ *ΕΙΜΙ* (δηλονότι[c] [d] προηγουμένων τῶν προρρηθεισῶν[e] λέξεων, ἐπεί[f] τὸ 'ἀνθρώπου[g] εἰμί' οὐκ ἐγκλίνεται καὶ τὸ[h] 'οὖν εἰμί', ὡς ἔφημεν, οὐκ ἐγκλίνεται) καὶ τὸ δεύτερον πρόσωπον *ΕΙΣ*, 'αἵματός[i] εἰς ἀγαθοῖο'.[j] καὶ ταῦτα οὐ πρὸς διάφορον σημαινόμενον ἐγκλίνεται,[k] ἀλλὰ πρὸς εὐπρεπείαν[l] φασὶν οὕτως ἀρέσαι[m] τοῖς παλαιοῖς. τὸ δὲ *ΕΙ* οὐκ ἐγκλίνεται, εἴτε ἀπὸ τοῦ *ΕΙΜΙ* ἐστιν[n] διὰ τὸ πάθος εἴτε ἑτέρωθεν, ἀλλ' ὀρθοτονεῖται καὶ[o] ἐν τῷ 'ἄνθρωπος εἶ'. τὸ[p] δὲ *ΕΣΣΙ* καὶ τὸ *ΕΣΤΙ* τρίτον πρόσωπον καὶ[q] αὐτὰ κατὰ τὸν λόγον ἐγκλίνεται, 'ἄνθρωπός ἐστι, 'σχέτλιός[r] ἔσσι γεραιέ'. τὸ[s] [t] δὲ *ΕΣΤΙ* εἰς πολλὰ παρέβη τὴν ἀκολουθίαν. ἐν ἀρχῇ γὰρ[u] ἄλλης λέξεως μὴ ἐγκλινομένης ἐγκλίνεται τῇ ἰδίᾳ ἀρχῇ τὸν τόνον ἀναπέμπον,[v] ὡς[w] ἐν τῷ 'ἔστι πόλις Ἐφύρη',[x] καὶ[y] ἐπὶ πάντων ὁμοίως. κάτω δὲ ὑπάρχον, προηγουμένων αὐτοῦ τινων λέξεων ὀξυνομένων, παρέβη τὴν ἔγκλισιν. ἔδει γὰρ ἐπὶ πάντων ἀναβιβάζειν τὸν τόνον τῇ πρὸ αὐτοῦ[z] λέξει ὀξυτόνῳ οὔσῃ, ὡς ἐν[aa] τῷ 'ἐμός ἐστι', 'καλός ἐστιν'. εἰς τὴν ἰδίαν δὲ[bb] ἀρχὴν ἀναβιβάζει ἐπί τινων καὶ ἐπὶ τῆς *ΟΥ*, 'οὐκ ἔστιν οὐδὲν δεινόν', καὶ ἐπὶ τοῦ *ΚΑΙ*, 'καὶ ἔστι', καὶ ἐπὶ τοῦ *ΩΣ*, 'ὡς ἔστι'. ταῦτα[cc]

§m
[a] δύο μόνα εἰς μι *ΦΗΒΛw₂N*: δύο μόνα *Gρ*
[b] φημὶ καὶ εἰμὶ *ΦΗΒΛy₂y₃N*: τὸ φημί καὶ εἰμί *K*: τὸ εἰμί καὶ φημί *ρ*: εἰμὶ καὶ φημὶ *G*: φημί καὶ εἰμί ἐγώ φημι ἐγώ εἰμι *V*
[c] δηλονότι — 'οὖν εἰμί' deest in **n**
[d] δηλονότι *ΦΗΒΛNρ*: καὶ δηλονότι *w₂*: καὶ ταῦτα δηλονότι *G*
[e] προρρηθεισῶν *w₁y₃ρ*: προηγηθεισῶν *y₂N*
[f] ἐπεὶ *w₁y₃Nr*: ἐπὶ *y₂*
[g] ἀνθρώπου *w₁y₃Nr*: ἄνθρωπος *y₂*
[h] τὸ (τὸ deest in **x**) οὖν εἰμὶ ὡς ἔφημεν οὐκ (οὐκ deest in **N**) ἐγκλίνεται καὶ (καὶ deest in **x**) τὸ δεύτερον πρόσωπον *ΕΙΣ* x*Λy₂y₃N*: τὸ οὖν εἰμί ὡς ἔφημεν καὶ τὸ δεύτερον πρόσωπον εἶς **BK**: τὸ οὖν εἰμί. τοῦ δὲ εἰμὶ ἐγκλίνεται καὶ τὸ δεύτερον πρόσωπον εἶς **Ald.**: τὸ δὲ εἰμί, οὐκ ἐγκλίνεται καὶ τὸ β᾽ πρόσωπον **n**
[i] αἵματός εἰς **Ald.**: αἵματος εἶς **K**: εἰς αἵματος εἶς **B**: αἵματος εἶς *GΛ***n**: αἵματος εἶς *y₂*: οἷον αἵματός εἰς **N**: αἵματος εἰς *y₃*: αἵματος *ΦΗ*
[j] ἀγαθοῖο *w₁y₂y₃Nr*: ἀγαθοῦ **n**
[k] ἐγκλίνεται *Φy₂Nρ*: ἐγκλίνονται *HGBΛy₃*
[l] εὐπρεπείαν φασὶν scripsimus: εὐπρεπῆ φράσιν x*BLₓ***K**: εὐπρεπῆ φάσιν **Ald.**: εὐτρεπῆ φράσιν *Λy₂***LN***Σ*: εὐτερπῆ φράσιν **JS**
[m] ἀρέσαι *ΦΗΒΛy₃Nρ*: ἀρέσαν *G*: ἀρέσει *y₂*
[n] ἐστὶ διὰ τὸ πάθος *w₁w₂N*: ὂν διὰ τὸ πάθος *ρ*
[o] καὶ ἐν τῷ *ΦΗΛw₂ρ*: ὡς ἐν τῷ **G**: ἐν τῷ *G*: ὡς ἐν τῷ **N**
[p] τὸ δὲ *ΕΣΣΙ* καὶ τὸ *ΕΣΤΙ* τρίτον πρόσωπον scripsimus: τὸ τρίτον πρόσωπον τὸ ἐστὶ *y₂*: τὸ τρίτον πρόσωπον τὸ ἔσσι *ΦΗΒΛy₃N*: τὸ δὲ *ΕΣΤΙ* τρίτον πρόσωπον *ρ*: τὸ δὲ ἔσσι *G*
[q] καὶ αὐτὰ (αὐτὰ scripsimus: αὐτὸ *w₁w₂***N**) κατὰ τὸν (τὸν deest in *y₂*) λόγον ἐγκλίνεται *w₁w₂***N**: καὶ αὐτὸ κατὰ τὸν λόγον ἐγκλινόμενον τυγχάνει *ρ*
[r] ἄνθρωπός ἐστι σχέτλιός ἔσσι γεραιέ (γηραιέ **B**) *Bw₂N*: ἄνθρωπος ἔσσι· σχέτλιος ἔσσι γεραιὲ **x**: ἄνθρωπός ἔσσι σχέτλιος *Λ*: ἄνθρωπός ἐστιν *ρ*
[s] τὸ δὲ *ΕΣΤΙ* — usque ad finem (§w) deest in *Λ*
[t] τὸ δὲ *ΕΣΤΙ* εἰς πολλὰ παρέβη *w₁w₂N*: εἰς πολλὰ δὲ αὐτὸ παρέβη *ρ*
[u] γὰρ *ΦΗΒy₂y₃N*: μὲν γὰρ *Gρ*
[v] ἀναπέμπον *GΘy₃Nζ*: ἀναπέμπουσα **B**: ἀποπέμπον **r**: ἀπαπέμπον (sic) **S**: ἀναπέμπων *ΦΗΥ*
[w] ὡς ἐν τῷ **x**: ὡς καὶ ἐν τῷ *By₂*: ὡς καὶ ἐν *y₃*: ὡς ἐν **N**: deest in *ρ*
[x] Ἐφύρη *w₁w₂N*: Ἐφύρη· καὶ μετὰ τοῦ οὐ (οὐ deest in **Ald.**) οὐκ ἔστι ταῦτα *ρ*
[y] καὶ ἐπὶ πάντων — ταῦτα περὶ τοῦ *ΕΣΤΙΝ* deest in *ρ*
[z] αὐτοῦ scripsimus: αὐτοῦ *w₁w₂N*
[aa] ἐν τῷ *Bw₂N*: τὸ **x**
[bb] δὲ *w₂N*: deest in x**B**
[cc] ταῦτα περὶ τοῦ *ΕΣΤΙΝ ΦΗN*: ταῦτα δὲ περὶ τοῦ ἐστὶν **B**: ταῦτά περ τουτέστιν *w₂*: deest in **G**

§m Among the verbs none throws back its accent except for two alone ending in -μι, *ΦΗΜΙ* and *'ΕΙΜΙ* (I mean when the aforementioned words precede, because [the *'ΕΙΜΙ* of] ἀνθρώπου εἰμί[258] does not throw its accent back, and nor does [the *'ΕΙΜΙ* of] οὖν εἰμι,[259] as we said) and the second person *'ΕΙΣ* [is also enclitic], as in αἵματός εἰς ἀγαθοῖο.[260] And these are enclitic not to express a different meaning, but they say that it pleased the ancients like this for seemliness. But *'ΕΙ* is not an enclitic, whether it comes from *'ΕΙΜΙ* by a modification or from somewhere else, but it is orthotonic even in ἄνθρωπος εἶ.[261] And *'ΕΣΣΙ* and the third person form *'ΕΣΤΙ* too throw back their accent according to the rule: ἄνθρωπός ἐστι, σχέτλιός ἐσσι γεραιέ.[262] But *'ΕΣΤΙ* in many cases contravenes regularity. For in initial position, where other words do not throw back their accent, it throws its accent back by sending it back to its own first syllable, as in ἔστι πόλις 'Εφύρη,[263] and similarly in all instances. But when it is found further down [the clause], with certain oxytone words preceding it, it violates [the rules of] enclisis. For it should in all instances have retracted its accent onto the preceding word, if this was oxytone, as in ἐμός ἐστι, καλός ἐστιν.[264] But in some cases, including that of *'ΟΥ*, it retracts the accent onto its own first syllable, as in οὐκ ἔστιν οὐδὲν δεινόν,[265] and in the case of ΚΑΙ, as in καὶ ἔστι,[266] and in the case of *'ΩΣ*, as in ὡς ἔστι.[267] So much then

---

[258] 'I belong to a person'.
[259] '...therefore I am'.
[260] *Od.* 4.611: 'You are of good lineage'.
[261] 'You are a person'.
[262] 'He/she is a person'; *Il.* 10.164: 'you're unstoppable, old man'.
[263] *Il.* 6.152: 'There is a city, Ephurē'.
[264] 'Is mine'; 'is beautiful'.
[265] Euripides, *Orestes* 1: 'There is no terrible thing ...'.
[266] 'And there is'/'And...is'.
[267] 'That there is'/'That he/she/it is'.

περὶ τοῦ ΕΣΤΙΝ. ἐγκλίνεται δὲ καὶ τὸ[dd] ΕΣΤΟΝ δυϊκόν, 'οἵ[ee] μοι φίλτατοί
ἐστον'. (οὕτως[ff] ἔχει καὶ ἡ ἀνάγνωσις, μὴ πεισθεῖσα τοῖς ἐναντιουμένοις, φημὶ
δὲ Τηλέφῳ Περγαμηνῷ.) καὶ[gg] τὰ πληθυντικὰ ὁμοίως[hh] κατὰ τὸν λόγον
ἐγκλίνονται, 'ἄνθρωποί ἐσμεν', 'ἄνθρωποί ἐστε', 'ἄνθρωποί εἰσιν'. ταῦτα[ii] μὲν
περὶ τοῦ ΕΙΜΙ.

§n τὸ[a] δὲ ΦΗΜΙ κατὰ τὸ[b] πρῶτον πρόσωπον ἀκολουθεῖ[c] τῷ λόγῳ, 'ἄνθρωπόν[d]
φημι'. τινὲς[e] δὲ ἔλεγον αὐτὸ μὴ ἐγκλίνεσθαι, ὡς ὁ προειρημένος Τήλεφος, ᾧ
οὐκ ἐπείσθη ἡ χρῆσις. τὸ[f] δὲ ΦΗΙΣ τὸ δεύτερον οὐκ ἐγκλίνεται, μήποτε[g] ⟨διὰ⟩[h]
τὸ[i] πλεόνασμα τοῦ Ι. ἀλλ' οὐδὲ τὸ ἀπ' αὐτοῦ γεγονὸς κατ' ἀποβολὴν τοῦ[j] φ
ΗΜΙ ἐγκλίνεται. τινὲς δὲ λέγουσι μὴ[k] εἶναι αὐτὸ ἀπ'[l] αὐτοῦ, διότι ἐνήλλαξε
τὴν συζυγίαν (τὸ γὰρ ΦΗΜΙ δευτέρας, τὸ δὲ ΗΜΙ[m] πρώτης[n]), κακῶς[o]
λέγοντες· ἰδοὺ[p] γὰρ τὸ 'καυχῶ καυχᾷς' δευτέρας ὂν συζυγίας ἐν τῇ ἀποβολῇ
τοῦ κάππα πρώτης[q] ἐγένετο 'αὐχῶ[r] αὐχεῖς'.[s] τὸ[t] τρίτον ἐγκλίνεται τὸ

[dd] τὸ deest in **ΦΗ**
[ee] οἵ μοι φίλτατοί ἐστον deest in ρ
[ff] οὕτως ἔχει — φημὶ δὲ (δὴ **xB**) Τηλέφῳ (deest in **B**) Περγαμηνῷ (περγαμινῶ **y₂y₃N**: deest in **B**)
w₁w₂N: εἰ καὶ ἄλλως Τήλεφος ὁ γραμματικός φρονεῖ ρ
[gg] καὶ **w₁w₂N**: ἔτι καὶ ρ
[hh] ὁμοίως κατὰ τὸν λόγον ἐγκλίνονται **w₁w₂N**: deest in ρ
[ii] ταῦτα μὲν (μὲν deest in **GB**) περὶ τοῦ ΕΙΜΙ **w₁Yy₃N**: deest in **V**ρ

§n
[a] τὸ δὲ ΦΗΜΙ — ἀκολουθεῖ τῷ λόγῳ **w₁w₂N**: ἔτι καὶ τὸ φημί ἐγκλίνεται ρ
[b] τὸ deest in **ΦΗ**
[c] ἀκολουθεῖ] ἀκολούθως **ΦΗ**
[d] ἄνθρωπόν **w₁w₂N**: ἄνθρωπός ρ
[e] τινὲς δὲ ἔλεγον — ἐπείσθη ἡ χρῆσις **w₁w₂N**: deest in ρ
[f] τὸ δὲ ΦΗΙΣ τὸ δεύτερον **xN**: τὸ δὲ φῇς δεύτερον ρ: τοῦ δὲ φημὶ τὸ δεύτερον **B**: τοῦ δὲ φῇς τὸ
δεύτερον **w₂**: τὸ δὲ β[ον] τὸ φης **V**
[g] μήποτε — αὐχῶ αὐχεῖς deest in ρ
[h] διὰ Bekker: δὲ **xBy₃N**: deest in y₂
[i] τὸ πλεόνασμα τοῦ Ι **w₂N**: τὸ πλεόνασμα τὸ ι **B**: διὰ τὸν τοῦ ι πλεονασμὸν τὸ γ[ον] ἐγκλίνεται τὸ
φησίν· αὐτός φησιν **G**: κατὰ πλεονασμὸν τοῦ ι **ΦΗ**
[j] τοῦ φ ΗΜΙ **N**: τοῦ φ **B**: τοῦ φημὶ **y₃**: φημὶ **y₂**: τοῦ φ εἰμὶ **ΦΗ**: deest in **G**: ἡμί Bekker
[k] μὴ **ΦΗΒVN**: μηδὲ **w₂**
[l] ἀπ' **ΦΗΒy₁N**: ἐπ' **y₂**
[m] ΗΜΙ **Βy₁N**: εἰμὶ **ΦΗy₂**
[n] πρώτης **xBy₂**: πρώτη **y₁**: α **N**
[o] κακῶς **Βw₂N**: οὐ καλῶς **G**: καλῶς **ΦΗ**
[p] ἰδοὺ **xBy₁N**: ἰδών **y₂**
[q] πρώτης ἐγένετο **xBy₁N**: ἐγένετο **y₂**
[r] αὐχῶ αὐχεῖς — usque ad finem (§w) deest in **G**
[s] αὐχεῖς **ΦΗΒy₁N**: αὐχεῖς τὸ δεύτερον **y₂**: deest in **G**
[t] τὸ τρίτον ἐγκλίνεται τὸ ΦΗΣΙΝ **ΦΗy₃N**: τὸ δὲ φησί ἐγκλίνεται ρ: ἐγκλίνεται τὸ φησὶ **y₂**: τὸ
τρίτον πρόσωπον ἐγκλίνεται, ἤτοι τὸ φησὶν **B**: τὸ γ[ον] ἐγκλίνεται **V**

for *'ΕΣΤΙΝ*. The dual *'ΕΣΤΟΝ* is also enclitic, as in <u>οἵ μοι φίλτατοί ἐστον</u>.[268] (For this is the [usual] reading, which has not been influenced by those who take a different view, I mean by Telephus of Pergamon.)[269] The plural forms too are likewise enclitic according to the rule, as in <u>ἄνθρωποί ἐσμεν, ἄνθρωποί ἐστε, ἄνθρωποί εἰσιν</u>.[270] So much then for *'ΕΙΜΙ*.

§n And *ΦΗΜΙ* follows the rule in the first person, as in *ἄνθρωπόν φημι*.[271] But some have said that it is not enclitic, for example the aforementioned Telephus, by whom usage has not been influenced. But the second person *ΦΗΙΣ* is not an enclitic, perhaps due to the insertion of *ι*. Nor is the *'ΗΜΙ* that is made from it by the deletion of [the letter] *φ* enclitic. And some say that *'ΗΜΙ* does not come from *ΦΗΜΙ*, because it has changed its conjugation (for *ΦΗΜΙ* belongs to the second conjugation, while *'ΗΜΙ* belongs to the first), but they are wrong. For *καυχῶ καυχᾶς*, which belongs to the second conjugation, came to belong to the first with the dropping of the *Κ*: *αὐχῶ αὐχεῖς*. The third person form

---

[268] 'Who are dearest to me': an approximate quotation of *Il.* 9.198 (οἵ μοι σκυζομένῳ περ Ἀχαιῶν φίλτατοί ἐστον).

[269] On the grammarian Telephus, of the second century AD, see Pagani (2015). The reference to those opposed to the reading οἵ μοι φίλτατοί ἐστον probably hints at a reading of *Il.* 9.198 with φιλτάτω, known to Didymus as the reading of 'some people' (see the Didyman scholion Sch. *Il.* 9.198*b* (A^ii)). If Didymus preferred φίλτατοί, Telephus of Pergamon's support for φιλτάτω may have been aimed against Didymus in particular; for another point on which Telephus attacked Didymus, see Sch. *Il.* 10.53*a*¹ (A) with Pagani (2015). Charax makes a special point of the reading not only because he likes to attack Telephus (as he does again just below) but because φίλτατοί ἐστον suits his purpose better than φιλτάτω ἐστόν: the second accent on φίλτατοί and the lack of accent on ἐστον make the enclitic character of *'ΕΣΤΟΝ* clear.

[270] 'We are people'; 'they are people'.

[271] 'I say that a person...'.

ΦΗΣΙΝ, 'ἄνθρωπόν[u] φησι'.[v] τὰ[w] ⟨δὲ⟩ πληθυντικὰ οὐκ ἐξωμάλισται, ἀλλὰ παρὰ μὲν τοῖς πολλοῖς καὶ μάλιστα τοῖς ἀκριβέσιν ἐγκλίνεται, 'ἄνθρωπόν φαμεν', 'ἄνθρωπόν φατε', 'ἄνθρωπόν φασι', παρά τισι δ' οὔ, οἷς ⟨ἡ⟩ ἀκριβὴς ἀνάγνωσις οὐκ ἐπείσθη.

§0 αὐτὴ[a] δὲ ἡ ἀντωνυμία πρὸς διάφορον σημαινόμενον ὡς[b] καὶ τὸ ὄνομα πῇ[c] μὲν ὀρθοτονεῖται, πῇ δὲ ἐγκλίνεται. ἀλλ'[d] οὔτε[e] ἐκεῖ πάντα τὰ ὀνόματα, οὔτε[f] ἐνταῦθα ὅλαι αἱ ἀντωνυμίαι. ἀλλ' οὐδὲ τὴν αὐτὴν διαφορὰν τοῦ σημαινομένου ἔχουσι τά τε ὀνόματα καὶ αἱ ἀντωνυμίαι ὀρθοτονούμεναι[g] καὶ ἐγκλινόμεναι. ἀλλ' ἐν τοῖς ὀνόμασιν, ὡς ἔφημεν, πυσματικὰ τὰ[h] ὀρθοτονούμενα, ἀορίστων[i] δὲ σημασίαν ποιοῦσιν ἀποφαντικὴν[j] ἐγκλινόμενα. ἐν[k] δὲ ταῖς ἀντωνυμίαις αἱ ἐγκλινόμεναι ἀπόλυτον σημασίαν ποιοῦσιν, αἱ δὲ ἀντιδιαστολὴν[l] ⟨ποιοῦσαι⟩[m] ὀρθοτονοῦνται.[n] οὐ πάντως γὰρ ὀρθοτονούμεναι ἀντιδιαστολὴν ποιοῦσιν· [εἰσὶ[o] γὰρ πολλαί, αἷ[p] ἀπόλυτον σημασίαν ἔχουσι[q] καὶ ὁ τόπος οὐκ ἀπαιτεῖ αὐτὰς ἐγκλίνεσθαι, ὡς ἐν ἀρχῇ. Καὶ αἱ βαρύτονοι.] πολλάκις γὰρ καὶ ἀπόλυτον σημασίαν ἔχουσαι οὐ δύνανται ἐγκλιθῆναι.[r] ἁπλῶς οὖν οὐδεμία[s] κτητικὴ[t] ἐγκλίνεται. καὶ εὐλόγως, ὅτι παράγονται καὶ προσλαμβάνουσι φωνήν τινα ἐν παραγωγῇ, 'ἐμοῦ ἐμός'· οὐδεμία δὲ παραγωγὴ ἐγκλίνεται. λοιπὸν περὶ πρωτοτύπων[u] ὁ λόγος.

[u] 'ἄνθρωπόν φησι' ρ: ἄνθρωπός φησι **Bw₂N**: αὐτός φησι **ΦΗ**
[v] post φησι verba ἔτι καὶ τὰ δυϊκά praebet ρ
[w] τὰ ⟨δὲ⟩ (add. Bekker: deest in **w₁w₂N**) πληθυντικὰ οὐκ (οὐκ **ΦΗΒ**: οὐ **L**: οὐ τοῖς **N**: οὖ **y₂**: deest in **V**) ἐξωμάλισται (ἐξωμάλισται Bekker: ἔξω μάλιστα **w₁w₂N**) ἀλλὰ παρὰ μὲν τοῖς πολλοῖς καὶ μάλιστα τοῖς (ἐν τοῖς **H**) ἀκριβέσιν ἐγκλίνεται (ἐγκλίνεται **y₂N**: ἐγκλίνονται **ΦΗΒy₁**) 'ἄνθρωπόν φαμεν', 'ἄνθρωπόν (ἄνθρωποί **ΦΗ**) φατε', 'ἄνθρωπόν (ἄνθρωποί **H**) φασι', παρά τισι δ' (παρά τισι δ' Bekker: παρά δέ τισιν **N**: παρά τισιν **w₁w₂**) οὔ, οἷς ⟨ἡ⟩ (ἡ Bekker: deest in **w₁w₂N**) ἀκριβὴς ἀνάγνωσις οὐκ ἐπείσθη **w₁w₂N**: καὶ πληθυντικὰ κατὰ τὴν χρῆσιν τῶν παλαιῶν, εἰ καί τινες τοὐναντίον φρονοῦσιν ρ

§0
[a] αὐτὴ δὲ (δὲ καὶ **ζ**) ἡ ἀντωνυμία ρ: αὔτη δὲ ἡ ἀντωνυμία **ΦΗw₂N**: ἡ δὲ ἀντωνυμία **B**
[b] ὡς καὶ τὸ ὄνομα **B**: καὶ τὸ ὄνομα **w₂N**: καὶ ὄνομα **ΦΗ**: deest in ρ: καθὰ τὸ ὄνομα Bekker
[c] πῇ...πῇ **w₁w₂NnK**: τῇ...τῇ **Ald.**
[d] ἀλλ' — περὶ πρωτοτύπων ὁ λόγος deest in ρ
[e] οὔτε...οὔτε Bekker: οὐδὲ (οὐδ' **Φ**)...οὐδὲ **ΦΗw₂N**: οὐδὲ...οὐδὲν **B**
[f] οὔτε ἐνταῦθα ὅλαι αἱ ἀντωνυμίαι] καὶ αἱ ἀντωνυμίαι **ΦΗ**
[g] ὀρθοτονούμεναι καὶ ἐγκλινόμεναι] ὀρθοτονούμενον καὶ ἐγκλινόμενον **ΦΗ**
[h] τὰ ὀρθοτονούμενα — usque ad finem (§w) deest in **ΦΗ**
[i] ἀορίστων...σημασίαν **y₂**: ἀορίστῳ...σημασίᾳ **B**: ἀορισ[τ]...σημασίαν **N**: ἀορίστῳ...σημασίαν **y₁**
[j] ἀποφαντικὴν **By₁N**: ἀποφαντικὸν **y₂**
[k] ἐν Bekker: deest in **Bw₂N**
[l] ἀντιδιαστολὴν **w₂**: διαστολὴν **B**: πρὸς ἀντιδιαστολὴν **N**
[m] ποιοῦσαι addidimus
[n] ὀρθοτονοῦνται **Bw₂**: ὀρθοτονούμεναι **N**
[o] εἰσὶ γὰρ πολλαί — καὶ αἱ βαρύτονοι delevimus
[p] αἷ Bekker: καὶ **Bw₂N**
[q] ἔχουσι (ἔχουσι **y₃N**: ἔχουσαι **BV**) καὶ ὁ τόπος οὐκ ἀπαιτεῖ αὐτὰς ἐγκλίνεσθαι ὡς ἐν ἀρχῇ καὶ αἱ βαρύτονοι (αἱ βαρύτονοι **By₁**: βαρύτονος **N**)· πολλάκις γὰρ καὶ ἀπόλυτον σημασίαν ἔχουσαι **By₁N**: ἔχουσαι **y₂**
[r] ἐγκλιθῆναι **Bw₂**: ἐγκλίνεσθαι **N**
[s] οὐδεμία **VN**: οὐδὲ **Bw₂**
[t] κτητικὴ **By₁N**: κλητικὴ **y₂**
[u] πρωτοτύπων **w₂N**: τῶν πρωτοτύπων **B**

ΦΗΣΙΝ is enclitic, as in ἄνθρωπόν φησι.[272] And the plural forms are not treated uniformly: in the usage of most people and especially those who are strict, they are enclitic, as in ἄνθρωπόν φαμεν, ἄνθρωπόν φατε, ἄνθρωπόν φασι,[273] but in the usage of some they are not; but the strict way of reading has not been influenced by them.

§0 And the pronoun, just like the nominal, is sometimes orthotonic and sometimes enclitic with a view to a different meaning. But the nominals did not all [appear] above, nor do all the pronouns [appear] here. Nor do the nominals and the pronouns have the same difference of meaning when they are orthotonic and when they are enclitic. But among the nominals, as we said, the interrogatives are orthotonic, while the enclitics give rise to the declaratory [i.e. non-interrogative] meaning of indefinites. But among the pronouns the enclitics give rise to a non-contrastive meaning, while those conveying a distinction are orthotonic. For the orthotonic ones do not in all cases indicate a distinction.[274] For often even though they have a non-contrastive meaning they nevertheless cannot throw their accent back. So, quite simply, no possessive pronoun [i.e. ἐμός etc.] is enclitic. And this is reasonable, because they are derived and they acquire some additional sound through derivation, as ἐμοῦ [makes the derivative] ἐμός, and no derivative is enclitic. From now on we will deal with underived pronouns.

---

[272] 'He/she says that a person'.
[273] 'We say that a person'; 'you say that a person'; 'they say that a person'.
[274] Charax here explains why he has said αἱ δὲ ἀντιδιαστολὴν ⟨ποιοῦσαι⟩ ὀρθοτονοῦνται rather than αἱ δὲ ὀρθοτονούμεναι ἀντιδιαστολὴν ποιοῦσι, as might have been expected after αἱ ἐγκλινόμεναι ἀπόλυτον σημασίαν ποιοῦσιν.

§p οὐδεμία[a] εὐθεῖα[b] ἀντωνυμίας ἐγκλίνεται· τὰ γὰρ ῥήματα ἀναπληροῦσι τὴν χρείαν αὐτῶν, ὡς δείκνυται ἐν τῷ Περὶ ἀντωνυμίας. ἀντωνυμία ἐν ἀρχῇ ἐγκλίνεται οὐδεμία. βαρύτονος φύσει οὐκ[c] ἐγκλίνεται. εἴπομεν δὲ 'φύσει βαρύτονος', ὡς ὅτι εἰσί τινες κατὰ πάθος[d] βαρυνόμεναι καὶ ἐγκλινόμεναι, ὡς τὸ 'ἡμέων' κατὰ διαίρεσιν. καὶ γὰρ ἐβαρύνθη οὐ φύσει. καὶ τὸ 'ΣΕΟ' παρὰ[e] τὸ[f] 'σοῦ' ἐνεκλίθη,[g] ὡς[h] ἐπὶ[i] τοῦ Πάριδος 'ὡς σεο νῦν ἔραμαι'. ἐπὶ[j] [k] γὰρ τοῦ Διὸς ὀρθοτονεῖται· ἀντιδιαστολὴν γὰρ ἔχει πρὸς ἄλλας γυναῖκας,[l] ἐπὶ δὲ τοῦ Πάριδος οὐκ ἔστι διαστολὴ πρὸς ἄλλην. ἐν τοῖς δυϊκοῖς τοῦ πρώτου καὶ δευτέρου προσώπου ἀεὶ ὀρθοτονοῦνται, ὅτι ἀεὶ βαρύνονται, κἂν περισπασθῶσι,[m] νῶν,[n] σφῶν. ὥσπερ τοὐναντίον[o] εἴπομεν ἐπὶ τοῦ 'ἡμέων', ὅτι ἐγκλίνεται· οὐ γὰρ φύσει[p] βαρύνεται. ἐγκλίνονται δὲ[q] ἀεὶ αἱ τοῦ τρίτου[r] δυϊκαί, 'ἀλλ᾽ εἴπ᾽[s] εἰ σφῶϊν καταλύσομεν ὠκέας ἵππους', 'τίς[t] τάρ[u] σφωε θεῶν ἔριδι'.[v] καὶ[w] ἐν τοῖς πληθυντικοῖς τοῦ τρίτου προσώπου 'σφίσι', 'σφέας' ἀναβιβάζεται ὁ τόνος τῇ[x] πρώτῃ λέξει, 'ἐπεὶ οὔ σφισι', 'καί σφεας φωνήσας', ἐπεὶ οὐ φύσει ἐβαρύνοντο, ἀλλὰ κατὰ πάθος, 'σφίν[y] σφίσιν', 'σφᾶς σφέας'. ἔφαμεν δὲ ὅτι ἐν τῷ πρώτῳ καὶ δευτέρῳ προσώπῳ[z] κἂν συσταλῶσι καὶ γένωνται[aa] τρίχρονοι, ἡμῖν[bb]

---

§p
[a] ante οὐδεμία verba αἱ πρωτότυποι δὲ ἐγκλίνονται οὕτως praebet ρ
[b] εὐθεῖα ἀντωνυμίας Bw₂ρ: εὐθείας ἀντωνυμία ζ: εὐθεῖα ἀντωνυμιῶν N
[c] οὐκ deest in y₂
[d] πάθος BVρ: τὸ πάθος y₂y₃N
[e] παρὰ Bw₂N: δὲ παρὰ ρ
[f] τὸ Bekker: τοῦ Bw₂Nρ
[g] ἐνεκλίθη Bw₂Nζ Ald.: ἐνεκλίνη (sic) SK
[h] ὡς ἐπὶ τοῦ πάριδος deest in ρ
[i] ἐπὶ Bekker: ἀπὸ Bw₂N
[j] ἐπὶ γὰρ — πρὸς ἄλλην deest in ρ
[k] ἐπὶ Bekker: ἀπὸ By₂y₃N
[l] γυναῖκας By₃N: γενικάς y₂
[m] περισπασθῶσι By₁N: περισπῶσι y₂ρ
[n] νῶν, σφῶν scripsimus: νῶϊν, σφῶϊν Bw₂Nρ
[o] τοὐναντίον ρ: τὸ ἐναντίον Bw₂N
[p] φύσει BVNJ Ald.: οὐ φύσει w₂ΣSK
[q] δὲ Ald.: deest in By₂y₃NnK
[r] τρίτου y₃Nρ: τρίτου προσώπου B: δευτέρου y₂
[s] εἴπ᾽ K: εἰπὲ By₂y₃Nn
[t] τίς By₂y₃N: καὶ τίς ρ
[u] τάρ BΣ: τ᾽ ἄρ w₂K Ald.: τὰρ S: γὰρ NJ
[v] ἔριδι By₃ρ: ἔριδι ξυνέηκε N: ἔριδι ξυνέεικε μαχεσθαι Σ: deest in y₂
[w] καὶ ρ: deest in By₂y₃N
[x] τῇ πρώτῃ By₂y₃NnK: τῇ τρίτῃ Ald.
[y] σφίν By₃nK: σφῖν N Ald.: σφῦς y₂
[z] προσώπῳ deest in y₂
[aa] γένωνται BYL᷿N: γίνονται ρ: γένονται ΘL
[bb] ἡμῖν ἥμιν ὑμῖν ὕμιν Bekker: ὑμῖν ὕμιν B: ἥμιν ὕμιν y₃NnK: ἡμῖν ἥμιν ὑμῖν ὕμιν Ald.: ἡμῖν ἥμιν y₂

§p No nominative of a pronoun is enclitic; for the verbs make up for the lack of them, as shown in the *On the Pronoun*. No pronoun is enclitic in initial position. One that is barytone by nature [i.e. has its natural accent on a non-final syllable] is not enclitic. And we said 'barytone by nature' because some are barytone through an alteration and are enclitic, like ἡμέων through resolution: for this is not barytone by nature. And *ΣΕΟ* from σοῦ is enclitic, as in ὥς σεο νῦν ἔραμαι in relation to Paris.[275] For in relation to Zeus it is orthotonic; for it conveys a contrast with other women, while in the case of Paris there is no contrast with another woman. In the dual of the first and second person, pronouns are always orthotonic because they are always barytone, even if they are perispomenon, as in νῶν, σφῶν[276]—just as we said about ἡμέων, on the other hand, that it is enclitic, for it is not barytone by nature. But the duals of the third person are always enclitic, as in ἀλλ᾽ εἴπ᾽ εἴ σφωϊν καταλύσομεν ὠκέας ἵππους[277] and τίς τάρ σφωε θεῶν ἔριδι.[278] And in the plurals of the third person, σφίσι and σφέας, the accent is thrown back onto the first word, as in ἐπεὶ οὔ σφισι[279] and καί σφεας φωνήσας,[280] because these are barytone not by nature but through a modification, as σφίν [is modified to] σφίσιν and σφᾶς [is modified to] σφέας. And we said that in the first and second person, even if they are shortened and come to have three units of time, as in ἡμῖν [being shortened to]

---

[275] I.e. at *Il.* 3.446, where this phrase is spoken by Paris: 'as I love you now', by contrast with *Il.* 14.328, where the same phrase is spoken by Zeus. For the thought, see n. 150.

[276] The forms νῶν and σφῶν are here taken to be derived by contraction from νῶϊν and σφῶϊν; the latter constitute the forms with 'natural accents', and are barytone, that is to say their final syllables are unaccented. Since 'naturally barytone' forms cannot be enclitics, it follows that νῶν and σφῶν are always orthotonic. In this analysis the forms νῶν and σφῶν behave as opposites of ἡμέων. The latter is taken to be derived from ἡμῶν, by the resolution of one vowel into two; the form with the 'natural accent' is thus ἡμῶν, which is not barytone. As a result, barytonesis does not stand in the way of *ΗΜΕΩΝ* behaving as an enclitic.

[277] *Od.* 4.28: 'But say whether we should unyoke their swift horses for them.'

[278] *Il.* 1.8: 'Who of the gods, then, [threw] the two of them [together to quarrel] with strife?'

[279] *Il.* 9.425: 'since [this one is] not [available] to them.'

[280] E.g. *Il.* 4.284: 'and speaking [he addressed winged words to] them.'

ἡμῖν, ὑμῖν ὑμῖν, οὐκ ἀναβιβάζουσι τῇ^{cc} πρώτῃ λέξει, ἀλλ᾽ ἐν τῇ ἰδίᾳ ἀρχῇ
ἔχουσιν ἔγκλισιν,^{dd} καὶ δέχονται^{ee} ἢ^{ff} ὑποστιγμὴν ἢ στιγμήν ⟨πρὸ^{gg} αὐτῶν. αἱ
γὰρ ἄλλαι ἐγκλινόμεναι οὐ δέχονται πρὸ αὐτῶν ὑποστιγμὴν ἢ στιγμήν. διὸ
οὐδέποτε αἱ ἐγκλινόμεναι μετὰ κλητικῆς τίθενται,⟩ εἰ μή που^{hh} φιλοφρονητικὴ
εἴη ἡ φράσις, ʽΠάτροκλέ μοιⁱⁱ δειλῇʼ καὶ^{jj} ἄλλαι τοιαῦται.

§q φασὶ δὲ τὰς ἐχούσας χαρακτῆρα καταλήξεως μὴ ἐγκλίνεσθαι, ὡς^a ἡ
ʽἐκεῖνοςʼ καὶ ʽοὗτοςʼ, ἀλλὰ μόνον ἡ ʽαὐτόςʼ κατὰ αἰτιατικὴν παρέβη, ʽκόψε^b γάρ^c
αὐτόνʼ. οὐ καλὸς δέ τοι^d ὁ λόγος· ὡς γὰρ βαρύτονοι οὖσαι οὐκ ἐγκλίνονται,
ʽἐκεῖνος ἐκείνουʼ, ʽοὗτος τούτουʼ. τὸ ʽαὐτόνʼ ὀξύνεται. ἀλλὰ πρὸς τούτοις^e φασὶν
ʽδιατί^f ἡ "αὐτοῦ" ἢ "αὐτῷ" οὐκ ἐγκλίνεται,^g οὐδ᾽^h ὡς τετράχρονοι εἰς τὴν ἰδίαν
ἀρχὴν τὸν τόνον ἀναπέμπουσι;ʼ πρὸς οὓς φαμεν ὅτιⁱ διὰ τὸ μὴ συνεμπεσεῖν^j
τοῖς Αἰολεῦσι^k βαρυτόνως λέγουσιν ʽαὐτουʼ^l καὶ ʽαὐτῷʼ. ἡ δὲ αἰτιατικὴ οὐ
συνενέπεσεν·^m ἐγκλινομένη γὰρ εἰς τὴν πρὸ αὐτῆςⁿ λέξιν τὸν τόνον ἀναπέμπει,
ʽκόψε^o γάρ αὐτον ἔχονταʼ, τὸ δὲ^p Αἰολικὸν εἰς τὴν ἀρχήν, ʽαὐτονʼ.

^{cc} τῇ Bekker: ἐν τῇ **By₂y₃Nρ**
^{dd} ἔγκλισιν scripsimus: κλητικὴν **By₃Nζ**: κλιτικήν **Sr**: ἐγκλιτικήν **y₂**
^{ee} δέχονται scripsimus: δέχεται **By₂y₃Nρ**
^{ff} ἢ (ἢ om. **N**) ὑποστιγμὴν ἢ στιγμήν **By₂y₃N**: ὑποστιγμὴν **ρ**
^{gg} Lacunam statuimus et ita complevimus exempli gratia, coll. Ap. Dysc., *Pron.* 53.16–19
^{hh} που **W**: πω **By₂y₃Nρ**
ⁱⁱ μοι δειλῇ (δειλῆ **y₃**: δειλὴ **N**: δηλῇ **B**) **By₃N**: μοι **y₂ρ**
^{jj} καὶ ἄλλαι τοιαῦται **B**: καὶ ἄλλαι αὗται **y₂y₃N**: deest in **ρ**

§q
^a ὡς ἡ ʽἐκεῖνοςʼ καὶ ʽοὗτοςʼ **By₂y₃Nρ**: ἀλλ᾽ ὡς οἱ ἐκεῖνοι καὶ οὗτοι (οἷτοι sic **Σ**) **ζ**
^b κόψε **By₂y₃NnK**: κόψαι **Ald.**
^c γάρ αὐτον **BLρ**: γὰρ αὐτὸν **y₂NΣ**: γὰρ τὸν **Lᵥ**
^d τοι **ρ**: τε **By₂y₃**: ἔστιν **N**
^e τούτοις **Θ**: τοῦτο **B**: τούτους **Yy₃Nρ**
^f διατὶ ἡ αὐτοῦ ἢ αὐτῷ **y₃N**: διατὶ ἡ αὐτοῦ καὶ αὐτῷ **B**: διατὶ ἡ αὐτοῦ αὐτῷ **ζ**: διὰ ἡ αὐτοῦ ἢ αὐτῶ **y₂**: διὰ τί ἡ αὐτοῦ αὐτῷ **SK**: ὅτι ἡ αὐτοῦ αὐτῷ **Ald.**
^g ἐγκλίνεται **y₂**: ἐγκλίνονται **By₃Nρ**
^h οὐδ᾽ scripsimus (cf. Ap. Dysc., *Pron.* 62.10–11): ἀλλ᾽ **Ald.**: deest in **Bw₂NnK**
ⁱ ὅτι διὰ τὸ μὴ **By₃Nρ**: ὅτι μὴ διὰ τὸ **y₂**
^j συνεμπεσεῖν **Nρ**: συνεμπέσειν **y₃**: συμπέσειν (sic) **y₂**: ἐμπεσεῖν **B**
^k Αἰολεῦσι **Bρ**: αἰολεῖς **y₃**: αἰολοῖς (sic) **y₂N**
^l αὐτου **By₃Nρ**: αὐτον **y₂**
^m συνενέπεσεν Bekker: συνέπεσεν **By₂y₃N**: συνέμπεσεν **nK**: σινέμπεσεν (sic) **Ald.**
ⁿ αὐτῆς scripsimus: αὐτῆς **Ald.**: ταύτης **By₂y₃N**: ταύτην **nK**
^o κόψε **By₂y₃N**: κόψαι **ρ**
^p δέ deest in **r**

ἡμιν and ὑμῖν [being shortened to] ῦμιν, they do not throw the accent back onto the first word but have the throwing back of the accent on their own first syllables, and they accept either a weak or a strong punctuation mark before themselves. For other enclitics do not accept a weak or strong punctuation mark before themselves. Hence enclitics are never placed after vocatives, unless the phrase is rather friendly, as in *Πάτροκλέ μοι δειλῇ* and other similar phrases.[281]

§q And they say that those pronouns with a typical form of termination, like *ἐκεῖνος* and *οὗτος*, are not enclitic, and that only *αὐτός* is an exception in the accusative, as in *κόψε γάρ αὐτον*.[282] But the argument is not good. For the reason why *ἐκεῖνος ἐκείνου* and *οὗτος τούτου* are not enclitic is because they are barytone, whereas *αὐτόν* is oxytone. To these points they say, 'why do *αὐτοῦ* and *αὐτῷ* not throw their accent back, nor send it back to their own first syllable as [we would expect for] forms with four units of time?' To these people we say that this is so that the forms do not fall together with the [ones used by the] Aeolians, who say *αὖτου* and *αὖτῳ* with barytone accents. But the accusative has not fallen together [with its Aeolic counterpart]; for when it throws its accent back it sends it back to the word before itself, as in *κόψε γάρ αὐτον ἔχοντα*,[283] but the Aeolic form throws it back to its first syllable: *αὖτον*.

---

[281] *Il.* 19.287: 'Patroklos [most dear to the heart] to unhappy me'.

[282] *Il.* 12.204 (reading *αὐτον*, not *αὖ τὸν*): 'For it [the snake] struck it [the eagle]'.

[283] *Il.* 12.204 (again reading *αὐτον*): 'For it [the snake] struck it [the eagle] as it [the eagle] held it [the snake]'.

§r πάλιν αἱ ἔχουσαι ἐπιφορὰν[a] τὴν[b] ἐπιταγματικὴν ὀρθοτονοῦνται, 'σὲ[c] αὐτόν', 'σὲ[d] δὲ αὐτὴν παντί', 'ἀλλὰ σὲ αὐτόν', εἰ μή που ποιητικῶς ἐγκλιθῶσιν, 'ἀλλά οἱ αὐτῷ'· οὐκ ὤφειλεν ἡ *ΟΙ* ἐγκλιθῆναι· ἔχει γὰρ τὴν ἐπιταγματικήν. τινὲς δέ φασι καὶ ἵνα μὴ νομισθῇ ἄρθρον, ὅπερ ψευδές· ἀντωνυμία γὰρ[e] οὖσα περισπᾶται,[f] οἷα[g] ἄρθρον δὲ ὀξύνεται. ὥστε ποιητικῶς ἐνεκλίθη.[h]

§s αἱ λοιπαί, ὥσπερ προείπομεν, πρὸς διάφορον σημαινόμενον πῇ μὲν ἐγκλίνονται, πῇ δὲ ὀρθοτονοῦνται. ἐγκλινόμεναι οὖν ἀπόλυτον σημασίαν σημαίνουσιν, ἀντιδιαστολὴν[a] δὲ[b] ὀρθοτονούμεναι, ἐάν, ὥσπερ[c] προείπομεν, προηγῶνται[d] αἱ παραφυλακαί.

§t ὀλίγαι δὲ παρέβησαν τὸν λόγον, οἷον τὸ[a] 'ἔσαν', 'ἔνθ' ἔσάν οἱ πέπλοι'. καὶ πάλιν ἐνταῦθα ⟨φασίν⟩[b] ἵνα μὴ νομισθῇ τὸ[c] *ΟΙ* ἄρθρον, ὅπερ ἄκαιρον· ὡς εἴπομεν γάρ, ὁ τόνος διέστειλε.[d] καὶ πάλιν 'ἵνά[e] σφισιν ἀγορή τε θέμις τε'. καὶ πάλιν 'ὅτέ σφεας εἰσαφίκηται', 'ἦρχε δ' ἄρά σφιν'. αὗται παραλόγως ἐνεκλίθησαν,[f] μὴ προηγουμένων ἢ ὀξυτόνων ἢ τροχαϊκῶν. καὶ παρὰ Καλλιμάχῳ[g] δὲ 'τόξού[h] σφεών τις ἄριστα[i] Κυδωνίου'· σπονδεῖος γὰρ βαρύτονος προηγεῖται. παραλόγως οὖν ἐπὶ τούτων ἐπεκράτησεν ἡ ἔγκλισις. ταῦτα περὶ τῶν[j] ἀντωνυμιῶν ἐν συντόμῳ· ἐν[k] ἑτέροις γὰρ ἐν πλάτει.

§r
a   ἐπιφορὰν **By₂y₃NSr**: ἀναφορὰν **ζ**
b   τὴν deest in **Νζ**
c   σὲ αὐτόν Bekker: σεαυτὸν **By₂y₃Νρ**
d   σὲ δὲ αὐτὴν παντί **w₂**: σεαυτὴν **B**: σὲ δὲ αὐτον, οὐ **Ald.**: σὲ δὲ αὐτὸν **nK**: σεαυτὴν παντὶ **N**
e   γὰρ οὖσα **By₂y₃N**: γὰρ **Lρ**
f   περισπᾶται **y₂LᵥΝρ**: περιεσπᾶτο **BL**
g   οἷα ἄρθρον δὲ ὀξύνεται **By₃**: οι δὲ ἄρθρον ὀξύνεται **Ald.**: οἷα δὲ ἄρθρον **nK**: οἷα δὲ ἄρθρον ὀξύτονος **N**: οἷον ἄρθρον δὲ ὀξύνεται **y₂**: ἄρθρον δὲ ὂν ὀξύνεται Bekker
h   ἐνεκλίθη **By₂y₃NJ**: ἐνεγκλιθῶσιν **Ald.**: ἐνεγκλίθη **SK**: ἀναγκλίθη **Σ**

§s
a   ἀντιδιαστολὴν **ρ**: ἀντιδιαστολῆς **B**: ἀντιδιαστολῇ **y₂y₃**: ἀντιδιαστο^λ **N**
b   δὲ **ρ**: εἰ δὲ **By₂y₃N**
c   ὥσπερ **By₃ρ**: ὡς **N**: ὡς περὶ **y₂**
d   προηγῶνται **Ald.**: προηγοῦνται **Bw₂NnK**

§t
a   τὸ **By₂y₃N**: deest in **ρ**
b   φασίν addidimus
c   τὸ deest in **r**
d   διέστειλε **y₂n**: διέστελλε **BLᵥN**: διέστελε **Lr**
e   ἵνά σφισιν — καὶ πάλιν om. **BN**
f   ἐνεκλίθησαν **By₂y₃N Ald.**: ἐκλίθησαν **nK**
g   Καλλιμάχῳ δὲ **By₂y₃nK**: καλλιμάχῳ **N Ald.**
h   τόξού σφεών **y₃Νρ**: τόξοις σφεῶν **B**: τόξον σφεῶν **y₂**
i   ἄριστα **By₃Νρ**: ἄρα **y₂**
j   τῶν ἀντωνυμιῶν **By₂y₃N**: ἀντωνυμιῶν **ρ**
k   ἐν ἑτέροις γὰρ ἐν πλάτει **By₂y₃N**: deest in **ρ**

§r Next, those pronouns that have a subsidiary appendage are orthotonic, as in σὲ αὐτόν,[284] σὲ δὲ αὐτὴν παντί,[285] or ἀλλὰ σὲ αὐτόν,[286] unless they become enclitic by poetic licence, ἀλλά οἱ αὐτῷ[287] (the pronoun ῾ΟΙ should not have been enclitic; for it has a subsidiary appendage). And some say in addition that [it throws its accent back] so that it is not taken to be the article.[288] But this is wrong: for when it is a pronoun it is perispomenon, but as an article it is oxytone. Thus, it is by poetic licence that it has thrown its accent back.

§s And the other pronouns, as we have said already, are sometimes enclitic and sometimes orthotonic with a view to a different meaning. When they are enclitic, then, they convey a non-contrastive meaning, while when they are orthotonic they convey a contrast, if, as we have said already, the conditions are presupposed.

§t And a few are exceptions to the rule: for example, the ἔσαν in ἔνθ᾿ ἔσάν οἱ πέπλοι.[289] And here again they say [this happens] so that the ῾ΟΙ is not thought to be the article, but this is an unfitting explanation. For as we have said, the accent distinguishes them.[290] Another example is ἵνά σφισιν ἀγορή τε θέμις τε,[291] and further examples are ὅτέ σφεας εἰσαφίκηται[292] and ἦρχε δ᾿ ἄρά σφιν.[293] These [enclitics] have thrown their accent back irregularly, with neither oxytone nor trochaic words preceding. And [another example is] τόξού σφεών τις ἄριστα Κυδωνίου[294] in Callimachus: for a barytone spondee precedes. Enclisis has prevailed irregularly, then, in these cases. So much for the pronouns, in short compass; for in other works [they are treated] at length.

---

[284] 'You yourself'.
[285] 'But you [make] yourself [like] everything': an approximate quotation of *Od.* 13.313 (σὲ γὰρ αὐτὴν παντί).
[286] 'But you yourself'.
[287] *Od.* 4.667: 'But [may Zeus destroy] his [vigour]'.
[288] Compare §t and section 2.7.3, on the phrase ἔνθ᾿ ἔσάν οἱ πέπλοι.
[289] *Il.* 6.289 and *Od.* 15.105: 'where she had robes'.
[290] On Charax's argument here, see section 2.7.3.
[291] 'Where their meeting-place and place of justice [were]': an approximate quotation of *Il.* 11.807 (ἵνά σφ᾿ ἀγορή τε θέμις τε).
[292] *Od.* 12.40, *Od.* 16.228, and *Od.* 20.188: 'whenever one comes to them'; ὅτέ is an ancient variant for the standard reading ὅτίς.
[293] E.g. *Il.* 5.592: 'And [Arēs and revered Enūō] led them'.
[294] Callimachus, fr. 560 Pfeiffer: 'someone ... of them ... excellently ... the Cydonian bow'.

§u πολλοὶ δὲ τρόποι εἰσὶν ὀρθοτονοῦντες καὶ προηγουμένης τῆς ὀφειλούσης[a] δέξασθαι[b] τὴν ἔγκλισιν. οἷον αἱ προθέσεις ὀξύνονται, καὶ ὅμως αἱ μετὰ τούτων[c] ἀντωνυμίαι ὀρθοτονοῦνται, 'περὶ ἐμοῦ,[d] 'κατ᾽[e] ἐμοῦ, 'σὺν ἐμοί,[f] 'ὑπὲρ[g] ἐμοῦ. ὅθεν παρὰ Μενάνδρῳ σημειοῦται[h] τὸ 'πρός με' ἐγκλιθέν· οἱ δὲ ἐξηγηταὶ μετὰ[i] τοῦ Ε προφέρονται[j] αὐτό,[k] 'πρὸς[l] ἐμέ. αἱ μετὰ τῶν[m] συμπλεκτικῶν καὶ διαζευκτικῶν ὀρθοτονοῦνται. τὸ[n] γὰρ 'ἢ 'μὲ ἀνάειρε' τὸ ΜΕ[o] συνεκεράσθη[p] μετὰ τοῦ[q] Η, 'ἢ ἐμέ – ἢ 'μέ, καὶ τὴν ὀξεῖαν εἰς τὸ[r] ΜΕ φυλάττομεν. τὸ δὲ 'καί[s] μοι ὑποστήτω' ὑπερβατόν ἐστι, 'καὶ ὑποστήτω μοι, ὡς δείκνυμεν ἐν τῇ ἀντωνυμίᾳ. καὶ εὐλόγως ὀρθοτονοῦνται,[t] ἐπειδὴ[u] ἀντιδιαστολὴν πάντως[v] εἰσφέρουσιν αὗται αἱ συντάξεις. καὶ μετὰ τοῦ[w] 'οὕνεκα' καὶ 'ἔνεκα' ὀρθοτονοῦνται,[x] 'ἔνεκα σοῦ,[y] 'οὕνεκα[z] σοῦ, 'ἔνεκεν[aa] σοῦ· κακῶς γὰρ[bb] ἐγκλίνουσιν. ταῦτα[cc] περὶ τούτων.

§u
[a] ὀφειλούσης **B**y$_2$y$_3$**Nn**: ὀφελούσης **K Ald.**
[b] δέξασθαι **B**y$_2$y$_3$**N**ρ: δείξασθαι ζ
[c] τούτων ἀντωνυμίαι **B**y$_3$**N**ρ: τουτωνυμίαι y$_2$
[d] ἐμοῦ **B**y$_2$y$_3$**NnK**: μοῦ **Ald.**
[e] κατ᾽ ἐμοῦ **B**y$_2$y$_3$**NnK**: κατὰ σοῦ· μετὰ μοῦ **Ald.**
[f] ἐμοί **B**y$_2$y$_3$**NnK**: μοί **Ald.**
[g] ὑπὲρ ἐμοῦ **B**y$_2$y$_3$**NnK**: ὑπὲρ μοῦ **Ald.**
[h] σημειοῦται **B Ald.**: σημειοῦνται y$_2$y$_3$**NnK**
[i] μετὰ τοῦ Ε **B**y$_2$**N**: μετὰ τοῦ τε y$_3$: ἀντὶ τοῦ τε ρ
[j] προφέρονται w$_2$ρ: προσφέρονται **BJ**: προφέρουσιν **N**
[k] αὐτὸ deest in ρ
[l] πρὸς ἐμέ **B**y$_2$y$_3$**N**: ἀντὶ πρὸς ἐμέ ρ
[m] τῶν συμπλεκτικῶν **B**y$_2$y$_3$**N**: συμπλεκτικῶν ρ
[n] τὸ **B**y$_2$y$_3$**NS**ρ: καὶ ζ
[o] ΜΕ **BΘLN**: ε **YL**$_v$ρ
[p] συνεκεράσθη **B**y$_2$y$_3$**N**: συνεκράθη **S**ρ: συνεκρατήθη ζ
[q] τοῦ Η deest in ρ
[r] τὸ ΜΕ y$_3$**N**ρ: τὸ Ε y$_2$**J**: τὴν μὲ **B**
[s] καί μοι ὑποστήτω **Bekker**: ὑποστήτω **B**y$_2$y$_3$**N**: ὑπερστήτω μοι **Ald.**: ὑπερστήτω **nK**
[t] ὀρθοτονοῦνται **Ald.**: ὀρθοτονοῦνται μετὰ τούτων **B**y$_2$y$_3$**NnK**
[u] ἐπειδὴ **BN Ald.**: ἐπεὶ δὲ w$_2$**nK**
[v] πάντως **B**y$_2$y$_3$**Σ**: πάντα **r**: πάντας **J**: πάντες **S**: deest in **N**
[w] τοῦ **B**: deest in y$_2$y$_3$**N**ρ
[x] ὀρθοτονοῦνται **Bekker**: ὀρθοτονουμένην **B**y$_2$y$_3$ρ: ὀρθοτονουμένων **N**
[y] σοῦ **Bekker Ald.**: σου **B**y$_2$y$_3$**NnK**
[z] οὕνεκα σοῦ **Ald.**: οὕνεκά σου **SK**: om. **B**y$_2$y$_3$**N**ζ
[aa] ἔνεκεν σοῦ **Ald.**: ἔνεκέν σου **B**y$_3$**NnK**: om. y$_2$
[bb] γὰρ deest in ρ
[cc] ταῦτα **B**y$_2$y$_3$**N**: ἀλλὰ ταῦτα μὲν ρ

§u And many circumstances cause orthotonesis even when a word that ought to accept the throwing back of an accent is the first in the sequence. For example, prepositions are oxytone, and yet pronouns with them are orthotonic, as in περὶ ἐμοῦ, κατ᾽ ἐμοῦ, σὺν ἐμοί, ὑπὲρ ἐμοῦ.[295] Thus in Menander [the με in] πρός με[296] is noted as an exception, in being enclitic. But the commentators produce it with *E*: πρὸς ἐμέ. Pronouns with copulative and disjunctive conjunctions are orthotonic. For as regards ἢ ᾽μὲ ἀνάειρε,[297] the *E* has coalesced with *H*, i.e. ἢ ἐμέ [gives] ἢ ᾽μέ, and we keep the acute on the *ME*. But καί μοι ὑποστήτω[298] is a transposition [for] καὶ ὑποστήτω μοι, as we show in our discussion of pronouns. And it is reasonable that [pronouns with prepositions and with copulative and disjunctive conjunctions] are orthotonic, because these arrangements give rise to a distinction in all cases. And [pronouns] are orthotonic with οὕνεκα and ἕνεκα, as in ἕνεκα σοῦ, οὕνεκα σοῦ, ἕνεκεν σοῦ:[299] for people wrongly make these enclitic. So much for these matters.

---

[295] 'About me', 'against me', 'with me', 'on behalf of me'.

[296] Menander, *Aspis* 391, *Perikeiromenē* 336, and *Samia* 454: 'towards me'.

[297] *Il.* 23.724: 'Either lift me up, [or I will lift you up]'. The Homeric phrase, ἤ μ᾽ ἀνάειρ᾽, contains two elisions that are disregarded here.

[298] *Il.* 9.160: 'And let him submit to me'.

[299] All three phrases mean 'on account of you'.

§v ὀλίγα δέ[a] καὶ ἐν τῷ ἐπιρρήματι ἐγκλίνονται καὶ ὀρθοτονοῦνται, ὥσπερ ἐπὶ τοῦ *ΤΙΣ* εἴπομεν καὶ τοῦ *ΤΙΝΟΣ* καὶ[b] τοῦ *ΤΟΥ* καὶ τοῦ *ΤΩΙ*, ὅτι ὀρθοτονούμενα πυσματικά εἰσιν, ἐγκλινόμενα δὲ ἀποφαντικῶς ἀόριστα. οἷον 'πόθεν ἦλθε' πύσμα, 'ἦλθέ ποθεν'[c] ἀόριστον·[d] 'πότε ἔγραψας', 'ἔγραψάς ποτε'. ὁμοίως καὶ τὸ *ΠΟΘΙ*, ⟨…⟩,[e] 'ἐπεὶ[f] οὔ ποθι'. καὶ τὸ[g] 'ποῦ ἀπῆλθεν;' 'ἀπῆλθέ που' {αἴ κε[h] ποθι Ζεύς}.[i] καὶ[j] τὸ *ΠΩΣ*, 'πῶς ἦλθεν;'[k] 'ἦλθέ[l] πως'. καὶ τὸ *ΠΩ*, ⟨…⟩,[m] 'οὔ πώ με γινώσκεις'. καὶ τὸ *ΠΗΙ* ὁμοίως. ταῦτα δέ τινες τὰ μονοσύλλαβα καὶ τὸ *ΠΟΘΙ* ἔλεγον[n] συνδέσμους κακῶς, καὶ[o] Ἡρωδιανὸς μετὰ αὐτῶν· Ἀπολλώνιος δὲ ἐν[p] πλάτει καλῶς ἀνατρέπει αὐτά. ταῦτ' οὖν ἐν ἐπιρρήμασιν.

§v
[a]   δὲ deest in **Bw₂N**
[b]   καὶ τοῦ *ΤΟΥ* καὶ τοῦ *ΤΩΙ* **Bw₂N**: καὶ τῶν ἄλλων ρ
[c]   ποθεν **Bw₂N Ald.**: ποτε **nK**
[d]   ἀόριστον **Ald.**: deest in **Bw₂NnK**
[e]   lacunam statuimus; locus cum interrogativo ποθι probabiliter excidit
[f]   ἐπεὶ **Bw₂NnK**: ἐπὶ **Ald.**
[g]   τὸ deest in ρ
[h]   κέ **Bw₂NJS**: καί **r**: θέ (sic) *Σ*
[i]   αἴ κέ ποθι Ζεύς delevimus
[j]   καὶ **Bw₂N**: καὶ ἔτι ρ
[k]   ἦλθεν **Bw₂N**: ἦλθες ρ
[l]   ἦλθέ **Bw₂N**: ἦλθές **nK**: ἦθές (sic) **Ald.**
[m]   Cf. Ap. Dysc., *Adv.* 185.15; 190.21
[n]   ἔλεγον συνδέσμους — μετὰ αὐτῶν Bekker: μετὰ αὐτῶν ἔλεγον συνδέσμους κακῶς καὶ Ἡρωδιανὸς μετὰ αὐτῶν **w₂**: μετὰ αὐτῶν ἔλεγον συνδέσμους, κακῶς· ὁ Ἡρωδιανὸς δὲ καὶ **V**: μετὰ τῶν αὐτῶν ἔλεγον κακῶς ρ: μετὰ αὐτῶν **N**
[o]   καὶ Ἡρωδιανὸς — ἐν ἐπιρρήμασιν deest in ρ
[p]   ἐν **By₂Nρ**: ἐκ **y₁**

§v And a few words coming under the adverb are both enclitic and orthotonic, just as we said about *TIΣ* and *TINOΣ* and *TOY* and *TΩI* that they are inter-rogative when orthotonic, but declaratively [i.e. non-interrogatively] indefinite when enclitic. For example, πόθεν ἦλθε is a question, while ἦλθέ ποθεν is indefin-ite;[300] [similarly] πότε ἔγραψας [is a question but] ἔγραψάς ποτε [is indefinite].[301] And similarly *ΠΟΘΙ*, as in … [but] ἐπεὶ οὔ ποθι.[302] And [*ΠΟΥ* as in] ποῦ ἀπῆλθεν [but] ἀπῆλθέ που.[303] And *ΠΩΣ*, as in πῶς ἦλθεν [but] ἦλθέ πως.[304] And *ΠΩ*, as in … [but] οὔ πώ με γινώσκεις.[305] And similarly *ΠΗΙ*. And some have wrongly called these monosyllables and *ΠΟΘΙ* conjunctions, and Herodian among them; but Apollonius refutes these [ideas] well in detail. These then [are the enclitics] among adverbs.

[300] 'From where did he come?'; 'he came from somewhere'.
[301] 'When did you write?'; 'you once wrote'.
[302] *Il.* 13.309: 'since [I do] not [think that the long-haired Achaeans are so unequal to the fight] anywhere [else]'.
[303] 'Where did he/she go off?'; 'he/she went off somewhere'.
[304] 'How did he/she come?'; 'somehow he/she came'.
[305] 'You do not yet recognize me'.

§w οἷ[a] σύνδεσμοι ὁμοίως, ὁ *ΤΕ*,[b] 'καί τε χαλιφρονέοντα'[c] Ἀρκεσίλαός τε'· ὁ[d] *ΓΕ*,
'τοῦτό γέ μοι χάρισαι'· ὁ[e] *ΠΕΡ*, 'μὴ δ' οὕτως[f] ἀγαθός περ ἐών'· ὁ[g] [h] *ΤΟΙ*, 'μή νύ
τοι[i] οὐ χραίσμῃ'· ὁ[j] *ῬΑ*, 'ὅς[k] ῥα παρὰ[l] Κρονίωνι'· ὁ[m] *ΝΥ*, 'οὐ νύ μοι'· ὁ[n] *ΘΗΝ*, 'οὔ[o]
θην[p] δ' αὐτός'· ὁ[q] *ΚΕΝ*, '{ἢ}[r] καί κεν ἐλέγχιστος'.[s] ὁ[t] *ΟΥΝ* μετὰ μόνης τῆς *ΟΥ*
παραπληρωματικὸς[u] ὢν ἐγκλίνεται, 'οὔκουν', συλλογιστικὸς δὲ ὢν ὀρθοτονεῖται,
'οὔκουν τόδε[v] καὶ τόδε ἐγένετο'. καὶ τὸ *ΝΥΝ* ἐπίρρημα ὂν[w] περισπᾶται, σύνδεσμος
δὲ[x] ὂν καὶ συστέλλεται καὶ[y] ἐγκλίνεται, 'πρῶτά νυν Ὀρφῆος[z] μνησώμεθα'. καὶ
οὗτοι μέν, ὅτε ἔχουσι τὰς προειρημένας[aa] λέξεις τὰς δεχομένας τοὺς τόνους τῶν[bb]
ἐγκλινομένων, ἀναπέμπουσι τοὺς τόνους, 'τοῦτό γε', "Ὅμηρόν[cc] τε', 'ἄνδρά τε'. εἰ δὲ
μή, ὡς εἴπομεν περὶ μονοσυλλάβων, οὔτε ἀναβιβάζουσιν οὔτε φυλάττουσιν,[dd]
οἷον *ΤΟΥΤΟΥ ΓΕ*· οὔτε[ee] εἰς τὸ *ΤΟΥ* ἡ ὀξεῖα, οὔτε εἰς τὸ[ff] *ΓΕ*, ἀλλ' εἰς τὴν
πρώτην συλλαβήν, 'τούτου γε'. οὐ γὰρ πειστέον[gg] τοῖς λέγουσιν ὅτι ἑκάστῃ[hh] λέξει
ἀναπέμπουσι τὸν τόνον. καὶ[ii] [jj] ταῦτα μὲν περὶ τούτων.

§w

[a] οἱ σύνδεσμοι ὁμοίως **ρ**: οἱ (ἱ sic **N**) σύνδεσμοι **w₂N**: ἐν δὲ τῷ συνδέσμῳ **B**
[b] *ΤΕ* **Βρ**: δὲ τε **w₂N**
[c] χαλιφρονέοντα Ἀρκεσίλαός τε **Βy₃**: γὰρ φρονέοντα ἀρκεσίλαός τε **N**: χαλιφρονέοντε ἀρκεσίλαός τε **y₂**: deest in **ρ**
[d] ὁ *ΓΕ* **Βρ**: γε **y₂y₃N**
[e] ὁ *ΠΕΡ* **ρ**: περ **y₂y₃N**: πέρ· καὶ ὁ περ **B**
[f] οὕτως **ΒΝρ**: οὗτος **y₂y₃**
[g] ὁ *ΤΟΙ* μή νύ τοι οὐ χραίσμῃ deest in **y₂**
[h] ὁ: καὶ ὁ **B**: deest in **y₃N**
[i] τοι οὐ χραίσμῃ **N**: τοι οὐ χρέσμωσι **B**: τοι οὐ χραίσμωσι **y₃**: τοι οὐ χραίς μοι **Σ**: τοι **ρ**
[j] ὁ **ρ**: deest in **Βy₂y₃N**
[k] ὅς ῥα **y₃ρ**: ὥς ῥα **Βy₂N**
[l] παρὰ Κρονίωνι **Βy₂y₃N**: deest in **ρ**
[m] ὁ deest in **y₂**
[n] ὁ *ΘΗΝ* **ρ**: θην **Βy₂y₃N**
[o] οὔ **Βy₂y₃Nn**: καί **Ald.**
[p] θην δ' αὐτὸς **Βy₂y₃N**: θην **ρ**
[q] ὁ **ρ**: deest in **Βy₂y₃N**
[r] ἢ delevimus
[s] ἐλέγχιστος **y₃Νρ**: ἐλάχιστος **B**: deest in **y₂**
[t] ὁ **ρ**: τὸ **Βw₂N**
[u] παραπληρωματικὸς ὢν Bekker: παραπληρωματικὸς οὖν **w₂N**: παραπληρωματικὸς **ρ**: ἀποφατικοῦ **B**
[v] τόδε καὶ τόδε ἐγένετο καὶ τὸ **Βw₂N**: αἰσχρὸν τόδε. καὶ τὸ **ρ**
[w] ὂν **Βw₂NS**: οὐ **ζΚ**: deest in **Ald.**
[x] δὲ ὂν **Sr**: δὲ ὢν **w₂J**: ὂν **ΒΝ**: ὢν **Σ**
[y] καὶ **Βw₂NnΚ**: τὸ **Ald.**
[z] Ὀρφῆος μνησώμεθα **ρ**: Ὀρφῆος μνησόμεθα **y₂**: ὀρφῇ ὑμνησώμεθα **N**: Ὀρφῆϊ μνησόμεθα **B**: ὀρφῆοιμνησόμεθα (sic) **y₁**
[aa] προειρημένας **Βw₂ΝnΚ**: προηιρημένας **Ald.**
[bb] τῶν ἐγκλινομένων ἀναπέμπουσι τοὺς τόνους deest in **ρ**
[cc] Ὅμηρόν τε deest in **ρ**
[dd] φυλάττουσιν Bekker: ἀναφυλάττουσιν **Βw₂ΝnΚ**: ἀναφυλάπτουσιν **Ald.**
[ee] οὔτε...οὔτε Bekker: οὐδὲ...οὐδὲ **Βw₂Νρ**
[ff] τὸ **Βy₂Νρ**: τὸν **y₁**
[gg] πειστέον **S**: πιστέον **Βw₂Νζr**
[hh] ἑκάστῃ **ρ**: κατὰ ἑκάστη **N**: ἐν ἑκάστῃ **V**: καὶ τὰ ἑκαστη **Βy₂y₃**
[ii] καὶ ταῦτα μὲν περὶ τούτων deest in **y₂**
[jj] καὶ ταῦτα μὲν **B**: καὶ ταῦτα **V**: ἀλλὰ ταῦτα μὲν **ρ**: ταῦτα **y₃**

§w The conjunctions similarly [include enclitics]: so *TE*, as in καί τε χαλιφρονέοντα,[306] Ἀρκεσίλαός τε.[307] *ΓE*, as in τοῦτό γέ μοι χάρισαι.[308] $\overline{ΠΕΡ}$, as in μὴ δ' οὕτως ἀγαθός περ ἐών.[309] *TOI*, as in μή νύ τοι οὐ χραίσμῃ.[310] 'PA, as in ὅς ῥα παρὰ Κρονίωνι.[311] *NY*, as in οὔ νύ μοι.[312] *ΘΗΝ*, as in οὔ θην δ' αὐτός.[313] *KEN*, as in καί κεν ἐλέγχιστος.[314] [The conjunction] οὖν is enclitic only when it is a filler with οὔ, in οὔκουν, while it is orthotonic when inferential, as in οὐκοῦν τόδε καὶ τόδε ἐγένετο.[315] And νῦν is perispomenon when it is an adverb, but when it is a conjunction it has a short vowel and is enclitic, as in πρῶτά νυν Ὀρφῆος μνησώμεθα.[316] And these conjunctions, when they have [in front of them] the aforementioned words that accept the accents of enclitics, throw their accents back, as in τοῦτό γε, Ὅμηρόν τε, ἄνδρά τε.[317] But if they do not, as we said in [our discussion of] monosyllables, they neither throw their accent back nor keep it, as in *ΤΟΥΤΟΥ ΓΕ*.[318] The acute falls neither on the [second] *ΤΟΥ* nor on the *ΓΕ*, but on the first syllable: τούτου γε. For one must not believe those who say that they throw back their accent onto every word. And so much for these matters.

[306] *Od.* 23.13: 'and [they bring] a foolish person [to sense]'.
[307] *Il.* 2.495: 'And Arkesilaos'.
[308] Callimachus, fr. 728 Pfeiffer: 'do me this favour'.
[309] *Il.* 1.131 = *Il.* 19.155: 'Great though you are, do not thus…'.
[310] E.g. *Il.* 1.28: 'lest [the staff and wreath of the god] don't help you'.
[311] *Il.* 1.405: 'He [sat down] by the son of Kronos'.
[312] 'Not…for me'. Cf. *Il.* 3.164 οὔ τί μοι 'not at all to me'.
[313] 'Truly not even you yourself': an approximate quotation of *Il.* 16.852 (οὔ θην οὐδ' αὐτός).
[314] *Il.* 4.171: 'And [I would come to very thirsty Argos] utterly worthy of reproach'.
[315] 'Therefore this and this happened'. Cf. e.g. ἐπειδὴ ἔπραξα τόδε καὶ τόδε, καὶ γέγονε τόδε καὶ τόδε…ἀποβήσεται τόδε 'Since I did this and this, and this and this happened…this will happen', an example of a sentence with a causal conjunction at Gregory of Corinth, Περὶ συντάξεως λόγου 24 Donnet.
[316] Apollonius Rhodius, *Argonautica* 1.23: 'First, then, let us mention Orpheus'.
[317] 'This at any rate'; 'and Homer'; 'and a man'.
[318] 'Of this at any rate'.

2.5 *About* 'ΕΣΤΙΝ

Transmitted in some manuscripts under the title *Περὶ τοῦ* 'ΕΣΤΙΝ, the text we call *About* 'ΕΣΤΙΝ is an extremely brief introduction to the behaviour of one particular enclitic, 'ΕΣΤΙ(Ν). The first paragraph deals with the circumstances under which 'ΕΣΤΙ(Ν) is an enclitic and those under which it is non-enclitic, and will be of particular interest to us in Chapter 3. The remaining two paragraphs deal with the circumstances under which 'ΕΣΤΙ(Ν) throws its accent back, and the circumstances under which it is accented on its own last syllable, ἐστί(ν). The principles laid out here comprise a version of those applying to disyllabic enclitics in general, but are presented with reference to 'ΕΣΤΙ(Ν) in particular.

About 'ΕΣΤΙΝ is best known as the last few sentences of the second section on enclitics to appear as an intrusion into Pseudo-Arcadius' epitome of Herodian's *Περὶ καθολικῆς προσῳδίας* (see section 2.1). Outside the tradition of Pseudo-Arcadius, however, *About* 'ΕΣΤΙΝ is transmitted as a short independent text, and this is the form in which we present it.

2.5.1 Sources and stemma

About 'ΕΣΤΙΝ is transmitted in the following manuscripts and early printed books, listed here according to the main families and sub-families that we posit.

Family α
S_a (10th cent.): Moscow, State Historical Museum, Sinod. Gr. 21 (Vlad. 124), folios 295v–296r, copied by a scribe named *Κωνσταντῖνος*. (See Dobrynina 2013: 136–41.)

B (14th cent.): Milan, Biblioteca Ambrosiana, Ambrosianus G 27 sup. = Martini-Bassi 389, folios 84v–85r.

L (14th cent.): Florence, Biblioteca Medicea Laurenziana, Laurentianus Plut. 57.26, folio 68r–v.

N (late 13th cent.): Florence, Biblioteca Medicea Laurenziana, Laurentianus Plut. 58.25, folio 10r–v, copied by Cyriacus Prasianus (?), in southern Italy (see Crostini 2019: 147–8).

Family φ
A_1 (15th cent.): Milan, Biblioteca Ambrosiana, Ambrosianus D 30 sup. = Martini-Bassi 225, folio 66r–v.

T (15th cent.): Madrid, Biblioteca Nacional de España, Matritensis 4635 = de Andrés 92 (previously N 114), folio 127v.

Family ξ: manuscripts of Pseudo-Arcadius

R (15th cent.): Madrid, Biblioteca Nacional de España, Matritensis 4575 = de Andrés 32 (previously N 38), folio 44r, copied by Konstantinos Laskaris in Messina (see Roussou 2018*a*: 83–4).

F (1495): Oxford, Bodleian Library, Baroccianus 179, folio 49r, copied by Leon Chalkiopoulos in Messina (see Roussou 2018*a*: 84–5).

K₁ (15th cent.): Copenhagen, Det Kongelige Bibliotek, Hauniensis regius GKS 1965 4°, pp. 154–5, copied by Urbano Bolzanio. This copy of the text is derived from the copy in **R** (see section 2.1.1). This manuscript also transmits a second copy of *About* 'ΕΣΤΙΝ, independently of the text of Pseudo-Arcadius (see **K₂** under family **m**, sub-family **q**, later in this list).

Δ (16th cent.): Paris, Bibliothèque Nationale de France, Parisinus Graecus 2603, folio 54r (see Roussou 2018*a*: 85). This copy of the text is derived from the copy in **R** (cf. Roussou 2018*a*: 91–8 and section 2.1.1).

Z (16th cent.): Paris, Bibliothèque Nationale de France, Parisinus Graecus 2102, folio 200r–v, copied by Jacob Diassorinus (see Roussou 2018*a*: 86). Following work in progress by Maria Giovanna Sandri we take this copy of the text to be derived from the one in **Δ** (see section 2.1.1).

Family m, manuscript Φ

Φ (13th–14th cent.): Vatican City, Biblioteca Apostolica Vaticana, Vaticanus Graecus 2226, folio 168r–v.

Family m, manuscript Ψ

Ψ (15th cent.): Vatican City, Biblioteca Apostolica Vaticana, Vaticanus Pal. Gr. 360, folio 256r–v.

Family m, manuscript Vₐ

Vₐ (15th cent.): Vatican City, Biblioteca Apostolica Vaticana, Vaticanus Graecus 887, folio 22r–v.

Family m, sub-family μ

O (1469): London, British Library, Londiniensis Add. 10064, folio 159r–v, copied by Iohannes Rhosos in Venice.

Ω (15th cent.): Vatican City, Biblioteca Apostolica Vaticana, Vaticanus Reginensis Graecus 104, folios 127v–128v.

A₂ (15th cent.): Milan, Biblioteca Ambrosiana, Ambrosianus D 30 sup. = Martini-Bassi 225, folio 72r–v.

J (16th cent.): El Escorial, Real Biblioteca del Monasterio de San Lorenzo, Escorialensis Ψ.IV.23 = de Andrés 497, folios 150v–151r.

Σ (15th–16th cent.): Vatican City, Biblioteca Apostolica Vaticana, Vaticanus Graecus 1751, folios 301v–302r, copied by a scribe named Μανουήλ.

Family m, sub-family q

K₂ (15th cent.): Copenhagen, Det Kongelige Bibliotek, Hauniensis regius GKS 1965 4°, pp. 255bis-255/2,[319] copied by Urbano Bolzanio (see Roussou 2018*a*: 85). This manuscript also transmits a second copy of *About* ᾽*EΣTIN*, as part of the text of Pseudo-Arcadius (see **K₁** under family *ξ*, earlier in this list).

Y (1493): Paris, Bibliothèque Nationale de France, Parisinus Graecus 1773, folios 19v–20r, copied by Bartolomeo Comparini da Prato at Padua.

Ald. (1496): *Thesaurus: Cornu copiae et Horti Adonidis*, printed by the Aldine Press in Venice (for further details, see the bibliography under Aldus 1496), folios 225v–226r. Copies of the text derived from **Ald.** appear in further early printed books including the work listed in the bibliography as Curio (1522) (at quire Θ, folio iiiir), and the following whose copies derive from Curio (1522): de Gourmont (1523) (at folios 6v–7r, in the fourth of five sequences of folio numbers this book contains), Froben (1524) (at quire V, folio 4v), Aldus (1524) (quire M, folio vi recto, i.e. folio 94r in the second of two series of folio numbers this book contains), and Sessa and de Ravanis (1525) (at quire G, folio i r–v). Four further copies derived ultimately from **Ald.** are listed immediately below.

Rome, Biblioteca Casanatense, Casanatensis 1710 (16th cent.), folios 69v–70v, copied by Petros Hypsilas. This is a copy of **Ald.**

᾽*Ερωτήματα τοῦ Χρυσολωρᾶ*, **printed by the Aldine Press in Venice in 1512** (for further details, see the bibliography under Aldus 1512), pp. 272–3. This is a copy of **Ald.**, and features a number of alterations in a classicizing vein, possibly due to Marcus Musurus (see section 2.2.1): an example from Demosthenes (ὡς ἔστι τῶν αἰσχρῶν, *Olynthiac 2*, 2) is substituted for ὡς ἔστι κακὸν ἀμαθία (§a, lines 4–5), and δοῖδυξ 'pestle' is introduced as a more recherché example of a word ending in a consonant cluster than Ald.'s κῆρυξ (§b, note c and §c, note f) or φοῖνιξ (§c, note l). **Ald.**'s example Θωμᾶς is replaced by φῶς 'light' (§b, note c), possibly because the name Θωμᾶς has Christian and hence post-classical associations. Copies of the text derived from Aldus (1512) appear in further early printed books, including those listed in the bibliography as de Brocar (1514) (at quire T, folio viii verso–quire U, folio i recto), Junta (1515) (at pp. 245–7), and Aldus (1517) (at pp. 272–3). The two sixteenth-century manuscripts listed next contain further copies derived ultimately from Aldus (1512).

Venice, Biblioteca Nazionale Marciana, Marcianus Gr. XI. 26 = coll. 1322 (16th cent.), folio 89v. This is ultimately derived from Aldus (1512), via an intermediate source shared with the manuscript listed immediately below.

---

[319] On the page numbering problem in this part of this manuscript, see n. 95. *About* ᾽*EΣTIN* begins on the page after 255, which we call 255bis, and ends on the following page, which we call 255/2.

Athens, Σπουδαστήριον Βυζαντινῆς καὶ Νεοελληνικῆς Φιλολογίας, **Atheniensis 25** (16th cent.), folios 206v–207r, copied by Pachomios Rousanos (see n. 97). This is ultimately derived from Aldus (1512), via an intermediate source shared with the manuscript listed immediately above.

We reconstruct the stemma for *About ἘΣΤΙΝ* as shown in Figure 2.7.[320]

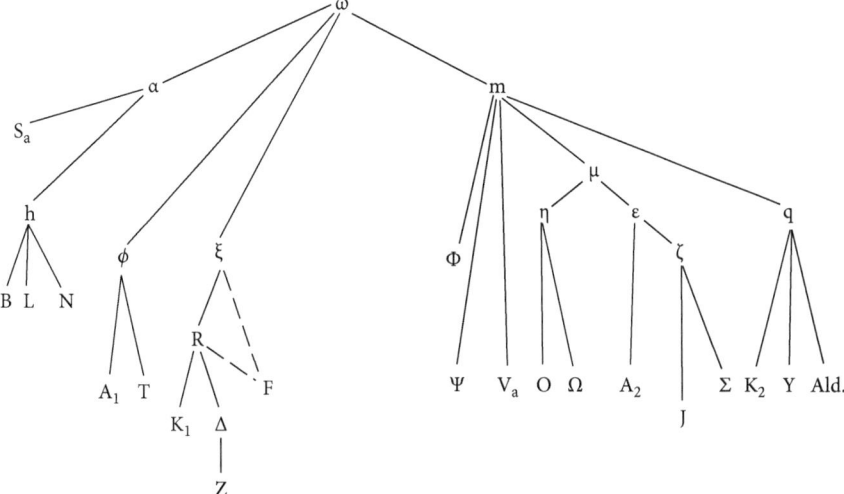

Fig. 2.7 Stemma for *About ἘΣΤΙΝ*

Since *About ἘΣΤΙΝ* is a very short treatise, the textual evidence it can provide for the relationships between witnesses is limited; such evidence as we have is consistent with the stemma reconstructed here, and will be laid out shortly. In addition, almost all manuscripts that transmit *About ἘΣΤΙΝ* also transmit one or more other texts on enclitics, in a way that helps to support the main families and sub-families reconstructed here. In each of the four families, *About ἘΣΤΙΝ* belongs to a block of two or three treatises that almost always appear in the same order, are almost always contiguous, and appear to have been transmitted together. The precise selection of treatises varies from one family to another, and within each family, the relationships between the witnesses to the other treatise(s) in the same block help support the stemma proposed here for *About ἘΣΤΙΝ*. The details can be laid out as follows:

---

[320] For the reasons given in section 2.1.1, our stemma for this treatise differs slightly from that of Roussou (2018a: 100) with respect to the witnesses belonging to family ξ (the Pseudo-Arcadius manuscripts).

Family α: *Charax* then *About* Ἐ*ΣΤΙΝ*

B   *Charax*: folios 76r–84v
        About Ἐ*ΣΤΙΝ*: folios 84v–85r

L   *Charax*: folios 51r–57v
        About Ἐ*ΣΤΙΝ*: folio 68r–v
        (In this manuscript, a copy of another treatise on accents intervenes
        between *Charax* and *About* Ἐ*ΣΤΙΝ*: John Philoponus' *De uocabulis*
        quae diuersum significatum exhibent secundum differentiam accentus.)

N   *Charax*: folios 7r–10r
        About Ἐ*ΣΤΙΝ*: folio 10r–v

Manuscript S_a transmits only *About* Ἐ*ΣΤΙΝ* (folios 295v–296r).

   The texts of *Charax* found in this family of manuscripts are related to each other
only insofar as they all descend from the archetype of *Charax* (see section 2.4.1).
Since **B**, **L**, and **N** are among the earliest manuscripts of *Charax* that we have, their
copies of *Charax* and *About* Ἐ*ΣΤΙΝ* might well derive from a manuscript whose
copy of *Charax* is close to the archetype, but whose copy of *About* Ἐ*ΣΤΙΝ* is
already more distinct from other versions of that text of which evidence comes
down to us. This said, the text of *About* Ἐ*ΣΤΙΝ* as we reconstruct it is close to
that of α—or to put this differently, we do not take α to have diverged from the
archetype by very much. (For the clearest instance of an innovation we take to
characterize α, see section 2.5.1.1, Table 2.34.)

   The oldest witness to *About* Ἐ*ΣΤΙΝ* known to us is the tenth-century manuscript S_a, which belongs to family α but transmits *About* Ἐ*ΣΤΙΝ* without *Charax*.
We tentatively posit a hyparchetype **h** shared by **B**, **L**, and **N**, but not S_a; on this
hypothesis the appearance of *Charax* alongside *About* Ἐ*ΣΤΙΝ* was inherited
from **h** but not necessarily from α. Decisive textual evidence for the hyparchetype
h is lacking, however: **B**, **L**, and **N** occasionally agree against S_a, but in no case can
an innovation on the part of S_a be ruled out.

   Be this as it may, a passage of Eustathius—quoted here as (2.1)—provides a
piece of evidence to suggest that *Charax* circulated alongside *About* Ἐ*ΣΤΙΝ*
already in the twelfth century. Eustathius' wording here is very close to that of
About Ἐ*ΣΤΙΝ* §§a–b, as Lehrs (1837: 125) in effect pointed out; under (2.1) we
show parallel wording via underlining (although for the avoidance of circularity,
we note that καὶ ἔστιν at *About* Ἐ*ΣΤΙΝ*, §a is our supplement and is based on
Eustathius). Eustathius suggests that he is drawing on Charax here, yet his wording is closer to that of *About* Ἐ*ΣΤΙΝ* than to that of the treatise attributed to
Charax.[321] However, the arrangement of *Charax* and *About* Ἐ*ΣΤΙΝ* in the four-
teenth-century manuscript **B** and the late thirteenth-century manuscript **N**

---

[321]   Cf. Lehrs (1837: 125); Lentz (1867–70: i. 553, on line 10).

(i.e. where *Charax* is followed immediately by *About 'ΕΣΤΙΝ*) leaves it unclear whether the attribution to Charax is meant to apply to *About 'ΕΣΤΙΝ* as well. We suggest that Eustathius knew both treatises from a manuscript in which they were arranged in this way, and that for this reason he mentions Charax while drawing from *About 'ΕΣΤΙΝ*. This indirect witness to *About 'ΕΣΤΙΝ* can confidently be dated to the twelfth century, especially as we are lucky enough to have two surviving manuscripts of the *Odyssey* commentary in Eustathius' own hand.[322]

(2.1) πρὸς τοῖς εἰρημένοις δὲ ἰστέον ἐν τῷ 'οὐκ ἔστ' οὐδὲ ἔοικεν', ὅτι τὸ ἔστιν οὐχ ἁπλῶς ἐνταῦθα παροξύνεται ἀλλὰ κατὰ παρατήρησιν ἀρχαίαν, τοιαύτην. τὸ ἔστιν ἡνίκα ἄρχεται λόγου ἢ ὑποτάσσεται τῇ 'ΟΥ ἀποφάσει ἢ τῷ ΚΑΙ συνδέσμῳ ἢ τῷ 'ΩΣ ἐπιρρήματι, παροξύνεται. οἷον, 'ἔστι πόλις Ἐφύρη', 'οὐκ ἔστ' οὐδὲ ἔοικε', 'καὶ ἔστιν', 'ὡς ἔστι δεινόν'. εἰ δὲ ὑποτάσσεται ὀξυτόνῳ λέξει ἢ περισπωμένῃ ἢ τροχαίῳ προπερισπωμένῳ ἢ προπαροξυνομένῃ λέξει, ἐγκλίνεται κατὰ τοὺς κανόνας τοῦ Χάρακος. οἷον 'ἀγαθός ἐστιν', 'Ἑρμῆς ἐστι', 'κῆπός ἐστιν'. (Eustathius, *In Odysseam* 1600.15–19 = i. 302.38–44 Stallbaum)

'In addition to what has been said, one must know that in οὐκ ἔστ' οὐδὲ ἔοικεν[323] the word ἔστιν is not *straightforwardly* paroxytone here but follows an ancient observation of the following sort: When ἔστιν begins its clause, or when it is placed after the negation 'ΟΥ, or the conjunction ΚΑΙ, or the adverb 'ΩΣ, then it is paroxytone, as in ἔστι πόλις Ἐφύρη[324] or οὐκ ἔστ' οὐδὲ ἔοικε[325] or καὶ ἔστιν or ὡς ἔστι δεινόν.[326] But if it is placed after an oxytone word or a perispomenon one, or a properispomenon trochee or a proparoxytone word, it throws back its accent according to the rules of Charax. As in ἀγαθός ἐστιν or Ἑρμῆς ἐστι or κῆπός ἐστιν.'[327]

Family φ: *On enclitics 1* then *About 'ΕΣΤΙΝ*

A₁ *On enclitics 1* (version A₁): folios 63r–66r
    About 'ΕΣΤΙΝ (version A₁): folio 66r–v
    (In this manuscript, these treatises are followed by other treatises on enclitics in the following sequence: *On enclitics 1* version A₂, at folios 66v–67v; *On enclitics 3*, at folios 67v–68v; *On enclitics 2*, at folios 69r–72r; *About 'ΕΣΤΙΝ* version A₂, at folio 72r–v.)

T   *On enclitics 1* (version T₂): folios 125v–127v
    About 'ΕΣΤΙΝ: folio 127v

---

[322] For extensive discussion and further bibliography, see Cullhed (2012).
[323] *Il.* 14.212 = *Od.* 8.358: 'It is not possible, nor is it seemly'.
[324] *Il.* 6.152: 'There is a city, Ephurē'.
[325] *Il.* 14.212 = *Od.* 8.358: 'It is not possible, nor is it seemly'.
[326] 'And it is' / 'and there is'; 'that it is a terrible thing'.
[327] '. . . is good'; 'Hermes is'; 'a garden is'.

(In this manuscript, these treatises are preceded by *On enclitics 1* version **T₁**, at folio 123r–v and *On enclitics 3*, at folios 124r–125v, and followed by *Charax*, at folios 128r–132v.)

Within this family, the texts of *On enclitics 1* (and not only those of *About* 'ΕΣΤΙΝ) are closely related to each other: see section 2.1.1.

Family ξ: *On enclitics 3* then *On enclitics 1*, moving seamlessly into *About* 'ΕΣΤΙΝ, all presented as part of the text of Pseudo-Arcadius

R   *On enclitics 3*: folios 41r–42r
         On enclitics 1: folios 42r–44r
         About 'ΕΣΤΙΝ: folio 44r

F   *On enclitics 3*: folios 46r–47r
         On enclitics 1: folios 47r–49r
         About 'ΕΣΤΙΝ: folio 49r

K₁   *On enclitics 3*: pp. 144–8
         On enclitics 1: pp. 148–54
         About 'ΕΣΤΙΝ (version **K₁**): pp. 154–5
         (This manuscript also transmits *About* 'ΕΣΤΙΝ version **K₂**, *On enclitics 2*, and *Charax*, independently of the text of Pseudo-Arcadius: see **K₂** under family **m**, later in this list.)

Δ   *On enclitics 3*: folios 51v–52r
         On enclitics 1: folios 52r–54r
         About 'ΕΣΤΙΝ: folio 54r

Z   *On enclitics 3*: folios 192v–194v
         On enclitics 1: folios 194v–200r
         About 'ΕΣΤΙΝ: folio 200r–v

The texts of *On enclitics 3* transmitted within the text of Pseudo-Arcadius, in manuscripts of this family, are closely related to one another, as are those of *On enclitics 1* which manuscripts of this family transmit in the same way: see sections 2.3.1, 2.1.1.

Family m (all manuscripts except Ψ and Va): *On enclitics 2*, *About* 'ΕΣΤΙΝ, and possibly *Charax*, mostly in this order

Φ   *About* 'ΕΣΤΙΝ: folio 168r–v
         On enclitics 2: folios 168v–169v
         Charax: folios 190v–191v
         (In this manuscript only, the text of *About* 'ΕΣΤΙΝ precedes that of *On enclitics 2*, and a grammatical text on a different topic intervenes between *On enclitics 2* and *Charax*: Michael Syncellus' Μέθοδος συντάξεως.)

O   *On enclitics 2*: folios 155v–158v
         About 'ΕΣΤΙΝ: folio 159r–v

Ω   *On enclitics 2*: folios 124r–127v
    About Ἐ*ΣΤΙΝ*: folios 127v–128v

A₂   *On enclitics 2*: folios 69r–72r
    About Ἐ*ΣΤΙΝ* (version **A₂**): folio 72r–v
    (In this manuscript, these treatises are preceded by other treatises on enclitics in the following sequence: *On enclitics 1* version **A₁**, at folios 63r–66r; *About* Ἐ*ΣΤΙΝ* version **A₁**, at folio 66r–v; *On enclitics 1* version **A₂**, at folios 66v–67v; *On enclitics 3*, at folios 67v–68v.)

J   *On enclitics 2*: folios 147r–150r
    About Ἐ*ΣΤΙΝ*: folios 150v–151r
    Charax: folios 151r–156v

Σ   *On enclitics 2*: 299r–301v
    About Ἐ*ΣΤΙΝ*: folios 301v–302r
    Charax: folios 302r–306r

K₂   *On enclitics 2*: pp. 251–6
    About Ἐ*ΣΤΙΝ* (version **K₂**): pp. 256–7
    Charax: pp. 257–66
    (This manuscript also transmits *On enclitics 3*; *On enclitics 1*; and *About* Ἐ*ΣΤΙΝ* version **K₁**, all as part of the text of Pseudo-Arcadius: see **K₁** under family ξ, earlier in this list.)

Y   *On enclitics 2*: folios 17v–19v
    About Ἐ*ΣΤΙΝ*: folios 19v–20r
    (This manuscript also transmits *Charax* and *On enclitics 4*, but on much later folios, copied by a different scribe: *Charax* appears at folios 284v–288r, and *On enclitics 4* at folio 288v.)

Ald.   *On enclitics 2*: folios 223v–225v
    About Ἐ*ΣΤΙΝ*: folios 225v–226r
    Charax: folios 226r–229v
    (The Aldine *Thesaurus* (Aldus 1496) also transmits *On enclitics 4*, at folio 229v; *On enclitics 3*, at folios 229v–230v; *On enclitics 1* version **Ald.₁**, at folios 231r–232r; and *On enclitics 1* version **Ald.₂**, at folios 232r–234v.)

Manuscript **Vₐ** transmits only *About* Ἐ*ΣΤΙΝ* (folio 22r–v).
Manuscript **Ψ** transmits only *About* Ἐ*ΣΤΙΝ* (folio 168r–v).

The texts of *On enclitics 2* transmitted by manuscripts of this family comprise all copies of *On enclitics 2* known to us. Within the tradition of *On enclitics 2*, manuscript **Φ** forms a branch by itself, manuscripts O*Ω*AJ*Σ* form a family divided into two sub-families (O*Ω* and AJ*Σ*), and **K**, **Y**, and **Ald.** comprise a further family (see section 2.2.1). Our stemma for *About* Ἐ*ΣΤΙΝ* posits the same relationships among the copies of *About* ’Ε*ΣΤΙΝ* comprising family **m**, with the addition of two further branches consisting of manuscripts **Ψ** and **V**$_a$.

In four of the manuscripts of family **m** (or rather, in three manuscripts and one early printed book), *About* ’Ε*ΣΤΙΝ* is followed immediately by *Charax*: we call the relevant texts of *About* ’Ε*ΣΤΙΝ* **K**$_2$, **Ald.**, **J**, and **Σ**, and those of *Charax* are **K**, **Ald.**, **J**, and **Σ**. Of these versions of *Charax*, **K** and **Ald.** are closely related, as are **J** and **Σ** (see section 2.4.1). These relationships too reappear in the stemma we reconstruct for *About* ’Ε*ΣΤΙΝ*.

Manuscript **Φ** also contains a text of *Charax* in the vicinity of *About* ’Ε*ΣΤΙΝ* (although the two texts are not contiguous, nor ordered in the same way as in the other manuscripts of this family). The text of *Charax* in **Φ** is only distantly related to copies **K**, **Ald.**, **J**, and **Σ** of the same treatise (see section 2.4.1), and this relationship too is paralleled by the position of **Φ** within family **m** of *About* ’Ε*ΣΤΙΝ*.

The following subsection lays out briefly the clearest pieces of textual evidence which can be gained from the text of *About* ’Ε*ΣΤΙΝ* itself, for the four main families *α*, *ϕ*, *ξ*, and **m**.

2.5.1.1 Evidence for families *α*, *ϕ*, *ξ*, and **m**

Tables 2.34–2.37 show the clearest instances of innovations specific to families *ϕ*, **h**, *ξ*, and **m** respectively.

The text of **V**$_a$ diverges considerably from that of the other witnesses belonging to family **m**. Like the particularly striking example discussed in Table 2.37 (under §b, notes b–c), the divergences are all compatible with rewriting of the text in **V**$_a$, preceded by corruption in an intermediate source—although we cannot rule out the possibility that **V**$_a$ is a sister rather than a daughter of **m**. For transparency on this point, our apparatus records individual readings of **V**$_a$, even where the reading of **m** can confidently be reconstructed.

Table 2.34 Evidence for family *α* (comprising manuscripts **S**$_a$**BLN**)

Reading of family *α*	Reading(s) of the rest of the tradition
§c, note f: παροξύτονος διὰ τὸ φύλλά ἐστιν S$_a$LN (B has παροξύτονος) We take the reading of the archetype to be παροξύτονος, and διὰ τὸ φύλλά ἐστιν to be an explanatory addition in *α*. B removed this phrase, while **m** adds different material.	παροξύτονος *ϕ*ξ**V**$_a$: παροξύτονος οἷον μάντις, πόρνος (πόρνος deest in A$_2$), ἢ προπερισπώμενος μέν, ἔχων (ἔχει **ε**) δὲ (δὲ deest in **Φ**) τὴν τελευταίαν θέσει μακράν, ὡς ἔχει τὸ φοῖνιξ, κῆρυξ **m** (**V**$_a$ simplifies **m**'s presentation at this point, but adds the words καὶ ἐὰν ἔχῃ ὁ τροχαῖος τὴν τελευτέαν θέσει μακρὰν· ὁποῖος ἂν ᾖ· οἷον κῆρυξ ἐστὶν· φοίνιξ ἐστὶν to the end of the treatise.)

Table 2.35 Evidence for family φ

Reading of sub-family φ (A₁T)	Reading(s) of the rest of the tradition
§a, notes k–r: ἔστι πόλις **A₁T** We take the archetype to have had a reading close to that of **m** or **α** (cf. also the parallel passage of Eustathius quoted in section 2.5.1 as (2.1)). In φ and ξ the series of examples was cut down to one, but in slightly different ways, so that the example takes the form ἔστι πόλις in φ and ἔστι πόλις Ἐφύρη in ξ. (**Vₐ** adjusts the series of examples in a different way of its own.)	ἔστι πόλις Ἐφύρη μυχῷ Ἄργεος ἱπποβότοιο, οὐκ ἔστ᾽ οὐδὲ ἔοικε τεὸν ἔπος ἀρνήσασθαι, ὡς ἔστι κακὸν ἀμαθία **m**: ἔστι πόλις Ἐφύρη μυχῷ Ἄργεος ἱπποβότοιο, οὐκ ἔστ᾽ οὐδὲ ἔοικε τεὸν ἔπος (τέον δέπως **Sₐ**) ἀρνήσασθαι **α**: ἔστι πόλις Ἐφύρη **ξ**: ἔστι πόλις Ἐφύρη οὐκ ἔσται οὐδὲ ἔοικε καὶ οὐκ ἔστιν ἄρχων ὡς ἔστιν κακὸν ἀμαθία **Vₐ**
§c, note d: πρόσκειται **A₁T** We take πρόκειται to be the reading of the archetype; this was variously corrected and further corrupted, but only φ has the specific corruption πρόσκειται, with the prefix taking the form πρόσ-.	προκέηται **ΦΨΩΖ**: πρόκειται **αξVₐ A₂**: προκῆται **Ald.**: προκέκται **OK₂Y**

Table 2.36 Evidence for family ξ (comprising the Pseudo-Arcadius manuscripts **RF**)

Reading of family ξ	Reading(s) of the rest of the tradition
§a, notes k–r: ἔστι πόλις Ἐφύρη **RF** As noted in Table 2.35 under §a, notes k–r, we take the archetype to have had a reading close to that of **m** or **α**, which was cut down to a single example in ξ and φ—but in slightly different ways, so that the example takes the form ἔστι πόλις Ἐφύρη in ξ and ἔστι πόλις in φ. (Again, **Vₐ** adjusts the series of examples in a different way of its own.)	ἔστι πόλις Ἐφύρη μυχῷ Ἄργεος ἱπποβότοιο, οὐκ ἔστ᾽ οὐδὲ ἔοικε τεὸν ἔπος ἀρνήσασθαι, ὡς ἔστι κακὸν ἀμαθία **m**: ἔστι πόλις Ἐφύρη μυχῷ Ἄργεος ἱπποβότοιο, οὐκ ἔστ᾽ οὐδὲ ἔοικε τεὸν ἔπος (τέον δέπως **Sₐ**) ἀρνήσασθαι **α**: ἔστι πόλις **φ**: ἔστι πόλις Ἐφύρη οὐκ ἔσται οὐδὲ ἔοικε καὶ οὐκ ἔστιν ἄρχων ὡς ἔστιν κακὸν ἀμαθία **Vₐ**
§b, notes d, f: examples omitted in **RF**	Ἑρμῆς ἐστιν **φ**: Ἑρμῆς ἐστιν Ἡρακλῆς ἐστιν **SₐBL**: Ἡρακλῆς ἐστιν Ἑρμῆς ἐστιν **N** (**m** substantially rewrites paragraph §b—see §b, note c and Table 2.37—but its reading also includes the example Ἑρμῆς ἐστιν.)
§b, note g: omission of a parenthetical explanation plus the following two words in **RF**	(διὰ τὸ φύλλα ἐστίν· παροξύτονος γὰρ οὗτος ὁ τροχαῖος, οὐχὶ προπερισπώμενος) ἢ προπαροξυτόνῳ **αφ** (**m** substantially rewrites paragraph §b—see §b, note c and Table 2.37—but still preserves the words διὰ τὸ ʻφύλλα ἐστίν· παροξύτονος γὰρ οὗτος ὁ τροχαῖος, οὐχὶ προπερισπώμενος.)

Continued

Table 2.36 *Continued*

Reading of family ξ	Reading(s) of the rest of the tradition
§c, note e: αὐτῷ **RF**	αὐτοῦ **αφξm**
§c, note l: Additional material added to the end of the treatise in **RF**, to provide a transition to the next topic to be treated in the text of Pseudo-Arcadius:	The treatise ends at the end of the preceding sentence in **αφξm**
καὶ ταῦτα μὲν περὶ τοῦ τόνου τῶν ὀνομάτων· ἔτι καὶ περὶ τῶν ἐγκλινομένων μορίων· ἕπεται δὲ εἰπεῖν περὶ τόνου τῶν ῥημάτων καὶ τῶν ἄλλων μερῶν τοῦ λόγου	

Table 2.37 Evidence for family **m** (comprising $\Phi \Psi V_a \mu q$)

Reading of family m	Reading(s) of the rest of the tradition
§a, note d: word not present in $\Phi \Psi V_a \mu q$	ὅτε **αφξ**
§b, notes b–c:	ἐὰν δὲ ὑποτάττηται — ἄδικός ἐστι
ἐὰν δὲ ὑποτάττηται ὀξυτόνῳ λέξει ἢ περισπωμένη, ἐγκλίνεται, οἷον 'καλός ἐστιν', 'Ἑρμῆς ἐστιν', ἢ τροχαίῳ μὴ παροξυτόνῳ ἀλλὰ προπερισπωμένῳ, οἷον 'οἶκός ἐστι', 'δῆμός ἐστι'. δεῖ προσθεῖναι, 'εἰ μὴ ἔχοι τὴν τελευταίαν συλλαβὴν ὁ τροχαῖος θέσει μακράν', ὡς ἔχει τὸ 'Φοῖνιξ ἐστί', 'κῆρυξ ἐστί'· διὰ γὰρ τὴν τοῦ Ξ ἐπιφορὰν οὐ γίνεται ἔγκλισις. 'μὴ παροξυτόνῳ' δὲ εἶπον διὰ τὸ 'φύλλα ἐστίν'· παροξύτονος γὰρ οὗτος ὁ τροχαῖος, οὐχὶ προπερισπώμενος, καὶ διὰ τοῦτο τὸ ΕΣΤΙΝ οὐκ ἐγκλίνεται, ἀλλ' ἐπὶ τοῦ Ι ἔχει τὴν ὀξεῖαν. γίνεται οὖν ἡ ἔγκλισις ὀξυτόνῳ μὲν λέξει, 'καλός ἐστι', προπαροξυτόνῳ δέ, 'ἄκακός ἐστι', περισπωμένῃ δέ, 'Θωμᾶς ἐστι', προπερισπωμένῃ δέ, 'φαῦλός ἐστιν'. καὶ γὰρ ἐπαναγωγὴν τῶν αὐτῶν πεποιήμεθα διὰ σαφεστέραν γνῶσιν. $\Phi \Psi \mu q$ (with minor variants noted in the critical apparatus): ἢ προπαροξυτόνῳ ἢ περισπωμένη ἢ προπερισπομένη (sic) ἐγκλίνεται· ὀξυτόνῳ μὲν οἷον μωρός ἐστι σοφός ἐστι καλός ἐστι· προπαροξυτόνῳ δὲ ἄκακος ἐστι περισπωμένη δὲ οἷον Θωμᾶς ἐστι· Ἑρμῆς ἐστι Ἡρακλῆς ἐστι· προπερισπωμένη δὲ οἷον κῆπος ἐστι· δῆμος ἐστι· φαῦλος ἐστι V_a	(The text we print appears in **αφξ**, with minor variations as noted in the critical apparatus; **m**'s text reflects a significant reworking of this material.)
We take the reading of **m** to be that inherited (with minor variations) by $\Phi \Psi \mu q$, and the reading of V_a to derive from this in two stages. First, a *saut du même au même* (καλός ἐστιν — καλός ἐστιν) in an intermediate source yielded the following:	
ἐὰν δὲ ὑποτάττηται ὀξυτόνῳ λέξει ἢ περισπωμένη, ἐγκλίνεται, οἷον καλός ἐστιν, προπαροξυτόνῳ δέ, ἄκακός ἐστι, περισπωμένῃ δέ, Θωμᾶς ἐστι, προπερισπωμένῃ δέ, φαῦλός ἐστιν. καὶ γὰρ ἐπαναγωγὴν τῶν αὐτῶν πεποιήμεθα διὰ σαφεστέραν γνῶσιν.	

Reading of family m	Reading(s) of the rest of the tradition

Then, a subsequent scribe made some additions (shown in triangular brackets below) so that oxytone, proparoxytone, perispomenon, and properispomenon words are mentioned in the same order as the new sequence of examples καλός ἐστιν, ἄκακός ἐστι, Θωμᾶς ἐστι, φαῦλός ἐστιν. He also added a few more stock examples, and deleted the sentence καὶ γὰρ ἐπαναγωγὴν — γνῶσιν, which now made little sense (we show the deletion in double square brackets):

ἐὰν δὲ ὑποτάττηται ὀξυτόνῳ λέξει ⟨ἢ προπαροξυτόνῳ⟩ ἢ περισπωμένῃ ⟨ἢ προπερισπωμένῃ⟩, ἐγκλίνεται· ⟨ὀξυτόνῳ μὲν⟩ οἷον ⟨μωρός ἐστι, σοφός ἐστι⟩, καλός ἐστι· προπαροξυτόνῳ δέ, ἄκακος ἐστι· περισπωμένῃ δέ, ⟨οἷον⟩ Θωμᾶς ἐστι· ῾Ερμῆς ἐστι· ῾Ηρακλῆς ἐστι)· προπερισπωμένῃ δέ, ⟨οἷον κῆπος ἐστι· δῆμος ἐστι⟩· φαῦλος ἐστι. [[καὶ γὰρ ἐπαναγωγὴν τῶν αὐτῶν πεποιήμεθα διὰ σαφεστέραν γνῶσιν.]]

§c, notes a–c:

ἔχῃ (ἔχει **η**) ἤγουν (εἴγουν **K₂Y**: ἤγουν deest in **A₂**) ὡς προτέτακται τὴν ὀξεῖαν ἐπὶ τοῦ ι δέχεται **ΦΨμq**: ὡς προτέτακται ἐστὶν τὴν ὀξείαν ἐπὶ τοῦ ι ἔχει **Vₐ**

I.e. **m** adds ὡς προτέτακται 'as just stated'.

ἔχῃ (ἔχει **Sₐ**) τὴν ὀξεῖαν ἐπὶ τοῦ ι δέχεται **αφξ**

2.5.2 Previous editions

Like *On enclitics 1* and *On enclitics 3*, *About* ʾΕΣΤΙΝ is printed by Barker (1820: 147–8), Schmidt (1860: 169), and Roussou (2018a: 308) as part of the text of Pseudo-Arcadius, on the basis of manuscripts belonging to family **ξ** (the Pseudo-Arcadius manuscripts). In these editions, as in the manuscripts of this family, the text of *About* ʾΕΣΤΙΝ is presented as the very end of the treatise we call *On enclitics 1*, and ends with a transition back to Pseudo-Arcadius' next topic, the accentuation of verbs (see Table 2.36 under §c, note l).

Bekker printed a self-standing text of *About* ʾΕΣΤΙΝ in the third volume of his *Anecdota Graeca* (Bekker 1821: 1148–9), on the basis especially of **Ald.**, although he also consulted **Y** and a second Aldine edition likely to be Aldus (1524) (see section 2.1.2). Because Bekker's sources belong to family **m**, his text gives a good impression of the form this treatise took after extensive rewriting by **m**, as well as including some further innovations made by **Ald.**

As mentioned already (sections 2.1.2, 2.2.2), Lentz (1867–70: i. 551–64) combines material from *On enclitics 1*, *On enclitics 2*, and *About* ʾΕΣΤΙΝ into one text entitled ῾Εκ τῶν ῾Ηρωδιανοῦ περὶ ἐγκλινομένων. Within this text, a portion corresponding to *About* ʾΕΣΤΙΝ appears at p. 553, line 10–p. 554, line 12, and is based on Bekker's text. In section 3.2 we will consider some of the conclusions which have been drawn from the text as presented by Lentz, and in particular from some innovations in **Ald.** which are—in essence—taken over into Bekker's text and from Bekker into Lentz (see also Chapter 3, n. 11).

2.5.3 *About* ’ΕΣΤΙΝ: text and translation

§a *Περὶ*[a] *τοῦ* ’ΕΣΤΙΝ

Τὸ ’ΕΣΤΙΝ ἡνίκα ἄρχει[b] λόγου,[c] ἢ ὅτε[d] ὑποτάττεται[e] τῇ ’ΟΥ ἀποφάσει ἢ τῷ ΚΑΙ[f] συνδέσμῳ ἢ τῷ ’ΩΣ ἐπιρρήματι,[g] τηνικαῦτα[h] τὴν ὀξεῖαν ἔχει ἐπὶ τοῦ[i] Ε, οἷον[j] ‘ἔστι πόλις Ἐφύρη[k] μυχῷ[l] [m] Ἄργεος ἱπποβότοιο’, ‘οὐκ ἔστ’[n] οὐδὲ[o] ἔοικε[p] τεὸν ἔπος ἀρνήσασθαι’, ⟨‘καὶ ἔστιν’⟩,[q] ‘ὡς[r] ἔστι κακὸν ἀμαθία’.[s]

---

§a

[a] *Περὶ τοῦ ἔστιν* **aA₁ζK₂ Ald.**: *περὶ τοῦ ἔστιν τοῦ αὐτοῦ* **ηY**: Ἡρωδιανοῦ *περὶ τοῦ ἔστιν* **Ψ**: *περὶ τὸ ἔστιν* **V_a**: *sine titulo* **TξΦA₂**

[b] *ἄρχει* **ΦΨ**: *ἄρχῃ* **S_aB_μ Ald.**: *ἀρχῇ* **LA₁**: *ἀρχή* **TξV_a**: *ἀρχ* **N**: *ἄρχηται* **Σ**: *ἄρχεται* Lentz (1867–70: i: 553), coll. Sch. *Il.* 1.63c et Sch. *Il.* 6.152

[c] *λόγου* **aφξΦΨV_aζ**: *λόγον* **OA₂q**: *λόγων* **Ω**

[d] *ὅτε* **aφξ**: *deest in* **m**

[e] *ὑποτάττεται* **S_aNTΨηA₂q**: *ὑποτάσσεται* **LJ**: *ὑποτάττηται* **A₁ξ**: *ὑποτάσσηται* **BΣ**: *ἀποτάττεται* **Φ**: *ὑποτάττῃ τὲ* **V_a**

[f] *post* ΚΑΙ *verba* ἢ εἰ ἢ ἀλλὰ *praebet* **Ald.**

[g] *post* ἐπιρρήματι *verba* ἢ τῷ τοῦτο *praebet* **Ald.**

[h] *τηνικαῦτα* **ω**: *τοινικαῦτα* (sic) **η**

[i] *τοῦ* **aφm**: *τῷ* **ξ**

[j] *οἷον deest in* **ξ**

[k] Ἐφύρη — κακὸν ἀμαθία *deest in* **φ**

[l] μυχῷ Ἄργεος ἱπποβότοιο — κακὸν ἀμαθία *deest in* **ξ**

[m] μυχῷ Ἄργεος ἱπποβότοιο *deest in* **V_a**

[n] ἔστ’] ἔσται **V_a**

[o] οὐδὲ **S_am**: οὐδ’ **h**

[p] ἔοικε τεὸν ἔπος ἀρνήσασθαι] ἔοικε τέον δέπως ἀρνήσασθαι **S_a**: ἔοικε καὶ οὐκ ἔστιν ἄρχων **V_a**

[q] καὶ ἔστιν *addidimus collato* Eustathio *In Odysseam* 1600.15–19 = i. 302.38–46 Stallbaum

[r] ὡς ἔστι κακὸν ἀμαθία *deest in* **a**

[s] *post* ἀμαθία *verba* εἰ ἔστιν οὕτως ἀλλ’ ἔστιν εἰπεῖν τοῦτ’ ἔστιν ἁμάρτημα *leguntur in* **Ald.**

§a About ἘΣΤΙΝ

When ἘΣΤΙΝ begins a clause,[328] or when it is placed after the negation ὈΥ, or after the conjunction ΚΑΙ, or the adverb ὩΣ, then it has the acute accent on its E, as in ἔστι πόλις Ἐφύρη μυχῷ Ἄργεος ἱπποβότοιο,[329] or οὐκ ἔστ᾽ οὐδὲ ἔοικε τεὸν ἔπος ἀρνήσασθαι,[330] or καὶ ἔστιν,[331] or ὡς ἔστι κακὸν ἀμαθία.[332]

[328] See n. 25.
[329] Il. 6.152: 'There is a city, Ephurē, at a remote point of the horse-nourishing Argolid'.
[330] Il. 14.212 = Od. 8.358: 'It is not possible, nor is it seemly, to refuse your bidding'.
[331] 'And there is' / 'and...is'.
[332] 'That ignorance is a bad thing', or 'how ignorance is a bad thing!'. Cf. Sophocles, fr. 924 Radt: ὡς δυσπάλαιστόν ἐστιν ἀμαθία κακόν 'that ignorance is an evil hard to wrestle with', or 'how intractable an evil is ignorance!'.

§b ἐὰν δὲ[a] ὑποτάττηται ὀξυτόνῳ λέξει ἢ[b] περισπωμένη, οἷον[c] [d] "Ἑρμῆς[e] [f] ἐστιν', ἢ τροχαίῳ μὴ παροξυτόνῳ ἀλλὰ προπερισπωμένῳ (διὰ[g] [h] τὸ 'φύλλα[i] ἐστίν'· παροξύτονος γὰρ οὗτος ὁ τροχαῖος, οὐχὶ[j] προπερισπώμενος), ἢ προπαροξυτόνῳ,[k] τηνικαῦτα[l] ἐγκλίνεται, οἷον 'ἀγαθός ἐστι', 'κακός[m] ἐστι', 'κῆπός[n] ἐστι', 'ἄδικός ἐστι'.

§b
a δὲ deest in **ΦΨ**
b ἢ περισπωμένη — ἄδικός ἐστι] ἢ προπαροξυτόνῳ ἢ περισπωμένη ἢ προπερισπομένη (sic) ἐγκλίνεται· ὀξυτόνῳ μὲν οἷον μωρός ἐστι σοφός ἐστι καλός ἐστι· προπαροξυτόνῳ δὲ ἄκακος ἐστι· περισπωμένη δὲ οἷον Θωμᾶς ἐστι· Ἑρμῆς ἐστι· Ἡρακλῆς ἐστι· προπερισπωμένη δὲ οἷον κῆπος ἐστι· δῆμος ἐστι· φαῦλος ἐστι **V**ₐ
c οἷον — ἄδικός ἐστι] ἐγκλίνεται, οἷον 'καλός (κακός **Φ**) ἐστιν', Ἑρμῆς ἐστιν', ἢ τροχαίῳ μὴ παροξυτόνῳ ἀλλὰ προπερισπωμένῳ, οἷον 'οἶκός ἐστι', 'δῆμός ἐστι' (δῆμός ἐστι deest in **K₂ Ald.**). δεῖ προσθεῖναι (προσθῆναι **ζ**), 'εἰ μὴ ἔχοι (ἔχει **Ψˢˡ ζ**) τὴν τελευταίαν συλλαβὴν ὁ τροχαῖος θέσει μακράν', ὡς ἔχει τὸ 'Φοῖνιξ ἐστί', 'κῆρυξ ἐστί'· διὰ γὰρ τὴν τοῦ Ξ ἐπιφορὰν οὐ γίνεται ἔγκλισις. 'μὴ παροξυτόνῳ (παροξύτονων **ηζ**: προπαροξυτόνῳ **Φ**)' δὲ εἶπον διὰ τὸ 'φύλλα ἐστίν'· παροξύτονος γὰρ οὗτος ὁ τροχαῖος, οὐχὶ προπερισπώμενος, καὶ διὰ τοῦτο τὸ 'ΕΣΤΙΝ οὐκ ἐγκλίνεται, ἀλλ' ἐπὶ τοῦ Ι ἔχει τὴν ὀξεῖαν. γίνεται οὖν ἡ ἔγκλισις ὀξυτόνῳ μὲν λέξει, 'καλός (κακός **K₂ Ald.**) ἐστι', προπαροξυτόνῳ (παροξυτόνῳ **ΦK₂ Ald.**) δέ, 'ἄκακός ἐστι', περισπωμένη δέ, 'Θωμᾶς (Ἑρμῆς **ε**) ἐστι', προπερισπωμένη δέ, 'φαῦλός ἐστι'. καὶ γὰρ ἐπαναγωγὴν τῶν αὐτῶν πεποιήμεθα (ποιούμεθα **ε**) διὰ σαφεστέραν γνῶσιν. **ΦΨμq**: de **V**ₐ vide §b, notam b
d οἷον Ἑρμῆς ἐστιν deest in **ξ**
e Ἑρμῆς ἐστιν] fortasse excidit exemplum vocis oxytoni cum enclitico
f Ἑρμῆς ἐστιν **φ**: Ἑρμῆς ἐστιν Ἡρακλῆς ἐστιν **S**ₐ**BL**: Ἡρακλῆς ἐστιν Ἑρμῆς ἐστιν **N**: de **V**ₐ vide §b, notam b
g διὰ τὸ — ἢ προπαροξυτόνῳ deest in **ξ**
h διὰ **LNφ**: εἴπομεν διὰ **B**
i φύλλα] φύλα **S**ₐ
j οὐχὶ **S**ₐ**LNφ**: οὐχὶ δὲ **B**
k προπαροξυτόνῳ **S**ₐ**BLA₁**ᵖ·ᶜ·: προπαροξύτονος **N**: παροξυτόνῳ **A₁**ᵃ·ᶜ·**T**
l τηνικαῦτα — ἄδικός ἐστι] οἷον ἄδικός ἐστι **B**
m κακός ἐστι **S**ₐ**φξ**: κακός ἐστιν οἰκός ἐστι **LN**
n κῆπός ἐστι, ἄδικός ἐστι **LN**: ἄδικός ἐστιν· κῆπός ἐστιν **φ**: deest in **S**ₐ**ξ**

§b But if it is placed after an oxytone or perispomenon word, as in Ἑρμῆς ἐστιν,[333] or after a trochaic word that is not paroxytone but properispomenon (because of φύλλα ἐστίν,[334] since this trochaic word is paroxytone, not properispomenon), or a proparoxytone word, in that case it throws its accent back, as in ἀγαθός ἐστι, κακός ἐστι, κῆπός ἐστι, ἄδικός ἐστι.[335]

---

[333] 'Hermes is'.
[334] 'Leaves are'.
[335] 'Is good'; 'is bad'; 'a garden is'; 'is unjust'.

§c ἐὰν δὲ μὴ οὕτως ἔχῃ,[a] [b] τὴν[c] ὀξεῖαν ἐπὶ τοῦ I δέχεται, καὶ ἐὰν προκέηται[d] αὐτοῦ[e] ἢ τροχαῖος παροξύτονος,[f] ἢ[g] πυρρίχιος παροξύτονος ἢ σπονδεῖος ὁμοίως[h] παροξύτονος, ἢ ἴαμβος πάλιν[i] παροξύτονος, τηνικαῦτα τὸν[j] τόνον ἐπὶ τοῦ I προσδέχεται,[k] οἷον[l] ‘φίλος ἐστίν’· ‘Ἀγαμέμνων ἐστίν’· ‘ἥρως ἐστίν’· ‘ἔρως ἐστίν’.

§c

[a] ἔχῃ τὴν ὀξεῖαν ἐπὶ τοῦ ι δέχεται] ὡς προτέτακται ἐστὶν τὴν ὀξεῖαν ἐπὶ τοῦ ι ἔχει **V**a

[b] ἔχῃ **BNφξ**: ἔχει **S**a**L**: ἔχῃ (ἔχει η**Y**a.c.) ἤγουν (εἴγουν **K₂Y**: ἤγουν deest in **A₂**) ὡς προτέτακται **ΦΨμq**: de **V**a vide §c, notam a

[c] τὴν ὀξεῖαν ἐπὶ τοῦ I δέχεται **αφξΦΨηq**: τὴν ὀξεῖαν ἔχει ἐπὶ τοῦ ι **ϵ**: de **V**a vide §c, notam a

[d] προκέηται **ΦΨΩζ**: πρόκειται **αξV**a**A₂**: προκῆται Ald.: πρόσκειται **φ**: προκέκται **OK₂Y**

[e] αὐτοῦ **αφm**: αὐτῷ **ξ**

[f] παροξύτονος **BφξV**a: παροξύτονος διὰ τὸ φύλλά ἐστιν **S**a**LN**: παροξύτονος οἷον μάντις, πόρνος (πόρνος deest in **A₂**), ἢ προπερισπώμενος μέν, ἔχων (ἔχει **ϵ**) δὲ (δὲ deest in **Φ**) τὴν τελευταίαν θέσει μακράν, ὡς ἔχει τὸ φοῖνιξ, κῆρυξ **ΦΨμq**

[g] ἢ πυρρίχιος παροξύτονος ἢ σπονδεῖος **h**: ἢ πυρρίχιος παροξύτονος **S**a: ἢ πυρρίχιος· ὅμοιος· σπονδεῖος **V**a: ἢ σπονδεῖος **φξΦΨμq**

[h] ὁμοίως παροξύτονος **hφξ**: ὥσπερ τὸ ἥρως, εἴλως **ΦΨμq**: deest in **S**a et **V**a

[i] πάλιν παροξύτονος **αφξ**: ὡς τὸ ἔρως, γέλως, ἢ πυρρίχιος, καθάπερ τὸ λόγος, πόνος **ΦΨμq**: ὅμοιος **V**a

[j] τὸν τόνον ἐπὶ τοῦ I προσδέχεται] ὀξύνεται **V**a

[k] προσδέχεται **S**a**φξ**: δέχεται **hΦΨμq**: de **V**a vide §c, notam j

[l] οἷον φίλος ἐστίν· Ἀγαμέμνων ἐστίν· ἥρως ἐστίν· ἔρως ἐστίν **αφ**: οἷον φίλος ἐστὶν ἥρως ἐστὶν ἔρως ἐστὶν (ἔρως ἐστὶν deest in λ) Ἀγαμέμνων ἐστίν. καὶ ταῦτα μὲν περὶ τοῦ τόνου τῶν ὀνομάτων· ἔτι καὶ περὶ τῶν ἐγκλινομένων μορίων· ἔπεται δὲ εἰπεῖν περὶ τόνου τῶν ῥημάτων καὶ τῶν ἄλλων μερῶν τοῦ λόγου **ξ**: οἷον μάντις ἐστί, φοῖνιξ ἐστί, ἥρως ἐστί, γέλως ἐστί, λόγος ἐστί **ΦΨμq**: οἷον ἔργον ἐστίν· φίλος ἐστίν· ἥρως ἐστίν· ἔρως ἐστίν· καὶ ἐὰν ἔχῃ ὁ τροχαῖος τὴν τελευτέαν (sic) θέσει μακρὰν· ὁποῖος ἂν ᾖ· οἷον κῆρυξ ἐστίν· φοῖνιξ ἐστίν **V**a

§c And if the situation is not like this, the word receives the acute accent on the *I*, whether a paroxytone trochee precedes it, or a paroxytone pyrrhic or a spondee that is likewise paroxytone, or an iamb that is again paroxytone, in that case the word gets the accent on the *I*, as in φίλος ἐστίν, Ἀγαμέμνων ἐστίν, ἥρως ἐστίν, ἔρως ἐστίν.[336]

---

[336] 'A friend is'; 'Agamemnon is'; 'a hero is'; 'love is'.

2.6 *On enclitics 4*

On enclitics 4 is a very brief, condensed treatise on enclitics, concentrating almost entirely on laying out which word forms are enclitics; the work reads like a summary of material on this topic to be found in other treatises (compare especially *On enclitics 1*, §§a–j). In the last paragraph, *On enclitics 4* moves onto the circumstances under which enclitics throw their accents back, but the treatise breaks off after mentioning only enclitics after spondaic words (paroxytone spondaic words in particular are meant, but 'paroxytone' is not specified).

In one manuscript (our *Ξ*ₐ), *On enclitics 4* is transmitted as part of the so-called London commentary on the *Τέχνη γραμματική* attributed to Dionysius Thrax. But *On enclitics 4* is absent from codex Londiniensis Add. 5118 (London, British Library), which contains the other and fuller text of the London commentary on which Hilgard's edition is based, and our treatise is otherwise transmitted independently of commentaries on (Ps.)-Dionysius Thrax. *On enclitics 4* appears to be a pre-existing text inserted into the London commentary on the *Τέχνη γραμματική*, along with some material on other grammatical topics (see Hilgard 1901: xxxvi).

A notable feature of *On enclitics 4* is that a New Testament quotation features among its examples of phrases with enclitics (ἁμαρτωλός εἰμι 'I am a sinful (man)' at §c, from Luke 5:8).[337]

2.6.1 Sources and stemma

On enclitics 4 is transmitted in the following manuscripts and early printed books, listed here according to the main families and sub-families that we posit:

Family β

Y (15th cent.): Paris, Bibliothèque Nationale de France, Parisinus Graecus 1773, folio 288v.

Yₐ (15th cent.): Paris, Bibliothèque Nationale de France, Parisinus Graecus 2047, folio 1r.

Y_b (15th–16th cent.): Paris, Bibliothèque Nationale de France, Paris. suppl. Gr. 58, folio 16v.

Y_c (16th cent.): Vatican City, Biblioteca Apostolica Vaticana, Vaticanus Graecus 1745, folios 139v–140r.

Y_d (16th cent.): Vatican City, Biblioteca Apostolica Vaticana, Vaticanus Graecus 2246, folios 57v–58v.

---

[337] Manuscript **D** adds a further example with Christian content, τοῦ θεοῦ ὕπο εὐεργετοῦμαι 'I am treated kindly by God' (see §d, note f). Compare an example used by Gregory of Corinth to illustrate anastrophe of prepositions: τοῦ Θεοῦ μου ὕπο εὐεργετοῦμαι 'I am treated kindly by my God' (*Περὶ συντάξεως λόγου* 102 Donnet).

Family i

$\varXi_d$ (13th cent.): Athens, Ἐθνική Βιβλιοθήκη της Ἑλλάδος (*EBE*; National Library of Greece), 1089, folio 86r.

B (14th cent.): Milan, Biblioteca Ambrosiana, Ambrosianus G 27 sup. = Martini-Bassi 389, folios 196v–197v.

$\varXi_b$ (14th cent.): Paris, Bibliothèque Nationale de France, Paris. suppl. Gr. 202, folios 113r–114r.

$\varXi_c$ (14th cent.): Vatican City, Biblioteca Apostolica Vaticana, Vaticanus Reginensis Graecus Pio II 54, folio 470v.

$\varXi$ (15th cent.): Cambridge, University Library, Cantabrigiensis Gg.I.2 = 1397, folio 66r–v.

$\varXi_a$ (15th cent.): Madrid, Biblioteca Nacional de España, Matritensis 4613 = de Andrés 70 (previously N 81), folio 34r–v.

Ald. (1496): *Thesaurus: Cornu copiae et Horti Adonidis*, printed by the Aldine Press in Venice (see the bibliography under Aldus 1496), folio 229v. Copies of the text derived from **Ald.** appear in further early printed books including the work listed in the bibliography as Curio (1522) (at quire Θ, folio v verso), and the following works whose copies derive from Curio (1522): de Gourmont (1523) (at folio 8v, in the fourth of five sequences of folio numbers this book contains); Froben (1524) (at quire V, folio 6r); Aldus (1524) (at quire M, folio vii recto–verso, i.e. folio 95r–v in the second of two series of folio numbers this book contains); Sessa and de Ravanis (1525) (at quire G, folio ii verso). The two sixteenth-century manuscripts listed next contain further copies derived from printed books.

Rome, Biblioteca Casanatense, Casanatensis 1710 (16th cent.), folios 76v–77r, copied by Petros Hypsilas. This is a copy of **Ald.**

Turin, Biblioteca Nazionale Universitaria, Taurinensis B VI 8 = Zuretti 10 (16th cent.), folio 5a–b. This is a copy of the text in Aldus (1524).

Manuscript D

D (15th cent.): Oxford, Bodleian Library, Baroccianus 76, folio 294r–v, copied by Michael Lyzigos. A copy almost identical to that in **D** appears in the 15th-century codex Mutinensis α.W.5.5 (165 Puntoni), folio 215r; this came to our attention too late for incorporation into the stemma and apparatus, but the text we print would be unaffected.

In addition to these witnesses, Maria Giovanna Sandri points out to us that Codex Alexandrinus 364 is likely to contain a copy of *On Enclitics 4* belonging to our family i: the information given by Moschonas (1965: 215–16) suggests that folios 124v–144r of this manuscript transmit material similar to that found in our manuscript $\varXi_b$, at folios 57r–116v. The Secretary of the Patriarchate of Alexandria informs us that the manuscript cannot be accessed for the time being.

We reconstruct the stemma for *On enclitics 4* as shown in Figure 2.8.

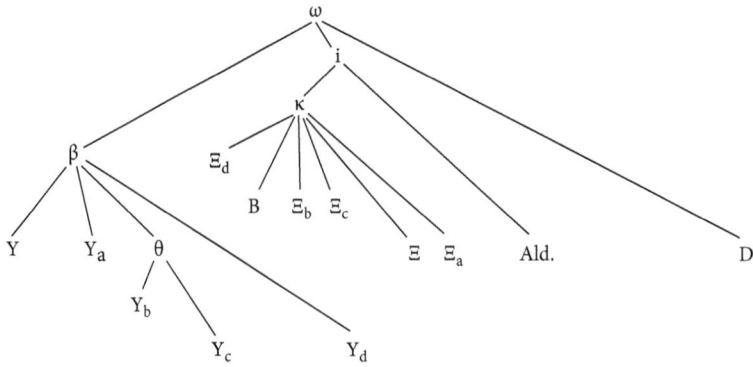

Fig. 2.8 Stemma for *On enclitics 4*

The following subsection explains our reasons for positing families β and **i** (but not the reasoning behind the hyparchetypes *θ* and *κ*, which are of little significance for the reconstruction of the text).

2.6.1.1 Evidence for families β and i

We consider all manuscripts of *On enclitics 4* except **D** to belong to one of two families, which we call β and **i**. Given the short compass of *On enclitics 4*, the textual evidence for these groupings is necessarily limited, and there are no clear errors shared by all and only the witnesses we place under β, or by all and only those we place under **i**. But in a few places manuscript **D** agrees in phraseology with family **i** against β, and we suspect an innovation on the part of β. In a few other places **D** agrees in phraseology with family β against **i**, and we suspect an innovation on the part of **i**. Tables 2.38 and 2.39 lay out this evidence, such as it is.

2.6.2 Previous editions

Bekker printed this treatise in the third volume of his *Anecdota Graeca* (Bekker 1821: 1155–6), on the basis of **Ald.** and **Y** (see section 2.1.2).

As mentioned in section 2.6, manuscript *Ξ*ₐ transmits *On enclitics 4* as part of the London commentary on the *Τέχνη γραμματική* attributed to Dionysius Thrax, and for this reason Hilgard (1901: 466) printed *On enclitics 4* as part of his edition of that commentary—albeit in small print, to mark its status as an interpolation. Hilgard's text is based mainly on manuscript *Ξ*ₐ, but he also consulted **Ald.** and Bekker's text (see Hilgard 1901: 466, note to lines 3–21). Hilgard does not record variant readings for *On enclitics 4*, but he brackets two points in the text for deletion. (We adopt the first of these deletions at §a, note b, and the second concerns a καί that is only read in *Ξ*ₐ: see §e, note b.)

Table 2.38 Evidence for family β

Reading of family β (comprising manuscripts Y Y_a Y_b Y_c Y_d)	Reading(s) of the rest of the tradition (comprising family i and manuscript D)
§d, note d: example(s) omitted in Y Y_a Y_b Y_c Y_d We take the archetype to have had the example καί μιν φωνήσας (shared by D and i), with or without the additional example καί οἱ ἐπευχόμενος found only in i.	καί μιν φωνήσας **D**: καί οἱ ἐπευχόμενος (ἐπευχόμενοι **Ald.**) καί μιν φωνήσας **i**
§d, note f: ἕνεκά σου, ἕνεκά μου καὶ αἱ προθέσεις περί σου καὶ διά σε Y Y_a Y_b Y_c Y_d We take the reading of the archetype to be close to that of **i**, whose sense and phrasing overlaps significantly with that of **D**; note especially the shared phrases μετὰ (δὲ) τοῦ ἕνεκεν and μετὰ προθέσεως.	μετὰ δὲ τοῦ (οὖ $Ξ_a$) ἕνεκεν (ἕνεκεν $Ξ_d$ **B**: ἕνεκε $Ξ_b$ $Ξ_c$ $Ξ$ $Ξ_a$) τὸν οἰκεῖον φυλάττουσι τόνον (τόνον φυλάττουσι $Ξ_a$) ταῦτα· ἕνεκα σοῦ ἕνεκα ἐμοῦ (ἐμοῦ $Ξ_d$ **B** $Ξ_b$ $Ξ_c$ $Ξ$ $Ξ_a$: εἰμοῦ **Ald.**)· καὶ μετὰ προθέσεως περὶ σοῦ διὰ σὲ καὶ τὰ τοιαῦτα **i**: ἔτι οὐδὲ μετὰ τοῦ ἕνεκεν ἐγκλίνονται, οἷον ἕνεκα σοῦ, ἕνεκα ἐμοῦ, οὐδὲ μετὰ προθέσεως, οἷον περὶ ἐμοῦ, κατὰ σοῦ. σημείωσαι δὲ ὅτι πολλάκις ὅταν ἐπάγωνται μετὰ τὰ ὀνόματα δισύλλαβοι προθέσεις ἀναβιβάζουσι τὸν τόνον οἷον τοῦ θεοῦ ὕπο εὐεργετοῦμαι, τοῦ φίλου πέρι λαλῶ **D**
§g, note a: φυλακτέον Y Y_a Y_b Y_c Y_d ($Ξ_d$ also has φυλακτέον, but this is probably an individual error.)	παραφυλακτέον (παρατηρητέον **B**: φυλακτέον $Ξ_d$) **iD**

Table 2.39 Evidence for family i

Reading of family i (comprising $Ξ_d$ B $Ξ_b$ $Ξ_c$ $Ξ$ $Ξ_a$ Ald.)	Reading(s) of the rest of the tradition (comprising family β and manuscript D)
§a, note c: ὀνόματα, ῥήματα, ἀντωνυμίαι, ἐπιρρήματα καὶ σύνδεσμοι (ὄνομα ῥῆμα σύνδεσμος ἀντωνυμία ἐπίρρημα $Ξ_d$) **B** $Ξ_b$ $Ξ_c$ $Ξ$ $Ξ_a$ **Ald.** (We take the reading in $Ξ_d$ to be an innovation.)	ὄνομα, ῥῆμα, ἀντωνυμία, ἐπίρρημα καὶ σύνδεσμος **βD**
§b, note a: ὄνομα ἤτοι ὡς ὄνομα $Ξ_d$ **B** $Ξ_b$ $Ξ_c$ $Ξ$ $Ξ_a$ **Ald.**	ὄνομα μέν, ὡς **βD**
§c, note a: ῥήματα τὸ εἰμί (ἠμί **Ald.**) **B** $Ξ_b$ $Ξ_c$ $Ξ$ $Ξ_a$ **Ald.**: ῥῆμα τὸ εἰμί $Ξ_d$ We take ῥήματα δὲ τὸ εἰμί to be the reading of the archetype, inherited by YY_aY_d. D and (independently) θ changed this to ῥῆμα δὲ ὡς τὸ εἰμί to follow the pattern of ὄνομα μέν, ὡς τὸ at the beginning of §b (and Y_c removed the ὡς), while i removed the δὲ to give ῥήματα τὸ εἰμί (and $Ξ_d$ further turned ῥήματα into ῥῆμα).	ῥήματα δὲ τὸ εἰμί YY_aY_d: ῥῆμα δὲ ὡς τὸ εἰμί Y_bD: ῥῆμα δὲ τὸ εἰμί Y_c

2.6.3 *On enclitics 4*: text and translation

§a *Περὶ*[a] *ἐγκλινομένων*

Ἐγκλίνονται, ἤγουν ἀναβιβάζουσι τὸν τόνον {ὅτε[b] καλεῖ ἀπὸ} τῶν τοῦ λόγου μερῶν πέντε, ὄνομα,[c] ῥῆμα, ἀντωνυμία, ἐπίρρημα καὶ σύνδεσμος.

§b ὄνομα μέν,[a] ὡς τὸ *ΤΙΣ*[b] καὶ αἱ[c] τούτου πτώσεις καὶ οἱ ἀριθμοὶ καὶ τὸ[d] οὐδέτερον *ΤΙ·* οἷον 'οἶκός[e] [f] τις', 'ἔμαθόν[g] τινος', 'ἦλθόν τινες', 'ἤκουσά τινων', 'ἔμαθόν[h] τι' καὶ τὰ[i] ἰσοδυναμοῦντα τούτοις τὸ *ΤΟΥ* καὶ τὸ *ΤΩΙ·* 'ἤκουσά του', 'δέδωκά[j] τῳ' καὶ τὰ τοιαῦτα.[k]

§c ῥήματα[a] δὲ τὸ *ΕΙΜΙ, ΦΗΜΙ,* οἷον[b] 'ἁμαρτωλός[c] εἰμι', 'ἐγώ φημι'. τὸ[d] δεύτερον *ΦΗΙΣ* ἀνέγκλιτον. τὸ[e] τρίτον *ΦΗΣΙΝ* ἐγκλίνεται, οἷον[f] 'αὐτός φησι'·[g] καὶ[h] τὰ πληθυντικὰ 'αὐτοί φαμεν', 'τί φατε', τί φασι'· καὶ τὰ πληθυντικὰ τοῦ *ΕΙΜΙ* 'ἄνθρωποί ἐσμεν', 'ἄνθρωποί εἰσιν', 'ἄνθρωποί ἐστε' καὶ τὰ ὅμοια.

---

§a

[a] *Περὶ ἐγκλινομένων* YY[d]κD: *Περὶ ἐγκλινομένων ἐκ τῶν τοῦ Χειροβοσκοῦ* **Ald.**: *Παύλου Αἰγινήτου ἰατρικὰ* **Y**[a]: sine titulo *θ*

[b] ὅτε καλεῖ ἀπὸ del. Hilgard

[c] ὄνομα — καὶ σύνδεσμος **βD**: ὀνόματα, ῥήματα, ἀντωνυμίαι, ἐπιρρήματα καὶ σύνδεσμοι **i**: ὄνομα ῥῆμα σύνδεσμος ἀντωνυμία ἐπίρρημα **Ξ**[d]

§b

[a] μέν, ὡς **βD**: ἤτοι ὡς ὄνομα **i**

[b] τίς — οὐδέτερον τί· οἷον deest in **D**

[c] αἱ **βκ**: deest in **Ald.**

[d] τὸ **κ**: deest in **β Ald.**

[e] οἶκός τις — ἔμαθόν τι] ἤκουσά τινος, ἦλθέ τις, εἶδόν τινα, ἔδωκά τινι **D**

[f] οἶκός τις] εἰκός τις *θ*

[g] 'ἔμαθόν τινος' — 'ἤκουσά τινων' iteravit **Ξ**[a]

[h] ἔμαθόν **β Ald.**: ἔπαθόν **κ**

[i] τὰ ἰσοδυναμοῦντα τούτοις τὸ *ΤΟΥ* καὶ τὸ *ΤΩΙ* deest in **D**

[j] δέδωκά **βΞ**[d]**BΞ**[b]**Ξ**[c]**Ξ Ald.**: καὶ δέδωκά **Ξ**[a]: ἔδωκά **D**

[k] τοιαῦτα **βi**: ὅμοια **D**

§c

[a] ῥήματα δὲ τὸ εἰμί YY[a]Y[d]: ῥήματα τὸ εἰμί **κ**: ῥήματα τὸ ἠμί **Ald.**: ῥῆμα δὲ ὡς τὸ εἰμί Y[b]**D**: ῥῆμα δὲ τὸ εἰμί Y[c]: ῥῆμα τὸ εἰμί **Ξ**[d]

[b] οἷον **βD**: deest in **i**

[c] ἁμαρτωλός εἰμι, ἐγώ φημι **βi**: ἐγώ εἰμι, ἐγώ φημι **D**

[d] τὸ δεύτερον *ΦΗΙΣ* ἀνέγκλιτον **βi**: τὰ δὲ δεύτερα οὐκ ἐγκλίνονται οἷον σὺ εἶς σὺ φῆς **D**

[e] τὸ τρίτον *ΦΗΣΙΝ* ἐγκλίνεται **Ξ**[d]**BΞΞ**[a] **Ald.**: τὸ τρίτον φησίν τοῦτο ἐγκλίνεται **β**: τὰ δὲ τρίτα ἐγκλίνονται **D**: τὸ τρίτον φης ἐγκλίνεται **Ξ**[b]**Ξ**[c]

[f] οἷον] ὡς τὸ **Ξ**[d]: deest in **BΞ**[b]**Ξ**[c]**ΞΞ**[a]

[g] post φησι add. ἐκεῖνός ἐστι **D**

[h] καὶ τὰ πληθυντικὰ — καὶ τὰ πληθυντικὰ τοῦ *ΕΙΜΙ* (τοῦ εἰς μι i.t. **Ξ**[c]: γρ τοῦ εἰμι i.m. **Ξ**[c]) 'ἄνθρωποί ἐσμεν', 'ἄνθρωποί εἰσιν', 'ἄνθρωποί ἐστε' καὶ τὰ ὅμοια ('ἄνθρωποί εἰσιν', 'ἄνθρωποί ἐστε' καὶ τὰ ὅμοια YY[a]*θ*: ἄνθρωποί ἐστε ἄνθρωποί εἰσι καὶ τὰ ὅμοια Y[d]: ἄνθρωποί εἰσιν, ἄνθρωποί ἐστε **BΞ**[b]**Ξ**[c]**ΞΞ**[a]: ἄνθρωποί ἐστε ἄνθρωποί εἰσιν **Ξ**[d] **Ald.**) **βi**: καὶ τὰ πληθυντικὰ αὐτοί ἐστε ἡμεῖς φαμεν καὶ τὰ λοιπά. τὰ δὲ δυϊκὰ μᾶλλον οὐκ ἐγκλίνονται οἷον νῶϊν ἐστον σφῶϊν οὐκ ἔστον **D**

§a On enclitics

Five of the parts of speech lean back, that is to say throw their accent back: noun, verb, pronoun, adverb, and conjunction.

§b Noun, as in *ΤΙΣ* and its cases and numbers and the neuter *ΤΙ*. For example, οἶκός τις, ἔμαθόν τινος, ἦλθόν τινες, ἤκουσά τινων, ἔμαθόν τι,[338] and their equivalents *ΤΟΥ* and *ΤΩΙ*: ἤκουσά του, δέδωκά τῳ,[339] and such examples.

§c And the verbs [are] *ΕΙΜΙ* and *ΦΗΜΙ*, as in ἁμαρτωλός εἰμι,[340] ἐγώ φημι.[341] The second person form *ΦΗΙΣ* is not enclitic. The third person form *ΦΗΣΙΝ* is an enclitic, as in αὐτός φησι, and the plurals, [as in] αὐτοί φαμεν, τί φατε, τί φασι, and the plurals of *ΕΙΜΙ*, [as in] ἄνθρωποί ἐσμεν, ἄνθρωποί εἰσιν, ἄνθρωποί ἐστε, and the like.[342]

---

[338] 'A certain house'; 'I learned from someone'; 'some people came'; 'I heard from some people'; 'I learned something'.
[339] 'I heard from someone'; 'I gave to someone'.
[340] New Testament, Luke 5:8: 'I am a sinful (man)'.
[341] 'I say'.
[342] 'He himself says'; 'we ourselves say'; 'what do you (pl.) say?'; 'what do they say?'; 'we are people'; 'they are people'; 'you (pl.) are people'.

§d καὶ[a] αἱ ἀντωνυμίαι 'ἔδωκάς μοι,'[b] 'ἔτυψάς με,' 'ἤκουσά σου,' 'παρέσχόν[c] σοι,' 'καὶ[d][e] μιν φωνήσας'. μετὰ[f] δὲ τοῦ ΕΝΕΚΑ τὸν οἰκεῖον φυλάττουσι τόνον ταῦτα· 'ἕνεκα σοῦ,' 'ἕνεκα ἐμοῦ'· καὶ μετὰ προθέσεως 'περὶ σοῦ,' 'διὰ σέ' καὶ τὰ τοιαῦτα.

§e ἐπίρρημα[a] τὸ ΠΟΤΕ, οἷον 'σύ ποτε,' 'ἐγώ ποτε'· καὶ τὸ ΠΟΘΕΝ, οἷον 'ἦλθέ ποθεν'· καὶ τὸ ΠΩΣ, ΠΗ, ΠΟΥ τὰ[b] ὡς ἐπιρρήματα 'ἦλθέ πως,' 'ἀπῆλθέ που,' 'ἀνεχώρησέ πη'.

§f σύνδεσμοι[a] δὲ ἐγκλίνονται ΜΕΝ, ΔΕ, ΤΕ, ΓΑΡ· οἷον 'ἐγώ μεν,' 'σύ δε,' 'αὐτός τε,' 'ἄλλός γαρ' καὶ τὰ τοιαῦτα.

§g ἐκεῖνο δὲ παραφυλακτέον[a] ὅτι, ἐὰν[b] σπονδειακὴ πρόκειται λέξις, ἤγουν δισύλλαβος, τὸν ἴδιον φυλάττει τόνον, οἷον 'ἤδη φαμέν,' 'οὕτως ἐστίν,' 'οὕτω[c] [d] ποτέ' καὶ τὰ ὅμοια.[e]

§d

[a] καὶ αἱ ἀντωνυμίαι β: καὶ τῶν ἀντωνυμιῶν ἐκεῖναι i: ἀντωνυμία D

[b] ἔδωκάς μοι — ἤκουσά (ἤκουσάς Y_d **Ald.**) σου β𝛯_d𝛯𝛯_a **Ald.**: ἔδωκάς μοι ἔτυψά σε ἤκουσά σου B𝛯_b𝛯_c: ἤκουσά σου, ἔδωκάς μοι, ἔτυψά σε D

[c] παρέσχόν (πάρεσχόν YY_a: παρέσχον B𝛯_b𝛯𝛯_a: παρεσχον Y_b: παρεσόν Y_c: πάρεσχον 𝛯_c) σοι YY_aθκD: ἔλεγόν σοι Y_d: deest in 𝛯_d **Ald.**

[d] καὶ μιν φωνήσας D: καὶ οἱ ἐπευχόμενοι καὶ μιν φωνήσας 𝛯_d𝛯_c **Ald.**: καὶ οἱ ἐπευχόμενος καὶ μιν φωνήσας B𝛯_b𝛯_a: deest in β

[e] post καὶ μιν φωνήσας verba αἱ δὲ εὐθεῖαι οὐκ ἐγκλίνονται praebet D

[f] μετὰ δὲ τοῦ (οὗ 𝛯_a) ἕνεκεν (ἕνεκεν 𝛯_dB: ἕνεκε 𝛯_b𝛯_c𝛯𝛯_a) τὸν οἰκεῖον φυλάττουσι τόνον (τόνον φυλάττουσι 𝛯_a) ταῦτα· ἕνεκα σοῦ ἕνεκα (ἕνεκεν 𝛯_d) ἐμοῦ (ἐμοῦ κ: εἰμοῦ **Ald.**)· καὶ μετὰ προθέσεως περὶ σοῦ διὰ σέ καὶ τὰ τοιαῦτα (καὶ τὰ τοιαῦτα om. 𝛯_d) i: ἔτι οὐδὲ μετὰ τοῦ ἕνεκεν ἐγκλίνονται, οἷον ἕνεκα σοῦ, ἕνεκα ἐμοῦ, οὐδὲ μετὰ προθέσεως, οἷον περὶ ἐμοῦ, κατὰ σοῦ. σημείωσαι δὲ ὅτι πολλάκις ὅταν ἐπάγωνται μετὰ τὰ ὀνόματα δισύλλαβοι προθέσεις ἀναβιβάζουσι τὸν τόνον οἷον τοῦ θεοῦ ὕπο εὐεργετοῦμαι, τοῦ φίλου πέρι λαλῶ D: ἕνεκά σου, ἕνεκά μου καὶ αἱ προθέσεις περί σου καὶ διά σε β

§e

[a] ἐπίρρημα — ἀνεχώρησε πη (sed ἐγώ ποτε iteravit 𝛯_a) B𝛯_b𝛯_c𝛯𝛯_a **Ald.**: ἐπίρρημα οἷον τὸ ποτέ, σύ ποτε, ἐγώ ποτε· καὶ τὸ πόθεν οἷον ἦλθέ ποθεν· καὶ τὸ πῶς οἷον ἦλθέ πως· καὶ τὸ ποῦ ἀπῆλθέ (οἷον ἀπῆλθέ Y_d: ἀπελθέ Y_c) που ἀναχωρῆσαί (ἀνεχώρησέ θY_d) που β: ἐπίρρημα τὸ ποτέ ἦλθέ πως ἀπῆλθέ που ἀνεχώρησέ πη 𝛯_d: ἐπίρρημα οἷον τὸ ποτέ τὸ πόθεν τὸ πῶς τὸ ποῦ καὶ τὰ ὅμοια· οἷον ἦλθέ ποτε ἀφίκετό ποθεν καὶ πως ἦλθεν ἀπῆλθέ που D

[b] τὰ B𝛯_b𝛯_c𝛯 **Ald.**: καὶ τὰ 𝛯_a

§f

[a] σύνδεσμοι (οἱ σύνδεσμοι β) δὲ (δὲ om. 𝛯_d) ἐγκλίνονται ΜΕΝ, ΔΕ, (ΜΕΝ, ΔΕ deest in Y_d) ΤΕ, ΓΑΡ (γε Y_d)· οἷον 'ἐγώ μεν,' (ἐγώ μεν deest in Y_d) 'σύ δε' (δε i: γε β), 'αὐτός τε' (τε i: γε β), 'ἄλλός' (ἄλλός β𝛯_dB𝛯_b𝛯𝛯_a: ἄλλως 𝛯_c: ἄλλοί **Ald.**: deest in Y_d) γαρ' (γαρ deest in Y_d) καὶ τὰ τοιαῦτα (καὶ τὰ τοιαῦτα om. 𝛯_d) βi: σύνδεσμος οἷον μὲν δὲ τε γὰρ οἷον ἐγώ μεν σύ δε αὐτός τε ἄλλος γαρ καὶ τὰ ὅμοια D

§g

[a] παραφυλακτέον iD: φυλακτέον β𝛯_d: παρατηρητέον B

[b] ἐὰν σπονδειακὴ (σπονδαϊκὴ θ) πρόκειται λέξις, ἤγουν δισύλλαβος, τὸν ἴδιον φυλάττει τόνον YY_aθ **Ald.**: ἐὰν σπονδειακὴ (σπονδιακὴ 𝛯) πρόκειται (πρόκηται B^s.l.) λέξις ἤγουν δισύλλαβος μακρὰς ἔχουσα καὶ τὰς δύο ἐπιφέρηται δὲ ἐγκλινομένη δισύλλαβος τὸν ἴδιον φυλάττει τόνον κ: εἰ σπονδιακὴ δισύλλαβος ἡ λέξις ἐστὶν ἡ προτέρα, οὐ γίνεται ἔγκλισις D: ἐὰν σπονδεῖος πρόκειται ἢ πυρρίχιος ἢ ἴαμβος τὸν ἴδιον φυλάττει τόνον Y_d

[c] οὕτω ποτὲ καὶ τὰ ὅμοια] φίλος ἐστί λέων ἐστί Σόλων εἰμί καὶ τὰ ὅμοια Y_d

[d] οὕτω] οὗτο θ

[e] post ὅμοια verba καὶ ἰαμβικὴ Σόλων εἰμί praebet Y

§d And the pronouns: ἔδωκάς μοι, ἔτυψάς με, ἤκουσά σου, παρέσχόν σοι, καί μιν φωνήσας.³⁴³ But with *ΕΝΕΚΑ* these keep their own accent: ἕνεκα σοῦ, ἕνεκα ἐμοῦ.³⁴⁴ And with a preposition: περὶ σοῦ, διὰ σέ,³⁴⁵ and the like.

§e An adverb [is] *ΠΟΤΕ*, as in σύ ποτε, ἐγώ ποτε, and *ΠΟΘΕΝ*, as in ἦλθέ ποθεν, and the *ΠΩΣ*, *ΠΗ*, and *ΠΟΥ* that are used as adverbs: ἦλθέ πως, ἀπῆλθέ που, ἀνεχώρησέ πη.³⁴⁶

§f And the conjunctions *ΜΕΝ*, *ΔΕ*, *ΤΕ*, and *ΓΑΡ* are enclitic,³⁴⁷ as in ἐγώ μεν, σύ δε, αὐτός τε, ἄλλός γαρ, and the like.³⁴⁸

§g And one must be aware that if a spondaic word, that is to say a disyllabic one, precedes, then [the enclitic] keeps its own accent, as in ἤδη φαμέν, οὕτως ἐστίν, οὕτω ποτέ,³⁴⁹ and the like.

³⁴³ 'You gave to me'; 'you hit me'; 'I heard you'; 'I provided to you'; e.g. *Il.* 1.201: 'and speaking [he addressed winged words to] her'.
³⁴⁴ 'For your sake'; 'for my sake'.
³⁴⁵ 'About you'; 'because of you'.
³⁴⁶ 'You at some time'; 'I at some time'; 'he/she came from somewhere'; 'somehow he/she has come'; 'he/she went off somewhere'; 'he/she withdrew somewhere/in some way'.
³⁴⁷ We are not aware of other sources for the claim that *ΜΕΝ*, *ΔΕ*, and *ΓΑΡ* are enclitics.
³⁴⁸ 'I on the one hand'; 'but you'; 'and he himself'; 'for another'.
³⁴⁹ 'We already say'; 'it is so'; 'thus at some time'.

2.7 Ideas reflected in the Byzantine treatises

The treatises presented in sections 2.1–2.6 can be considered broadly Byzantine in date, and we have seen that they deal with two main questions: (a) how are we to accent sequences of words that include enclitics, and (b) which words are enclitics (and under what circumstances)? The following subsections will try to unpack the main doctrines bearing on the first of these questions, and an aspect of the second question will concern us in Chapter 3. In section 2.7.1 we begin by laying out some general features of ancient terminology and thought on the Greek accent system, knowledge of which is presupposed by our texts on enclitics. Many of these features have been inherited into our own learning and teaching of ancient Greek accentuation, but we will see that some differences are worth appreciating too.[350]

2.7.1 Ancient terminology and thought on Greek accents

From the Hellenistic period onwards, mainstream Greek theory of prosody operates with the concept that there were three accent marks, each of them with its own sign:

- an acute or 'high' accent, ὀξεῖα (προσῳδία): ´
- a circumflex or 'drawn around' accent, περισπωμένη (προσῳδία): ^
- a grave or 'low' accent, βαρεῖα (προσῳδία): `

From an ancient point of view the acute and circumflex have a different status from the grave, and are sometimes said to be 'accents' in the proper sense of the word.[351] The acute represents an accent on a short vowel or on the second half (or 'mora') of a long vowel or diphthong, while the circumflex represents what we would call an accent on the first mora of the long vowel or diphthong. In ancient terms, the circumflex represents an acute followed by a grave on a single syllable (as the shape ^ suggests)[352]—a point which brings us to the original meaning of the grave accent.

Ancient scholars considered that any syllable that does not have an acute or a circumflex accent has a grave accent, and could theoretically be written with a grave.[353] The grave accent thus conveys the absence of an acute or circumflex: it is

---

[350] The following discussion overlaps with the discussion at Probert (2019: 47–51), where more detail can be found.

[351] See e.g. Sch. D. Thr. 294.5.

[352] See e.g. Dionysius of Halicarnassus, *De compositione uerborum* 11.16, and cf. section 2.8.2 with passages (2.15) and (2.16).

[353] See e.g. (Ps.)-Dionysius Thrax, Supplement Περὶ προσῳδιῶν 110.5–6.

equivalent to our notion of lack of accent. This point may come as a surprise to readers familiar with the way in which we use the grave accent mark in writing ancient Greek today—exclusively as a replacement for an acute accent on a final syllable, appearing in most contexts that arise in connected speech. This specialized use of the written grave accent mark had been developed by late antiquity, but conceptually a final syllable with this kind of grave was a special case of an unaccented syllable, and *any* unaccented syllable was describable as having a grave accent.[354]

A series of ancient technical terms for words with accents on particular syllables is familiar from our own tradition:

- ὀξύτονος 'oxytone' means 'having an acute on the last syllable', as in καλός.
- παροξύτονος 'paroxytone' means 'having an acute on the penultimate syllable', as in Ἰωάννης.
- προπαροξύτονος 'proparoxytone' means 'having an acute on the antepenultimate syllable', as in Θεόδωρος.
- περισπώμενος 'perispomenon' means 'having a circumflex on the final syllable', as in Λουκᾶς.
- προπερισπώμενος 'properispomenon' means 'having a circumflex on the penultimate syllable', as in κῆπος.

This terminology takes the final syllable as its reference point. For example, the term ὀξύτονος literally means 'high-pitched' or 'with the acute accent', but in most contexts ὀξύτονος signals an acute accent on the final syllable in particular.[355] The term παροξύτονος literally means 'with an acute accent adjacent'; the concept of the final syllable is again left understood, so that we understand

---

[354] It does not necessarily follow that a syllable with a contextual grave accent was indistinguishable in pronunciation from other unaccented syllables. Moore-Blunt (1978) and Mazzucchi (1979) show that in early accented papyri, syllables that ancient grammarians consider to have a contextual grave accent are sometimes written with an acute, sometimes (and according to Mazzucchi considerably more often) with a grave, and most often without any accent mark at all. The vacillation seen here could have various origins: (a) hesitation over whether to indicate the 'natural' or the contextual accent (on 'natural accents' see below); (b) hesitation over whether to categorize syllables with a reduced accent as accented or unaccented; (c) hesitation over whether to consider a particular instance of an oxytone word to be followed by a pause (see on the 'lulling rule', later in this section); (d) in certain contexts, hesitation over whether to consider the following word an enclitic (again see on the 'lulling rule'); (e) a feel for the influence of contextual factors beyond those mentioned in grammatical texts. These possibilities need not be mutually exclusive.

[355] Less commonly, ὀξύτονος and the related ὀξύνω and ὀξυτονέω 'give an acute accent' are used in relation to any syllable with an acute accent, but unless the syllable is the last one in a word the context usually makes clear which syllable is meant. See for example *On enclitics 1*, §f: καὶ αἱ πληθυντικαὶ τοῦ τε πρώτου καὶ δευτέρου, ἡμῶν, ὑμῶν, ἡμῖν, ὑμῖν, ἡμᾶς, ὑμᾶς, τετράχρονοι οὖσαι, ἐπειδὰν ἐγκλίνωνται τὴν πρώτην συλλαβὴν ὀξύνουσιν 'And the plural pronouns of the first and second [person], ἡμῶν, ὑμῶν, ἡμῖν, ὑμῖν, ἡμᾶς, ὑμᾶς, since they contain four units of time, give their first syllables an acute accent when they throw back their accents'. For a scholion that we take to contain an exception, perhaps because a longer discussion has been compressed, see passage (3.13).

'with an acute accent on the syllable adjacent to the final one'. Similarly, προπαροξύτονος literally means 'with an acute accent pre-adjacent', but we understand 'with an acute accent on the syllable before the one adjacent to the final syllable'. The term περισπώμενος literally means 'having a circumflex accent', but in most contexts the term signals a circumflex on the final syllable in particular;[356] and so on.

In a similar vein, but less familiar to us, is a term βαρύτονος, literally meaning 'with a grave accent'. In most contexts this term and the related verbs βαρύνω and βαρυτονέω ('give a grave accent') are used in relation to forms whose final syllable in particular has a grave accent.[357] Since the grave accent stands for lack of either acute or circumflex accent, a βαρύτονος word is one with neither an acute nor a circumflex on its final syllable.[358]

Ancient scholars operate with a distinction between a word's 'natural' or 'own' accent (κατὰ φύσιν τόνος, ἴδιος τόνος, οἰκεῖος τόνος, or κύριος τόνος) on the one hand,[359] and on the other hand the way the word is accented in connected speech.[360] The 'natural' accent is either an acute or a circumflex, and is similar to our concept of the accent with which a word is listed in a dictionary. But whereas we consider the dictionary forms of some ancient Greek words to lack any accent (e.g. οὐ, ἐκ, εἰ, γε, πω), for ancient scholars every single Greek word has an acute or circumflex as its natural accent (οὔ, ἔκ, εἴ, γέ, πῶ). To arrrive at the correct form in context, ancient scholars require us to know firstly the form with the natural accent, and secondly a set of rules that will add, delete, or alter accents under certain conditions. For example, we have already alluded to a rule affecting words whose natural accent is an acute on the final syllable, like καλός 'beautiful'. Following an ancient metaphor we call this the 'lulling rule':[361]

The 'lulling rule':[362]

An acute on a final syllable is turned—or 'lulled'—into a grave in connected speech (καλός → καλὸς ἀνήρ), except under the following conditions:

---

[356] For the possibility of using the word περισπώμενος, or the related verb περισπάω 'give a circumflex accent', in relation to a penultimate syllable, where the context makes clear that this is the intended syllable, see e.g. John Philoponus, *Praecepta Tonica* 20 Xenis (ἐν τῷ 'ἀλλοῖος' ἡ μὲν μέση περισπᾶται 'in the word ἀλλοῖος the middle syllable has a circumflex').

[357] For uses in relation to syllables other than the final one, with contexts making clear which syllable is intended, see again John Philoponus, *Praecepta Tonica* 20 Xenis.

[358] In practice, this term is most often used for an accent falling as far from the end of the word as the usual limitations on the position of the Greek accent allow: what modern scholars would call a 'recessive' accent. However, the term βαρύτονος is not restricted to recessive accents, either as explicitly defined or as used in practice. For further detail see Probert (2015: 939–41).

[359] For the term κατὰ φύσιν τόνος, see *On enclitics 1*, §c; *Charax*, §b. For ἴδιος τόνος (or e.g. ἰδία ὀξεῖα), see *On enclitics 1*, §s; *On enclitics 2*, §b; *On enclitics 3*, §§e, f; *On enclitics 4*, §g. For οἰκεῖος τόνος, see *On enclitics 4*, §d. For κύριος τόνος in this use, see e.g. *Ep. Hom. alph.* η 18.27 Dyck.

[360] For more details, see Probert (2019: 51–8).

[361] For the 'lulling' metaphor (and a converse 'waking up' metaphor), see further section 2.7.4.

[362] The lulling rule is laid out in detail, with all the conditions we mention here, in *On enclitics 3*, §d. For briefer allusions to the rule in our texts on enclitics, see *On enclitics 2*, §a; *Charax*, §§j, l.

(i) When the word with an acute on its final syllable is followed by punctuation: καλός·

(ii) When the word with an acute on its final syllable is followed by an enclitic (in this situation the enclitic loses what is considered to be its own natural accent): καλός γέ → καλός γε.

(iii) When the word with an acute on its final syllable is the interrogative τίς or τί.

With these general features of ancient thought on Greek accents in mind, we now turn to what our texts on enclitics have to say on the accentuation of sequences of words that include enclitics.

2.7.2 The natural accent of an enclitic

Two of our texts on enclitics[363] tell us explicitly that every enclitic was considered to have an acute or circumflex on its final or only syllable as its natural accent, and none of our texts contradicts this doctrine. When we are told that an enclitic 'throws its accent back' under certain circumstances, we are to understand that the accent of the enclitic is conceived as starting out on its final or only syllable.

2.7.3 Accenting a word followed by an enclitic: the main doctrines

All of our texts lay out some rules governing the accentuation of an ordinary word followed by an enclitic in an actual sentence. The main rules apply to enclitics comprising at most two syllables, of which at most one is long.[364] (A category of enclitics comprising two long syllables is recognized on occasion,[365] with the enclitic status of these words affecting their own accentuation but not that of the preceding word.) These rules are similar but not identical to the ones we usually learn today (for which see Chapter 1), and may be summarized as follows.

---

[363] *On enclitics 1*, §a; *Charax*, §e; cf. also *Charax*, §p; *On enclitics 3*, §f. Charax in both passages adds the detail that an apparently barytone word (i.e. one whose final syllable has neither an acute nor a circumflex) can be an enclitic if the word is barytone only as a result of a modification—as in the case of σφέας, considered to derive from σφᾶς via an operation resolving the long vowel ᾱ into two vowels. In such cases the word's ultimate 'natural' accent is on its final syllable. Cf. already Ap. Dysc., *Pron.* 90.16–17.

[364] In modern scholarly work (and especially in linguistically inclined work) it is customary to distinguish between heavy and light syllables, and to reserve the terms 'long' and 'short' for vowels. Our focus is on ancient and medieval thought, however, and to represent the ancient and medieval tradition more accurately we use the terms 'long' and 'short' for both vowels and syllables.

[365] *On enclitics 1*, §§f, l; *On enclitics 3*, §b; *Charax*, §§h, p. Compare already Apollonius Dyscolus in passage (2.16), and contrast *On enclitics 2*, §e.

I. If the word preceding the enclitic is naturally oxytone or perispomenon, the oxytone or perispomenon word retains its own accent while the enclitic loses its accent, as follows:[366]

natural accents		accents in context
πατήρ φησίν	→	πατήρ φησιν
καλοῦ τινός	→	καλοῦ τινος

II. If the word preceding the enclitic is naturally properispomenon or proparoxytone, it retains its own accent and receives an additional acute on its last syllable. At the same time, the accent of the enclitic disappears from the enclitic itself.[367]

natural accents		accents in context
γυναῖκες εἰσί	→	γυναῖκές εἰσι 'women are'
ἄνθρωποι εἰσί	→	ἄνθρωποί εἰσι 'people are'

III. If the word preceding an enclitic is naturally paroxytone, then:
i. if this word ends in a trochaic sequence (long syllable followed by short syllable), it retains its accent and acquires an additional acute on its last syllable. The accent of the enclitic again disappears from the enclitic itself:[368]

natural accents		accents in context
ἔνθα ποτέ	→	ἔνθά ποτε

ii. if the word preceding the enclitic ends in any other kind of sequence (pyrrhic, iambic, or spondaic), it simply retains its accent before an enclitic. If the enclitic is monosyllabic it loses its own accent, although no additional accent appears on the preceding word.[369] If the enclitic is disyllabic it retains its own accent:[370]

natural accents		accents in context
λέγε τί	→	λέγε τι
λέβης τίς	→	λέβης τις
παίδων τινῶν	→	παίδων τινῶν

---

[366] See *On enclitics 1*, §q; *On enclitics 3*, §d; *About* ἘΣΤΙΝ, §§b–c. On oxytone words with and without following enclitics, see also *Charax*, §§f, g, j, m.

[367] See *On enclitics 1*, §§n–o; *On enclitics 2*, §§b, e; *On enclitics 3*, §c; *Charax*, §§f, g, w; *About* ἘΣΤΙΝ, §§b–c.

[368] See *On enclitics 1*, §p; *On enclitics 2*, §e; *On enclitics 3*, §c; *Charax*, §f. But contrast *Charax*, §g, and *About* ἘΣΤΙΝ, §§b–c.

[369] See *On enclitics 1*, §t; *On enclitics 2*, §e; *On enclitics 3*, §e; *Charax*, §§i, w.

[370] See *On enclitics 1*, §u; *On enclitics 3*, §e; *About* ἘΣΤΙΝ, §c; *On enclitics 4*, §g; and cf. *Charax*, §i, with discussion in section 2.7.4.

Our texts on enclitics present three curious exceptions to the principles just laid out. Firstly, naturally properispomenon words whose final syllable is 'long by position' (i.e. the vowel of that syllable is followed by two consonants) are said to be exceptions to principle II: a word such as κῆρυξ 'herald' does not receive an additional accent from a following enclitic.[371] Secondly, enclitics beginning with σφ- induce an additional accent on the preceding word even if that word is paroxytone and ends in a non-trochaic sequence.[372] Thirdly, in the Homeric phrase ἔνθ᾿ ἔσάν οἱ πέπλοι 'where she had robes' the enclitic οἱ ('to her') induces a second accent on ἔσαν, despite the pyrrhic shape of ἔσαν.[373]

The first exception makes a certain amount of sense if at least some ancient scholars thought—and *Charax* appears to suggest this[374]—that properispomenon as well as paroxytone words needed to end in a trochaic sequence in order to receive an additional accent from a following enclitic. The second exception is more puzzling: an enclitic beginning with σφ- does not help to make the preceding sequence trochaic, and it is difficult to see what kind of linguistic principle could be at work. Charax (§t) suggests that some explained the third exception on the basis that the accentuation ἔσάν οἱ prevents οἱ being taken as the nominative plural masculine form of the definite article. Charax disapproves of the explanation himself, but on grounds which are difficult to accept.[375] The phrase had plausibly come to be written or spoken in a way that stretched the rules under which enclitics induce a second accent on the preceding word, in order to make it clear that οἱ here is an enclitic—and therefore that it is the enclitic pronoun form οἱ meaning 'to him/her', not a definite article to be taken with πέπλοι 'robes'.[376]

As well as laying out all the principles and exceptions just given, our texts on enclitics suggest that there were differences of opinion about some of the details. Some of the disagreements concern the precise ways in which various metaphors

---

[371] See *On enclitics 3*, §c (and also manuscript family *m*'s version of *About* ᾿ΕΣΤΙΝ: see *About* ᾿ΕΣΤΙΝ, §b, note c and §c, note f). The enclitic itself is treated as under III.ii in the scheme just given: hence κῆρύξ μοι 'a herald to me', κῆρυξ ἐστί 'a herald is' (the treatment of disyllabic enclitics here is spelled out most explicitly in family *m*'s version of *About* ᾿ΕΣΤΙΝ, §c). In connection with this principle it is to be understood that the consonants making the final syllable of the first word 'long by position' both belong to that word, although for metrical purposes a consonant belonging to the following word would also be relevant to syllable weight.

[372] *On enclitics 1*, §m; *On enclitics 2*, §e; *On enclitics 3*, §e; *Charax*, §t.

[373] *On enclitics 1*, §l; *Charax*, §t.

[374] *Charax*, §f, and cf. *Charax*, §§g, i, t.

[375] He suggests that even if the accent were not thrown back, the naturally perispomenon pronoun form οἱ would still be distinguished from the (in ancient terms) naturally oxytone article form οἵ. He alludes here to a similar argument he had made at §r, but in its new context at §t the argument misses the point that ἔσάν οἱ is to be contrasted not with ἔσαν οἵ but with ἔσαν οἱ, where the enclitic (not orthotonic) pronoun form ᾿ΟΙ obeys the usual rule for enclitics following paroxytone words with a pyrrhic termination.

[376] For another circumstance under which an accent rule is said to be stretched when this helps to avoid an ambiguity, see John Philoponus, *Praecepta Tonica* 130 Xenis.

for enclitic behaviour should be used, while others are substantive disagreements concerning the actual locations of accents. In section 2.7.4 we take a look at the metaphors for enclitic behaviour, along with differences of opinion that we take to concern their proper uses, and then section 2.7.5 will turn to the most significant disagreement on a more substantive point.

2.7.4 Metaphors for enclitic behaviour

Conspicuous among our texts' metaphors for enclitic behaviour is the use of the verb ἐγκλίνομαι, literally meaning 'lean back', along with its derivatives ἔγκλισις, ἐγκλιτικός, and (at least as a textual variant) ἐγκλιματικός.[377] Charax attempts to explain the idea as follows: 'We say that a word is *ortho-tonic* (ὀρθοτονεῖσθαι) when it keeps its regular and natural accent, and that it is *enclitic* (ἐγκλίνεσθαι) when it causes the accent to go up (τὸν τόνον ἀναβιβάζει) onto the word before itself, as from the metaphor of those who lean their bodies backwards'.[378] While the use of one metaphor (ἀναβιβάζει) to explain another does not make the thought very easy to follow, the idea that an enclitic 'leans back' conveys some sort of interaction between the enclitic and the preceding word.

In practice, the verb ἐγκλίνομαι (and its derivatives) is sometimes used in a broad sense for 'be an enclitic', and sometimes in a narrower sense for 'tangibly affect the accentuation of the preceding word'. (For the sake of a less clumsy translation, in sections 2.1–2.6 we render this narrower sense with 'throw its accent back', using a metaphor familiar from our own didactic tradition.) Using the word in its broad sense, the treatise *On enclitics 1* (for example) says ἐγκλίνεται δὲ ἀεὶ καὶ ἡ *MIN* 'and *MIN* too is always an enclitic'.[379] The point here is not that *MIN* always affects the accentuation of the preceding word—that will depend on the shape of the preceding word, after all—but that *MIN* is always an enclitic. Using the word in its narrower sense, the same treatise explains further on that enclitics οὐχ ὡς ἔτυχε...ἐγκλίνονται, ἀλλὰ κατά τινα παρατήρησιν τῆς πρὸ αὐτῶν λέξεως 'do not affect the accentuation of the preceding word at random, but on the basis of a certain observation of the preceding word'.[380] This time ἐγκλίνονται does not mean simply 'be an enclitic' but 'tangibly affect the accentuation of the preceding word': the whole point is that to know when an enclitic does this we need to observe the shape of the preceding word.

---

[377] For ἐγκλιματικός, see manuscript family **q**'s reading at *On enclitics 2*, §j, note d; the reading of **w₂B** at *Charax*, §a, note c; and the reading of **y₂** at *Charax*, §d, note c.
[378] *Charax*, §b.
[379] *On enclitics 1*, §g.
[380] *On enclitics 1*, §k.

In many contexts, it makes little practical difference whether ἐγκλίνομαι is taken in the broader or the narrower of these senses. In *On enclitics 1* (§c), for example, the statement ἐν μὲν οὖν ὀνόμασι τὸ *ΤΙΣ* μόνον ἐγκλίνεται conveys that *ΤΙΣ* is the only enclitic among the ὀνόματα (nouns and adjectives), and for this purpose it makes little difference whether ἐγκλίνεται is taken to mean 'is enclitic' or 'affects the accentuation of the preceding word (i.e. under appropriate circumstances)'. Even when ἐγκλίνομαι is readily understood as 'be an enclitic', the idea that a specific word is an enclitic tends to be backed up by one or more examples that show the enclitic actually affecting the accentuation of the preceding word. So in *On enclitics 1* the idea that *MIN* is an enclitic is supported by the example καί μιν φωνήσας,[381] and the idea that indefinite *ΤΙΣ* and its inflected forms are enclitics is supported by the examples οἶκός τις, ἔμαθόν τινος, ἔδωκά τινι, ἐδίδαξά τινα, ἔμαθόν τι, ἤκουσά του λέγοντος, and ἔλεξά τῳ φράσοντι.[382] Such examples make it easy to see that a word is indeed an enclitic, but they also reinforce the sense that what enclitics prototypically do is to have certain tangible effects on the accentuation of the preceding word.

Two further metaphors for enclitic behaviour reflect two different ways of conceptualizing the precise effect of an enclitic on the preceding word. With the first of these, an enclitic 'wakes up' (ἐγείρει) a grave accent on the syllable preceding itself,[383] or turns a grave on this syllable into an acute.[384] With the second, an enclitic transfers its own accent to the last syllable of the preceding word. In the texts presented in sections 2.1–2.6, several verbs are used to convey the transferring of an accent: ἀναπέμπω 'send up' (with a spatial metaphor that translates better into English as 'send back'),[385] παραπέμπω 'send on',[386] παρέχω 'pass on',[387] and ἀναβιβάζω 'cause to go up'.[388]

Two somewhat different uses of the 'waking up' metaphor can be distinguished, although they appear alongside one another in our texts. In some instances, an enclitic is said to 'wake up' a grave accent falling on the final syllable of a (naturally) oxytone word, like the final syllable of πατήρ (in the form πατὴρ). We understand that the 'natural' acute of the oxytone word is first put to sleep by the lulling rule, and then woken up again by the enclitic. This way of thinking about the effect of an enclitic on a preceding oxytone word is actually found more often

---

[381] *On enclitics 1*, §g.
[382] *On enclitics 1*, §c.
[383] *On enclitics 1*, §§l, n, o, q, t. *On enclitics 2*, §§c, g, j, k, l, m, n. *Charax*, §d.
[384] *On enclitics 2*, §b (τὴν προκειμένην βαρεῖαν εἰς ὀξεῖαν μεθίστησιν).
[385] *On enclitics 1*, §l (here in relation to enclitics consisting of two long syllables and sending their accents back onto their own first syllables: on these cf. section 2.7.3); *On enclitics 2*, §§e, f; *On enclitics 3*, §§b, c, e; *Charax*, §§m (in relation to *ΕΣΤΙΝ* transferring its accent to its own first syllable), q, w.
[386] *On enclitics 3*, §f.
[387] *Charax*, §i.
[388] *Charax*, §§b, h, i, m, p, w.

in our texts on enclitics than the one we gave in section 2.7.3, in which an oxytone word simply retains its acute accent before an enclitic—but both accounts are found.[389] They start from identical starting points and give identical results, but via two different routes:

Enclitics following naturally oxytone words:
Idea that the enclitic reverses 'lulling':   πατήρ φησίν → πατὴρ φησίν → πατὴρ φησιν
Idea that the enclitic prevents 'lulling':   πατήρ φησίν   →   πατὴρ φησιν
                                  natural accents   accents in context

Alongside the idea that an enclitic can wake up a sleeping acute accent on a naturally oxytone word, we find an idea that, under the right circumstances, an enclitic can wake up the theoretical grave accent (i.e. lack of accent) on a naturally unaccented final syllable. In *On enclitics 1* (§n), for example, the grave accent on the final syllable of ἄνθρωπος is said to be woken up by a following indefinite *ΤΙΣ*, giving ἄνθρωπός τις.

The idea that a grave accent is a sleeping acute, with the potential to be woken up, possibly began with grave accents on the final syllables of naturally oxytone words. From the notion that the natural accent of an oxytone word can be 'lulled', it is a small step to the idea that this accent can be woken up again. But the 'waking up' metaphor was extended also to other grave accents on final syllables, even when these cannot be thought to result from the lulling rule.

The 'transfer of an accent' metaphor too turns out to have more and less straightforward manifestations. At their most straightforward, expressions conveying the transfer of an accent apply to sequences involving an enclitic preceded by a proparoxytone or properispomenon word, or by a paroxytone word ending in a trochaic sequence. In such sequences the enclitic is conceived of as losing its 'natural accent' and the preceding word as gaining a second accent, and the accent lost by the enclitic can readily be understood as the one gained by the preceding word:

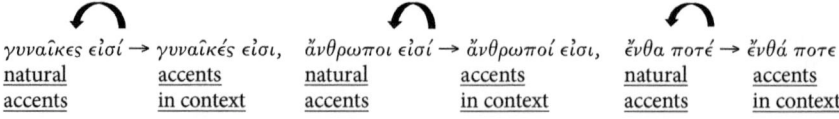

γυναῖκες εἰσί → γυναῖκές εἰσι,   ἄνθρωποι εἰσί → ἄνθρωποί εἰσι,   ἔνθα ποτέ → ἔνθά ποτε
natural   accents   natural   accents   natural   accents
accents   in context   accents   in context   accents   in context

The author of *On enclitics 2* (§e) insists that an enclitic only 'sends its accent up' (ἀναπέμπει) in sequences of these kinds, and that it does not do so after a perispomenon word, nor after a paroxytone word with a spondaic, iambic, or pyrrhic

---

[389] For the idea that an enclitic prevents lulling of the acute accent of a preceding oxytone word, so that the acute accent is simply retained, see *On enclitics 3*, §d.

termination. At first sight, he is simply expressing what we have just seen: the idea that an enclitic transfers its accent to the preceding word makes most sense if the preceding word is properispomenon or proparoxytone, or is paroxytone and ends in a trochaic sequence. But he possibly considers it a moot point whether an enclitic can be said to 'send its accent up' after a naturally *oxytone* word: he omits to mention enclitics after oxytone words both when listing sequences in which the enclitic 'sends its accent up' and when listing those in which it fails to do so. More explicitly, Charax (§m) suggests that we expect an enclitic 'to cause its accent to go up' (ἀναβιβάζειν τὸν τόνον) onto the preceding word if that word is oxytone. If the accent that disappears from the enclitic is conceived of as ending up on the last syllable of the oxytone word, we can perhaps understand that it gives that syllable the additional element of accentedness needed to either 'wake up' the acute of that syllable or prevent this acute from being lulled in the first place:

Enclitics following oxytone words:

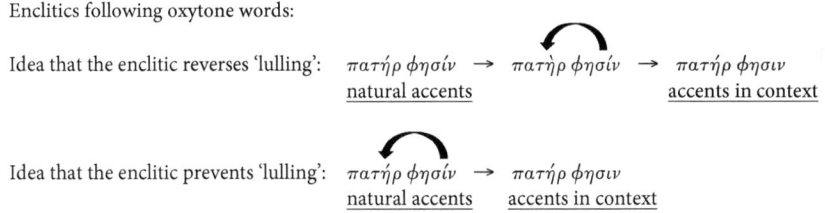

Idea that the enclitic reverses 'lulling':   πατήρ φησίν   →   πατὴρ φησίν   →   πατήρ φησιν
                      natural accents   accents in context

Idea that the enclitic prevents 'lulling':   πατήρ φησίν   →   πατήρ φησιν
                      natural accents   accents in context

The idea that an enclitic physically transfers its accent to the preceding word appears to be applied least often to an enclitic following either a perispomenon word or a paroxytone word ending in a non-trochaic sequence. But in one passage Charax (§i) takes issue with Romanus and unnamed others for thinking that enclitics 'pass on' (παρέχουσι) their accents to the preceding word under one or more of these circumstances too. Did Charax and the people he disagrees with here take different views about the way certain sequences should be accented in practice, or about the limits within which the 'transfer of an accent' metaphor was applicable? To try to answer this question, it is worth taking a closer look at the text and interpretation of this passage, in which Charax draws a contrast between the behaviour of disyllabic enclitics and that of monosyllabic ones.

Charax starts off the discussion by claiming that disyllabic enclitics unambiguously either 'cause their accents to go up' or 'keep' them, and then gives three examples: ἤκουσά τινος, ἀνθρώπου τινός, and a third example consisting of the letters ΑΦΟΥΤΙΝΟΣ. If we leave this third example to one side for a moment, the first two unproblematically illustrate an enclitic transferring its accent to the preceding word (ἤκουσά τινος) and an enclitic keeping its accent instead (ἀνθρώπου τινός). In ἤκουσά τινος, no accent appears on the enclitic and an additional accent appears on the preceding word; in ἀνθρώπου τινός, an accent appears on the second syllable of the enclitic and there is no additional accent on the preceding word.

Turning to monosyllabic enclitics, Charax suggests that an enclitic like μου should not really occur at all after a word that cannot receive an additional accent: ἀνθρώπου μου should have been ἀνθρώπου ἐμοῦ, and μέλει μοι should have been μέλει ἐμοί. The idea appears to be that an enclitic should not logically get itself into a position where it can neither retain its accent nor transfer it to the preceding word. Acknowledging that in practice phrases like ΑΝΘΡΩΠΟΥ ΜΟΥ do occur, however, Charax lays out his opinion that in such phrases the enclitics 'neither throw their accent back nor maintain it, but the accent is placed as if the word were one, as in ἀνθρώπου μου'. In Charax's view it is wrong to analyse a phrase of this kind in terms of an abstract starting point with two 'natural accents': the phrase simply has one accent, the way a single word has a single accent. One might object that the rules for assigning an accent to a phrase like ἀνθρώπου μου cannot be quite the same as those for assigning an accent to a single word (a single word cannot normally have an acute on its antepenultimate syllable if the vowel of the final syllable is long), but Charax does not appear to worry about this point. His view is perhaps not that phrases like this should actually be considered single words, but that they behave similarly to single words insofar as they have one accent, not two.

Romanus and some others apparently took a different view—but what view exactly? At this point, a discussion of the text of the passage is in order; we will see that textual decisions matter. In Bekker's text, Charax's discussion of Romanus' view reads as follows:

(2.2)   Ἄλλοι δέ τινες συγχέουσιν, ὡς καὶ Ῥωμανὸς λέγων, εἰ περισπωμένη προηγεῖται, οὐ παρέχουσι τὸν τόνον αὐτῇ, οἷον καλοῦ μοῦ· εἰ δὲ ἄλλος τόνος εἴη, παρέχουσι τὸν τόνον, οἷον πόθεν τις, ὅθεν με. ψευδὲς δὲ λίαν ἐστίν· εἷς γὰρ ὁ τόνος ἐστὶ καὶ τίθεται, καὶ οὐ παρέχουσι τὸν τόνον, ὡς εἴπομεν, ταῖς προηγουμέναις, εἰ μὴ εἴη προπαροξύτονος ἢ ὀξύτονος ἢ τροχαϊκή. (Charax, §i, text of Bekker 1821: 1150, lines 22–7)

> 'But some others cause confusion, including Romanus, who says that if a perispomenon word precedes, enclitics do not pass their accent on to it, as in καλοῦ μοῦ. But if the accent [of the preceding word] is different they pass on their accent, as in πόθεν τις, ὅθεν με. But this is very wrong. For the accent is one and is placed as such; and as we have said, enclitics do not pass their accent on to preceding words unless the preceding word is proparoxytone or oxytone or trochaic.'

In this version of the passage, Charax thought that an enclitic did not 'pass its accent on' in a sequence like ΚΑΛΟΥ ΜΟΥ ('of my beautiful'), but did so in

ΠΟΘΕΝ ΤΙΣ ('from where does someone...?') and *'ΟΘΕΝ ΜΕ* ('from where... me'). By printing these examples as καλοῦ μοῦ, πόθεν τις, and ὅθεν με, Bekker implies that the crucial difference between an enclitic 'not passing its accent on' and one 'passing its accent on', in Romanus' view, is that the former is accented in actual practice (καλοῦ μοῦ) while the latter is not (πόθεν τις, ὅθεν με).[390] Differently, Gaisford (1842: 21) printed the examples as καλοῦ μου, πόθέν τις, and ὅθέν με, so that an enclitic 'not passing its accent on' fails to cause an additional accent on the preceding word (καλοῦ μου) while one 'passing its accent on' causes an additional accent (πόθέν τις).[391] However, we are not aware of other evidence of any Greek grammarians thinking either that sequences comparable to *ΚΑΛΟΥ ΜΟΥ* were accented καλοῦ μοῦ, or that sequences comparable to *ΠΟΘΕΝ ΤΙΣ* and *'ΟΘΕΝ ΜΕ* were accented πόθέν τις and ὅθέν με.

Moreover, the words αὐτῇ, οἷον καλοῦ μοῦ· εἰ δὲ ἄλλος τόνος εἴη, παρέχουσι τὸν τόνον, οἷον reflect an insertion into the text made at one point in the tradition. By taking the whole tradition into account, we can reconstruct the following text for the archetype of all the manuscripts known to us:

(2.3)   ἄλλοι δέ τινες συγχέουσιν, ὡς καὶ ὁ 'Ρωμανὸς λέγων, εἰ περισπωμένη προηγεῖται οὐ παρέχουσι τὸν τόνον, 'πόθεν τις', 'ὅθεν με'. ψευδὲς δέ ἐστιν· εἷς γὰρ ὁ τόνος τίθεται, καὶ οὐ παρέχουσι τὸν τόνον ταῖς προηγουμέναις, εἰ μὴ ὦσιν, ὡς εἴπομεν, προπαροξύτονος ἢ ὀξύτονος ἢ τροχαϊκή. (*Charax*, §i, reconstructed text of the archetype **ω**)

> 'But some others cause confusion, including Romanus, who says that if a perispomenon word precedes, enclitics do not pass on their accent, as in πόθεν τις, ὅθεν με. But this is wrong. For the accent that is placed is one; and enclitics do not pass their accent on to preceding words unless, as we have said, the preceding word is proparoxytone or oxytone or trochaic.'

In most manuscripts, the text remains close to this version. But this version is nonsensical as it stands. Firstly, πόθεν τις and ὅθεν με cannot serve as examples for a situation in which a perispomenon word precedes the enclitic. Secondly, Charax's objection 'enclitics do not pass their accent on to preceding words unless, as we have said, the preceding word is proparoxytone or oxytone or trochaic'

---

[390] Cf. Lehrs (1837: 107).
[391] However, it is unclear whether Gaisford thought this was in fact the view that Charax takes issue with: Gaisford also prints the material οἷον πόθεν τις, καὶ ὅθέν με, δέον πόθεν τις λέγειν, καὶ ὅθεν με, found in only one sub-family of manuscripts (see *Charax*, §i, note w), and his text of the passage makes little sense.

makes no sense unless Romanus' view included some additional circumstance in which enclitics do pass their accents on.

The scribe responsible for manuscript **N** (or a precedessor of his) saw both problems, and attempted to repair the text. Taking some words to have fallen out after παρέχουσι τὸν τόνον, he inserted words designed firstly to supply a suitable example in which 'a perispomenon word precedes', and secondly to make Romanus think enclitics did pass their accents on in some situations for which Charax insisted otherwise:

(2.4)   ἄλλοι δέ τινες συγχέουσιν, ὡς καὶ ὁ Ῥωμανὸς λέγων, εἰ περισπωμένη
       προηγεῖται οὐ παρέχουσι τὸν τόνον ⟨αὐτῇ, 'καλοῦ μου'· εἰ δὲ ἄλλος
       τόνος εἴη, παρέχουσι τὸν τόνον,⟩ 'πόθεν τις', 'ὅθεν με'. ψευδές ἐστιν· εἰς
       γὰρ ὁ τόνος τίθεται, καὶ οὐ παρέχουσι τὸν τόνον ταῖς προηγουμέναις,
       εἰ μὴ ὦσιν, ὡς εἴπομεν, προπαροξύτονος ἢ ὀξύτονος ἢ τροχαϊκός.
       (*Charax*, §i, as emended by manuscript **N** or a source of this manuscript)

> 'But some others cause confusion, including Romanus, who says that if a perispomenon word precedes, enclitics do not pass their accent on ⟨to it, as in καλοῦ μου. But if there should be another accent, they pass on their accent⟩, as in πόθεν τις, ὅθεν με. This is wrong. For the accent that is placed is one; and enclitics do not pass their accent on to preceding words unless, as we have said, the preceding word is proparoxytone or oxytone or trochaic.'

This insertion was taken over into manuscript **V** and into subfamily **c**, both of which are likely to have been influenced by **N**.[392] In subfamily **c**, the insertion was adopted with the minor addition of οἷον before καλοῦ μου and again before πόθεν τις. Bekker's text (our passage (2.2)) here reflects the version in manuscript **X** of sub-family **c**,[393] with the accentuation καλοῦ μοῦ further reflecting Bekker's efforts to make sense of the passage.

A different attempt to repair the text, or perhaps this time a simple error, appears in manuscripts **ΦH**, and can be attributed to the hyparchetype of sub-family **x**. In this branch of the tradition, the words 'πόθεν τις', 'ὅθεν με'. ψευδὲς δέ ἐστιν· εἰς γὰρ ὁ τόνος τίθεται, καὶ οὐ παρέχουσι τὸν τόνον are omitted (*Charax*, §i, note bb), either because the scribe's eye jumped from the first transmitted instance of παρέχουσι τὸν τόνον to the second or because he saw the unsuitability of the examples πόθεν τις, ὅθεν με after εἰ περισπωμένη προηγεῖται. If he emended the text deliberately, he decided to omit the offending examples along with what followed them, in such a way that οὐ παρέχουσι τὸν τόνον came to be followed by ταῖς προηγουμέναις. The words οὐ παρέχουσι τὸν τόνον ταῖς

---

[392] See section 2.4.1.4.
[393] For Bekker's sources for the text of *Charax*, see section 2.4.2.

προηγουμέναις make some sense in themselves ('they do not pass their accent on to the preceding words'), even if the passage as a whole now amounts to a nonsensical blend between Romanus' view and Charax's objection:

(2.5) ἄλλοι δέ τινες συγχέουσιν, ὡς καὶ ὁ Ῥωμανὸς λέγει, εἰ περισπωμένη προηγεῖται οὐ παρέχουσι τὸν τόνον {material deleted here} ταῖς προηγουμέναις, εἰ μὴ ὦσιν, ὡς εἴπομεν, προπαροξύτονος ἢ ὀξύτονος ἢ τροχαϊκή. (*Charax*, §i, as deliberately or accidentally altered in the hyparchetype of sub-family **x**)

'But some others cause confusion, in the way that Romanus too says that if a perispomenon word precedes, enclitics do not pass their accent on to preceding words unless, as we have said, the preceding word is proparoxytone or oxytone or trochaic.'

A yet further attempt to repair the text appears in manuscript **G** (also belonging to sub-family **x**), where the whole passage is recast so that the details of Romanus' view are left unspecified (see *Charax*, §i, note t).

In our view, better sense can be made of the passage with a different solution. Starting with the text that we reconstruct for the archetype of the whole tradition (2.3), we suggest that material has fallen out after εἰ περισπωμένη προηγεῖται. Passage (2.6) gives our version of the text, with the approximate words we take to be missing. In honour of the scribe responsible for the conjecture in manuscripts **NVUX**, who put his finger on the problems with the transmitted text, our version includes the example καλοῦ μου, but any perispomenon word followed by a monosyllabic enclitic could have stood here:

(2.6) ἄλλοι δέ τινες συγχέουσιν, ὡς καὶ ὁ Ῥωμανὸς λέγων, εἰ περισπωμένη προηγεῖται, ⟨παρέχουσι τὸν τόνον, 'καλοῦ μου'. εἰ δὲ παροξύτονος προηγεῖται⟩ οὐ παρέχουσι τὸν τόνον, 'πόθεν τις', 'ὅθεν με'. ψευδὲς δέ ἐστιν· εἷς γὰρ ὁ τόνος τίθεται, καὶ οὐ παρέχουσι τὸν τόνον ταῖς προηγουμέναις, εἰ μὴ ὦσιν, ὡς εἴπομεν, προπαροξύτονος ἢ ὀξύτονος ἢ τροχαϊκή. (*Charax*, §i, our text)

'But some others cause confusion, including Romanus, who says that if a perispomenon word precedes, enclitics pass their accent on to it, as in καλοῦ μου. But if a paroxytone word precedes, they do not pass on their accent, as in πόθεν τις, ὅθεν με. But this is wrong. For the accent that is placed is one; and enclitics do not pass their accent on to preceding words unless, as we have said, the preceding word is proparoxytone or oxytone or trochaic.'

With this solution, the omission in the archetype has a straightforward explanation: a scribe's eye jumped from one instance of προηγεῖται to the next. This version also does not require anyone to have had an otherwise unattested view about the accentuation of καλοῦ μου, πόθεν τις, or ὅθεν με. In our view, the dispute did not concern how any of these sequences should actually be accented, but the appropriate use of the 'transfer of an accent' metaphor. Romanus and others thought one could speak of an accent being transferred from a monosyllabic enclitic to a preceding perispomenon word, as in καλοῦ μου, but not from a monosyllabic enclitic to a word like πόθεν or ὅθεν. For sequences of the type καλοῦ μου, the idea requires us to understand that the transferred accent ends up coalescing with the natural accent of the preceding word:

καλοῦ μοῦ   →   καλοῦ μου
<u>natural accents</u>   <u>accents in context</u>

The same logic does not encourage the 'transfer of an accent' metaphor for phrases like πόθεν τις and ὅθεν με, where the syllable preceding the enclitic manifestly lacks an accent.

Charax here opposes the idea that καλοῦ μου should be analysed differently from πόθεν τις and ὅθεν με, and the idea that the 'transfer of an accent' metaphor is suitable for sequences like καλοῦ μου. At least where monosyllabic enclitics are concerned, Charax takes the 'transfer of an accent' metaphor to be appropriate only where the preceding word is proparoxytone (ἄνθρωπός μου), oxytone (μαθητής μου), or 'trochaic' (which for Charax is a shorthand for sequences like δοῦλός μου and those like ἄλλός μοι). As we have seen, these situations can all be conceptualized fairly straightforwardly in terms of an accent being lost from the enclitic and added to the preceding word. For sequences of the type καλοῦ μου, as well as for those of the type πόθεν τις, Charax prefers to think in terms of sequences with only a single 'natural accent': even at an abstract level, there is no second accent whose disappearance needs to be accounted for.

At this point, it is worth returning to Charax's third example involving a disyllabic enclitic. The sequence ΑΦΟΥΤΙΝΟΣ is most straightforwardly interpreted as ἀφ' οὗ τινος 'from whoever/whichever'—that is to say ἀφ' οὗτινος, with τινος clearly understood as a separate enclitic word.[394] But did Charax think that this sequence was accented ἀφ' οὗ τινος or ἀφ' οὗ τινός? On the one hand, his claim that disyllabic enclitics unambiguously either 'cause their accents to go up' or

---

[394] Alternatively, the sequence could be read ἀφοῦ τινος 'let go [aorist imperative] of something'. But it is difficult to see the resemblance of ΟΥΤΙΝΟΣ to the genitive οὗ τινος as purely accidental, especially after what could plausibly be a preposition taking the genitive.

'keep' them might seem to speak for ἀφ' οὗ τινός, with the enclitic keeping its accent and no additional accent appearing on the preceding word (since οὗ already has a circumflex as its natural accent). On the other hand, the treatise *About ἘΣΤΙΝ* strongly implies that ἘΣΤΙΝ appears without an accent in the phrase Ἑρμῆς ἐστιν,[395] and we suggest that sense can also be made of our passage if Charax similarly accented his third example ἀφ' οὗ τινος. If so, he thought that in this instance the accent of the enclitic 'goes up' onto the preceding word, where it coalesces with the preceding word's natural accent:

$$\overset{\frown}{}$$
ἀφ' οὗ τινός   →   ἀφ' οὗ τινος
<u>natural accents</u>   <u>accents in context</u>

This is precisely the type of analysis Charax opposes for sequences of the type καλοῦ μου, involving a monosyllabic enclitic. But the essence of his contrast between disyllabic and monosyllabic enclitics is that when a disyllabic enclitic is involved, an accent *always* appears either on the second syllable of the enclitic or on the final syllable of the preceding word. When a monosyllabic enclitic is involved the same cannot be said, because of ἀνθρώπου μου, μέλει μοι, etc. He considers these sequences to have a single natural accent, and he considers it logical to apply the same analysis to sequences of type καλοῦ μου, for the sake of a consistent analysis of sequences involving monosyllabic enclitics. But sequences of the type ἀφ' οὗ τινος involve a *disyllabic* enclitic, and this time Charax offers an analysis involving the transfer of an accent, for consistency with other sequences involving disyllabic enclitics.

If this suggestion is correct, Charax offers a contradictory analysis of disyllabic enclitics after perispomenon words later on, at least on our reading of a different textually problematic passage: at §m, recalling his view that enclitics only 'throw back their accents' after proparoxytone, oxytone, or 'trochaic' words, he offers ἀνθρώπου εἰμί and οὖν εἰμι as examples of phrases in which ἘΙΜΙ does not 'throw back' its accent. In so doing, he now treats disyllabic enclitics after perispomenon words in the same way as he has treated monosyllabic enclitics in the same position. The contradiction with his analysis of ἀφ' οὗ τινος would be mild, however, since the suggestion that ΤΙΝΟΣ can be considered to 'throw back its accent' in this phrase was made only implicitly at §i.

Ultimately, we cannot be sure whether Charax thought in terms of the accentuation ἀφ' οὗ τινος: what we have shown is that a coherent set of views can be reconstructed for paragraph §i if he did. If so, then although he suggests that an

---

[395] *About ἘΣΤΙΝ*, §b. The phrase Ἑρμῆς ἐστιν is adduced as an example in which ἘΣΤΙΝ ἐγκλίνεται, and §§b–c together envisage an opposition between ἐγκλίνεται and 'gets the accent on the Γ.

enclitic transfers its accent to a preceding proparoxytone, oxytone, or 'trochaic' word (*Charax*, §f), at §i it is only in the case of monosyllabic enclitics that he considers the transfer of the accent strictly limited to these circumstances: in the analysis we suggest he offers at this point in the treatise, a disyllabic enclitic also transfers its accent to a preceding perispomenon word.

Returning to firmer ground, we have argued that the accentuation of sequences like καλοῦ μου and πόθεν τις was not in dispute. But there were differences of opinion about how best to think and talk about the accentuation of such sequences. Romanus (along with unnamed others) thought about sequences of the type καλοῦ μου in terms of the 'transfer of an accent' metaphor, although this could not easily be extended to sequences like πόθεν τις. Charax had a different way of thinking about sequences like καλοῦ μου, under which he could also account for sequences like πόθεν τις.

A difference of opinion between Charax and others surfaces again in the closing remarks of his treatise (§w), where he insists that those who think enclitics 'send up' (ἀναπέμπουσι) their accents onto *every* word are wrong. If this is more than a reference back to the disagreement mentioned earlier, with an element of hyperbole (the grammarians mentioned at §i applied the 'transfer of an accent' metaphor more broadly than Charax, but not to *all* sequences with enclitics), we should probably think of people who used expressions for 'transfer their accents' in a broadest possible sense, as equivalents for 'behave as enclitics'.

In their narrower uses, then, expressions for 'transfer an accent' require a clear place where the accent started off and a clear place where it ended up, but there is room for some hesitation about what constitutes a clear place where the accent ends up. An enclitic following a perispomenon word constitutes something of a borderline case: the natural accent of the enclitic can be seen as transferred to the last syllable of the perispomenon word, but only with the implicit help of the idea that it coalesces there with that word's natural accent. Romanus applied this metaphor to sequences of the type καλοῦ μου, while Charax did not, although both scholars possibly applied it to sequences of the type ἀφ' οὗ τινος (in Charax's case at least at one point in his treatise). In addition, the expressions for 'transfer an accent' may have acquired a very broad use in which they stand for enclitic behaviour in general. In this use they are applicable whether or not the enclitic actually appears to have lost its 'natural accent', and whether or not the preceding word appears to have gained any additional accent.

Metaphors naturally weaken with use, and at least two of the metaphors for enclitic behaviour probably owe their broader uses to this kind of process. The 'waking up' metaphor weakened so that it could convey the action of an enclitic in turning any preceding grave accent into an acute, even where there was no particular reason to think of the grave as a sleeping acute. And the 'transfer of an accent' metaphor perhaps weakened so that it could stand for enclitic behaviour in general, even where it made little sense to think of an accent being transferred from one syllable to another. It is less clear whether the 'leaning back' metaphor was originally used in its narrower sense ('tangibly affect the accent of the preceding word') or its broader one ('be closely associated with the preceding word', and hence 'be an enclitic').[396] If the narrower sense came first, the broader one could again be owed to weakening of the metaphor over time, or if the broader sense came first the narrower one could be owed to influence from the 'waking up' metaphor and the 'transfer of an accent' metaphor.

2.7.5 Differences of opinion on sequences of the type ἘΝΘΑ ΜΟΙ

As well as differences of opinion surrounding the appropriate use of particular metaphors for enclitic behaviour, there were also some substantive differences of opinion about how to accent particular sequences involving enclitics. The main debate concerns sequences of the type ἘΝΘΑ ΜΟΙ, where an enclitic follows a paroxytone word ending in a trochaic sequence; once again the differences of opinion emerge most clearly from the treatise ascribed to Charax.

After first laying out the usual main rules governing the accent of words followed by enclitics (the ones laid out in section 2.7.3), Charax explains why enclitics do not cause an additional accent to appear on a preceding paroxytone word ending in a non-trochaic sequence: 'the ancients did not seek to give two acute accents in succession to a single word, for they produce an unpleasant sound'.[397] This explanation raises an obvious question: why did the ancients' aversion to successive acute accents not apply also to sequences like ἄλλός μοι or ἔνθά μοι? Implicitly acknowledging this question, Charax offers an answer: in fact 'those who are precise' (οἱ ἀκριβεῖς) do not approve of successive acute accents in such sequences either. In this connection he claims that Aristarchus refused to accent the first two words of the *Odyssey* as ἄνδρά μοι, apparently insisting on ἄνδρα μοι, an idea we shall return to in section 2.8.3. Later on in his treatise, Charax reverts to the usual view that paroxytone words ending in a trochaic sequence behave differently before enclitics from those ending in a non-trochaic sequence.[398] The treatise *About* ἘΣΤΙΝ, on the other hand, takes the same position as Charax

---

[396] For an early witness to the idea that enclitics are closely associated with a preceding word (regardless of whether they tangibly affect its accent), see Ap. Dysc., *Pron.* 49.19–23: enclitic pronoun forms are always 'juxtaposed to some word' (μετά τινος μέρους λόγου παρατίθενται), never pronounced 'by themselves' (κατ᾽ ἰδίαν).

[397] *Charax*, §g.

[398] *Charax*, §§t, w (with the example ἄνδρά τε).

ascribes to 'those who are precise,'[399] this time without reference to any debate on the subject.[400]

Our texts on enclitics thus show that by the Byzantine period there were differences of opinion about the accentuation of sequences like *ἘΝΘΑ ΜΟΙ*. In section 2.8.3 we shall see that the idea that such sequences are to be accented ἔνθά μοι goes back at least to the second century AD, and probably to the Hellenistic period. We shall also see that there are no clear indications of any real debate on the subject at this early period, and a careful reading of Charax's story about Aristarchus will suggest that Aristarchus is being used rather tendentiously here.

Charax mentions further debates about the enclitic or non-enclitic status of particular forms (*ΦΗΜΙ, ΦΑΜΕΝ, ΦΑΤΕ, ΦΑΣΙ*)[401] and about whether to use non-enclitic or enclitic personal pronoun forms with οὕνεκα and ἕνεκα.[402] In addition, our texts on enclitics present us with various apparently incompatible doctrines on the accent patterns associated with two or more enclitics in sequence—but without explicitly signalling their incompatibility or suggesting that they were the subject of any debate. These doctrines turn out to be of considerable interest, and will be taken up in Chapter 4.

2.8 Earlier stages of the tradition

As already mentioned, particularly helpful sources for a relatively early stage of the tradition on enclitic accents are the surviving works of Apollonius Dyscolus, and Homeric scholia likely to derive from the work of his son Herodian. In fact most of the doctrines found in the texts presented in sections 2.1–2.6 can be found in the surviving works of Apollonius, and some of the wording found in those texts echoes Apollonius closely enough to suggest that work of his fed into the Byzantine tradition. Some caution is needed here, because on occasion an apparent verbal correspondence may be due to an interpolation into the text of Apollonius from the work of a later author.[403] It is notoriously difficult to know when to take the text of Apollonius Dyscolus at face value and when to recognize an interpolation, and we shall not be wading into this arena. But since we would like to use Apollonius as a robust chronological anchor, except where otherwise

---

[399] *About* ἘΣΤΙΝ, §b, and implicitly §c.

[400] Differently, Lehrs (1837: 104) takes it that ἘΣΤΙΝ behaved in an exceptional way after paroxytone words ending in a trochaic sequence, so that the accentuation prescribed here for the phrase *ΦΥΛΛΑ ἘΣΤΙΝ* ('leaves are'), namely φύλλα ἐστίν, should not be applied to sequences involving enclitics other than ἘΣΤΙΝ.

[401] *Charax*, §n.

[402] *Charax*, §u.

[403] For this possibility see especially Maas (1907).

specified our discussion will be based on passages that to our knowledge have not been thought interpolated.

Not only are most of the doctrines that we find in our Byzantine treatises already attested in the surviving works of Apollonius Dyscolus, but almost all those not attested in Apollonius are visible in the Herodianic scholia to Homer: they therefore appear to go back at least as far as Apollonius' son Herodian. Our evidence is much more patchy for stages of the tradition before Apollonius and Herodian, but we shall see that some doctrines can be traced back to the Hellenistic period with more or less confidence.

2.8.1 Ancient thought on Greek accents: general features and the 'lulling rule'

Apollonius' work already makes use of the same basic system of notation and terminology for accents as our Byzantine texts, and it is clear that this system has its origins in Hellenistic scholarship.[404] Apollonius too works with the notion that every word has an acute or circumflex as its 'natural accent' or 'accent of its own',[405] and with a system of rules that can add, remove, or alter an accent to give a word its correct form for its context. We shall concentrate here on a rule that is of particular importance to ancient discussions of enclitic accents: the 'lulling rule'.

Like our Byzantine treatises, Apollonius operates with a category of words whose natural accent was an acute on the final syllable (the words we call 'oxytone', following ancient tradition) and with a rule 'lulling' the accent of these words to a grave in connected speech.[406] Also like the Byzantine treatises, he demonstrably assumes that the lulling rule either fails to apply or is reversed when the oxytone word is followed by punctuation and when that word is followed by an enclitic. In addition, in one passage he perhaps also has in mind the idea that the lulling rule fails to apply or is reversed when the oxytone word consists of interrogative τίς or τί—the third condition mentioned by the Byzantine treatises. Since all three points are hinted at rather than directly stated, the main evidence is worth briefly laying out.

---

[404] This system is visible not only in the considerable body of surviving fragments of Hellenistic scholarship (see for example Schironi 2018: 109–15, 378–412) but also in its influence on the Latin grammatical tradition on Latin accentuation, which received significant impetus from Greek thought in the first century BC (see Probert 2019: 1–4).

[405] It is clear from Ap. Dysc., *Pron.* 60.13–19, that this principle was already taken for granted by Trypho in the first century BC.

[406] In addition to the passages to be quoted shortly, see also Ap. Dysc., *Pron.* 36.1–3, where the word ἐγκλινόμενον denotes an oxytone word subject to the lulling rule (as also in *On enclitics 2*, §§a, d; cf. *Charax*, §j). Note, however, Maas's (1907) argument that this material belongs to an interpolation; cf. Maas (1903: 61; 1911: 32–3); Thierfelder (1935: 23–4, 26–7).

To begin with the presence of punctuation, in passage (2.7) Apollonius says that the lulling rule applies to an oxytone word 'in juxtaposition with' another word:

(2.7)   . . . πᾶσαι αἱ ὀξύτονοι ἐκφοραὶ ἐν παραθέσει οὖσαι ἑτέρων λέξεων εἰς βαρεῖαν μετατίθενται, ὡς ἐν τῷ 'εἰ μὴ μητρυιὴ' καὶ τοῖς ὁμοίοις. (Ap. Dysc., Constr. 480.5–8)

'. . . all oxytone pronunciations are changed to a grave in juxtaposition with other words, as in εἰ μὴ μητρυιή[407] and the like.'

From his treatment of enclitics, we can deduce that Apollonius understands παράθεσις 'juxtaposition' to imply the absence of intervening punctuation. He holds that enclitic pronoun forms are always 'juxtaposed to some word' (μετά τινος μέρους λόγου παρατίθενται), never pronounced 'by themselves' (κατ' ἰδίαν),[408] and that an enclitic never follows a vocative because a vocative is 'complete in itself' (αὐτοτελής) and therefore needs to be followed by punctuation (στιγμὴν ἀπαιτεῖ).[409] The property of being always 'juxtaposed to some word' appears to prevent enclitics from coming after words that have to be followed by punctuation. That is to say, παράθεσις 'juxtaposition' is disrupted if punctuation intervenes, and so passage (2.7) implies that the lulling rule was blocked when an oxytone word was followed by punctuation.

To turn to the role of an enclitic following an oxytone word, clear evidence that Apollonius thought that a following enclitic reverses the action of the lulling rule comes from passages (2.8) and (2.9).[410] In passage (2.8), Apollonius is discussing alternative analyses of *Iliad* 23.387. One analysis features orthotonic ΌΙ (taken to be a possessive pronoun form meaning 'his', in the nominative plural masculine), while another features enclitic ΌΙ (a third-person-singular personal pronoun form in the dative). The idea that ΌΙ is an enclitic on the second analysis is expressed with the help of the idea that in this case an acute accent falls on the preceding δέ, that is to say on a word considered oxytone:

(2.8)   δι' ὃ κἀκεῖνο τὸ ἀνάγνωσμα οὐκ ἐγκλινόμενον τὴν κτητικὴν ἀντωνυμίαν σημαίνει, 'οἱ δὲ οἳ ἐβλάφθησαν'· ἐγκλιτικῶς γε μὴν ἀναγνωσθέν, ἡνίκα

---

[407] *Il.* 5.389: 'had not their stepmother'. (The Homeric line continues with περικαλλὴς Ἠερίβοια 'very beautiful Eriboia'; like εἰ and μή, μητρυιή is probably considered a naturally oxytone word 'in juxtaposition with other words' here, although some modern editors of Homer print μητρυιή followed by a comma.) The same example illustrates the lulling rule at *On enclitics 2*, §a, and *Charax*, §j.

[408] Ap. Dysc., *Pron.* 49.19–23. Cf. Ap. Dysc., *Constr.* 477.5–8: articles are also not produced κατ' ἰδίαν, but always in juxtaposition with case forms (ἐν παραθέσει οὖσι τῶν πτωτικῶν).

[409] Ap. Dysc., *Pron.* 53.16–19. Like Charax (§p), Apollonius makes an exception for the 'friendly' use of μοι illustrated by Πάτροκλέ μοι δειλῇ 'Patroklos [most dear to the heart to] unhappy me' (*Il.* 19.287).

[410] See also passage (2.20), where the quotation καί μοι ταῦτ' ἀγόρευσον provides an example of an enclitic shifting its accent, as if leaning its weight onto another body.

ὀξύνομεν τὴν ΔΕ συλλαβήν, ἔθος τηρεῖ Ὁμηρικὸν τὸ δοτικὴν ἀντὶ
γενικῆς παρειλῆφθαι. (Ap. Dysc., *Constr.* 314.7–11)

'For this reason the reading without enclisis conveys the possessive pronoun in οἱ δὲ οἳ ἐβλάφθησαν.[411] But when it is read enclitically, when we
give the syllable ΔΕ an acute [i.e. οἱ δέ οἱ ἐβλάφθησαν], it observes the
Homeric habit that a dative is used instead of a genitive.'

In passage (2.9), Apollonius engages with an argument due to Trypho, in the
context of a discussion about whether the accusative pronoun form αὐτόν is
enclitic in some contexts (Trypho thought not, while Apollonius took the
opposite view).[412] Trypho explains that if the enclitic pronoun forms ἑο and οἱ
are replaced by the corresponding forms of αὐτός (i.e. αὐτοῦ and αὐτῷ), at *Od.*
14.461 and *Il.* 21.121 respectively, these replacement forms will not take on the
accentual behaviour of ἑο and οἱ, that is to say they will not cause the preceding
ἐπεί and καί to appear with an acute rather than a grave accent in context.
Apollonius goes on to take issue with one of Trypho's assumptions (the idea
that αὐτοῦ and αὐτῷ can fairly be compared to αὐτόν), but he implicitly accepts
the basic point that matters for us here: unlike αὐτοῦ and αὐτῷ, the forms ἑο
and οἱ reverse the action of the lulling rule on a preceding oxytone word such as
ἐπεί or καί. The point due to Trypho (whose words may or may not be quoted
directly) is shown here between double quotation marks,[413] while the phrase
οὐκ ἤγειρε τὴν ὑπερκειμένην συλλαβὴν εἰς ὀξεῖαν belongs to Apollonius' own
argumentation:

(2.9) "οὐχ ὑγιὲς λέγειν, ἐπεὶ τὸ Ἑ ἐγκλίνεται, εὐθέως καὶ τὸ
μεταλαμβανόμενον ΑΥΤΟΝ. ἰδοὺ γὰρ τὸ 'ἐπεί ἑο κήδετο λίην' καὶ τὸ
'καί οἱ ἐπευχόμενος'· καὶ τὰ μεταλαμβανόμενα ταύτης τῆς τάσεως οὐ
τυγχάνει." ἅπερ οὐκ ἤγειρε τὴν ὑπερκειμένην συλλαβὴν εἰς ὀξεῖαν,
ὁμοίως τῇ 'αὐτόν' αἰτιατικῇ, ἐπεὶ τοῖς τετραχρόνοις τὸ ἐγλιτικὸν οὐ
παρείπετο· (Ap. Dysc., *Pron.* 62.3–10)

'"It is not correct to say that because Ἑ is an enclitic, it follows automatic-
ally that its substitute ΑΥΤΟΝ is an enclitic too. For consider the
examples ἐπεί ἑο κήδετο λίην[414] and καί οἱ ἐπευχόμενος.[415] The substi-
tutes [i.e. αὐτοῦ and αὐτῷ, in hypothetical examples ἐπεί αὐτοῦ κήδετο
λίην and καί αὐτῷ ἐπευχόμενος] do not partake of this accentuation." But

---

[411] *Il.* 23.387: 'but his were hindered'. West (1998–2000) prints the ancient variant ἑοί.
[412] For the idea that αὐτόν can be enclitic compare *Charax*, §q (a passage which has further parallels with Apollonius' discussion, going beyond the extract we quote here).
[413] These are due to Schneider (1878 *ad loc.*), followed by Brandenburg (2005 *ad loc.*).
[414] *Od.* 14.461: 'since he cared about him very much'.
[415] *Il.* 16.829 and *Il.* 21.121: 'And gloating over him'.

those forms [i.e. αὐτοῦ and αὐτῷ] do not wake up the preceding syllable to an acute like the accusative αὐτόν, because enclitic behaviour does not characterize forms with four units of time [i.e. as opposed to αὐτόν, with only three units of time].'

The third exception to the lulling rule is that the accent of interrogative τίς and τί is never lulled. Once again, Apollonius does not explicitly say that these interrogative forms are exempt from the lulling rule—but in passing he makes a point that also appears in Charax's treatise (§1), where it serves to explain why interrogative τίς and τί are exempt from the lulling rule. Apollonius' comment belongs to an argument as to why interrogative forms are never enclitic, and runs as follows:

(2.10)   καὶ ἔνθεν δείκνυται ὅτι τὸ ΤΙΣ ἀοριστούμενον μᾶλλον ὀξύτονόν ἐστιν, πευστικὸν δὲ καθεστὼς τῷ λόγῳ[416] τῆς ἀρχούσης ὀξύνεται. (Ap. Dysc., Constr. 187.11–12)

'And hence it is apparent that indefinite ΤΙΣ is more properly oxytone, but when it is interrogative it has an acute by the principle of the first syllable [i.e. by the principle that the first syllable in the word has the accent].'

The idea is that unlike indefinite ΤΙΣ (which is 'naturally' oxytone and therefore capable of being enclitic), interrogative ΤΙΣ is not 'really' oxytone, because we should consider it accented on its first syllable, not its last. The lone syllable of ΤΙΣ has to do duty for both the 'first' syllable and the 'last'[417]—but since most other Greek direct interrogative forms are accented on their *first* syllables,[418] the single syllable of interrogative τίς should be considered accented in its capacity as

---

[416] Uhlig (followed by Lallot 1997 *ad loc.*) conjectured πευστικὸν δὲ καθεστὼς τῷ λόγῳ ⟨ἐπὶ⟩ τῆς ἀρχούσης ὀξύνεται 'but on becoming interrogative it has an acute on the first syllable, by the general principle', but (as noted by Probert 2019: 57 n. 18) the transmitted text makes good sense and is supported by the identical wording τῷ λόγῳ τῆς ἀρχούσης in *Charax* (§1).

[417] Compare Ap. Dysc., *Adv.* 172.20–3, in connection with perispomenon interrogatives such as πῶς: τὰ πύσματα ἢ φύσει θέλει βαρύνεσθαι ἢ δυνάμει. τὰ γοῦν ὑπὲρ μίαν συλλαβήν, ἔχοντα τόπον τῆς βαρείας, πάντα βαρύνεται· τὰ δὲ μονοσύλλαβα, οὐ δυνάμενα ἐκτὸς τῆς ὀξείας γενέσθαι, δυνάμει ἐβαρύνθη περισπασθέντα 'Interrogatives are barytone [i.e. accented on a non-final syllable] either actually or in effect. For those with more than one syllable, having space for the grave [i.e. on the final syllable], are all barytone. But the monosyllables, not being able to escape from the acute, are barytone in effect by having a circumflex'.

[418] Compare Ap. Dysc., *Pron.* 28.18–19, where the generalization is framed so as to exclude monosyllables: τὰ πύσματα πρὸς πάντων Ἑλλήνων βαρύνεται, ὑπὲρ μίαν συλλαβὴν ὄντα, ὑπεξαιρουμένου τοῦ 'ποδαπός' διὰ τὸν τύπον '[direct] interrogative forms are made "barytone" [i.e. accented on a non-final syllable] by all the Greeks, as long as they have more than one syllable—with the exception of ποδαπός, because of its form'. On our passage (2.10) see also Lallot (1997: ii. 117), who notes the relevance of the oblique case forms τίνα, τίνος, etc. in motivating the idea that interrogative τίς is in principle accented on its 'first' syllable.

an initial syllable, not in its capacity as a final syllable. This point helps to explain why interrogative *TIΣ* is not enclitic, since enclitics are all considered 'naturally' oxytone or perispomenon (for this point in Apollonius Dyscolus, see section 2.8.2), but Apollonius perhaps also had in mind the further point that Charax makes explicit—that this is why interrogative τίς fails to undergo the lulling rule. The phrase τῷ λόγῳ τῆς ἀρχούσης recurs verbatim in Charax,[419] and suggests that Charax depends directly or indirectly on Apollonius' thought here; conceivably Charax's point was already made explicitly in Apollonius' lost work on accents.[420]

In scholarship earlier than Apollonius, one of the clearest pieces of evidence for the lulling rule comes from a Latin text. In his *Institutio oratoria*, Quintilian complains about a fashion for giving certain Latin words an acute accent on the final syllable, against the normal principles of accentuation for Latin.[421] The relevant words are what we would call proclitics, and in ordinary contexts they had no audible accent at all; an example was the preposition *circum* 'around', which was unaccented in a phrase like Vergil's *circum lítora* 'around the shores' (*Aeneid* 4.254). The acute accent that some people assigned to the second syllable of such words (*circúm*) provided a way of thinking about this lack of audible accent, since it enabled them to think of these words as undergoing a Greek-style lulling rule (hence *circùm lítora*). The passage has been discussed by one of us elsewhere,[422] and will not be re-discussed in detail here, but it demonstrates that the Greek lulling rule was a sufficiently well-established doctrine to have influenced Latin grammatical thought by the time Quintilian was writing in the 90s AD.

It is more difficult to find traces of the lulling rule in scholarship earlier than Quintilian, but there are some hints. A clear mention of the rule that might or might not be Hellenistic in date comes from the scholia vetera to Euripides:

(2.11)   μεταβάλλεται μὲν γὰρ εἰς βαρεῖαν ὡς ἐν τῇ συνεπείᾳ, ἀποτίθεται ⟨δὲ⟩ παντελῶς ἐν τοῖς ἐγκλινομένοις, ὡς τὸ 'ἐγώ εἰμι,' 'ἐγώ φημι'· (Scholia vetera in Eur., *Andr.* 250)

'For it [i.e. the acute accent] is transformed into a grave in connected discourse, and it is altogether thrown off in the case of enclitics, as in ἐγώ εἰμι, ἐγώ φημι.'[423]

---

[419] *Charax*, §1. The phrase turns up a few more times in grammatical works, but in other contexts: see Probert (2019: 57–8 n. 19).

[420] See Apollonius' reference to this work at *Constr.* 182.11.

[421] Quintilian, *Inst.* 1.5.25–9.

[422] Probert (2019: 119–31).

[423] 'I am', 'I say'.

The material in these scholia derives for the most part from Alexandrian scholar-ship (see Dickey 2007: 32), but there can be no certainty that any individual com-ment is Hellenistic in date.[424]

Two comments in the Homeric scholia deriving from Herodian suggest that both Ptolemy of Ascalon (first century BC) and Aristarchus (second century BC) gave grave accents to specific monosyllabic words in Homeric passages. The easier passage to interpret is the one concerning Ptolemy of Ascalon:

(2.12)   ἀλλ' ὅτε δὴ ῥ̇· τὸ πλῆρές ἐστι 'δή ῥα', οὐχ ὡς οἴεται ὁ Ἀσκαλωνίτης ὅτι τὸ 'δή' ἐπλεόνασε τῷ 'ῥ'· διὸ βαρύνει. (Sch. Il. 5.334a (A))

'ἀλλ' ὅτε δὴ ῥ̇':[425] The full expression is δή ῥα, not what Ptolemy of Ascalon thinks, i.e. that the δή has an additional ρ. For this reason he gives the form [i.e. δήρ] a grave accent.'

The relevant line of the Iliad runs (in West's text) ἀλλ' ὅτε δὴ ῥ' ἐκίχανε...'But when he had reached her...'. According to Herodian, Ptolemy of Ascalon thought that instead of two words δή ῥα, of which the second was enclitic, there was a single non-enclitic word δήρ, and so in context he gave the word a grave accent: δὴρ. The comment implies that Ptolemy of Ascalon operated with the concept that words like δή and the hypothetical δήρ carry an acute accent before an enclitic and a grave accent before a non-enclitic word. This does not necessarily mean that he conceptualized this alternation in terms of a 'lulling rule', for which the form with the acute accent provided the starting point, although he might well have done so.[426]

A similar conclusion should probably be drawn from the comment concerning Aristarchus, although this comment is more difficult to interpret:

(2.13)   φθὰν δὲ μέγ' ἱππήων ⟨ἐπὶ τάφρῳ κοσμηθέντες⟩· ὁ Ἀρίσταρχος βαρύνει, καὶ δῆλον ὅτι ὑγιῶς· κοιμίζεται γὰρ ἡ ὀξεῖα ἐν τῇ συνεπείᾳ· 'Ζεὺς δ' ἐπεὶ οὖν Τρῶάς τε'. (Sch. Il. 11.51b (A))

---

[424] The sentence we quote as passage (2.11) is followed by the claim that the negation 'ΟΥ always has an acute, never a grave, because of the way the head is moved upwards when one says 'ΟΥ 'no'. We are not aware of any parallel for this idea, and it is difficult to see it as going back to a very early date—but it is also tangential to the discussion at hand, and could be late without passage (2.11) necessarily being late too.

[425] Il. 5.334: 'But when indeed'.

[426] Compare Sch. Il. 6.260a¹ (A), suggesting that Ptolemy of Ascalon's view that ἔπειτα δέ κ' αὐτὸς was to be read at Il. 6.260 (with the κ' as elided κε, rather than by crasis for καί) was expressed by prescribing a 'revived' acute for the δέ, while those who read ἔπειτα δὲ καὐτὸς, with the κ- by crasis for καί, expressed this view by giving δὲ a grave accent.

'φθὰν δὲ μέγ' ἱππήων ἐπὶ τάφρῳ κοσμηθέντες:'[427] Aristarchus puts a grave accent, and it's clear that he's right. For the acute accent is lulled in connected discourse, as in Ζεὺς δ' ἐπεὶ οὖν Τρῶάς τε.'[428]

We are not told here where exactly Aristarchus put a grave accent, only that he put one in a place that Herodian considered correct in the light of the lulling rule. Erbse (*ad loc.*) suggested that Aristarchus assigned a grave accent to the word φθάν (i.e. φθὰν), and that this was his way of expressing the reading φθὰν δὲ (as two words) rather than φθάνδε or φθᾶνδε.[429] The late Martin West once suggested to one of us that the point could be, instead, Aristarchus' judgement that φθάν had a short alpha rather than a long one; in this case φθὰν δὲ would be opposed to φθᾶν δὲ rather than φθάνδε or φθᾶνδε. As West (if we have understood him rightly) recognized, however, the supporting statement κοιμίζεται γὰρ ἡ ὀξεῖα ἐν τῇ συνεπείᾳ would suggest that Herodian understood Aristarchus' thought in the same way as Erbse. Either way, Aristarchus probably assigned a grave accent to φθάν in this line. Strictly speaking, Herodian's comment does not prove that Aristarchus thought in terms of a 'lulling rule' in which φθάν counted as the start-ing point, although in the absence of evidence to the contrary it is most econom-ical to think that he did—but in one way or another, it appears that Aristarchus already operated with the idea that a word like φθάν/φθὰν carried a grave accent when followed immediately by another non-enclitic word.

2.8.2 The natural accent of an enclitic

Apollonius Dyscolus makes it clear in several passages that—like our Byzantine treatises on enclitics—he considers enclitics all either 'oxytone' or 'perispomenon', and that this oxytone or perispomenon accentuation provides the starting point for rules throwing the accent off the final syllable of the enclitic. His most explicit statements of the idea that *all* enclitics are 'oxytone' or 'perispomenon' appear in passages (2.14) and (2.15):[430]

(2.14)   αἱ δυϊκαὶ τοῦ πρώτου καὶ δευτέρου πάσης πτώσεως ὀρθοτονοῦνται. ὑπὲρ μὲν οὖν τῆς εὐθείας οὐ χρὴ παλιλλογεῖν, ὑπὲρ δὲ τῶν λειπομένων

---

[427] *Il.* 11.51: 'And they (the foot-soldiers) were drawn up at the ditch far in front of the chariot-fighters'.

[428] *Il.* 13.1: 'And when Zeus had [brought] the Trojans [and Hektor to the ships]'.

[429] Cf. Probert (2015: 937); Schironi (2018: 113).

[430] Compare the following passages, in which Apollonius mentions that an enclitic cannot be 'barytone': *Pron.* 90.13–18; *Constr.* 136.12–137.2; *Constr.* 187.4–8; *Constr.* 373.10.

ἐκεῖνο ἂν αἴτιον εἴη, τὸ πᾶν μόριον ἐγκλιτικὸν ἤτοι ἀπὸ περισπωμένου ἢ
ἀπὸ ὀξυτόνου ἐγκεκλίσθαι· ἀπὸ γὰρ βαρυτόνου ἀδύνατον· 'πῶς', 'ἦλθέ
πως', 'Ἀρίσταρχός ποτε', 'ἄνθρωποί εἰσι'· καὶ ἐπὶ τῶν ὑπολειπομένων τὸ
αὐτό. εὐλόγως οὖν διὰ τὴν ἐπὶ τέλους βαρύτητα ἡ ἔγκλισις οὐκ ἦν. καὶ
γὰρ κατὰ τοῦτον τὸν λόγον ἡ 'ἐκεῖνος' καὶ 'οὗτος' πάλιν μόνως
ὀρθοτονοῦνται...(Ap. Dysc., *Pron.* 38.9–16)[431]

'The duals of the first and second person are orthotonic in every case
form. As regards the nominative there is no need for a repeat discussion, but as regards the remaining forms [νῶϊν, σφῶϊν] the reason
would be that every enclitic item throws back its accent starting from
either a perispomenon or an oxytone form. For starting from a barytone form it is impossible. So πῶς [i.e. indefinite ΠΩΣ, considered to
have a circumflex as its 'natural accent'] gives ἦλθέ πως, [and simi-
larly] Ἀρίσταρχός ποτε, ἄνθρωποί εἰσι,[432] and similarly for the rest.
So it stands to reason that there was no enclisis [in genitive/dative
first- and second-person dual pronoun forms], because of the grave
accent on the final syllable. And for the same reason ἐκεῖνος and οὗτος
are also exclusively orthotonic...'

(2.15)   προευθέτισται γὰρ τὰ ἐγκλιτικὰ μόρια ἐπὶ τέλους ἔχειν τὴν ὀξεῖαν, ἢ
φύσει ἢ δυνάμει (λέγω δὲ δυνάμει διὰ τὰ περισπώμενα), ἵνα ἡ τοῦ
τόνου ὑποστροφὴ τὸ μὲν προκείμενον ὀξύνῃ, αὐτὸ δὲ μεταστήσῃ εἰς
βαρεῖαν τάσιν· (Ap. Dysc., *Constr.* 186.15–187.1)

'For enclitic items are predisposed[433] to have an acute on the last syllable,
either actually or in effect (I say 'in effect' because of the perispomenon
words), so that the throwing back of the accent puts an acute accent on
the preceding word, and changes the enclitic itself to having a grave
accent [i.e. on its final syllable].'

The idea that perispomenon words have an acute on the last syllable 'in effect'
(δυνάμει) depends on the idea that a circumflex represents a combination of
acute and grave accents on a single syllable.[434] A syllable with a circumflex does
not 'actually' (φύσει) have an acute accent, insofar as the acute and circumflex are
considered different accents from one another, but it has one 'in effect', insofar as a

---

[431] The ideas expressed in passage (2.14) are repeated soon afterwards at *Pron.* 39.7–11; on this
basis Skrzeczka (1847: 12, followed by Schneider 1878: 39 and Brandenburg 2005: 324) suggested that
the latter passage was an intrusion based on the former, while Maas (1911: 36) suggested that the
repetition pointed to the existence of successive redactions of the text.
[432] 'He came in some way'; 'Aristarchus once'; 'people are'.
[433] For the sense of προευθέτισται see Lallot (1997: ii. 116).
[434] Cf. section 2.7.1.

circumflex effectively contains an acute. This point is made more explicitly in passage (2.16). In this passage the discussion is limited to pronouns, but a comparison with passages (2.14) and (2.15) shows that the point 'their last syllable...has an acute accent either actually or in effect' is meant to be valid for enclitics in general.

(2.16)   συμβέβηκε τῶν ἀντωνυμιῶν ἃς μὲν ὀρθοτονεῖσθαι, τουτέστι τὸν κατὰ
         φύσιν τόνον ἔχειν, ἃς δὲ ἐγκλίνεσθαι, ὧν τὸ τέλος, λέγω δὴ τῶν
         ἐγκλινομένων, ἢ φύσει ὀξύνεται ἢ δυνάμει, ὡς τὰ περισπώμενα. ἐν
         αὐτοῖς γὰρ ἔχει ὀξεῖαν. ἥτις μεθίσταται κατὰ τὴν ἄρχουσαν
         συλλαβήν, ὡς ἐπὶ τῶν τετραχρόνων, 'ἥρπασέ τις ἥμων', ἢ κατὰ τὸ
         τέλος τῆς ὑπερκειμένης λέξεως, ὡς ἐπὶ τῶν ἐλάττονας χρόνους
         ἀναδεξαμένων, τοῦ τονικοῦ οὐκ ἐμποδίζοντος, 'ἀνθρώποις μοι', 'τίς τάρ
         σφωε'. (Ap. Dysc., *Pron.* 35.7–14)

> 'It is characteristic of pronouns that some are orthotonic, that is to say
> they have their natural accent, while some are enclitic; their last syl-
> lable (I mean that of the enclitics) has an acute accent either actually
> or in effect—the latter in the case of the perispomena. For they have an
> acute accent within themselves. That moves onto the initial syllable, as
> in the case of those enclitics with four units of time (e.g. ἥρπασέ τις
> ἥμων[435]), or onto the end of the preceding word, as in the case of those
> which have received fewer units of time (as long as the accent rule
> does not stand in the way, as it does in ἀνθρώποις μοι[436]): τίς τάρ
> σφωε.'[437]

For scholarship earlier than Apollonius, we are not aware of evidence that every enclitic was thought of as having a natural accent on its final or only syllable, nor of evidence to the contrary. The doctrine is likely to have been a standard one by the time Apollonius was writing, since he invokes it repeatedly without suggesting that it is original to him, but more cannot be said on this point.

2.8.3 Accenting a word followed by an enclitic: the main doctrines

As far as we can piece together his assumptions about the accentuation of a word followed by an enclitic, Apollonius Dyscolus works with principles that coincide very closely with those we have seen in our Byzantine treatises. We have already

---

[435] 'One of us snatched'.
[436] 'People [dative] me [dative]'.
[437] *Il.* 1.8: 'Who [of the gods], then, [threw] the two of them [together to quarrel with strife]?'

seen that he regarded enclitics as causing an acute rather than grave accent to appear on the final syllable of a preceding oxytone word (passages (2.8) and (2.9)), and he also took it for granted that an enclitic left a preceding perispomenon word unchanged:[438]

(2.17)   αἱ ἀντωνυμίαι τὴν περισπωμένην ὑπερκειμένην φυλάσσουσι, ʽπῶς μοι, ʽκαλῶς μοι· (Ap. Dysc., *Pron.* 34.23–4)

'[Enclitic] pronouns keep a preceding circumflex as it is, as in πῶς μοι, καλῶς μοι.'[439]

(2.18)   εἴπερ ἄρα δύο μέρη λόγου τὸ ʽὤμοι' ἦν, καὶ πάντως ἡ τοῦ ʽὤ' περισπωμένη ἐσώζετο, εἴγε ἀμετάθετοι αἱ περισπώμεναι, κἂν ἐγκλιτικὸν ἐπιφέρηται κἂν ἀνέγκλιτον. (Ap. Dysc., *Adv.* 127.24–6)

'If ὤμοι were two words, the circumflex of the ὤ would certainly be preserved, given that circumflexes are immutable, whether an enclitic or a non-enclitic word follows.'

Beyond this, Apollonius works with the rules deriving Ὅμηρός ἐστι from the starting point Ὅμηρος ἐστί, and γυναῖκές εἰσι from γυναῖκες εἰσί. In passage (2.19), for example, he is commenting on the -δε that combines with an accusative to express motion towards something, and has the accentual effects of an enclitic in many (but not all) combinations. He envisages a starting point Οὔλυμπον δέ giving rise to Οὐλυμπόνδε 'to Olympus', and likewise a starting point οἶκον δέ giving rise to οἰκόνδε 'to home':

(2.19)   τὸ γὰρ ʽοἶκον' προπερισπᾶται, καὶ πάλιν ἐν τῇ προσθέσει τοῦ ʽδέ' μένει ὁ αὐτὸς τόνος, ʽοἶκον δέ, μετὰ τοῦ καὶ τὴν ὀξεῖαν ἐπὶ τέλους εἶναι. ὁ αὐτὸς λόγος ἐπὶ τοῦ ʽὌλυμπον' καὶ ʽΟὔλυμπον δέ. (Ap. Dysc., *Adv.* 177.26–8)

'For the word οἶκον is properispomenon, and the same accent remains with the addition of δέ, giving οἶκον δέ, along with the acute going on the last syllable [i.e. the eventual form is οἰκόνδε]. And the same applies to Ὄλυμπον and Οὔλυμπον δέ [i.e. the eventual form is Οὐλυμπόνδε].'[440]

---

[438] In addition to the passages cited here, cf. Ap. Dysc., *Pron.* 43.11, but note Maas's (1911: 39) judgement that the relevant comment is an interpolation here.

[439] 'How to me'; 'well to me'.

[440] Cf. passage (2.14) and Ap. Dysc., *Constr.* 179.4–6. Compare also Ap. Dysc., *Pron.* 36.4–5, but note again Maas's reasoned view that this material belongs to an interpolation (see n. 406). For a different interpretation of passage (2.19), see Dumarty (2021: 426–7).

Passage (2.16), already quoted, hints at the further point that at least some paroxytone words fail to receive a second accent when an enclitic follows: this appears to be the sense of the comment τοῦ τονικοῦ οὐκ ἐμποδίζοντος 'as long as the accent rule does not stand in the way', and of the example ἀνθρώποις μοι.

In Apollonius we find no evidence of the idea that a paroxytone word with a trochaic termination does after all receive a second accent from a following enclitic (so ἔνθά τε), nor of the idea that an enclitic fails to throw its accent back onto a preceding properispomenon word if this has a final consonant cluster (so κῆρυξ ἐστί, despite γυναῖκές εἰσι). We also find no evidence of the curious exception for the Homeric phrase ἔνθ᾽ ἔσάν οἱ πέπλοι, nor for paroxytone words followed by enclitic pronouns beginning with σφ-. We do not know whether Apollonius operated with any of these ideas too, but the backbone of the system we see in the Byzantine treatises is clearly known to him already.

Furthermore, the idea that paroxytone words ending in a trochaic sequence receive a second accent when followed by an enclitic is visible in the Homeric scholia deriving from Herodian,[441] as is the idea that ἔσαν receives a second accent before enclitic οἱ,[442] and the idea that paroxytone words receive a second accent before enclitic pronoun forms beginning with σφ-.[443] These notions therefore go back at least as far as Apollonius' son, who also adds two further points that we have not seen in the Byzantine treatises. Firstly, he suggests that in two contexts a paroxytone word receives a second accent before an enclitic despite ending in a spondaic sequence: γενέσθαί τε[444] at Iliad 7.199 and λοέσσαί τε[445] at Odyssey 19.320.[446] Herodian apparently justified both instances on the basis that the additional accent helped to avoid an ambiguity, although modern scholars have suspected that in reality the sequences counted as 'trochaic' because

---

[441] This point is implied collectively by the following scholia, which between them make clear that paroxytone words normally fail to receive a second accent before an enclitic if they end in a pyrrhic, iambic, or spondaic sequence (by implication it is necessary to specify these metrical shapes because not all paroxytone words behave in the same way, and the only two-syllable metrical shape left unaccounted for is the trochee): Sch. Il. 2.255b (AT) (paroxytone words ending in two short syllables fail to receive a second accent before an enclitic, with the exception of the ΕΣΑΝ in ἔνθ᾽ ἔσάν οἱ πέπλοι); Sch. Il. 6.289a¹ (A) (specifying that the first word of ἔσάν οἱ is to be read with two accents, despite its pyrrhic shape); Sch. Il. 7.199b (A) (γενέσθαι at Il. 7.199 and λοέσσαι at Od. 19.320 receive a second accent before τε despite ending in spondaic sequences); Sch. Od. 1.170a Pontani (HMᵃ) (because of its pyrrhic shape, πόθεν does not receive a second accent before enclitic εἰς); Sch. Od. 12.40 (H) (paroxytone words receive a second accent before an enclitic pronoun beginning with σφ- even if they end in a spondaic, pyrrhic, or iambic sequence). Also relevant are Sch. Od. 7.200a Pontani (HP¹) (ἄλλο should have been given a second accent before enclitic τι), where the sequence preceding the enclitic is trochaic; Sch. Od. 1.1a Pontani (MᵃO), to be discussed shortly; and our passages (4.9) and (4.10), to be discussed in section 4.2.3.

[442] Sch. Il. 2.255b (AT); Sch. Il. 6.289a¹ (A); Sch. Il. 6.289a² (T); Sch. Od. 15.105 (H) (but note that the line is numbered 106 in Dindorf 1855). For the Herodianic origins of Sch. Od. 15.105 (H), see Ludwich (1877: 194).

[443] Sch. Il. 2.255b (AT); Sch. Il. 6.367b (A); Sch. Od. 12.40 (H); cf. Lehrs (1837: 106-7).

[444] 'To have been born and [brought up]'.

[445] 'Both wash [him and rub him with oil]'.

[446] Sch. Il. 7.199b (A) (on the origins of this scholion see Erbse 1960: 394, against Laum 1928: 242).

the final -αι of the infinitives counted 'short' for the purposes of the accent.[447] Secondly, and more enigmatically, Herodian appears to have held that the exception for enclitic pronoun forms beginning with σφ- had its own sub-exception: in the verse οὐ γάρ τ' οἶδ' εἰ ἔτι σφιν ὑπότροπος ἵξομαι αὖτις,[448] he apparently held that the word ἔτι exceptionally fails to receive a second accent before the enclitic σφιν.[449]

Returning to the system as a whole, crucial elements of this system can also be glimpsed in the extant fragments of scholarship earlier than Apollonius Dyscolus. One of the *Iliad* scholia deriving from Herodian suggests that Ptolemy of Ascalon and Aristarchus expressed their reading κελεύετέ μ' αὐτὸν ἑλέσθαι[450] at *Iliad* 10.242 (as opposed to κελεύετ' ἐμαυτὸν ἑλέσθαι) by putting an acute accent on the syllable -τε.[451] In a similar vein, some sources report that Aristarchus read κεῖνός θ' ὣς ἀγόρευε[452] (rather than κεῖνος τὼς ἀγόρευε) at *Iliad* 2.330, and one of these suggests that he expressed this (at least in part) in terms of the syllable -νός requiring an acute accent because of the enclitic τε.[453] It appears, then, that Aristarchus already operated with the principle that proparoxytone and properispomenon words received a second accent when followed by an enclitic. To our knowledge, we lack evidence that would show quite how he conceptualized this principle (whether he thought in terms of the enclitic throwing back its accent, for example), but in one way or another he took the principle itself for granted.

An enigmatic story about Aristarchus bears on the status in the Hellenistic period of what we might call the 'trochaic principle'—the idea that paroxytone words receive a second accent before an enclitic if they end in a trochaic sequence. We have already mentioned[454] Charax's claim that Aristarchus refused to apply the special rule for paroxytone words with a trochaic termination to the first line of the *Odyssey*.[455] The story appears to have some sort of tradition behind it: it is found not only in Charax but also in a scholion to the *Odyssey* that in Pontani's judgement goes back to Herodian.[456] Charax and the scholion each offer an explanation for Aristarchus' rejection of the accentuation

---

[447] So West (1966: 440); Probert (2003: 149–50).

[448] *Il.* 6.367: 'For I do not know whether I will come back to them any more'.

[449] So Sch. *Il.* 6.367b (A); Sch. *Od.* 12.40 (H).

[450] 'You urge me to choose [a companion] for myself'.

[451] Sch. *Il.* 10.242b¹ (A).

[452] 'Thus he spoke'.

[453] Sch. *Il.* 2.330a (bT), a version of Aristarchus, fr. 13 Schironi (for versions holding that κεῖνός θ' ὣς ἀγόρευε was Herodian's reading, not Aristarchus', and for the likelihood that it should be ascribed to Aristarchus, see Schironi 2004: 131–7). Compare also the Herodianic scholion Sch. *Il.* 16.207a (A), which makes it likely that Aristarchus prescribed an acute accent on the syllable TA as a way of expressing the idea that ME is an enclitic in ταῦτά μ' ἀγειρόμενοι (cf. also Laum 1928: 243).

[454] Section 2.7.5.

[455] *Charax*, §g.

[456] Sch. *Od.* 1.1a Pontani (MᵃO), with Pontani *ad loc.*

ἄνδρά μοι. The scholion claims that the point was to avoid a harsh sound at the beginning of the poem (διὰ τὸ μὴ ἐν τῇ εἰσβολῇ κακοφωνίαν ποιῆσαι), while Charax quotes what purport to be Aristarchus' own words: ἐν ἀρχῇ ποιήσεως παράλογον οὐ μὴ ποιήσω 'at the beginning of the poem I will not create an irregularity'. Since these explanations diverge from each other it is tempting to dismiss both of them, retaining only the idea that Aristarchus accented the first two words of the *Odyssey* as ἄνδρα μοι. In that case, one might think either that the trochaic principle was unknown to Aristarchus or that he rejected it entirely—and if he knew of the principle but rejected it, the debate known to our Byzantine sources could date back to the Hellenistic period. Yet both sources for the story agree that Aristarchus singled out the beginning of the poem for special treatment. In so doing both presuppose that Aristarchus knew of the trochaic principle and thought that it normally applied—otherwise there would be no point in making a special exception for this particular line. In Charax's version, moreover, this presupposition comes through even though it is actually unhelpful to his case that the ἀκριβεῖς disapproved of the trochaic principle. Cautiously, we take it that Aristarchus did indeed take the trochaic principle for granted, and that for some reason he treated the beginning of the poem as an exception.[457]

2.8.4 Metaphors

We saw in section 2.7.4 that three metaphors for enclitic behaviour turn up in our Byzantine treatises: enclitics lean back, transfer their accents to the preceding word, or wake up sleeping accents. All three metaphors can be found in Apollonius Dyscolus, the earliest author whose use of language for accents is available to us in any detail.

In passage (2.20) Apollonius explains the 'leaning back' metaphor, and links it to the 'transfer of an accent' metaphor: an enclitic passes its accent onto another word like someone who transfers weight onto another body by leaning onto it.

(2.20) καλοῦνται αἱ ἐντελεῖς κατὰ τὴν φωνὴν καὶ τὸν διεγηγερμένον τόνον ὀρθοτονούμεναι, τάχα συνωνυμοῦντος τοῦ ὀρθοῦ καὶ τοῦ ὑγιοῦς· αἱ δὲ τὸν τόνον μετατιθεῖσαι ὡσπερεὶ βάρος ἀπὸ τῶν ἐγκλινόντων τὰ βάρη ἐφ᾽ ἕτερον σῶμα ἐγκλιτικαί· εἴγε τὸ ʽσοὶ μὲν ἐγώ, σὺ δ᾽ ἐμοίʼ μετὰ τῆς ἐντελοῦς γραφῆς καὶ τὸν ἴδιον τόνον ἔχει, τὸ δὲ ʽκαί μοι ταῦτ᾽ ἀγόρευσονʼ παρῆκεν μὲν τὴν γραφήν, μετέθηκεν δὲ καὶ τὸν τόνον. (Ap. Dysc., *Constr.* 133.9–16)

---

[457] Quite why he did this is another question. Perhaps he thought that the opening words of the *Odyssey* should be delivered slowly and carefully, and perhaps in this style of delivery the word ἄνδρα was produced as a unit independent of what followed (ἄνδρα…μοι ἔννεπε).

'Words that are intact as regards their production and their awake accent are called "orthotonic" [literally "straight-accented"], with "straight" and "healthy" being virtually synonymous. But those that shift their accent, as if it were a weight, are called "enclitics" [literally "leaners"] after those who lean weights onto another body. So while [the ἐμοί of] σοὶ μὲν ἐγώ, σὺ δ' ἐμοί⁴⁵⁸ has its own accent along with its intact spelling, [the μοι of] καί μοι ταῦτ' ἀγόρευσον⁴⁵⁹ has both let go of its spelling and changed the place of its accent.'

The reference to transferring something to another body (ἐφ' ἕτερον σῶμα) suggests that Apollonius thinks of enclitics as words that prototypically transfer their accents to the preceding word.⁴⁶⁰ But he recognizes that enclitics fail to transfer their accents when the accent of the preceding word prevents it, and he also recognizes a category of enclitics consisting of two long syllables, which transfer their accents only onto their own first syllables.⁴⁶¹ In practice he generally uses the verb ἐγκλίνομαι and its derivatives to signal that a word is an enclitic, whether or not he draws attention to an example involving a clear transfer of accent.

In two passages (our (2.9) and (2.21)) Apollonius also makes use of the 'waking up' metaphor, in which an enclitic is conceived as waking up a grave accent on the syllable preceding itself. It is clear from passage (2.9) that he considered this metaphor usable in connection with an enclitic 'waking up' the grave accent on the final syllable of an oxytone word (as in ἐπεί ἑο and καί οἱ). It is less clear whether he also considered the metaphor usable in connection with enclitics 'waking up' the potential acute accent on the final syllable of any other words, but passage (2.21) probably suggests that he did:

(2.21)   ἴσως τις φήσει, 'ἰδοὺ ἡ "ἡμέων" βαρυτονουμένη ἐγκλιτική ἐστι.' πρῶτον οὐ φύσει βαρύνεται, διῄρηται δὲ ἐκ περισπωμένου· διόπερ ἀκωλύτως τὴν ἔγκλισιν ἀνεδέξατο. ἔπειτα τὰ ἐγκλιτικὰ λεγόμενα τὴν τῆς ὑπερκειμένης λέξεως ὀξεῖαν ἐγείρει. (Ap. Dysc., *Pron.* 90.16–19)

'Perhaps someone will say, "There now, the barytone word ἡμέων is an enclitic." Firstly, it is not barytone by nature, but has been resolved from a perispomenon form; for this reason it has admitted the throwing back of the accent without hindrance. Secondly, the words called 'enclitics' wake up the acute accent of the word preceding themselves [i.e. unlike ἡμέων, whose accent has been transferred to its own first syllable].'

⁴⁵⁸ *Il.* 4.63: 'I to you, and you to me'.
⁴⁵⁹ *Od.* 13.232: 'And tell me these things' (with the known variant reading ταῦτ' rather than τοῦτ').
⁴⁶⁰ Cf. Ap. Dysc., *Pron.* 39.24–5; 90.18–19; *Constr.* 177.17–178.3; 180.4–5; 183.1–4; 228.4.
⁴⁶¹ For both points see, for example, passage (2.16).

Enclitics are here portrayed as words that prototypically 'wake up the acute accent of the word preceding themselves'. We have just seen that Apollonius also regarded enclitics as words that prototypically transfer their accents to the preceding word, and in this light it is most likely that he thought of the two concepts as equivalent. That is to say, enclitics 'wake up' a latent acute on the last syllable of the preceding word wherever they are in a position to cause an acute to end up on that syllable. If the 'waking up' metaphor originated with the 'waking up' of the acute accent of an oxytone word, as we suggested tentatively in section 2.7.4, its use had probably been extended to further contexts by Apollonius' time.

A related metaphor appears in passage (2.22). When an enclitic causes an acute accent to appear on the preceding syllable, the acute of this syllable is this time said to have 'risen up':

(2.22) πᾶν μόριον ἐγκλιτικὸν λέξις ἐστίν, 'ἦλθέ τις', 'ἄνθρωπός εἰμι'·
πάμπολλοι δέ εἰσιν οἱ παραπληρωματικοὶ ἐν ἐγκλίσει, ὡς ὁ ΓΕ, ὁ ΡΑ,
ὁ ΘΗΝ, ⟨ὁ⟩ ΝΥ. δύο λέξεων ἢ τριῶν οὐσῶν ἀκώλυτον τὸ ἐπάλληλον
τῆς ὀξείας· καὶ κατὰ τοῦτο οὖν λέξεις τὰ προκείμενα μόρια· ἰδοὺ γὰρ
ἐν τῷ 'ἦ νύ σέ που δέος ἴσχει' καθ' ἓν ἕκαστον μέρος λόγου ἡ ὀξεῖα
ἀνέστη. (Ap. Dysc., Conj. 249.14–20)

'Every enclitic item is a word, as in ἦλθέ τις and ἄνθρωπός εἰμι.[462] There are very many filler particles that are enclitic: e.g. ΓΕ, ΡΑ, ΘΗΝ, and ΝΥ. When there are two [such] words or three, the succession of acute accents is unimpeded. And for this reason the items in question are words. Thus in ἦ νύ σέ που δέος ἴσχει[463] the acute accent has risen up on each word individually.'

Dalimier (2001: 393) notes that the concept of an accent 'rising up' is reminiscent of the concept of an ὀρθὸς τόνος 'upright accent':[464] a natural accent that survives without alteration to the form actually produced in context. In connection with the action of an enclitic, the idea that an accent 'rises up' is also reminiscent of the idea that it can be 'woken up'.[465] Nevertheless, we are aware of only one parallel for Apollonius' use of ἀνίστημι in this connection, in the prolegomena to the 'Vatican scholia' on the Τέχνη γραμματική attributed to Dionysius Thrax,[466] and at least one scholar has thought passage (2.22) an interpolation into the text of Apollonius (Laum 1928: 488 with n. 1). The passage will be of interest to us in

---

[462] 'Someone came', 'I am a person'.
[463] Il. 5.812: 'or perhaps fear has got hold of you'.
[464] E.g. Ap. Dysc., Pron. 36.10; 39.15.
[465] For the use of intransitive forms of ἀνίστημι in connection with rising from bed or sleep, see LSJ s.v. ἀνίστημι, B. I. 2.
[466] Sch. D. Thr. 153.18.

connection with the history of thought on sequences of enclitics, and we shall return to this question in that context (section 4.2.6, with 4.2.1).

2.9 Conclusions

The broadly Byzantine texts we present in sections 2.1–2.6 provide us with continuous discussions of enclitics and their accentual effects. To reconstruct earlier stages in the tradition, we rely on scattered comments in works on other topics, but a considerable amount can be gleaned not least from the works of Apollonius Dyscolus, and from Homeric scholia deriving from his son Herodian. The Byzantine treatises lay out a system that was already in place, in its outlines and in many of its details, by the time these scholars were writing in the second century AD. Many of the ideas are likely to derive from Hellenistic scholarship, although the scarcity of our evidence for Hellenistic scholarship on accents means that many details must remain obscure.

3

The accent of ἘΣΤΙ

3.1 Introduction

At Aristophanes, *Wasps* 28–9, where Sosias says of his recent dream, 'but it's big: for it's about the city', Sommerstein (1983) prints ἀλλ' ἔστιν μέγα. | περὶ τῆς πόλεως γάρ ἐστι, while Wilson (2007a) prints ἀλλ' ἐστὶν μέγα. | περὶ τῆς πόλεως γάρ ἐστι. At *Wasps* 64, both editors print ἀλλ' ἔστιν ἡμῖν λογίδιον γνώμην ἔχον ('but we have a little story with meaning'). Two of the three instances of ἘΣΤΙ(Ν) (for simplicity we shall call the form ἘΣΤΙ) appearing in these quotations are accented in the same way by both editors, but one is accented differently. Why does editorial practice vary, and what is the correct rule?

The first of these questions is the easier to answer. In essence there are two modern views:[1]

(a) Non-enclitic ἔστι occurs at the beginning of the clause or verse, and under circumstances that vary from one modern scholar to another but usually involve a preceding οὐ, καί, εἰ, ἀλλά, ὡς, or perhaps τοῦτο. For at least some scholars holding this view, non-enclitic ἔστι occurs in clause-initial or verse-initial position and specifically when the *only* preceding word in the clause is οὐ, καί, εἰ, ἀλλά, ὡς, or (perhaps) τοῦτο. With the possible exception of τοῦτο, these words are understood as standing outside the clause proper, in some sense, so that one can talk about 'initial and quasi-initial position'.[2] Martin West considered that non-enclitic ἔστι occured in

---

[1] One could attempt to formulate both views in more precise linguistic terms. For instance, one could consider whether the environment under which the first view takes non-enclitic ἔστι to appear is best defined in syntactic or prosodic terms: does non-enclitic ἔστι appear when ἘΣΤΙ is the first word in some syntactic unit ('clause proper') or when it is the first word in some intonational unit? Is the important point about the words οὐ, καί, and so on their syntactic status or—as per West—their prosodic status as proclitics? Is the answer necessarily the same for οὐ and (for example) for καί? We leave these questions open, since these views simply provide a starting point for our own discussion; we shall not ultimately be arguing that either tells the whole story.

[2] This form of the doctrine is foreshadowed by Wackernagel (1877: 466–7), who held that non-enclitic ἔστι occurs in initial position and after οὐ, καί, εἰ, ἀλλά, ὡς, or τοῦτο, with some of these words being incapable of hosting an enclitic and others standing outside the clause proper, and with the sequence τοῦτ' ἐστι(ν) perhaps representing a further unrelated situation. (Wackernagel's formulation also recognizes a point that will become important for us in section 3.2: that some ancient sources mention only οὐ in this connection, and some only οὐ, καί, and ὡς.) Barrett (1964: 425–6), followed by Kahn 1973: 420–4, esp. 422) speaks explicitly of non-enclitic ἔστι occurring in initial and 'quasi-initial' position.

Ancient and Medieval Thought on Greek Enclitics. Stephanie Roussou & Philomen Probert, Oxford University Press. © Stephanie Roussou and Philomen Probert 2023.
DOI: 10.1093/oso/9780192871671.003.0003

initial or quasi-initial position in a verse or in a colon, in the sense of Fraenkel (1933; 1964)—a unit likely to have been set off intonationally. He also considered that the important unifying feature of οὐ, καί, εἰ, ἀλλά, and ὡς was their proclitic status: that is to say, these are words likely to have formed an accentual unit with what follows them.[3] It should follow from his view that the same principle is extendable to other proclitics, and he accordingly prints line- and utterance-initial οὐδ᾽ ἔστιν at *Prometheus Bound* 769.[4] We shall call this view (in its various manifestations) the 'initial and quasi-initial' view.

(b) Non-enclitic ἔστι occurs when the word is not just the copula (that is to say, when it does more than just join a subject and predicate), and is not omissible (Hermann 1801: 84–90). This view is normally now taken to mean that non-enclitic ἔστι occurs at the beginning of the clause or verse, and otherwise when the word indicates existence or possibility (when it is translatable as 'exists', 'there is', 'it is possible', or 'it is allowed').[5] We shall call this the 'existential' view (although we shall revisit Hermann's original version briefly in section 3.5.2).

In practice, these approaches produce different results under some circumstances but not others. At Aristophanes, *Wasps* 28, Sommerstein's ἀλλ᾽ ἔστιν μέγα reflects the 'initial and quasi-initial' view, and Wilson's ἀλλ᾽ ἐστὶν μέγα the 'existential' view. On the first, what matters is the position of 'EΣTI after ἀλλ(ά), and on the second its function as a simple copula ('but [the dream] is big'). At *Wasps* 29, both views call for περὶ τῆς πόλεως γάρ ἐστι, but for different reasons: because of the 'non-quasi-initial' position of 'EΣTI after γάρ, or because of its function as a simple copula ('for [the dream] is about the city'). At *Wasps* 64, both views call for ἀλλ᾽ ἔστιν ἡμῖν λογίδιον γνώμην ἔχον: either because 'EΣTI once again follows ἀλλ(ά), or because this time its meaning is existential (literally 'but there is to us a little story with meaning'). In practice, editors may combine the two approaches, and it is not our purpose to provide a complete description of the editorial practice of Sommerstein or of Wilson—but the point that both approaches produce the same results some of the time will be an important theme for this chapter.

---

[3] See West (1990: xxxi): 'EΣTI is enclitic 'nisi primum locum in versu sive in colo syntactico occupat, vel solo proclitico (οὐκ, καί, εἰ, ἀλλά, ὡς) praeceditur'. For καί, ἀλλά, and ὡς as elements that may stand outside the colon proper (or form 'short cola'), see Fraenkel (1933: 341–2 n. 1, 345 n. 4; 1964: 135–6).

[4] Because West regarded the colon rather than the clause as the unit within which orthotonic ἔστι(ν) must come first or second, he printed οὐκ ἔστι(ν) in a variety of places that would not normally be considered 'clause-initial', but where a new syntactic unit begins with the οὐκ (so τόθεν οὐκ ἔστιν...at *Persae* 100; χωρίς τε γένους οὐκ ἔστιν ὅτῳ...at *Prometheus Bound* 291). In fact West's editions of Aeschylus and of Homer always feature non-enclitic ἔστι, never enclitic ἐστι, after οὐκ, presumably because all the instances allow the οὐκ to be interpreted as beginning a colon. West does not comment on the sequence τοῦτ᾽ ἔστι, but prints τοῦτ᾽ ἔστιν at *Il.* 1.564.

[5] In this form the view was defended by Probert (2003: 144–6); cf. Wilson (2007b: 80).

Both main approaches are based on the information provided by ancient and medieval grammatical texts. At this point, one might ask whether we could not investigate the distribution of enclitic and non-enclitic 'ΕΣΤΙ more directly, by finding out for ourselves where enclitic and non-enclitic 'ΕΣΤΙ turn up in ancient literary texts. Unfortunately, we cannot distinguish between enclitic and non-enclitic 'ΕΣΤΙ unless we already know how 'ΕΣΤΙ was accented in a particular context—and ancient literary texts do not come down to us with accent marks going back to the authors. For this reason, 'ΕΣΤΙ differs from an enclitic such as ΜΕ, whose non-enclitic counterpart 'ΕΜΕ can be distinguished from ΜΕ even in the absence of reliable accent marks. In the case of 'ΕΣΤΙ the grammatical tradition must play the central role, and so it has.

The 'existential' view became well established in the nineteenth century after it was put forward by Hermann (1801), until it was challenged by Wackernagel (1877: 466–7) and subsequent scholars.[6] Today the existential view has largely fallen out of favour in scholarly treatments of the subject,[7] although it remains prominent in didactic works on ancient Greek,[8] where it is sometimes combined with the 'initial and quasi-initial' view.[9]

The basis on which the 'existential' view has fallen from favour is that the evidence for this view is less plentiful, and is taken to be less ancient, than the evidence for the 'initial and quasi-initial' view. Indeed, proponents of the 'initial and quasi-initial' view tend to call this the doctrine of the older Greek grammarians (Wackernagel 1877: 466) or simply Herodian's doctrine (Barrett 1964: 426; Kahn 1973: 420–3). In addition, some scholars have argued that no distinction is to be made between a 'copular' and an 'existential' meaning for Greek εἶναι—that emphasis on existence arises from aspects of some of the contexts in which εἶναι is used, not from a separate meaning of the verb.[10] If this view is correct, it is not immediately obvious that a

---

[6] See nn. 2–3.

[7] Kahn (1973: 420) writes as if the matter ought to be considered settled: 'Since Hermann's theory continues to exert an influence by way of handbooks, school tradition, and even text editions, and since it has been taken for granted by many Hellenists including some of the best, a discussion of the matter is called for here.'

[8] For example, Chase and Phillips (1961: 41–2) and (very concisely) Abbott and Mansfield (1977: 133) simply prescribe the 'existential' view.

[9] One method of combining the two views is to prescribe orthotonic ἔστι(ν) in clause-initial position and perhaps after οὐ, καί, εἰ, ἀλλά, ὡς, or τοῦτο (or some variant of this list), but to claim at the same time that in at least some of these positions ἔστι(ν) is emphatic and/or expresses existence or possibility: so Mastronarde (2013: 85); Hansen and Quinn (1992: ii. 612; cf. i. 440); Luschnig (2007: 46). Differently, some works prescribe orthotonic ἔστι(ν) under all the circumstances under which this accentuation would result either from the 'initial and quasi-initial' view or from the existential view: so Goodwin (1894: 32); North and Hillard (1927: 241 n. 1); Pharr (1959: 214); McKay (1974: 15); van Emde Boas, Rijksbaron, Huitink, and de Bakker (2019: 290). More cautiously, Morwood (2001: 93) prescribes orthotonic ἔστι(ν) at the beginning of a sentence and after οὐκ, μή, εἰ, ὡς, καί, ἀλλά, and τοῦτο, and allows for the *possibility* of orthotonic ἔστι(ν) in existential meaning.

[10] See Burnyeat (2003: 9–17) and Kahn (2009b), and cf. Kahn (1981). This rejection of a dichotomy between copular and existential εἶναι is related to a wider debate in philosophy and semantics as to the semantic distinction, if any, that should be made between copular and existential verbs in any language (see e.g. Kahn 2009b: 111 with n. 4, 114). However, those who argue for a unified semantics

distinction in accentuation could have correlated with a semantic distinction that did not actually exist (this is, however, a topic to which we shall return).

This chapter takes a new look at the ancient and medieval evidence on which the two modern views are based. We shall see that the tradition supporting the 'initial and quasi-initial' was known to Herodian, but possibly in a more limited form than has been assumed, and that the foundations for the 'existential' view are probably older than has been suggested. It will be argued that a situation in which both traditions are partly right is linguistically plausible and may well be correct.

3.2 Ancient support for the 'initial and quasi-initial' view

Our texts *On enclitics 1* (§d), *Charax* (§m), and *About* 'ΕΣΤΙΝ (§a) all support a version of the 'initial and quasi-initial' view, and they present a consistent picture: the form ἔστι occurs in initial position (in some sense) and after 'ΟΥ, ΚΑΙ, or 'ΩΣ. Or rather, these texts *as printed by us* present this picture—but once again (cf. section 2.7.4), textual decisions matter. An important source for the longer list of preceding words 'ΟΥ, ΚΑΙ, 'ΕΙ, 'ΑΛΛΑ, 'ΩΣ, and ΤΟΥΤΟ that features in modern discussions is the passage of *About* 'ΕΣΤΙΝ just mentioned, but in a form that ultimately derives from the version printed in the Aldine *Thesaurus: Cornu copiae et Horti Adonidis* (Aldus 1496).[11] Our version is shown as passage (3.1), and the Aldine version as (3.2). Words that appear in our version but not the Aldine version are underlined in (3.1), while the more significant material appearing in the Aldine version but not in ours is underlined in (3.2). (We do not underline the parenthetical comment διὰ τὸ 'φύλλα ἐστίν' in (3.1), nor the mention of proparoxytone words, because these occur in the Aldine version, although slightly later than the extract reproduced in (3.2): see *About* 'ΕΣΤΙΝ, §b, note c.)

(3.1)   Τὸ 'ΕΣΤΙΝ ἡνίκα ἄρχει λόγου, <u>ἢ ὅτε</u> ὑποτάττεται τῇ 'ΟΥ ἀποφάσει ἢ τῷ ΚΑΙ συνδέσμῳ ἢ τῷ 'ΩΣ ἐπιρρήματι, τηνικαῦτα τὴν ὀξεῖαν ἔχει ἐπὶ

---

for Greek εἶναι do not necessarily argue against a semantic distinction between copula and existential verb for all languages (see Burnyeat 2003: 16, 18).

[11] This treatise has entered modern discussion via Bekker's text (1821: 1148, line 13–1149, line 6); as explained in section 2.5.2, Bekker consulted both Aldus (1496) (and a second Aldine edition whose text of this treatise ultimately derives from that of Aldus 1496) and manuscript Parisinus Graecus 1773 (our Y). His text of this passage (Bekker 1821: 1148, lines 14–23) is largely identical to the Aldine text, minor differences apart, but he prints ἢ ἄλλῳ συνδέσμῳ 'or another conjunction' rather than ἢ ἀλλὰ συνδέσμῳ 'or the conjunction 'ΑΛΛΑ'. Lehrs (1837: 125) proposes ἀλλά rather than ἄλλῳ (as if by conjecture, although this represents a return to the Aldine text), and with this reading Lentz incorporates the passage into his reconstruction of Herodian's works (Lentz 1867–70: i. 553, lines 10–18). In his challenge to the 'existential view' of non-enclitic 'ΕΣΤΙ, Wackernagel (1877: 466) relies on Lentz's text, and Wackernagel's treatment of the subject has in turn fed into subsequent discussion.

τοῦ Ε, οἷον 'ἔστι πόλις Ἐφύρη μυχῷ Ἄργεος ἱπποβότοιο', 'οὐκ ἔστ' οὐδὲ
ἔοικε τεὸν ἔπος ἀρνήσασθαι', ⟨'καὶ ἔστιν'⟩, 'ὡς ἔστι κακὸν ἀμαθία'.

    ἐὰν δὲ ὑποτάττηται ὀξυτόνῳ λέξει ἢ περισπωμένη, οἷον Ἑρμῆς
ἐστιν', ἢ τροχαίῳ μὴ παροξυτόνῳ ἀλλὰ προπερισπωμένῳ (διὰ τὸ 'φύλλα
ἐστίν'· παροξύτονος γὰρ οὗτος ὁ τροχαῖος, οὐχὶ προπερισπώμενος), ἢ
προπαροξυτόνῳ, τηνικαῦτα ἐγκλίνεται, οἷον 'ἀγαθός ἐστι', 'κακός ἐστι',
'κῆπός ἐστι', 'ἄδικός ἐστι'. (About ΕΣΤΙΝ, §§a–b, our text)

'When ΕΣΤΙΝ begins a clause, or when it is placed after the negation
ΟΥ, or after the conjunction ΚΑΙ, or the adverb ΩΣ, then it has the acute
accent on its Ε, as in ἔστι πόλις Ἐφύρη μυχῷ Ἄργεος ἱπποβότοιο,[12] or
οὐκ ἔστ' οὐδὲ ἔοικε τεὸν ἔπος ἀρνήσασθαι,[13] or καὶ ἔστιν,[14] or ὡς ἔστι
κακὸν ἀμαθία.[15]

But if it is placed after an oxytone or perispomenon word, as in Ἑρμῆς
ἐστιν,[16] or after a trochaic word that is not paroxytone but properispomenon
(because of φύλλα ἐστίν,[17] since this trochaic word is paroxytone, not
properispomenon), or a proparoxytone word, in that case it throws its
accent back, as in ἀγαθός ἐστι, κακός ἐστι, κῆπός ἐστι, ἄδικός ἐστι.'[18]

(3.2)   Τὸ ἔστιν ἡνίκα ἄρχῃ λόγον, ἢ ὑποτάττεται τῇ οὖ ἀποφάσει ἢ τῷ καὶ ἢ εἰ
ἢ ἀλλὰ συνδέσμῳ ἢ τῷ ὡς ἐπιρρήματι ἢ τῷ τοῦτο, τηνικαῦτα τὴν ὀξεῖαν
ἔχει ἐπὶ τοῦ ε, οἷον ἔστι πόλις ἐφύρη μυχῷ ἄργεος ἱπποβότοιο· οὐκ ἔστ'
οὐδὲ ἔοικε τεὸν ἔπος ἀρνήσασθαι· ὡς ἔστι κακὸν ἀμαθία· εἰ ἔστιν οὕτως·
ἀλλ' ἔστιν εἰπεῖν· τοῦτ' ἔστιν ἁμάρτημα.

    ἐὰν δὲ ὑποτάττηται ὀξυτόνῳ λέξει, ἢ περισπωμένη, ἐγκλίνεται· οἷον
καλός ἐστιν· ἑρμῆς ἐστιν· ἢ τροχαίῳ μὴ παροξυτόνῳ ἀλλὰ
προπερισπωμένῳ· οἷον οἶκός ἐστι· (About ΕΣΤΙΝ, §§a–b, as printed in
Aldus (1496), fol. 225v, lines 20–7)

'When ΕΣΤΙ begins its clause, or when it is placed after the negation ΟΥ,
or after ΚΑΙ, or ΕΙ, or the conjunction ΑΛΛΑ, or the adverb ΩΣ, or
ΤΟΥΤΟ, then it has the acute accent on its Ε, as in ἔστι πόλις Ἐφύρη
μυχῷ Ἄργεος ἱπποβότοιο, or οὐκ ἔστ' οὐδὲ ἔοικε τεὸν ἔπος ἀρνήσασθαι,
or ὡς ἔστι κακὸν ἀμαθία, or εἰ ἔστιν οὕτως, or ἀλλ' ἔστιν εἰπεῖν, or τοῦτ'
ἔστιν ἁμάρτημα.'[19]

---

[12] *Il.* 6.152: 'There is a city, Ephurē, at a remote point of the horse-nourishing Argolid'.
[13] *Il.* 14.212 = *Od.* 8.358: 'It is not possible, nor is it seemly, to refuse your bidding'.
[14] 'And there is' / 'and ...is'.
[15] 'That ignorance is a bad thing', or 'how ignorance is a bad thing!'.   [16] 'Hermes is'.
[17] 'Leaves are'.   [18] 'Is good'; 'is bad'; 'a garden is'; 'is unjust'.
[19] The last three quotations mean 'if it is so'; 'but it is possible to say'; 'this is a mistake'. (For translations of the quotations that also appear in (3.1), see nn. 12, 13, 15, 16.)

But if it is placed after an oxytone or perispomenon word, it throws back its accent, as in καλός ἐστιν[20] or Ἑρμῆς ἐστιν, or after a trochaic word that is not paroxytone but properispomenon, as in οἶκός ἐστι.[21]

The additional elements ἢ εἴ ἢ ἀλλά and εἰ ἔστιν οὕτως· ἀλλ᾽ ἔστιν εἰπεῖν· τοῦτ᾽ ἔστιν ἁμάρτημα found in the Aldine *Thesaurus* are otherwise found only in later versions of the text deriving ultimately from the text in the *Thesaurus* (see section 2.5.1). The idea that *ΈΣΤΙ* was non-enclitic after *ΈΙ*, *ΆΛΛΑ*, or *ΤΟΥΤΟ*, with examples to match, appears to be an addition made in the *Thesaurus* or in a lost source thereof. In the rest of the *About ΈΣΤΙΝ* tradition (and in the indirect witness quoted in section 2.5.1 as passage (2.1)), *ΈΣΤΙ* is paroxytone in initial position and after *ΌΥ*, *ΚΑΙ*, or *ῺΣ*. While it is of some interest to wonder when someone added *ΈΙ*, *ΆΛΛΑ*, and *ΤΟΥΤΟ* to the list of words that could precede paroxytone ἔστι, and on what basis, the text *About ΈΣΤΙΝ* does not provide evidence for any early version of the doctrine in which these words were included in the list.

A further source for the modern idea that *ΈΣΤΙ* was non-enclitic after *ΤΟΥΤΟ* is Charax, in the form in which the treatise attributed to him is printed by Bekker (1821: 1149–55).[22] Passage (3.3) gives our text of the relevant discussion, while (3.4) gives Bekker's text. In both versions, underlining points out the relevant difference in wording:

(3.3)   τὸ δὲ *ΈΣΣΙ* καὶ τὸ *ΈΣΤΙ* τρίτον πρόσωπον καὶ αὐτὰ κατὰ τὸν λόγον ἐγκλίνεται, ʻἄνθρωπός ἐστιʼ, ʻσχέτλιός ἔσσι γεραιέʼ. τὸ δὲ *ΈΣΤΙ* εἰς πολλὰ παρέβη τὴν ἀκολουθίαν. ἐν ἀρχῇ γὰρ ἄλλης λέξεως μὴ ἐγκλινομένης ἐγκλίνεται τῇ ἰδίᾳ ἀρχῇ τὸν τόνον ἀναπέμπον, ὡς ἐν τῷ ʻἔστι πόλις Ἐφύρηʼ, καὶ ἐπὶ πάντων ὁμοίως. κάτω δὲ ὑπάρχον, προηγουμένων αὐτοῦ τινων λέξεων ὀξυνομένων, παρέβη τὴν ἔγκλισιν. ἔδει γὰρ ἐπὶ πάντων ἀναβιβάζειν τὸν τόνον τῇ πρὸ αὐτοῦ λέξει ὀξυτόνῳ οὔσῃ, ὡς ἐν τῷ ʻἐμός ἐστιʼ, ʻκαλός ἐστινʼ. εἰς τὴν ἰδίαν δὲ ἀρχὴν ἀναβιβάζει ἐπί τινων καὶ ἐπὶ τῆς *ΌΥ*, ʻοὐκ ἔστιν οὐδὲν δεινόνʼ, καὶ ἐπὶ τοῦ *ΚΑΙ*, ʻκαὶ ἔστιʼ, καὶ ἐπὶ τοῦ *ῺΣ*, ʻὡς ἔστιʼ. <u>ταῦτα περὶ τοῦ ΈΣΤΙΝ</u>. (Charax, §m, our text)

ʻAnd *ΈΣΣΙ* and the third person form *ΈΣΤΙ* too throw back their accent according to the rule: ἄνθρωπός ἐστι, σχέτλιός ἔσσι γεραιέ.[23] But *ΈΣΤΙ* in many cases contravenes regularity. For in initial position, where other

---

[22] Again (cf. n. 11) Bekker's text is based in part on the text printed in the Aldine *Thesaurus* (Aldus 1496), but Bekker's text of this passage differs significantly from the Aldine one; the phrase ταυτάπερ τουτέστι, which is of particular interest to us here, comes not from Aldus (1496) but from the manuscript Parisinus Graecus 1773 (our **Y**). On Bekker's sources for *Charax*, see section 2.4.2.
[23] ʻHe/she is a personʼ; *Il.* 10.164: ʻyou're unstoppable, old manʼ.

words do not throw back their accent, it throws its accent back by sending it back to its own first syllable, as in ἔστι πόλις Ἐφύρη,[24] and similarly in all instances. But when it is found further down [the clause], with certain oxytone words preceding it, it violates [the rules of] enclisis. For it should in all instances have retracted its accent onto the preceding word, if this was oxytone, as in ἐμός ἐστι, καλός ἐστιν.[25] But in some cases, including that of 'OY, it retracts the accent onto its own first syllable, as in οὐκ ἔστιν οὐδὲν δεινόν,[26] and in the case of KAI, as in καὶ ἔστι,[27] and ΩΣ as in ὡς ἔστι.[28] So much then for 'ΕΣΤΙΝ.'

(3.4) Τὸ δὲ ἔστι τρίτον πρόσωπον καὶ αὐτὸ κατὰ τὸν λόγον ἐγκλίνεται, ἄνθρωπός ἐστιν. εἰς πολλὰ δὲ αὐτὸ παρέβη τὴν ἀκολουθίαν. ἐν ἀρχῇ μὲν γὰρ ἄλλης λέξεως μὴ ἐγκλινομένης ἐγκλίνεται τῇ ἰδίᾳ ἀρχῇ τὸν τόνον ἀναπέμπον, ἔστι πόλις Ἐφύρη, καὶ ἐπὶ πάντων ὁμοίως. κάτω δὲ ὑπάρχον, προηγουμένων αὐτοῦ τινῶν λέξεων ὀξυνομένων, παρέβη τὴν ἔγκλισιν. ἔδει γὰρ ἐπὶ πάντων ἀναβιβάζειν τὸν τόνον τῇ πρὸ αὐτοῦ λέξει ὀξυτόνῳ οὔσῃ, ὡς ἐν τῷ ἐμός ἐστι, καλός ἐστιν. εἰς τὴν ἰδίαν δὲ ἀρχὴν ἀναβιβάζει ἐπί τινων καὶ ἐπὶ τῆς οὔ,
 οὐκ ἔστιν οὐδὲν δεινόν,
καὶ ἐπὶ τοῦ καί, καὶ ἔστι, καὶ ἐπὶ τοῦ ὡς, ὡς ἔστι ταυτάπερ τουτέστι.
(*Charax*, §m, text of Bekker 1821: 1151, lines 26–36)

'And the third person form 'ΕΣΤΙ too throws back its accent according to the rule: ἄνθρωπός ἐστιν. But in many cases it contravenes regularity. For in initial position, where other words do not throw back their accent, it throws its accent back by sending it back to its own first syllable, as in ἔστι πόλις Ἐφύρη, and similarly in all instances. But when it is found further down [the clause], with certain oxytone words preceding it, it violates [the rules of] enclisis. For it should in all instances have retracted its accent onto the preceding word, if this was oxytone, as in ἐμός ἐστι, καλός ἐστιν. But in some cases, including that of 'OY, it retracts the accent onto its own first syllable, as in οὐκ ἔστιν οὐδὲν δεινόν, and in the case of KAI, as in καὶ ἔστι, and 'ΩΣ, as in ὡς ἔστι, ?? ταυτάπερ ?? τουτέστι.'

This passage is present down to the last sentence quoted in manuscripts **Φ**, **H**, **B**, **Θ**, **Y**, **L**, **L**ᵥ, and **N**, of which **Φ**, **H**, and **B** represent family w₁ for this passage, **Θ**, **Y**, **L**, and **L**ᵥ represent family w₂, and **N** stands outside both families (see section 2.4.1). **Φ**, **H**, and **N** round off this discussion with ταῦτα περὶ τοῦ ἐστιν, **B** has the minor variant ταῦτα δὲ περὶ τοῦ ἐστίν, while the representatives of

---

[24] *Il.* 6.152: 'There is a city, Ephurē'.   [25] 'Is mine'; 'is beautiful'.
[26] Euripides, *Orestes* 1: 'There is no terrible thing...'.
[27] 'And there is' / 'And...is'.   [28] 'That there is' / 'That he/she/it is'.

family **w₂** have ταῦτά περ τοῦτέστιν. The reading of **w₂** makes little sense, and is clearly a corrupt version of the rounding-off sentence found in **w₁** and **N**: 'So much then for '*ΕΣΤΙΝ*'.

In the light of what can now be said about the text of the relevant passages, then, *On enclitics 1* (§d), *Charax* (§m), and *About* '*ΕΣΤΙΝ* (§a) present a consistent picture to the effect that '*ΕΣΤΙ* is paroxytone in initial position and after '*ΟΥ*, *ΚΑΙ*, or *ΏΣ*. But various questions arise. Do any other texts provide support for the 'initial and quasi-initial' view, and if so do they present us with the same picture as these three texts, or with something different? And can we reconstruct the history of the doctrine?

To start with the last question, Lehrs (1837: 104–5 n. 2) followed by Lentz (1867–70: i. 553, on line 10) considered it clear that *About* '*ΕΣΤΙΝ* derives from Herodian, because of the close verbal similarities between this text and part of Pseudo-Arcadius' epitome of Herodian's Περὶ καθολικῆς προσῳδίας. But the relevant passage of Pseudo-Arcadius (308.6–15 Roussou) belongs to the second of two sections on enclitics which are evidently intrusions into the text of Pseudo-Arcadius—for the most part a version of *On enclitics 1*, but ending with a version of *About* '*ΕΣΤΙΝ* (see section 2.1). Lehrs was quite right to notice the close similarities between this last part and the treatise *About* '*ΕΣΤΙΝ*, but it does not follow that anything very similar to *About* '*ΕΣΤΙΝ* was penned by Herodian.

On the other hand, a more limited doctrine is ascribable to Herodian with some confidence on the basis of its appearance in one of the 'A' scholia to the *Iliad*. These derive primarily from the work of Aristonicus, Didymus, Herodian, and Nicanor, with comments on prosody being attributable to Herodian.[29] Here we are told that '*ΕΣΤΙ* is paroxytone when initial and when it follows '*ΟΥ*:

(3.5)   ἔστι {πόλις}· τὸ ἔστι ἐπὶ τῆς πρώτης συλλαβῆς ἔχει τὴν ὀξεῖαν, ὅταν ἄρχηται, 'ἔστι δέ τις προπάροιθε πόλιος', καὶ ὅταν ὑποτάσσηται τῇ οὐ ἀποφάσει, 'ὡς οὐκ ἔσθ' ὅδε μῦθος'. εἰ μέντοι γε μὴ εἴη τὸ τοιοῦτο, οὐκέτι ἐπὶ τῆς πρώτης συλλαβῆς ἔχει τὴν ὀξεῖαν, οἷον 'ὃ δὴ τετελεσμένον ἐστίν'. (Sch. *Il.* 6.152a (A))

'ἔστι: '*ΕΣΤΙ* has the acute on the first syllable when the word comes first, as in ἔστι δέ τις προπάροιθε πόλιος,[30] and when it is placed after the negation οὐ, as in ὡς οὐκ ἔσθ' ὅδε μῦθος.[31] But when this sort of thing does not apply, it no longer has the acute on the first syllable, as in ὃ δὴ τετελεσμένον ἐστίν.[32]'

---

[29] For an accessible introduction to the various groups of *Iliad* scholia and their sources, see Schironi (2018: 6–14).

[30] *Il.* 2.811: 'There is in front of the city a ...'.

[31] 'As this story is not ...': an approximate quotation or variant of *Od.* 23.62 (καὶ οὐκ ἔσθ' ὅδε μῦθος).

[32] 'Which has indeed been fulfilled': an approximate quotation of *Il.* 14.196 = *Il.* 18.427 = *Od.* 5.90 (εἰ τετελεσμένον ἐστίν).

This more limited doctrine is also found in the bT scholia, which include some Herodianic material related to that in the A scholia, and in the *Epimerismi Homerici*, which again include Herodianic material (see Dyck 1983: 29):

(3.6)   ⟨ἐκ Διός ἐστιν·⟩ τὸ ᾽ΕΣΤΙΝ ἐγκλιτικόν ἐστιν, εἰ μὴ ἄρχεται ἢ προηγεῖται αὐτοῦ ἡ ᾽ΟΥ ἀπόφασις. (Sch. *Il.* 1.63c (bT))

'ἐκ Διός ἐστιν:[33] ᾽ΕΣΤΙΝ is enclitic if it does not come first and if the negation ᾽ΟΥ does not precede.'

(3.7)   ὅτε δὲ ἀρκτικόν ἐστιν, ἀναβιβάζει τὸν τόνον, ῾ἔστι πόλις ᾽Εφύρη᾽. ὑποτασσομένη δὲ ὀξύνεται· καὶ ὅτε τῇ ᾽ΟΥ ἀποφάσει ὑποτάσσεται, ἀναβιβάζει· ῾οὐκ ἔστ{ιν} οὐδὲ ἔοικε᾽. ἀμφίβολον τὸ ῾ἡ δέ τοι οὐ θνητή, ἀλλ᾽ ἀθάνατον κακόν ἐστιν᾽. (*Ep. Hom. alph.* ε 103.22–8 Dyck (s.v. ἔστιν))

'And when the word comes first, it retracts its accent: ἔστι πόλις ᾽Εφύρη.[34] But when it is placed after [other words] it is oxytone. And when it is placed after the negation ᾽ΟΥ, it retracts its accent: οὐκ ἔστ᾽ οὐδὲ ἔοικε.[35] The case of ἡ δέ τοι οὐ θνητή, ἀλλ᾽ ἀθάνατον κακόν ἐστιν[36] is doubtful.'[37]

In the scholia to the *Odyssey*, which again include Herodianic material,[38] we find a comment limited to what is relevant to the verse at hand, namely the accentuation of ᾽ΕΣΤΙ at verse-initial position:

(3.8)   ἔστ᾽ ἄφενος· ὅτε ἐστὶν ἐν ἀρχῇ στίχου, παροξύνεται. (Sch. *Od.* 14.99 (H))

'ἔστ᾽ ἄφενος:[39] When it [i.e. ᾽ΕΣΤΙ] is at the beginning of a verse, it is paroxytone.'

As well as these witnesses to a more restricted version of the doctrine that supports the 'initial and quasi-initial' view, we are aware of two witnesses to a version more similar to the one found in the Aldine text of *About ᾽ΕΣΤΙΝ*.[40] The first comes, once again, from the Aldine *Thesaurus* (Aldus 1496), but this time from one of its two versions of *On enclitics 1*:

---

[33] *Il.* 1.63: '...comes from Zeus'.   [34] *Il.* 6.152: 'There is a city, Ephurē'.

[35] *Il.* 14.212 = *Od.* 8.358: 'It is not possible, nor is it seemly...'.

[36] *Od.* 12.118: 'She is not mortal, but an immortal evil'.

[37] The problem posed by this last example appears to be that ᾽ΕΣΤΙΝ here follows οὐ, but not immediately. At some stage, therefore, there was doubt as to how exactly to interpret the rule that οὐ(κ) is followed by ἔστι(ν). To our knowledge there are no other ancient discussions of *Od.* 12.118 in this light, and so we do not know how early this problem was felt.

[38] Cf. Lentz's (1867–70: ii. 156) inclusion of this scholion in his collection of fragments from Herodian's Περὶ ᾽Οδυσσειακῆς προσῳδίας.

[39] *Od.* 14.99 'there is wealth'. In context, the meaning is '[Not even twenty mortals together] have [so much] wealth'.

[40] See on passages (3.1) and (3.2).

(3.9)   τοῦτο δὲ τὸ ἐ̄στιν ἐν ταῖς ἀρχαῖς τῶν λόγων βαρύνεται, ἔστι πόλις
ἐφύρη· καὶ μετὰ τοῦ ὡς ἐπιρρήματος· ὡς ἔστιν εἰπεῖν· καὶ μετὰ τοῦ
ἀλλά· ἀλλ᾽ ἔστι, καὶ μετὰ τοῦ τοῦτο τοῦτ᾽ ἔστι· καὶ μετάγεται εἰς
ἐπίρρημα τουτέστι· καὶ μετὰ τοῦ καὶ· καὶ ἔστι, καὶ μετὰ τοῦ οὐκ· οὐκ
ἔστι...(On enclitics 1, §d, text of **Ald.**₁, from Aldus (1496), fol. 231r,
lines 17–21)

'And this word, 'ΕΣΤΙΝ, is barytone at the beginnings of clauses, as in
ἔστι πόλις 'Εφύρη,[41] and with the adverb 'ΩΣ, as in ὡς ἔστιν εἰπεῖν,[42] and
with ΑΛΛΑ, as in ἀλλ᾽ ἔστι, and with ΤΟΥΤΟ, as in τοῦτ᾽ ἔστι. And this
goes over to being an adverb, τουτέστι. And with ΚΑΙ, as in καὶ ἔστι, and
with 'ΟΥΚ, as in οὐκ ἔστι...'

In a pattern familiar already from passage (3.2), the material καὶ μετὰ τοῦ
ἀλλά—μετάγεται εἰς ἐπίρρημα τουτέστι appears only in copy **Ald.**₁ of this treatise, and in later copies ultimately derived from **Ald.**₁ (cf. On enclitics 1, §d,
note x). As well as including ΑΛΛΑ and ΤΟΥΤΟ among the words after which
'ΕΣΤΙ is non-enclitic, this additional material includes an observation on non-
enclitic 'ΕΣΤΙ after ΤΟΥΤΟ: 'and this goes over to being an adverb, τουτέστι'.
This comment alludes to the idiomatic expression τουτέστι(ν) 'i.e.', which goes
back to antiquity and survives into formal registers of modern Greek, where it
continues to be stressed on the penultimate syllable. The idea that 'ΕΣΤΙ was
non-enclitic after ΤΟΥΤΟ may well be based entirely on this 'adverb' τουτέστι,
whose penultimate-syllable accent may be due in some way to the semantic weakening of ΤΟΥΤ(Ο). It need not follow that other uses of the combination
ΤΟΥΤ(Ο) 'ΕΣΤΙ ever prompted non-enclitic 'ΕΣΤΙ.

Our last (but chronologically a little earlier) source giving more than three
words after which 'ΕΣΤΙ is non-enclitic is a passage of the *Etymologicum
Magnum*, a work put together on the basis of pre-existing sources in the twelfth
century.[43]

(3.10)   τὸ 'ΕΣΤΙ κατ᾽ ἀρχὰς[44] τιθέμενον βαρύνεται· ὡς τὸ 'ἔστι πόλις'.
βαρύνεται δὲ καὶ μετὰ τοῦ 'ΩΣ, καὶ μετὰ τοῦ ΜΗ ἀπαγορευτικοῦ· καὶ
μετὰ τοῦ ΑΛΛΑ· καὶ μετὰ τοῦ ΚΑΙ· καὶ μετὰ τοῦ ΤΟΥΤΟ.
(*Etymologicum Magnum* 301.3–5).

''ΕΣΤΙ when placed at the beginning is recessive, as in ἔστι πόλις.[45] And
it is also recessive with 'ΩΣ, and with the prohibitive ΜΗ, and with
ΑΛΛΑ, and with ΚΑΙ, and with ΤΟΥΤΟ.'

---

[41] *Il.* 6.152: 'There is a city, Ephurē'.   [42] 'As it is possible to say'.
[43] See Lasserre and Livadaras (1976: xvii–xviii); Dickey (2007: 91–2), with bibliography.
[44] Gaisford reads καταρχὰς.   [45] *Il.* 6.152: 'There is a city'.

The relationship between this passage and others we have quoted is difficult to establish, and a modern edition of the *Etymologicum Magnum* remains a desideratum, but available digitized manuscripts make it possible to verify that the list *ΩΣ, MH, ΑΛΛΑ, KAI*, and *TOYTO* is part of the tradition at least as early as the thirteenth century.[46] As far as we have been able to verify, no list of words preceding non-enclitic *ΕΣΤΙ* appears in the surviving earlier etymological works that fed into the *Etymologicum Magnum;*[47] the list that appears in the *Etymologicum Magnum* is most likely to be a recent addition to the etymological tradition.

Be this as it may, passages (3.2), (3.9), and (3.10), taken together, show that at some point various lists of more than three words preceding non-enclitic *ΕΣΤΙ* gained currency. One of these lists—the one in the Aldine version of the *About ΕΣΤΙΝ* passage, our (3.2)—has been influential on modern discussion of the subject. But the mainstream Byzantine tradition appears to have recognized a list consisting of the three words *ΟΥΚ, KAI*, and *ΩΣ*. And the doctrine that can be reconstructed for Herodian with some confidence is more limited still: *ΕΣΤΙ* was non-enclitic in initial position and after *ΟΥ* (or in practice *ΟΥΚ*).

3.3 Ancient support for the 'existential' view

We saw in section 3.1 that some of the time, the two main modern approaches to the accent of *ΕΣΤΙ* produce the same result. At Aristophanes, *Wasps* 64 (ἀλλ' ἔστιν ἡμῖν λογίδιον γνώμην ἔχον 'but we have a little story with meaning'), once again, modern editors print ἔστιν regardless of whether they consider *ΕΣΤΙ* paroxytone after *ΑΛΛ(Α)* or paroxytone when existential. Hermann's (1801: 84–90) view that *ΕΣΤΙ* is orthotonic when not just the copula, and when not omissible, is based to a large extent on passages (already quoted) which ostensibly support the 'initial and quasi-initial' view, the idea being that the authors of those passages were really trying to describe *ΕΣΤΙ* when it was existential, contrastive, or

---

[46] The passage can be seen at f. 81v, lines 33–4 of Parisinus Graecus 2654 (13th century), via <https://gallica.bnf.fr/ark:/12148/btv1b10724062z>, and at f. 121v, lines 1–2 of Venetus Marcianus Gr. Z. 530 (late 13th century) via <www.internetculturale.it/jmms/iccuviewer/iccu.jsp?id=oai%3A19 3.206.197.121%3A18%3AVE0049%3ACSTOR.240.10258>.

[47] On the works that fed into the *Etymologicum Magnum*, see Berger (1972: ix–xxviii); Lasserre and Livadaras (1976: xvii); Cunningham (2003: 13–14, 22, 23); Schironi (2004: 13). If we are not mistaken, no such list appears in any of the following: (a) Cunningham's edition of the Συναγωγὴ λέξεων χρησίμων; (b) manuscript A of the *Etymologicum Genuinum* (codex Vaticanus Graecus 1818, <https://digi.vatlib.it/view/MSS_Vat.gr.1818>; other material related to the passage containing our (3.10) appears on folios 120v–121r); (c) manuscript B of the *Etymologicum Genuinum* (codex Laurentianus S. Marco 304; other material related to the passage containing our (3.10) appears on fol. 91r; see also E. Miller's (1868: 1–318) comparison with Gaisford's text of the *Etymologicum Magnum*); (d) the *Etymologicum Gudianum* (for relevant entries see *Et. Gud.* 421.16–423.6 de Stefani); (e) Dyck's edition of the *Lexicon Αἱμωδεῖν*; (f) Pintaudi's edition of the *Etymologicum Parvum*; (g) Baldi's edition of the *Etymologicum Symeonis*, γ–ε.

otherwise beefed up.[48] In attempting to do so, according to Hermann, they seized on 'ΕΣΤΙ in certain positions—at the beginning of its clause or after 'ΟΥ, ΚΑΙ, etc.—because existential, contrastive, or otherwise beefed-up 'ΕΣΤΙ just happens to appear frequently in those positions. Indeed, many of the specific examples of paroxytone ἔστι adduced in the passages already quoted have an 'ΕΣΤΙ that is most naturally translatable with 'there is' (e.g. ἔστι πόλις Ἐφύρη) or 'it is possible' (e.g. οὐκ ἔστ' οὐδὲ ἔοικε τεὸν ἔπος ἀρνήσασθαι), or have an 'ΕΣΤΙ that one can imagine being given emphasis (e.g. ὡς ἔστι κακὸν ἀμαθία: perhaps 'that ignorance really is a bad thing' or 'how ignorance really is a bad thing!'). Thus, the position-based principle given especially in passages (3.1), (3.3), and (3.10) (paroxytone ἔστι occurs in initial position and after certain words) conceivably aimed at identifying 'ΕΣΤΙ when it does more than just link a subject and predicate. But two sources directly attest an analysis much closer to Hermann's:

(3.11)   'ΕΣΤΙΝ· ἡ πρώτη ὀξεῖα, ἐπειδὰν ἀποφαινώμεθα αὐτοὶ περὶ τοῦ
         ὑπάρχειν τι· 'ἔστι πόλις Ἐφύρη'. ὅταν δὲ πρὸς ἐρώτησιν ἀποκρινώμεθα,
         τὴν ὑστέραν ὀξυτονητέον. (Photius, Lexicon ε 2030 Theodoridis)

         "ΕΣΤΙΝ: The first syllable is acute, when we ourselves make a declaration
         about something's existence: ἔστι πόλις Ἐφύρη.[49] But when we answer to
         a question, the second syllable is to be given the acute.'

(3.12)   ἰστέον δὲ ὅτι περὶ τοῦ 'ΕΣΤΙΝ οὕτω φασὶν οἱ παλαιοί. τοῦ 'ΕΣΤΙΝ ἡ
         πρώτη ὀξύνεται, ἐπειδὰν ἀποφαινώμεθα περὶ του ὡς ὑπάρχει, οἷον
         'ἔστι πόλις Ἐφύρη' καὶ τὰ τοιαῦτα. ὅταν δέ, φασί, πρὸς ἐρώτησιν
         ἀποκρινώμεθα, τὴν ὑστέραν ὀξυτονητέον. (Eustathius, In Iliadem
         880.22–4 = iii. 311.11–14 van der Valk)

         'And one must know that the ancients pronounce as follows about 'ΕΣΤΙ:
         The first syllable of 'ΕΣΤΙ has an acute accent when we declare about
         something that it exists, as in ἔστι πόλις Ἐφύρη and the like. But, they
         say, when we answer to a question, the second syllable is to be given
         the acute.'

An apparently related idea appears in two scholia to the *Iliad*, although these do not mention 'ΕΣΤΙ expressing 'existence' but being used ἐπαγγελτικῶς 'in a proclamatory way'.[50]

---

[48] We borrow the phrase 'beefed up' from Lesley Brown, to whom we are very grateful for discussion of meanings and uses of 'ΕΣΤΙ.

[49] *Il.* 6.152: 'There is a city, Ephurë'.

[50] Cf. van der Valk (1963–4: i. 522), who takes it as 'obvious that bT wishes to say that ἐστιν is not an auxiliary verb'.

(3.13) ἔστι τοι ⟨ἐν κλισίη χρυσὸς πολύς, ἔστι δὲ χαλκός⟩· ἐπαγγελτικῶς τὸ
ἔστι· διὸ ὀξέως. (Sch. Il. 23.549 (T))

'ἔστι τοι ἐν κλισίη χρυσὸς πολύς, ἔστι δὲ χαλκός:[51] The ἘΣΤΙ is [used/
produced] in a proclamatory way. Therefore with an acute [on the first
syllable].'

(3.14) ἄλλως· γόοιο μὲν ἔστι ⟨καὶ ἆσαι⟩· ἐπαγγελτικῶς προενεκτέον τὸ ἔστι,
ὡς 'ἔστι τοι ἐν κλισίη χρυσὸς πολύς, ἔστι δὲ χαλκός'. (Sch. Il. 23.157c (T))

'Differently: γόοιο μὲν ἔστι καὶ ἆσαι:[52] The ἘΣΤΙ is to be pronounced in
a proclamatory way, as in ἔστι τοι ἐν κλισίη χρυσὸς πολύς, ἔστι δὲ
χαλκός.[53]

These scholia suggest that a category of 'proclamatory' ἘΣΤΙ was recognized,
and the examples suggest that this category corresponds to or overlaps with what
we might call 'existential' ἘΣΤΙ. Proclamatory ἘΣΤΙ was to be pronounced in a
specific way, which had something to do with the accent. Strictly speaking these
scholia do not make it clear quite what accent was considered appropriate for
proclamatory ἘΣΤΙ. In our translation of scholion (3.13), '[on the first syllable]'
is a clarification that we take to be necessary, in the light of the evidence that
ἘΣΤΙ should be accented on its first syllable in clause-initial position (see section 3.2). On this position-based view, we would expect both instances of ἘΣΤΙ
to be paroxytone in the example ἔστι τοι ἐν κλισίη χρυσὸς πολύς, ἔστι δὲ
χαλκός. We tentatively take the scholia (3.13) and (3.14) to evidence a different
way of thinking about the reasons for paroxytone accentuation here, rather than
prescribing a different accentuation.

Be this as it may, Photius in passage (3.11) and Eustathius in (3.12) make clear
that ἘΣΤΙ is paroxytone when it expresses existence. They have very similar
wording to one another, and Eustathius ascribes the doctrine to οἱ παλαιοί 'the
ancients'. This term has a wide range of meaning in Eustathius; it is often used
when Eustathius' sources are Homeric scholia,[54] but other sources concealed
behind this term include Suetonius, Strabo, Stephanus of Byzantium, and even
sources as late as the *Etymologicum Magnum* and the *Suda*.[55] It is very unlikely,
however, that Eustathius' source is Photius, not so much because of the term
παλαιοί but because Eustathius does not appear to have used Photius as a source
(van der Valk 1971–87: i. lxvii). Theodoridis (1982–: ii. 195) suggests that the
source for both Photius in (3.11) and Eustathius in (3.12) might have been the

[51] Il. 23.549: 'You have in your hut much gold; you have bronze'.
[52] Il. 23.157: 'It is possible to have one's fill of weeping'.
[53] Il. 23.549: 'You have in your hut much gold; you have bronze'.
[54] See Schrader (1879: 244–5).
[55] Van der Valk (1963–4: i. 8 n. 31, 187 n. 266, 603); Cribiore (2008: 108–9).

second-century AD Atticist lexicographer Aelius Dionysius. Aelius Dionysius was a source for both Photius and Eustathius and is often named by Eustathius where Photius has similar wording,[56] and the surviving fragments demonstrate that he had an interest in accentuation.[57] Theodoridis' identification of Aelius Dionysius as the source for passages (3.11) and (3.12) is necessarily tentative, but it is likely as long as a late date is not assumed a priori for the 'existential' tradition.

3.4 Preliminary conclusions

To sum up the argument so far, the doctrine supporting the 'initial and quasi-initial' view can be ascribed with some confidence to Herodian in the second century AD, although in a more limited form than has sometimes been thought: in this version of the doctrine, 'ΕΣΤΙ is paroxytone in initial position and after 'OYK. A terminus ante quem of the second century AD can also be assigned, albeit tentatively, to the tradition supporting the 'existential' view. This tradition may therefore be much earlier than has been assumed, indeed also contemporary with Herodian.

Which tradition is right? In the following we argue that both traditions are most plausibly interpreted as simplifications of a complex linguistic situation: that both traditions are partly right.

3.5 The linguistic plausibility of both ancient traditions being partly right

As noted in section 3.1, current opinion favours the view that paroxytone ἔστι is restricted to initial and quasi-initial position, and one at least implicit reason is that the 'existential' view is considered linguistically implausible. We shall consider firstly the plausibility of the view that ἔστι is restricted to initial and quasi-initial position, along the lines suggested by the passages quoted in section 3.2, and secondly the linguistic plausibility of the 'existential' view, along the lines suggested by the passages quoted in section 3.3.

---

[56] Cf. Wentzel (1895: 482); Reitzenstein (1907: xii, lii); Erbse (1950: 27–30); Theodoridis (1982–: i. lxxiii).

[57] Cf. Erbse (1950: 28). Aelius Dionysius' interest in accentuation is what makes him a more likely source for passages (3.11) and (3.12) than his contemporary Pausanias, another Atticist lexicographer who was likewise excerpted by both Photius and Eustathius. Material from the Atticist lexicographers also appears in the bT scholia to the *Iliad* (see van der Valk 1963–4: i. 450), so conceivably the material in passages (3.13) and (3.14) also goes back to an Atticist lexicon.

3.5.1 The linguistic plausibility of ἔστι in initial and quasi-initial position

It is to be expected that an enclitic does not occur in sentence-initial position. By definition, enclitics require a preceding host word within the same sentence.[58] Enclitics may, however, have non-enclitic counterparts, whose placement does not require a host word. Non-enclitic ἔστι is certainly to be expected in sentence-initial position, and in modern scholarship there is widespread agreement on this point.

It is also entirely plausible that, in addition to being excluded from the beginning of a sentence, an enclitic should be excluded from what we might call 'clause-initial' position, with the proviso that certain words may need to be ignored when 'clause-initial position' is calculated. The proper linguistic interpretation of such facts is fiercely disputed (e.g. how much of a role is played by phonological facts and how much by syntactic facts), but, as noticed by Wilson (2007b: 80), Serbian provides an instructive illustration.[59]

In Serbian, the present tense forms of the verb *biti*, 'to be', have enclitic and non-enclitic variants. The enclitic variants are excluded from clause-initial position, where the non-enclitic variants occur instead. Contrast example (3.15), with an enclitic form *je*, and the interrogative example (3.16), with orthotonic *jesi* in initial position:[60]

(3.15) *Ona je   moja   sestra*
        She   is[ENCL.]   my   sister
        'She is my sister' (example and translation from Hammond 2005: 62)

(3.16) *Jesi   li   bila   na pijaci   danas?*
        Are[2.SG. ORTH.]   INTERROG.   been[SG.]   to market   today
        'Have you been to the market today?' (example and translation from Hammond 2005: 62)

---

[58] Strictly speaking, 'by definition' is an exaggeration, since some languages have unstressed words which normally behave as enclitics but behave as proclitics instead under some circumstances, even appearing in sentence-initial position (see Halpern 1995: 43; Toman 1996). In other words, behaviour that prompts us to label a word 'enclitic' need not make it an enclitic always and by definition; nor need it be replaced by an independently accented counterpart for non-enclitic behaviour to occur. But words that always behave as enclitics unless replaced by an independently accented counterpart are widespread, and the grammatical texts quoted suggest that Greek ’ΕΣΤΙ behaves in this way (see especially passages (3.1), (3.3), (3.6)).

[59] As will be clear from the sources cited, some of the Serbian sentences we quote are taken from grammars of Serbian, others are from (older) grammars of Serbo-Croatian, and others were given to one of us by Ana Kotarcic. We use the term 'Serbian' because we have checked all these examples with Ana Kotarcic, who is a first-language speaker of Serbian.

[60] We use the following abbreviations in glossing examples: 2.SG. = (familiar) second person singular; POL.2.SG. = polite second person singular; 2.PL. = second person plural; ENCL. = enclitic; ORTH. = orthotonic (i.e. non-enclitic); INTERROG. = interrogative particle.

Crucially, most co-ordinating conjunctions that join clauses are ignored when 'clause-initial' position is calculated. Thus, when clauses are combined with *a* 'but' or *i* 'and', this conjunction is not followed by any enclitic, but it may be followed by a non-enclitic form of *biti*:

(3.17)   *A   jeste   bili   y   Pisy?*
         And   are[2.PL. ORTH.]   been[PL.]   to   Pisa
         'And have you been to Pisa?' (from Ana Kotarcic)

Serbian thus provides a parallel for non-enclitic ἔστι in sentence-initial position and after a co-ordinating conjunction such as καί:

(3.18)   ἔστι δέ τις προπάροιθε πόλιος αἰπεῖα κολώνη (*Il.* 2.811, quoted in passage (3.5))

         'There is a steep hill in front of the city'

(3.19)   καὶ ἔστι μέν γ᾽, ἦν δ᾽ ἐγώ, τοιοῦτος ὁ τιμοκρατικὸς νεανίας…(Plato, *Republic* 549b9)

         'And the timocratic young man is of such a character, I said…'

In the mainstream Byzantine tradition (see section 3.2), καί is the co-ordinating conjunction most consistently mentioned as inducing paroxytone accentuation on a following 'ΕΣΤΙ. There is little evidence that any other clause-initial co-ordinating conjunctions were thought to behave in the same way, although ἀλλά makes a marginal appearance in passage (3.10), and was inserted into Aldine versions of *About 'ΕΣΤΙΝ* and *On enclitics 1* (passages (3.2) and (3.9)). Be this as it may, consistency between different conjunctions is not necessarily to be expected. In Serbian two co-ordinating conjunctions—*ali* 'but' and *pa* 'and then, and so'—may be followed by enclitics, as in example (3.20).[61]

(3.20)   *Nije   dobar,   ali   je   lep*
         Is-not[3.SG.]   good   but   is[3.SG. ENCL.]   beautiful
         'He's not good, but he's beautiful.' (from Ana Kotarcic)

The mainstream Byzantine tradition suggests that Greek also required non-enclitic ἔστι after at least one subordinating conjunction, namely ὡς 'that, since, because, as'. The word ὡς can also introduce an exclamatory main clause,[62] but

---

[61] See Zec and Inkelas (1990: 368); Taylor (1996: 497–8).
[62] This may be relevant for the other illustration which our treatises provide for ὡς followed by non-enclitic ἔστι (leaving aside illustrations consisting only of the words ὡς ἔστι, and examples that were demonstrably added at a late stage of the tradition): ὡς ἔστι κακὸν ἀμαθία 'that ignorance is a bad thing' or 'how ignorance is a bad thing!' (*About 'ΕΣΤΙΝ*, §a).

On enclitics 1 provides an example in which the ὡς is much more likely to be intended as introducing a subordinate clause (readers will notice that the ἘΣΤΙΝ expresses possibility here, but our treatise holds the ὡς responsible for the non-enclitic ἔστι, and it is the plausibility of this view that we wish to consider at this point):

(3.21)   ὡς ἔστιν εἰπεῖν *(On enclitics 1, §d)*

'as it is possible to say'

In Serbian, subordinating conjunctions can host enclitics, but some languages with enclitics provide closer parallels for a situation in which at least one enclitic (ἐστι) was excluded from the position after at least one subordinating conjunction (ὡς). Modern standard Dutch, for example, does not allow subordinating conjunctions to host enclitic object pronouns.[63] If enclitic ἐστί was excluded from the position after ὡς 'that, since, because, as', there would be nothing to prevent non-enclitic ἔστι appearing in this position.

A second strand of evidence can be adduced for the linguistic plausibility of the idea that in relatively conversational Greek of the Roman period, certain enclitics were excluded from positions following certain words that fall early on in what we might normally consider to be the 'clause'. This second strand of evidence comes from the behaviour of some other Greek words that can more confidently be recognized as enclitics, without our already having to know how particular instances should be accented. For example, the forms of indefinite τις are always enclitics; they can therefore be readily recognized as such, as long as we can distinguish on contextual grounds between indefinite and interrogative ΤΙΣ. The pronoun forms με, μου, and μοι can readily be recognized as enclitics because they are clearly distinct from non-enclitic ἐμέ, ἐμοῦ, and ἐμοί, in respects that go beyond their accentuation. With some caution, many other pronoun forms can be recognized as enclitic when they are used unemphatically.

Taylor (1996: 498–500) considers the placement of indefinite τις (in all cases) and of enclitic pronoun forms in Homer, Herodotus, Plato, the *Pastor Hermae* (probably second century AD), and a selection of papyrus letters from the first three centuries AD. She finds that in Homer these enclitics often follow co-ordinating conjunctions (3.22); less often they are placed after the following word instead (3.23):

(3.22)   ...καί οἱ πείθονται Ἀχαιοί *(Il. 1.79)*

'...and the Achaeans obey him'

---

[63] See Fontana (1996: 58); Zwart (1997: 35).

(3.23)   καὶ λίην σε πάρος γ᾽ οὔτ᾽ εἴρομαι οὔτε μεταλλῶ...(*Il.* 1.553)

'I've not at all asked or questioned you in the past...'

However, she finds that the pattern in (3.22) decreases in frequency between Homer and the classical period (with a corresponding increase in the pattern in (3.23)), and is not found at all in her sample of Roman-period texts.

Taylor also finds that the same enclitics often follow subordinating conjunctions in Homer; more rarely, they are placed after the following word instead:

(3.24)   Τυδέα δ᾽ οὐ μέμνημαι, ἐπεί μ᾽ ἔτι τυτθὸν ἐόντα
   κάλλιφ᾽...(*Il.* 6.222–3)

'But I do not remember Tydeus, since he left me behind when I was still small.'

(3.25)   τοῖο δ᾽ Ἀπόλλων
   εὐξαμένου ἤκουσεν, ἐπεὶ μάλα οἱ φίλος ἦεν (*Il.* 1.380–1)

'And Apollo heard him as he prayed, since he was very dear to him.'

Once again, she finds that there is a decrease between Homer and the classical period (albeit a less striking one this time) in the incidence of the pattern found in (3.24). By the Roman period the pattern in (3.24) appears to have become somewhat literary: the *Pastor Hermae* uses this pattern roughly as frequently as Herodotus and Plato, whereas the papyrus letters Taylor considers use it considerably less frequently.

This is not the place to discuss possible linguistic interpretations of the decrease in the patterns seen in examples (3.22) and (3.24).[64] What matters for present purposes is that in conversational speech of the Roman period, certain enclitics appear not to have been placed readily in the position after a co-ordinating or subordinating conjunction. When speakers wanted to use the enclitic, they placed it after the following word instead. But in contexts where the non-enclitic variant was appropriate, this variant could be placed (among other possibilities) immediately after the conjunction. In the *Pastor Hermae*, for example, where the pattern seen in example (3.22) is not found, we do find clauses such as (3.26)–(3.28):

(3.26)   καὶ ἐμὲ ἀνέκλιναν εἰς [τὸ μέσον αὐτ]ῶν (*Pastor Hermae* 88.7)

'and they laid me down in the middle of them'

(3.27)   καὶ ἐμοὶ ἡ ἐξουσία τῆς μετανοίας ταύτης ἐδόθη (*Pastor Hermae* 31.5)

'and the opportunity for this repentance was given to me.'

---

[64] For discussion in the context of a larger debate about the nature of various kinds of clitic behaviour, see Taylor (1996: 500–1).

(3.28)   καὶ ἐμοὶ λίαν ἤρεσεν (Pastor Hermae 55.7)

'and he pleased me very much.'

Speakers for whom 'ΕΣΤΙ behaved in a similar way might well have felt that where the combination ΚΑΙ 'ΕΣΤΙ appeared, even in older literary texts, the 'ΕΣΤΙ should be taken as the non-enclitic variant ἔστι.

A similar argument can be made for 'ΕΣΤΙ after clause-initial and near-clause-initial 'ΟΥΚ. In Homer, if clause-negating 'ΟΥΙ'ΟΥΚΙ'ΟΥΧ comes near the beginning of its clause, and the clause also contains an enclitic pronoun, the enclitic pronoun often comes immediately after the negative, as in examples (3.29) and (3.30) (see Taylor 1990: 43–5):

(3.29)   οὔ μιν ἐγώ γε
         φεύξομαι ἐκ πολέμοιο δυσηχέος (Il. 18.306-7)

'I shall not run away from him, out of the terrible-sounding war'

(3.30)   ἐπεὶ οὔ σφι θαλάσσια ἔργα μεμήλει. (Il. 2.614)

'since the affairs of the sea had not been of interest to them.'

In the Pastor Hermae, we count sixteen instances of a clause negated by 'ΟΥ and including an enclitic pronoun or an unemphatic form of αὐτός as a complement of the verb.[65] In none of these examples does the enclitic pronoun or the unemphatic form of αὐτός immediately follow the negative.[66] A similar picture emerges from Hunt and Edgar's selection of eighty-one Greek papyrus letters ranging from the third century BC to the sixth or seventh century AD (Hunt and Edgar 1932: 268–395),[67] in which we count nine clauses negated by 'ΟΥ and including an enclitic pronoun or an unemphatic form of αὐτός as a complement

---

[65] At 1.7 (x2), 1.8, 3.1, 7.1, 9.9, 10.8, 25.3, 30.2, 37.3, 37.4, 46.5, 50.3, 62.7, 64.3, 78.2. We exclude clauses negated by the stronger combination οὐ μή.

[66] All but two examples conform to the scheme '(conjunction)—negative—intervening word—enclitic/unemphatic pronoun' (where parentheses mean that the conjunction may or may not be present): ἢ οὐ δοκεῖ σοι ἀνδρὶ δικαίῳ πονηρὸν πρᾶγμα εἶναι ἐὰν...'Or does it not seem to you to be a wicked thing for a just man if...' (Pastor Hermae, 1.8). The intervening word is usually the verb (a pattern already found in Homer: see Taylor 1990: 45), but other possibilities are also found: the emphatic adverb πάντοτε 'altogether' (two consecutive examples at Pastor Hermae, 1.7), and (perhaps surprisingly, in the light of its own postpositive status) the modal particle ἄν (Pastor Hermae, 64.3). Of the two examples that do not conform to the scheme just mentioned, one is a minor variant of it (Pastor Hermae, 3.1: ἀλλ' οὐχ ἕνεκα τούτου σοι ὀργίζεται ὁ θεός 'But it is not because of this that God is angry with you') while the remaining example has οὐκ immediately before the verb at the end of the clause (a possibility also found in Homer: see Taylor 1990: 45): καὶ ὅλως ἀνάπαυσιν αὐτοῖς οὐκ ἐδίδει 'and altogether he did not give them respite' (Pastor Hermae, 62.7).

[67] The figure of eighty-one is arrived at by excluding Hunt and Edgar's no. 122, which is in Latin.

of the verb.[68] Again, none of these has the enclitic pronoun or unemphatic form of αὐτός immediately after the negative.[69]

A series of glosses from Hesychius' lexicon further suggests an implicit awareness at some stage that the patterns shown in (3.29) and (3.30) had become unnatural. In each case the lemma consists of a literary phrase with ᾿ΟΥ followed by a plausibly (and in some instances certainly) enclitic pronoun form. In the gloss, the word order is changed and/or ᾿ΟΥ is replaced by οὐδαμῶς, or in one instance (3.36) an additional word is inserted, so that the version presented as more natural does not feature ᾿ΟΥ followed immediately by an enclitic. In some instances the whole point of the gloss appears to be the rephrasing of ᾿ΟΥ followed by an enclitic pronoun form; in other instances this type of sequence appears to be rephrased incidentally, in a gloss whose main point is to paraphrase a literary word or phrase with a more widely known equivalent:

(3.31)   ἐπεὶ οὔ τοι·[70] ἐπεὶ οὐδαμῶς σοι (Hesychius, ε 4343 Latte-Cunningham)

(3.32)   οὔ ἕθεν·[71] οὐδαμῶς αὐτῆς (Hesychius, ο 1600 Latte-Cunningham)

(3.33)   οὔ μ᾽ εἴας·[72] οὐ συνεχώρεις με (Hesychius, ο 1766 Latte-Cunningham)

(3.34)   οὔ με γάμος δέ·[73] οὐδαμῶς δὲ γάμος με (Hesychius, ο 1769 Latte-Cunningham)

(3.35)   οὔ οἱ·[74] οὐδαμῶς αὐτῷ (Hesychius, ο 1797 Latte-Cunningham)

(3.36)   οὔ σε·[75] οὐ δή σε (Hesychius, ο 1873 Latte-Cunningham)

A similar entry has the negative ΜΗ rather than ᾿ΟΥ, and another has the conjunction ΚΑΙ:

---

[68] At no. 100 (= P.Paris 47 = UPZ i, no. 70), lines 4–5 (οὐκ ἄν με ἴδες…); no. 114 (= P.Flor. 332), line 3 (οὐ λανθάνει σε…); no. 115 (= P.Giss. i 17), line 10 (ὅτι οὐ βλέπομέν σε…); no. 124 (= P.Oxy. xii 1482), lines 4–6 (καὶ οὐ οὕτως αὐτὴν λελικμήκαμεν μετὰ κόπου); no. 129 (P.Oxy. x 1295), lines 3–4 (ἰδοὺ μὲν ἐγὼ οὐκ ἐμιμησάμην σε τοῦ ἀπ⟨οσπ⟩ᾶν…); no. 133 (= Rev. Ég. 1919, p. 201), line 7 (οὐκ ἔγραψάς μοι…); no. 138 (= P.Oxy. vii 1065), lines 6–7 (ὥσπερ [ο]ἱ θεοὶ οὐκ ἐφίσαντό μ[ο]υ); no. 147 (= P.Flor. 367), line 3 (ἐγὼ δὲ οὐ μειμήσομαί σε…); no. 159 (= P.Oxy. i 123), lines 8–9 (διότι οὐκ ἐδεξάμην σου γράμματα).

[69] Six examples again conform to the scheme '(conjunction)—negative—intervening word—enclitic/unemphatic pronoun'. In the remaining three, the subject of the clause precedes the negative but the negative is still followed by a non-enclitic word, itself followed by the clitic or unemphatic pronoun form: ὥσπερ [ο]ἱ θεοὶ οὐκ ἐφίσαντό μ[ο]υ 'as the gods have not spared me…' (Hunt and Edgar 1932, no. 138, lines 6–7); ἐγὼ δὲ οὐ μειμήσομαί σε…'I will not imitate you' (Hunt and Edgar 1932, no. 147, line 3); ἐγὼ οὐκ ἐμιμησάμην σε τοῦ ἀπ⟨οσπ⟩ᾶν…'I have not imitated you in your taking away…' (Hunt and Edgar 1932, no. 129, lines 3–4; the words quoted are preceded by ἰδοὺ μέν 'Look!', which we take to function for present purposes as a clause of its own).

[70] E.g. Il. 1.515: 'since you have no [fear]'.   [71] Il. 1.114: '[she is] not [inferior] to her'.

[72] Il. 5.819: 'you did not allow me'.

[73] Gregory Nazianzen, Carmina 2.1.1.63 (= Patrologia Graeca 37, p. 974, line 13): 'And marriage did not [bind] me'.

[74] E.g. Il. 2.392: 'not for him'.   [75] E.g. Od. 16.202: '[it is] not [fitting for] you'.

(3.37)   μή με·⁷⁶ μηδαμῶς με (Hesychius, μ 1209 Latte-Cunningham)

(3.38)   καί με πρὸς μῦθον ἔειπε·⁷⁷ καὶ προσεῖπέ με τῷ λόγῳ (Hesychius, κ 235 Latte-Cunningham)

Hesychius' work is ultimately based on Diogenianus' lexicon of the second century A D, but at least some of these entries are certainly later; in (3.34), for example, the lemma is a quotation from the fourth-century figure Gregory Nazianzen. But Hesychius provides us with some supporting evidence that at some point, turning poetic phrases into natural Greek came to involve rephrasing things so as to avoid sequences like οὔ με.

The point to retain from this discussion is that in fairly conversational Greek of the Roman period and later, certain enclitics appear to have been avoided after co-ordinating and subordinating conjunctions, and after a clause-negating 'OY near the beginning of the clause. We cannot prove that enclitic ἐστί was also disfavoured in the same positions (once again we cannot simply read the intended accent of 'EΣTI off ancient texts), but the behaviour of some other enclitics makes this a distinct possibility. If enclitic ἐστί was indeed disfavoured in such positions, non-enclitic ἔστι might nevertheless appear. Or to put the same point from a different perspective, literary instances of 'EΣTI in these positions would naturally be interpreted as involving non-enclitic ἔστι.

None of this proves that the 'initial and quasi-initial' view of non-enclitic 'EΣTI is necessarily correct. What we hope to have shown, however, is that the behaviour of 'EΣTI on this view is not implausible. Parallels can be adduced from other languages, and from the behaviour of some other enclitics in Roman-period Greek.

3.5.2   The linguistic plausibility of ἔστι as existential, contrastive, and emphatic

Many languages, like Greek, have verbs translatable sometimes with 'is' and sometimes with 'exists'. Philosophers and semanticists are far from agreed as to how many genuinely different senses these verbs have, and whether any such different senses are systematically related to one another or not.⁷⁸ As noted in section 3.1, those who have discussed Greek εἶναι in recent decades incline towards the view that, at least for this verb in Greek, no semantic distinction is to be made between 'copular' and 'existential' meanings. It is not our purpose either to defend or argue against this view (which philosophers and semanticists are

---

⁷⁶ E.g. *Il.* 3.438: 'Do not [attack] me.'   ⁷⁷ *Il.* 2.59: 'and addressed a speech to me'.
⁷⁸ For a reasonably accessible introduction, see B. Miller (2009).

much more competent to discuss), but let us suppose for argument's sake that it is right. For present purposes the important consequence is that it would be difficult to see how an accentual distinction between copular and existential 'ΕΣΤΙ could have been made.

However, it is important not to conclude from the difficulty (on this view) of an accentual distinction between 'copular' and 'existential' 'ΕΣΤΙ that there could not have been a distinction that was somewhat similar to this—one for which it was reasonable enough (even if it was an approximation) to speak of a special accentuation for an 'existential' meaning or use of 'ΕΣΤΙ.

Russian provides a nice illustration of this point. The Russian verb *byt'* 'to be' does not have an expressed present tense in most contexts; sentences like 'John is in the kitchen' normally take the form 'John (is) in the kitchen', with no overt form corresponding to the English 'is'. But we learn from basic grammars of Russian that a third person singular present form *ést'* is used in the meaning 'there is':

> Although the present tense of **быть** as a link-verb is not normally used in Russian, the 3rd person, singular and plural, **есть** (is) and **суть** (are) exist. The latter is very seldom used. **Есть** is used with the meaning of "there is", "there are", when "is" and "are" indicate actual "being" or "presence" (cf. French *il y a*), e.g.
>
> В ко́мнате есть окно́. There is a window in the room.
> В ко́мнате есть о́кна. There are windows in the room.
>
> (Semeonoff 1958: 34)

More advanced treatments of Russian grammar, however, reveal that the situation is far less simple. If we think in terms of a distinction between 'copular' and 'existential' *byt'*, it turns out that overt *ést'* is found in both copular and existential contexts, and the absence of any overt form corresponding to 'is' is also found in both copular and existential contexts. Wade (2020: 257–8) explains that 'Есть, a relic of a former verb conjugation, may be used for emphasis' and that *ést'* is particularly common '(i) In questions (and positive answers to questions)', '(ii) In contexts where the verb is heavily emphasized', '(iii) When "to be" means "to exist"', and '(iv)…in definitions'. Wade's examples include the following:[79]

(3.39)   In questions and answers:
　　　　–　*Papirósi*　**ést'**?　　　–　**Ést'**!
　　　　　cigarettes　is　　　　　　Is
　　　　'–　Are there any cigarettes?'　–　Yes, there are.'

---

[79] Wade presents examples in Cyrillic script; we have transliterated them but preserved Wade's use of bold face and the stress mark ′. (In the Russian examples, bold face draws attention to the form of particular interest; in the English translations, bold face conveys emphatic stress. On a polysyllabic Russian word such as *papirósi*, ′ marks the position of the word stress. On the form *est'* / *ést'*, ′ conveys emphatic stress.) The word-by-word glosses are ours but the translations are Wade's.

(3.40)   With heavy emphasis on the verb:
–   *Nûžno   spravedlívoe   rešénie.*   –   *Náše   resénie   i*
necessary   equitable   solution   our   solution   really

ést'   spravedlívoe.
is   equitable
'–   We need an equitable solution.   –   Our solution **is** equitable.'

(3.41)   In existential contexts:
Est'   takíe   ljúdi,   kotórie   ne   ljúbjat   ikrý
Is   such   people   who   not   like   caviar
'There are people who do not like caviar.'

(3.42)   In definitions:
Prjamája   línija   est'   kratčájšee   rasstojánie   mèždu
straight   line   is   shortest   distance   between

dvumjá   tóčkami
two   points
'A straight line is the shortest distance between two points.'

Wade also provides alternative versions of an existential sentence with and with-out an expressed verb (a dash may appear in Russian orthography where there is no expressed verb):

(3.43)   *Na   stené   –   kartína.*   OR   *Na   stené   est'   kartína.*
on   wall   picture   on   wall   is   picture
'There is a picture on the wall.'

In addition to providing more detail than Semeonoff, Wade gives pride of place to emphasis, rather than existential use, as the main determinant of expressed *est'*. This difference is not solely due to the more advanced nature of Wade's grammar. According to another advanced Russian grammar, Offord (1993: 377), 'In the modern language есть means *there is, there are*, but it may still be used in the sense of *is* in a very restricted way…'. Further on, Offord (1993: 383) gives a spe-cific context in which *est'* may be used in the sense of 'is': 'When the subject and the complement are the same then *is* may be rendered by есть.' An example with identical subject and complement is also given by Wade (2020: 258), who, how-ever, classifies it as an example with heavy emphasis on the verb:

(3.44)   *Zakón   est'   zakón.*
law   is   law
'The law is the law.'

Scholarly treatments of Russian 'to be' make clear that the conditions under which *est'* does and does not appear are extremely complex and difficult to describe adequately (see Chvany 1975). Both elementary and more advanced grammar handbooks are concerned with producing some helpful rules in a graspable form and in a compass that is reasonable, given the aims and scope of the grammar. Different paths may be taken here, but in the case of Russian, one helpful first approximation is that *est'* appears when the meaning is 'there is' or 'there are'.

Thus scholars who hold that Greek εἶναι has a unified semantics, without separate copular and existential meanings, need not also hold that the 'existential' view of non-enclitic ἔστι is simply wrong. Perhaps the passages supporting this view instead provide a reasonable simplification of a situation in which ʾΕΣΤΙ was paroxytone in a range of contexts including, but not limited to, ones that can at least informally be considered existential. When linguistic phenomena are complex, approximations are to be expected. Moreover, the passages that support the 'existential' tradition themselves hint at a picture more complex than it may at first sight appear.

Firstly, passages (3.11) and (3.12) do not contrast 'existential' ʾΕΣΤΙ with 'copular' ʾΕΣΤΙ, but 'existential' ʾΕΣΤΙ with ʾΕΣΤΙ used in the reply to a question. Since all sorts of Greek expressions can constitute replies to questions, something more specific is likely to be meant here, but it is difficult to see quite what.[80] Be this as it may, the uses of ʾΕΣΤΙ are very far from being exhausted when ʾΕΣΤΙ in existential contexts and ʾΕΣΤΙ in a reply have been considered: passages (3.11) and (3.12) cannot be intended as exhaustive discussions of the subject but only as cursory allusions. Possibly these passages derive from a source that presented a fuller picture, but possibly even the παλαιοί (whoever they might have been) whom Eustathius mentions in passage (3.12) only alluded to the subject in a way that was never intended to be complete.

Secondly, as noted earlier, passages (3.13) and (3.14) do not say that ʾΕΣΤΙ means 'exists' but that it is used or is to be pronounced ἐπαγγελτικῶς 'in a proclamatory way'. Although the examples appearing in these passages suggest that the same distinction is being made as in (3.11) and (3.12), the term ἐπαγγελτικῶς hints at a wider distinction between emphatic and unemphatic ʾΕΣΤΙ, rather than a narrower one between existential and non-existential ʾΕΣΤΙ.

Thus a tradition claiming that existential and non-existential ʾΕΣΤΙ were accentually distinguished would be a plausible simplification of a linguistic situation in which ʾΕΣΤΙ was paroxytone in a messy range of contexts involving such things as emphasis, contrast, and something like existentiality. In modern times,

---

[80] One might wonder whether answers consisting of ʾΕΣΤΙΝ all by itself are meant (e.g. Plato, *Phaedo* 93d7–8: –ἔστιν οὕτως; –ʾΕΣΤΙΝ.'–Is it so? –It is.'), but if so it is puzzling that the form should receive the accentuation ἐστίν rather than the usual non-enclitic accentuation ἔστιν.

the idea that ’EΣTI is paroxytone when it conveys existence or possibility is itself a simplification of Hermann's more nuanced discussion, according to which paroxytone ἔστι occurs when the word is not just the copula and is not omissible (see Hermann 1801: 84–90). In fact the ancient and medieval witnesses supporting the 'existential' view already hint that ’EΣTI was paroxytone in a more complex range of contexts than our distillation 'existential' might suggest. When understood in this way, the 'existential' view is linguistically plausible and has parallels in other languages including Russian.

3.5.3 Serbian again: the linguistic plausibility of ἔστι in initial and quasi-initial position *and* when existential, contrastive, or emphatic

We saw in section 3.5.1 that Serbian provides a nice illustration of how a language that excludes enclitics from initial and quasi-initial positions, and has enclitic and orthotonic variants of the verb 'to be', has the non-enclitic variant in sentence-initial position and after certain conjunctions. However, the non-enclitic forms of Serbian *biti* 'to be' are also used in various emphatic, contrastive, or strongly assertive contexts:[81]

(3.45)   *Marko*   *jeste*   *dobar.*
       Mark   is [ORTH.]   good.
       '[Is Mark good?] Mark *is* good [but he's lazy].' (example from Lord 1956: 18; context from Ana Kotarcic)

(3.46)   – *Jeste*   *li*   *umorni?* *Ja*   *jesam,*
          Are [POL.2.SG.ORTH.]   INTERROG.   tired   I   am [ORTH.]
          ali   *Anđela*   *nije.*
          but   Angela   is-not.
          'Are you tired? Yes, *I* am, but Angela is not.' (example from Hawkesworth with Ćalić 2006: 14)

(3.47)   *Jesi*   *lep.*
       Are [2.SG. ORTH.]   beautiful
       'You *are* beautiful.' (as a very strong compliment) (from Ana Kotarcic)

Existential sentences are not regularly formed in Serbian with *biti* 'to be', but with *imati* 'to have'; existence may also be expressed with a specialized verb meaning

---

[81] Ana Kotarcic tells us that when the orthotonic forms are not clause-initial, there is usually a strongly implied 'yes' or 'on the contrary', and that in (3.46) the overt pronoun *Ja* 'I' also puts emphasis on this word.

'to exist'. However, the existence of a person can be asserted using *biti* 'to be', and in such sentences the non-enclitic forms are used:

(3.48) *Ja   jesam.*
      I   exist [1.SG. ORTH.]
      'I exist.' (from Ana Kotarcic)

Thus Serbian would provide a fairly close typological parallel for a situation in which the verb 'to be' is non-enclitic in initial and quasi-initial position and in various emphatic contexts. In addition, Serbian allows us to see how such a situation can be simplified for didactic purposes. Hammond gives the following account of the use of the non-enclitic present forms of *biti*:

> This form is quite restricted in its use and is generally only used when the verb occurs as the first word of a sentence or phrase, often in posing a question, when it is followed by the interrogative enclitic ли/**li**. It is also used in response to a question, often on its own, denoting an affirmative response.
>
> (Hammond 2005: 62)

Prince concentrates on the same facts but does not refer directly to sentence- or clause-initial position, only to the circumstances under which initial *biti* is normally found:

> The longer form **jèsam,** etc., is only used independently, as 'are you there?'; **jèsam** 'I am'; or in questions; as, **jèste-li tamo** 'are you there'?
>
> (Prince 1945: 59)

Other grammars make reference both to initial and emphatic *biti*:

> The long accented forms…are used a) when the verb comes first in the sentence, or b) for emphasis. The verb comes first in the sentence most frequently in interrogative sentences not introduced by an interrogative conjunction such as kàd, when, or gdè, where: e.g. jèsi li (enclitic interrogative particle) dòbar, are you good?…Emphasis is given to the verb by using the long form: e.g. Mârko jèste dòbar, Mark *is* good.'
>
> (Lord 1956: 18)

Thus it may be a mistake to ask which ancient tradition on Greek *ἜΣΤΙ* is correct. Both traditions could represent simplifications of a complex situation somewhat like the one found in modern Serbian. Some simplification may well have occurred in the process of transmission, but some may have been there since the beginning.

3.6 Conclusion

In this chapter, we set out to re-examine the foundations for the two main modern views on the conditions under which 'ΕΣΤΙ is non-enclitic: the 'initial and quasi-initial' view and the 'existential' view. A first result concerns the 'initial and quasi-initial' view, most often understood to mean that non-enclitic ἔστι occurs at the beginning of its clause or verse, and when preceded in its clause only by οὐ, καί, εἰ, ἀλλά, ὡς, or perhaps τοῦτο. A new examination of the textual evidence underpinning this view shows that in the Byzantine period the list of words followed by non-enclitic ἔστι regularly has three members: οὐ, καί, and ὡς. There is only scant evidence for other members of this list. This does not mean that other words could not have been followed by non-enclitic ἔστι, but Wackernagel (1877: 466) already found τοῦτο anomalous in this context. Following a hint in an Aldine version of *On enclitics 1*, we suggest that the basis for including τοῦτο in the list of words prompting non-enclitic ἔστι was limited to the idiomatic expression τουτέστι 'i.e.', and our reassessment of the textual evidence suggests that τοῦτο was in any case a late and weakly attested addition to the list.

Contrary to the current consensus that the tradition supporting the 'initial and quasi-initial' view is ancient and the one supporting the 'existential' view emerged later, we have found that the first of these traditions can be traced back to the second century AD only in a somewhat limited form ('ΕΣΤΙ was non-enclitic in initial position and after 'ΟΥΚ), and the second tradition is also likely to have been in existence by that date.

Parallels from other languages suggest that each view is linguistically plausible in itself. More interestingly, both views could plausibly be partly right, with each being a reasonable simplification of a more complex reality. Grammars and didactic works on Serbian (and older works on Serbo-Croatian) provide a typological comparison for different reasonable simplifications of a complex reality of this type.

For those wanting a simple and correct rule for the accentuation of 'ΕΣΤΙ, for example for the purposes of editing a text, we cannot offer quite this. If the surviving evidence consists of various simplifications of a complex reality, as we suggest, it is unrealistic to think that we can recover all the details of the complex reality itself. For the same reason, we cannot attempt an explicit modern linguistic analysis of the syntactic behaviour of enclitic 'ΕΣΤΙ, such as has been offered for some other Greek enclitics.[82] Such an analysis would need to rest on a set of reasonably clear empirical facts: with some caveats connected to the transmission of texts, such empirical facts are available for those enclitics that can be identified independently of their accentuation, for instance the particle ΓΕ (always enclitic), the enclitic pronoun form ΜΕ (distinct from non-enclitic 'ΕΜΕ in ways that go

---

[82] See especially Taylor (1990; 1996); Goldstein (2016).

beyond accentuation), or indefinite *ΤΙΣ* (distinguishable from interrogative *ΤΙΣ* wherever the meaning can be determined from the context). For 'ΕΣΤΙ, we depend on what can be gleaned from the grammatical tradition—and since this does not stretch to a complete set of empirical facts, the conclusions we can offer are more modest. We can, however, suggest that the modern didactic works that attempt to combine the two traditions on non-enclitic ἔστι (see n. 9) may not be far wrong. We can also suggest that whatever principle we follow, we are likely to be right some of the time: as we have seen (sections 3.1, 3.3), the different approaches currently on offer produce the same results as each other some of the time. On the other hand, regardless of which principle we follow we are also likely to be wrong some of the time. With this in mind, we encourage scholars to exercise tolerance towards each other's practices in accenting 'ΕΣΤΙ.

4

εἴ πέρ τίς σέ μοι φησίν ποτε

Accenting sequences of enclitics

4.1 Introduction

When two or more enclitics follow one another in succession in ancient Greek, we traditionally learn that each enclitic receives an accent—normally an acute—on its final syllable, except that the last enclitic is unaccented: hence αἰδοῖός τέ μοί ἐσσι 'you are respected in my eyes' (*Il.* 3.172) or εἴ πού τίς τινα ἴδοι 'if by chance anyone saw anyone' (Thucydides 4.47.3).[1] This is normally said to be the main view found in the ancient grammatical tradition.[2]

Some modern scholars have doubted this rule[3] and have proposed alternatives, or have claimed that alternative systems are found in some manuscripts[4] and/or hinted at in the grammatical tradition.[5] The best-known alternative was originally put forward by Karl Göttling, and later popularized by W. S. Barrett;[6] we shall call this the 'Göttling-Barrett system'. In the Göttling-Barrett system, with each addition of an enclitic the resulting sequence is treated as a new word, to which the rules for adding a single enclitic can be applied again. As Barrett (1964: 427) puts this, 'ἤγγειλέ γε ; then ἤγγειλέ-γε μοι like λέγε μοι ; then ἤγγειλέ-γε-μοί ποτε like λέγεταί ποτε ; and so on'. An example will be worked out in more detail shortly.

In this chapter, we shall see that evidence from several directions comes together to suggest that ancient and medieval scholars operated—implicitly—with what is in essence the Göttling-Barrett system, but not quite in the form that

---

[1] See e.g. Chandler (1881: 280); Probert (2003: 152–3).

[2] E.g. Kühner and Blass (1890–2: i. 343); Wackernagel (1893: 21); Vendryes (1904: 87); West (1990: xxxii).

[3] The main point made against the traditional view has been that acute accents on successive syllables are implausible, but evidence for their implausibility has not been produced. Devine and Stephens (1994: 373–4) point out somewhat similar phenomena in some modern languages, while West (1990: xxxii) points out that acute accents also appear on successive syllables in sequences such as τί λέγεις.

[4] Lipsius (1863: 50–5); La Roche (1866: 414–16); Vendryes (1904: 88–9); Kühner and Blass (1890–2: i. 343); Barrett (1964: 427); Devine and Stephens (1994: 373). For doubts as to whether a consistent alternative to the traditional view is really found in manuscripts, see Chandler (1881: 281–2).

[5] Göttling (1835: 405); La Roche (1866: 414–15); Kühner and Blass (1890–2: i. 343); Vendryes (1904: 89).

[6] Göttling (1835: 405); Barrett (1964: 426–7). Cf. also also Kühner and Blass (1890–2: i. 343).

Ancient and Medieval Thought on Greek Enclitics. Stephanie Roussou & Philomen Probert, Oxford University Press. © Stephanie Roussou and Philomen Probert 2023.
DOI: 10.1093/oso/9780192871671.003.0004

Göttling or Barrett envisaged. The crucial difference lies in the precise rules to be applied repeatedly: what 'rules for adding a single enclitic' are applied on each addition of a new enclitic?

From the examples which Göttling and Barrett provide,[7] it is clear that they think in terms of the 'rules for adding a single enclitic' that we normally learn today—the ones we set out in Chapter 1. In order to think of these as rules that can be applied repeatedly, it will be convenient to formulate them as follows:

Göttling-Barrett system

I

If the sequence preceding the new enclitic would have an acute or circumflex on its last syllable in isolation, this sequence retains its accent (and any preceding accents) before an enclitic, with no change of an acute to a grave. No accent appears on the new enclitic.

II

If the last accent on the sequence preceding the new enclitic is a circumflex on its second-to-last syllable, or an acute on its third-to-last syllable, the sequence retains this accent (and any preceding accents) and acquires an additional acute on its last syllable before an enclitic. No accent appears on the new enclitic.

III

If the last accent on the sequence preceding the new enclitic is an acute on its penultimate syllable, the sequence simply retains this accent (and any preceding accents) before the new enclitic. If the enclitic is monosyllabic it appears without an accent; if the enclitic is disyllabic it appears with an acute on its second syllable (or grave, if a non-enclitic word follows without intervening punctuation), or a circumflex in the case of τινοῖν or τινῶν.

Suppose we want to apply this system to our example ἈΙΔΟΙΟΣ ΤΕ ΜΟΙ᾽ΕΣΣΙ (*Il.* 3.172). First, we need to consider what should happen to the naturally properispomenon word αἰδοῖος before the first enclitic *ΤΕ*. By principle II of the Göttling-Barrett system, αἰδοῖος retains its circumflex accent and acquires an additional acute accent on its final syllable, and no accent appears on the enclitic; the resulting sequence is αἰδοῖός τε. Now, what should happen to αἰδοῖός τε before the new

---

[7] In particular, Göttling's example ἤ νυ σέ που (and implicitly εἴ πέρ τίς σε μοί φησί ποτε) and Barrett's εἴ τί μοι show that these scholars did not operate with a particular modification of these principles that is necessary (as we shall see) for making sense of the ancient and medieval evidence.

enclitic *ΜΟΙ*? The last accent of αἰδοῖός τε is an acute on the penultimate syllable: so by principle III, αἰδοῖός τε simply retains this acute accent (and the preceding circumflex) before the new enclitic. No new accent appears on the τε, nor does the new enclitic *ΜΟΙ* receive an accent at this stage. The result, then, is αἰδοῖός τε μοι. Lastly, we need to ask what happens to αἰδοῖός τε μοι before the further enclitic *ΕΣΣΙ*. The last accent of αἰδοῖός τε μοι is an acute on the third-to-last syllable, so by principle II this sequence receives an additional acute accent on its last syllable. No accent appears on the new enclitic, so the result is αἰδοῖός τε μοί ἐσσι.

In the system that will become central to this chapter (we shall call it the 'revised Göttling-Barrett system'), the rules that we need to apply repeatedly are slightly different:

Revised Göttling-Barrett system

I

If the sequence preceding the new enclitic would have an acute or circumflex on its last syllable in isolation, this sequence retains its accent (and any preceding accents) before an enclitic, with no change of an acute to a grave. No accent appears on the new enclitic.

II

If the last accent on the sequence preceding the new enclitic is a circumflex on its second-to-last syllable, or an acute on its third-to-last syllable, the sequence retains this accent (and any preceding accents) and acquires an additional acute on its last syllable before an enclitic. No accent appears on the new enclitic.

III

If the last accent of the sequence preceding the new enclitic is an acute on its penultimate syllable, then

   i. if this sequence ends in a trochaic pattern (before the addition of the new enclitic), it retains this accent (and any preceding accents) and acquires an additional acute on its last syllable before an enclitic. No accent appears on the new enclitic.

   ii. otherwise, the sequence simply retains this accent (and any preceding accents) before the new enclitic. If the enclitic is monosyllabic it appears without an accent; if the enclitic is disyllabic it appears with an acute on its second syllable (or grave, if a non-enclitic word follows without intervening punctuation), or a circumflex in the case of τινοῖν or τινῶν. (Sections 4.2.4, 4.2.5, and 4.3 will add the qualification that if the new enclitic begins with σφ-, the sequence is treated as under III.i.)

The crucial difference between this system on the one hand, and Göttling and Barrett's original system on the other, consists of principle III.i, which follows from the ancient doctrine concerning sequences like ἔνθά τε (see sections 2.7.3, 2.8.3): a paroxytone word *does* receive a new accent before an enclitic if the paroxytone word ends in a trochaic sequence.

Suppose we want to apply the revised Göttling-Barrett system to our example *ΑΙΔΟΙΟΣ ΤΕ ΜΟΙ ΈΣΣΙ*. Once again, we first consider what should happen to αἰδοῖος before *TE*. By principle II, αἰδοῖος once again retains its circumflex accent and acquires an additional acute accent on its final syllable, and no accent appears on the enclitic; the result is αἰδοῖός τε. But when we consider what happens to αἰδοῖός τε before *MOI*, the revised Göttling-Barrett system yields a different answer from the one we saw just now. The sequence αἰδοῖός τε has an acute on its penultimate syllable and (importantly) ends in a trochaic pattern. So by principle III.i, this sequence acquires an additional accent on its last syllable. No accent appears on the monosyllabic enclitic, so the result is αἰδοῖός τέ μοι. This new sequence again has an acute on its penultimate syllable, but this time it does not end in a trochaic pattern. So by principle III.ii, no new accent appears on the μοι before *ΈΣΣΙ*, and an acute (or grave, as the case may be[8]) appears on the second syllable of the disyllabic enclitic. The result is αἰδοῖός τέ μοι ἐσσί.

Göttling and Barrett's original system and our revised version do not always produce different outcomes from each other. For example (and as readers will be able to verify), both systems produce εἴ που τίς τινα ἴδοι at Thucydides 4.47.3. It will in fact be a recurring theme of this chapter that different systems (of ancient, medieval, or modern origin) do not always produce different results. But some of the time, as illustrated by *ΑΙΔΟΙΟΣ ΤΕ ΜΟΙ ΈΣΣΙ*, the original Göttling-Barrett system and the revised one do give different results. These differences will turn out to matter.

Before we go on, the concept 'trochaic termination' requires a bit more comment. In a sequence like *ΑΙ ΚΕΝ ΠΩΣ* 'if by chance' (*Il.* 1.66), the word αἴ (which from an ancient point of view counts as naturally oxytone) keeps its acute accent before the enclitic *ΚΕΝ*, but does αἴ κεν count as ending in a trochaic sequence or not? That is to say, does the final -ν of κεν cause this to count as a long syllable? Does it matter that the enclitic which is to follow begins with a consonant? The answer will be that αἴ κεν counts as ending in a trochaic sequence. For the purposes of applying the revised Göttling-Barrett system, what matters is the shape that a sequence has *before the addition of the next enclitic*: so the shape of αἴ κεν needs to be considered in isolation, without regard to the fact that *ΠΩΣ* begins with a consonant. In addition, for present purposes a single consonant at the end of the sequence under consideration does not count as making the

---

[8] At *Il.* 3.172 itself, modern editors normally print a comma after ἐσσί and before the following vocative φίλε ἑκυρέ 'dear father-in-law'. In this context the revised Göttling-Barrett system gives rise to ἐσσί with an acute.

preceding syllable long. (In the same way, our texts on enclitics consider ἄλλος a 'trochaic' word, even when it is followed by an enclitic like τις.[9]) On the other hand, a word-final consonant is only ignored if it falls at the very end of the sequence being considered, not if it falls in the middle. For this reason, ὠχρός τε counts as ending in a trochaic sequence for the purposes of the revised Göttling-Barrett system: adding the further enclitic μιν gives ὠχρός τέ μιν. For the same reason again, under some circumstances a syllable counts as short at one step of the process and then long at the next step. Suppose, for example, that we want to accent the sequence ΈΙ ΠΕΡ ΤΙΣ ΣΕ 'if anybody…you' according to the revised Göttling-Barrett system. ΈΙ 'if' counts as an oxytone word for ancient grammarians, and so adding the enclitic ΠΕΡ gives εἴ περ. This sequence εἴ περ counts as trochaic, with ΠΕΡ counting as a short syllable, and so adding the further enclitic ΤΙΣ gives εἴ πέρ τις. This sequence εἴ πέρ τις also counts as ending in a trochaic sequence, with ΠΕΡ now counting as a long syllable, and so adding the further enclitic ΣΕ gives εἴ πέρ τίς σε.

But why should we think that any of this has any basis in ancient thought or practice? This chapter will consider evidence from three different directions: grammatical texts, accented papyri, and the accents in the *Iliad* manuscript Venetus A. Evidence from these sources will turn out to come together in a way that has not been noticed before, and that points strongly in the direction of our revised Göttling-Barrett system.

4.2 Grammatical texts

Ancient grammatical texts preserve three different doctrines relating to sequences of enclitics. The following subsections lay these out, beginning with the ancient counterpart of the system we normally learn (we shall call this the 'traditional' view or system), to the effect that every enclitic except the last gets an accent (an acute, except for enclitic τινῶν or τινοῖν) on its last or only syllable.

4.2.1 The traditional view

At least at first sight, the earliest fairly clear allusion to the 'traditional' view on accenting sequences of enclitics appears in a passage of Apollonius Dyscolus, quoted earlier as passage (2.22), on the problem of identifying words as opposed to parts of words:

---

[9] See *On enclitics 1*, §p (on ἄλλός τις) and Charax, §f (on ἄλλός μοι). But see also *On enclitics 2*, §e (where the transmitted text calls the word πάρος 'iambic' in the sequence πάρος γε), with Chapter 2, n. 113.

(4.1)   πᾶν μόριον ἐγκλιτικὸν λέξις ἐστίν, 'ἦλθέ τις', 'ἄνθρωπός εἰμι'· πάμπολλοι
δέ εἰσιν οἱ παραπληρωματικοὶ ἐν ἐγκλίσει, ὡς ὁ ΓΕ, ὁ 'ΡΑ, ὁ ΘΗΝ, ⟨ὁ⟩
ΝΥ. δύο λέξεων ἢ τριῶν οὐσῶν ἀκώλυτον τὸ ἐπάλληλον τῆς ὀξείας· καὶ
κατὰ τοῦτο οὖν λέξεις τὰ προκείμενα μόρια· ἰδοὺ γὰρ ἐν τῷ 'ἤ νύ σέ που
δέος ἴσχει' καθ' ἓν ἕκαστον μέρος λόγου ἡ ὀξεῖα ἀνέστη. (Ap. Dysc.,
Conj. 249.14–20)

'Every enclitic item is a word, as in ἦλθέ τις and ἄνθρωπός εἰμι.[10] There
are very many filler particles that are enclitic: e.g. ΓΕ, 'ΡΑ, ΘΗΝ, and
ΝΥ. When there are two [such] words or three, the succession of acute
accents is unimpeded. And for this reason the items in question are words.
Thus in ἤ νύ σέ που δέος ἴσχει[11] the acute accent has risen up on each
word individually.'

This passage should be taken together with passage (4.2), which also deals with
the example ἤ νύ σέ που δέος ἴσχει. By explicitly mentioning an acute accent on
the ΣΕ, this passage—it seems—helps to confirm that Apollonius thought the
succession of acute accents extended as far as the ΣΕ:

(4.2)   αἱ μὲν οὖν ὀρθὸν τόνον εἰληχυῖαι τὸ πλέον ἕνεκα σημαινομένου
ὀρθοτονοῦνται, ἔσθ' ὅτε δὲ ἢ σύνταξις ἢ τόπος ἢ ποιητικὴ ἄδεια
ὀρθοτονοῦσι τὰς ἀντωνυμίας· καὶ ἐπὶ μὲν συντάξεως 'ἤ νύ σέ που δέος
ἴσχει'· τὸ γὰρ ΠΟΥ ἐγκλιτικὸν αἴτιον τοῦ τὴν ΣΕ ὀξύνεσθαι. (Ap.
Dysc., Pron. 39.14–19)

'Those [pronouns] which have an unmodified accent [i.e. are accented,
not enclitic] usually have it because of their meaning, but sometimes
either the syntax or the placement [of the pronoun] or poetic licence gives
pronouns an unmodified accent. In the case of syntax e.g. ἤ νύ σέ που δέος
ἴσχει: for the enclitic ΠΟΥ is the reason why the ΣΕ has an acute accent.'

The clearest statements of the principle appear in On enclitics 1 and On enclitics 2:

(4.3)   ἐὰν οὖν συμβῇ πλείονα ἐφεξῆς ἐγκλιτικὰ εἶναι, πολλαὶ ἔσονται καὶ
παράλληλοι αἱ ὀξεῖαι, ὡς παρ' Ὁμήρῳ· 'ἤ νύ σέ που δέος ἴσχει ἀκήριον'.
τρεῖς γάρ εἰσιν ἐφεξῆς αἱ ὀξεῖαι. δυνατὸν δὲ καὶ πλείονας ἐπινοῆσαι,
οἷον· 'εἴ πέρ τίς σέ μοί φησίν ποτε'. τὸ μὲν γὰρ ΕΙ ὀξύνεται διὰ τὴν
ἐπιφορὰν τοῦ ΠΕΡ ἐγκλιτικοῦ· τὸ δὲ ΠΕΡ διὰ τὸ ΤΙΣ, τὸ δὲ ΤΙΣ
διὰ τὸ ΣΕ, τὸ δὲ ΣΕ διὰ τὸ ΜΟΙ, τὸ δὲ ΜΟΙ διὰ τὸ ΦΗΣΙΝ, τὸ δὲ
ΦΗΣΙΝ διὰ τὸ ΠΟΤΕ. ὥστε ἐφεξῆς εἶναι ὀξείας ἕξ, εἰ καὶ σπάνιον τὸ

---

[10] 'Someone came', 'I am a person'.   [11] Il. 5.812: 'or perhaps fear has got hold of you'.

τοιοῦτον διὰ τὴν τοῦ πνεύματος συνέχειαν δεομένην ἀναπαύσεως. (*On Enclitics 1*, §r)

'If several enclitics happen to occur in a row, the acute accents will be many and consecutive, as in Homer's ἤ νύ σέ που δέος ἴσχει ἀκήριον.[12] For the acutes are three in a row. And it is possible to think of more, as in εἴ πέρ τίς σέ μοί φησίν ποτε.[13] For the *ΕΙ* has an acute because of the addition of the enclitic *ΠΕΡ*, and the *ΠΕΡ* because of the *ΤΙΣ*, and the *ΤΙΣ* because of the *ΣΕ*, and the *ΣΕ* because of the *ΜΟΙ*, and the *ΜΟΙ* because of the *ΦΗΣΙΝ*, and the *ΦΗΣΙΝ* because of the *ΠΟΤΕ*, with the result that there are six acutes in a row—even if this happens rarely, because of the fact that the continuity of the breath needs a break.'

(4.4) συνεγκλιτικὸν δέ ἐστι σύνταξις δυοῖν ἢ πλειόνων μορίων ἐγκλιτικῶν ἐπαλλήλων ὀξυνομένων, ὡς ἔχει τὰ τοιαῦτα· 'ἤ νύ σέ που δέος ἴσχει. ὁ μὲν γὰρ Ἤ ὀξύνεται διὰ τὸ ΝΥ ἐγκλιτικόν, τὸ δὲ ΝΥ διὰ τὴν ἀντωνυμίαν τὴν ΣΕ, ἡ δὲ ΣΕ ἀντωνυμία διὰ τὸν ΠΟΥ παραπληρωματικὸν σύνδεσμον. (*On Enclitics 2*, §c)

'*Synenclitic* is the putting together of two or more enclitic items that are oxytone in succession, as in the following sort of example: ἤ νύ σέ που δέος ἴσχει.[14] For the *Ἤ* is oxytone because of the enclitic *ΝΥ*, and the *ΝΥ* because of the pronoun *ΣΕ*, and the pronoun *ΣΕ* because of the filler conjunction *ΠΟΥ*.'

The same doctrine turns up in the *Etymologicum Gudianum* (and in an almost identical form in the *Etymologicum Magnum*, which derives some of its material from the *Etymologicum Gudianum*[15]). The formulation closely resembles the beginning of passage (4.3), including the almost identical wording πολλαὶ ἔσονται καὶ παράλληλοι ὀξεῖαι, although a different Homeric example appears:

(4.5) οὔ θήν μιν· οὐδαμῶς δὴ αὐτόν. πόσοι τόνοι; δύο· διατί; ἡνίκα εὑρεθῶσιν ἐγκλιτικὰ ἐφεξῆς ἀλλήλων κείμενα, πολλαὶ ἔσονται καὶ παράλληλοι ὀξεῖαι· ἤ ῥά νύ μοί τι πίθοιο Λυκάονος υἱὲ δαΐφρον' (*Et. Gud.* 439.45–8 Sturz; almost identically *Etymologicum Magnum* 638.15–17)

'οὔ θήν μιν[16] [means] οὐδαμῶς δὴ αὐτόν.[17] How many accents? Two. Why? When enclitics are found placed next to one another, acute accents

---

[12] *Il.* 5.812: 'or perhaps spiritless fear has got hold of you'.
[13] 'If ever anyone says to me that you'.
[14] *Il.* 5.812: 'or perhaps fear has got hold of you'.   [15] See Lasserre and Livadaras (1976: xvii).
[16] *Il.* 2.276: '[His manly heart will] surely not [spur] him [on again]'.
[17] 'On no account…him'.

will be many and consecutive, as in ἦ ῥά νύ μοί τι πίθοιο Λυκάονος υἱὲ
δαΐφρον.'[18]

Statements (4.3), (4.4), and (4.5) all look related not only to one another, but also
to Apollonius' discussions (4.1) and (4.2). The phrases πολλαὶ ἔσονται καὶ
παράλληλοι αἱ ὀξεῖαι (passage (4.3), and almost identically in (4.5)) and
ἐπαλλήλων ὀξυνομένων (passage (4.4)) are reminiscent of Apollonius' ἀκώλυτον
τὸ ἐπάλληλον τῆς ὀξείας (passage (4.1)), while σύνταξις δυοῖν ἢ πλειόνων
μορίων ἐγκλιτικῶν (passage (4.4)) is reminiscent of Apollonius' δύο λέξεων ἢ
τριῶν οὐσῶν (passage (4.1)). Apollonius' example ἤ νύ σέ που δέος ἴσχει (passages (4.1) and (4.2)) reappears in passages (4.3) and (4.4).

On the face of it, then, the traditional view was held by Apollonius (although
we shall return to this point in section 4.2.6), and at first sight it is tempting to
suspect that this was also the view of his son Herodian.[19] Material from Herodian's
works on prosody found its way into the Byzantine etymological lexica,[20] and into
all manner of late antique and medieval works relating to prosody. The similarities between passages (4.3), (4.4), and (4.5), and more distantly between all of
these and passage (4.1), would be readily explained if Herodian expressed the
same view as his father, in terms at least somewhat influenced by those of his
father, and if Herodian's statement was an ultimate source for passages (4.3), (4.4),
and (4.5).

Curiously, however, the Homeric scholia that derived a considerable quantity
of material on prosody from Herodian[21] never state the traditional principle.
They do comment on the accentuation of sequences of enclitics, but they either
lay out different principles, as we shall see, or they simply note the accentuation of
specific words in specific sequences. Even notes of the latter kind are never
demonstrably based on the straightforward 'traditional' system, as we shall see in
section 4.2.5.

Statements of the traditional view are thus distributed in a curious way. The
view is laid out (i) in Apollonius Dyscolus, (ii) in the short treatises giving us passages (4.3) and (4.4), and (iii) in the Byzantine etymological lexica, giving us passage (4.5). Since the etymological lexica are known to have derived material from
Herodian, and passages (4.3), (4.4), and (4.5) look related to one another, the
obvious inference is that Herodian followed his father in laying out the traditional

---

[18] *Il.* 4.93: 'Might you listen to me now, brave son of Lycaon?'

[19] Readers will recall that the treatise to which passage (4.3) belongs is transmitted as part of
Pseudo-Arcadius' epitome of Herodian's Περὶ καθολικῆς προσῳδίας, as well as being transmitted
independently, but once again this does not entitle us to ascribe the doctrine to Herodian with any
confidence (see section 3.2).

[20] See Schironi (2004: 11–13).

[21] That is to say, the A scholia to the *Iliad*; material of a similar kind where this turns up in the bT
scholia; and *Odyssey* scholia similar in kind to the A scholia to the *Iliad* (see Dickey 2007: 18–19, 21,
with bibliography).

view. But if this is so, one might expect this view to turn up in the Homeric scholia derived from Herodian too. We shall return to this pattern of distribution in sections 4.2.4 and 4.2.5.

4.2.2 The traditional view with an exception for *ΠΟΥ, ΠΗ(Ι), ΠΩΣ, ΠΩ*, and perhaps others

We have presented passage (4.3) as a representative of the 'traditional' view, but this passage is followed immediately by a discussion making an exception for certain enclitics, including *ΠΟΥ, ΠΗ(Ι)*, and *ΠΩΣ*:

(4.6)   εἰ δέ, παραλλήλων ὄντων ἐγκλιτικῶν, ἐν τῷ μεταξὺ περισπώμενον εἴη, ὡς ἐπὶ τοῦ *ΠΟΥ, ΠΗ, ΠΩΣ*, καὶ μετὰ τοῦτο ἐπιφέροιτο ἕτερον ἐγκλιτικόν, τοῦτο τὸ περισπώμενον οὔτε περισπᾶται διὰ τὸ ἐγκλῖναι τὸν ἴδιον τόνον, οὔτε ὀξύνεται, ἐπεὶ μὴ πέφυκεν ἡ περισπωμένη κατὰ τὸ κοινὸν ἔθος συστολῆς μὴ παρακολουθούσης εἰς ὀξεῖαν μετατίθεσθαι, οἷον· ʽοὔ πως ἐστ᾽, Ἀγέλαεʼ (ἐν γὰρ τῇ *ΟΥ* διφθόγγῳ μόνον ἡ ὀξεῖα), ʽἤ που τίς σφιν εἶπεν᾽ (ἐν τῷ *Η* καὶ ἐν τῷ *ΤΙΣ* ἡ ὀξεῖα), ʽἄνθρωπόν τινά που φησὶ μελῳδεῖν᾽ (πάλιν ἐν τῇ *ΠΟΝ* συλλαβῇ καὶ τῇ *ΝΑ* ἡ ὀξεῖα). (*On enclitics 1*, §s)

'But if there are enclitics next to one another, and one in the middle is ['naturally'] perispomenon, like [indefinite] *ΠΟΥ, ΠΗ*, and *ΠΩΣ*, and after this there is another enclitic, the perispomenon one neither gets a circumflex (because it has thrown its own ['natural'] accent off) nor gets an acute (because a circumflex is not normally exchanged for an acute unless a vowel is shortened). For example: ʽοὔ πως ἐστ᾽, Ἀγέλαεʼ[22] (with an acute only on the diphthong *ΟΥ*); ʽἤ που τίς σφιν εἶπεν᾽[23] (with an acute on *Η* and *ΤΙΣ*); ʽἄνθρωπόν τινά που φησὶ μελῳδεῖν᾽[24] (again the acute goes on the syllable *-ΠΟΝ* and on *-ΝΑ*).'

In his edition of Pseudo-Arcadius' epitome of Herodian's *Περὶ καθολικῆς προσῳδίας*, Schmidt (1860: 168) printed a text of this passage that made little sense, as had Barker (1820: 146–7) before him,[25] but the logic of the passage was

---

[22] *Od.* 22.136: 'I suppose it's not possible, Agelaos'. The treatise assumes that ἐστ᾽ is an enclitic here.

[23] 'Either I suppose somebody said to them' (cf. *Il.* 6.438).

[24] 'I suppose he says that some person sings'.

[25] As a result, although Göttling (1835: 405) and Vendryes (1904: 89) both saw that the passage is relevant to the question of accenting sequences of enclitics, neither scholar understood it correctly. Göttling thought the idea was that an enclitic whose 'own' or 'natural' accent was a circumflex should receive an acute, not a circumflex, when accented because of a following enclitic, but the text argues against either an acute or a circumflex for the relevant enclitics. Vendryes thought the idea was that an

seen already by Lehrs (1837: 129). The idea is that an enclitic whose 'own' or 'natural' accent is a circumflex can receive neither an acute nor a circumflex when followed by a further enclitic.[26] At this point we need to recall that unlike modern scholars, who normally cite monosyllabic enclitics in isolation without an accent, ancient grammarians considered *all* enclitics 'naturally' accented on their final or only syllables (see sections 2.7.1–2.7.2); this idea is attested as early as Apollonius Dyscolus, along with the idea that in some instances this 'natural' accent is a circumflex.[27] Enclitics whose 'natural' accent is a circumflex will always have a long vowel or diphthong in their final or only syllable, because only long vowels and diphthongs can have a circumflex accent. On the other hand, not all enclitics whose final syllable has a long vowel or diphthong need have had a circumflex as their theoretical 'natural' accent, but passage (4.6) suggests that *ΠΟΥ*, *ΠΗ(Ι)*, and *ΠΩΣ* were examples of enclitics that did.

Our passage argues against either an acute or a circumflex for the relevant enclitics. A circumflex is said to be impossible because the 'naturally perispomenon' enclitic has given up its own accent (διὰ τὸ ἐγκλῖναι τὸν ἴδιον τόνον). An acute is said to be impossible too, on the following grounds. If the 'naturally' perispomenon enclitic were to receive an acute from the following enclitic this would involve exchanging a circumflex for an acute, but circumflexes are not normally exchanged for acutes except where a vowel has been shortened (ἐπεὶ μὴ πέφυκεν ἡ περισπωμένη κατὰ τὸ κοινὸν ἔθος συστολῆς μὴ παρακολουθούσης εἰς ὀξεῖαν μετατίθεσθαι). According to passage (4.6), then, enclitics that the grammarians considered to have a circumflex on the final syllable as their 'own' or 'natural' accent, and only those enclitics, fail to receive an accent when they stand in a sequence of enclitics, with at least one more enclitic following.

A pair of closely related scholia to *Iliad* 20.464 suggest that *ΠΩ* and—once again—*ΠΩΣ* were exceptions to what we have been calling the 'traditional' rule for accenting sequences of enclitics. Both seem to suggest that enclitic *ΠΩΣ* and *ΠΩ* 'often' fail to have an acute when other enclitics follow, or do not 'necessarily' have this acute:

(4.7) ΕΙ ΠΩΣ ΕΥ πεφίδοιτο· ἡ ΕΥ ἀντωνυμία ἐν τῇ συντάξει ἐνέκλινε τὸν τόνον· ἔστι γὰρ ἀπόλυτος. οὐχ ὃν τρόπον δ' οἴεται ὁ Ἀσκαλωνίτης τὸ ΠΩΣ πάντως ὀξυτονηθήσεται, ἐπεὶ ἤδη ἐμελέτησε καὶ ἄλλων ἐγκλιτικῶν ἐπιφερομένων τὸ ΠΩ καὶ τὸ ΠΩΣ τοῦτο μὴ πάσχειν· 'οὔ πως ἐστ', Ἀγέλαε διοτρεφές'· 'μή πως με προϊδών'· 'μή πω μ' ἐς θρόνον ἴζε, διοτρεφές'· 'οὔ πω μίν φασιν φαγέμεν'. οὕτως οὖν καὶ τὸ ΕΙ ΠΩΣ

---

enclitic with a long vowel should be left unaccented in a sequence of enclitics, but the text does not make vowel length as such the determining factor.

[26] Cf. Kühner and Blass (1890–2: i. 343 n. 3); Wackernagel (1893: 21); Donnet (1967: 32).

[27] See section 2.8.2, with the passages quoted there.

ΕΥ πεφίδοιτο· οὐκ ἀναγκαστικὴν ἕξει τὴν ἐπὶ τοῦ ΠΩΣ ὀξεῖαν. ὁ
μέντοι Ἀρίσταρχος γενόμενος κατὰ ταύτην τὴν προσῳδίαν τοῦτο
μόνον ἀπεφήνατο ἐγκλίνοντα δεῖν τῷ τόνῳ καὶ δασύνοντα λέγειν τὴν
τρίτην συλλαβήν· σημαίνει γὰρ ʽεἴ πως αὐτοῦʼ. (Sch. Il. 20.464a¹ (A))²⁸

ʼΕΙ ΠΩΣ εὑ πεφίδοιτο:²⁹ The pronoun ΕΥ loses its accent [i.e. is an
enclitic] in context, because it's non-contrastive. It's not the case that
ΠΩΣ will necessarily have an acute accent, as Ptolemy of Ascalon thinks,
since when other enclitics follow too, ΠΩ and ΠΩΣ are already accus-
tomed not to undergo this: so οὔ πως ἐστ᾽, Ἀγέλαε διοτρεφές,³⁰ and μή
πως με προϊδών,³¹ and μή πω μ᾽ ἐς θρόνον ἵζε, διοτρεφές,³² and οὔ πω
μίν φασι⟨ν⟩ φαγέμεν.³³ Similarly, then, ΕΙ ΠΩΣ ΕΥ πεφίδοιτο will not
necessarily have the acute on the ΠΩΣ. But in discussing this question of
prosody Aristarchus only said that one should pronounce the third
syllable [i.e. the ΕΥ] making it lean back as to its accent [i.e. treating it as
an enclitic] and giving it a rough breathing. For the meaning is εἴ
πως αὐτοῦ.

(4.8) ΕΙ ΠΩΣ ΕΥ πεφίδοιτο· ἡ μὲν ΕΥ ἐγκλίνεται, τὸ δὲ ΠΩΣ οὐ πάντως
ὀξυνθήσεται. καὶ ἐμελέτησε πολλάκις ἐγκλιτικῶν ἐπιφερομένων μὴ
ὀξύνεσθαι, ʽοὔ πως ἔστ᾽, Ἀγέλαεʼ, ʽμή πως με προϊδώνʼ, ʽοὔ πω μίν φασιν
φαγέμενʼ. οὕτως οὖν καὶ τὸ ΕΙ ΠΩΣ ΕΥ οὐκ ἀναγκαστικὴν ἕξει τὴν
ἐπὶ τοῦ ΠΩΣ ὀξεῖαν. ὁ μέντοι Ἀρίσταρχος γενόμενος κατ᾽ αὐτὴν τὴν
προσῳδίαν τοῦτο μόνον ἀπεφήνατο· ἐγκλίνειν δεῖ τῷ τόνῳ καὶ δασύνειν
τὴν τρίτην συλλαβήν· δηλοῖ γὰρ ʽεἴ πως αὐτοῦʼ. (Sch. Il. 20.464a² (T))³⁴

ʼΕΙ ΠΩΣ ΕΥ πεφίδοιτο: The ΕΥ is enclitic, but the ΠΩΣ will not
necessarily have an acute. And it's in the habit of often not having an acute
when enclitics follow, [as in] οὔ πως ἔστ᾽, Ἀγέλαε, and μή πως με
προϊδών, and οὔ πω μίν φασιν φαγέμεν. In the same way, then, ΕΙ ΠΩΣ
ΕΥ too will not necessarily have the acute on the ΠΩΣ. But in discussing
this question of prosody Aristarchus only said this: one must make the

---

²⁸ In addition to putting expressions whose accentuation is in question in capitals (without accents)
we make the following adjustments to Erbse's presentation of the text: (i) In the lemma we give
ʼΕΙ ΠΩΣ, Erbse ΕΙΠΩΣ. (ii) In the quotations we give οὔ πως, μή πως, μή πω, οὔ πω, ΕΙ ΠΩΣ,
Erbse οὔπως, μήπως, μήπω, οὔπω, εἴπως.
²⁹ Il. 20.464: ʽ[to see] if by chance he might spare himʼ.
³⁰ Od. 22.136: ʽI suppose it's not possible, Agelaos nourished by Zeus...ʼ
³¹ Od. 4.396: ʽlest by chance, seeing me beforehandʼ.
³² Il. 24.553: ʽDo not seat me on the seat yet, o you who are nourished by Zeus...ʼ.
³³ Od. 16.143: ʽThey say that he has not eaten yetʼ.
³⁴ In addition to putting expressions whose accentuation is in question in capitals (without accents)
we make the following adjustments to Erbse's presentation of the text: (i) In the lemma we give ʼΕΙ
ΠΩΣ ΕΥ, Erbse εἰ πῶς εὖ (sic). (ii) In the quotations we give οὔ πως, μή πως, οὔ πω, ΕΙ ΠΩΣ,
Erbse οὔπως, μήπως, οὔπω, εἴπως.

third syllable [i.e. the Ἐ𝘠] lean back as to its accent [i.e. treat it as an enclitic] and give it a rough breathing. For the meaning is εἴ πως αὐτοῦ.

These scholia have attracted some scholarly discussion. Laum (1928: 245–6) thought that one could reconstruct from them a doctrine of Ptolemy of Ascalon that the compiler of the scholia had misunderstood and garbled. In Laum's view, Ptolemy of Ascalon thought the phrase in the lemma should be accented εἴ πώς εὐ πεφίδοιτο, while the examples cited further on should all contain unaccented ΠΩΣ or ΠΩ. Laum thought it crucial that in all these further examples the ΠΩΣ or ΠΩ is preceded by οὐ or μή, and that οὔπως, οὔπω, μήπως, and μήπω were treated as single words with an acute accent on the penultimate syllable:³⁵ in his view one should write οὔπως ἐστ', Ἀγέλαε διοτρεφές, and so on. But he thought that the compiler of the scholia failed to understand that this was the reason for the unaccented ΠΩΣ or ΠΩ in these examples. Laum took the phrase καὶ ἄλλων ἐγκλιτικῶν ἐπιφερομένων in (4.7) to mean 'even when other enclitics (i.e. apart from pronouns) follow', and to suggest that the compiler wrongly thought the identity of the enclitic following the ΠΩΣ or ΠΩ relevant to the discussion. In Laum's view, the compiler's confusion was clear because three of the four examples for the situation 'even when other enclitics follow' actually have a pronoun after the ΠΩΣ or ΠΩ (μήπως με…, μήπω μ'…, οὔπω μίν φασιν…), just like the phrase in the lemma (εἴ πώς εὐ…).

Erbse (1960: 388–90) pointed out that Laum had misunderstood these scholia, which do not in fact ascribe the examples 'οὔπως ἐστ', Ἀγέλαε διοτρεφές', 'μήπως με προϊδών', 'μήπω μ' ἐς θρόνον ἵζε, διοτρεφές', and 'οὔπω μίν φασιν φαγέμεν' to Ptolemy of Ascalon. They ascribe to Ptolemy the view that enclitic ΠΩΣ necessarily (πάντως) has an acute at Il. 20.464, and they argue that this is not necessarily (ἀναγκαστικήν) the case, because there are other instances in which ΠΩ and ΠΩΣ fail to have an acute before another enclitic.³⁶ Erbse thought καὶ ἄλλων ἐγκλιτικῶν ἐπιφερομένων in (4.7) meant 'also when other enclitics (i.e. apart from Ἐ𝘠) follow'. He agreed with Laum, however, in thinking that the real reason for unaccented ΠΩ and ΠΩΣ in the four examples adduced was the presence of οὐ or μή before the ΠΩ or ΠΩΣ, with the combinations οὔπως, μήπως, μήπω, and οὔπω being treated as single words. He also agreed with Laum in thinking that the compiler of the scholia had not understood this point, and that the compiler therefore inferred wrongly that the ΠΩΣ of Ἐ𝘐 ΠΩΣ Ἐ𝘠 πεφίδοιτο did not necessarily have an acute.

But let us postpone for the time being the question of whether we can discern any linguistic principles that were not understood by the compilers of the

---

³⁵ This idea was partly anticipated by La Roche (1866: 415), although he raised the suggestion only to reject it.
³⁶ Cf. Kühner and Blass (1890–2: i. 343).

scholia—a question to which we shall return briefly in section 4.2.4. If we concentrate in the meantime on what texts (4.7) and (4.8) actually say, the doctrine fits extremely well with that of passage (4.6), where two of the three examples have a word other than $οὐ$ or $μή$ before the relevant enclitic ($ἤ$ $που$ $τίς$ $σφιν$ $εἶπεν$, $ἄνθρωπόν$ $τινά$ $που$ $φησὶ$ $μελῳδεῖν$). Like passage (4.6), the scholia (4.7) and (4.8) prescribe that certain enclitics appear without an accent when followed by a further enclitic. Like passage (4.6), they specify that enclitic $ΠΩΣ$ is one of these enclitics. Unlike passage (4.6), they do not offer any explanation for this exceptional behaviour, nor do they mention the enclitics $ΠΟΥ$ or $ΠΗ$, but they add the enclitic $ΠΩ$ to the list of exceptional enclitics (in the case of passage (4.8) this is done implicitly, via the example $οὔ$ $πω$ $μίν$ $φασιν$ $φαγέμεν$).

However, there is also a difference between the doctrine found in passages (4.7) and (4.8) and that found in passage (4.6). Passage (4.6) simply claims that enclitics in the exceptional category come out as unaccented before another enclitic, while passages (4.7) and (4.8) suggest that the exceptional enclitics do not *necessarily* have an acute before another enclitic; instead they *often* ($πολλάκις$, (4.8)) fail to have an acute 'also when other enclitics follow' ($καὶ$ $ἄλλων$ $ἐγκλιτικῶν$ $ἐπιφερομένων$, (4.7)) or simply 'when enclitics follow' ($ἐγκλιτικῶν$ $ἐπιφερομένων$, (4.8)). Kühner and Blass (1890–2: i. 343) suggest that the point was that a certain freedom was assumed here, both when it came to accenting poetry and when it came to living speech. In section 4.2.4 we shall offer a different explanation for the qualified manner in which passages (4.7) and (4.8) exempt $ΠΩΣ$ and $ΠΩ$ from the 'traditional' rule.

Passage (4.6) offers no guidance as to whether any further enclitics were thought to have a circumflex as their 'natural' accent, beyond $ΠΟΥ$, $ΠΗ(Ι)$, and $ΠΩΣ$, and the $ΠΩ$ added by passages (4.7) and (4.8). For $ΠΟΥ$, $ΠΗ(Ι)$, and $ΠΩΣ$ the existence of interrogative counterparts $ποῦ$, $πῆ(ι)$, and $πῶς$ is likely to have encouraged the notion that the 'natural' accent of the indefinite forms was also a circumflex,[37] and $ΠΩ$ might have been considered an obvious further member of the same set.[38] Be this as it may, passages (4.6), (4.7), and (4.8) together prescribe that certain enclitics are exempt—or according to passages (4.7) and (4.8) 'often' exempt—from the rule giving each enclitic except the last an accent (normally an acute) on its only or final syllable. These enclitics include $ΠΟΥ$, $ΠΗ(Ι)$, and $ΠΩΣ$, and $ΠΩ$, and any other enclitics considered to have a circumflex as their 'natural' accent.

---

[37] Indefinites and their interrogative counterparts can be discussed in terms that suggest they had different natural accents from one another (see e.g. *On enclitics 1*, §i). But there is a co-existing conception on which the obvious accent of the interrogative is also the natural accent of the indefinite (see e.g. *On enclitics 1*, §c.).

[38] There was also a Doric interrogative $πῶ$ 'where?', known to ancient grammarians; see e.g. Ap. Dysc., *Adv.* 185.15; 190.21.

It is tempting to ascribe this variant on the traditional system to Herodian. The 'A' scholia to the *Iliad* are known to have derived material on prosody from Herodian's *Περὶ Ἰλιακῆς προσῳδίας*; the obvious inference from the subject matter of passage (4.7) is that this is indeed one of the scholia deriving from Herodian, and in Erbse's judgement this was indeed the case.[39] Laum (1928: 245) thought that the appearance of almost identical material in manuscript T (passage (4.8)) argued against a Herodianic origin, but there is no good basis for this conclusion: material found in the 'A' scholia sometimes turns up in a very similar form in the bT tradition, owing to the use of related sources in both traditions.[40] However, if our variant on the 'traditional' system is indeed due to Herodian, it needs to be asked whether the 'traditional' system itself can also be the view of Herodian: we return to this question in section 4.2.4.

4.2.3 The traditional rule with an exception for pyrrhic and iambic sequences

An apparently quite different doctrine is hinted at in two scholia to the *Odyssey*. Both scholia suggest that under certain rhythmic conditions, an enclitic fails to induce an accent on a preceding enclitic. These include a condition that in some way involves two short syllables, and one that involves an iambic sequence:

(4.9)   τί νυ οἱ τόσον· μία μόνη ὀξεῖα τὸ 'τί νυ οἷ'· τὰ γὰρ παράλληλα ἐγκλιτικά, καὶ μάλιστα ὅταν εἰς φωνῆεν λήγῃ, προφάσει τῶν δύο βραχειῶν οὐκ ἐγείρει τὸν τόνον. (Sch. *Od.* 1.62*b* Pontani (H¹MᵃO))

'τί νυ οἷ τόσον: There is only one acute on τί νυ οἷ. For consecutive enclitics, and especially when they end in a vowel, do not raise up the accent on account of the two short syllables.'

(4.10)   ⟨ἄλλο δέ *TOI* τι⟩· οὐ δύναται τὸ *TOI* ὀξύνεσθαι· ἴαμβος γάρ ἐστι τὸ δέ *TOI*. (Sch. *Od.* 15.27 (H))

'ἄλλο δέ *TOI* τι: the *TOI* cannot have an acute, because the δέ *TOI* is an iamb.'

Both of these scholia discuss sequences in which the first enclitic is monosyllabic and follows a word whose accent is an acute on the final syllable. The addition of this first enclitic thus creates a sequence with an acute accent on its penultimate syllable. The references to a sequence of two short syllables in passage (4.9), and

---

[39] Erbse (1960: 389; 1969–88 *ad loc.*).
[40] See Erbse (1960: 373, 389 n. 1, 393–4); Dickey (2007: 18–19).

Table 4.1 Principle for adding a single enclitic after a paroxytone sequence

Possible sequences of two syllables preceding an enclitic	If the first of these syllables has an acute accent, does the enclitic give rise to an additional acute accent on the second?
1. Both syllables short (pyrrhic sequence)	No
2. First syllable short, second long (iambic sequence)	No
3. Both syllables long (spondaic sequence)	No
4. First syllable long, second short (trochaic sequence)	Yes

to an iambic sequence in passage (4.10), are strongly reminiscent of the ancient rules for adding a single enclitic after a word with an acute accent on its penultimate syllable: words with an acute on the penultimate syllable acquired a second accent before an enclitic if they ended in a trochaic sequence, but not otherwise (see sections 2.7.3, 2.8.3). Our main sources for this doctrine express it by considering each of the four possible shapes that a sequence of two syllables may take, and laying out whether a sequence of this shape with an acute on the first syllable gains another acute on its second syllable if an enclitic follows (see Table 4.1).[41]

Between them, our two scholia dealing with the addition of a second enclitic mention two of the three types of non-trochaic sequence (types 1 and 2). Their interest in the rhythmic shape of a paroxytone sequence of two syllables followed by an enclitic, together with the agreement between their doctrines and those applying to a single enclitic, might well lead us to think in terms of the application of this doctrine to sequences of more than one enclitic, and hence in terms of our 'revised Göttling-Barrett system' (section 4.1).

However, there is a conceptual gulf between the revised Göttling-Barrett system, in the form we have given it, and what the two scholia actually say. The scholia do not suggest that any care is needed about how the metrical shape of a sequence is calculated (contrast our discussion in section 4.1), and we suspect that no careful calculation was envisaged. On a more straightforward interpretation, sequences were to be considered pyrrhic or iambic if this is what they seemed to be, in the fully formed sequence of enclitics at hand. In the examples which the two scholia actually provide, τί νυ οἱ and (ἄλλο) δέ τοι τι, we do not have to think the last enclitic away in order to conclude that τί νυ and δέ τοι make (respectively) a pyrrhic and an iambic sequence: they simply make a pyrrhic and iambic sequence. We can clarify the procedure to be followed (according to these scholia) when accenting sequences of enclitics, in a way that keeps closely to what

---

[41] *On enclitics 1*, §§l, p; *On enclitics 2*, §e; *On enclitics 3*, §§c, e.

the scholia actually say, as follows: apply the 'traditional' system, but avoid acute accents on successive syllables in any pyrrhic or iambic sequence, by leaving the second of the relevant syllables unaccented.

In many cases, this procedure will yield the same result as our revised Göttling-Barrett system: not only for the sequences τί νυ οἱ and (ἄλλο) δέ τοι τι themselves, but also (for instance) for the sequence ΑΙΔΟΙΟΣ ΤΕ ΜΟΙ ᾽ΕΣΣΙ (*Il.* 3.172) that we worked through in section 4.1. The result will be αἰδοῖός τέ μοι ἐσσί by the procedure applied there, but the outcome will be the same if we start with the traditional system (αἰδοῖός τέ μοί ἐσσι) and then adjust the result by removing the second consecutive acute accent from the iambic sequence *TE MOI*. (We can take it that ᾽ΕΣΣΙ will also end up with an accent on its second syllable, once an unaccented syllable precedes.)

In this light, the absence from our evidence of a similar exception for spondaic sequences may not be merely accidental. Recall that under the revised Göttling-Barrett system, we envisage that a sequence such as ΑΙ ΚΕΝ ΠΩΣ 'if by chance' is accented αἴ κέν πως (section 4.1). At the point when the system requires us to decide whether to give *KEN* an accent, the sequence *ΑΙ ΚΕΝ* counts as trochaic, just as ἄλλος counts as a 'trochaic' word even before an enclitic like τις. But if the sequence *ΑΙ ΚΕΝ ΠΩΣ* is considered as a whole, the first two syllables are more readily considered to make a spondee. Suppose, then, that the conception underlying the two *Odyssey* scholia is that the traditional system is to be applied, but successive acute accents are to be avoided on pyrrhic and iambic sequences only. The result will be identical to that of the revised Göttling-Barrett system not only for sequences like τί νυ οἱ, ἄλλο δέ τοι τι, and αἰδοῖός τέ μοι ἐσσί, but also for sequences like αἴ κέν πως, and syllable quantities can be calculated straightforwardly from the sequence as a whole: for example the *ΑΙ ΚΕΝ* in *ΑΙ ΚΕΝ ΠΩΣ* can happily be considered a spondee.

If this is indeed the conception underlying the two *Odyssey* scholia, it will not always yield identical results to our revised Göttling-Barrett system. For example, the revised Göttling-Barrett system gives εἴ που τίς τινα ἴδοι at Thucydides 4.47.3, as noted in section 4.1, but the traditional system with exceptions for pyrrhic and iambic sequences will give εἴ πού τίς τινα ἴδοι. We shall return to this point in section 4.2.4.

It is tempting to ascribe the idea behind the scholia (4.9) and (4.10) to Herodian. Although it is more difficult to identify the origins of different groups of *Odyssey* scholia than it is for *Iliad* scholia, some *Odyssey* scholia are similar in kind to the 'A' scholia to the *Iliad*, and are likely to derive from similar sources (see Dickey 2007: 21). Our two scholia belong to a group of *Odyssey* scholia that pronounce on the accentuation of particular phrases, with appeals to more general rules of accentuation; they are likely to derive from Herodian's Περὶ Ὀδυσσειακῆς προσῳδίας, just as the *Iliad* scholia of a similar kind can be derived with some confidence from his Περὶ Ἰλιακῆς προσῳδίας. Pontani accordingly designates the scholion (4.9) as possibly Herodianic ('Hrd.?'). But if the idea behind these scholia derives from Herodian, it needs to be asked whether he can also have been resposible for the 'traditional' system, and for the variant excepting certain enclitics including *ΠΟΥ*, *ΠΗ(Ι)*, *ΠΩΣ*, and *ΠΩ*. We now turn to this question.

4.2.4 The three ancient systems: incompatible and yet compatible

We have seen evidence for three different systems in ancient grammatical sources: (i) the 'traditional' system; (ii) the 'traditional' system with an exception for enclitic *ΠΟΥ*, *ΠΗ(Ι)*, *ΠΩΣ*, and *ΠΩ*, along with any further enclitics thought to have a circumflex as their 'natural' accent; and (iii) the 'traditional' system, with exceptions designed to avoid successive acute accents on pyrrhic and iambic sequences.

There are reasons to ascribe all three systems to Herodian, as we have seen, and yet the three systems are genuinely different from each other in that they make different predictions in some instances. For example, for *Il.* 1.154, systems (i) and (iii) give γάρ πώ ποτ' (where underlined words are enclitics), while system (ii) gives γάρ πω ποτ'. For *Il.* 1.124, systems (i) and (ii) give οὐδέ τί που, while system (iii) gives οὐδέ τι που. For *Il.* 1.542, system (i) gives οὐδέ τί πώ μοι, system (ii) οὐδέ τί πω μοι, and system (iii) οὐδέ τι πώ μοι.

Although the three systems can make different predictions, they fit together in an intriguing way, and this is where the revised Göttling-Barrett system comes in. If we take system (i) and bolt on the exceptions prescribed both by system (ii) and by system (iii), the results (although not the way of arriving at them) are identical to those of the revised Göttling-Barrett system for the vast majority of sequences of enclitics actually occurring in works of ancient literature.

To illustrate this point, Table 4.2 shows the first hundred sequences of more than one enclitic appearing in West's edition of the *Iliad* (West 1998–2000), accented according to five different principles: (i) the 'traditional' system; (ii) the 'traditional' system except that indefinite *ΠΟΥ*, *ΠΗ(Ι)*, *ΠΩΣ*, and *ΠΩ* are left unaccented; (iii) the 'traditional' system except that consecutive acute accents are avoided on pyrrhic or iambic sequences by working forwards (i.e. towards the end of the word) from the word preceding the first enclitic, and leaving a syllable unaccented after a short syllable to which an acute accent has already been assigned; (iv) the 'traditional' system except that indefinite *ΠΟΥ*, *ΠΗ(Ι)*, *ΠΩΣ*, and *ΠΩ* are left unaccented AND consecutive acute accents are avoided on pyrrhic or iambic sequences (as for (iii)); (v) the revised Göttling-Barrett system (for which see section 4.1).[42]

---

[42] In order to produce this table, some decisions on what to count as an enclitic were necessary. We take the following to count as single non-enclitic words: the conjunction ὅτι, temporal ὅτε, and αὖτε. For present purposes we do not count the -δε that conveys motion towards as an enclitic, although in some combinations it behaves accentually as one—but synchronically opaque combinations such as οἴκαδε 'homeward', at the very least, are likely to have become fossilized simply as words (cf. the

In the table, shading draws attention to sequences of enclitics accented in ways that do not coincide with the results of the revised Göttling-Barrett system. A point that emerges immediately is that such instances are rarer than one might expect. Systems (i)–(iv) each produce the same results as the revised Göttling-Barrett system more than half the time, and increasingly so as we move from the left-hand side of the table to the right: system (i) produces the same results as system (v) in 65 instances out of 100; system (ii) in 67 instances out of 100; system (iii) in 92 instances out of 100; and system (iv) in 93 instances out of 100.

The suspicion arises that an implicit awareness of the revised Göttling-Barrett system lies behind the whole variety of apparently incompatible doctrines on accenting sequences of enclitics that we find in the grammatical tradition. Each of these doctrines, including the 'traditional' system, can be seen as a rule of thumb intended to yield the same outcome as the revised Göttling-Barrett system more often than not. But the incidence of matching outcomes is highest when the 'traditional' system is applied in combination with the exception for indefinite $ΠΟΥ$, $ΠΗ(Ι)$, $ΠΩΣ$, $ΠΩ$ and also the exception for pyrrhic and iambic sequences.

The revised Göttling-Barrett system itself would have been difficult for ancient authors to describe, because of what we can call, in modern terms, its recursive character: at each step we need to think about the metrical shape of a sequence before the addition of the next enclitic, and a syllable that counts short at one step may count long at the next step (see section 4.1). The apparently disparate doctrines we find in the grammatical tradition give us a way of achieving identical results in the vast majority of instances, without the need for a recursive calculation.

At this point, we can be explicit about what makes indefinite $ΠΟΥ$, $ΠΗ(Ι)$, $ΠΩΣ$, and $ΠΩ$ special. Because these enclitics each contain a long vowel, in combination with a preceding syllable they make either an iamb or a spondee. When they make an iamb, the avoidance of successive acutes on pyrrhic or iambic sequences will apply. What is more interesting is what happens when they make a spondee, like $ΜΗ \ ΠΩΣ$ or $ΓΑΡ \ ΠΩ$. These sequences are spondaic regardless of the following syllable; in this respect they differ from sequences like $ΑΙ \ ΚΕΝ$, and are treated differently by the revised Göttling-Barrett system. But the exception for $ΠΟΥ$, $ΠΗ(Ι)$, $ΠΩΣ$, and $ΠΩ$ allows us to treat (for example) the $ΜΗ \ ΠΩΣ$ of μή πως οἱ differently from the $ΑΙ \ ΚΕΝ$ of αἴ κέν τοι, without

---

analytical difficulties faced by Apollonius Dyscolus, *Adv.* 177.13–181.31, a discussion which includes our passage (2.19)). On the other hand, we take the second elements of οὔ τις, οὔ τι, and οὔτε to count as enclitics, on the basis of the consistent picture presented by the accents of the first elements (οὔ τις, οὔ τι, οὔτε, not οὗτις, οὗτι, οὗτε). We count the second element in forms of ὅστις and ὅτις as an enclitic, on the basis of forms such as ἥτις (not ἧτις). We treat the second element of οὔ πω, μή πω (and in principle οὔ πως and μή πως) as an enclitic (cf. section 4.2.2), and likewise both elements of πώ ποτε 'ever yet'. In accordance with these decisions we treat the forms ὍΤΤΙ (nominative-accusative neuter singular of ὅστις), ὍΤΙΣ, and ὌΥΤΕ as comprising a non-enclitic word form Ὅ(Τ), Ὅ, or ὌΥ followed by enclitic ΤΙ, ΤΙΣ, or ΤΕ, although West prints these forms as single words as per the usual modern convention.

Table 4.2 The first 100 sequences of more than one enclitic appearing in West's edition of the *Iliad* (West 1998–2000), accented according to five different principles. The word preceding the first enclitic is included, and enclitics themselves are underlined. For the forms *ʹΟΤΤΙ* (nominative-accusative neuter singular of *ὅστις*), *ʹΟΤΙΣ*, and *ʹΟΥΤΕ* (see n. 42), a hyphen separates the enclitic from what precedes. Shading indicates a way of accenting a sequence that differs from the result of the revised Göttling-Barrett system.

Line of *Iliad*	(i) 'Traditional' system: give every enclitic except the last an accent (normally an acute) on its last or only syllable	(ii) 'Traditional' system but leave indefinite *ΠΟΥ, ΠΗ(Ι), ΠΩΣ, ΠΗ(Ι), ΠΩ* and *ΠΩ* unaccented	(iii) 'Traditional' system but avoid consecutive acute accents on pyrrhic or iambic sequences (work forwards from the word preceding the first enclitic)	(iv) 'Traditional' system but leave indefinite *ΠΟΥ, ΠΗ(Ι), ΠΩΣ, ΠΗ(Ι)* and *ΠΩ* unaccented AND avoid consecutive acute accents on pyrrhic or iambic sequences (work forwards from the word preceding the first enclitic)	(v) Revised Göttling-Barrett system (apply the ancient rules for a single enclitic, each time a new enclitic is added)
1.8	τίς τάρ σφωε	τίς τάρ σφωε	τίς τάρ σφωε	τίς τάρ σφωε	τίς τάρ σφωε
1.28	μή νύ τοι	μή νύ τοι	μή νύ τοι	μή νύ τοι	μή νύ τοι
1.39	εἴ ποτέ τοι	εἴ ποτέ τοι	εἴ ποτέ τοι	εἴ ποτέ τοι	εἴ ποτέ τοι
1.40	δή ποτέ τοι	δή ποτέ τοι	δή ποτέ τοι	δή ποτέ τοι	δή ποτέ τοι
1.66	αἴ κέν πως	αἴ κέν πως	αἴ κέν πως	αἴ κέν πως	αἴ κέν πως
1.100	τότε κέν μιν	τότε κέν μιν	τότε κέν μιν	τότε κέν μιν	τότε κέν μιν
1.106	οὔ πώ ποτέ μοι	οὔ πω ποτέ μοι	οὔ πώ ποτέ μοι	οὔ πω ποτέ μοι	οὔ πω ποτέ μοι
1.108	οὔ-τέ τί πω	οὔ-τέ τί πω	οὔ-τέ τι πω	οὔ-τέ τι πω	οὔ-τέ τι πω
1.114	οὔ ἑθέν ἐστι	οὔ ἑθέν ἐστι	οὔ ἑθέν ἐστι	οὔ ἑθέν ἐστι	οὔ ἑθέν ἐστι
1.115	οὔ-τέ τι	οὔ-τέ τι	οὔ-τέ τι	οὔ-τέ τι	οὔ-τέ τι
1.123	πῶς τάρ τοι	πῶς τάρ τοι	πῶς τάρ τοι	πῶς τάρ τοι	πῶς τάρ τοι
1.124	οὐδέ τί που	οὐδέ τί που	οὐδέ τι που	οὐδέ τι που	οὐδέ τι που

Continued

Table 4.2 *Continued*

Line of *Iliad*	(i) 'Traditional' system: give every enclitic except the last an accent (normally an acute) on its last or only syllable	(ii) 'Traditional' system but leave indefinite *ΠΟΥ, ΠΗ(Ι), ΠΩΣ,* and *ΠΩ* unaccented	(iii) 'Traditional' system but avoid consecutive acute accents on pyrrhic or iambic sequences (work forwards from the word preceding the first enclitic)	(iv) 'Traditional' system but leave indefinite *ΠΟΥ, ΠΗ(Ι), ΠΩΣ,* and *ΠΩ* unaccented AND avoid consecutive acute accents on pyrrhic or iambic sequences (work forwards from the word preceding the first enclitic)	(v) Revised Göttling-Barrett system (apply the ancient rules for a single enclitic, each time a new enclitic is added)
1.128	αἴ κέ ποθι	αἴ κέ ποθι	αἴ κέ ποθι	αἴ κέ ποθι	αἴ κέ ποθι
1.150	πῶς τίς τοι	πῶς τίς τοι	πῶς τίς τοι	πῶς τίς τοι	πῶς τίς τοι
1.153	οὔ τί μοι	οὔ τί μοι	οὔ τί μοι	οὔ τί μοι	οὔ τί μοι
1.154	γάρ πώ ποτ'	γάρ πω ποτ'	γάρ πώ ποτ'	γάρ πω ποτ'	γάρ πω ποτ'
1.175	οἵ κέ με	οἵ κέ με	οἵ κέ με	οἵ κέ με	οἵ κέ με
1.176	δέ μοί ἐσσι	δέ μοί ἐσσι	δέ μοι ἐσσί	δέ μοι ἐσσί	δέ μοι ἐσσὶ
1.213	καί ποτέ τοι	καί ποτέ τοι	καί ποτέ τοι	καί ποτέ τοι	καί ποτέ τοι
1.226	οὔ-τέ ποτ'	οὔ-τέ ποτ'	οὔ-τέ ποτ'	οὔ-τέ ποτ'	οὔ-τέ ποτ'
1.236	γάρ ῥά ἑ	γάρ ῥά ἑ	γάρ ῥά ἑ	γάρ ῥά ἑ	γάρ ῥά ἑ
1.261	οὔ ποτέ μ'	οὔ ποτέ μ'	οὔ ποτέ μ'	οὔ ποτέ μ'	οὔ ποτέ μ'
1.294	ὅτ-τί κεν	ὅτ-τί κεν	ὅτ-τί κεν	ὅτ-τί κεν	ὅτ-τί κεν
1.299	οὔ-τέ τῳ	οὔ-τέ τῳ	οὔ-τέ τῳ	οὔ-τέ τῳ	οὔ-τέ τῳ
1.300	ἅ μοί ἐστι	ἅ μοί ἐστι	ἅ μοι ἐστί	ἅ μοι ἐστί	ἅ μοι ἐστὶ
1.332	οὐδέ τί μιν	οὐδέ τί μιν	οὐδέ τί μιν	οὐδέ τι μιν	οὐδέ τι μιν
1.335	οὔ τί μοι	οὔ τί μοι	οὔ τί μοι	οὔ τί μοι	οὔ τί μοι
1.353	τιμήν πέρ μοι	τιμήν πέρ μοι	τιμήν πέρ μοι	τιμήν πέρ μοι	τιμήν πέρ μοι

	1	2	3	4	5
1.361	χειρί τέ μιν	χειρί τέ μιν	χειρί τε μιν	χειρί τε μιν	χειρί τε μιν
1.408	αἴ κέν πως	αἴ κέν πως	αἴ κέν πως	αἴ κέν πως	αἴ κέν πως
1.414	τί νύ σ'	τί νύ σ'	τί νύ σ'	τί νυ σ'	τί νυ σ'
1.416	ἐπεί νύ τοι	ἐπεί νύ τοι	ἐπεί νύ τοι	ἐπεί νύ τοι	ἐπεί νύ τοι
1.490	οὔ-τέ ποτ'	οὔ-τέ ποτ'	οὔ-τέ ποτ'	οὔ-τέ ποτ'	οὔ-τέ ποτ'
1.491	οὔ-τέ ποτ'	οὔ-τέ ποτ'	οὔ-τέ ποτ'	οὔ-τέ ποτ'	οὔ-τέ ποτ'
1.508	σύ πέρ μιν	σύ πέρ μιν	σύ περ μιν	σύ περ μιν	σύ περ μιν
1.510	ὀφέλλωσίν τέ ἑ	ὀφέλλωσίν τέ ἑ	ὀφέλλωσίν τέ ἑ	ὀφέλλωσίν τέ ἑ	ὀφέλλωσίν τέ ἑ
1.518	ὅ τέ μ'	ὅ τέ μ'	ὅ τέ μ'	ὅ τε μ'	ὅ τε μ'
1.521	καί τέ μέ φησι	καί τέ μέ φησι	καί τέ με φησί	καί τέ με φησὶ	καί τέ με φησὶ
1.527	ὅ τι κεν	ὅ τι κεν	ὅ τι κεν	ὅ τι κεν	ὅ τι κεν
1.542	οὐδέ τί πώ μοι	οὐδέ τί πω μοι	οὐδέ τι πώ μοι	οὐδέ τι πω μοι	οὐδέ τι πώ μοι
1.566	μή νύ τοι	μή νύ τοι	μή νύ τοι	μή νύ τοι	μή νύ τοι
1.567	ὅτε κέν τοι	ὅτε κέν τοι	ὅτε κέν τοι	ὅτε κέν τοι	ὅτε κέν τοι
2.72	αἴ κέν πως	αἴ κέν πως	αἴ κέν πως	αἴ κέν πως	αἴ κέν πως
2.83	αἴ κέν πως	αἴ κέν πως	αἴ κέν πως	αἴ κέν πως	αἴ κέν πως
2.119a	τόδε γ' ἐστί	τόδε γ' ἐστί	τόδε γ' ἐστὶ	τόδε γ' ἐστὶ	τόδε γ' ἐστὶ
2.122	οὔ πώ τι	οὔ πώ τι	οὔ πώ τι	οὔ πω τι	οὔ πω τι
2.202	οὔ-τέ ποτ'	οὔ-τέ ποτ'	οὔ-τέ ποτ'	οὔ-τέ ποτ'	οὔ-τέ ποτ'
2.215	ὅ τί οἱ	ὅ τί οἱ	ὅ τι οἱ	ὅ τι οἱ	ὅ τι οἱ
2.229	ὅν κέ τις	ὅν κέ τις	ὅν κέ τις	ὅν κέ τις	ὅν κέ τις
2.238	ἦ ῥά τι οἱ	ἦ ῥά τι οἱ	ἦ ῥά τι οἱ	ἦ ῥά τι οἱ	ἦ ῥά τι οἱ
2.252	οὐδέ τι πω	οὐδέ τι πω	οὐδέ τι πω	οὐδέ τι πω	οὐδέ τι πω

Continued

Table 4.2 *Continued*

Line of *Iliad*	(i) 'Traditional' system: give every enclitic except the last an accent (normally an acute) on its last or only syllable	(ii) 'Traditional' system but indefinite *ΠΟΥ, ΠΗ(Ι), ΠΩΣ*, and *ΠΩ* unaccented	(iii) 'Traditional' system but avoid consecutive acute accents on pyrrhic or iambic sequences (work forwards from the word preceding the first enclitic)	(iv) 'Traditional' system but leave indefinite *ΠΟΥ, ΠΗ(Ι), ΠΩΣ*, and *ΠΩ* unaccented AND avoid consecutive acute accents on pyrrhic or iambic sequences (work forwards from the word preceding the first enclitic)	(v) Revised Göttling-Barrett system (apply the ancient rules for a single enclitic, each time a new enclitic is added)
2.258	ὥς νύ περ	ὥς νύ περ	ὥς νύ περ	ὥς νύ περ	ὥς νύ περ
2.276	οὔ θήν μιν	οὔ θήν μιν	οὔ θήν μιν	οὔ θήν μιν	οὔ θήν μιν
2.292	γάρ τίς τ'	γάρ τίς τ'	γάρ τίς τ'	γάρ τίς τ'	γάρ τίς τ'
2.361	ὅτ-τί κεν	ὅτ-τί κεν	ὅτ-τί κεν	ὅτ-τί κεν	ὅτ-τί κεν
2.365	ὅς τέ νυ	ὅς τέ νυ	ὅς τέ νυ	ὅς τέ νυ	ὅς τέ νυ
2.419	ἄρα πώ οἱ	ἄρα πω οἱ	ἄρα πώ οἱ	ἄρα πω οἱ	ἄρα πώ οἱ
2.553	οὔ πώ τις	οὔ πω τις	οὔ πώ τις	οὔ πω τις	οὔ πω τις
2.687	ὅς τίς σφιν	ὅς τίς σφιν	ὅς τίς σφιν	ὅς τίς σφιν	ὅς τίς σφιν
2.754	ἀλλά τέ μιν	ἀλλά τέ μιν	ἀλλά τε μιν	ἀλλά τε μιν	ἀλλά τε μιν
2.873	οὐδέ τί οἱ	οὐδέ τί οἱ	οὐδέ τι οἱ	οὐδέ τι οἱ	οὐδέ τι οἱ
3.12	τόσσόν τίς τ'	τόσσόν τίς τ'	τόσσόν τίς τ'	τόσσόν τίς τ'	τόσσόν τίς τ'
3.33	ὅτε τίς τε	ὅτε τίς τε	ὅτε τίς τε	ὅτε τίς τε	ὅτε τίς τε
3.35	ὠχρός τέ μιν	ὠχρός τέ μιν	ὠχρός τέ μιν	ὠχρός τέ μιν	ὠχρός τέ μιν
3.56	ἦ τέ κεν	ἦ τέ κεν	ἦ τέ κεν	ἦ τέ κεν	ἦ τέ κεν
3.61	ὅς ῥά τε	ὅς ῥά τε	ὅς ῥά τε	ὅς ῥά τε	ὅς ῥά τε
3.164	οὔ τί μοι	οὔ τί μοι	οὔ τί μοι	οὔ τί μοι	οὔ τί μοι
3.164	θεοί νύ μοι	θεοί νύ μοι	θεοί νύ μοι	θεοί νύ μοι	θεοί νύ μοι

Line	Col 1	Col 2	Col 3	Col 4	Col 5
3.172	αἰδοῖός τέ μοι ἔσσι	αἰδοῖός τέ μοι ἔσσι	αἰδοῖός τέ μοι ἔσσι	αἰδοῖός τέ μοι ἔσσι	αἰδοῖός τέ μοι ἔσσι
3.183	ἦ ῥά νύ τοι	ἦ ῥά νύ τοι	ἦ ῥά νύ τοι	ἦ ῥά νυ τοι	ἦ ῥά νυ τοι
3.220	ζάκοτόν τέ τιν'	ζάκοτόν τέ τιν'	ζάκοτόν τέ τιν'	ζάκοτόν τέ τιν'	ζάκοτόν τέ τιν'
3.242	ἅ μοί ἐστιν	ἅ μοί ἐστιν	ἅ μοι ἐστίν	ἅ μοι ἐστίν	ἅ μοι ἐστίν
3.279	ὅ-τίς κ'	ὅ-τίς κ'	ὅ-τις κ'	ὅ-τις κ'	ὅ-τις κ'
3.302	ἄρα πώ σφιν	ἄρα πω σφιν	ἄρα πω σφιν	ἄρα πω σφιν	ἄρα πώ σφιν
3.373	καί νύ κεν	καί νύ κεν	καί νύ κεν	καί νύ κεν	καί νύ κεν
3.400	ἦ πῇ με	ἦ πῇ με	ἦ πῇ με	ἦ πῇ με	ἦ πῇ με
3.402	εἴ τίς τοι	εἴ τίς τοι	εἴ τίς τοι	εἴ τίς τοι	εἴ τίς τοι
3.409	ὅ κε σ'	ὅ κε σ'	ὅ κε σ'	ὅ κε σ'	ὅ κε σ'
3.442	γάρ πώ ποτέ μ'	γάρ πω ποτέ μ'	γάρ πώ ποτέ μ'	γάρ πω ποτέ μ'	γάρ πω ποτέ μ'
4.31	τί νύ σε	τί νύ σε	τί νύ σε	τί νυ σε	τί νυ σε
4.48	γάρ μοί ποτε	γάρ μοί ποτε	γάρ μοί ποτε	γάρ μοί ποτε	γάρ μοί ποτε
4.93	ἦ ῥά νύ μοί τι	ἦ ῥά νύ μοί τι	ἦ ῥά νυ μοί τι	ἦ ῥά νυ μοί τι	ἦ ῥά νυ μοί τι
4.106	ὅν ῥά ποτ'	ὅν ῥά ποτ'	ὅν ῥά ποτ'	ὅν ῥά ποτ'	ὅν ῥά ποτ'
4.141	ὅτε τίς τ'	ὅτε τίς τ'	ὅτε τίς τ'	ὅτε τίς τ'	ὅτε τίς τ'
4.143	πολέες τέ μιν	πολέες τέ μιν	πολέες τέ μιν	πολέες τέ μιν	πολέες τέ μιν
4.155	θάνατόν νύ τοι	θάνατόν νύ τοι	θάνατόν νύ τοι	θάνατόν νύ τοι	θάνατόν νύ τοι
4.176	καί κέ τις	καί κέ τις	καί κέ τις	καί κέ τις	καί κέ τις
4.182	ὡς ποτέ τις	ὡς ποτέ τις	ὡς ποτέ τις	ὡς ποτέ τις	ὡς ποτέ τις
4.184	μηδέ τί πω	μηδέ τί πω	μηδέ τι πω	μηδέ τι πω	μηδέ τι πω
4.219	τά οἱ ποτὲ	τά οἱ ποτὲ	τά οἱ ποτὲ	τά οἱ ποτὲ	τά οἱ ποτὲ

Continued

Table 4.2 *Continued*

Line of *Iliad*	(i) 'Traditional' system: give every enclitic except the last an accent (normally an acute) on its last or only syllable	(ii) 'Traditional' system but leave indefinite *ΠΟΥ, ΠΗ(Ι), ΠΩΣ,* and *ΠΩ* unaccented	(iii) 'Traditional' system but avoid consecutive acute accents on pyrrhic or iambic sequences (work forwards from the word preceding the first enclitic)	(iv) 'Traditional' system but leave indefinite *ΠΟΥ, ΠΗ(Ι), ΠΩΣ,* and *ΠΩ* unaccented AND avoid consecutive acute accents on pyrrhic or iambic sequences (work forwards from the word preceding the first enclitic)	(v) Revised Göttling-Barrett system (apply the ancient rules for a single enclitic, each time a new enclitic is added)
4.229	ὁππότε κέν μιν	ὁππότε κέν μιν	ὁππότε κέν μιν	ὁππότε κέν μιν	ὁππότε κέν μιν
4.234	μή πώ τι	μή πω τι	μή πώ τι	μή πω τι	μή πω τι
4.245	ἄρα τίς σφι	ἄρα τίς σφι	ἄρα τίς σφι	ἄρα τίς σφι	ἄρα τίς σφι
4.259	ὅτε πέρ τε	ὅτε πέρ τε	ὅτε πέρ τε	ὅτε πέρ τε	ὅτε πέρ τε
4.331	γάρ πώ σφιν	γάρ πω σφιν	γάρ πώ σφιν	γάρ πω σφιν	γάρ πώ σφιν (see below)
4.353	αἴ κέν τοι	αἴ κέν τοι	αἴ κέν τοι	αἴ κέν τοι	αἴ κέν τοι
4.359	οὔ-τέ σε	οὔ-τέ σε	οὔ-τέ σε	οὔ-τέ σε	οὔ-τέ σε
4.483	ἤ ῥά τ'	ἤ ῥά τ'	ἤ ῥά τ'	ἤ ῥά τ'	ἤ ῥά τ'
4.484	ἀτάρ τέ οἱ	ἀτάρ τέ οἱ	ἀτάρ τέ οἱ	ἀτάρ τέ οἱ	ἀτάρ τέ οἱ
5.103	οὐδέ ἕ φημι	οὐδέ ἕ φημι	οὐδέ ἕ φημί	οὐδέ ἕ φημί	οὐδέ ἕ φημί
Results identical to those of system (v) (out of 100)	65	67	92	93	

[a] Elision (with the accentual effects laid out in section 4.3) is treated as applying after the relevant system has been applied to the unelided sequence *ΤΟΔΕ ΓΕ ΈΣΤΙ*.

the need to calculate syllable quantities recursively. We can think of both sequences as beginning with a spondee, and being treated differently from one another because indefinite *ΠΩΣ* is subject to a special exception.

Seen as a way of replicating the results of the revised Göttling-Barrett system, the system of rules of thumb is not perfect. In part, this may be due to the limitations of our evidence. At *Il.* 2.276, the revised Göttling-Barrett system requires οὔ θην μιν but the rules of thumb we have point to οὔ θήν μιν. Might *ΘΗΝ* have been considered naturally perispomenon, like *ΠΟΥ*, *ΠΗ(Ι)*, *ΠΩΣ*, and *ΠΩ* (recall that we left open whether any further enclitics were considered to belong under this heading)? Or might *ΘΗΝ* have been considered subject to an individual exception of its own? Be this as it may, the exception for *ΠΟΥ*, *ΠΗ(Ι)*, *ΠΩΣ*, and *ΠΩ* will also not always yield results matching those of the revised Göttling-Barrett system, if applied to every sequence containing one of these enclitics. At *Il.* 1.542, for example, the revised Göttling-Barrett system requires οὐδέ τι πώ μοι, with an accent on the *ΠΩ*, because at the point when *MOI* is to be added the preceding sequence is proparoxytone: οὐδέ τι πω. Even allowing for gaps in our evidence, the rules of thumb probably never gave a perfect match with the results of the revised Göttling-Barrett system, although they came remarkably close.

In the light of all this, we can return to the wording of the scholia (4.7) and (4.8), according to which *ΠΩ* and *ΠΩΣ* do not *necessarily* have an acute accent when other enclitics follow, or *often* fail to have an acute accent when other enclitics follow. Differently from previous scholarship (on which see section 4.2.2), we suggest that nothing has been garbled here. Instead, we suggest that these comments go back to someone with an instinct for where accents went on sequences of enclitics, and whose instinct was guided—implicitly—by the revised Göttling-Barrett system. Along with this instinct came a sense that indefinite *ΠΩ* and *ΠΩΣ* should often, *but not always*, be left unaccented before another enclitic. In our sample of 100 sequences of enclitics, six have unaccented indefinite *ΠΩΣ* or *ΠΩ* before another enclitic under the revised Göttling-Barrett system: *Il.* 1.106 (οὔ πω ποτέ μοι), *Il.* 1.154 (γάρ πω ποτ᾽), *Il.* 2.122 (οὔ πω τι), *Il.* 2.553 (οὔ πω τις), *Il.* 3.442 (γάρ πω ποτέ μ᾽), *Il.* 4.234 (μή πω τι). For another three sequences, the same system straightforwardly requires an accent on indefinite *ΠΩΣ* or *ΠΩ*: *Il.* 1.542 (οὐδέ τι πώ μοι), as already noted, along with *Il.* 2.419 (ἄρα πώ οἱ) and *Il.* 3.302 (ἄρα πώ σφιν). For a further sequence, *ΓΑΡ ΠΩ ΣΦΙΝ* at *Il.* 4.331, we suggest that a consistent recursive application of the ancient principles applying to single enclitics should result in γάρ πώ σφιν, with an enclitic beginning with σφ- inducing an additional accent regardless of the metrical shape of the preceding sequence (see section 2.7.3)—but we shall return to this topic in more detail in section 4.2.5. For now the important point is that when seen as an attempt to replicate the results of the revised Göttling-Barrett system, the rule of thumb about leaving certain enclitics unaccented is best deployed in combination with a feel for the limits within which it is valid.

We have noted indications pointing to Herodian as a source of each of the three doctrines we find in the grammatical tradition. If these doctrines fit together in the way we have suggested, Herodian could indeed be a source for all three: a person with a feel for the recursive principle, and a way of conveying it, or at least a good approximation, via various rules of thumb. But does the recursive principle really go back to Herodian's time? We believe that it does, and that this point is confirmed firstly by further evidence from the Homeric scholia, and secondly by accented papyri. The next section is devoted to the evidence from the scholia, and we will turn to accented papyri in section 4.3.

4.2.5   Homeric scholia on sequences of enclitics

Every time one of the scholia vetera ('old' scholia) to Homer pronounces on the accentuation of a specific sequence of enclitics, what is said about this specific sequence is consistent with the revised Göttling-Barrett system—even where no explanation is given for the accents mentioned, or an explanation is given in terms conceptually quite different from those of our revised Göttling-Barrett system. To demonstrate this point, we collect here the scholia vetera to Homer mentioning accents on specific sequences of enclitics.

Let us begin with scholia concerning sequences of enclitics to which the 'trochaic principle' applies: the second enclitic is added to a paroxytone sequence ending in a trochaic pattern, when syllable quantities are calculated before the addition of the second enclitic (see section 4.1). Our first such scholion clearly prescribes the accentuation κρατερόν ῥά ἑ πένθος:

(4.11)   *ΚΡΑΤΕΡΟΝ ῬΑ ῝Ε ΠΕΝΘΟΣ· ὁ ῬΑ σύνδεσμος ἐγκλιτικὸς ὢν φυλάξει τὴν ἰδίαν ὀξεῖαν διὰ τὴν ῝Ε ἀντωνυμίαν νῦν ἐγκλιτικὴν οὖσαν.* (Sch. *Il.* 11.249 (A))

'*ΚΡΑΤΕΡΟΝ ῬΑ ῝Ε ΠΕΝΘΟΣ:*[43] The conjunction *ῬΑ*, which is enclitic, will keep its own acute because of the pronoun *῝Ε*, which is enclitic here.'

No rule is cited to justify this accentuation, and as it happens any of the ancient principles we have considered would do the job: the 'traditional' system, the traditional system with an (irrelevant) exception for *ΠΟΥ, ΠΗ(Ι), ΠΩΣ,* and *ΠΩ,* or the traditional system with an (again irrelevant) exception for pyrrhic and iambic sequences. But for present purposes the important point is that κρατερόν ῥά ἑ πένθος is also the accentuation required by the revised Göttling-Barrett system.

---

[43]   *Il.* 11.249: 'strong grief [covered] him [as to his eyes]'.

Under this system the oxytone form κρατερόν retains its acute accent before the enclitic 'PA, and the trochaic sequence (κρατε)ρόν ῥα then receives an acute accent on its final syllable before the further enclitic 'E, with the end result κρατερόν ῥά ἐ.

The *Odyssey* scholion (4.12) mentions various alternative readings and interpretations of the phrase in the lemma. The first of these involves a sequence of enclitics, and on this reading the accentuation is clearly taken to be καί κέ τεο:[44]

(4.12)   *KAI KE*[45] *TEO·* τὸ *TEO*[46] ἀόριστον. διὸ καὶ ἐπὶ τοῦ *KE* ὁ τόνος. ὁ δὲ Ἀσκαλωνίτης 'ἐτεοδμώων', τῶν ἀγαθῶν θεραπόντων. τινὲς δὲ οὕτως, 'ἐτεοδμώων',[47] τῶν ὄντων ἡμετέρων δούλων. (Sch. *Od.* 16.305 (H.Q.))

'*KAI KE TEO*:[48] the *TEO* is indefinite. Therefore the accent also falls on the *KE*. But Ptolemy of Ascalon read ἐτεοδμώων, "good servants". And some take it like this: ἐτεοδμώων, "those who are really our servants".'

The revised Göttling-Barrett system again gives the same result. The oxytone form καί retains its accent before the enclitic *KE*, and the trochaic sequence καί κε then receives an acute accent on its final syllable before the further enclitic *TEO*, with the end result καί κέ τεο.

The *Iliad* scholion (4.13) contemplates two possible readings of the sequence of letters *OYKETI*: 'OYK 'ETI 'no longer' (accented οὐκ ἔτι) and 'OY KE TI.

(4.13)   ἔνθά κεν *OYKETI* ἔργον ⟨ἀνὴρ ὀνόσαιτο μετελθών⟩· ὅτι περισσὸς ὁ *KEN*, καὶ ὅτι ῥῆμα καὶ χρόνος ἐνήλλακται. ἰστέον δὲ ὅτι ὁ Ἀσκαλωνίτης βαρύνει τὴν 'OY ἀπόφασιν, 'οὐκ ἔτι',[49] ἵνα ᾖ τὸ ἑξῆς ἀρχὴ 'ἔτι'. φέρεται δὲ καὶ ἑτέρα ἀνάγνωσις {ἐν παραλλήλοις} οὔ κέ τι, ἐν παραλλήλοις δύο ὀξείαις, ἵνα τρία μέρη λόγου γένηται, 'OY καὶ ὁ *KE* σύνδεσμος καὶ τὸ *TI*, ἵνα τὸ ἑξῆς ᾖ 'οὐκ ἂν ὀνόσαιτο καὶ φανέντα'...(Sch. *Il.* 4.539a (A))

'ἔνθά κεν *OYKETI* ἔργον ἀνὴρ ὀνόσαιτο μετελθών.'[50] The *KEN* is superfluous, and the verb form and time period have been changed [i.e.

---

[44] So also Laum (1928: 244), but we reject his view that the absence of any mention of the accent on καί is a sign of abbreviation.

[45] Dindorf (1855) prints the lemma as καί τε τέο, but it is clear from the text of the scholion that κε is the intended reading.

[46] As transmitted—and as printed by Dindorf (1855)—the scholion has τε here, but this is clearly an error for τεο: see Buttmann (1821: 472), whose note on this point is reproduced by Dindorf, and cf. Laum (1928: 244).

[47] Dindorf (1855) reads ὅτεο δμώων here, but following Lentz (1867–70: ii. 159, line 31) we read ἐτεοδμώων, on the basis of the gloss τῶν ὄντων ἡμετέρων δούλων.

[48] *Od.* 16.305: 'And let us [yet test] one and another [of the manservants]'.

[49] Erbse presents the text with οὐκέτι, but what follows suggests that ἔτι should here be considered a fresh word.

[50] *Il.* 4.539: 'Then a man going into the midst would no longer find fault with the work'.

future potential $\kappa\epsilon...\dot{o}\nu\acute{o}\sigma\alpha\iota\tau o$ 'stands for' past counterfactual $\mathring{a}\nu$ $\mathring{\omega}\nu\acute{o}\sigma\alpha\tau o$]. And one must know that Ptolemy of Ascalon makes the negative $\text{'}OY$ unaccented, as in $o\mathring{v}\kappa\ \mathring{\epsilon}\tau\iota$, so that what follows is the new word $\mathring{\epsilon}\tau\iota$. And there is another reading $o\mathring{v}\ \kappa\acute{\epsilon}\ \tau\iota$, with two consecutive acutes, making three words: the $\text{'}OY$, the conjunction KE, and the TI, so that the natural sequence is $o\mathring{v}\kappa\ \mathring{a}\nu\ \dot{o}\nu\acute{o}\sigma\alpha\iota\tau o\ \kappa\alpha\grave{\iota}\ \phi\alpha\nu\acute{\epsilon}\nu\tau\alpha...$'

Only the reading $\text{'}OY\ KE\ TI$ is relevant for us, since only this one involves a sequence of enclitics. It is clear from the comment $\mathring{\epsilon}\nu\ \pi\alpha\rho\alpha\lambda\lambda\acute{\eta}\lambda o\iota s\ \delta\acute{v}o\ \mathring{o}\xi\epsilon\acute{\iota}\alpha\iota s$, 'with two consecutive acutes' that if this reading is adopted, acute accents are considered to fall on both the $\text{'}OY$ and the KE, i.e. $o\mathring{v}\ \kappa\acute{\epsilon}\ \tau\iota$. Once again, this is also the result of applying the revised Göttling-Barrett system. From an ancient point of view $\text{'}OY$ has an acute as its natural accent, and retains this acute before an enclitic. The trochaic sequence $o\mathring{v}\ \kappa\epsilon$ then receives an acute on its second syllable when a further enclitic is added, with the end result $o\mathring{v}\ \kappa\acute{\epsilon}\ \tau\iota$.

The scholion (4.14) deals with the sequence $\text{'}H\ NY\ \Sigma E\ \Pi OY$:

(4.14) $\text{'}H\ NY\ \Sigma E\ \Pi OY\cdot\ \dot{o}\ \text{'}H\ \mathring{o}\xi\acute{v}\nu\epsilon\tau\alpha\iota\cdot\ \delta\iota\alpha\zeta\epsilon\upsilon\kappa\tau\iota\kappa\grave{o}s\ \gamma\acute{a}\rho.\ \phi\upsilon\lambda\acute{a}\sigma\sigma\epsilon\tau\alpha\iota\ \delta\grave{\epsilon}\ \mathring{\eta}$
$\mathring{o}\xi\epsilon\hat{\iota}\alpha\ \delta\iota\grave{a}\ \tau\grave{o}\ \mathring{\epsilon}\pi\iota\phi\epsilon\rho\acute{o}\mu\epsilon\nu o\nu\ NY\ \mathring{\epsilon}\gamma\kappa\lambda\iota\tau\iota\kappa\acute{o}\nu,\ \mathring{o}\ \kappa\alpha\grave{\iota}\ \alpha\mathring{v}\tau\grave{o}\ \mathring{\epsilon}\sigma\chi\epsilon\nu\ \mathring{o}\xi\epsilon\hat{\iota}\alpha\nu\ \delta\iota\grave{a}$
$\tau\grave{\eta}\nu\ \Sigma E\ \mathring{\epsilon}\gamma\kappa\lambda\iota\tau\iota\kappa\grave{\eta}\nu\ o\mathring{v}\sigma\alpha\nu.$ (Sch. Il. 5.812a (A))

'$\text{'}H\ NY\ \Sigma E\ \Pi OY$.[51] the $\text{'}H$ has an acute, for it is disjunctive. And the acute is retained because of the following enclitic NY, which has an acute itself too because of the ΣE, which is enclitic.'

Erbse presents the lemma as $\mathring{\eta}\ \nu\acute{v}\ \sigma\acute{\epsilon}\ \pi o\upsilon$. In support of this as the intended accentuation for the sequence he adduces our passages (4.1) and (4.2), from Apollonius Dyscolus (to whom we shall return in section 4.2.6), as well as (4.3) and (4.4), from On enclitics 1 and On enclitics 2.[52] Differently, Laum (1928: 243–4) argues that the accentuation intended by the scholion is $\mathring{\eta}\ \nu\acute{v}\ \sigma\epsilon\ \pi o\upsilon$. Since the scholion says nothing about the accented or unaccented status of the ΣE (cf. Erbse 1960: 400), it does not itself provide enough information to decide between the two views. Nevertheless, like the other Homeric scholia commenting on the accentuation of specific sequences of enclitics, what the scholion does say is at least compatible with the result of applying the revised Göttling-Barrett system, namely $\mathring{\eta}\ \nu\acute{v}\ \sigma\epsilon\ \pi o\upsilon$. Under this system the oxytone form $\mathring{\eta}$ retains its acute accent before NY, the trochaic sequence $\mathring{\eta}\ \nu\upsilon$ receives an acute on its second syllable when a further enclitic is added (hence $\mathring{\eta}\ \nu\acute{v}\ \sigma\epsilon$), the pyrrhic sequence $\nu\acute{v}\ \sigma\epsilon$ receives no further accent when one final enclitic is added, and so the end result is $\mathring{\eta}\ \nu\acute{v}\ \sigma\epsilon\ \pi o\upsilon$.

---

[51] Il. 5.812: 'or perhaps [fear has got hold of] you'.
[52] See Erbse (1960: 366; 1969–88 ad loc.).

We now turn to scholia discussing sequences of enclitics in which the second enclitic is added to a paroxytone sequence ending in a non-trochaic pattern, when syllable quantities are calculated (once again) before the addition of the next enclitic. Under the revised Göttling-Barrett system, the syllable preceding the second enclitic should not receive an acute accent in these sequences.

The pair of related scholia (4.15) and (4.16) deals with the sequence 'ΟΥΔΕ ΤΙ ΠΩ ΜΟΙ:

(4.15)   ⟨'ΟΥΔΕ ΤΙ ΠΩ ΜΟΙ·⟩ τὸ δὲ ΠΩ ὀξύνεται διὰ τὴν ΜΟΙ ἀντωνυμίαν, ἥτις νῦν ἐγκλιτική ἐστιν. (Sch. Il. 1.542c¹ (Aᶦⁿᵗ))

'ΟΥΔΕ ΤΙ ΠΩ ΜΟΙ:[53] The ΠΩ has an acute because of the pronoun ΜΟΙ, which is enclitic here.'

(4.16)   'ΟΥΔΕ ΤΙ ΠΩ ΜΟΙ· ὀξυντέον τὸ ΠΩ διὰ τὴν ΜΟΙ. (Sch. Il. 1.542c² (T))

'ΟΥΔΕ ΤΙ ΠΩ ΜΟΙ: The ΠΩ should have an acute because of the ΜΟΙ.'

Erbse presents the lemma for scholion (4.15) as οὐδέ τί πώ μοι, while Laum (1928: 245) thought that the intended accentuation was οὐδε (sic) τι πώ μοι. These scholia are silent about the presence or absence of any accent on the ΤΙ (and on the 'ΟΥΔΕ), but what they do say is once again compatible with the result of applying the revised Göttling-Barrett system, namely οὐδέ τι πώ μοι. Under this system the oxytone form οὐδέ retains its accent before the enclitic ΤΙ, the pyrrhic sequence (οὐ)δέ τι does not receive any additional accent before the enclitic ΠΩ, and the proparoxytone sequence (οὐ)δέ τι πω then receives an acute on its final syllable before ΜΟΙ: hence οὐδέ τι πώ μοι.

The scholion (4.17) deals with the words 'ΟΥ ΓΑΡ ΠΩ ΤΙ Μ':

(4.17)   'ΟΥ ΓΑΡ ΠΩ ΤΙ Μ' 'ΕΦΗ· ὀφείλει τὸ ΤΙ ὀξύνεσθαι διὰ τὴν ΜΕ ἀντωνυμίαν νῦν ἐγκλιτικὴν οὖσαν. (Sch. Il. 11.719a (A))

'ΟΥ ΓΑΡ ΠΩ ΤΙ Μ' 'ΕΦΗ:[54] The ΤΙ ought to have an acute accent because of the pronoun ΜΕ, which is enclitic here.'

Erbse presents the lemma as οὐ γάρ πώ τί μ' ἔφη, while Laum (1928: 244–5) thought the intended accentuation was οὔ γαρ πω τί μ' ἔφη. It is very unlikely that the non-enclitic word ΓΑΡ was considered unaccented,[55] but the scholion offers no information on the accented or unaccented status of the ΠΩ. Once

---

[53] Il. 1.542: 'And never yet to me'.
[54] Il. 11.719: 'For he said that I did not yet [know the affairs of war]'.
[55] Even Laum, who thought in general that the distinction between acute and grave accents on the final syllables of oxytone words was purely graphic, allowed that this distinction was linguistically real

again, what it tells us is compatible with the accentuation required by the revised Göttling-Barrett system, οὐ γάρ πω τί μ' ἔφη. Under this system the oxytone form γάρ retains its accent before enclitic ΠΩ, the spondaic sequence γάρ πω acquires no additional accent before enclitic ΤΙ, and finally the proparoxytone sequence γάρ πω τι receives an additional acute before the enclitic Μ(Ε): hence οὐ γάρ πω τί μ' ἔφη.

The scholion (4.18) deals with the sequence ᾽ΕΠΕΙ ῾ΕΥ ΦΗΜΙ:

(4.18)   ᾽ΕΠΕΙ ῾ΕΥ {ΦΗΜΙ}· καὶ ἐπὶ τούτου ἐγκλιτική ἐστιν ἡ ἀντωνυμία καὶ ἀπόλυτος· διὸ τὸν ᾽ΕΠΕΙ σύνδεσμον ὀξυτονητέον ὁμοφώνως τῷ ῾καί εὐ κράτος ἐστὶ μέγιστον᾽. (Sch. Il. 15.165a[1] (A))

᾽ΕΠΕΙ ῾ΕΥ:[56] Here too the pronoun is enclitic and non-contrastive. Therefore one should give the conjunction ᾽ΕΠΕΙ an acute on its last syllable, just like [the ΚΑΙ in] καί εὐ κράτος ἐστὶ μέγιστον᾽.[57]

Laum (1928: 244) took this scholion to prescribe ἐπεί εὐ φημι.[58] The ᾽ΕΠΕΙ is explicitly said to have an acute on its last syllable, but nothing is said about any accent on the ῾ΕΥ (cf. Erbse 1960: 400). The point of interest is to distinguish between enclitic and non-enclitic ῾ΕΥ, rather than to lay out the accentuation of the whole sequence. However, what is said is compatible with the accentuation ἐπεί εὐ φημί (or in context ἐπεί εὐ φημὶ), and this corresponds to the most likely interpretation of the related scholion (4.19), on the same sequence:

(4.19)   ᾽ΕΠΕΙ ῾ΕΥ ὁμοίως τῷ ῾καί εὐ κράτος ἐστὶ μέγιστον᾽. (Sch. Il. 15.165a[2] (T[il]))

᾽ΕΠΕΙ ῾ΕΥ [is accented] like [the καί εὐ in] καί εὐ κράτος ἐστὶ μέγιστον᾽.

Once again the accentuation ἐπεί εὐ φημί is what the revised Göttling-Barrett system gives: the oxytone form ἐπεί retains its accent before enclitic ῾ΕΥ, the spondaic sequence (ἐπ)εί εὐ receives no additional accent before ΦΗΜΙ, and finally the disyllabic enclitic ΦΗΜΙ receives an acute (or grave, as in this instance) on its final syllable after an unaccented enclitic: hence ἐπεί εὐ φημί.

---

for monosyllables, and that monosyllabic words (including γάρ) had an acute accent before enclitics: see Laum (1928: 154–5).

[56] Il. 15.165: 'Since [I say that I am much greater in might] than him'.

[57] Il. 24.293 and Il. 24.311: 'and its power is the greatest'.

[58] He expressed some hesitation, on the grounds that the scholia do not pronounce on the enclitic status of ΦΗΜΙ, but in the absence of evidence to the contrary we should assume that ΦΗΜΙ was taken to be normally enclitic. Compare On enclitics 1, §d; On enclitics 2, §h; On enclitics 3, §a; Charax, §§m, n (with reference to some debate on the enclitic status of ΦΗΜΙ); On enclitics 4, §c.

The pair of related scholia Sch. *Il.* 20.464*a*¹ and Sch. *Il.* 20.464*a*² have already been quoted as passages (4.7) and (4.8). These scholia give the examples ’*OY ΠΩΣ ’ΕΣΤ’, ΜΗ ΠΩΣ ΜΕ, ΜΗ ΠΩ Μ’*, and ’*OY ΠΩ ΜΙΝ ΦΑΣΙΝ*, and in each case the *ΠΩΣ* or *ΠΩ* is said to be unaccented. In each case the lack of accent on *ΠΩΣ* or *ΠΩ* is as required by the revised Göttling-Barrett system, which gives οὔ πως ἐστ’, μή πως με, μή πω μ’, and οὔ πω μίν φασιν. The lemma has the sequence ’*ΕΙ ΠΩΣ ’ΕΥ*, and the scholia argue that accentuation εἴ πως εὖ is at least a possibility. This too is the accentuation we expect under the revised Göttling-Barrett system.

The two *Odyssey* scholia Sch. *Od.* 1.62*b* Pontani and Sch. *Od.* 15.27 have already been quoted as passages (4.9) and (4.10). These scholia comment on the sequences τί νυ οἱ (where τί is interrogative) and δέ τοι τι, and require these to be accented as shown here. Since these two scholia come close to hinting at the revised Göttling-Barrett system (see section 4.2.3), it is not too surprising that their ways of accenting these sequences are as required by that system.

The pair of closely related scholia (4.20) and (4.21) concern a sequence of enclitics in which the second enclitic follows a sequence that is properispomenon before the addition of this second enclitic. The accentuation prescribed is clearly ἢ πή με:

(4.20) ’*Η ΠΗ ΜΕ·* τὸν ’*Η* σύνδεσμον περισπαστέον, τὸ δὲ *ΠΗ* ὀξυτονητέον διὰ τὸ *ΜΕ* ἐγκλιτικόν· ἐνθάδε γὰρ τὸ *ΠΗ* οὐ πύσμα, ἀλλὰ ἀόριστον. (Sch. *Il.* 3.400*a*¹ (A))

’*Η ΠΗ ΜΕ*:[59] one must give the conjunction ’*Η* a circumflex, and the *ΠΗ* an acute because of the enclitic *ΜΕ*. For the *ΠΗ* is not interrogative here, but indefinite.’

(4.21) ’*Η ΠΗ ΜΕ·* τὸ ἢ περισπαστέον, τὸ δὲ πή ὀξυντέον διὰ τὸ μέ· οὐ γάρ ἐστι νῦν ἐρωτηματικὸν τὸ *ΠΗ*, ἀλλὰ ἀόριστον. (Sch. *Il.* 3.400*a*² (bT))

’*Η ΠΗ ΜΕ*: one must give the ’*Η* a circumflex, and the *ΠΗ* an acute because of the *ΜΕ*. For the *ΠΗ* is not interrogative here, but indefinite.’

Once again, ἢ πή με is also what the revised Göttling-Barrett system gives. Under this system the perispomenon form ἢ retains its circumflex accent before the enclitic *ΠΗ*, and the properispomenon sequence ἢ πη then receives an additional acute accent before the enclitic *ΜΕ*: hence ἢ πή με.

Our final scholion, (4.22), concerns the words ’*ΑΛΛ’ ’Η ΤΟΙ ΣΦΕΑΣ*, where *ΤΟΙ* and *ΣΦΕΑΣ* should probably both be seen as enclitics (regardless of whether ’*ΗΤΟΙ* is written as one word or two):

[59] *Il.* 3.400: '[Are you going to take] me somewhere...?'

(4.22)   ⟨ἈΛΛ᾽ Ἦ ΤΟΙ ΣΦΕΑΣ·⟩ ἐγκλιτικὴ ἡ ΣΦΕΑΣ· διὸ τὴν ΤΟΙ
συλλαβὴν ἐγερτέον. (Sch. Od. 13.276 (H))

ἈΛΛ᾽ Ἦ ΤΟΙ ΣΦΕΑΣ:[60] The ΣΦΕΑΣ is enclitic. Therefore the syllable ΤΟΙ must be woken up [i.e. must have an acute].'

An acute is prescribed for τοί—but is ἀλλ᾽ ἦ τοί σφεας envisaged, or ἀλλ᾽ ἤ τοί
σφεας? Editorial practice varies, but ancient discussions hint that Ἦ ΤΟΙ (or
ἨΤΟΙ) should be accented ἤτοι regardless of function: when ἤτοι is emphatic (as
here) as well as when the meaning is disjunctive ('either'/'or').[61] Homeric manuscripts also normally have ἤτοι, regardless of function,[62] and the accented Iliad
papyrus P.Lond.Lit. 28—with ἈΛΛ᾽ἨΤΟΙ at Il. 24.490 and ἨΤΟΙ at Il. 24.629—
helps to confirm that this practice goes back to antiquity. If we therefore take the
Homeric scholion (and its likely source, Herodian) to envisage an acute accent for
ἤ, our sequence becomes ἀλλ᾽ ἤ τοί σφεας. This time the final enclitic has trig-
gered an acute accent on a preceding paroxytone sequence that is not trochaic but
spondaic (ἤ τοι)—something that would normally be counter to the revised
Göttling-Barrett system. But as already noted in passing (section 4.2.4), the revised
Göttling-Barrett system is based on the concept that on each addition of a new
enclitic, the ancient principles for accenting a word followed by a single enclitic are
applied again—and according to the full ancient principles, enclitics beginning
with σφ- induce an additional accent on a preceding paroxytone word, regardless
of its metrical shape (see section 2.7.3). If the revised Göttling-Barrett system is to
apply this principle recursively, along with the other ancient principles that apply
when a single enclitic is added, then ἤ τοι should receive an additional accent
before σφεας: hence ἤ τοί σφεας. Notably, this is the only sequence for which the
Homeric scholia suggest that an enclitic induced an accent on a preceding paroxytone sequence with non-trochaic shape—and it is not a random exception but one
with a basis in the ancient rules for accenting sequences with single enclitics.

To sum up, all the comments on the accentuation of specific sequences of enclitics that we find in the scholia vetera to Homer are consistently compatible with the
revised Göttling-Barrett system. This is so even though some of these scholia offer
an explanation in terms of one of the rules of thumb we have identified, and some
others prescribe accents that might seem to contradict one of these rules of thumb.
In particular, the scholia (4.7) and (4.8) offer an explanation in terms of the

---

[60]   Od. 13.276: 'But truly [the force of the wind drove] them…'.
[61]   See Wackernagel (1893: 20–1); differently Laum (1928: 244).
[62]   See Dalimier (2001: 433), and cf. Wackernagel (1893: 21). We have been able to verify this claim
for the medieval Iliad manuscripts 'Venetus A' (Marcianus Graecus 822 = Z.454), using the images
made available by the Homer Multitext Project at <www.homermultitext.org/facsimiles/venetus-
a-2020/pages>; and 'Venetus B' (Marcianus Graecus 821 = Z.453), using the images available at
<www.internetculturale.it/jmms/iccuviewer/iccu.jsp?id=oai%3A193.206.197.121%3A18%3AVE004
9%3ACSTOR.240.10163>.

exceptional status of *ΠΩ* and *ΠΩΣ*, while (4.15) and (4.16) prescribe an accent on an instance of enclitic *ΠΩ*, and (4.20) and (4.21) similarly prescribe an accent on an instance of enclitic *ΠΗ*. But all these scholia yield specific sequences compatible with the revised Göttling-Barrett system. This point helps to confirm the reason for the apparent indecisiveness with which (4.7) and (4.8) suggest that *ΠΩ* and *ΠΩΣ* do not 'necessarily' receive an accent from a following enclitic: when taken together, the Homeric scholia suggest that *ΠΩ* and *ΠΩΣ* do indeed fail to receive an accent in a sequence like εἴ πως εὖ πεφίδοιτο, but not in a sequence like οὐδέ τι πώ μοι.

The comments on sequences of enclitics in the Homeric scholia bear the hallmarks of comments going back to Herodian: they appear in the A scholia to the *Iliad*, in related material in bT scholia, and in material of a similar character in scholia to the *Odyssey*. The consistent picture they present helps to confirm that Herodian's sense for accents on sequences of enclitics was guided by the revised Göttling-Barrett system.

4.2.6 The grammatical tradition: conclusion and a remaining puzzle

As we have seen, the various doctrines on accenting sequences of enclitics that we find in the grammatical tradition can be understood as rules of thumb whose goal is to produce results close to those of the revised Göttling-Barrett system. The point that we are dealing with rules of thumb makes it possible to reconcile the reasons for thinking that each of the three doctrines goes back to Herodian with the difficulty of seeing how all three could represent the views of one person.

The comments on the accentuation of specific sequences of enclitics in the scholia vetera to Homer strengthen the conclusion that Herodian operated implicitly with the revised Göttling-Barrett system, and that he offered various rules of thumb aimed at producing similar results—either because he did not have the principle fully worked out in theory, or because he thought a rules-of-thumb style presentation more helpful to his audience.

Since the Homeric scholia are likely to be our best source of evidence for Herodian's views on the accentuation of sequences involving enclitics,[63] it is worth emphasizing that they provide us with evidence for two of the three ancient doctrines we have discussed: the exceptional status of *ΠΩ* and *ΠΩΣ* (passages (4.7) and (4.8)) and the need to avoid consecutive acute accents on pyrrhic and iambic sequences (passages (4.9) and (4.10)). The Homeric scholia never give us any statements of the 'traditional' system, to the effect that every enclitic except the last gets an accent on its last or only syllable. However, passages (4.7)–(4.10) amount to

---

[63] On the status of the sections on enclitics transmitted as part of Pseudo-Arcadius' epitome of Herodian's *Περὶ καθολικῆς προσῳδίας*, see the introduction to Chapter 2 together with sections 2.1, 2.3, and 2.5.

statements that under some circumstances an enclitic *fails* to receive an accent from a following enclitic. We suggest that Herodian might well have said that an enclitic generally receives an accent from a following enclitic, but that this rule was subject to various exceptions. It is tempting to conclude that the 'traditional' system was never intended to be exceptionless: that this was itself a rule of thumb, intended to be useful up to a point but subject to various exceptions.

This view of the 'traditional' system is challenged by five passages of grammatical texts falling outside the Homeric scholia tradition, in which accents contrary to the revised Göttling-Barrett system are prescribed for the following specific sequences:

ἤ νύ σέ που δέος: passages (4.1), (4.2), (4.3), (4.4)
εἴπέρ τίς σέ μοί φησίν ποτε: passage (4.3)
ἤ ῥά νύ μοί τι πίθοιο: passage (4.5)

As far as passages (4.3), (4.4), and (4.5) are concerned, one might think in terms of a late exaggeration of the scope of the traditional principle. But passages (4.1) and (4.2) come from Apollonius Dyscolus: did he have a different view from his son on the accentuation of sequences of enclitics? Or does the system that we can extract with remarkable consistency from the Homeric scholia not, after all, go back to Herodian? Or have the passages of Apollonius suffered interference at a late date?

Laum (1928: 488 with n. 1) had already suggested that both passages (4.1) and (4.2) are of Byzantine origin. Laum's interpretation of the Homeric scholia was different from ours,[64] but like us he also thought that these two passages of 'Apollonius' contradict the picture gained from the scholia. This remains true on our interpretation of the scholia, and we too are led to suspect that passages (4.1) and (4.2) have been influenced in transmission by the Byzantine tradition on enclitics: that the apparent verbal echoes of Apollonius which we have noted in passages (4.3)–(4.5) (see section 4.2.1) are actually verbal echoes of the Byzantine treatises in the text of Apollonius as it comes down to us.[65] In section 2.8.4 we noted the unusual use of ἀνέστη in passage (4.1) (= (2.22)), for which the only parallel known to us comes from the 'Vatican scholia' on the *Τέχνη γραμματική* attributed to Dionysius Thrax—a source of broadly Byzantine date. The presence of the same unusual usage in Apollonius Dyscolus and a Byzantine text certainly

---

[64]   Laum (1928: 243–6, 307–12, 326) took the scholia to point to a variant of the traditional system in which enclitic pronoun forms, apart from forms of indefinite *ΤΙΣ* (on which see Laum 1928: 311–12), failed to acquire an accent when followed by an enclitic. His reasoning was partly based on a misinterpretation of scholia in which the terms ἐγκλιτική and ἐγκλιτικῶς are applied to pronouns (see Erbse 1960: 400). On the other hand, Laum thought that his view was supported by the scholia (4.14) and (4.18), and we too consider unaccented pronoun forms to be intended for the specific sequences of enclitics discussed here—but for reasons that do not imply any general exception for pronouns.

[65]   Compare Maas's (1907) suspicion that a different discussion of enclitics in the text of Apollonius, *Pron.* 35.22–36.5, was interpolated on the basis of the discussion at *On enclitics* 2, §d.

does not prove that the Byzantine tradition has influenced our text of Apollonius. On the other hand, if passage (4.1) has its origins in the Byzantine period we find it just conceivable that a well-known use of ἀνέστη in Christian contexts played a role in the choice of word:[66] should we think of the accent being resurrected?

Be this as it may, the evidence from the grammatical tradition points strongly towards the revised Göttling-Barrett system as the way Herodian implicitly took sequences of enclitics to be accented. In the next section, we shall see that the evidence of accented papyri strengthens this conclusion and further suggests that Herodian's practice was the normal one in his day.

4.3 Accented papyri

If we want to know how sequences of enclitics were accented in antiquity, it is natural to ask how they are treated on accented papyri. The question is easier to ask than to answer. The marking of accents in papyri is almost always sporadic, and always unpredictable. For this reason, while an accent mark can be taken as a positive indication of the accentuation the writer had in mind, on any given occasion the absence of an accent mark need not imply that the writer considered a particular syllable unaccented. In addition, individual examples cannot by themselves tell us what system lies behind them; we will need to work from a systematic collection of examples and see if any larger picture emerges.

With all this in mind we have collected sequences of more than one enclitic, plus the preceding word, from all the accented literary papyri published in *P.Oxy.*, volumes I–LXXXIV, and from three further long and generously accented literary papyri: *P.Lond.Lit.* 25 (the 'Harris Homer roll'), *P.Lond.Lit.* 28 (the 'Bankes Homer') and *P.Lond.Lit.* 46 ('Bacchylides papyrus A').[67] In total, these papyri yield seventy usable sequences of enclitics, once we have discounted all sequences for which no accent mark appears on any enclitic or on the preceding word. (Even on papyri in which accent marks are frequently deployed, a completely unaccented sequence is unremarkable and does not help

---

[66] E.g. New Testament, 1 Thessalonians 4:14: Ἰησοῦς ἀπέθανεν καὶ ἀνέστη 'Jesus died and rose again'.

[67] For the literary papyri published in the *P.Oxy.* volumes, we primarily made use of the diplomatic transcripts published alongside interpretative transcripts there; on occasion we also consulted later editions of the texts and/or published photographs of the papyri to clarify our understanding. For *P.Lond.Lit.* 25, we worked from Thompson and Warner's (1881: 2–6) transcription, and then checked readings against the images available at <www.bl.uk/manuscripts/Viewer.aspx?ref=papyrus_107_f001r> (in no case did the images prompt us to diverge from Thompson and Warner's reading). For *P.Lond.Lit.* 28, we first compiled a list of sequences of enclitics in the relevant portion of *Iliad* 24 (lines 127–804) on the basis of West's edition (including readings of this papyrus recorded in his apparatus), and then consulted the images available at <www.bl.uk/manuscripts/Viewer.aspx?ref=papyrus_114_f001ar>. For *P.Lond.Lit.* 46, we worked from the diplomatic transcript published alongside an interpretative transcript by Kenyon (1897), and compared the readings of interest to us with the images available at <www.bl.uk/manuscripts/Viewer.aspx?ref=papyrus_733>.

with our question.)[68] Most of these examples come from papyri dating to the second or third century AD; sixteen come from papyri that may date to the first century AD (but fourteen of these come from *P.Lond.Lit.* 25, on which many of the accents may have been added considerably later than the original copying of the text[69]), and two from papyri of the fifth century AD. In many instances accents have been added by a second hand, but since papyri tended to have a relatively short working life,[70] the accents too will mostly date from the second and third centuries AD.

Table 4.3 lists our sequences of enclitics, and shows for comparison how the same sequences would be accented by the revised Göttling-Barrett system. When we compare the accents on the papyri to those predicted by this system, a striking fact emerges. Although a papyrus may lack an accent mark where the revised Göttling-Barrett system requires an accent (this is hardly surprising, given the sporadic nature of accents in papyri), in our sample of papyri we never find an accent mark on a syllable that the revised Göttling-Barrett system would make unaccented. The structure of the evidence makes it very unlikely that this is a mere coincidence. In order to see why this is so, we will turn shortly to the structural characteristics of the collection of examples as a whole. But three examples raise questions about details of the revised Göttling-Barrett system, and it will be convenient to take these first.

The first sequence to require some discussion is item 24 in Table 4.3: τά ρά σφ (for τά ῥά σφ'). How should the revised Göttling-Barrett system treat this sequence? First of all, the oxytone form τά will retain its accent before the enclitic ῥα, and then τά ῥα makes a paroxytone pyrrhic sequence. Normally, such a sequence does not acquire an additional accent before another enclitic, on the revised Göttling-Barrett system. But once again (see sections 4.2.4, 4.2.5), the ancient principles governing the accentuation of a word followed by a single enclitic include the idea that enclitics beginning with σφ- induce an accent on a preceding paroxytone sequence, regardless of its metrical shape. If this principle is to be applied recursively, along with the other ancient principles applying to

---

[68] We have also omitted sequences such as αρ' σέ γε at *Il.* 24.288 on *P.Lond.Lit.* 28, where the σέ may well have been taken as orthotonic (as in West's edition, where the preceding word is printed ἄρ), and sequences for which the papyrus itself provides evidence that a word we might think enclitic was taken as orthotonic. Examples of the latter kind include οὐδ' ἔτι οἱ at *Il.* 24.414 on *P.Lond.Lit.* 28, where the scribe responsible for the apostrophe had in mind οὐδ' ἔτι οἱ rather than οὐδέ τι οἱ; and ἠὲ σε γ at *Od.* 11.399 on *P.Oxy.* xlix 3442, where the grave accent on ἠὲ suggests orthotonic σέ. For *P.Lond.Lit.* 46, we omit the sequence ἧράτις at Bacchylides 5.165, on the basis that ἧρα may be a contraction of ἤ and non-enclitic ἄρα—although in literary Doric this sequence is difficult to distinguish from ἤ plus enclitic ῥα (see Denniston 1950: 284).

[69] See Thompson and Warner (1881: 1).

[70] Johnson (2009: 272–7) shows that evidence for multiple annotators of a literary text need not point to a papyrus roll being passed from generation to generation—although as Johnson also notes, there are known instances of literary papyri being passed from one generation to another (see e.g. Bagnall 1992).

Table 4.3 Sequences of enclitics (plus the preceding non-enclitic word) from accented literary papyri published in *P.Oxy.*, volumes i–lxxxiv, and from *P.Lond.Lit.* 25, *P.Lond.Lit.* 28, and *P.Lond.Lit.* 46. Sequences are included if at least one enclitic and/or the preceding word carries an accent mark on the papyrus. The last column shows how the same sequence would be accented by the revised Göttling-Barrett system; in this column, hyphens are used as in Table 4.2.

Papyrus	Place in the text	Date of the papyrus (not necessarily of the accent marks)[a]	Sequence of enclitics plus preceding word, showing accents on the papyrus. (Word divisions are not necessarily on the papyrus.)	Same sequence showing accents as per the revised Göttling-Barrett system
1. P.Oxy. i 21	*Il.* 2.754	1st–2nd cent. AD	ἅ τε μιν[b]	ἅ τε μιν
2. P.Oxy. ii 223	*Il.* 5.103	AD 186–224	οὐδέ ἑ φῂμί	οὐδέ ἑ φημί
3. P.Oxy. ii 223	*Il.* 5.116	AD 186–224	ει ποτέ μοι	εἴ ποτέ μοι
4. P.Oxy. ii 223	*Il.* 5.118	AD 186–224	δέ τε μ᾽	δέ τε μ᾽
5. P.Oxy. ii 223	*Il.* 5.119	AD 186–224	οὐδέ με φῇσιν	οὐδέ με φησίν
6. P.Oxy. ii 223	*Il.* 5.137	AD 186–224	ὅν ῥά τε	ὅν ῥά τε
7. P.Oxy. ii 223	*Il.* 5.170	AD 186–224	επος τέ μιν	ἔπος τέ μιν
8. P.Oxy. ii 223	*Il.* 5.172	AD 186–224	ου τίς τοι	οὔ τίς τοι
9. P.Oxy. ii 223	*Il.* 5.191	AD 186–224	θεος νύ τις εσ[τ]ι	θεός νύ τις ἐστὶ
10. P.Oxy. ii 223	*Il.* 5.298	AD 186–224	μή πως ὁι	μή πως οἱ
11. P.Oxy. ii 223	*Il.* 5.359	AD 186–224	κ[ο]μί[σ]αι τέ με	κόμισαί τέ με
12. P.Oxy. iii 448	*Od.* 22.40	3rd cent. AD	[ο]υτέ τιν᾽	οὔ-τέ τιν᾽
13. P.Oxy. iii 448	*Od.* 22.252	3rd cent. AD	αι κέ ποθι	αἴ κέ ποθι
14. P.Oxy. v 841	Pindar, *Paean* 4.42	AD 100–150	χθόνα τοί ποτε	χθόνα τοί ποτε
15. P.Oxy. viii 1091	Bacchylides 17.53	2nd cent. AD	εἰ πέρ με	εἴ πέρ με
16. P.Oxy. x 1231	Sappho 23.8 V.[c]	2nd cent. AD	πάισαν κε με	παῖσαν κέ με[d]
17. P.Oxy. xiii 1618	Theocritus 7.105	5th cent. AD	εἴτε τις	εἴ-τέ τις
18. P.Oxy. xvii 2091	Hesiod, *Opera* 330	3rd cent. AD	[ὅς] τέ τευ	ὅς τέ τευ
19. P.Oxy. xix 2211	Callimachus, *Aetia* fr. 63, line 9[e]	3rd cent. AD	ὁν πως εστιν	ὅν πως ἐστὶν

Continued

Table 4.3 *Continued*

Papyrus	Date of the papyrus (not necessarily of the accent marks)[a]	Place in the text	Sequence of enclitics plus preceding word, showing accents on the papyrus. (Word divisions are not necessarily on the papyrus.)	Same sequence showing accents as per the revised Göttling-Barrett system
20. *P.Oxy.* xxi 2290	2nd–3rd cent. AD	Sappho 88a.23 V[f]	ὅττί σ᾽	ὤτ–τί σ᾽
21. *P.Oxy.* xxi 2299	1st cent. AD?	Sappho or Alcaeus, *incerti auctoris* fr. 33.2 V[g]	οττινά τοι	ὄτ–τινά τοι
22. *P.Oxy.* xxiii 2362 fr.1	AD 150–250	Bacchylides fr. 20D, line 10[h]	[θ]ηκέν τέ νιν	θῆκέν τέ νιν
23. *P.Schub.* 22, fr. 2[i]	AD 400–450	Menander, *Misoumenos* 139	τίς ποτ᾽ εστιν	τίς ποτ᾽ ἐστίν
24. *P.Oxy.* xliv 3155	2nd–3rd cent. AD	*Il.* 15.388	τά ρά σφ	See discussion
25. *P.Oxy.* xliv 3155	2nd–3rd cent. AD	*Il.* 15.403	ει κέν όι	εἴ κέν οἱ
26. *P.Oxy.* xlix 3441	2nd cent. AD	*Od.* 10.3	δέ τε μιν	δέ τε μιν
27. *P.Oxy.* lii 3663	AD 150–250	*Il.* 18.269	εὐ νύ τις	εὖ νύ τις
28. *P.Oxy.* lvi 3825	AD 100–150	*Il.* 1.66	αἱ κέν πως	αἴ κέν πως
29. *P.Oxy.* lvi 3825	AD 100–150	*Il.* 1.108	ούτέ τι πω	οὔ–τέ τι πω
30. *P.Oxy.* lxviii 4653	3rd cent. AD	Hesiod, *Theogony* 418	πολλ]ή τέ οι	πολλή τέ οἱ
31. *P.Oxy.* lxxxiv 5426	AD 100–150	Apollonius Rhodius, *Argonautica* 4.1305	κἀι νύ κεν	καί νύ κεν
32. *P.Lond.Lit.* 25	1st–2nd cent. AD	*Il.* 18.9	ὥς ποτέ μοι	ὥς ποτέ μοι
33. *P.Lond.Lit.* 25	1st–2nd cent. AD	*Il.* 18.62	ουδέ τι οἱ	οὐδέ τι οἱ
34. *P.Lond.Lit.* 25	1st–2nd cent. AD	*Il.* 18.64	ὅττι νυἰ	ὅτ–τί νιν
35. *P.Lond.Lit.* 25	See n. k	*Il.* 18.132	ουδέ ἑ φημμ[k]	οὐδέ ἑ φημί
36. *P.Lond.Lit.* 25	1st–2nd cent. AD	*Il.* 18.199	α[ἱ] κέ σ᾽	αἴ κέ σ᾽
37. *P.Lond.Lit.* 25	1st–2nd cent. AD	*Il.* 18.213	ἄι κέν πως	αἴ κέν πως
38. *P.Lond.Lit.* 25	1st–2nd cent. AD	*Il.* 18.319	ὡι ῥά θ᾽	ᾧ ῥά θ᾽

		Date	Il.		
39.	*PLond.Lit.* 25	1st–2nd cent. AD	*Il.* 18.358	ἦ ῥά νν	ἦ ῥά νν
40.	*PLond.Lit.* 25	1st–2nd cent. AD	*Il.* 18.362	δή που τις	δή που τις
41.	*PLond.Lit.* 25	1st–2nd cent. AD	*Il.* 18.363	θνητός τ᾽ ἐστι	θνητός τ᾽ ἐστι
42.	*PLond.Lit.* 25	1st–2nd cent. AD	*Il.* 18.392	Θέτις νύ τι	Θέτις νύ τι
43.	*PLond.Lit.* 25	1st–2nd cent. AD	*Il.* 18.394	ἦ ῥά νν μ[οι]	ἦ ῥά νν μοι
44.	*PLond.Lit.* 25	1st–2nd cent. AD	*Il.* 18.443	οὐδέ τι οἱ	οὐδέ τι οἱ
45.	*PLond.Lit.* 25	1st–2nd cent. AD	*Il.* 18.454	καί νύ κεν	καί νύ κεν
46.	*PLond.Lit.* 28	2nd cent. AD	*Il.* 24.134	σκύζ[εσθ]άι σοι φησὶ	σκύζ[εσθ]αι σοι φησὶ
47.	*PLond.Lit.* 28	2nd cent. AD	*Il.* 24.149	κῆρυξ τίς οἱ	κῆρυξ τίς οἱ[m]
48.	*PLond.Lit.* 28	2nd cent. AD	*Il.* 24.178	κῆρυξ τίς τοι	κῆρυξ τίς τοι
49.	*PLond.Lit.* 28	2nd cent. AD	*Il.* 24.205	σιδήρειον νύ τοι	σιδήρειόν νύ τοι
50.	*PLond.Lit.* 28	2nd cent. AD	*Il.* 24.208	οὐδέ τι σ᾽[n]	οὐδέ τι σ᾽
51.	*PLond.Lit.* 28	2nd cent. AD	*Il.* 24.256	οὔ τινα φημι	οὔ τινά φημι
52.	*PLond.Lit.* 28	2nd cent. AD	*Il.* 24.278	τοὺς ῥά ποτε	τοὺς ῥά ποτε
53.	*PLond.Lit.* 28	2nd cent. AD	*Il.* 24.366	εἴ τις σε	εἴ τις σε
54.	*PLond.Lit.* 28	2nd cent. AD	*Il.* 24.415	αἴ ῥά τε	αἴ ῥά τε
55.	*PLond.Lit.* 28	2nd cent. AD	*Il.* 24.439	ἀν τις τοι[o]	ἀν τίς τοι
56.	*PLond.Lit.* 28	2nd cent. AD	*Il.* 24.494	οὔ τινα φημὶ	οὔ τινά φημι
57.	*PLond.Lit.* 28	2nd cent. AD	*Il.* 24.505	οὔ πω τις	οὔ πω τις
58.	*PLond.Lit.* 28	2nd cent. AD	*Il.* 24.521	σιδήρειόν νύ τοι	σιδήρειόν νύ τοι
59.	*PLond.Lit.* 28	2nd cent. AD	*Il.* 24.538	ὅτ᾽ τί οἱ	ὅτ᾽ τί οἱ
60.	*PLond.Lit.* 28	2nd cent. AD	*Il.* 24.553	μή με πω	μή με πω
61.	*PLond.Lit.* 28	2nd cent. AD	*Il.* 24.651	οἴ τέ μοι	οἴ τέ μοι
62.	*PLond.Lit.* 28	2nd cent. AD	*Il.* 24.653	εἴ τις σε	εἴ τίς σε
63.	*PLond.Lit.* 28	2nd cent. AD	*Il.* 24.661	ὧδέ κε μοι	ὧδέ κε μοι
64.	*PLond.Lit.* 28	2nd cent. AD	*Il.* 24.683	οὐ νύ τι[p]	οὐ νύ τι
65.	*PLond.Lit.* 28	2nd cent. AD	*Il.* 24.713	καί νύ κε	καί νύ κε
66.	*PLond.Lit.* 28	2nd cent. AD	*Il.* 24.729	ὅς τέ μιν	ὅς τέ μιν
67.	*PLond.Lit.* 28	2nd cent. AD	*Il.* 24.744	οὔ τέ κεν	οὔ τέ κεν

Continued

Table 4.3 *Continued*

Papyrus	Date of the papyrus (not necessarily of the accent marks)[a]	Place in the text	Sequence of enclitics plus preceding word, showing accents on the papyrus. (Word divisions are not necessarily on the papyrus.)	Same sequence showing accents as per the revised Göttling-Barrett system
68. *P.Lond.Lit.* 46	2nd cent. AD	Bacchylides 5.43	ὅν πω νυν	οὔ πω νυν
69. *P.Lond.Lit.* 46	2nd cent. AD	Bacchylides 17.18	καρδίαν τε οι	καρδίαν τέ οἱ
70. *P.Lond.Lit.* 46	2nd cent. AD	Bacchylides 20.9	ιππους τέ οι	ἵππους τέ οἱ

^a Dates are those given in <www.trismegistos.org>.

^b The standard reading here is ἀλλά τε μιν, but the papyrus has [αλ]λ ἄ τε μιν.

^c = fr. 14, line 8 of the papyrus. One might wonder whether papyri of Lesbian poets can be treated as part of the same body of evidence as other literary papyri, given that Lesbian accentuation (as reflected in the papyri of Lesbian poets) was significantly different from that of other dialects, with most words being assigned a recessive accent. But in general enclitics appear to be treated in the same ways on papyri of Lesbian poets as they are on other literary papyri. A priori we thus expect the same to be true for enclitics in sequence, so we see no need to exclude the three examples that come from Sappho or Alcaeus papyri.

^d παίσαν is the Lesbian feminine genitive plural of πᾶς 'all', with a Lesbian recessive accent. The -α- of the final syllable is long, and so παίσαν has a spondaic shape.

^e = fragment 1v, line 6 of the papyrus. Harder (2012: ii 510) discusses whether *ΕΣΤΙΝ* should be considered enclitic or orthotonic in this line of Callimachus, but our concern is simply with how this sequence of enclitics is accented on the papyrus, given that the scribe who added the accents here considered the *ΕΣΤΙΝ* enclitic. (The writing ἐστὶν is unlikely to represent paroxytone ἔστιν, although on papyri a grave accent mark may appear on syllables *preceding* the one carrying the main word accent.)

^f = fr. (a), line 23 of the papyrus.

^g = fr. 7, line 2 of the papyrus.

^h = fr. 1, col. ii, line 9 of the papyrus.

ⁱ Included here on the basis of the republication at *P.Oxy.* xxxiii, p. 18.

^j A correction of νυν to μιν was made via the addition of μ above the line. Since both νυν and μιν are enclitics of the same shape, the choice between these does not affect the points of interest to us.

^k This line (like some others on this papyrus) was omitted by the original scribe, and is added in the top margin by a later hand.

^l The first hand wrote σοι, but a second (who perhaps also added the accent) made a correction to οἱ (cf. already Lewis 1832: 180).

^m For κῆρυξ rather than κήρυξ as the form prescribed by our Greek grammatical texts before even one enclitic, see section 2.7.3.

ⁿ Laum (1928: 312) claims that the papyrus has οὐδέ τί σ' here (col. 2, line 40 of the papyrus), but the absence of an accent mark on τι is clear on the photograph. (Laum also suggests that the papyrus has οὐδέ τί σ' at *Il.* 24.414 = col. 7, line 28, but at this point it has οὐδ' ἔτι οἱ: see n. 68.)

^o The scribe wrote ου κέν τις τοι (with or without the accent) before correction to ουκ ἀν τις τοι. According to Lewis (1832: 183) the correction was made by a second hand (more neutrally West 1998–2000), apparatus criticus *ad loc.*); since most accents were also added by a second hand, the accent should probably be taken to go with the corrected reading. The involvement of more than one hand is difficult to verify from the photograph in this instance, as the photograph is unclear just here.

^p With the following two words, the papyrus has οἱ νύ τι σοί γε. Conceivably ΣΟΙ is taken to be enclitic, so that we have a sequence of four enclitics, accented exactly as predicted by the revised Göttling-Barrett principle. But given the emphasis lent to the preceding word by γε, it is perhaps more likely that ΣΟΙ is taken to be orthotonic here.

sequences with a single enclitic, then τά ῥά σφ' is the expected accentuation. In our sample of accented papyri, this is the only instance in which a papyrus marks an accent induced by an enclitic on a preceding paroxytone sequence with non-trochaic shape. Our evidence from the Homeric scholia also turned up one example of such a sequence, again involving an enclitic beginning with σφ- (see section 4.2.5, on passage (4.22)). The similarly isolated appearance of τά ῥά σφ in our sample of accented papyri strengthens the conclusion that these are not random exceptions.

The other two examples that require discussion are θνητός τ' εστι (Table 4.3, item 41) and τίς ποτ' εστιν (Table 4.3, item 23). In both examples, the first of two consecutive enclitics has lost its last or only vowel by elision. If this vowel were not elided, we would expect the revised Göttling-Barrett system to give θνητός τέ ἐστι and τίς ποτέ ἐστιν. But what should we expect from the same system when elision does occur? Since the revised Göttling-Barrett system consists of a recursive application of the rules that apply when there is a single enclitic, the most important question here is what happens when even a single enclitic loses its last or only vowel by elision. Where the enclitic is monosyllabic, the standard principle is clear: the enclitic ends up unaccented and has the same effect (or lack of effect) on the accent of the preceding word as it would if not elided.[71] According to the tradition we have inherited from medieval manuscripts, and which we take to be probably ancient, the same is true for the disyllabic enclitics τιν(ά) and ποτ(έ).[72] On this basis we should expect our two sequences to begin θνητός τ' and τίς ποτ'. It is less clear whether a further enclitic *following* an elided one should be accented as if the preceding enclitic were not elided. In the sequence ΘΝΗΤΟΣ Τ' 'ΕΣΤΙ, the 'ΕΣΤΙ follows a syllable with an acute accent both 'before elision' (i.e. in unelided θνητός τέ ἐστι) and 'after elision'

---

[71] See e.g. *On enclitics 1*, §m (on the example ἵνά σφ' ἀγορή τε θέμις τε) and *On enclitics 2*, §e (on the example Φοίβῳ θ' ἱερὴν ἑκατόμβην).

[72] In this respect, indefinite *TINA* and *ΠΟΤΕ* belong to a group of exceptions to the principle that the accent of a non-monosyllabic word considered oxytone shifts to the penultimate syllable if its final vowel is elided (e.g. δειλέ 'unhappy man' (vocative) → δειλ'). For the full list of forms traditionally treated as exceptions to this principle, see Probert (2003: 39, 152). As noted there, all the relevant words are either proclitics or enclitics, but not all disyllabic *enclitics* have traditionally been treated in the same way. To our knowledge, explicit ancient statements relevant to the idea that certain oxytone words simply lose their accent if the accented vowel is elided all focus on prepositions (see Sch. *Il.* 2.6a (A); Sch. *Il.* 2.150b¹ (A) and b² (bT); Sch. *Il.* 4.97a (AbT); Sch. *Il.* 7.167a (A); Sch. *Il.* 8.163a (A); Sch. *Il.* 9.456b (A); Sch. *Il.* 9.582 (A); Sch. *Il.* 10.273b (A); Sch. *Il.* 15.144; Sch. *Il.* 18.191a (A) and b (AbT); Sch. *Il.* 18.244a (A); Sch. *Il.* 18.400a¹ (A) and b (bT); Sch. *Il.* 21.588 b¹ (A) and b² (T); Sch. *Od.* 4.311a Pontani (H); Sch. *Od.* 16.19 (H); John Philoponus, *Praecepta Tonica* 130 Xenis). The earliest evidence for the application of this idea to indefinite τιν(ά) and ποτ(έ) is likely to come from accented papyri, and we have not attempted a study of the papyrological evidence on this point, but we are not aware of any evidence to suggest that any different principle applied to these words at an early date.

(i.e. in $\theta\nu\eta\tau\acute{o}s$ τ' $\dot{\epsilon}\sigma\tau\iota$); the outcome will therefore be $\theta\nu\eta\tau\acute{o}s$ τ' $\dot{\epsilon}\sigma\tau\iota$ regardless of whether the treatment of $\text{'}E\Sigma TI$ is determined 'before' or 'after' the elision. At Menander, *Misoumenos* 139, we tentatively give the expected accentuation as $\tau\acute{\iota}s$ $\pi o\tau$' $\dot{\epsilon}\sigma\tau\acute{\iota}\nu$ (rather than $\tau\acute{\iota}s$ $\pi o\tau$' $\dot{\epsilon}\sigma\tau\iota\nu$), with a disyllabic enclitic at the end of a sequence receiving an accent if preceded by any unaccented syllable—but the argument will not depend on the treatment of a disyllabic enclitic at the end of a sequence.

To return to our collection of examples as a whole, Table 4.4 shows the same sequences of enclitics as Table 4.3, but groups them so as to show the relationship between the following two points: (i) whether the papyrus shows an accent on the first enclitic of the sequence, and (ii) whether we expect the first enclitic to be accented under the revised Göttling-Barrett system. Since most of the sequences in our collection contain precisely two enclitics (and since the last enclitic in most sequences is unaccented, regardless of the precise principle being applied), the main way in which we can hope to see what principle (if any) the writers of these papyri had in mind is to look at the treatment of the first enclitic in each sequence.

In addition to showing (once again) that in our sample we never find an accent mark on a syllable that the revised Göttling-Barrett system would make unaccented, Table 4.4 shows that this is very unlikely to be a mere coincidence. Of the seventy sequences of enclitics in our sample altogether, forty-two (60%) are

Table 4.4 The sequences of enclitics (plus the preceding non-enclitic word) listed in Table 4.3, grouped according to whether the first enclitic has an accent mark and whether we expect that enclitic to be accented under the revised Göttling-Barrett system. Sequences are numbered as in Table 4.3.

	The first enclitic would be accented by the revised Göttling-Barrett system	The first enclitic would not be accented by the revised Göttling-Barrett system
The papyrus shows an accent on the first enclitic	42 3. $\epsilon\iota$ $\pi o\tau\acute{\epsilon}$ $\mu o\iota$ 6. $\acute{o}\nu$ $\rho\acute{a}$ $\tau\epsilon$ 7. $\epsilon\pi os$ $\tau\acute{\epsilon}$ $\mu\iota\nu$ 8. $o\upsilon$ $\tau\acute{\iota}s$ $\tau o\iota$ 9. $\theta\epsilon os$ $\nu\acute{\upsilon}$ $\tau\iota s$ $\epsilon\sigma[\tau]\iota$ 11. $\kappa[o]\mu\iota[\sigma]\alpha\iota$ $\tau\acute{\epsilon}$ $\mu\epsilon$ 12. $[o]\upsilon\tau\acute{\epsilon}$ $\tau\iota\nu$' 13. $\alpha\iota$ $\kappa\acute{\epsilon}$ $\pi o\theta\iota$ 14. $\chi\theta\acute{o}\nu a$ $\tau\acute{o}\iota$ $\pi o\tau\epsilon$ 15. $\epsilon\acute{\iota}$ $\pi\acute{\epsilon}\rho$ $\mu\epsilon$ 18. $[\acute{o}s]$ $\tau\acute{\epsilon}$ $\tau\epsilon\upsilon$ 20. $\acute{\omega}\tau\tau\acute{\iota}$ σ' 21. $\rho\tau\tau\iota\nu\acute{a}$ $\tau o\iota$ 22. $[\theta]\eta\kappa\acute{\epsilon}\nu$ $\tau\acute{\epsilon}$ $\nu\iota\nu$	0

	The first enclitic would be accented by the revised Göttling-Barrett system	The first enclitic would not be accented by the revised Göttling-Barrett system
	24. τά ρά σφ 25. ει κέν ὁι 27. εὐ νύ τις 28. άι κέν πως 29. ούτέ τι πω 30. πολλ]η τέ οι 31. ϙάι νύ κεν 32. ὡς ποτέ μοι 36. α[ι] κέ σ᾽ 37. ἄι κέν πως 38. ὡι ρά θ᾽ 39. ἦ ρά νυ 42. Θέτις νύ τι 43. ἦ ρά νυ μ[οι] 45. καί νύ κεν 47. κηρυξ τίς οἱ 48. κηρυξ τίς τοι 49. σιδήρειον νύ τοι 52. τούς ρά ποτε 54. αἱ ρά τε 58. σιδήρειον νύ τοι 59. ὅτ᾽ τί οἱ 61. οἱ τέ μοι 64. ού νύ τι 65. καί νύ κε 66. ὅς τέ μιν 67. ού τέ κεν 70. ιππους τέ οἱ	
The papyrus does not show an accent on the first enclitic	**10** 16. πάισαν κε με 17. είτε τις 34. ὅττι νιν 51. ού τινα φημι 53. έι τις σε 55. άν τις τοι 56. ού τινα φημί 60. μή με πω 62. εί τις σε 69. καρδίαν τε οι	**18** 1. ἄ τε μιν 2. ουδέ ἑ φὴμι 4. δέ τε μ᾽ 5. ουδέ με φὴσιν 10. μή πως ὁι 19. όν πως εστὶν 23. τίς ποτ᾽ εστιν 26. δέ τε μιν 33. ουδέ τι οι 35. ουδέ ἑ φημι 40. δή που τις 41. θνητός τ᾽ εστι 44. ουδέ τι ὁι 46. σκυζ[εσθ]άι σοι φησὶ 50. ουδέ τι σ᾽ 57. ού πω τις 63. ὡδέ κε μοι 68. όν πω νιν

shown with an accent mark on the first enclitic. If the writers of the papyri had the 'traditional' system in mind (every enclitic except the last gets an accent on its last or only syllable), we should expect these accent marks to be distributed more or less evenly between the sequences for which the revised Göttling-Barrett system predicts an accent on the first enclitic and those for which it predicts no accent on that enclitic. Instead, out of fifty-two sequences for which the revised Göttling-Barrett system predicts an accent on the first enclitic, forty-two (81%) have an accent mark on that enclitic on the papyrus, but out of eighteen sequences for which the same system predicts no accent on the first enclitic, none (0%) have an accent mark on that enclitic.[73]

In addition, our sample includes three sequences containing three enclitics: θεος νύ τις εσ[τ]ι (Table 4.3, item 9), ούτέ τι πω (Table 4.3, item 29), and ἢ ῥά νυ μ[οι] (Table 4.3, item 43). For all three sequences, the second as well as the first enclitic is treated in accordance with the revised Göttling-Barrett system. In each instance, what is needed is an accent on the first enclitic and then no accent on the second, since ἢ ῥα makes a properispomenon sequence, (θε)ός νυ and ού-τε make paroxytone trochaic sequences, and νύ τις, -τέ τι, and ῥά νυ make paroxytone pyrrhic sequences. While the more plentiful and hence more important evidence comes from the treatment of the first enclitic in each sequence, the treatment of these longer sequences strengthens the conclusion that the writers of papyri had in mind either the revised Göttling-Barrett system or a system whose results were almost identical: either the revised Göttling-Barrett system or something like Herodian's rules of thumb. The evidence of accented papyri therefore confirms that the revised Göttling-Barrett system was in use around and after Herodian's day, via an implicit awareness of the system as such or via Herodian's approximation.

4.4 Venetus A

Our final piece of evidence for the revised Göttling-Barrett system is the tenth-century *Iliad* manuscript Marcianus Graecus 822 (Z.454), or 'Venetus A.'[74] We have already seen that the revised Göttling-Barrett system lies behind the accents prescribed for sequences of enclitics in the Homeric scholia deriving from Herodian, many of which come down to us as marginal notes in this manuscript.

---

[73] A Pearson's chi-squared test with one degree of freedom, using the figures shown in bold in Table 4.4 as a 2 × 2 contingency table, gives a p-value of 1.7×10^{-9}—a highly significant result.

[74] Our discussion of Venetus A is based on the images made available by the Homer Multitext Project at <www.homermultitext.org/facsimiles/venetus-a-2020/pages>. Readings are based on our own inspection of the images; at the time of writing, they do not always agree with the transcriptions made available by the Homer Multitext Project, but in these cases we have shared our readings with the Homer Multitext Project.

In this section, we consider what principle guided the location of actual accent marks on the text of Venetus A.

To determine what principle the scribe might have had in mind, it would be ideal if we could formulate a hypothesis (e.g. 'sequences of enclitics in Venetus A are accented according to the revised Göttling-Barrett system'), and find that the accents of Venetus A always match those predicted by our hypothesis. Surprisingly, something like this actually worked for the sample of accented literary papyri considered in section 4.3.[75] For the accents written on the text of Venetus A, however, it is fairly clear that no system was deployed with absolute consistency, since identical sequences of enclitics are sometimes accented differently on different occasions. For example, the sequence 'OY TI MOI (where the underlined words are enclitics) appears as οὔ τί μοι at Il. 1.153 and Il. 3.164, but as οὔ τι μοι at Il. 1.335; 'H 'PA TIΣ 'EΣTI appears as ἦ ῥά τίς ἐστι at Il. 7.446, but as ἦ ῥά τις ἐστὶ at Il. 23.103. To see what (if any) principle the scribe had in mind, we therefore need to test hypotheses against one another: what principle, if any, gives us the best match for the accents the scribe has actually written? We claim that the answer is either the revised Göttling-Barrett system itself or an approximation to this system deriving from Herodian's rules of thumb. Since Herodian's rules of thumb gave very similar results to those of the revised Göttling-Barrett system (this was the whole point of the rules of thumb), deciding between these two possibilities will be an interesting problem. But first we need to show why we take a system of one form or the other to have guided the accent marks in this manuscript in the first place.

As a sample against which to test hypotheses, we have taken the first 250 sequences[76] of enclitics that appear in Venetus A, omitting those folios of Venetus

---

[75] Nevertheless, the conclusions of section 4.3 do not depend crucially on the absolute consistency with which our sample of accented papyri turned out to be consistent with the hypothesis tested there, i.e. that the acutes and circumflexes written on sequences of enclitics (plus the preceding word) on papyri never contradict those predicted by the revised Göttling-Barrett system. We would not be surprised if a reader soon found a counter-example from an accented literary papyrus outside our sample, and it would take more than the occasional counter-example to suggest that the accentuation of sequences of enclitics has nothing to do with the revised Göttling-Barrett system. But counter-examples would hold out the possibility of formulating alternative hypotheses and finding out which gives the best account of the evidence.

[76] It is clear that this is a large enough sample to give robust results, because the percentage success rates we give for the various hypotheses we test (to be laid out shortly) are broadly similar to those obtained from smaller sub-sets of this sample; most importantly, the success rates of the different hypotheses relative to one another are broadly similar in smaller subsets of the sample. For example, the first set of percentage success rates given in the last row of Table Ap.1 runs (from left to right) 62%, 62%, 74%, 74%, 74%, and 76%; if only the first 100 sequences of enclitics in that table had been considered, the success rates would have been 66%, 64%, 80%, 77%, 79%, and 82%. Similarly, the first set of percentage success rates given in the last row of Table Ap.2 runs 67%, 65%, 69%, 45%, 48%, 43%, 26%, and 60%; if only the first 100 sequences of enclitics had been considered, the success rates would have been 70%, 69%, 74%, 42%, 47%, 45%, 25%, and 65%. Our analysis could thus have been based on 100 sequences of enclitics rather than 250 without the results being substantially different. We base the briefer analysis of Venetus B in Appendix B on 100 sequences.

A for which we have only a fifteenth-century replacement for the originals.[77] Decisions on what to count as a sequence of enclitics are those laid out at n. 42,[78] but we have disregarded places where Venetus A's text does not involve a sequence of more than one enclitic, or may well not be intended to involve one.[79]

The results of our investigation are presented in Appendix A, in two tables. The first of these (Table Ap.1) compares Venetus A's accentuation of our 250 sequences with the ways in which those same sequences would be accented under the five systems discussed in section 4.2.4: (i) the 'traditional' system; (ii) the 'traditional' system except that indefinite $ΠΟΥ$, $ΠΗ(Ι)$, $ΠΩΣ$, and $ΠΩ$ are left unaccented; (iii) the 'traditional' system except that consecutive acute accents are avoided on pyrrhic or iambic sequences by working forwards from the word preceding the first enclitic, and leaving a syllable unaccented after a short syllable to which an acute accent has already been assigned; (iv) the 'traditional' system except that indefinite $ΠΟΥ$, $ΠΗ(Ι)$, $ΠΩΣ$, and $ΠΩ$ are left unaccented AND consecutive acute accents are avoided on pyrrhic or iambic sequences (as for (iii)); and (v) the revised Göttling-Barrett system. (Column (vi) adds a further hypothesis, which we leave out of account for the time being.) As can be seen from the figures given in the last row of Table Ap.1, systems (i) and (ii) correctly 'predict' Venetus A's accentuation of a sequence of enclitics 62% of the time, while systems (iii)–(v) do so 74% of the time. Each of the systems (i)–(v) thus correctly 'predicts' Venetus A's accentuation of a sequence of enclitics considerably more than half the time. But systems (iii)–(v) do noticeably better in this respect than (i)–(ii), and the three systems with the higher success rate comprise the revised Göttling-Barrett system and two of the approximations to this system.

All this makes it much more likely that the scribe of Venetus A has either the revised Göttling-Barrett system or some (or all) of Herodian's rules of thumb in mind than that he is being guided by the traditional system. But could he have had in mind a different system altogether: is there a system that correctly predicts

---

[77] See West (1998–2000: vol. i, p. xi). For our sample, this means that we omit sequences of enclitics from the part of the poem beginning at *Il.* 5.336 and ending at *Il.* 5.635.

[78] In addition to the decisions laid out there, we disregard ὍΤΕ Μ' at *Il.* 1.518, since the scribe probably took ὅτε as a single non-enclitic word; and ΕΙΣ Ὁ ΚΕ Σ' at *Il.* 3.409 and ΕΙΣ Ὁ ΚΕ ΠΕΡ at *Il.* 9.46, since Venetus A presents εἰσόκε as one word (although it is possible that *ΚΕ* was nevertheless taken to be the enclitic).

[79] E.g. *Il.* 6.18, where West reads ὅς ῥά οἱ but Venetus A has ὅς ῥα τοθ', and *Il.* 9.73, where West reads πᾶσά τοί ἐσθ' but Venetus A's πᾶσά τοι ἔσθ' suggests strongly that ΕΣΤ(Ι) is being considered orthotonic. We disregard ΟΥ ΠΩ ΠΟΤΕ ΜΟΙ at *Il.* 1.106, where Venetus A has οὐ πώποτε μοι, since the lack of acute accent on the οὐ suggests the scribe thought of πώποτε as a single non-enclitic word. We likewise disregard *Il.* 1.154 and *Il.* 3.442, where Venetus A has γαρ πώποτ' and γαρ πώποτέ μ' respectively: the lack of accent on γαρ is again consistent with a non-enclitic-word analysis of πώποτε. We also disregard sequences such as ΟΥΔΕ ΝΥ ΣΟΙ ΠΕΡ at *Il.* 8.201, where ΣΟΙ is plausibly taken to be orthotonic. (West's view that ΣΟΙ is orthotonic here is clear from his accentuation οὐδέ νυ σοί περ, since he follows the traditional rule that in a sequence of enclitics, each enclitic except the last gets an accent on its last or only syllable. Venetus A also presents the sequence as οὐδέ νυ σοί περ, and this is compatible with the same view, although other explanations would also be possible.)

Venetus A's accentuation more than 74% of the time? To answer this question, we have further tested Venetus A's accentuation of our 250 sequences of enclitics against the claims to be listed shortly, all of which can either be found in existing scholarly literature or are our attempts to make existing claims precise enough to be testable.[80] For those who would like to understand the source of each claim, this information is laid out in the footnotes attached to the list below. Some of the ideas in question have been presented as claims about the 'real' ancient rule, and some as claims to the effect that the systems in question are hinted at in the grammatical tradition and/or implemented in some manuscripts. Manuscripts about which claims have been made include Venetus A itself, the eleventh-century *Iliad* manuscript known as 'Venetus B' (Marcianus Graecus 821 = Z.453), and other often unspecified manuscripts. Our aim here is to see whether any of these claims help to shed light on the practice of Venetus A, regardless of whether they are valid for other manuscripts for which they might have been designed. Given the place which Venetus B has also occupied in scholarship on this subject, however, in Appendix B we analyse a sample of sequences of enclitics from Venetus B. But for now our focus is on Venetus A, and the further hypotheses against which we test the practice of this manuscript are the following:

(A)   Further claims to the effect that the traditional system applies, subject to certain exceptions:

(Ai)   A monosyllabic enclitic is unaccented if an unelided disyllabic one follows.[81]

e.g. εἴ πέρ τίς σέ μοι φησίν ποτε

(Aii)   Enclitic pronoun forms are always unaccented, except forms of indefinite *ΤΙΣ*.[82]

---

[80] In practice, these claims have not always been clearly distinguished from one another. For example, Vendryes (1904: 88) suggests that the Homeric manuscript Venetus B (Marcianus Graecus 821= Z.453) accents every other enclitic, and then continues as if this comes to the same thing as Göttling's (1835: 405) suggestion. In support of his own system, which does agree with Göttling's suggestion, Barrett (1964: 427 n. 4) cites not Göttling but Vendryes (1904: 88–9).

[81] Lipsius (1863: 50–5) claims that biblical manuscripts follow the traditional system under most circumstances, but that a monosyllabic enclitic is unaccented before a disyllabic enclitic, and the disyllabic enclitic 'keeps its own accent' under these circumstances (cf. Kühner and Blass 1890–2: i. 343). We add the specification 'unelided', which is consistent with Lipsius' examples and gives more matches between the predictions of his system and the practice of Venetus A—a desirable outcome, since we wish to see how close any system can come to producing the results we actually see in Venetus A.

[82] Laum (1928: 243–6, 307–12, 326). In addition to his view on enclitic pronoun forms, Laum himself (1928: 245–6) thought that 'ΟΥΠΩ(Σ) and ΜΗΠΩ(Σ) were single words and that for this reason ΠΩΣ and ΠΩ were left unaccented in these sequences before an enclitic. In our view the evidence from multiple directions does indeed point to unaccented ΠΩΣ or ΠΩ after 'ΟΥ or ΜΗ and before a further enclitic, not for the reason Laum gave but because this is the accentuation required by the revised Göttling-Barrett system (see section 4.2.2). It will be most helpful for our discussion to test hypothesis (Aii) as it stands, without adding a requirement to implement Laum's view on 'ΟΥΠΩ(Σ) and ΜΗΠΩ(Σ), in order to make clear the independent effect of his view on the treatment of enclitic pronoun forms. We note, however, that with the addition of a requirement to leave ΠΩΣ and ΠΩ

e.g. *εἴ πέρ τίς σε μοι φησίν ποτε*

(Aiii) The following are left unaccented: (a) a monosyllabic enclitic ending in a short vowel, after a syllable ending in a short accented
vowel; (b) the enclitics *ΠΩ* and *ΠΩΣ*.[83]

e.g. *εἴ πέρ τίς σέ μοί φησίν ποτε, οὐδέ τι μοι, οὔ πω μοι, οὔ
πω φησίν*

(B) A claim to the effect that accents fell on alternate enclitics.[84] In order to
implement this idea, we distinguish between five ways in which it
might work:

(Bi) Begin the alternation by accenting the first enclitic to be accentable
without causing accents on successive syllables (after also avoiding
accents on successive syllables on the word preceding the first
enclitic), and then work forwards:

*εἴ περ τίς σε μοί φησιν ποτέ, πῶς τις τοι, οὔ θην μιν, αἰδοῖος τέ
μοι ἐσσί, ἄλλος κέν τις*

---

unaccented after *ΟΥ* or *ΜΗ*, the success rate of hypothesis (Aii) at predicting the practice of Venetus
A would go up from 66% to 68%. As regards Laum's view on the treatment of enclitic pronoun forms,
this was partly based on a misinterpretation of Homeric scholia, as noted at n. 64. Laum also found
some evidence for his view in accented papyri, although Erbse (1960: 400–1) dismissed this as too
scanty to be significant, and our own investigation of accented papyri turned up two misreadings of
his by chance (see Table 4.3, note n); Laum himself noted that accented papyri do not always bear out
his view of the status of indefinite *ΤΙΣ* (Laum 1928: 312 with n. 2). In spite of these limitations to his
approach, Laum's view on the status of enclitic pronoun forms (as well as his view on *ΟΥΠΩ(Σ)* and
ΜΗΠΩ(Σ)) produces results that often coincide with our own, and with the practice of Venetus A;
the reasons for this will be discussed further on.
[83] La Roche (1866: 414–16) claims that ancient grammatical texts mention certain exceptions to
the traditional system, and that these are observed in the *Iliad* manuscript Venetus A. Although the
precise claims are not made fully clear, he appears to intend the exceptions to the traditional principle
that we give as (a) and (b).
[84] Vendryes (1904: 88) claims that enclitics are accented 'de deux en deux' in the *Iliad* manuscript
Venetus B (Marcianus Graecus 821 = Z.453) and in 'manuscrits anciens de la bible'; as examples he
gives *ἤ νυ σέ που* and *εἴ περ τίς σε μοί φησι* (the first of these is a Homeric example, from *Il.* 5.812, but
in Venetus B it is in fact accented *ἤ, νύ σέ που*). His examples leave it unclear how he thought the
position of the first accented enclitic was calculated, but systems (Bi)–(Biii) are worth considering
since some take Greek to have avoided accents that are in some sense too close together, at least within
a unit consisting of a full word or a full word plus following enclitics; compare Göttling's (1835: 405–6)
notion that the rules of Greek accentuation do not normally allow 'dass zwei Sylben unmittelbar
neben einander in einem Worte betont werden'. On the other hand a principle of alternation need not
have been motivated by any avoidance of successive accents. Devine and Stephens (1994: 373) claim
that the practice of Venetus B is to place accents on alternate enclitics, beginning with the second
enclitic from the end (they too give the example *ἤ νυ σέ που*). This idea requires a decision to be made
about what happens to the word preceding the first enclitic if there is an even number of enclitics.
Since claims about accents on alternating enclitics are said to derive from Venetus B, some support for
system (Biv) might be seen in accentuations such as *μὴ νύ τοι* in Venetus B (in the sample considered
in Appendix B, *μὴ νύ τοι* occurs at *Il.* 1.28 and 1.566), and some accentuations of this type also occur
in Venetus A (for example, *μὴ νύ τοι* occurs there at *Il.* 1.28, but not at *Il.* 1.566). (For our own conclusion on Venetus B, which will ultimately be a different one, see Appendix B.) Both in Venetus B and in
Venetus A we also find accentuations of the type *αἴ κέν πως*, which cannot reflect system (Biv) but
could reflect system (Bv) (as well as, in this instance, numerous other systems); for this reason, we
consider system (Bv) worth testing too.

(Bii) Begin the alternation by accenting the first enclitic to be accentable without causing *acutes* on successive syllables (after also avoiding acutes on successive syllables on the word preceding the first enclitic), and then work forwards:

εἴ περ τίς σε μοί φησιν ποτέ, πῶς τίς τοι, οὔ θην μιν, αἰδοῖός τε μοί ἐσσι, ἄλλος κέν τις

(Biii) Begin the alternation by accenting the first enclitic to be accentable without causing accents on successive morae (after also avoiding accents on successive morae on the word preceding the first enclitic), and then work forwards. A circumflex counts as an accent on the first mora of a long vowel or diphthong; an acute on a long vowel or diphthong counts as an accent on the second mora.[85]

εἴ περ τίς σε μοί φησιν ποτέ, πῶς τίς τοι, οὔ θήν μιν, αἰδοῖός τε μοί ἐσσι, ἄλλος κέν τις

(Biv) Begin the alternation by accenting the second enclitic from the end, and then work backwards. If there is an even number of enclitics, do not allow the first enclitic to affect the accent of the preceding word (so do not add any additional accent, and do not change a grave to an acute):

εἰ (= εἴ)[86] πέρ τις σέ μοι φησίν ποτε, πῶς τίς τοι, ἄλλος κέν τις, αἰδοῖός τε μοί ἐσσι

(Bv) Begin the alternation by accenting the second enclitic from the end, and then work backwards. But regardless of the number of enclitics, accent the word preceding the first enclitic in accordance with the normal ancient rules applying to words followed by a single enclitic.

εἴ πέρ τις σέ μοι φησίν ποτε, πῶς τίς τοι, ἄλλός κέν τις, αἰδοῖός τε μοί ἐσσι

(C) Göttling and Barrett's original system, for which see section 4.1:[87]

εἴ περ τίς σε μοί φησίν ποτε, πῶς τίς τοι, οὔ θην μιν, αἰδοῖός τε μοί ἐσσι, ἄλλος κέν τις

For all 250 sequences of enclitics in our sample, this system gives the same result as system (Bii), and in Table Ap.2 we therefore devote a single column to the results of both these systems. The two systems are nevertheless different in principle, as there exist sequences for which they would give

---

[85] We evaluate this possibility on the basis that all long vowels and diphthongs have two morae for the purposes of calculating whether accents fall on successive morae or not (for the possibility that the -οι of μοι, σοι, and τοι counted 'short for accentuation', see the end of this section). The effect of this decision is very small, but it slightly increases the number of instances in which systems (Bii) and (Biii) give different results from one another.

[86] We write (for example) εἰ rather than εἴ in contexts where ΈΙ does not have an acute, and similarly for other words which are today normally written without an accent mark in such contexts. This is also the usual practice of Venetus A, in common with most manuscripts.

[87] Göttling (1835: 405); Barrett (1964: 426–7).

different results: in addition to εἴ περ τίς σε μοί φησίν ποτε (system C) / εἴ περ τίς σε μοί φησιν ποτέ (system Bii), compare e.g. τυραννεῖν μέ φᾱσί τινες[88] (system C) / τυραννεῖν μέ φᾱσι τινές (system Bii)

The results of this investigation are presented in the second table in Appendix A (Table Ap.2). A first headline is that none of our alternative hypotheses does as well at predicting the practice of Venetus A as systems (iii), (iv), and (v) of Table Ap.1 (the revised Göttling-Barrett system and two of the approximations to this system), with their success rates of 74%. But there is a second point of interest: the success rates of some of the alternative hypotheses come fairly close to this. In particular, systems (Ai), (Aii), and (Aiii) correctly predict the practice of Venetus A 65%–69% of the time. In effect, these three systems amount to further approximations to the revised Göttling-Barrett system, and it is worth pausing for a moment on why this should be so.

The answer to this question is most immediately apparent for system (Aiii), because this system captures a subset of the deviations from the traditional system that are also captured by the ancient approximations to the revised Göttling-Barrett system (i.e. by system (iv) of Table Ap.1). Firstly, by leaving a monosyllabic enclitic ending in a short vowel unaccented after a syllable ending in a short accented vowel, system (Aiii) avoids successive acute accents on some pyrrhic sequences, while leaving iambic sequences and other pyrrhic sequences to follow the traditional rule. Secondly, by leaving indefinite ΠΩΣ and ΠΩ unaccented, system (Aiii) achieves a more limited version of the effect that is achieved by leaving indefinite ΠΟΥ, ΠΗ(Ι), ΠΩΣ, and ΠΩ unaccented. System (Aiii) was formulated by La Roche as an account of the practice of Venetus A itself (see n. 83), and credit is due to him for being on very much the right lines.

At first sight, it is more surprising that systems (Ai) and (Aii) should amount to further approximations to the revised Göttling-Barrett system. Both systems give different outcomes from the traditional system for some sequences, and for some of these (Ai) or (Aii) gives the same outcome as the revised Göttling-Barrett system, but for other sequences it is the traditional system that gives the same outcome as the revised Göttling-Barrett system. All this can be visualized from the four middle columns of Table 4.5. These give the sequences in our Homeric sample for which system (Ai) and/or (Aii) gives a different result from that of the traditional system, showing how these are accented according to the traditional system, system (Ai), system (Aii), and the revised Göttling-Barrett system. Shading draws attention to sequences accented in ways that differ from the results of the revised Göttling-Barrett system. Where a sequence is shaded for the traditional system but unshaded for system (Ai) and/or (Aii), then,

---

[88]   Dio Chrysostom, *Oratio* 47.18: 'Some say that I am behaving as a tyrant'.

Table 4.5 Sequences of enclitics for which system (Ai) and/or (Aii) gives a different result from that of the traditional system (out of the 250 Homeric sequences of enclitics considered in Appendix A), accented according to four different systems and as in Venetus A. The word preceding the first enclitic in the sequence is included, and enclitics are underlined. Shading indicates a way of accenting a sequence that differs from the result of the revised Göttling-Barrett system.

Line of *Iliad*	'Traditional' system: give every enclitic except the last an accent (normally an acute) on its last or only syllable	System (Ai): 'Traditional' system but a monosyllabic enclitic is unaccented if a non-elided disyllabic one follows	System (Aii): 'Traditional' system but enclitic pronoun forms are unaccented, except forms of indefinite *ΤΙΣ*	Revised Göttling-Barrett system (apply the ancient rules for a single enclitic, each time a new enclitic is added)	Venetus A
1.8	τίς τάρ σφωε	τίς ταρ σφωε	τίς τάρ σφωε	τίς τάρ σφωε	τίς τάρ σφωε
1.114	οὔ ἕθέν ἐστι	οὔ ἕθέν ἐστι	οὔ ἕθέν ἐστί	οὔ ἕθέν ἐστι	οὔ ἕθέν ἐστι
1.128	αἴ κέ πόθι	αἴ κε πόθι	αἴ κέ πόθι	αἴ κέ πόθι	αἴ κέ ποθι
1.176	δέ μοί ἐσσί	δέ μοι ἐσσί	δέ μοι ἐσσί	δέ μοι ἐσσί	δέ μοι ἐσσί
1.300	ἄ μοί ἐστί	ἄ μοι ἐστί	ἄ μοι ἐστί	ἄ μοι ἐστί	ἄ μοι ἐστί
1.521	καί τέ μέ φησί	καί τέ με φησί	καί τέ με φησί	καί τέ με φησί	καί τέ με φησί
1.557	γάρ σοί γε	γάρ σοί γε	γάρ σοι γε	γάρ σοι γε	γάρ σοί γε
2.238	ἤ ῥά τί οἱ	ἤ ῥά τί οἱ	ἤ ῥά τί οἱ	ἤ ῥά τι οἱ	ἤ ῥά τι οἱ
3.172	αἰδοῖός τέ μοί ἐσσί	αἰδοῖός τέ μοι ἐσσί	αἰδοῖός τέ μοι ἐσσί	αἰδοῖός τέ μοι ἐσσί	αἰδοῖός τέ μοι ἐσσί
3.242	ἄ μοί ἐστίν	ἄ μοι ἐστίν	ἄ μοι ἐστίν	ἄ μοι ἐστίν	ἄ μοι ἐστίν
4.48	γάρ μοί ποτέ	γάρ μοι ποτέ	γάρ μοι ποτέ	γάρ μοι ποτέ	γάρ μοί ποτε
4.93	ἤ ῥά νύ μοί τι	ἤ ῥά νύ μοί τι	ἤ ῥά νύ μοί τι	ἤ ῥά νυ μοί τι	ἤ ῥά νύ μοί τι
4.219	τά οἱ ποτέ	τά οἱ ποτέ	τά οἱ ποτέ	τά οἱ ποτέ	τά οἱ ποτέ
5.103	οὐδέ ἑ φημί	οὐδέ ἑ φημί	οὐδέ ἑ φημί	οὐδέ ἑ φημί	οὐδέ ἑ φημί

Continued

Table 4.5 *Continued*

Line of *Iliad*	'Traditional' system: give every enclitic except the last an accent (normally an acute) on its last or only syllable	System (Ai): 'Traditional' system but a monosyllabic enclitic is unaccented if a non-elided disyllabic one follows	System (Aii): 'Traditional' system but enclitic pronoun forms are unaccented, except forms of indefinite *ΤΙΣ*	Revised Göttling-Barrett system (apply the ancient rules for a single enclitic, each time a new enclitic is added)	Venetus A
5.119	οὐδέ μέ φησι	οὐδέ μέ φησι	οὐδέ με φησί	οὐδέ με φησί	οὐδέ με φησὶ
5.191	θεός νύ τίς ἐστι	θεός νύ τις ἐστὶ	θεός νύ τίς ἐστι	θεός νύ τις ἐστὶ	θεός νύ τίς ἐστι
5.700	οὔ-τέ ποτε	οὔ-τε ποτὲ	οὔ-τέ ποτε	οὔ-τέ ποτε	οὔτέ ποτε
5.812	ἤ νύ σέ που	ἤ νύ σέ που	ἤ νύ σε που	ἤ νύ σε που	ἤ νύ σέ που
5.890	δέ μοί ἐσσι	δέ μοι ἐσσὶ	δέ μοι ἐσσὶ	δέ μοι ἐσσὶ	δέ μοι ἐσσὶ
6.100	ὅν πέρ φασι	ὅν περ φασὶ	ὅν πέρ φασι	ὅν πέρ φασι	ὅν πέρ φασι
6.142	δέ τίς ἐσσι	δέ τις ἐσσὶ	δέ τίς ἐσσι	δέ τις ἐσσὶ	δέ τις ἐσσι
6.267	οὐδέ πῆ ἐστι	οὐδέ πῆ ἐστὶ	οὐδέ πῆ ἐστι	οὐδέ πῃ ἐστὶ	οὐδέ πῃ ἐστὶ
6.413	οὐδέ μοί ἐστι	οὐδέ μοί ἐστι	οὐδέ μοι ἐστὶ	οὐδέ μοι ἐστὶ	οὐδέ μοι ἐστι
6.429	σύ μοί ἐσσι	σύ μοι ἐσσὶ	σύ μοι ἐσσὶ	σύ μοι ἐσσὶ	σύ μοι ἐσσὶ
6.486	μή μοί τι	μή μοί τι	μή μοι τι	μή μοι τι	μή μοί τι
6.526	αἴ κέ ποθι	αἴ κε ποθὶ	αἴ κέ ποθι	αἴ κέ ποθι	αἴ κέ ποθι
7.28	εἴ μοί τι	εἴ μοί τι	εἴ μοι τι	εἴ μοί τι	εἴ μοί τι
7.48	ἤ ῥά νύ μοί τι	ἤ ῥά νύ μοί τι	ἤ ῥά νύ μοι τι	ἤ ῥά νυ μοί τι	ἤ ῥά νύ μοί τι
7.48	δέ τοι εἰμί	δέ τοι εἰμί	δέ τοι εἰμί	δέ τοι εἰμί	δέ τοι εἰμί
7.239	τό μοί ἐστι	τό μοί ἐστι	τό μοι ἐστὶ	τό μοι ἐστὶ	τό μοι ἐστὶ

7.446	ἦ ῥά τίς ἐστι	ἦ ῥά τις ἐστι	ἦ ῥά τίς ἐστι	ἦ ῥά τίς ἐστι
9.144	δέ μοί εἰσὶ	δέ μοι εἰσὶ	δέ μοι εἰσὶ	δέ μοι εἰσὶ
9.286	δέ οἱ εἰσὶ	δέ οἱ εἰσὶ	δέ οἱ εἰσὶ	δέ οἱ εἰσὶ
9.410	γάρ τέ μέ φῇσι	γάρ τέ με φῇσι	γάρ τέ με φῇσι	γάρ τέ με φῇσι
9.495	ἵνα μοί ποτ'	ἵνα μοί ποτ'	ἵνα μοί ποτ'	ἵνα μοί ποτ'
9.640	δέ τοι εἰμέν	δέ τοι εἰμέν	δέ τοι εἰμέν	δέ τοι εἰμέν
10.186	ἀπό τε σφισιν	ἀπό τε σφισιν	ἀπό τέ σφισιν[a]	ἀπό τέ σφισιν[b]

[a] For the ancient principle that enclitics beginning with σφ- induce an additional accent on a paroxytone word of any shape, see section 2.7.3. For the point that under the revised Göttling-Barrett system (qua iterative application of the ancient rules applying to sequences with a single enclitic), enclitics beginning with σφ- induce an additional accent on a paroxytone *sequence* of any shape, see sections 4.2.5 and 4.3.

[b] We take the accent mark to be intended as falling on the τε, although conceivably it was meant to fall on the πο.

system (Ai) or (Aii) causes the accentuation to coincide with that of the revised Göttling-Barrett system where the traditional system did not. Where a sequence is shaded for system (Ai) and/or (Aii) but unshaded for the traditional system, on the other hand, the traditional system causes the accentuation to coincide with that of the revised Göttling-Barrett system but system (Ai) and/or (Aii) causes a deviation. Both situations occur, so if we think for a moment of systems (Ai) and (Aii) as attempts to 'improve' on the extent to which the traditional system yields the same results as the revised Göttling-Barrett system, systems (Ai) and (Aii) achieve this result for some sequences, but they are (as it were) counter-productive for others.

However, because sequences of enclitics with some characteristics are better represented in Homer than others—for reasons that are partly metrical, partly syntactic, and partly stylistic—more sequences are shaded for the traditional system and unshaded for (Ai) than vice versa, and likewise more sequences are shaded for the traditional system and unshaded for (Aii) than vice versa. When applied to sequences of enclitics actually occurring in Homer, then, systems (Ai) and (Aii) both yield a net increase in coincidences with the results of the revised Göttling-Barrett system, by comparison with the traditional system. This effect is driven almost entirely by the use of enclitic forms of ᾽EIMI 'I am' or ΦHMI 'I say', with a long first syllable and short second syllable. The metrical shape of these forms makes them liable to be placed in the hexameter at the beginning of a foot, where they are most often preceded by two short syllables, as in ΚAI TE ME ΦHΣI. In some instances, this pattern is achieved with the help of epic correption (short scansion of a long vowel or diphthong before another vowel), as in ΔE MOI ᾽EΣΣI. For the purposes of accentuation (for which we do not expect epic correption to be taken into account), the enclitic verb form is preceded by a pyrrhic or iambic sequence, and the revised Göttling-Barrett system will give accentuations such as καί τέ με φησί and δέ μοι ἐσσί. Interestingly, these same sequences (with two syllables counting as short in the hexameter, followed by an unelided enclitic verb form) also play the main role in the extent to which system (Aii) causes a net increase in coincidences with the revised Göttling-Barrett system, because the enclitic preceding the disyllabic verb form is most often a personal pronoun form: δέ μοι ἐσσί, ἅ μοι ἐστί, καί τέ με φησί, etc.

The right-hand column of Table 4.5 shows how Venetus A accents the sequences listed here, and shading again draws attention to deviations from the results of the revised Göttling-Barrett system. This column serves as a reminder that the practice of Venetus A and the result of the revised Göttling-Barrett system are not always identical, and we shall return to some specific types of deviation between the two. But systems (Ai) and (Aii) 'predict' the practice of Venetus A more successfully than the traditional system by achieving a closer match with the results of the revised Göttling-Barrett system,[89] which in turn comes even closer to the actual practice of Venetus A.

As regards the remaining hypotheses we have tested against the practice of Venetus A, most of those involving accents on alternate enclitics make correct predictions for Venetus A less than half the time—and the same is true for Göttling and Barrett's original system, whose results always coincide in our sample with those of system (Bii). Only system (Bv) achieves a higher success rate of 60%, but even this is less impressive than the success rate of other systems we have considered: the revised Göttling-Barrett system and approximations (i)–(iv) from Table Ap.1, and systems (Ai)–(Aiii) from Table Ap.2.

One might ask, however, whether we are demanding too much of an 'alternate enclitics' system by distinguishing strictly between system (Biv) (which gives rise, for example, to μὴ νύ τοι) and system (Bv) (which gives rise to μή νύ τοι). Was the scribe primarily interested in accenting every other enclitic, working from the second-to-last enclitic towards the beginning of the sequence, and less worried about how to accent the word preceding the first enclitic? If we count how many sequences in our sample have accents in Venetus A that conform to the predictions of system (Biv) *and/or* system (Bv), the total is 174/250, or 70%. But even under this generous definition, this alternate-enclitics system predicts the practice of Venetus A less well than the revised Göttling-Barrett system or approximation (iii) or (iv) from Table Ap.1.

Moreover, by calculating the combined success rate of systems (Biv) and (Bv), we are effectively allowing for some variation in the way the scribe accents the word preceding the first enclitic. Normally he accents this word following the normal ancient rules for words followed by enclitics (μή νύ τοι), but sometimes he accents it as if a non-enclitic word were coming up (μὴ νύ τοι). If we ascribe the treatment of the word preceding the first enclitic in sequences like μὴ νύ τοι to a momentary failure to spot the enclitic coming up, and if we count such sequences together with their otherwise identical counterparts (μή νύ τοι), the success rate of all our hypotheses goes up, as shown by the last set of figures at the bottom of Tables Ap.1 and Ap.2. But the highest success rates (now 80%–81%) are still those of systems (iii)–(v) from Table Ap.1 (recall that we are leaving column (vi) out of account for the time being): the revised Göttling-Barrett system and two ways of approximating that system.

We may conclude that the main guiding principle behind the accentuation of sequences of enclitics in Venetus A was either the revised Göttling-Barrett system or something very much like Herodian's rules of thumb. But can we say which of these the scribe was in fact aiming at? In terms of absolute number of occurrences in our

---

[89] Note in this connection that of the sequences listed in Table 4.5, only one is accented in Venetus A in a way that differs from that of the revised Göttling-Barrett system but matches that of system (Ai) or (Aii), where the relevant accentuation is not also that of the traditional system: ὅν περ φασὶ at *Il.* 6.100.

sample (and not only in terms of rounded percentages), the success rate of system (v) is identical to that of systems (iii) and (iv),[90] or marginally better when sequences of the type $μὴ$ $νύ$ $τοι$ are counted along with their counterparts like $μή$ $νύ$ $τοι$.[91] But this identity or marginal difference in absolute numbers is not informative by itself, and would fluctuate if we varied the precise extent of our sample. What is more interesting is that there are twenty-two sequences of enclitics altogether in our sample for which systems (iii), (iv), and (v) do not all yield the same result. It is worth taking a closer look at these sequences, to see if they can shed light on the procedure being followed by the scribe of Venetus A. To this end, Table 4.6 shows how these sequences are accented under systems (iii), (iv), and (v), and in Venetus A.

Twenty-one of these twenty-two sequences include an enclitic containing a long vowel or diphthong, somewhere other than the end of the sequence. (The exception is the last sequence in the table, for which the revised Göttling-Barrett system yields $ἀπό$ $τέ$ $σφισιν$ by the ancient principle governing the behaviour of enclitics beginning with $σφ$-: see section 4.2.5, on passage (4.22), and section 4.3.) For these twenty-one sequences, system (iii) consistently puts an accent on the enclitic containing a long vowel or diphthong: in the relevant sequences this accent does not cause acute accents on consecutive syllables in a pyrrhic or iambic pattern. System (iv) consistently leaves the same enclitic unaccented if it belongs to the set $ΠΟΥ$, $ΠΗ(Ι)$, $ΠΩΣ$, $ΠΩ$, and puts an accent on it otherwise. System (v) puts an accent on this enclitic in some instances and not in others, depending whether the sequence that ends with this enclitic is paroxytone (in the relevant sequences it is always non-trochaic) at the point when the following enclitic is about to be added, and also depending whether the following enclitic begins with $σφ$-. What is striking is that where the enclitic containing a long vowel or diphthong belongs to the set $ΠΟΥ$, $ΠΗ(Ι)$, $ΠΩΣ$, $ΠΩ$, in almost all instances Venetus A has the same outcome as system (v), the revised Göttling-Barrett system: $οὐδέ$ $τι$ $πώ$ $μοι$, $οὔ$ $πω$ $τι$, $ἄρα$ $πώ$ $οἱ$, $οὔ$ $πω$ $τις$, $ἄρα$ $πώ$ $σφιν$, $ἦ$ $πῆι$ $με$, $μή$ $πω$ $τι$, $γάρ$ $πώ$ $σφιν$, $μή$ $πως$ $οἱ$, $ἤ$ $που$ $τί⟨ς⟩$ $σφιν$, $γάρ$ $πω$ $τοι$, $οὔ$ $πω$ $τις$, and $ὅσα$ $πού$ $νῦν$. (The sequence $θεός$ $πού$ $σοι$ is an exception, and one occurrence of $ΟΥ$ $ΠΩ$ $ΤΙΣ$ has a stray accent on the *last* enclitic of the sequence.) The other six sequences each involve one of the enclitics $ΘΗΝ$, $ΜΟΙ$, and $ΣΟΙ$, in a position for which the revised Göttling-Barrett system leaves this enclitic unaccented: at the point when the following enclitic is to be added, this enclitic ends a paroxytone and spondaic sequence. For all six sequences, Venetus A agrees not with the revised Göttling-Barrett system but with systems (iii) and (iv): $γάρ$ $σοί$ $γε$, $οὔ$ $θήν$ $μιν$, $γάρ$ $μοί$ $ποτε$, $μή$ $μοί$ $τι$, $εἴ$ $μοί$ $τι$, and $Πηλεύς$ $θήν$ $μοι$. So, the scribe of

---

[90] All three systems (iii)–(v) correctly predict Venetus A's accentuation of 184 sequences in our sample, although for no two of these systems is the list of 184 sequences identical.

[91] On this basis system (v) (the revised Göttling-Barrett system) correctly predicts Venetus A's accentuation of 202 sequences in our sample, while the approximations (iii) and (iv) correctly predict Venetus A's accentuation of 201 sequences.

Table 4.6 Sequences of enclitics for which system (iii), (iv), and (v) from Table Ap.1 do not all give the same result (out of the 250 Homeric sequences of enclitics considered in Appendix A), accented according to these three systems and as in Venetus A. The word preceding the first enclitic in the sequence is included, and enclitics are underlined. Shading indicates a way of accenting a sequence that differs from the accentuation found in Venetus A.

Line of *Iliad*	(iii) 'Traditional' system but avoid consecutive acute accents on pyrrhic or iambic sequences (work forwards from the word preceding the first enclitic)	(iv) 'Traditional' system but leave indefinite *ΠΟΥ, ΠΗ(Ι), ΠΩΣ,* and *ΠΩ* unaccented AND avoid consecutive acute accents on pyrrhic or iambic sequences (work forwards from the word preceding the first enclitic)	(v) Revised Göttling-Barrett system (apply the ancient rules for a single enclitic, each time a new enclitic is added).	Venetus A
1.178	θεός πού σοι	θεός που σοι	θεός που σοι	θεός πού σοι
1.542	οὐδέ τι πώ μοι	οὐδέ τι πω μοι	οὐδέ τι πώ μοι	οὐδέ τι πώ μοι
1.557	γάρ σοί γε	γάρ σοί γε	γάρ σοι γε	γάρ σοί γε
2.122	οὔ πώ τι	οὔ πω τι	οὔ πω τι	οὔ πω τι
2.276	οὔ θήν μιν	οὔ θήν μιν	οὔ θην μιν	οὔ θήν μιν
2.419	ἄρα πώ οἱ	ἄρα πω οἱ	ἄρα πώ οἱ	ἄρα πώ οἱ
2.553	οὔ πώ τις	οὔ πω τις	οὔ πω τις	οὔ πω τις
3.302	ἄρα πώ σφιν	ἄρα πω σφιν	ἄρα πώ σφιν	ἄρα πώ σφιν
3.400	ἦ πή με	ἦ πη με	ἦ πή με	ἦ πήι με
4.48	γάρ μοί ποτε	γάρ μοί ποτε	γάρ μοι ποτέ	γάρ μοί ποτε
4.234	μή πώ τι	μή πω τι	μή πω τι	μή πω τι
4.331	γάρ πώ σφιν	γάρ πω σφιν	γάρ πώ σφιν	γάρ πώ σφιν
5.298	μή πώς οἱ	μή πως οἱ	μή πως οἱ	μή πως οἱ
6.438	ἦ πού τίς σφιν	ἦ που τίς σφιν	ἦ που τίς σφιν	ἦ που τί (for τίς) σφιν
6.486	μή μοί τι	μή μοί τι	μή μοι τι	μή μοί τι
7.28	εἴ μοί τι	εἴ μοί τι	εἴ μοι τι	εἴ μοί τι
7.52	γάρ πώ τοι	γάρ πω τοι	γάρ πω τοι	γάρ πω τοι
9.148	οὔ πώ τις	οὔ πω τις	οὔ πω τις	οὔ πω τις
9.290	οὔ πώ τις	οὔ πω τις	οὔ πω τις	οὔ πω τίς
9.394	Πηλεύς θήν μοι	Πηλεύς θήν μοι	Πηλεύς θην μοι	Πηλεύς θήν μοι
10.105	ὅσα πού νυν	ὅσα που νυν	ὅσα πού νυν	ὅσα πού νῦν
10.186	ἀπό τε σφισὶν	ἀπό τε σφισὶν	ἀπό τέ σφισιν	ἀπο τέ σφισιν[a]

[a] As noted at Table 4.5, note b, we take the accent mark to be intended as falling on the τε, although conceivably it was meant to fall on the πο. For the purposes of calculating which systems produce the same accentuation as we find in Venetus A, we treat ἀπο as equivalent to ἀπό.

Venetus A leaves *ΠΟΥ*, *ΠΗ(Ι)*, *ΠΩΣ*, and *ΠΩ* unaccented where these end a paroxytone and spondaic sequence (at the point when the following enclitic is to be added), but accents other enclitics with a long vowel or diphthong under similar circumstances. The special treatment of *ΠΟΥ*, *ΠΗ(Ι)*, *ΠΩΣ*, and *ΠΩ* might suggest that the scribe is following Herodian's rules of thumb rather than the revised Göttling-Barrett system itself. And yet the scribe regularly gives an accent to enclitics belonging to the set *ΠΟΥ/ΠΗ(Ι)/ΠΩΣ/ΠΩ* where this is what the revised Göttling-Barrett system requires: οὐδέ τι πώ μοι, ἄρα πώ οἱ, ἄρα πώ σφιν, ἦ πή ἱ με, γάρ πώ σφιν (here the crucial factor is the enclitic beginning with σφ), ὅσα πού νῦν. He may well be following Herodian's rules of thumb, but if so he has an implicit or explicit awareness of the limits within which to apply the rule of thumb about *ΠΟΥ*, *ΠΗ(Ι)*, *ΠΩΣ*, and *ΠΩ*: these enclitics should be left unaccented before another enclitic *if they are preceded by a syllable with an acute accent. And even then, only if the following enclitic does not begin with σφ-*.

An alternative possibility is worth contemplating at least briefly in connection with *MOI* and other enclitic personal pronoun forms ending in -οι (the part of the poem beyond our sample confirms that Venetus A's usual practice is to give these an accent when they end a paroxytone and spondaic sequence, at the point when a further enclitic is about to be added[92]). In Greek, in some morphological categories word-final -αι and -οι behave for the purposes of accentuation as if they were short vowels (see section 2.8.3). In most contexts it makes no difference whether enclitic pronoun forms like *MOI* are considered to have a final -οι that counts long for the purposes of the accent or one that counts short. However, the acute rather than circumflex accent of the non-enclitic forms ἐμοί and σοί (by contrast with datives in -ῷ and old locatives such as Ἰσθμοῖ) makes it possible that the -οι of *MOI*, *ΣOI*, and *TOI* (like the -οι and -αι of nominative plural forms, for example) counted 'short for accentuation'. In this case we would expect the revised Göttling-Barrett principle to yield (for example) γάρ μοί ποτε, on the basis that the paroxytone sequence γάρ μοι counts as 'trochaic for the accent'; we have seen that when a single enclitic is involved, the same idea is likely to lie behind the second acute that we are told appears on γενέσθαί τε and λοέσσαί τε (see section 2.8.3).

In fact, we suspect that no such idea lies behind the scribe's treatment of enclitic pronoun forms ending in -*OI*. Firstly, the idea is more difficult to apply to enclitic Ὅ*I*: Venetus A appears to treat this enclitic in the same way as *MOI* and *TOI*, to judge from γάρ οἵ τις at *Il.* 14.521 and *Il.* 22.438, but its non-enclitic counterpart οἷ has a circumflex accent suggesting that this diphthong counted

---

[92] Five instances of *MOI*, *TOI*, or Ὅ*I* in a relevant position occur beyond our sample (again disregarding portions of the poem for which we have Venetus A only as a fifteenth-century replacement), and four of these are again given an accent. As accented in Venetus A, the examples are γάρ οἵ τις (*Il.* 14.521); μή τοί τι (*Il.* 2.358); γάρ οἵ τις (*Il.* 22.438; γάρ here is a scribal correction for γὰρ); γάρ μοί ποτε (*Il.* 24.69); and the exception οὔ τοι τι (*Il.* 13.811). (We leave the form *ΣOI* aside in this context, because it is only sometimes possible to distinguish between a *ΣOI* that the scribe considered enclitic and one that he considered orthotonic: cf. n. 79 and Table 4.3, note p.)

'long for accentuation'. Secondly, the enclitic *ΘΗΝ* neither belongs to the set *ΠΟΥ/ΠΗ(I)/ΠΩΣ/ΠΩ* nor ends in *-OI*, but appears to have been treated like *MOI*. Unfortunately the instances of *ΘΗΝ* at *Il.* 2.276 (Venetus A's οὔ θήν μιν) and *Il.* 9.394 (Venetus A's Πηλεύς θήν μοι) are the only instances in the poem where *ΘΗΝ* occurs before another enclitic and ends a paroxytone and spondaic sequence, at the point when the further enclitic is about to be added.[93] This last point rests on slight evidence, then, but such evidence as we have suggests that the scribe of Venetus A was using, in essence, Herodian's rules of thumb. But it was a nuanced version of these rules of thumb, which did not leave *ΠΟΥ*, *ΠΗ(I)*, *ΠΩΣ*, and *ΠΩ* unaccented indiscriminately before another enclitic, but only after a syllable with an acute accent, and even then only if the following enclitic did not begin with σφ-. Our final hypothesis on the principles guiding the scribe of Venetus A can be formulated in full as follows:

Final hypothesis on Venetus A: a nuanced version of Herodian's rule of thumb
Give every enclitic except the last an accent (normally an acute) on its last or only syllable, but leave indefinite *ΠΟΥ*, *ΠΗ(I)*, *ΠΩΣ*, and *ΠΩ* unaccented after a syllable with an acute accent, unless an enclitic beginning with σφ- follows, AND ALSO avoid consecutive acute accents on pyrrhic or iambic sequences (work forwards from the word preceding the first enclitic), unless an enclitic beginning with σφ- follows.

Column (vi) of Table Ap.1 shows how the application of this hypothesis to our whole sample successfully predicts the practice of Venetus A 76% of the time, as compared with a 74% success rate for the revised Göttling-Barrett system or for less nuanced versions of Herodian's rules of thumb. When sequences of the type καὶ νύ κεν are counted together with those of the type καί νύ κεν, the success rate goes up to 83%, as opposed to 81% for the revised Göttling-Barrett system itself. The differences in success rate are small, because these systems yield different results in only a small proportion of Homeric sequences of enclitics. That is to say, Herodian's rules of thumb do exactly what they were designed to do.

4.5 Conclusions and some further questions

This chapter has examined the evidence for the accentuation of sequences of enclitics from sources of several different kinds: direct evidence in the form of statements in Greek grammatical texts; indirect evidence from comments on

---

[93] There are four further occurrences of *ΘΗΝ* in sequences of enclitics, but all of these are preceded by a syllable with a circumflex. As accented in Venetus A, the examples are ῆ θήν σ' (*Il.* 11.365), ῆ θήν που τοι (*Il.* 13.813), ῆ θήν μιν (*Il.* 15.288), and ῆ θήν σ' (*Il.* 20.452).

specific sequences of enclitics in the Homeric scholia; the practice of accented papyri; and the practice of the tenth-century *Iliad* manuscript Venetus A.

On the face of it, Greek grammatical texts present us with the system that we traditionally learn today (every enclitic except the last gets an accent on its last or only syllable), plus an apparently unlikely assortment of exceptions. But when these exceptions are bolted on to the 'traditional' system, they yield results very close to those of a system based on a consistent and plausible principle: apply the rules for sequences with a single enclitic, recursively, each time a new enclitic is added. Conceptually, this was the system put forward by Karl Göttling and further popularized by W. S. Barrett (see section 4.1), but we have tweaked the details by insisting that the rules to be applied recursively are the full ancient principles applying to sequences with a single enclitic, including the 'trochaic principle' that gives (for example) ἔνθά τε but λέγε τι. It is in this form (the 'revised Göttling-Barrett system') that the idea allows us to see what the apparently disparate doctrines we find in the grammatical tradition are all about: they are rules of thumb, designed to allow users to accent sequences of enclitics correctly in the vast majority of cases.

The revised Göttling-Barrett system turns out to lurk behind not only the explicit instructions which Greek grammatical texts give on accenting sequences of enclitics, but also the locations of accents prescribed for specific sequences of enclitics in the Homeric scholia deriving from Herodian, and the accent marks actually written on sequences of enclitics on accented papyri. Remarkably, the revised Göttling-Barrett system also lurks behind the accents in the tenth-century *Iliad* manuscript known as Venetus A (and in Appendix B, we argue that the same is true for the eleventh-century *Iliad* manuscript known as Venetus B): in some quarters, the principle is still—or again?—reflected in practice at this period.

Nevertheless, it is not clear that anybody in antiquity or the Middle Ages ever formulated the recursive principle explicitly. In all likelihood, explicit formulations always took the form of rules of thumb such as the ones that have come down to us. And yet we have repeatedly seen evidence that these rules of thumb were used with the help of an implicit feel for the limits within which they ought to be applied. In particular, it was always understood that while *ΠΟΥ, ΠΗ(Ι), ΠΩΣ*, and *ΠΩ* should often be left unaccented before another enclitic, this did not extend to the *ΠΩ* in a sequence like οὐδέ τι πώ μοι.

Was the revised Göttling-Barrett system a linguistically real rule—one based in speakers' natural competence in their own language—or was it somebody's artificial extrapolation from the rules applying to a single enclitic? The use of enclitics themselves is much reduced in informal Greek of the Roman period, compared to the situation in Homer or in classical Attic literature:[94] how much of a feel for *sequences* of enclitics could Herodian or his contemporaries really

---

[94] See e.g. Mayser (1934: 123, 153, 155–6) on γε, περ, and τε; Blomqvist (1969: 129, 143–4) on γε and περ; Blass, Debrunner, and Rehkopf (1979: 84 with nn. 1–2, 364–5) on γε, νυν, περ, τοι, and particles in general (including non-enclitic ones); Clarysse (2010: 39–40) on γε.

have had? In this connection, three observations might be made. Firstly, although the rules of thumb can be attributed to Herodian, they need not have originated with him: we have much less evidence for Hellenistic scholarship on accentuation than we do for Herodian's day, and on this point we simply lack evidence for periods earlier than the second century AD. Secondly, as long as consecutive enclitics continued to occur, on occasion, in spoken Greek, a way of accenting them is likely to have been a living part of the language. Thirdly, if the recursive principle had been worked out by extrapolating from the rules applying to single enclitics, one would expect it to be formulated in terms that reflected the underlying principle. Instead, the use of apparently disparate rules of thumb suggests a principle for which some speakers had a feel, rather than one they had worked out in theory. For this last reason above all, we suggest that the revised Göttling-Barrett system has a serious claim to being a linguistically real system, perhaps in use in the Hellenistic period and perhaps still in use in the second century AD, and passed down into the medieval period as a complex series of rules of thumb.

These findings raise a number of questions that we have not attempted to answer. A first set of questions arises from the scope of the concept 'trochaic sequence' in the revised Göttling-Barrett system. In connection with single enclitics, modern scholars have long suspected that the ancient 'trochaic principle' was originally meant to apply only to enclitics after trochaic sequences whose long syllable ended in a liquid consonant (λ, ρ), nasal consonant (μ, ν,), or possibly σ, as in ἄλλός τις, ἔνθά ποτε, and possibly τόσσόν τις.[95] This suspicion is based on the idea that in such sequences the sequence of short vowel plus liquid or nasal consonant (or possibly σ) might have counted as a diphthong, so that the accent was effectively a circumflex (although written as an acute) because it fell on the first half of a diphthong. On this view, a sequence such as ἔνθά ποτε was accented on the same basis as γυναῖκές εἰσι. But if the revised Göttling-Barrett system is ancient and linguistically real, this view will need rethinking: for the purposes of this system, not only does a sequence like ὄν ῥα count as ending in a trochee, but so do sequences like αἴ κεν or καί νυ. This point is integral to the way the rules of thumb work, and is reflected on accented papyri via accentuations like ἅι κέν πως, καί νύ κε, and εἴ πέρ με (Table 4.3, items 28, 65, and 15). It would be difficult to argue that the first syllable of these sequences counts as being accented on the first member of a diphthong, because the first syllable contains an *ordinary* diphthong: if it counted as being accented on its first member, we would expect the accent to be considered a circumflex, and to be written as such.

If the current scholarly consensus on the basis for the trochaic principle needs rethinking, this may cast a new light on the tradition that properispomenon

---

[95] For general discussion see Probert (2003: 148–50), with bibliography. On the position of the liquid or nasal consonant (or σ) in syllable structure, and on possible pitch changes on resonant consonants in fragments of ancient Greek music, see Devine and Stephens (1994: 193, 371).

words with a final consonant cluster, like κῆρυξ 'herald', fail to receive an additional accent from a following enclitic. In section 2.7.3, we suggested that this doctrine reflects a view that properispomenon as well as paroxytone words needed to end in a trochaic sequence in order to receive an additional accent from a following enclitic. If the linguistic basis for the trochaic principle has to do with syllables ending in certain consonants counting as diphthongs, it is difficult to see why a final consonant cluster on a properispomenon word should make any difference.[96] On the other hand, if the trochaic principle has nothing to do with syllables ending in certain consonants counting as diphthongs, this opens up the possibility that the trochaic principle has a linguistic basis which genuinely prevented words like κῆρυξ from getting an additional accent before an enclitic. We leave open for further work the question of what this linguistic basis might have been, and we note that any attempt to answer this question will also need to grapple with the sequence ἤ πή με at *Il.* 3.400, for which the accentuation shown here is clearly prescribed by the (closely related) scholia (4.20) and (4.21): if the rules pertaining to sequences with one enclitic were re-applied on each addition of a new enclitic, and if the spondaic shape of κῆρυξ prevented it getting an additional accent before an enclitic, why should the spondaic shape of ἤ πη not prevent this sequence getting an additional accent before an enclitic?

Answers to these questions will best be attempted as part of an explicit linguistic account of the phonological principles from which the revised Göttling-Barrett system as a whole would follow, together with other aspects of the ancient Greek accent system. An account of this kind could realistically be attempted, because the empirical facts we take to comprise the revised Göttling-Barrett system are to a large extent clear; in this respect the situation is different from that of enclitic and non-enclitic ἘΣΤΙ (see section 3.6). Such a phonological account is beyond the scope of this book, but some first steps towards one are offered in Probert (in preparation).

A quite different set of questions has to do with the influence of the revised Göttling-Barrett system in later centuries. How does the practice of Venetus A (and Venetus B) compare with that of other manuscripts of the same period, and what happens over the subsequent centuries? In this connection, an intriguing possibility arises from a passage of Pasor's *Libellus de Graecis Novi Testamenti accentibus* (1646: 38), in which we find an anticipation of Laum's (1928: 243–6, 307–12, 326) view that an enclitic pronoun form was left unaccented before another enclitic, unless it was a form of indefinite *ΤΙΣ*. After first laying out the 'traditional' system, Pasor adds, 'Excipe μοῦ, σοῦ, οὗ, μοὶ, &c.' A series of examples from the New Testament follows, with the accents Pasor considered these to have;

---

[96] West (1990: xlviii) argued that the correct accentuation was in fact κήρυξ, but the logic of *On enclitics 3*, §c requires κῆρυξ (as does manuscript family **m**'s version of *About* ἘΣΤΙΝ: see *About* ἘΣΤΙΝ, §b, note c and §c, note f); see also Probert (2003: 84).

these examples include the forms μου, μοι, σοι, and με left unaccented before further enclitics, and appear to confirm that by 'μοῦ, σοῦ, οὗ, μοὶ, &c.', Pasor meant enclitic personal pronoun forms. The passage suggests that some of the results of the revised Göttling-Barrett system continued to be known, but gave rise to new attempts to produce rules of thumb. If the 'right' way to accent sequences such as δέ μοι ἐσσί and καί τέ με φησί was known from manuscripts, but the recursive principle was long forgotten (if it had ever been known explicitly), and the idea that consecutive acute accents should be avoided in iambic or pyrrhic sequences was forgotten too, one might well try attributing the unaccentedness of *MOI* and *ME* in these sequences to the fact that these enclitics are personal pronoun forms. As we have seen (section 4.4, on system Aii), this approach can function as a very decent approximation to the revised Göttling-Barrett system.[97] By definition, no rules of thumb are perfect, and this idea too does not capture earlier practice perfectly. But it could have been reified in the writing of accents in texts, if it was ever used as a prescriptive principle for this purpose. It would be worth investigating whether the rule Pasor gives was ever implemented as such, in printed texts or manuscripts of the early modern period.

To sum up, much remains to be done on the linguistic basis for the principles governing the accentuation of sequences involving even one enclitic, and on the afterlife of the revised Göttling-Barrett system from the tenth century AD to our own times. In the meantime, evidence from several different directions converges to suggest that the revised Göttling-Barrett system makes consistent sense of ancient theory and practice.

For those wanting to know how we should accent sequences of ancient Greek enclitics today, there is no simple answer. We have made a case for the 'revised Göttling-Barrett system' as an ancient and probably linguistically real system, while the 'traditional' system has the advantage of familiarity from our modern tradition. For those wishing to stick to our modern tradition, we offer the thought that Herodian already treated our 'traditional' rule as a first rule of thumb that would yield correct results more often than not. At a distance of about two millennia, if we can accent sequences of enclitics in a way that counted as a decent first approximation in antiquity, we are perhaps not doing too badly.

---

[97] The extent to which an approximation yields passable results will depend, however, on the texts to which it is being applied: do the kinds of sequences for which this approximation is a good one outnumber those for which it is counter-productive? In section 4.4 we considered this question for the sequences that occur in practice in Homer. We leave the investigation of such questions for other authors open for future work.

5

Conclusions

This book began with an introduction to our ancient and medieval sources for the accentual effects of Greek enclitics, which includes new editions and translations of the texts that provide the most continuous surviving discussions of the subject. None of these texts is precisely dateable (indeed, the tenth-century witness to *About 'ΕΣΤΙΝ* and the twelfth-century witness to *On enclitics 1* are of particular interest because they make clear that texts which are recognizably these were in circulation in the Middle Ages), but we have seen that the main doctrines were known already to Apollonius Dyscolus and Herodian in the second century AD, along with the main conceptual apparatus and metaphors deployed to think and talk about the accentual effects of enclitics. Our evidence for still earlier stages of the tradition is extremely patchy, but on rare occasions we are able to trace a doctrine back to Hellenistic scholarship; a case in point concerns the 'trochaic principle' giving ἔνθά τε rather than ἔνθα τε (see sections 2.8.1–2.8.3).

Chapters 3 and 4 took up two questions which have long worried classicists: when was 'ΕΣΤΙ non-enclitic, and how were sequences of enclitics accented? Until now the debate about 'ΕΣΤΙ has been framed as a contest between two views: beyond its appearance in sentence-initial and unequivocal clause-initial position (which is not in doubt), where else did non-enclitic ἔστι appear? Were further occurrences of non-enclitic ἔστι conditioned by its position after certain words (understood by modern scholars as a 'quasi-initial' position, in some syntactic or phonological sense), or by its conveying existence or possibility? In recent scholarship the first of these views has tended to be favoured on the basis that it rests on more plentiful and more ancient evidence, but a re-examination of the textual basis for both views has shown that the first can be traced back to the second century AD only in a limited form, and that foundations for the 'existential' view can probably be traced back to this date too. We have also seen that in asking which view is right, scholars may well have been asking the wrong question. Parallels from modern languages, and notably Serbian, suggest that the situation might plausibly have been a complex one that both approaches capture in part. Furthermore, a look at didactic presentations of Serbian shows that the same complex situation can be simplified in different ways, with alternative presentations of the Serbian facts bearing a remarkable resemblance to the two traditions on non-enclitic 'ΕΣΤΙ. If our account of non-enclitic 'ΕΣΤΙ is on the right lines, the two approaches that come down to us were never meant to be opposed to one

Ancient and Medieval Thought on Greek Enclitics. Stephanie Roussou & Philomen Probert, Oxford University Press. © Stephanie Roussou and Philomen Probert 2023.
DOI: 10.1093/oso/9780192871671.003.0005

another. They are different reasonable simplifications of the same complex reality, or different rules of thumb.

Rules of thumb hold the key to our ancient and medieval sources on sequences of enclitics too. On the face of it, grammatical texts present us with three mutually incompatible doctrines: the rule we traditionally learn, the same rule plus an odd set of exceptions, and the same rule plus a different odd set of exceptions. But these doctrines come together in a remarkable way if we take all the exceptions and bolt them onto the traditional rule, and apply this system to series of enclitics that occur in texts. The results approximate remarkably closely to those of a coherent rule that makes linguistic sense: the recursive principle we call the revised Göttling-Barrett system. We have argued that this system underlies not only the doctrines found in grammatical texts, but also the accents written on accented papyri, and at a much later date the accents written in the tenth-century *Iliad* manuscript Venetus A (and the eleventh-century *Iliad* manuscript Venetus B). It is not clear that the recursive principle was ever formulated explicitly, and this point above all leads us to conclude that the recursive principle was a linguistically real one for which some speakers of Herodian's day had a feel—even though their attempts to formulate it amounted to a sort of Ptolemy's epicycles approach to accenting sequences of enclitics.

When one of us learned French, she was taught in the first instance that verbs which take *avoir* as their auxiliary make the passé composé using a non-agreeing, invariable form of the past participle, while those taking *être* use a past participle that agrees in gender and number with the subject. At a more advanced stage, a set of exceptions was introduced: the past participle of a verb taking *avoir* agrees with its direct object if the direct object precedes the verb. A more advanced stage still brought yet more refinements, to do with reflexive verbs. When scholars of the future try to reconstruct the grammar of French at the turn of the third mil- lennium AD, they may happen upon some of the descriptive works that we use today. To make sense of the variety of doctrines they contain, it will be helpful to understand that some of these doctrines are rules of thumb: they allow their users to produce correct results most of the time but were never intended to be the whole story.

Descriptive works on French will probably not be the only sources of evidence available to our hypothetical scholars of the future. For ancient Greek accentu- ation we are in a different position, because we would know very little about the accent system if it were not for ancient and medieval grammarians. The accent marks that appear on papyri, manuscripts, and printed books are all dependent on the grammatical tradition reaching back to the Hellenistic period. For this rea- son, our own understanding of the accent system depends on our understanding what ancient grammarians said, and what they meant by it. This book has drawn attention to an under-appreciated component of ancient and medieval scholarly activity, the production of rules of thumb.

APPENDIX A

Sequences of enclitics in Venetus A

Table Ap.1 The first 250 sequences of more than one enclitic appearing in Venetus A (omitting folios of Venetus A for which we have only a fifteenth-century replacement for the original), accented according to the five principles shown in Table 4.2, the 'final hypothesis' laid out towards the end of section 4.4, and then as in Venetus A. The word preceding the first enclitic is included, and enclitics themselves are underlined. For the forms *'OTTI* (nominative-accusative neuter singular of ὅστις), *'OTTIΣ*, and *'OYTE*, a hyphen separates the enclitic from what precedes (see Chapter 4 , n. 42), except where we reproduce the reading of Venetus A. Shading indicates a way of accenting a sequence that differs from that of Venetus A, and an asterisk indicates a way of accenting a sequence differing from that of Venetus A only insofar as Venetus A accents the word preceding the first enclitic as if a non-enclitic word was to follow.

Line of *Iliad*	(i)	(ii)	(iii)	(iv)	(v)	(vi)	(vii)
	'Traditional' system: give every enclitic except the last an accent (usually an acute) on its last or only syllable	'Traditional' system but leave indefinite *ΠΟΥ, ΠΗ(Ι), ΠΩΣ*, and *ΠΩ* unaccented	'Traditional' system but avoid consecutive acute accents on pyrrhic or iambic sequences (work forwards from the word preceding the first enclitic)	'Traditional' system but leave indefinite *ΠΟΥ, ΠΗ(Ι), ΠΩΣ*, and *ΠΩ* unaccented AND avoid consecutive acute accents on pyrrhic or iambic sequences (work forwards from the word preceding the first enclitic)	Revised Göttling-Barrett system (apply the ancient rules for a single enclitic, each time a new enclitic is added).	Final hypothesis: 'Traditional' system but leave indefinite *ΠΟΥ, ΠΗ(Ι), ΠΩΣ*, and *ΠΩ* unaccented after a syllable with an acute accent, unless an enclitic beginning with σφ- follows, AND avoid consecutive acute accents on pyrrhic or iambic sequences (work forwards from the word preceding the first enclitic), unless an enclitic beginning with σφ- follows	Venetus A
1.8	τίς τάρ σφϣε	τίς τάρ σφϣε	τίς τάρ σφϣε	τίς τάρ σφϣε	τίς τάρ σφϣε	τίς τάρ σφϣε	τίς τάρ σφϣε
1.28	* μή νύ τοι	* μή νύ τοι	* μή νύ τοι	* μή νύ τοι	* μή νύ τοι	* μή νύ τοι	μὴ νύ τοι

Continued

Table Ap.1 *Continued*

Line of Iliad	(i)	(ii)	(iii)	(iv)	(v)	(vi)	(vii)
1.39	εἴ ποτέ τοι	εἴ ποτέ τοι	εἴ ποτέ τοι	εἴ ποτέ τοι	εἴ ποτέ τοι	εἴ ποτέ τοι	εἴ ποτέ τοι
1.40	δή ποτέ τοι	δή ποτέ τοι	δή ποτέ τοι	δή ποτέ τοι	δή ποτέ τοι	δή ποτέ τοι	δή ποτέ τοι
1.66	αἴ κέν πως	αἴ κέν πως	αἴ κέν πως	αἴ κέν πως	αἴ κέν πως	αἴ κέν πως	αἴ κέν πως
1.100	τότε κέν μιν	τότε κέν μιν	τότε κέν μιν	τότε κέν μιν	τότε κέν μιν	τότε κέν μιν	τότε κέν μιν
1.108	οὐδέ τί πω	οὐδέ τί πω	οὐδέ τι πω	οὐδέ τι πω	οὐδέ τι πω	οὐδέ τι πω	οὐδέ τι πω
1.114	οὐ ἔθέν ἐστι	οὐ ἔθέν ἐστι	οὐ ἔθέν ἐστι	οὐ ἔθέν ἐστι	οὐ ἔθέν ἐστι	οὐ ἔθέν ἐστι	οὐ ἔθέν ἐστι
1.115	* οὐ-τέ τι	* οὐ-τέ τι	* οὐ-τέ τι	* οὐ-τέ τι	* οὐ-τέ τι	* οὐ-τέ τι	οὐτέ τι
1.123	πῶς τάρ τοι	πῶς τάρ τοι	πῶς τάρ τοι	πῶς τάρ τοι	πῶς τάρ τοι	πῶς τάρ τοι	πῶς τάρ τοι
1.124	οὐδέ τί πω	οὐδέ τί πω	οὐδέ τι πω	οὐδέ τι πω	οὐδέ τι πω	οὐδέ τι πω	οὐδέ τι πω
1.128	αἴ κέ ποθι	αἴ κέ ποθι	αἴ κέ ποθι	αἴ κέ ποθι	αἴ κέ ποθι	αἴ κέ ποθι	αἴ κέ ποθι
1.150	πῶς τίς τοι	πῶς τίς τοι	πῶς τίς τοι	πῶς τίς τοι	πῶς τίς τοι	πῶς τίς τοι	πῶς τίς τοι
1.153	οὐ τί μοι	οὐ τί μοι	οὐ τί μοι	οὐ τί μοι	οὐ τί μοι	οὐ τί μοι	οὐ τί μοι
1.175	οἵ κέ με	οἵ κέ με	οἵ κέ με	οἵ κέ με	οἵ κέ με	οἵ κέ με	οἵ κέ με
1.176	δέ μοί ἐσσι	δέ μοί ἐσσι	δέ μοι ἐσσί	δέ μοι ἐσσί	δέ μοι ἐσσί	δέ μοι ἐσσί	δέ μοι ἐσσί
1.178	θεός πού σοι	θεός πού σοι	θεός πού σοι	θεός πού σοι	θεός που σοι	θεός που σοι	θεός που σοι
1.213	καί ποτέ τοι	καί ποτέ τοι	καί ποτέ τοι	καί ποτέ τοι	καί ποτέ τοι	καί ποτέ τοι	καί ποτέ τοι
1.226	οὐ-τέ ποτ'	οὐ-τέ ποτ'	οὐ-τέ ποτ'	οὐ-τέ ποτ'	οὐ-τέ ποτ'	οὐ-τέ ποτ'	οὔτέ ποτ'
1.236	γάρ ῥά ἑ	γάρ ῥά ἑ	γάρ ῥά ἑ	γάρ ῥά ἑ	γάρ ῥά ἑ	γάρ ῥά ἑ	γάρ ῥά ἑ
1.261	οὐ ποτέ μ'	οὐ ποτέ μ'	οὐ ποτέ μ'	οὐ ποτέ μ'	οὐ ποτέ μ'	οὐ ποτέ μ'	οὐ ποτέ μ'
1.294	ὅτ-τί κεν	ὅτ-τί κεν	ὅτ-τί κεν	ὅτ-τί κεν	ὅτ-τί κεν	ὅτ-τί κεν	ὅττι κεν
1.296	ἐγωγέ τι σοι	ἐγωγέ τι σοι	ἐγωγέ τι σοι	ἐγωγέ τι σοι	ἐγωγέ τι σοι	ἐγωγέ τι σοι	ἐγωγέ τι σοι

1.299	οὔ-τέ τῳ	οὔ-τέ τῳ	οὔ-τέ τῳ	οὔ-τέ τῳ	οὔ-τέ τῳ	οὔτέ τοι
1.300	ἅ μοι ἐστὶ	ἅ μοι ἐστὶ	ἅ μοι ἐστὶ	ἅ μοι ἐστὶ	ἅ μοι ἐστὶ	ἅ μοι ἐστὶ
1.332	οὐδέ τι μιν	οὐδέ τι μιν	οὐδέ τι μιν	οὐδέ τι μιν	οὐδέ τι μιν	οὐδέ τι μιν
1.335	οὔ τί μοι	οὔ τί μοι	οὔ τί μοι	οὔ τί μοι	οὔ τί μοι	οὔ τι μοι
1.353	τιμήν πέρ μοι	τιμήν πέρ μοι	τιμήν πέρ μοι	τιμήν πέρ μοι	τιμήν πέρ μοι	τιμήν πέρ μοι
1.361	Χειρί τέ μιν	Χειρί τέ μιν	Χειρί τε μιν	Χειρί τε μιν	Χειρί τε μιν	Χειρί τέ μιν[a]
1.408	αἴ κέν πως	αἴ κέν πως	αἴ κέν πως	αἴ κέν πως	αἴ κέν πως	αἴ κέν πως
1.414	τί νύ σ'	τί νύ σ'	τί νύ σ'	τί νυ σ'	τί νυ σ'	τί νύ σ'
1.416	ἐπεί νύ τοι	ἐπεί νύ τοι	ἐπεί νύ τοι	ἐπεί νύ τοι	ἐπεί νύ τοι	ἐπεί νύ τοι
1.490	οὔ-τέ ποτ'	οὔ-τέ ποτ'	οὔ-τέ ποτ'	οὔ-τέ ποτ'	οὔ-τέ ποτ'	οὔ-τέ ποτ'
1.491	οὔ-τέ ποτ'	οὔ-τέ ποτ'	οὔ-τέ ποτ'	οὔ-τέ ποτ'	οὔ-τέ ποτ'	οὔτέ ποτ'
1.508	σύ πέρ μιν	σύ πέρ μιν	σύ πέρ μιν	σύ πέρ μιν	σύ πέρ μιν	σύ πέρ μιν
1.510	* ὀφέλλωσίν τέ ἑ	* ὀφέλλωσίν τέ ἑ	* ὀφέλλωσίν τέ ἑ	* ὀφέλλωσίν τέ ἑ	* ὀφέλλωσίν τέ ἑ	ὀφέλλωσιν τέ ἑ
1.521	καί τέ μέ φησι	καί τέ μέ φησι	καί τέ με φησί	καί τέ με φησί	καί τέ με φησί	καί τέ με φησί
1.527	ὅ τι κεν	ὅ τι κεν	ὅ τι κεν	ὅ τι κεν	ὅ τι κεν	ὅ τι κεν
1.542	οὐδέ τί πώ μοι	οὐδέ τί πω μοι	οὐδέ τι πω μοι	οὐδέ τι πω μοι	οὐδέ τι πώ μοι	οὐδέ τι πώ μοι
1.557	γάρ σοί γε	γάρ σοί γε	γάρ σοί γε	γάρ σοί γε	γάρ σοί γε	γάρ σοί γε
1.566	μή νύ τοι	μή νύ τοι	μή νύ τοι	μή νύ τοι	μή νύ τοι	μή νοί (for νύ) τοι
1.567	ὅτε κέν τοι	ὅτε κέν τοι	ὅτε κέν τοι	ὅτε κέν τοι	ὅτε κέν τοι	ὅτε κέν τοι
2.72	αἴ κέν πως	αἴ κέν πως	αἴ κέν πως	αἴ κέν πως	αἴ κέν πως	αἴ κέν πως
2.83	αἴ κέν πως	αἴ κέν πως	αἴ κέν πως	αἴ κέν πως	αἴ κέν πως	αἴ κέν πως
2.119[b]	τόδε γ' ἐστὶ	τόδε γ' ἐστὶ	τόδε γ' ἐστὶ	τόδε γ' ἐστὶ	τόδε γ' ἐστὶ	τόδε γ' ἐστὶ

Continued

Line of Iliad	(i)	(ii)	(iii)	(iv)	(v)	(vi)	(vii)
2.122	οὔ πώ τι	οὔ πω τι	οὔ πώ τι	οὔ πω τι	οὔ πω τι	οὔ πω τι	οὔ πω τι
2.202	οὐ-τέ ποτ'	οὐ-τέ ποτ'	οὐ-τέ ποτ'	οὐ-τέ ποτ'	οὐ-τέ ποτ'	οὐ-τέ ποτ'	οὐ-τέ ποτ'
2.215	ὅ τί οἱ	ὅ τί οἱ	ὅ τί οἱ	ὅ τί οἱ	ὅ τί οἱ	ὅ τι οἱ	ὅ τι οἱ
2.229	ὄν κέ τις	ὄν κέ τις	ὄν κέ τις	ὄν κέ τις	ὄν κέ τις	ὄν κέ τις	ὄν κέ τις
2.238	ἦ ῥά τι οἱ	ἦ ῥά τι οἱ	ἦ ῥά τι οἱ	ἦ ῥά τι οἱ	ἦ ῥά τι οἱ	ἦ ῥά τι οἱ	ἦ ῥά τι οἱ
2.252	οὐδέ τί πω	οὐδέ τί πω	οὐδέ τι πω	οὐδέ τι πω	οὐδέ τι πω	οὐδέ τι πω	οὐδέ τι πω
2.258	* ὡς νύ περ	* ὡς νύ περ	* ὡς νύ περ	* ὡς νύ περ	* ὡς νύ περ	* ὡς νύ περ	ὡς νύ περ
2.276	οὐ θήν μιν	οὐ θήν μιν	οὐ θήν μιν	οὐ θήν μιν	οὐ θήν μιν	οὐ θήν μιν	οὐ θήν μιν
2.292	γάρ τίς τ'	γάρ τίς τ'	γάρ τίς τ'	γάρ τίς τ'	γάρ τίς τ'	γάρ τίς τ'	γάρ τις θ'
2.361	ὅτ-τί κεν	ὅτ-τί κεν	ὅτ-τί κεν	ὅτ-τί κεν	ὅτ-τί κεν	ὅτ-τί κεν	ὅττι κεν
2.365	ὅς τέ νυ	ὅς τέ νυ	ὅς τέ νυ	ὅς τέ νυ	ὅς τέ νυ	ὅς τέ νυ	ὅς τέ νυ
2.419	ἄρα πώ οἱ	ἄρα πω οἱ	ἄρα πώ οἱ	ἄρα πω οἱ	ἄρα πώ οἱ	ἄρα πώ οἱ	ἄρα πώ οἱ
2.553	οὐ πώ τις	οὐ πω τις	οὐ πω τις	οὐ πω τις	οὐ πω τις	οὐ πω τις	οὐ πω τις
2.687	ὅς τίς σφιν	ὅς τίς σφιν	ὅς τίς σφιν	ὅς τίς σφιν	ὅς τίς σφιν	ὅς τίς σφιν	ὅς τί (for τίς) σφιν
2.754	ἀλλά τέ μιν	ἀλλά τέ μιν	ἀλλά τε μιν	ἀλλά τε μιν	ἀλλά τε μιν	ἀλλά τε μιν	ἀλλά τε μιν
2.873	οὐδέ τί οἱ	οὐδέ τί οἱ	οὐδέ τι οἱ	οὐδέ τι οἱ	οὐδέ τι οἱ	οὐδέ τι οἱ	οὐδέ τι οἱ
3.12	τόσσον τίς τ'	τόσσον τίς τ'	τόσσον τίς τ'	τόσσον τίς τ'	τόσσον τίς τ'	τόσσον τίς τ'	τόσσον τις τ'
3.33	ὅτε τίς τε	ὅτε τίς τε	ὅτε τίς τε	ὅτε τίς τε	ὅτε τίς τε	ὅτε τίς τε	ὅτε τίς τε
3.35	ὦχρός τέ μιν	ὦχρός τέ μιν	ὦχρός τέ μιν	ὦχρός τέ μιν	ὦχρός τέ μιν	ὦχρός τέ μιν	ὦχρός τέ μιν
3.56	ἦ τέ κεν	ἦ τέ κεν	ἦ τέ κεν	ἦ τέ κεν	ἦ τέ κεν	ἦ τέ κεν	ἦ τέ κεν
3.61	ὅς ῥά τε	ὅς ῥά τε	ὅς ῥά τε	ὅς ῥά τε	ὅς ῥά τε	ὅς ῥά τε	ὅς ῥά τε

3.164	οὔ τί μοι	οὔ τί μοι	οὔ τί μοι	οὔ τί μοι	οὔ τί μοι	οὔ τί μοι	οὔ τί μοι	οὔ τί μοι
3.164	θεοί νύ μοι	θεοί νύ μοι	θεοί νύ μοι	θεοί νύ μοι	θεοί νύ μοι	θεοί νύ μοι	θεοί νύ μοι	θεοί νύ μοι
3.172	αἰδοῖός τέ μοι ἐσσι	αἰδοῖός τέ μοι ἐσσι	αἰδοῖός τέ μοι ἐσσι	αἰδοῖός τέ μοι ἐσσι	αἰδοῖός τέ μοι ἐσσι	αἰδοῖός τέ μοι ἐσσι	αἰδοῖός τέ μοι ἐσσι	αἰδοῖός τέ μοι ἐσσι
3.183	ἦ ῥά νύ τοι	ἦ ῥά νύ τοι	ἦ ῥά νύ τοι	ἦ ῥά νύ τοι	ἦ ῥά νύ τοι	ἦ ῥά νύ τοι	ἦ ῥά νύ τοι	ἦ ῥά νύ τοι
3.220	ζάκοτόν τέ τιν᾽	ζάκοτόν τέ τιν᾽	ζάκοτόν τέ τιν᾽	ζάκοτόν τέ τιν᾽	ζάκοτόν τέ τιν᾽	ζάκοτόν τέ τιν᾽	ζάκοτόν τέ τιν᾽	ζάκοτόν τέ τιν᾽
3.242	ἅ μοι ἐστὶν	ἅ μοι ἐστὶν	ἅ μοι ἐστὶν	ἅ μοι ἐστὶν	ἅ μοι ἐστὶν	ἅ μοι ἐστὶν	ἅ μοι ἐστὶν	ἅ μοι ἐστὶν
3.279	ὅ-τις κ᾽	ὅ-τις κ᾽	ὅ-τις κ᾽	ὅ-τις κ᾽	ὅ-τις κ᾽	ὅ-τις κ᾽	ὅ-τις κ᾽	ὅτις κ᾽
3.302	ἄρα πό σφιν	ἄρα πω σφιν	ἄρα πω σφιν	ἄρα πω σφιν	ἄρα πό σφιν	ἄρα πό σφιν	ἄρα πό σφιν	ἄρα πό σφιν
3.373	* καί νύ κεν	* καί νύ κεν	* καί νύ κεν	* καί νύ κεν	* καί νύ κεν	* καί νύ κεν	καί νύ κεν	καί νύ κεν
3.400	ἦ πή με	ἦ πή με	ἦ πή με	ἦ πή με	ἦ πή με	ἦ πή με	ἦ πή με	ἦ πή με
3.402	εἴ τίς τοι	εἴ τίς τοι	εἴ τίς τοι	εἴ τίς τοι	εἴ τίς τοι	εἴ τίς τοι	εἴ τίς τοι	εἴ τίς τοι
4.31	τί νύ σε	τί νύ σε	τί νύ σε	τί νύ σε	τί νύ σε	τί νύ σε	τί νύ σε	τί νύ σε
4.48	γάρ μοί ποτε	γάρ μοί ποτε	γάρ μοί ποτε	γάρ μοί ποτε	γάρ μοί ποτε	γάρ μοί ποτε	γάρ μοί ποτε	γάρ μοί ποτε
4.93	ἦ ῥά νυ μοί τι	ἦ ῥά νυ μοί τι	ἦ ῥά νυ μοί τι	ἦ ῥά νυ μοί τι	ἦ ῥά νυ μοί τι	ἦ ῥά νυ μοί τι	ἦ ῥά νυ μοί τι	ἦ ῥά νύ μοί τι
4.106	ὅν ῥά ποτ᾽	ὅν ῥά ποτ᾽	ὅν ῥά ποτ᾽	ὅν ῥά ποτ᾽	ὅν ῥά ποτ᾽	ὅν ῥά ποτ᾽	ὅν ῥά ποτ᾽	ὅν ῥά ποτ᾽
4.141	ὅτε τίς τ᾽	ὅτε τίς τ᾽	ὅτε τίς τ᾽	ὅτε τίς τ᾽	ὅτε τίς τ᾽	ὅτε τίς τ᾽	ὅτε τίς τ᾽	ὅτε τίς τ᾽
4.143	πολέες τέ μιν	πολέες τέ μιν	πολέες τέ μιν	πολέες τέ μιν	πολέες τέ μιν	πολέες τέ μιν	πολέες τέ μιν	πολέες τέ μιν
4.155	* θάνατόν νύ τοι	* θάνατόν νύ τοι	* θάνατόν νύ τοι	* θάνατόν νύ τοι	* θάνατόν νύ τοι	θάνατόν νύ τοι	* θάνατόν νύ τοι	θάνατόν νύ τοι
4.176	καί κέ τις	καί κέ τις	καί κέ τις	καί κέ τις	καί κέ τις	καί κέ τις	καί κέ τις	καί κέ τις[c]
4.182	ὥς ποτέ τις	ὥς ποτέ τις	ὥς ποτέ τις	ὥς ποτέ τις	ὥς ποτέ τις	ὥς ποτέ τις	ὥς ποτέ τις	ὥς ποτέ τις
4.184	δέ τι πω	δέ τι πω	δέ τι πω	δέ τι πω	δέ τι πω	δέ τι πω	δέ τι πω	δέ τι πω
4.219	τά οἱ ποτὲ	τά οἱ ποτὲ	τά οἱ ποτὲ	τά οἱ ποτὲ	τά οἱ ποτὲ	τά οἱ ποτὲ	τά οἱ ποτὲ	τά οἱ ποτὲ

Continued

Table Ap.1 Continued

Line of Iliad	(i)	(ii)	(iii)	(iv)	(v)	(vi)	(vii)
4.229	ὁππότε κέν μιν	ὁππότε κέν μιν	ὁππότε κέν μιν	ὁππότε κέν μιν	ὁππότε κέν μιν	ὁππότε κέν μιν	ὁππότε κέν μιν
4.234	μή πώ τι	μή πω τι	μή πώ τι	μή πω τι	μή πω τι	μή πω τι	μή πω τι
4.245	ἄρα τίς σφι	ἄρα τίς σφι	ἄρα τίς σφι	ἄρα τίς σφι	ἄρα τίς σφι	ἄρα τίς σφι	ἄρα τίς σφι
4.259	ὅτε πέρ τε	ὅτε πέρ τε	ὅτε πέρ τε	ὅτε πέρ τε	ὅτε πέρ τε	ὅτε πέρ τε	ὅτε πέρ τε
4.331	γάρ πώ σφιν	γάρ πω σφιν	γάρ πώ σφιν	γάρ πω σφιν	γάρ πώ σφιν^d	γάρ πώ σφιν	γάρ πώ σφιν
4.353	αἴ κέν τοι	αἴ κέν τοι	αἴ κέν τοι	αἴ κέν τοι	αἴ κέν τοι	αἴ κέν τοι	αἴ κέν τοι
4.359	οὐ-τέ σε	οὐ-τέ σε	οὐ-τέ σε	οὔ-τέ σε	οὔ-τέ σε	οὔ-τέ σε	οὔτέ σε
4.483	ἤ ῥά τ᾽	ἤ ῥά τ᾽	ἤ ῥά τ᾽	ἤ ῥά τ᾽	ἤ ῥά τ᾽	ἤ ῥά τ᾽	ἤ ῥά τ᾽
4.484	ἀτάρ τέ οἱ	ἀτάρ τέ οἱ	ἀτάρ τέ οἱ	ἀτάρ τέ οἱ	ἀτάρ τέ οἱ	ἀτάρ τέ οἱ	ἀτάρ τέ οἱ
4.539	οὐ κέ τι	οὐ κέ τι	οὐ κέ τι	οὐ κέ τι	οὐ κέ τι	οὐ κέ τι	οὐ κέ τι
5.103	οὐδέ ἕ φημὶ	οὐδέ ἕ φημὶ	οὐδέ ἕ φημὶ	οὐδέ ἕ φημὶ	οὐδέ ἕ φημὶ	οὐδέ ἕ φημὶ	οὐδέ ἕ φημὶ
5.116	εἴ ποτέ μοι	εἴ ποτέ μοι	εἴ ποτέ μοι	εἴ ποτέ μοι	εἴ ποτέ μοι	εἴ ποτέ μοι	εἴ ποτέ μοι
5.118	δέ τέ μ᾽	δέ τέ μ᾽	δέ τέ μ᾽	δέ τέ μ᾽	δέ τέ μ᾽	δέ τέ μ᾽	δέ τε μ᾽^e
5.119	οὐδέ μέ φησὶ	οὐδέ μέ φησὶ	οὐδέ μέ φησὶ	οὐδέ με φησὶ	οὐδέ με φησὶ	οὐδέ με φησὶ	οὐδέ με φησὶ
5.137	ὅν ῥά τε	ὅν ῥά τε	ὅν ῥά τε	ὅν ῥᾶ τε	ὅν ῥᾶ τε	ὅν ῥᾶ τε	ὅν ῥᾶ τε
5.170	ἔπος τέ μιν	ἔπος τέ μιν	ἔπος τέ μιν	ἔπος τέ μιν	ἔπος τέ μιν	ἔπος τέ μιν	ἔπος τέ μιν
5.172	οὐ τίς τοι	οὐ τίς τοι	οὐ τίς τοι	οὐ τίς τοι	οὐ τίς τοι	οὐ τίς τοι	οὐ τίς τοι
5.191	θεός νύ τις ἐστι	θεός νύ τις ἐστι	θεός νύ τις ἐστι	θεός νύ τις ἐστι	θεός νύ τις ἐστι	θεός νύ τις ἐστι	θεός νύ τις ἐστι
5.260	αἴ κέν μοι	αἴ κέν μοι	αἴ κέν μοι	αἴ κέν μοι	αἴ κέν μοι	αἴ κέν μοι	αἴ κέν μοι
5.298	μή πως οἱ	μή πως οἱ	μή πώς οἱ	μή πως οἱ	μή πως οἱ	μή πως οἱ	μή πως οἱ
5.306	δέ τέ μιν	δέ τέ μιν	δέ τε μιν	δέ τε μιν	δέ τε μιν	δέ τε μιν	δέ τε μιν

5.311	* καὶ νύ κεν	* καὶ νύ κεν	* καὶ νύ κεν	* καὶ νύ κεν	* καὶ νύ κεν	* καὶ νύ κεν	καὶ νὺ ἐκεν
5.638	οἷόν τινά φασι	οἷόν τινά φασι	οἷόν τινά φασι	οἷόν τινά φασι	οἷόν τινά φασι	οἷόν τινά φασι	οἷον τινα φασὶ
5.644	οὐδέ τί σε	οὐδέ τί σε	οὐδέ τι σε	οὐδέ τι σε	οὐδέ τι σε	οὐδέ τι σε	οὐδὲ τι σε
5.650	* ὅς ῥά μιν	* ὅς ῥά μιν	* ὅς ῥά μιν	* ὅς ῥά μιν	* ὅς ῥά μιν	* ὅς ῥά μιν	ὅς ῥά μιν[e]
5.679	* καὶ νύ κ'	* καὶ νύ κ'	* καὶ νύ κ'	* καὶ νύ κ'	* καὶ νύ κ'	* καὶ νύ κ'	καὶ νὺ κ'
5.700	οὔ-τέ ποτε	οὔ-τέ ποτε	οὔ-τέ ποτε	οὔ-τέ ποτε	οὔ-τέ ποτε	οὔ-τέ ποτε	οὔτέ ποτε
5.701	* οὔ-τέ ποτ'	* οὔ-τέ ποτ'	* οὔ-τέ ποτ'	* οὔ-τέ ποτ'	* οὔ-τέ ποτ'	* οὔ-τέ ποτ'	οὔτέ ποτ'
5.762	ἢ ῥά τί μοι	ἢ ῥά τί μοι	ἢ ῥά τι μοι	ἢ ῥά τι μοι	ἢ ῥά τι μοι	ἢ ῥά τι μοι	ἢ ῥά τί μοι
5.802	ὅτε πέρ μιν	ὅτε πέρ μιν	ὅτε πέρ μιν	ὅτε πέρ μιν	ὅτε πέρ μιν	ὅτε πέρ μιν	ὅτε πέρ μιν
5.812	ἤ νύ σε που	ἤ νύ σε που	ἤ νύ σε που	ἤ νύ σε που	ἤ νύ σε που	ἤ νύ σε που	ἤ νὺ σέ που
5.817	οὐ-τέ τί με	οὐ-τέ τί με	οὐ-τέ τι με	οὐ-τέ τι με	οὐ-τέ τι με	οὐ-τέ τι με	οὔτέ τι με
5.817	οὔ-τέ τις	οὔ-τέ τις	οὔ-τέ τις	οὔ-τέ τις	οὔ-τέ τις	οὔ-τέ τις	οὔτε τις
5.827	μή-τέ τιν'	μή-τέ τιν'	μή-τέ τιν'	μή-τέ τιν'	μή-τέ τιν'	μή-τέ τιν'	μή-τέ τιν'
5.858	τῇ ῥά μιν	τῇ ῥά μιν	τῇ ῥά μιν	τῇ ῥά μιν	τῇ ῥά μιν	τῇ ῥά μιν	τῆι ῥά μιν
5.879	οὔ-τέ τι	οὔ-τέ τι	οὐ-τέ τι	οὐ-τέ τι	οὐ-τέ τι	οὐ-τέ τι	οὔτέ τι
5.885	ἢ τέ κε	ἢ τέ κε	ἢ τέ κε	ἢ τέ κε	ἢ τέ κε	ἢ τέ κε	ἢ τέ κε
5.889	μή τί μοι	μή τί μοι	μή τί μοι	μή τί μοι	μή τί μοι	μή τί μοι	μή τί μοι
5.890	δέ μοί ἐσσι	δέ μοί ἐσσι	δέ μοί ἐσσι	δέ μοί ἐσσὶ	δέ μοι ἐσσὶ	δέ μοι ἐσσὶ	δέ μοι ἐσσὶ
6.49	τῶν κέν τοι	τῶν κέν τοι	τῶν κέν τοι	τῶν κέν τοι	τῶν κέν τοι	τῶν κέν τοι	τῶν κέν τοι
6.100	ὃν πέρ φασι	ὃν πέρ φασι	ὃν πέρ φασι	ὃν πέρ φασι	ὃν πέρ φασι	ὃν πέρ φασι	ὃν πέρ φασι
6.101	οὐδέ τίς οἱ	οὐδέ τίς οἱ	οὐδέ τις οἱ	οὐδέ τις οἱ	οὐδέ τις οἱ	οὐδέ τις οἱ	οὐδέ τι,σ οἱ
6.142	δέ τις ἐσσι	δέ τις ἐσσι	δέ τις ἐσσὶ	δέ τις ἐσσὶ	δέ τις ἐσσὶ	δέ τις ἐσσὶ	δέ τις ἐσσὶ
6.177	ὅτ-τί ῥά οἱ	ὅτ-τί ῥά οἱ	ὅτ-τί ῥα οἱ	ὅτ-τί ῥα οἱ	ὅτ-τί ῥα οἱ	ὅτ-τί ῥα οἱ	ὅτι ῥά ου

Continued

Table Ap.1 *Continued*

Line of Iliad	(i)	(ii)	(iii)	(iv)	(v)	(vi)	(vii)
6.215	ἦ ῥά νύ μοι	ἦ ῥά νύ μοι	ἦ ῥά νύ μοι	ἦ ῥά νύ μοι	ἦ ῥά νυ μοι	ἦ ῥά νυ μοι	ἦ ῥά νύ μοι
6.258	* ὄφρά κέ τοι	* ὄφρά κέ τοι	ὄφρά κε τοι	ὄφρά κε τοι	ὄφρά κε τοι	ὄφρά κε τοι	ὄφρά κέ τοι
6.267	οὐδέ πῄ ἐστί	οὐδέ πῃ ἐστί	οὐδέ πῃ ἐστί	οὐδέ πῃ ἐστί	οὐδέ πῃ ἐστί	οὐδέ πῃ ἐστί	οὐδέ πῃ ἐστί
6.271	ὅς τίς τοι	ὅς τίς τοι	ὅς τίς τοι	ὅς τίς τοι	ὅς τίς τοι	ὅς τίς τοι	ὅς τίς τοι
6.281	* ὡς κέ οἱ	* ὡς κέ οἱ	* ὡς κέ οἱ	* ὡς κέ οἱ	* ὡς κέ οἱ	* ὡς κέ οἱ	* ὡς κέ οἱ
6.330	εἴ τινά που	εἴ τινά που	εἴ τινά που	εἴ τινά που	εἴ τινά που	εἴ τινά που	εἴ τινά που
6.383	οὐ-τέ πῃ	οὐ-τέ πῃ	οὔ-τέ πῃ	οὔ-τέ πῃ	οὔ-τέ πῃ	οὔ-τέ πῃ	οὔ-τέ πῃ
6.413	οὐδέ μοί ἐστι	οὐδέ μοί ἐστι	οὐδέ μοι ἐστί	οὐδέ μοι ἐστί	οὐδέ μοι ἐστί	οὐδέ μοι ἐστί	οὐδέ μοι ἐστί
6.429	σύ μοί ἐσσι	σύ μοί ἔσσι	σύ μοι ἔσσι	σύ μοι ἐσσί	σύ μοι ἐσσί	σύ μοι ἐσσί	σύ μοι ἐσσί
6.438	ἦ πού τίς σφιν	ἦ πού τίς σφιν	ἦ πού τίς σφιν	ἦ πού τίς σφιν	ἦ πού τίς σφιν	ἦ πού τίς σφιν	ἦ πού τί (for τίς) σφιν
6.454	ὅτε κέν τις	ὅτε κέν τις	ὅτε κέν τις	ὅτε κέν τις	ὅτε κέν τις	ὅτε κέν τις	ὅτε κέν τις
6.459	καί ποτέ τις	καί ποτέ τις	καί ποτέ τις	καί ποτέ τις	καί ποτέ τις	καί ποτέ τις	καί ποτέ τις
6.462	ὥς ποτέ τις	ὥς ποτέ τις	ὥς ποτέ τις	ὥς ποτέ τις	ὥς ποτέ τις	ὥς ποτέ τις	ὥς ποτέ τις
6.465	πρίν γέ τι	πρίν γέ τι	πρίν γέ τι	πρίν γέ τι	πρίν γέ τι	πρίν γέ τι	πρίν γέ τι
6.479	καί ποτέ τις	καί ποτέ τις	καί ποτέ τις	καί ποτέ τις	καί ποτέ τις	καί ποτέ τις	καί ποτέ τις
6.485	χειρί τέ μιν	χειρί τέ μιν	χειρί τε μιν	χειρί τε μιν	χειρί τε μιν	χειρί τε μιν	χειρί τέ μιν
6.486	μή μοί τι	μή μοί τι	μή μοί τι	μή μοί τι	μή μοί τι	μή μοί τι	μή μοί τι
6.487	γάρ τίς μ'	γάρ τίς μ'	γάρ τίς μ'	γάρ τίς μ'	γάρ τίς μ'	γάρ τίς μ'	γάρ τίς μ'
6.488	οὔ τινά φημι	οὔ τινά φημι	οὔ τινά φημι	οὔ τινά φημι	οὔ τινά φημι	οὔ τινά φημι	οὔ τινα φημί
6.521	ἄν τίς τοι	ἄν τίς τοι	ἄν τίς τοι	ἄν τίς τοι	ἄν τίς τοι	ἄν τίς τοι	ἄν τίς τοι

6.526	αἴ κέ ποθι	αἴ κέ ποθι	αἴ κέ ποθι	αἴ κέ ποθι	αἴ κέ ποθι	αἴ κέ ποθι
7.28	εἴ μοί τι	εἴ μοί τι	εἴ μοί τι	εἴ μοί τι	εἴ μοί τι	εἴ μοί τι
7.39	ἤν τινά που	ἤν τινά που	ἤν τινά που	ἤν τινά που	ἤν τινά που	ἤν τινά που
7.48	ἦ ῥά νύ μοί τι	ἦ ῥά νύ μοί τι	ἦ ῥά νύ μοί τι	ἦ ῥά νύ μοί τι	ἦ ῥά νύ μοί τι	ἦ ῥά νύ μοί τι
7.48	δέ τοί εἰμι	δέ τοί εἰμι	δέ τοι εἰμί	δέ τοι εἰμί	δέ τοι εἰμί	δέ τοι εἰμί
7.52	γάρ πώ τοι	γάρ πώ τοι	γάρ πω τοι	γάρ πω τοι	γάρ πω τοι	γάρ πω τοι
7.86	σῆμά τέ οἱ	σῆμά τέ οἱ	σῆμά τε οἱ	σῆμά τε οἱ	σῆμά τε οἱ	σῆμά τέ οἱ
7.87	καί ποτέ τις	καί ποτέ τις	καί ποτέ τις	καί ποτέ τις	καί ποτέ τις	καί ποτέ τις[f]
7.91	* ὥς ποτέ τις	* ὥς ποτέ τις	* ὥς ποτέ τις	* ὥς ποτέ τις	* ὥς ποτέ τις	ὥς ποτέ τις
7.104	* ἔνθά κέ τοι	* ἔνθά κέ τοι	ἔνθά κε τοι	ἔνθά κε τοι	ἔνθά κε τοι	ἔνθα κέ τοι
7.109	οὐδέ τί σε	οὐδέ τί σε	οὐδέ τι σε	οὐδέ τι σε	οὐδέ τι σε	οὐδέ τι σε
7.117	ἀδευής τ' ἔστι	ἀδευής τ' ἔστι	ἀδευής τ' ἔστι	ἀδευής τ' ἔστι	ἀδευής τ' ἔστι	ἀδευής τ' ἔστι
7.127	ὅς ποτέ μ'	ὅς ποτέ μ'	ὅς ποτέ μ'	ὅς ποτέ μ'	ὅς ποτέ μ'	ὅς ποτέ μ'
7.197	γάρ τίς με	γάρ τίς με	γάρ τίς με	γάρ τίς με	γάρ τίς με	γάρ τις με
7.235	μή τί μεν	μή τί μεν	μή τί μεν	μή τί μεν	μή τί μεν	μή τί μεν
7.239	τό μοι ἐστὶ	τό μοι ἐστὶ	τό μοι ἐστὶ	τό μοι ἐστὶ	τό μοι ἐστὶ	τό μοι ἐστὶ
7.273	* καί νύ κε	* καί νύ κε	* καί νύ κε	* καί νύ κε	* καί νύ κε	καί νύ κε
7.298	αἴ τέ μοι	αἴ τέ μοι	αἴ τέ μοι	αἴ τέ μοι	αἴ τέ μοι	αἴ τέ μοι
7.352	οὐ νύ τι	οὐ νύ τι	οὐ νύ τι	οὐ νύ τι	οὐ νύ τι	οὐ νύ τι
7.387	αἴ κέ περ	αἴ κέ περ	αἴ κέ περ	αἴ κέ περ	αἴ κέ περ	αἴ κε περ
7.446	ἦ ῥά τίς ἐστι	ἦ ῥά τίς ἐστι	ἦ ῥά τις ἐστὶ	ἦ ῥά τις ἐστὶ	ἦ ῥά τις ἐστὶ	ἦ ῥά τίς ἐστι
7.456	ἄλλός κέν τις	ἄλλός κέν τις	ἄλλός κέν τις	ἄλλός κέν τις	ἄλλός κέν τις	ἄλλός κέν τις
7.463	ὡς κέν τοι	ὡς κέν τοι	ὡς κέν τοι	ὡς κέν τοι	ὡς κέν τοι	ὡς κέν τοι

Continued

Table Ap.1 *Continued*

Line of *Iliad*	(i)	(ii)	(iii)	(iv)	(v)	(vi)	(vii)
8.7	μή-τέ τις	μή-τέ τις	μή-τέ τις	μή-τέ τις	μή-τέ τις	μή-τέ τις	μή-τέ τις
8.7	* μή-τέ τις	* μή-τέ τις	* μή-τέ τις	* μή-τέ τις	* μή-τέ τις	* μή-τέ τις	μὴ-τέ τις
8.27	περί τ᾽ εἰμι	περί τ᾽ εἰμι	περί τ᾽ εἰμι	περί τ᾽ εἰμι	περί τ᾽ εἰμι	περί τ᾽ εἰμι	περί τ᾽ εἰμι
8.27	περί τ᾽ εἰμ᾽	περί τ᾽ εἰμ᾽	περί τ᾽ εἰμ᾽	περί τ᾽ εἰμ᾽	περί τ᾽ εἰμ᾽	περί τ᾽ εἰμ᾽	περί τ᾽ εἰμ᾽
8.39	οὖ νύ τι	οὖ νύ τι	οὖ νύ τι	οὖ νύ τι	οὖ νύ τι	οὖ νύ τι	οὖ νΰ τι
8.90	* καί νύ κεν	* καί νύ κεν	* καί νύ κεν	* καί νύ κεν	* καί νύ κεν	* καί νύ κεν	καί νύ κεν
8.95	μή τίς τοι	μή τίς τοι	μή τίς τοι	μή τίς τοι	μή τίς τοι	μή τίς τοι	μή τίς τοι
8.104	δέ νύ τοι	δέ νύ τοι	δέ νυ τοι	δέ νυ τοι	δέ νυ τοι	δέ νυ τοι	δέ νΰ τοι
8.131	καί νύ κε	καί νύ κε	καί νύ κε	καί νύ κε	καί νύ κε	καί νύ κε	καί νύ κε[g]
8.190	ὅς πέρ οἱ	ὅς πέρ οἱ	ὅς πέρ οἱ	ὅς πέρ οἱ	ὅς πέρ οἱ	ὅς πέρ οἱ	ὅς πέρ οἱ
8.217	* καί νύ κεν	* καί νύ κεν	* καί νύ κεν	* καί νύ κεν	* καί νύ κεν	* καί νύ κεν	καί νύ κεν
8.236	ἦ ῥά τιν᾽	ἦ ῥά τιν᾽	ἦ ῥά τιν᾽	ἦ ῥά τιν᾽	ἦ ῥά τιν᾽	ἦ ῥά τιν᾽	ἦ ῥά τιν᾽
8.238	δή ποτέ φημι	δή ποτέ φημι	δή ποτέ φημι	δή ποτέ φημι	δή ποτέ φημι	δή ποτέ φημι	δή ποτέ φημι[i]
8.242	τόδε πέρ μοι	τόδε πέρ μοι	τόδε πέρ μοι	τόδε πέρ μοι	τόδε πέρ μοι	τόδε πέρ μοι	τόδε πέρ μοι
8.282	αἴ κέν τι	αἴ κέν τι	αἴ κέν τι	αἴ κέν τι	αἴ κέν τι	αἴ κέν τι	αἴ κέν τι
8.287	αἴ κέν μοι	αἴ κέν μοι	αἴ κέν μοι	αἴ κέν μοι	αἴ κέν μοι	αἴ κέν μοι	αἴ κέν μοι
8.291	ἤ κέν τοι	ἤ κέν τοι	ἤ κέν τοι	ἤ κέν τοι	ἤ κέν τοι	ἤ κέν τοι	ἤ κέν τοι
8.338	ὅτε τίς τε	ὅτε τίς τε	ὅτε τίς τε	ὅτε τίς τε	ὅτε τίς τε	ὅτε τίς τε	ὅτε τίς τε
8.445	οὐδέ τι μιν	οὐδέ τι μιν	οὐδέ τι μιν	οὐδέ τι μιν	οὐδέ τι μιν	οὐδέ τι μιν	οὐδέ τι μιν
8.532	εἴ κέ μ᾽	εἴ κέ μ᾽	εἴ κέ μ᾽	εἴ κέ μ᾽	εἴ κέ μ᾽	εἴ κέ μ᾽	εἴ κέ μ᾽
9.55	οὖ τίς τοι	οὖ τίς τοι	οὖ τίς τοι	οὖ τίς τοι	οὖ τίς τοι	οὖ τίς τοι	οὖ τίς τοι

9.61	οὐδέ κέ τίς μοι	οὐδέ κέ τίς μοι	οὐδέ κε τίς μοι	οὐδέ κε τίς μοι	οὐδέ κε τίς μοι	οὐδέ κε τίς μοι	οὐδέ κε τίς μοι
9.102	ὅτ-τί κεν	ὅτ-τί κεν	ὅτ-τί κεν	ὅτ-τί κεν	ὅτ-τί κεν	ὅτ-τί κεν	ὅτ-τί κεν
9.112	ὥς κέν μιν	ὥς κέν μιν	ὥς κέν μιν	ὥς κέν μιν	ὥς κέν μιν	ὥς κέν μιν	ὥς κέν μιν
9.142	* γαμβρός κέν μοι	* γαμβρός κέν μοι	* γαμβρός κέν μοι	* γαμβρός κέν μοι	* γαμβρός κέν μοι	* γαμβρός κέν μοι	γαμβρός κέν μοι
9.144	δέ μοί εἶσι	δέ μοί εἶσι	δέ μοι εἶσὶ	δέ μοι εἶσὶ	δέ μοι εἶσὶ	δέ μοι εἶσὶ	δέ μοι εἶσὶ
9.148	οὐ πώ τις	οὐ πώ τις	οὐ πώ τις	οὐ πω τις	οὐ πω τις	οὐ πω τις	οὐ πω τις
9.155	οἴ κέ ἑ	οἴ κέ ἑ	οἴ κέ ἑ	οἴ κέ ἑ	οἴ κέ ἑ	οἴ κέ ἑ	οἴ κέ ἑ
9.157	* ταῦτά κέ οἱ	* ταῦτά κέ οἱ	ταῦτά κε οἱ	ταῦτά κε οἱ	ταῦτά κε οἱ	ταῦτά κε οἱ	ταῦτα κέ οἱ
9.262	δέ κέ τοι	δέ κέ τοι	δέ κε τοι	δέ κε τοι	δέ κε τοι	δέ κε τοι	δέ κε τοι
9.284	γαμβρός κέν οἱ	γαμβρός κέν οἱ	γαμβρός κέν οἱ	γαμβρός κέν οἱ	γαμβρός κέν οἱ	γαμβρός κέν οἱ	γαμβρός κέν οἱ
9.286	δέ οἱ εἶσι	δέ οἱ εἶσι	δέ οἱ εἶσὶ	δέ οἱ εἶσὶ	δέ οἱ εἶσὶ	δέ οι εἶσὶ	δέ οι εἶσὶ
9.290	οὐ πώ τις	οὐ πώ τις	οὐ πώ τις	οὐ πω τις	οὐ πω τις	οὐ πω τις	οὐ πω τις
9.297	οἴ κέ σε	οἴ κέ σε	οἴ κέ σε	οἴ κέ σε	οἴ κέ σε	οἴ κέ σε	οἴ κέ σε
9.299	* ταῦτά κέ τοι	* ταῦτά κέ τοι	ταῦτά κε τοι	ταῦτά κε τοι	ταῦτά κε τοι	ταῦτά κε τοι	ταῦτα κέ τοι
9.303	γάρ κέ σφι	γάρ κέ σφι	γάρ κέ σφι	γάρ κέ σφι	γάρ κέ σφι	γάρ κέ σφι	γάρ κέ σφι
9.305	οὔ τινά φησιν	οὔ τινά φησιν	οὔ τινά φησιν	οὔ τινά φησιν	οὔ τινά φησιν	οὔ τινά φησιν	οὔ τινα φησιν
9.324	δέ τέ οἱ	δέ τέ οἱ	δέ τε οἱ	δέ τε οἱ	δέ τε οἱ	δέ τε οἱ	δέ τε οἱ
9.359	αἴ κέν τοι	αἴ κέν τοι	αἴ κέν τοι	αἴ κέν τοι	αἴ κέν τοι	αἴ κέν τοι	αἴ κέν τοι
9.371	εἴ τινά που	εἴ τινά που	εἴ τινά που	εἴ τινά που	εἴ τινά που	εἴ τινά που	εἴ τινά που
9.380	* ὅσσά τέ οἱ	* ὅσσά τέ οἱ	ὅσσά τε οἱ	ὅσσά τε οἱ	ὅσσά τε οἱ	ὅσσά τε οἱ	ὅσσα τέ οἱ
9.394	Πηλεύς θήν μοι	Πηλεύς θήν μοι	Πηλεύς θήν μοι	Πηλεύς θην μοι	Πηλεύς θην μοι	Πηλεύς θην μοι	Πηλεύς θην μοι
9.410	γάρ τέ μέ φησια	γάρ τέ μέ φησια	γάρ τέ με φησὶ	γάρ τέ με φησὶ	γάρ τέ με φησὶ	γάρ τέ με φησὶ	γάρ τέ με φησὶ
9.416	οὐδέ κε μ'	οὐδέ κε μ'	οὐδέ κε μ'	οὐδέ κε μ'	οὐδέ κε μ'	οὐδέ κε μ'	οὐδέ κε μ'

Continued

Table Ap.1 *Continued*

Line of Iliad	(i)	(ii)	(iii)	(iv)	(v)	(vi)	(vii)
9.424	ἤ κέ σφιν	ἤ κέ σφιν	ἤ κέ σφιν	ἤ κέ σφιν	ἤ κέ σφιν	ἤ κέ σφιν	ἤ κέ σφιν
9.429	οὔ τί μιν	οὔ τί μιν	οὔ τί μιν	οὔ τί μιν	οὔ τί μιν	οὔ τί μιν	οὔ τί μιν
9.445	εἴ κέν μοι	εἴ κέν μοι	εἴ κέν μοι	εἴ κέν μοι	εἴ κέν μοι	εἴ κέν μοι	εἴ κέν μοι
9.495	ἵνα μοί ποτ'	ἵνα μοί ποτ'	ἵνα μοί ποτ'	ἵνα μοί ποτ'	ἵνα μοί ποτ'	ἵνα μοί ποτ'	ἵνα μοί ποτ'
9.496	οὐδέ τι σε	οὐδέ τί σε	οὐδέ τι σε	οὐδέ τι σε	οὐδέ τι σε	οὐδέ τι σε	οὐδέ τι σε
9.501	ὅτε κέν τις	ὅτε κέν τις	ὅτε κέν τις	ὅτε κέν τις	ὅτε κέν τις	ὅτε κέν τις	ὅτε κέν τις
9.504	αἱ ῥά τε	αἱ ῥά τε	αἱ ῥά τε	αἱ ῥά τε	αἱ ῥά τε	αἱ ῥά τε	αἱ ῥά τε
9.525	ὅτε κέν τιν'	ὅτε κέν τιν'	ὅτε κέν τιν'	ὅτε κέν τιν'	ὅτε κέν τιν'	ὅτε κέν τιν'	ὅτε κέν τιν'
9.607	οὔ τί με	οὔ τί με	οὔ τί με	οὔ τί με	οὔ τί με	οὔ τί με	οὔ τί με
9.613	οὐδέ τι σε	οὐδέ τί σε	οὐδέ τι σε	οὐδέ τι σε	οὐδέ τι σε	οὐδέ τι σε	οὐδέ τι σε
9.615	ὅς κέ με	ὅς κέ με	ὅς κέ με	ὅς κέ με	ὅς κέ με	ὅς κέ με	ὅς κέ με
9.632	μέν τίς τε	μέν τίς τε	μέν τίς τε	μέν τίς τε	μέν τίς τε	μέν τίς τε	μέν τίς τε
9.640	δέ τοι εἶμεν	δέ τοι εἶμεν	δέ τοι εἶμεν	δέ τοι εἶμεν	δέ τοι εἶμεν	δέ τοι εἶμεν	δέ τοι εἶμεν
9.645	* πάντά τί μοι	* πάντά τί μοι	πάντά τι μοι	πάντά τι μοι	πάντά τι μοι	πάντά τι μοι	πάντα τί μοι
9.692	οὔ τί μιν	οὔ τί μιν	οὔ τί μιν	οὔ τί μιν	οὔ τί μιν	οὔ τί μιν	οὔ τι μιν
9.702	ὁππότε κέν μιν	ὁππότε κέν μιν	ὁππότε κέν μιν	ὁππότε κέν μιν	ὁππότε κέν μιν	ὁππότε κέν μιν	ὁππότε κέν μιν
10.7	ὅτε πέρ τε	ὅτε πέρ τε	ὅτε πέρ τε	ὅτε πέρ τε	ὅτε πέρ τε	ὅτε πέρ τε	ὅτε πέρ τε
10.19	εἴ τινά οἱ	εἴ τινά οἱ	εἴ τινά οἱ	εἴ τινά οἱ	εἴ τινά οἱ	εἴ τινά οἱ	εἴ τινά οἱ
10.39	οὔ τίς τοι	οὔ τίς τοι	οὔ τίς τοι	οὔ τίς τοι	οὔ τίς τοι	οὔ τίς τοι	οὔ τίς τοι
10.44	ἤ τίς κεν	ἤ τίς κεν	ἤ τίς κεν	ἤ τίς κεν	ἤ τίς κεν	ἤ τίς κεν	ἤ τίς κεν
10.105	ὅσα πού νυν	ὅσα που νυν	ὅσα πού νυν	ὅσα που νυν	ὅσα πού νυν	ὅσα πού νυν	ὅσα πού νῦν

	Col 1	Col 2	Col 3	Col 4	Col 5	Col 6	Col 7
10.115	εἴ πέρ μοι	εἴ πέρ μοι	εἴ πέρ μοι	εἴ πέρ μοι	εἴ πέρ μοι	εἴ πέρ μοι	εἴ πέρ μοι
10.129	οὔ τίς οἱ	οὔ τίς οἱ	οὔ τίς οἱ	οὔ τίς οἱ	οὔ τίς οἱ	οὔ τίς οἱ	οὔ τίς οἱ
10.130	ὅτε κέν τιν'	ὅτε κέν τιν'	ὅτε κέν τιν'	ὅτε κέν τιν'	ὅτε κέν τιν'	ὅτε κέν τιν'	ὅτε κέν τιν'
10.171	τῶν κέν τις	τῶν κέν τις	τῶν κέν τις	τῶν κέν τις	τῶν κέν τις	τῶν κέν τις	τῶν κέν τις
10.186	* ἀπό τέ σφισιν	ἀπό τέ σφισιν	ἀπό τε σφισὶν	* ἀπό τέ σφισιν	ἀπό τε σφισὶν	* ἀπό τέ σφισιν[h]	ἀπο τέ σφισιν[i]
10.206	εἴ τινά που	εἴ τινά που	εἴ τινά που	εἴ τινά που	εἴ τινά που	εἴ τινά που	εἴ τινά που
10.207	ἤ τινά που	ἤ τινά που	ἤ τινά που	ἤ τινά που	ἤ τινά που	ἤ τινά που	ἤ τινά που
10.212	μέγα κέν οἱ	μέγα κέν οἱ	μέγα κέν οἱ	μέγα κέν οἱ	μέγα κέν οἱ	μέγα κέν οἱ	μέγα κέν οἱ
10.222	εἴ τίς μοι	εἴ τίς μοι	εἴ τίς μοι	εἴ τίς μοι	εἴ τίς μοι	εἴ τίς μοι	εἴ τίς μοι
10.225	εἴ πέρ τε	εἴ πέρ τε	εἴ πέρ τε	εἴ πέρ τε	εἴ πέρ τε	εἴ πέρ τε	εἴ πέρ τε
Number of sequences for which the accentuation matches that of Venetus A	154 (62%) or 178 (71%) with asterisked sequences included	156 (62%) or 180 (72%) with asterisked sequences included	184 (74%) or 201 (80%) with asterisked sequences included	184 (74%) or 201 (80%) with asterisked sequences included	184 (74%) or 201 (80%) with asterisked sequences included	184 (74%) or 202 (81%) with asterisked sequences included	190 (76%) or 208 (83%) with asterisked sequences included

^a χειρί is a scribal correction of χειρί.

^b On the treatment of elision here, see Table 4.2, note a.

^c καί is a scribal correction of καί.

^d For this as the expected accentuation under the revised Göttling-Barrett system, see section 4.2.4.

^e We treat the lack of accent mark on ὅς as the equivalent of what modern scholars would print as ὅς, i.e. ὅς with 'lulled' accent.

^f καί is a scribal correction of καί.

^g καί is a scribal correction of καί.

^h For this as the expected accentuation under the revised Göttling-Barrett system, see section 4.4, discussion of Table 4.6.

ⁱ As noted at Table 4.5, note b, we take the accent mark to be intended as falling on the τε, although conceivably it was meant to fall on the πο. Once again, for the purposes of calculating which systems produce the same accentuation as we find in Venetus A, we treat ἀπο as equivalent to ἀπό: there would be little difference in principle between the two, even if ἀπο is an unexpected writing in an accented medieval codex.

Table Ap.2 The first 250 sequences of more than one enclitic appearing in Venetus A (omitting folios of Venetus A for which we have only a fifteenth-century replacement for the original), accented according to eight further principles derived from the scholarly literature on enclitics, and then as in Venetus A. The word preceding the first enclitic is included, and enclitics themselves are underlined. Shading indicates a way of accenting a sequence that differs from that in Venetus A. In columns (Ai)–(Aiii) and (Bi)–(Biii), an asterisk indicates a way of accenting a sequence differing from that of Venetus A only insofar as Venetus A accents the word preceding the first enclitic as if a non-enclitic word was to follow.

Line of Iliad	(Ai)	(Aii)	(Aiii)	(Bi)	(Bii)	(Biii)	(Biv)	(Bv)	(D) Venetus A
	'Traditional' system but a monosyllabic enclitic is unaccented if a non-elided disyllabic one follows.	'Traditional' system but enclitic pronoun forms are unaccented, except forms of indefinite *ΤΙΣ*	'Traditional' system but the following are left unaccented: (a) a monosyllabic enclitic ending in a short vowel, after a syllable ending in a short accented vowel; (b) enclitic *ΠΩ* and *ΠΩΣ*	Accents on alternate enclitics: begin by accenting the first enclitic to be accentable without causing accents on successive syllables (after also avoiding accents on successive syllables on the word preceding the first enclitic).	Accents on alternate enclitics: begin by accenting the first enclitic to be accentable without causing *acutes* on successive syllables (after also avoiding *acutes* on successive syllables on the word preceding the first enclitic). OR (C) Göttling and Barrett's original system (see section 4.1).	Accents on alternate enclitics: begin by accenting the first enclitic to be accentable without causing accents on successive morae (after also avoiding accents on successive morae on the word preceding the first enclitic).	Accents on alternate enclitics: begin by accenting the second enclitic from the end. If an even number of enclitics, the first does not affect the accent of the preceding word.	Accents on alternate enclitics: begin by accenting the second enclitic from the end. The word preceding the first enclitic is accented following the normal ancient rules applying to a word followed by a single enclitic.	
1.8	* τίς τάρ σφωε	* τίς τάρ σφωε	τίς τάρ σφωε	τίς ταρ σφωε	τίς ταρ σφωε	τίς ταρ σφωε	τίς τάρ σφωε	τίς τάρ σφωε	τίς τάρ σφωε
1.28	* μή νύ τοι	* μή νύ τοι	* μή νύ τοι	μή νυ τοι	μή νυ τοι	μή νυ τοι	μή νύ τοι	μή νύ τοι	μή νύ τοι

1.39	εἴ ποτέ τοι	εἴ ποτέ τοι	εἴ ποτέ τοι	εἴ ποτέ τοι	εἴ ποτέ τοι	εἴ ποτέ τοι	εἴ ποτέ τοι	εἴ ποτέ τοι
1.40	δή ποτέ τοι	δή ποτέ τοι	δή ποτέ τοι	δή ποτέ τοι	δή ποτέ τοι	δή ποτέ τοι	δή ποτέ τοι	δή ποτέ τοι
1.66	αἴ κέν πως	αἴ κέν πως	αἴ κεν πως	αἴ κέν πως	αἴ κεν πως	αἴ κέν πως	αἴ κέν πως	αἴ κέν πως
1.100	τότε κέν μιν	τότε κέν μιν	τότε κέν μιν	τότε κέν μιν	τότε κέν μιν	τότε κέν μιν	τότε κέν μιν	τότε κέν μιν
1.108	οὐδέ τί πω	οὐδέ τί πω	οὐδέ τι πω	οὐδέ τι πω	οὐδέ τι πω	οὐδέ τί πω	οὐδέ τι πω	οὐδέ τι πω
1.114	οὐ ἔθέν ἐστί	οὐ ἔθέν ἐστί	οὐ ἔθέν ἐστι	οὐ ἔθέν ἐστι	οὐ ἔθέν ἐστι	οὐ ἔθέν ἐστι	οὐ ἔθέν ἐστι	οὐ ἔθέν ἐστι
1.115	* οὔ-τέ τι	* οὔ-τέ τι	* οὔ-τέ τι	οὔ-τέ τι	οὔ-τε τι	οὔ-τε τι	οὔ-τε τι	οὔ-τέ τι
1.123	πῶς τάρ τοι	πῶς τάρ τοι	πῶς τάρ τοι	πῶς ταρ τοι	πῶς τάρ τοι	πῶς τάρ τοι	πῶς τάρ τοι	πῶς τάρ τοι
1.124	οὐδέ τι πω	οὐδέ τί πω	οὐδέ τι πω	οὐδέ τι πω	οὐδέ τι πω	οὐδέ τί πω	οὐδέ τι πω	οὐδέ τι πω
1.128	αἴ κε ποθι	αἴ κέ ποθι	αἴ κε ποθι	αἴ κε ποθι	αἴ κε ποθι	αἴ κέ ποθι	αἴ κέ ποθι	αἴ κέ ποθι
1.150	πῶς τίς τοι	πῶς τίς τοι	πῶς τις τοι	πῶς τίς τοι	πῶς τίς τοι	πῶς τίς τοι	πῶς τίς τοι	πῶς τάρ τοι
1.153	οὐ τί μοι	οὐ τί μοι	οὐ τι μοι	οὐ τι μοι	οὐ τί μοι	οὐ τί μοι	οὐ τί μοι	οὐ τί μοι
1.175	οἴ κέ με	οἴ κέ με	οἴ κε με	οἴ κε με	οἴ κε με	οἴ κέ με	οἴ κέ με	οἴ κέ με
1.176	δέ μοι ἐσσί	δέ μοι ἐσσί	δέ μοι ἔσσι	δέ μοι ἔσσι	δέ μοι ἐσσι	δέ μοι ἐσσὶ	δέ μοι ἐσσὶ	δέ μοι ἐσσὶ
1.178	θεός πού σοι	θεός πού σοι	θεός πού σοι	θεός πού σοι	θεός που σοι	θεός πού σοι	θεός πού σοι	θεός πού σοι
1.213	καί ποτέ τοι	καί ποτέ τοι	καί ποτέ τοι	καί ποτέ τοι	καί ποτέ τοι	καί ποτέ τοι	καί ποτέ τοι	καί ποτέ τοι
1.226	οὔ-τέ ποτ'	οὔ-τέ ποτ'	οὔ-τε ποτ'	οὔ-τε ποτ'	οὔ-τε ποτ'	οὔ-τέ ποτ'	οὔ-τέ ποτ'	οὔ-τέ ποτ'
1.236	γάρ ῥά ἑ	γάρ ῥά ἑ	γάρ ῥά ἑ	γάρ ῥά ἑ	γάρ ῥα ἑ	γάρ ῥά ἑ	γάρ ῥά ἑ	γάρ ῥά ἑ
1.261	οὐ ποτέ μ'	οὐ ποτέ μ'	οὐ ποτέ μ'	οὐ ποτέ μ'	οὐ ποτέ μ'	οὐ ποτέ μ'	οὐ ποτέ μ'	οὐ ποτέ μ'
1.294	ὅτ-τί κεν	ὅτ-τί κεν	ὅτ-τι κεν	ὅτ-τι κεν	ὅτ-τι κεν	ὅτ-τί κεν	ὅττι κεν	ὅττι κεν
1.296	ἔγωγέ τι σοι	ἔγωγέ τι σοι	ἔγωγέ τι σοι	ἔγωγέ τι σοι	ἔγωγέ τι σοι	ἔγωγέ τι σοι	ἔγωγέ τι σοι	ἔγωγέ τι σοι
1.299	οὔ-τέ τῳ	οὔ-τέ τῳ	οὔ-τε τῳ	οὔ-τε τῳ	οὔ-τε τῳ	οὔ-τέ τῳ	οὔ-τε τῳ	οὔ-τέ τοι

Table Ap.2 *Continued*

Line of Iliad	(Ai)	(Aii)	(Aiii)	(Bi)	(Bii)	(Biii)	(Biv)	(Bv)	(D)
1.300	ἅ μοι ἐστὶ	ἅ μοι ἐστὶ	ἅ μοί ἐστι	ἅ μοι ἐστὶ	ἅ μοι ἐστὶ	ἅ μοί ἐστι	ἅ μοί ἐστι	ἅ μοί ἐστι	ἅ μοι ἐστὶ
1.332	οὐδέ τί μιν	οὐδέ τί μιν	οὐδέ τί μιν	οὐδέ τι μιν	οὐδέ τι μιν	οὐδέ τι μιν	οὐδέ τί μιν	οὐδέ τί μιν	οὐδέ τι μιν
1.335	οὔ τί μοι	οὔ τί μοι	οὔ τί μοι	οὐ τι μοι	οὔ τί μοι	οὔ τι μοι	οὔ τί μοι	οὔ τί μοι	οὔ τι μοι
1.353	τιμήν πέρ μοι	τιμήν πέρ μοι	τιμήν περ μοι	τιμήν περ μοι	τιμήν περ μοι	τιμήν περ μοι	τιμήν πέρ μοι	τιμήν πέρ μοι	τιμήν πέρ μοι
1.361	χειρί τέ μιν	χειρί τέ μιν	χειρί τε μιν	χειρί τε μιν	χειρί τε μιν	χειρί τε μιν	χειρί τε μιν	χειρί τέ μιν	χειρί τέ μιν[a]
1.408	αἴ κέν πως	αἴ κέν πως	αἴ κέν πως	αἴ κέν πως	αἴ κέν πως	αἴ κέν πως	αἴ κέν πως	αἴ κέν πως	αἴ κέν πως
1.414	τί νύ σ'	τί νύ σ'	τί νυ σ'	τί νυ σ'	τί νυ σ'	τί νυ σ'	τί νύ σ'	τί νύ σ'	τί νύ σ'
1.416	ἐπεί νύ τοι	ἐπεί νύ τοι	ἐπεί νύ τοι	ἐπεί νυ τοι	ἐπεί νυ τοι	ἐπεί νυ τοι	ἐπεί νύ τοι	ἐπεί νύ τοι	ἐπεί νύ τοι
1.490	οὔ-τέ ποτ'	οὔ-τέ ποτ'	οὔ-τέ ποτ'	οὔ-τέ ποτ'	οὔ-τε ποτ'	οὔ-τε ποτ'	οὔ-τέ ποτ'	οὔ-τέ ποτ'	οὔτέ ποτ'
1.491	οὔ-τέ ποτ'	οὔ-τέ ποτ'	οὔ-τέ ποτ'	οὔ-τέ ποτ'	οὔ-τε ποτ'	οὔ-τε ποτ'	οὔ-τέ ποτ'	οὔ-τέ ποτ'	οὔτέ ποτ'
1.508	σύ πέρ μιν	σύ πέρ μιν	σύ πέρ μιν	σύ περ μιν	σύ περ μιν	σύ περ μιν	σύ πέρ μιν	σύ πέρ μιν	σύ πέρ μιν
1.510	* ὀφέλλωσίν τέ ἑ	* ὀφέλλωσίν τέ ἑ	* ὀφέλλωσίν τέ ἑ	ὀφέλλωσίν τέ ἑ	ὀφέλλωσίν τε ἑ	ὀφέλλωσίν τε ἑ	ὀφέλλωσιν τέ ἑ	ὀφέλλωσιν τέ ἑ	ὀφέλλωσιν τέ ἑ
1.521	καί τέ με φῇσὶ	καί τέ με φῇσὶ	καί τέ με φῇσὶ	καί τε με φῇσὶ	καί τε με φῇσὶ	καί τε με φῇσὶ	καί τε με φῇσὶ	καί τε με φῇσὶ	καί τέ με φῇσὶ
1.527	ὅ τί κεν	ὅ τί κεν	ὅ τι κεν	ὅ τι κεν	ὅ τι κεν	ὅ τι κεν	ὅ τί κεν	ὅ τί κεν	ὅ τι κεν
1.542	οὐδέ τί πό μοι	οὐδέ τι πτω μοι	οὐδέ τι πτω μοι	οὐδέ τι πό μοι	οὐδέ τι πό μοι	οὐδέ τι πό μοι	οὐδέ τι πό μοι	οὐδέ τι πό μοι	οὐδέ τι πό μοι
1.557	γάρ σοί γε	γάρ σοι γε	γάρ σοί γε	γάρ σοί γε	γάρ σοί γε	γάρ σοί γε	γάρ σοί γε	γάρ σοί γε	γάρ σοί γε
1.566	μή νύ τοι	μή νύ τοι	μή νύ τοι	μή νυ τοι	μή νυ τοι	μή νυ τοι	μή νύ τοι	μή νύ τοι	μή νοι (for νυ) τοι
1.567	ὅτε κέν τοι	ὅτε κέν τοι	ὅτε κέν τοι	ὅτε κέν τοι	ὅτε κέν τοι	ὅτε κέν τοι	ὅτε κέν τοι	ὅτε κέν τοι	ὅτε κέν τοι
2.72	αἴ κέν πως	αἴ κέν πως	αἴ κέν πως	αἴ κέν πως	αἴ κέν πως	αἴ κέν πως	αἴ κέν πως	αἴ κέν πως	αἴ κέν πως
2.83	αἴ κέν πως	αἴ κέν πως	αἴ κέν πως	αἴ κέν πως	αἴ κέν πως	αἴ κέν πως	αἴ κέν πως	αἴ κέν πως	αἴ κέν πως
2.119[b]	τόδε γ' ἐστί	τόδε γ' ἐστί	τόδε γ' ἐστί	τόδε γ' ἐστί	τόδε γ' ἐστί	τόδε γ' ἐστί	τόδε γ' ἐστί	τόδε γ' ἐστί	τόδε γ' ἐστί

Line								
2.122	οὐ πώ τι	οὔ πώ τι	οὔ πώ τι	οὔ πώ τι	οὔ πώ τι	οὔ πω τι	οὔ πω τι	οὔ πω τι
2.202	οὐ-τέ ποτ'	οὐ-τέ ποτ'	οὐ-τέ ποτ'	οὐ-τέ ποτ'	οὐ-τέ ποτ'	οὔ-τε ποτ'	οὔ-τέ ποτ'	οὔ-τέ ποτ'
2.215	ὅ τί οἱ	ὅ τί οἱ	ὅ τι οἱ	ὅ τι οἱ	ὅ τι οἱ	ὅ τι οἱ	ὅ τι οἱ	ὅ τι οἱ
2.229	ὅν κέ τις	ὅν κέ τις	ὅν κε τις	ὅν κε τις	ὅν κε τις	ὅν κέ τις	ὅν κέ τις	ὅν κέ τις
2.238	ἤ ῥά τι οἱ	ἤ ῥά τι οἱ	ἤ ῥά τι οἱ	ἤ ῥά τι οἱ	ἤ ῥά τι οἱ	ἤ ῥά τι οἱ	ἤ ῥά τι οἱ	ἤ ῥά τι οἱ
2.252	οὐδέ τί πω	οὐδέ τί πω	οὐδέ τι πω	οὐδέ τι πω	οὐδέ τι πω	οὐδέ τι πω	οὐδέ τι πω	οὐδέ τι πω
2.258	* ὡς νύ περ	* ὡς νύ περ	ὡς νυ περ	ὡς νυ περ	ὡς νυ περ	ὡς νύ περ	ὡς νύ περ	
2.276	οὔ θήν μιν	οὔ θήν μιν	οὔ θήν μιν	οὔ θήν μιν	οὔ θήν μιν	οὔ θήν μιν	οὔ θήν μιν	
2.292	γάρ τίς τ'	γάρ τίς τ'	γάρ τίς θ'	γάρ τις θ'	γάρ τις θ'	γάρ τις τ'	γάρ τίς τ'	γάρ τις θ'
2.361	ὅτ-τί κεν	ὅτ-τί κεν	ὅτ-τι κεν	ὅτ-τι κεν	ὅτ-τι κεν	ὅτ-τι κεν	ὅτ-τί κεν	ὅττι κεν
2.365	ὅς τέ νυ	ὅς τέ νυ	ὅς τε νυ	ὅς τε νυ	ὅς τε νυ	ὅς τέ νυ	ὅς τέ νυ	ὅς τέ νυ
2.419	ἄρα πώ οἱ	ἄρα πώ οἱ	* ἄρα πω οἱ	ἄρα πω οἱ	ἄρα πώ οἱ	ἄρα πώ οἱ	ἄρα πώ οἱ	
2.553	οὔ πώ τις	οὔ πώ τις	οὔ πω τις	οὔ πω τις	οὔ πω τις	οὔ πό τις	οὔ πώ τις	οὔ πω τις
2.687	ὅς τίς σφιν	ὅς τίς σφιν	ὅς τις σφιν	ὅς τις σφιν	ὅς τις σφιν	ὅς τις σφιν	ὅς τίς σφιν	ὅς τί (for τίς) σφιν
2.754	ἀλλά τέ μιν	ἀλλά τέ μιν	ἀλλά τε μιν	ἀλλά τε μιν	ἀλλά τε μιν	ἀλλά τε μιν	ἀλλά τέ μιν	ἀλλά τε μιν
2.873	οὐδέ τι οἱ	οὐδέ τι οἱ	οὐδέ τι οἱ	οὐδέ τι οἱ	οὐδέ τι οἱ	οὐδέ τι οἱ	οὐδέ τι οἱ	οὐδέ τι οἱ
3.12	τόσσόν τίς τ'	τόσσόν τίς τ'	τόσσον τίς τ'	τόσσον τίς τ'	τόσσον τίς τ'	τόσσον τις τ'	τόσσόν τις τ'	τόσσόν τις τ'
3.33	ὅτε τίς τε	ὅτε τίς τε	ὅτε τίς τε	ὅτε τίς τε	ὅτε τίς τε	ὅτε τίς τε	ὅτε τίς τε	ὅτε τίς τε
3.35	ὣχρός τέ μιν	ὣχρός τέ μιν	ὣχρός τε μιν	ὣχρός τε μιν	ὣχρός τε μιν	ὣχρός τε μιν	ὣχρός τέ μιν	ὣχρός τε μιν
3.56	ἤ τέ κεν	ἤ τέ κεν	ἤ τέ κεν	ἤ τε κεν	ἤ τέ κεν	ἤ τέ κεν	ἤ τέ κεν	
3.61	ὅς ῥά τε	ὅς ῥά τε	ὅς ῥα τε	ὅς ῥα τε	ὅς ῥα τε	ὅς ῥα τε	ὅς ῥά τε	ὅς ῥά τε
3.164	οὔ τί μοι	οὔ τί μοι	οὔ τί μοι	οὔ τι μοι	οὔ τι μοι	οὔ τι μοι	οὔ τί μοι	οὔ τί μοι

Continued

Table Ap.2 *Continued*

Line of Iliad	(Ai)	(Aii)	(Aiii)	(Bi)	(Bii)	(Biii)	(Biv)	(Bv)	(D)
3.164	θεοί νύ μοι	θεοί νύ μοι	θεοί νύ μοι	θεοί νυ μοι	θεοί νυ μοι	θεοί νυ μοι	θεοί νύ μοι	θεοί νύ μοι	θεοί νύ μοι
3.172	αἰδοῖός τέ μοι ἐσσί	αἰδοῖός τέ μοι ἐσσί	αἰδοῖός τέ μοι ἐσσί	αἰδοῖός τέ μοι ἐσσί	αἰδοῖός τέ μοι ἐσσί	αἰδοῖός τέ μοι ἐσσί	αἰδοῖός τέ μοι ἐσσί	αἰδοῖός τέ μοι ἐσσί	αἰδοῖός τέ μοι ἐσσί
3.183	ἦ ῥά νύ τοι	ἦ ῥά νύ τοι	ἦ ῥά νύ τοι	ἦ ῥά νύ τοι	ἦ ῥά νύ τοι	ἦ ῥά νύ τοι	ἦ ῥά νύ τοι	ἦ ῥά νύ τοι	ἦ ῥά νύ τοι
3.220	ζάκοτόν τέ τιν’	ζάκοτόν τέ τιν’	ζάκοτόν τε τιν’	ζάκοτόν τε τιν’	ζάκοτόν τε τιν’	ζάκοτόν τέ τιν’	ζάκοτόν τέ τιν’	ζάκοτόν τέ τιν’	ζάκοτόν τέ τιν’
3.242	ἄ μοι ἐστίν	ἄ μοι ἐστίν	ἄ μοι ἐστίν	ἄ μοι ἐστιν	ἄ μοι ἐστιν	ἄ μοι ἐστιν	ἄ μοι ἐστιν	ἄ μοι ἐστιν	ἄ μοι ἐστιν
3.279	ὅ-τις κ’	ὅ-τις κ’	ὅ-τις κ’	ὅ-τις κ’	ὅ-τις κ’	ὅ-τις κ’	ὅ-τις κ’	ὅ-τις κ’	ὅτις κ’
3.302	ἄρα πιό σφιν	ἄρα πιό σφιν	ἄρα πιο σφιν	ἄρα πιό σφιν	ἄρα πιό σφιν	ἄρα πιό σφιν	ἄρα πιό σφιν	ἄρα πιό σφιν	ἄρα πιό σφιν
3.373	* καί νύ κεν	* καί νύ κεν	* καί νύ κεν	καί νύ κεν	καί νυ κεν	καί νυ κεν	καί νύ κεν	καί νύ κεν	καί νύ κεν
3.400	ἦ πῆ με	ἦ πῆ με	ἦ πῆ με	ἦ πῃ με	ἦ πῇ με	ἦ πῇ με	ἦ πῇ με	ἦ πῇ με	ἦ πῇ με
3.402	εἴ τίς τοι	εἴ τίς τοι	εἴ τίς τοι	εἴ τις τοι	εἴ τις τοι	εἴ τις τοι	εἴ τίς τοι	εἴ τίς τοι	εἴ τίς τοι
4.31	τί νύ σε	τί νύ σε	τί νυ σε	τί νυ σε	τί νυ σε	τί νυ σε	τί νύ σε	τί νύ σε	τί νύ σε
4.48	γάρ μοι ποτέ	γάρ μοι ποτέ	γάρ μοι ποτέ	γάρ μοι ποτε	γάρ μοι ποτε	γάρ ποτε	γάρ μοι ποτε	γάρ μοι ποτε	γάρ μοι ποτε
4.93	ἦ ῥά νύ μοί τι	ἦ ῥά νύ μοί τι	ἦ ῥά νύ μοί τι	ἦ ῥά νύ μοί τι	ἦ ῥά νύ μοί τι	ἦ ῥά νυ μοί τι	ἦ ῥά νυ μοί τι	ἦ ῥά νύ μοί τι	ἦ ῥά νύ μοί τι
4.106	ὅν ῥά ποτ’	ὅν ῥά ποτ’	ὅν ῥά ποτ’	ὅν ῥα ποτ’	ὅν ῥα ποτ’	ὅν ῥα ποτ’	ὅν ῥά ποτ’	ὅν ῥά ποτ’	ὅν ῥά ποτ’
4.141	ὅτε τίς τ’	ὅτε τίς τ’	ὅτε τίς τ’	ὅτε τίς τ’	ὅτε τίς τ’	ὅτε τίς τ’	ὅτε τίς τ’	ὅτε τίς τ’	ὅτε τίς τ’
4.143	πολέες τέ μιν	πολέες τέ μιν	πολέες τέ μιν	πολέες τέ μιν	πολέες τέ μιν	πολέες τέ μιν	πολέες τέ μιν	πολέες τέ μιν	πολέες τέ μιν
4.155	* θάνατόν νύ τοι	* θάνατόν νύ τοι	* θάνατόν νύ τοι	θάνατόν νυ τοι	θάνατόν νυ τοι	θάνατόν νυ τοι	θάνατον νύ τοι	θάνατον νύ τοι	θάνατον νύ τοι
4.176	καί κέ τις	καί κέ τις	καί κέ τις	καί κε τις	καί κε τις	καί κε τις	καί κέ τις	καί κέ τις	καί κέ τις[c]
4.182	ὡς ποτέ τις	ὡς ποτέ τις	ὡς ποτέ τις	ὡς ποτέ τις	ὡς ποτέ τις	ὡς ποτέ τις	ὡς ποτέ τις	ὡς ποτέ τις	ὡς ποτέ τις
4.184	δέ τί πω	δέ τί πω	δέ τι πω	δέ τι πω	δέ τι πω	δέ τι πω	δέ τι πω	δέ τι πω	δέ τι πω
4.219	τά οἱ ποτέ	τά οἱ ποτέ	τά οἱ ποτέ	τά οἱ ποτέ	τά οἱ ποτέ	τά οἱ ποτέ	τά οἱ ποτέ	τά οἱ ποτέ	τά οἱ ποτέ

	ὁππότε κέν μιν	ὁππότε κέν μιν	ὁππότε κέν μιν	ὁππότε κέν μιν	ὁππότε κέν μιν	ὁππότε κέν μιν	ὁππότε κέν μιν	ὁππότε κέν μιν	ὁππότε κέν μιν
4.229	μή πώ τι	μή πώ τι	μή πώ τι	μή πώ τι	μή πω τι	μή πω τι	μή πώ τι	μή πώ τι	μή πώ τι
4.234	ἄρα τίς σφι	ἄρα τίς σφι	ἄρα τίς σφι	ἄρα τίς σφι	ἄρα τίς σφι	ἄρα τίς σφι	ἄρα τίς σφι	ἄρα τίς σφι	ἄρα τίς σφι
4.245	ὅτε πέρ τε	ὅτε πέρ τε	ὅτε πέρ τε	ὅτε πέρ τε	ὅτε πέρ τε	ὅτε πέρ τε	ὅτε πέρ τε	ὅτε πέρ τε	ὅτε πέρ τε
4.259									
4.331	γάρ πώ σφιν	γάρ πω σφιν	γάρ πω σφιν	γάρ πώ σφιν	γάρ πω σφιν	γάρ πώ σφιν	γάρ πώ σφιν	γάρ πώ σφιν	γάρ πώ σφιν
4.353	αἴ κέν τοι	αἴ κέν τοι	αἴ κέν τοι	αἴ κέν τοι	αἴ κέν τοι	αἴ κέν τοι	αἴ κέν τοι	αἴ κέν τοι	αἴ κέν τοι
4.359	οὐ-τέ σε	οὐ-τε σε	οὐ-τε σε	οὔ-τε σε	οὔ-τε σε	οὐ-τέ σε	οὔ-τε σε	οὔ-τέ σε	οὔτέ σε
4.483	ἤ ῥά τ'	ἤ ῥά τ'	ἤ ῥά τ'	ἤ ῥά τ'	ἤ ῥά τ'	ἤ ῥά τ'	ἤ ῥά τ'	ἤ ῥά τ'	ἤ ῥά τ'
4.484	ἀτάρ τε οἱ	ἀτάρ τε οἱ	ἀτάρ τε οἱ	ἀτάρ τε οἱ	ἀτάρ τε οἱ	ἀτάρ τε οἱ	ἀτάρ τε οἱ	ἀτάρ τε οἱ	ἀτάρ τε οἱ
4.539	οὔ κέ τι	οὔ κε τι	οὔ κε τι	οὔ κέ τι	οὔ κε τι	οὔ κέ τι	οὔ κέ τι	οὔ κέ τι	οὔ κέ τι
5.103	οὐδέ ἕ φημι	οὐδέ ἕ φημι	οὐδέ ἕ φημι	οὐδέ ἕ φημι	οὐδέ ἕ φημι	οὐδέ ἕ φημι	οὐδέ ἕ φημι	οὐδέ ἕ φημι	οὐδέ ἕ φημι
5.116	εἴ ποτέ μοι	εἴ ποτέ μοι	εἴ ποτέ μοι	εἴ ποτέ μοι	εἴ ποτέ μοι	εἴ ποτέ μοι	εἴ ποτέ μοι	εἴ ποτέ μοι	εἴ ποτέ μοι
5.118	δέ τέ μ'	δέ τε μ'	δέ τε μ'	δέ τε μ'	δέ τε μ'	δέ τέ μ'	δέ τέ μ'	δέ τε μ'	δέ τε μ''
5.119	οὐδέ με φησὶ	οὐδέ με φησὶ	οὐδέ με φησι	οὐδέ με φησι	οὐδέ με φησι	οὐδέ με φησι	οὐδέ με φησι	οὐδέ με φησι	οὐδέ με φησι
5.137	ὅν ῥά τε	ὅν ῥά τε	ὅν ῥά τε	ὅν ῥά τε	ὅν ῥα τε	ὅν ῥά τε	ὅν ῥά τε	ὅν ῥά τε	ὅν ῥά τ
5.170	ἔπος τέ μιν	ἔπος τέ μιν	ἔπος τέ μιν	ἔπος τέ μιν	ἔπος τέ μιν	ἔπος τέ μιν	ἔπος τέ μιν	ἔπος τέ μιν	ἔπος τέ μιν
5.172	οὔ τίς τοι	οὔ τίς τοι	οὔ τις τοι	οὔ τίς τοι	οὔ τις τοι	οὔ τις τοι	οὔ τίς τοι	οὔ τις τοι	οὔ τίς τοι
5.191	θεός νύ τίς ἐστι	θεός νύ τίς ἐστι	θεός νυ τίς ἐστι	θεός νυ τίς ἐστι	θεός νυ τίς ἐστι	θεός νυ τίς ἐστι	θεός νυ τίς ἐστι	θεός νυ τίς ἐστι	θεός νυ τίς ἐστι
5.260	αἴ κέν μοι	αἴ κέν μοι	αἴ κέν μοι	αἴ κέν μοι	αἴ κέν μοι	αἴ κέν μοι	αἴ κέν μοι	αἴ κέν μοι	αἴ κέν μοι
5.298	μή πώς οἱ	μή πώς οἱ	μή πως οἱ	μή πώς οἱ	μή πός οἱ	μή πώς οἱ	μή πώς οἱ	μή πώς οἱ	μή πως οἱ
5.306	δέ τέ μιν	δέ τέ μιν	δέ τε μιν	δέ τε μιν	δέ τε μιν	δέ τε μιν	δέ τέ μιν	δέ τε μιν	δέ τε μιν
5.311	* καί νύ κεν	* καί νύ κεν	καί νύ κεν	καί νύ κεν	καί νυ κεν	καί νύ κεν	καί νύ κεν	καί νύ κεν	καί νύ κεν

Continued

Table Ap.2 Continued

Line of Iliad	(Ai)	(Aii)	(Aiii)	(Bi)	(Bii)	(Biii)	(Biv)	(Bv)	(D)
5.638	οἷόν τινά φασι σε	οἷόν τινά φασι σε	οἷόν τινά φασι σε	οἷόν τινά φασι σε	οἷόν τινά φασι σε	οἷόν τινά φασι σε	οἷόν τινά φασι σε	οἷόν τινά φασι σε	οἷόν τινα φασι σε
5.644	οὐδέ τί σε	οὐδέ τί σε	οὐδέ τί σε	οὐδέ τί σε	οὐδέ τί σε	οὐδέ τι σε	οὐδέ τι σε	οὐδέ τι σε	οὐδέ τι σε
5.650	* ὅς ῥά μιν	* ὅς ῥά μιν	* ὅς ῥά μιν	ὅς ῥα μιν	ὅς ῥα μιν	ὅς ῥα μιν	ὅς ῥά μιν	ὅς ῥα μιν	ὃς ῥά μιν
5.679	* καί νύ κ'	* καί νύ κ'	* καί νύ κ'	καί νυ κ'	καί νυ κ'	καί νυ κ'	καί νύ κ'	καί νύ κ'	καὶ νύ κ'
5.700	οὔ-τέ ποτε	οὔ-τέ ποτε	* οὔ-τέ ποτε	οὔ-τέ ποτέ	οὔ-τε ποτέ	οὔ-τέ ποτε	οὔ-τέ ποτε	οὔ-τέ ποτε	οὔτέ ποτ'
5.701	* οὔ-τέ ποτ'	* οὔ-τέ ποτ'	* οὔ-τέ ποτ'	οὔ-τέ ποτ'	οὔ-τε ποτ'	οὔ-τε ποτ'	οὔ-τέ ποτ'	οὔ-τέ ποτ'	οὔτε ποτ'
5.762	ἦ ῥά τί μοι	ἦ ῥά τί μοι	ἦ ῥά τι μοι	ἦ ῥά τι μοι	ἦ ῥά τι μοι	ἦ ῥά τι μοι	ἦ ῥα τί μοι	ἦ ῥα τί μοι	ἦ ῥά τί μοι
5.802	ὅτε πέρ μιν	ὅτε πέρ μιν	ὅτε πέρ μιν	ὅτε πέρ μιν	ὅτε πέρ μιν	ὅτε πέρ μιν	ὅτε πέρ μιν	ὅτε πέρ μιν	ὅτε πέρ μιν
5.812	ἤ νύ σέ που	ἤ νύ σέ που	ἤ νύ σε που	ἤ νυ σέ που	ἤ νυ σέ που	ἤ νυ σέ που	ἤ νυ σέ που	ἤ νυ σέ που	ἤ νύ σέ που
5.817	οὔ-τέ τί με	οὔ-τέ τί με	οὔ-τέ τι με	οὔ-τε τί με	οὔ-τε τί με	οὔ-τε τί με	οὔ-τε τί με	οὔ-τε τί με	οὔτέ τι με
5.817	οὔ-τέ τις	οὔ-τέ τις	οὔ-τέ τις	οὔ-τέ τις	οὔ-τε τις	οὔ-τε τις	οὔ-τέ τις	οὔ-τέ τις	οὔτέ τις
5.827	μή-τέ τιν'	μή-τέ τιν'	μή-τέ τιν'	μή-τε τιν'	μή-τε τιν'	μή-τε τιν'	μὴ-τέ τιν'	μή-τέ τιν'	μή-τέ τιν'
5.858	τῇ ῥά μιν	τῇ ῥά μιν	τῇ ῥά μιν	τῇ ῥά μιν	τῇ ῥά μιν	τῇ ῥά μιν	τῇ ῥά μιν	τῇ ῥά μιν	τῇ ῥά μιν
5.879	οὔ-τέ τι	οὔ-τέ τι	οὔ-τέ τι	οὔ-τέ τι	οὔ-τε τι	οὔ-τέ τι	οὔ-τέ τι	οὔ-τέ τι	οὔτέ τι
5.885	ἦ τέ κε	ἦ τέ κε	ἦ τέ κε	ἦ τέ κε	ἦ τέ κε	ἦ τέ κε	ἦ τέ κε	ἦ τέ κε	ἦ τέ κε
5.889	μή τί μοι	μή τί μοι	μή τί μοι	μή τι μοι	μή τι μοι	μή τι μοι	μή τί μοι	μή τί μοι	μή τί μοι
5.890	δέ μοί ἐσσι	δέ μοί ἐσσι	δέ μοί ἐσσι	δέ μοι ἐσσι	δέ μοί ἐσσι	δέ μοί ἐσσι	δέ μοί ἐσσι	δέ μοί ἐσσι	δέ μοι ἔσσι
6.49	τόν κέν τοι	τόν κέν τοι	τόν κέν τοι	τόν κέν τοι	τόν κέν τοι	τόν κέν τοι	τόν κέν τοι	τόν κέν τοι	τόν κέν τοι
6.100	ὃν πέρ φασι	ὃν πέρ φασι	ὃν πέρ φασι	ὃν περ φασι	ὃν περ φασι	ὃν περ φασι	ὃν πέρ φασι	ὃν πέρ φασι	ὃν πέρ φασι
6.101	οὐδέ τίς οἱ	οὐδέ τίς οἱ	οὐδέ τίς οἱ	οὐδέ τις οἱ	οὐδέ τις οἱ	οὐδέ τις οἱ	οὐδέ τίς οἱ	οὐδέ τίς οἱ	οὐδέ τι, σ οἱ[d]
6.142	δέ τίς ἐσσι	δέ τίς ἐσσι	δέ τίς ἐσσι	δέ τίς ἐσσι	δέ τις ἐσσι	δέ τις ἐσσι	δέ τίς ἐσσι	δέ τίς ἐσσι	δέ τίς ἔσσι
6.177	ὅτ-τί ῥά οἱ	ὅτ-τί ῥα οἱ	ὅτ-τί ῥα οἱ	ὅτ-τι ῥά οἱ	ὅτ-τι ῥά οἱ	ὅτ-τι ῥά οἱ	ὅτ-τι ῥά οἱ	ὅτ-τι ῥά οἱ	ὅττι ῥά οι

6.215	ἦ ῥά νύ μοι	ἦ ῥά νύ μοι	ἦ ῥά νύ μοι	ἦ ῥά νύ μοι	ἦ ῥά νύ μοι	ἦ ῥα νύ μοι	ἦ ῥά νύ μοι
6.258	* ὄφρά κέ τοι	* ὄφρά κέ τοι	ὄφρα κέ τοι	ὄφρά κέ τοι	ὄφρα κέ τοι	ὄφρά κέ τοι	ὄφρα κέ τοι
6.267	οὐδέ πῃ ἔστι	οὐδέ πῃ ἔστι	οὐδέ πῃ ἔστι	οὐδέ πῃ ἔστι	οὐδέ πῃ ἔστι	οὐδέ πῃ ἔστι	οὐδέ πῃ ἔστι
6.271	ὅς τίς τοι	ὅς τίς τοι	ὅς τις τοι	ὅς τις τοι	ὅς τίς τοι	ὅς τίς τοι	ὅς τίς τοι
6.281	* ὡς κέ οἱ	* ὡς κέ οἱ	ὡς κε οἱ	ὡς κέ οἱ	ὡς κέ οἱ	ὡς κέ οἱ	ὡς κέ οἱ
6.330	εἴ τινά που	εἴ τινά που	εἴ τινα που	εἴ τινά που	εἴ τινά που	εἴ τινά που	εἴ τινά που
6.383	οὐ-τέ πῃ	οὐ-τέ πῃ	οὐ-τε πῃ	οὐ-τέ πῃ	οὐ-τέ πῃ	οὐ-τέ πῃ	οὐτέ πῃ
6.413	οὐδέ μοί ἐστι	οὐδέ μοί ἐστι	οὐδέ μοί ἐστι	οὐδέ μοί ἐστι	οὐδέ μοί ἐστι	οὐδέ μοί ἐστι	οὐδέ μοί ἐστι
6.429	σύ μοι ἔσσι	σύ μοι ἔσσι	σύ μοι ἔσσί	σύ μοι ἔσσι	σύ μοι ἔσσι	σύ μοί ἔσσι	σύ μοι ἔσσι
6.438	ἦ πού τίς σφιν	ἦ πού τίς σφιν	ἦ πού τίς σφιν	ἦ πού τις σφιν	ἦ πού τίς σφιν	ἦ πού τίς σφιν	ἦ πού τί (for τίς) σφιν
6.454	ὅτε κέν τις	ὅτε κέν τις	ὅτε κέν τις	ὅτε κέν τις	ὅτε κέν τις	ὅτε κέν τις	ὅτε κέν τις
6.459	καί ποτέ τις	καί ποτέ τις	καί ποτέ τις	καί ποτέ τις	καί ποτέ τις	καὶ ποτέ τις	καί ποτέ τις
6.462	ὥς ποτέ τις	ὥς ποτέ τις	ὥς ποτέ τις	ὥς ποτέ τις	ὥς ποτέ τις	ὥς ποτέ τις	ὥς ποτέ τις
6.465	πρίν γέ τι	πρίν γέ τι	πρίν γέ τι	πρίν γέ τι	πρίν γε τι	πρίν γέ τι	πρίν γέ τι
6.479	καί ποτέ τις	καί ποτέ τις	καί ποτέ τις	καί ποτέ τις	καί ποτέ τις	καί ποτέ τις	καί ποτέ τις
6.485	χειρί τέ μιν	χειρί τέ μιν	χειρί τε μιν	χειρί τε μιν	χειρί τέ μιν	χειρί τέ μιν	χειρί τέ μιν
6.486	μή μοί τι	μή μοί τι	μή μοί τι	μή μοί τι	μή μοί τι	μή μοί τι	μή μοί τι
6.487	γάρ τις μ'	γάρ τίς μ'	γάρ τισ μ'	γάρ τις μ'	γάρ τις μ'	γάρ τις μ'	γάρ τίς μ'
6.488	οὐ τινά φημι	οὐ τινά φημι	οὐ τινά φημι	οὐ τινά φημι	οὐ τινά φημι	οὐ τινά φημι	οὐ τινα φημί
6.521	ἄν τίς τοι	ἄν τίς τοι	ἄν τίς τοι	ἄν τις τοι	ἄν τίς τοι	ἄν τις τοι	ἄν τίς τοι
6.526	αἴ κε πόθι	αἴ κε πόθι	αἴ κε πόθι	αἴ κε πόθι	αἴ κε πόθι	αἴ κε πόθι	αἴ κέ πόθι
7.28	εἴ μοί τι	εἴ μοί τι	εἴ μοί τι	εἴ μοί τι	εἴ μοί τι	εἴ μοί τι	εἴ μοί τι

Continued

Table Ap.2 *Continued*

Line of Iliad	(Ai)	(Aii)	(Aiii)	(Bi)	(Bii)	(Biii)	(Biv)	(Bv)	(D)
7.39	ἢν τινά που	ἢν τινά που	ἢν τινά που	ἢν τινά που	ἢν τινά που	ἢν τινά που	ἢν τινά που	ἢν τινά που	ἢν τινά που
7.48	ἢ ῥά νύ μοί τι	ἢ ῥά νύ μοί τι	ἢ ῥά νύ μοί τι	ἢ ῥα νύ μοί τι	ἢ ῥά νυ μοί τι	ἢ ῥά νυ μοί τι	ἢ ῥά νυ μοί τι	ἢ ῥά νυ μοί τι	ἢ ῥά νυ μοί τι
7.48	δέ τοι εἰμί	δέ τοι εἰμί	δέ τοι εἰμί	δέ τοι εἰμί	δέ τοι εἰμι	δέ τοι εἰμι	δέ τοι εἰμι	δέ τοι εἰμι	δέ τοι εἰμί
7.52	γάρ πώ τοι	γάρ πώ τοι	γάρ πω τοι	γάρ πω τοι	γάρ πω τοι	γάρ πώ τοι	γάρ πώ τοι	γάρ πώ τοι	γάρ πω τοι
7.86	σῆμά τε οἱ	σῆμά τε οἱ	σῆμά τε οἱ	σῆμα τέ οἱ	σῆμά τε οἱ	σῆμά τε οἱ	σῆμα τέ οἱ	σῆμα τέ οἱ	σῆμα τέ οἱ
7.87	καί ποτέ τις	καί ποτέ τις	καί ποτέ τις	καί ποτέ τις	καί ποτέ τις	καί ποτέ τις	καί ποτέ τις	καί ποτέ τις	καί ποτέ τις[e]
7.91	* ὥς ποτέ τις	* ὥς ποτέ τις	* ὥς ποτέ τις	* ὥς ποτέ τις	* ὥς ποτέ τις	* ὥς ποτέ τις	ὥς ποτέ τις	ὥς ποτέ τις	ὥς ποτέ τις
7.104	* ἔνθά κέ τοι	* ἔνθά κέ τοι	ἔνθά κε τοι	ἔνθα κέ τοι	ἔνθα κέ τοι	ἔνθα κέ τοι	ἔνθα κέ τοι	ἔνθα κέ τοι	ἔνθα κέ τοι
7.109	οὐδέ τι σε	οὐδέ τι σε	οὐδέ τι σε	οὐδέ τι σε	οὐδέ τι σε	οὐδέ τι σε	οὐδέ τι σε	οὐδέ τι σε	οὐδέ τι σε
7.117	ἀδευὴς τ' ἐστι	ἀδευὴς τ' ἐστι	ἀδευὴς τ' ἐστι	ἀδευὴς τ' ἐστι	ἀδευὴς τ' ἐστι	ἀδευὴς τ' ἐστί†	ἀδευὴς τ' ἐστι	ἀδευὴς τ' ἐστι	ἀδευὴς τ' ἐστι
7.127	ὅς ποτέ μ'	ὅς ποτέ μ'	ὅς ποτέ μ'	ὅς ποτέ μ'	ὅς ποτέ μ'	ὅς ποτέ μ'	ὅς ποτέ μ'	ὅς ποτέ μ'	ὅς ποτέ μ'
7.197	γάρ τίς με	γάρ τίς με	γάρ τίς με	γάρ τις με	γάρ τις με	γάρ τις με	γάρ τις με	γάρ τις με	γάρ τις με
7.235	μή τί μεν	μή τί μεν	μή τί μεν	μή τι μεν	μή τι μεν	μή τι μεν	μὴ τί μεν	μὴ τί μεν	μὴ τί μεν
7.239	τό μοι ἐστί	τό μοι ἐστὶ	τό μοι ἐστὶ	τό μοι ἐστὶ	τό μοι ἐστί	τό μοι ἐστί	τό μοι ἐστί	τό μοι ἐστί	τό μοι ἐστί
7.273	* καί νύ κε	* καί νύ κε	* καί νύ κε	καί νυ κε	καί νυ κε	καί νυ κε	καί νύ κε	καί νύ κε	καί νύ κε
7.298	αἴ τέ μοι	αἴ τέ μοι	αἴ τέ μοι	αἴ τε μοι	αἴ τε μοι	αἴ τε μοι	αἴ τέ μοι	αἴ τέ μοι	αἴ τε μοι
7.352	οὐ νύ τι	οὐ νύ τι	οὐ νύ τι	οὐ νυ τι	οὐ νυ τι	οὐ νυ τι	οὐ νύ τι	οὐ νύ τι	οὐ νύ τι
7.387	αἴ κέ περ	αἴ κέ περ	αἴ κέ περ	αἴ κε περ	αἴ κε περ	αἴ κε περ	αἴ κέ περ	αἴ κέ περ	αἴ κε περ
7.446	ἢ ῥά τίς ἐστι	ἢ ῥά τίς ἐστι	ἢ ῥά τίς ἐστι	ἢ ῥα τίς ἐστι	ἢ ῥά τις ἐστί	ἢ ῥά τις ἐστί	ἢ ῥά τις ἐστί	ἢ ῥά τις ἐστί	ἢ ῥά τίς ἐστι
7.456	ἄλλός κέν τις	ἄλλός κέν τις	ἄλλός κέν τις	ἄλλός κέν τις	ἄλλος κέν τις	ἄλλος κέν τις	ἄλλος κέν τις	ἄλλός κέν τις	ἄλλός κέν τις
7.463	ὡς κέν τοι	ὡς κέν τοι	ὡς κέν τοι	ὡς κεν τοι	ὡς κεν τοι	ὡς κεν τοι	ὡς κεν τοι	ὡς κεν τοι	ὡς κέν τοι
8.7	μή-τέ τις	μή-τέ τις	μή-τέ τις	μή-τε τις	μή-τε τις	μή-τε τις	μή-τε τις	μή-τέ τις	μή-τέ τις

8.7	* μή-τέ τις	* μή-τέ τις	* μή-τέ τις	μή-τε τις	μή-τε τις	μὴ-τέ τις	μή-τε τις	μή-τέ τις	μὴ-τέ τις
8.27	περί τ᾽ εἰμι	περί τ᾽ εἰμι	περί τ᾽ εἰμι	περί τ᾽ εἰμι	περί τ᾽ εἰμι	περί τ᾽ εἰμι[g]	περί τ᾽ εἰμι	περί τ᾽ εἰμι	περί τ᾽ εἰμι
8.27	περί τ᾽ εἰμ᾽	περί τ᾽ εἰμ᾽	περί τ᾽ εἰμ᾽	περί τ᾽ εἰμ᾽	περί τ᾽ εἰμ᾽	περί τ᾽ εἰμ᾽	περί τ᾽ εἰμ᾽	περί τ᾽ εἰμ᾽	περί τ᾽ εἰμ᾽
8.39	οὐ νύ τι	οὖ νύ τι	οὐ νύ τι	οὐ νύ τι	οὐ νύ τι	οὐ νύ τι	οὐ νύ τι	οὐ νύ τι	οὐ νύ᾽ τι
8.90	* καί νύ κεν	* καί νύ κεν	* καί νύ κεν	καί νυ κεν	καί νυ κεν	καὶ νυ κεν	καί νυ κεν	καί νυ κεν	καί νύ κεν
8.95	μή τις τοι	μή τίς τοι	μή τις τοι	μή τις τοι	μή τις τοι	μή τις τοι	μή τις τοι	μή τίς τοι	μή τίς τοι
8.104	δέ νύ τοι	δέ νύ τοι	δέ νυ τοι	δέ νυ τοι	δέ νυ τοι	δέ νυ τοι	δέ νυ τοι	δέ νύ τοι	δέ νύ τοι
8.131	καί νύ κε	καί νύ κε	ὅς πέρ οἱ	καί νυ κε	καί νυ κε	καί νυ κε	καί νυ κε	καί νυ κε	καί νύ κε[h]
8.190	ὅς πέρ οἱ	ὅς πέρ οἱ		ὅς πέρ οἱ	ὅς πέρ οἱ	ὅς πέρ οἱ	ὅς πέρ οἱ	ὅς πέρ οἱ	ὅς πέρ οἱ
8.217	* καί νύ κεν	* καί νύ κεν	* καί νύ κεν	καί νυ κεν	καί νυ κεν	καί νυ κεν	καί νυ κεν	καί νυ κεν	καί νύ κεν
8.236	ἤ ῥά τιν᾽	ἤ ῥά τιν᾽	ἤ ῥά τιν᾽	ἤ ῥά τιν᾽	ἤ ῥά τιν᾽	ἤ ῥά τιν᾽	ἤ ῥά τιν᾽	ἤ ῥά τιν᾽	ἤ ῥά τιν᾽
8.238	δή ποτέ φημι	δή ποτέ φημι	δή ποτέ φημι	δή ποτέ φημι	δή ποτέ φημι	δή ποτέ φημι	δή ποτέ φημι	δή ποτέ φημι	δή ποτε φημι
8.242	τόδε πέρ μοι	τόδε πέρ μοι	τόδε πέρ μοι	τόδε πέρ μοι	τόδε πέρ μοι	τόδε πέρ μοι	τόδε πέρ μοι	τόδε πέρ μοι	τόδε πέρ μοι
8.282	αἴ κέν τι	αἴ κέν τι	αἴ κέν τι	αἴ κέν τι	αἴ κέν τι	αἰ κέν τι	αἰ κέν τι	αἰ κέν τι	αἰ κέν τι
8.287	αἴ κέν μοι	αἴ κέν μοι	αἴ κέν μοι	αἴ κεν μοι	αἴ κεν μοι	αἰ κέν μοι	αἰ κέν μοι	αἰ κέν μοι	αἰ κέν μοι
8.291	ἤ κέν τοι	ἤ κέν τοι	ἤ κέν τοι	ἤ κέν τοι	ἤ κέν τοι	ἤ κέν τοι	ἤ κέν τοι	ἤ κέν τοι	ἤ κέν τοι
8.338	ὅτε τίς τε	ὅτε τίς τε	ὅτε τίς τε	ὅτε τίς τε	ὅτε τίς τε	ὅτε τίς τε	ὅτε τίς τε	ὅτε τίς τε	ὅτε τίς τε
8.445	οὐδέ τί μιν	οὐδέ τί μιν	οὐδέ τί μιν	οὐδέ τι μιν	οὐδέ τι μιν	οὐδέ τι μιν	οὐδέ τι μιν	οὐδέ τι μιν	οὐδέ τι μιν
8.532	εἴ κέ μ᾽	εἴ κέ μ᾽	εἴ κέ μ᾽	εἴ κε μ᾽	εἴ κε μ᾽	εἴ κε μ᾽	εἴ κε μ᾽	εἴ κέ μ᾽	εἴ κέ μ᾽
9.55	οὐ τίς τοι	οὐ τίς τοι	οὖ τις τοι	οὖ τις τοι	οὖ τις τοι	οὖ τις τοι	οὖ τις τοι	οὐ τίς τοι	οὐ τίς τοι
9.61	οὐδέ κέ τίς μοι	οὐδέ κέ τίς μοι	οὐδέ κε τίς μοι	οὐδέ κε τίς μοι	οὐδέ κε τίς μοι	οὐδέ κε τίς μοι	οὐδέ κε τίς μοι	οὐδέ κε τίς μοι	οὐδέ κε τίς μοι
9.102	ὅτ-τί κεν	ὅτ-τί κεν	ὅτ-τί κεν	ὅτ-τί κεν	ὅτ-τι κεν	ὅτ-τι κεν	ὅτ-τι κεν	ὅτ-τι κεν	ὅτ-τι κεν
9.112	ὥς κέν μιν	ὥς κέν μιν	ὥς κεν μιν	ὥς κεν μιν	ὥς κεν μιν	ὥς κεν μιν	ὥς κεν μιν	ὡς κέν μιν	ὡς κέν μιν

Continued

Table Ap.2 *Continued*

Line of Iliad	(Ai)	(Aii)	(Aiii)	(Bi)	(Bii)	(Biii)	(Biv)	(Bv)	(D)
9.142	* γαμβρός κέν οἱ	* γαμβρός κέν μοι	* γαμβρός κέν μοι	γαμβρός κέν μοι	γαμβρός κεν μοι	γαμβρός κέν μοι	γαμβρός κέν μοι	γαμβρός κέν μοι	γαμβρός κέν μοι
9.144	δέ μοί εἰσί	δέ μοί εἰσί	δέ μοί εἰσί	δέ μοι εἰσί	δέ μοί εἰσι	δέ μοί εἰσί	δέ μοί εἰσί	δέ μοί εἰσί	δέ μοί εἰσι
9.148	οὐ πώ τις	οὐ πώ τις	οὔ πω τις	οὔ πω τις	οὔ πω τις	οὔ πώ τις	οὐ πώ τις	οὐ πώ τις	οὔ πω τις
9.155	οἵ κέ ἑ	οἵ κέ ἑ	οἵ κέ ἑ	οἵ κέ ἑ	οἵ κέ ἑ	οἵ κέ ἑ	οἵ κέ ἑ	οἵ κέ ἑ	οἵ κέ ἑ
9.157	* ταῦτά κέ οἱ	* ταῦτά κέ οἱ	ταῦτά κε οἱ	ταῦτά κε οἱ	ταῦτά κέ οἱ	ταῦτά κε οἱ	ταῦτα κέ οἱ	ταῦτα κέ οἱ	ταῦτα κέ οἱ
9.262	δέ κε τοι	δέ κέ τοι	δέ κε τοι	δέ κε τοι	δέ κε τοι	δέ κε τοι	δέ κέ τοι	δέ κέ τοι	δέ κέ οἱ
9.284	γαμβρός κέν οἱ	γαμβρός κέν οἱ	γαμβρός κεν οἱ	γαμβρός κέν οἱ	γαμβρός κεν οἱ	γαμβρός κέν οἱ	γαμβρός κέν οἱ	γαμβρός κέν οἱ	γαμβρός κέν οἱ
9.286	δέ οἱ εἰσί	δέ οἱ εἰσί	δέ οἱ εἰσι	δέ οἱ εἰσί	δέ οἱ εἰσι	δέ οἱ εἰσί	δέ οἱ εἰσί	δέ οἱ εἰσί	δέ οἱ εἰσι
9.290	οὔ πώ τις	οὔ πώ τις	οὔ πω τις	οὔ πω τις	οὔ πω τις	οὔ πω τις	οὔ πω τις	οὔ πώ τις	οὔ πω τις
9.297	οἵ κέ σε	οἵ κέ σε	οἵ κέ σε	οἵ κε σε	οἵ κε σε	οἵ κε σε	οἵ κέ σε	οἵ κέ σε	οἵ κέ σε
9.299	* ταῦτά κε τοι	* ταῦτά κε τοι	ταῦτά κε τοι	ταῦτά κε τοι	ταῦτά κε τοι	ταῦτά κε τοι	ταῦτα κέ τοι	ταῦτα κέ τοι	ταῦτα κέ τοι
9.303	γάρ κέ σφι	γάρ κέ σφι	γάρ κέ σφι	γάρ κε σφι	γάρ κε σφι	γάρ κε σφι	γὰρ κέ σφι	γὰρ κέ σφι	γάρ κέ σφι
9.305	οὔ τινά φησιν	οὔ τινά φησιν	οὔ τινά φησιν	οὔ τινά φησαν	οὔ τινά φησαν	οὔ τινά φησαν	οὔ τινά φησὶν	οὔ τινά φησιν	οὔ τινα φησιν
9.324	δέ τέ οἱ	δέ τέ οἱ	δέ τε οἱ	δέ τε οἱ	δέ τε οἱ	δέ τε οἱ	δέ τέ οἱ	δέ τέ οἱ	δέ τε οἱ
9.359	αἰ κέν τοι	αἰ κέν τοι	αἰ κέν τοι	αἰ κεν τοι	αἰ κεν τοι	αἰ κεν τοι	αἰ κέν τοι	αἰ κέν τοι	αἰ κέν τοι
9.371	εἴ τινά που	εἴ τινά που	εἴ τινά που	εἴ τινά που	εἴ τινά που	εἴ τινά που	εἴ τινά που	εἴ τινά που	εἴ τινά που
9.380	* ὅσσά τέ οἱ	* ὅσσά τέ οἱ	ὅσσά τε οἱ	ὅσσά τε οἱ	ὅσσα τέ οἱ	ὅσσα τέ οἱ	ὅσσα τέ οἱ	ὅσσα τέ οἱ	ὅσσα τέ οἱ
9.394	Πηλεύς θήν μοι	Πηλεύς θήν μοι	Πηλεύς θην μοι	Πηλεύς θην μοι	Πηλεύς θην μοι	Πηλεύς θην μοι	Πηλεύς θην μοι	Πηλεύς θην μοι	Πηλεύς θην μοι
9.410	γάρ τέ με φησι	γάρ τέ με φησι	γάρ τέ με φησι	γάρ τε με φησι	γάρ τε με φησι	γάρ τε με φησι	γάρ τε με φησι	γάρ τε με φησι	γάρ τε με φησι
9.416	οὐδέ κε μ'	οὐδέ κέ μ'	οὐδέ κε μ'	οὐδέ κε μ'	οὐδέ κε μ'	οὐδέ κε μ'	οὐδέ κε μ'	οὐδέ κε μ'	οὐδέ κε μ'
9.424	ἤ κέ σφιν	ἤ κέ σφιν	ἤ κέ σφιν	ἤ κε σφιν	ἤ κε σφιν	ἤ κε σφιν	ἤ κέ σφιν	ἤ κέ σφιν	ἤ κέ σφιν
9.429	οὔ τί μιν	οὔ τί μιν	οὔ τί μιν	οὔ τι μιν	οὔ τι μιν	οὔ τι μιν	οὔ τί μιν	οὔ τί μιν	οὔ τι μιν

9.445	εἴ κέν μοι	εἴ κέν μοι	εἴ κέν μοι	εἴ κέν μοι	εἴ κέν μοι	εἴ κέν μοι	εἴ κέν μοι	εἴ κέν μοι	εἴ κέν μοι
9.495	ἵνα μοί ποτ'	ἵνα μοί ποτ'	ἵνα μοί ποτ'	ἵνα μοί ποτ'	ἵνα μοί ποτ'	ἵνα μοί ποτ'	ἵνα μοί ποτ'	ἵνα μοί ποτ'	ἵνα μοί ποτ'
9.496	οὐδέ τι σε	οὐδέ τί σε	οὐδέ τι σε	οὐδέ τι σε	οὐδέ τί σε	οὐδέ τι σε	οὐδέ τί σε	οὐδέ τι σε	οὐδέ τι σε
9.501	ὅτε κέν τις	ὅτε κέν τις	ὅτε κέν τις	ὅτε κέν τις	ὅτε κέν τις	ὅτε κέν τις	ὅτε κέν τις	ὅτε κέν τις	ὅτε κέν τις
9.504	αἴ ῥά τε	αἴ ῥά τε	αἴ ῥά τε	αἴ ῥά τε	αἴ ῥά τε	αἴ ῥά τε	αἴ ῥά τε	αἴ ῥά τε	αἴ ῥά τε
9.525	ὅτε κέν τιν'	ὅτε κέν τιν'	ὅτε κέν τιν'	ὅτε κέν τιν'	ὅτε κέν τιν'	ὅτε κέν τιν'	ὅτε κέν τιν'	ὅτε κέν τιν'	ὅτε κέν τιν'
9.607	οὔ τί με	οὔ τί με	οὔ τι με	οὔ τι με	οὔ τι με	οὔ τί με	οὔ τί με	οὔ τί με	οὔ τι με
9.613	οὐδέ τι σε	οὐδέ τι σε	οὐδέ τι σε	οὐδέ τι σε	οὐδέ τι σε	οὐδέ τι σε	οὐδέ τι σε	οὐδέ τι σε	οὐδέ τι σε
9.615	ὅς κέ με	ὅς κέ με	ὅς κε με	ὅς κε με	ὅς κέ με	ὅς κέ με	ὅς κέ με	ὅς κέ με	ὅς κέ με
9.632	μέν τίς τε	μέν τίς τε	μέν τίς τε	μέν τις τε	μέν τίς τε	μέν τίς τε	μέν τίς τε	μέν τίς τε	μέν τίς τε
9.640	δέ τοι εἰμὲν	δέ τοι εἰμὲν	δέ τοι εἰμὲν	δέ τοι εἰμὲν	δέ τοι εἰμὲν	δέ τοί εἰμεν	δέ τοί εἰμεν	δέ τοι εἰμὲν	δέ τοι εἰμὲν
9.645	* πάντά τί μοι	* πάντά τί μοι	πάντά τί μοι	πάντα τί μοι	πάντα τί μοι	πάντά τί μοι	πάντα τί μοι	πάντά τί μοι	πάντά τί μοι
9.692	οὔ τί μιν	οὔ τί μιν	οὔ τι μιν	οὔ τι μιν	οὔ τι μιν	οὔ τί μιν	οὔ τί μιν	οὔ τι μιν	οὔ τι μιν
9.702	ὅππότε κέν μιν	ὅππότε κέν μιν	ὅππότε κέν μιν	ὅππότε κέν μιν	ὅππότε κέν μιν	ὅππότε κέν μιν	ὅππότε κέν μιν	ὅππότε κέν μιν	ὅππότε κέν μιν
10.7	ὅτε πέρ τε	ὅτε πέρ τε	ὅτε πέρ τε	ὅτε πέρ τε	ὅτε πέρ τε	ὅτε πέρ τε	ὅτε πέρ τε	ὅτε πέρ τε	ὅτε πέρ τε
10.19	εἴ τινά οἱ	εἴ τινά οἱ	εἴ τινά οἱ	εἴ τινά οἱ	εἴ τινά οἱ	εἴ τινά οἱ	εἴ τινά οἱ	εἴ τινά οἱ	εἴ τινά οἱ
10.39	οὔ τίς τοι	οὔ τίς τοι	οὔ τίς τοι	οὔ τίς τοι	οὔ τις τοι	οὔ τίς τοι	οὔ τίς τοι	οὔ τίς τοι	οὔ τίς τοι
10.44	ἤ τίς κεν	ἤ τίς κεν	ἤ τις κεν	ἤ τις κεν	ἤ τίς κεν	ἤ τίς κεν	ἤ τίς κεν	ἤ τίς κεν	ἤ τίς κεν
10.105	ὅσα πού νυν	ὅσα πού νυν	ὅσα πού νυν	ὅσα πού νυν	ὅσσα πού νῦν	ὅσσα πού νῦν	ὅσσα πού νῦν	ὅσσα πού νῦν	ὅσσα πού νῦν
10.115	εἴ πέρ μοι	εἴ πέρ μοι	εἴ πέρ μοι	εἴ πέρ μοι	εἴ πέρ μοι	εἴ πέρ μοι	εἴ πέρ μοι	εἴ πέρ μοι	εἴ πέρ μοι
10.129	οὔ τίς οἱ	οὔ τίς οἱ	οὔ τις οἱ	οὔ τις οἱ	οὔ τίς οἱ	οὔ τις οἱ	οὔ τίς οἱ	οὔ τίς οἱ	οὔ τίς οἱ
10.130	ὅτε κέν τιν'	ὅτε κέν τιν'	ὅτε κέν τιν'	ὅτε κέν τιν'	ὅτε κέν τιν'	ὅτε κέν τιν'	ὅτε κέν τιν'	ὅτε κέν τιν'	ὅτε κέν τιν'

Continued

Table Ap.2 *Continued*

Line of Iliad	(Ai)	(Aii)	(Aiii)	(Bi)	(Bii)	(Biii)	(Biv)	(Bv)	(D)
10.171	τῶν κέν τις	τῶν κέν τις	τῶν κέν τις	τῶν κέν τις	τῶν κέν τις	τῶν κέν τις	τῶν κέν τις	τῶν κέν τις	τῶν κέν τις
10.186	ἀπό τέ σφισιν	*ἀπό τέ σφισιν	ἀπό τε σφισιν	ἀπό τε σφισιν	ἀπό τε σφισιν	ἀπό τε σφισιν	ἀπό τε σφισιν	ἀπό τέ σφισιν	ἀπό τέ σφισιν[i]
10.206	εἴ τινά που	εἴ τινά που	εἴ τινά που	εἴ τινά που	εἴ τινά που	εἴ τινά που	εἴ τινά που	εἴ τινά που	εἴ τινά που
10.207	ἤ τινά που	ἤ τινά που	ἤ τινά που	ἤ τινά που	ἤ τινά που	ἤ τινά που	ἤ τινά που	ἤ τινά που	ἤ τινά που
10.212	μέγα κέν οἱ	μέγα κέν οἱ	μέγα κέν οἱ	μέγα κέν οἱ	μέγα κέν οἱ	μέγα κέν οἱ	μέγα κέν οἱ	μέγα κέν οἱ	μέγα κέν οἱ
10.222	εἴ τίς μοι	εἴ τίς μοι	εἴ τίς μοι	εἴ τις μοι	εἴ τις μοι	εἴ τις μοι	εἴ τίς μοι	εἴ τίς μοι	εἴ τις μοι
10.225	εἴ πέρ τε	εἴ πέρ τε	εἴ πέρ τε	εἴ πέρ τε	εἴ περ τε	εἴ περ τε	εἴ πέρ τε	εἴ πέρ τε	εἴ πέρ τε
Number of sequences for which the accentuation matches that of Venetus A	167 (67%) or 190 (76%) with asterisked sequences included	162 (65%) or 186 (74%) with asterisked sequences included	172 (69%) or 189 (76%) with asterisked sequences included	112 (45%) or 113 (45%) with asterisked sequence included	120 (48%) or 121 (48%) with asterisked sequence included	108 (43%) or 109 (44%) with asterisked sequence included	64 (26%)	150 (60%)	

^a χειρί is a scribal correction of χεῖρι.

^b On the treatment of elision here, see Table 4.2, note a.

^c καί is a scribal correction of καὶ.

^d We treat the lack of accent mark on ὅς as the equivalent of what modern scholars would print as ὅς, i.e. ὅς with 'lulled' accent.

^e καί is a scribal correction of καὶ.

^f We give the word preceding the first enclitic as ἀδευῆς rather than ἀδευῇς here, in keeping with the general principle that elided monosyllabic enclitics affect (or fail to affect) the accent of the preceding word in the same way as if there were no elision (see section 4.3).

^g For περί rather than περὶ here and just below, see note f.

^h καί is a scribal correction of καὶ.

ⁱ As noted at Table 4.5, note b, we take the accent mark to be intended as falling on the τε, although conceivably it was meant to fall on the πο. Once again, for the purposes of calculating which systems produce the same accentuation as we find in Venetus A, we treat ἀπο as equivalent to ἀπό.

Sequences of enclitics in Venetus B

Table Ap.3 lays out the first hundred sequences of enclitics found in the eleventh-century manuscript Marcianus Graecus 821 (Z. 453) ('Venetus B'),[1] omitting the folios of Venetus B for which we have only a twelfth- or thirteenth-century replacement for the originals.[2] The last column shows the accents actually found in this manuscript (a small number of these accents are likely to be by the corrector who also supplied these missing parts of the text,[3] but most are by the first hand); the preceding six columns compare the outcomes of various systems for accenting sequences of enclitics, starting with the revised Göttling-Barrett system.

In this sample, Venetus B accents 56 out of 100 sequences of enclitics as predicted by the revised Göttling-Barrett system—a noticeably lower proportion than we found for Venetus A, where 74% of sequences of enclitics are accented as predicted by this system.

Since it has been claimed that Venetus B has a system in which accents fall on alternate enclitics (see Chapter 4, n. 84), Table Ap.3 also tests the manuscript's accentuation of sequences of enclitics in our sample against the five conceivable versions of this system laid out in section 4.4.[4] As can be seen from the table, none of these systems predicts the accentuation of sequences of enclitics in Venetus B any better than the revised Göttling-Barrett system. The 'alternate enclitics' systems that do best in this respect are (Bi) and (Bii), but even these do less well than the revised Göttling-Barrett system.

However, it is worth asking whether a possibility we ultimately rejected for Venetus A (section 4.4) could be relevant for Venetus B: are we right to distinguish strictly between systems (Biv) and (Bv), or could the scribe have been primarily interested in accenting every other enclitic, working backwards from the second-to-last enclitic, and less worried about how to accent the word preceding the first enclitic? If we count up how many sequences in our sample have accents conforming to system (Biv) *and/or* system (Bv), the total is 64 (64%). At first sight, this is a clear advance on the success rate of the revised Göttling-Barrett system for this manuscript.

And yet if we allow that the scribe of Venetus B might have been a bit flexible, hesitant, or sloppy about how to accent the word preceding the first enclitic, we ought to consider how this might also have affected the outcome if he was aiming at some other system. With

---

[1] Our readings are based on the images available at <http://www.internetculturale.it/jmms/ iccuviewer/iccu.jsp?id=oai%3A193.206.197.121%3A18%3AVE0049%3ACSTOR.240.10163>.

[2] See West (1998–2000: vol. i, p. xi). For our sample, this means that we omit sequences of enclitics from the portion of the text beginning at *Il.* 5.259 and ending at *Il.* 5.355. We also omit 'ΟΥ 'ΕΘΕΝ 'ΕΣΤΙ at *Il.* 1.114, since Venetus B's οὐ ἔθεν ἐστὶ suggests that 'ΕΘΕΝ is taken to be orthotonic; ΘΕΟΣ ΠΟΥ ΣΟΙ at *Il.* 1.178, since Venetus B's θεός που σοὶ suggests that ΣΟΙ is taken to be orthotonic (as also by West); 'ΟΤΕ Μ' at *Il.* 1.518, since the scribe probably took ὅτε as a single non-enclitic word; and 'ΕΙΣ 'Ο ΚΕ Σ' at *Il.* 3.409, since Venetus B presents εἰσόκε as a single word (cf. Chapter 4, n. 78). At *Il.* 2.258, West's (1998–2000) apparatus suggests that εἰ κέ τι is a scribal correction of εἰ κ' ἔτι or εἰ κ' ἔτι (the point is difficult to see on the photograph); we omit this sequence because the accent mark was written along with the original reading.

[3] See West (1998–2000: vol. i, p. xi).

[4] As in the case of Venetus A (see section 4.4), for our sample system (Bii) always produces the same results as Göttling and Barrett's original system (on which see section 4.1); this point is accordingly noted in Table Ap.3, at the top of the column for system (Bii).

this in mind, for all systems other than (Biv) and (Bv) (for which the combined results have just been discussed), Table Ap.3 gives an asterisk to sequences whose accentuation differs from that of Venetus B only insofar as Venetus B accents the word preceding the first enclitic as if a non-enclitic word was to follow. If we add the asterisked sequences to those whose accentuation is considered to match that of Venetus B, the number of matches increases only marginally for the 'alternate enclitics' systems (Bi)–(Biii) (see the last line of the table). But for the revised Göttling-Barrett system the number of matches goes up from 56 (56%) to 80 (80%). Not only is this much higher than the success rate of 'alternate enclitics' systems (Biv) and (Bv) combined, but it comes very close to the success rate of 81% which the same calculation yielded for Venetus A (see the last line of Table Ap.1, with section 4.4).

We conclude that the main guiding principle behind the accentuation of sequences of enclitics in Venetus B was once again the revised Göttling-Barrett system—either as such or, more likely, in a version of Herodian's rules of thumb (we do not attempt to test these possibilities against one another for Venetus B). On the face of it, the revised Göttling-Barrett system predicts Venetus B's accents on sequences of enclitics less well than Venetus A's, but this is because the scribe of Venetus B is more prone to the mistake of accenting a word in its usual way, even though an enclitic is coming up and an adjustment would have been in order—an additional accent, or an acute instead of a grave. A mistake of this type can happen to anybody, including the scribe of Venetus A, but it happens more frequently to the scribe of Venetus B.

Table Ap.3 The first 100 sequences of more than one enclitic appearing in Venetus B (omitting folios of Venetus B for which we have only a twelfth- or thirteenth-century replacement for the original), accented according to the revised Göttling-Barrett system, according to principles (Bi)–(Bv) laid out in section 4.4, and then as in Venetus B. The word preceding the first enclitic is included, and enclitics themselves are underlined. For the forms ʽΟΤΤΙ (nominative-accusative neuter singular of ὅστις), ʽΟΤΙΣ, and ʽΟΥΤΕ, a hyphen separates the enclitic from what precedes (see Chapter 4, n. 42), except where we reproduce the reading of Venetus B. Shading indicates a way of accenting a sequence that differs from that in Venetus B. In the columns for the revised Göttling-Barrett system and for systems (Bi)–(Biii), an asterisk indicates a way of accenting a sequence differing from that of Venetus B only insofar as Venetus B accents the word preceding the first enclitic as if a non-enclitic word was to follow.

Line of *Iliad*	Revised Göttling-Barrett system	(Bi)	(Bii)	(Biii)	(Biv)	(Bv)	Venetus B
		Accents on alternate enclitics: begin by accenting the first enclitic to be accentable without causing accents on successive syllables (after also avoiding accents on successive syllables on the word preceding the first enclitic).	Accents on alternate enclitics: begin by accenting the first enclitic to be accentable without causing *acutes* on successive syllables (after also avoiding acutes on successive syllables on the word preceding the first enclitic). OR (C) Göttling and Barrett's original system (see section 4.1).	Accents on alternate enclitics: begin by accenting the first enclitic to be accentable without causing accents on successive morae (after also avoiding accents on successive morae on the word preceding the first enclitic).	Accents on alternate enclitics: begin by accenting the second enclitic from the end. If an even number of enclitics, the first does not affect the accent of the preceding word.	Accents on alternate enclitics: begin by accenting the second enclitic from the end. The word preceding the first enclitic is accented following the normal ancient rules applying to a word followed by a single enclitic.	
1.28	* μή νύ τοι	μή νυ τοι	μή νυ τοι	μή νυ τοι	μὴ νύ τοι	μή νύ τοι	μὴ νύ τοι
1.39	εἴ ποτέ τοι	εἴ ποτέ τοι	εἴ ποτέ τοι	εἴ ποτέ τοι	εἴ ποτέ τοι	εἴ ποτέ τοι	εἴ ποτέ τοι
1.40	δή ποτέ τοι	δή ποτέ τοι	δή ποτέ τοι	δή ποτέ τοι	δὴ ποτέ τοι	δὴ ποτέ τοι	δή ποτέ τοι
1.66	αἴ κέν πως	αἴ κεν πως	αἴ κεν πως	αἴ κεν πως	αἴ κέν πως	αἴ κέν πως	αἴ κέν πως

Continued

Table Ap.3 *Continued*

Line of *Iliad*	Revised Göttling-Barrett system	(Bi)	(Bii)	(Biii)	(Biv)	(Bv)	Venetus B
1.100	τότε κέν μιν	τότε κέν μιν	τότε κέν μιν	τότε κέν μιν	τότε κέν μιν	τότε κέν μιν	τότε κέν μιν
1.108	οὔτέ τι πω	οὔ-τε τί πω	οὔ-τε τί πω	οὔ-τε τί πω	οὔ-τε τί πω	οὔ-τε τί πω	οὔτέ τι πω
1.115	οὔ-τέ τι	οὔ-τε τι	οὔ-τε τι	οὔ-τε τι	οὐ-τέ τι	οὔ-τέ τι	οὔτέ τι
1.124	οὐδέ τι πω	οὐδέ τι πω	οὐδέ τι πω	οὐδέ τι πω	οὐδέ τί πω	οὐδέ τί πω	οὐδέ τι πω
1.128	αἴ κέ ποθι	αἴ κε ποθι	αἴ κε ποθι	αἴ κε ποθι	αἴ κε ποθι	αἴ κέ ποθι	αἴ κέ ποθι
1.150	πῶς τίς τοι	πῶς τις τοι	πῶς τίς τοι	πῶς τίς τοι	πῶς τίς τοι	πῶς τίς τοι	πῶς τίς τοι
1.153	οὔ τί μοι	οὔ τι μοι	οὔ τι μοι	οὔ τι μοι	οὔ τί μοι	οὔ τί μοι	οὔ τί μοι
1.163	μέν σοι ποτέ	μέν σοι ποτέ	μέν σοι ποτέ	μέν σοι ποτέ	μέν σοί ποτε	μέν σοί ποτέ	μέν σοι ποτέ
1.175	* οἵ κέ με	οἵ κε με	οἵ κε με	οἵ κέ με	οἵ κέ με	οἵ κέ με	οἵ κέ με
1.176	δέ μοι ἐσσὶ	δέ μοι ἐσσὶ	δέ μοι ἐσσὶ	δέ μοι ἐσσὶ	δέ μοι ἐσσὶ	δέ μοι ἐσσὶ	δέ μοι ἐσσὶ
1.213	καί ποτέ τοι	καί ποτέ τοι	καί ποτέ τοι	καί ποτέ τοι	καί ποτέ τοι	καί ποτέ τοι	καί ποτέ τοι
1.226	οὔ-τέ ποτ'	οὔ-τέ ποτ'	οὔ-τέ ποτ'	οὔ-τέ ποτ'	οὔ-τέ ποτ'	οὔτέ ποτ'	οὔτέ ποτ'
1.236	* γάρ ῥά ἑ	γάρ ῥά ἑ	γάρ ῥά ἑ	γάρ ῥά ἑ	γάρ ῥά ἑ	γάρ ῥά ἑ	γάρ ῥά ἑ
1.261	οὔ ποτέ μ'	οὔ ποτέ μ'	οὔ ποτέ μ'	οὔ ποτέ μ'	οὔ ποτέ μ'	οὔ ποτέ μ'	οὔ ποτέ μ'
1.294	ὅτ-τί κεν	ὅττι κεν	ὅττι κεν	ὅττι κεν	ὅτ-τί κεν	ὅτ-τί κεν	ὅττι κεν
1.296	ἔγωγέ τι σοι	ἔγωγέ τι σοι	ἔγωγέ τι σοι	ἔγωγέ τι σοι	ἔγωγέ τί σοι	ἔγωγέ τί σοι	ἔγωγέ τι σοι[a]
1.299	οὔ-τέ τῳ	οὔ-τε τῳ	οὔ-τε τῳ	οὔ-τε τῳ	οὔ-τέ τῳ	οὔ-τέ τῳ	οὔτέ τοι
1.300	ἅ μοι ἐστὶ	ἅ μοι ἐστὶ	ἅ μοι ἐστὶ	ἅ μοι ἐστι	ἅ μοι ἐστὶ	ἅ μοι ἐστι	ἅ μοι ἐστὶ
1.332	οὐδέ τι μιν	οὐδέ τι μιν	οὐδέ τι μιν	οὐδέ τι μιν	οὐδέ τι μιν	οὐδέ τί μιν	οὐδέ τι μιν
1.335	οὔ τί μοι	οὔ τι μοι	οὔ τι μοι	οὔ τι μοι	οὔ τί μοι	οὔ τί μοι	οὔ τι μοι
1.353	* τιμήν πέρ μοι	τιμήν πέρ μοι	τιμήν πέρ μοι	τιμήν περ μοι	τιμήν πέρ μοι	τιμήν πέρ μοι	τιμήν πέρ μοι
1.361	χειρί τε μιν	χειρί τε μιν	χειρί τε μιν	χειρί τε μιν	χειρί τέ μιν	χειρί τέ μιν	χειρί τέ μιν

Continued

1.408	αἴ κέν πως	αἴ κέν πως	αἴ κέν πως	αἴ κέν πως	αἴ κέν πως	αἴ κέν πως	αἴ κέν πως
1.414	τί νυ σ'	τί νυ σ'	τί νυ σ'	τί νυ σ'	τί νύ σ'	τί νύ σ'	τί νύ σ'
1.416	* ἐπεί νύ τοι	ἐπεί νυ τοι	ἐπεί νυ τοι	ἐπεί νυ τοι	ἐπεί νύ τοι	ἐπεί νύ τοι	ἐπεί νύ τοι
1.490	οὔ-τέ ποτ'	οὔ-τε ποτ'	οὔ-τε ποτ'	οὔ-τε ποτ'	οὔ-τε ποτ'	οὐ-τέ ποτ'	οὔτέ ποτ'
1.491	οὔ-τέ ποτ'	οὔ-τε ποτ'	οὔ-τε ποτ'	οὔ-τε ποτ'	οὔ-τε ποτ'	οὐ-τέ ποτ'	οὔτέ ποτ'
1.508	σύ πέρ μιν	σύ πέρ μιν	σύ περ μιν	σύ πέρ μιν	σύ πέρ μιν	σύ πέρ μιν	σὺ πέρ μιν
1.510	* ὀφέλλωσιν τέ ἑ	ὀφέλλωσιν τε ἑ	ὀφέλλωσιν τέ ἑ	ὀφέλλωσιν τέ ἑ	ὀφέλλωσιν τέ ἑ	ὀφέλλωσιν τέ ἑ	ὀφέλλωσιν τέ ἑ
1.521	καί τε μέ φῃσι	καί τε μέ φῃσι	καί τε μέ φησι	καί τε μέ φῃσι	καί τε μέ φῃσι	καί τε μέ φῃσι	καί τε με φῃσι
1.527	ὅ τι κεν	ὅ τι κεν	ὅ τι κεν	ὅ τι κεν	ὅ τι κεν	ὅ τι κεν	ὅ τι κεν
1.542	οὐδέ τι πό μοι	οὐδέ τι πό μοι	οὐδέ τι πό μοι	οὐδέ τι πό μοι	οὐδέ τι πό μοι	οὐδέ τι πό μοι	οὐδέ τι πό μοι
1.566	* μή νύ τοι	μή νυ τοι	μή νυ τοι	μή νυ τοι	μή νύ τοι	μή νύ τοι	μὴ νύ τοι
1.567	ὅτε κέν τοι	ὅτε κέν τοι	ὅτε κέν τοι	ὅτε κέν τοι	ὅτε κέν τοι	ὅτε κέν τοι	ὅτε κέν τοι
2.72	αἴ κέν πως	αἴ κεν πως	αἴ κεν πως	αἴ κέν πως	αἴ κέν πως	αἴ κέν πως	αἴ κέν πως
2.83	αἴ κέν πως	αἴ κεν πως	αἴ κέν πως	αἴ κέν πως	αἴ κέν πως	αἴ κέν πως	αἴ κέν πως
2.122	οὔ πω τι	οὔ πω τι	οὔ πω τι	οὔ πω τι	οὐ πὸ τι	οὐ πὸ τι	οὐ πω τι
2.202	οὔ-τέ ποτ'	οὔ-τε ποτ'	οὔ-τε ποτ'	οὔ-τέ ποτ'	οὔ-τέ ποτ'	οὔ-τέ ποτ'	οὔτέ ποτ'
2.215	ὅ τι οἱ	ὅ τι οἱ	ὅ τι οἱ	ὅ τι οἱ	ὅ τι οἱ	ὅ τι οἱ	ὅ τι οἱ
2.229	* ὅν κέ τις	ὅν κε τις	ὅν κε τις	ὅν κέ τις	ὅν κέ τις	ὅν κέ τις	ὅν κέ τις
2.238	* ἤ ῥα τί οἱ	ἤ ῥα τί οἱ	ἤ ῥα τί οἱ	ἤ ῥα τί οἱ	ἤ ῥα τί οἱ	ἤ ῥα τι οἱ	ἤ ῥά τι οἱϸ
2.252	οὐδέ τι πω	οὐδέ τι πω	οὐδέ τι πω	οὐδέ τί πω	οὐδέ τί πω	οὐδέ τί πω	οὐδέ τι πω
2.258	* ὡς νύ περ	ὡς νυ περ	ὡς νυ περ	ὡς νύ περ	ὡς νύ περ	ὡς νύ περ	ὡς νύ περ
2.276	οὐ θήν μιν	οὐ θην μιν	* οὐ θήν μιν	οὐ θήν μιν	οὐ θήν μιν	οὐ θήν μιν	οὐ θήν μιν
2.292	γάρ τίς τ'	γάρ τις θ'	γάρ τις θ'	γάρ τις θ'	γάρ τίς τ'	γάρ τίς τ'	γάρ τις θ'

Table Ap.3 *Continued*

Line of *Iliad*	Revised Göttling-Barrett system	(Bi)	(Bii)	(Biii)	(Biv)	(Bv)	Venetus B
2.361	ὅτ-τί κεν	ὅτ-τι κεν	ὅτ-τι κεν	ὅτ-τι κεν	ὅτ-τί κεν	ὅτ-τί κεν	ὅττι κεν
2.365	* ὅς τε νυ	ὅς τε νυ	ὅς νυ	ὅς τε νυ	ὅς τέ νυ	ὅς τέ νυ	ὅς τέ νυ
2.419	ἄρα πώ οἱ	ἄρα πώ οἱ	ἄρα πώ οἱ	ἄρα πώ οἱ	ἄρα πώ οἱ	ἄρα πώ οἱ	ἄρα πώ οἱ
2.553	οὔ πω τίς	οὔ πω τίς	οὔ πω τις	οὔ πώ τις	οὔ πώ τις	οὔ πώ τίς	οὔ πω τίς
2.687	ὅς τίς σφιν	ὅς τις σφιν	ὅς τις σφιν	ὅς τις σφιν	ὅς τις σφιν	ὅς τίς σφιν	ὅς τίς σφιν
2.754	ἀλλά τε μιν	ἀλλά τε μιν	ἀλλά τε μιν	ἀλλά τε μιν	ἀλλά τέ μιν	ἀλλά τέ μιν	ἀλλά τέ μιν
2.873	οὐδέ τι οἱ	οὐδέ τι οἱ	οὐδέ τι οἱ	οὐδέ τι οἱ	οὐδέ τι οἱ	οὐδέ τι οἱ	οὐδέ τι οἱ
3.12	* τόσσόν τίς τ᾽	τόσσόν τίς τ᾽	τόσσον τίς τε	τόσσον τίς τ᾽	τόσσον τίς τ᾽	τόσσον τίς τ᾽	τόσσον τίς τ᾽
3.33	ὅτε τίς τε	ὅτε τίς τε	ὅτε τίς τε	ὅτε τίς τε	ὅτε τίς τε	ὅτε τίς τε	ὅτε τίς τε
3.35	* ὤχρός τέ μιν	ὤχρος τέ μιν	ὤχρός τε μιν	ὤχρος τε μιν	ὤχρος τέ μιν	ὤχρος τέ μιν	ὤχρος τέ μιν
3.56	ἤ τέ κεν	ἤ τε κεν	ἤ τέ κεν	ἤ τέ κεν	ἤ τέ κεν	ἤ τέ κεν	ἤ τέ κεν
3.61	* ὅς ῥά τε	ὅς ῥα τε	ὅς ῥα τε	ὅς ῥα τε	ὅς ῥά τε	ὅς ῥά τε	ὅς ῥά τε
3.164	οὔ τί μοι	οὔ τι μοι	οὔ τι μοι	οὔ τι μοι	οὔ τί μοι	οὔ τί μοι	οὔ τί μοι
3.164	* θεοί νύ μοι	θεοί νυ μοι	θεοί νυ μοι	θεοί νυ μοι	θεοί νύ μοι	θεοί νύ μοι	θεοί νύ μοι
3.172	* αἰδοῖός τέ μοι ἐσσί	αἰδοῖος τέ μοι ἐσσί	αἰδοῖος τε μοι ἐσσί	αἰδοῖος τε μοι ἐσσι	αἰδοῖός τε μοι ἐσσι	αἰδοῖός τε μοι ἐσσι	αἰδοῖός τέ μοι ἐσσί
3.183	ἤ ῥά νύ τοι	ἤ ῥα νύ τοι	ἤ ῥά νυ τοι	ἤ ῥά νυ τοι	ἤ ῥα νύ τοι	ἤ ῥα νύ τοι	ἤ ῥα νύ τοι
3.220	* ζάκοτόν τέ τιν᾽	ζάκοτόν τε τιν᾽	ζάκοτόν τε τιν᾽	ζάκοτόν τε τιν᾽	ζάκοτον τέ τιν᾽	ζάκοτον τέ τιν᾽	ζάκοτον τέ τιν᾽
3.242	ἅ μοι ἐστίν	ἅ μοι ἐστίν	ἅ μοι ἐστίν	ἅ μοι ἐστίν	ἅ μοι ἐστίν	ἅ μοι ἐστίν	ἅ μοι ἐστίν
3.302	ἄρα πώ σφιν	ἄρα πώ σφιν	ἄρα πώ σφιν	ἄρα πώ σφιν	ἄρα πώ σφιν	ἄρα πώ σφιν	ἄρα πώ σφιν
3.373	* καί νύ κεν	καί νυ κεν	καί νυ κεν	καί νυ κεν	καί νύ κεν	καί νύ κεν	καί νύ κεν

Continued

3.400	ἢ πή με	ἢ πή με	ἢ πή με	ἢ πή με	ἢ πή με	ἢ πή με
3.402	εἴ τίς τοι	εἴ τις τοι	εἴ τίς τοι	εἴ τίς τοι	εἴ τις τοι	εἴ τίς τοι
4.31	τί νύ σε	τί νυ σε	τί νύ σε	τί νυ σε	τί νύ σε	τί νύ σε
4.48	γάρ μοι ποτὲ	γάρ μοι ποτέ	γάρ μοι ποτὲ	γάρ μοι ποτὲ	γάρ μοί ποτε	γάρ μοι ποτὲ
4.93	ἤ ῥά νύ μοί τι	ἤ ῥά νυ μοι τι	ἤ ῥά νυ μοί τι	ἤ ῥά νυ μοι τι	ἤ ῥά νυ μοί τι	ἤ ῥά νύ μοι τί
4.106	ὅν ῥα ποτ᾽	ὅν ῥα ποτ᾽	ὅν ῥά ποτ᾽	ὅν ῥα ποτ᾽	ὅν ῥά ποτ᾽	ὅν ῥα πότ᾽
4.141	ὅτε τίς τ᾽	ὅτε τίς τ᾽	ὅτε τίς τ᾽	ὅτε τίς τ᾽	ὅτε τίς τ᾽	ὅτε τίς τ᾽
4.143	πολέες τέ μιν	πολέες τέ μιν	πολέες τέ μιν	πολέες τέ μιν	πολέες τέ μιν	πολέες τέ μιν
4.155	*θάνατόν νύ τοι	θάνατόν νυ τοι	θάνατόν νυ τοι	θάνατόν νύ τοι	θάνατόν νύ τοι	θάνατον νύ τοι
4.176	καί κέ τις	καί κε τις	καί κε τις	καί κέ τις	καί κέ τις	καί κέ τις
4.182	*ὥς ποτέ τις	*ὥς ποτέ τις	*ὥς ποτέ τις	ὥς ποτέ τις	ὥς ποτέ τις	ὥς ποτέ τις^c
4.184	δέ τι πω	δέ τι πω	δέ τι πω	δέ τι πω	δέ τί πω	δέ τί πω
4.219	τά οἱ ποτὲ	τά οἱ ποτὲ	τά οἱ ποτε	τά οἱ ποτε	τά οἱ ποτε	τά οἱ ποτε
4.229	ὅππότε κέν μιν	ὅππότε κέν μιν	ὅππότε κέν μιν	ὅππότε κέν μιν	ὅππότε κέν μιν	ὅππότε κέν μιν
4.234	μή πω τι	μή πω τι	μή πώ τι	μή πώ τι	μή πώ τι	μή πω τι
4.245	ἄρα τίς σφι	ἄρα τίς σφι	ἄρα τίς σφι	ἄρα τίς σφι	ἄρα τίς σφι	ἄρα τίς σφι^d
4.259	ὅτε πέρ τε	ὅτε πέρ τε	ὅτε πέρ τε	ὅτε πέρ τε	ὅτε πέρ τε	ὅτε πέρ τε
4.331	γάρ πώ σφιν^e	γάρ πω σφιν	γάρ πώ σφιν	γάρ πώ σφιν	γάρ πώ σφιν	γάρ πω σφιν
4.353	αἴ κέν τοι	αἴ κεν τοι	αἴ κεν τοι	αἴ κέν τοι	αἴ κέν τοι	αἴ κέν τοι
4.359	οὔ-τε σε	οὔ-τε σε	οὔ-τε σε	οὔ-τέ σε	οὔ-τέ σε	οὔ-τέ σε
4.483	*ἤ ῥά τ᾽	ἤ ῥά τ᾽	ἤ ῥά τ᾽	ἤ ῥά τ᾽	ἤ ῥά τ᾽	ἤ ῥά τ᾽
4.484	ἀτάρ τέ οἱ	ἀτάρ τε οἱ	ἀτάρ τε οἱ	ἀτάρ τέ οἱ	ἀτάρ τέ οἱ	ἀτάρ τε οἱ
5.103	οὐδέ ἕ φημὶ	οὐδέ ἕ φημί	οὐδέ ἕ φημί	οὐδέ ἕ φημί	οὐδέ ἕ φημι	οὐδέ ἕ φημὶ

Table Ap.3 *Continued*

Line of *Iliad*	Revised Göttling-Barrett system	(Bi)	(Bii)	(Biii)	(Biv)	(Bv)	Venetus B
5.116	εἴ ποτέ μοι	εἴ ποτέ μοι	εἴ ποτέ μοι	εἴ ποτέ μοι	εἴ ποτέ μοι	εἴ ποτέ μοι	εἴ ποτέ μοι
5.118	δέ τέ μ'	δέ τέ μ'	δέ τέ μ'	δέ τέ μ'	δέ τέ μ'	δέ τέ μ'	δέ τε μ'
5.119	οὐδέ με φησὶ	οὐδέ με φησὶ	οὐδέ με φησὶ	οὐδέ με φησὶ	οὐδέ μέ φησι	οὐδέ μέ φησι	οὐδέ με φησὶ
5.137	* ὅν ῥά τε	ὅν ῥα τε	ὅν ῥα τε	ὅν ῥα τε	ὅν ῥα τε	ὅν ῥα τε	ὅν ῥα τε
5.170	ἔπος τέ μιν	ἔπος τέ μιν	ἔπος τέ μιν	ἔπος τέ μιν	ἔπος τέ μιν	ἔπος τέ μιν	ἔπος τέ μιν
5.172	οὔ τίς τοι	οὔ τις τοι	οὔ τις τοι	οὔ τις τοι	οὔ τίς τοι	οὔ τίς τοι	οὔ τίς τοι
5.191	* θεός νύ τις	θεός νύ τις	θεός νυ τις	θεός νυ τις	θεός νύ τις	θεός νύ τις	θεός νύ τιςf
5.359	* κόμισαί τέ με	κόμισαί τε με	κόμισαί τε με	κόμισαί τε με	κόμισαί τέ με	κόμισαί τέ με	κόμισαί τέ με
Number of sequences accented as in Venetus B (out of 100)	56 (56%) or 80 (80%) with asterisked sequences included	50 (50%) or 51 (51%) with asterisked sequences included	50 (50%) or 51 (51%) with asterisked sequence included	41 (41%) or 43 (43%) with asterisked sequences included	43 (43%)	39 (39%)	

a This appears to be the reading before correction to ἔγω (*sic*) γ' ἔτι σοι. The accent marks appear to have been written with the original reading.

b For consistency with Venetus B's reading, we give the word preceding the first enclitic as ἤ rather than ἦ in all columns.

c Here we find it not certain that ποτέ rather than πότε is meant.

d Before correction the reading was ἄρα τί σφι.

e For this as the expected accentuation under the revised Göttling-Barrett system, see section 4.2.4.

f The following word ΕΣΤΙ appears in Venetus B as ἔστι, and is presumably taken to be orthotonic.

References

Abbott, E. and Mansfield, E. D. 1977. *A primer of Greek grammar*, 1st Duckworth edn. London: Duckworth.

Aldus 1496. *ΘΗΣΑΥΡΟΣ· Κέρας ἀμαλθείας, καὶ κῆποι Ἀδώνιδος. THESAVRVS Cornucopiae et Horti Adonidis. Τάδε ἔνεστι ἐν τῆδε τῇ βίβλῳ.* Printed by the Aldine Press in Venice. Available at https://bildsuche.digitale-sammlungen.de/index.html?c=viewer&bandnummer=bsb00049625&pimage=473&v=2p&nav=&l=it. Accessed 05/08/2022.

Aldus 1512. *Ἐρωτήματα τοῦ χρυσολωρᾶ. Περὶ ἀνωμάλων ῥημάτων. Περὶ σχηματισμοῦ τῶν χρόνων ἐκ τῶν χαλκονδύλου. Τὸ τέταρτον τοῦ γαζῆ, περὶ συντάξεως. Περὶ ἐγκλιτικῶν. Γνῶμαι μονόστιχοι ἐκ διαφόρων ποιητῶν. Erotemata chrysolorae. De anomalis uerbis. De formatione temporum ex libro chalcondylae. Quartus Gazae de constructione. De encliticis. Sententiae monostichi ex uariis poetis.* Printed by the Aldine Press in Venice.

Aldus 1517. *Ἐρωτήματα τοῦ Χρυσολωρᾶ. Περὶ ἀνωμάλων ῥημάτων. Περὶ σχηματισμοῦ τῶν χρόνων ἐκ τοῦ χαλκονδύλου. Τὸ τέταρτον τοῦ γαζῆ, περὶ συντάξεως. Περὶ ἐγκλητικῶν* (sic). *Γνῶμαι μονόστιχοι ἐκ διαφόρων ποιητῶν. Κάτων. Ἐρωτήματα τοῦ Γουαρίνου. Erotemata Chrysolorae. De anomalis uerbis. De formatione temporum ex libro Chalcondylae. Quartus Gazae De constructione. De encleticis* (sic). *Sententiae monostichi ex uariis poetis. Cato. Erotemata Guarini.* Published by the Aldine Press in Venice.

Aldus 1524. *DICTIONARIVM GRAECVM cum interpretatione latina, omnium, quae hactenus impressa sunt, copiosissimum. Collectio dictionum, quae differunt significatu, per ordinem literarum. Dictiones latinae graece redditae. Ammonius de similibus et differentibus dictionibus. Vetus instructio et denominationes praefectorum militum. Orbicius de nominibus ordinum militarium. Significata τοῦ ἦ καὶ ὧς. Io. Grammatici quaedam de proprietatibus linguarum. Eustathii quaedam de proprietatibus linguarum. Corinthus de proprietatibus linguarum apud Homerum. Verborum anomalorum declinationes secundum ordinem literarum. Herodiani quaedam de encliticis. Io. Grammatici Characis quaedam de encliticis. Choerobosci quaedam de encliticis. Thomae Magistri eclogae atticorum nominum et uerborum. Phrynichi ecloge atticorum nominum et uerborum. Emanuelis Moschopuli eclogae atticarum dictionum, nunc primum impressae.* Printed by the Aldine Press in Venice.

Bagnall, R. S. 1992. 'An owner of literary papyri'. *Classical Philology* 87: 137–40.

Bandini, A. M. 1768. *Catalogus codicum graecorum Bibliothecae Laurentianae*, ii. Florence: Typis Regiis.

Barker, E. H. 1820. *Ἀρκαδίου Περὶ τόνων* e codicibus parisinis primum edidit Edmund. Henr. Barkerus. Leipzig: apud Gerhardum Fleischerum.

Barrett, W. S. 1964. *Euripides: Hippolytos.* Oxford: Clarendon Press.

Bekker, I. 1821. *Anecdota graeca*, iii. Berlin: Reimer.

Berger, G. 1972. *Etymologicum Genuinum et Etymologicum Symeonis (β).* Meisenheim am Glan: Hain.

Blass, F., Debrunner, A., and Rehkopf, F. 1979. *Grammatik des neutestamentlichen Griechisch*, 15th edn. Göttingen: Vandenhoeck & Ruprecht.

Blomqvist, J. 1969. *Greek particles in Hellenistic prose.* Lund: Gleerup.

Botley, P. 2010. *Learning Greek in western Europe, 1396–1529: grammars, lexica, and classroom texts*. Philadelphia, PA: American Philosophical Society.

Bowen, A. 2013. *Aeschylus: Suppliant Women*. Oxford: Aris and Phillips.

Brandenburg, P. 2005. *Apollonios Dyskolos: Über das Pronomen*. Munich: Saur.

Burnyeat, M. F. 2003. 'Apology 30B 2-4: Socrates, money, and the grammar of γίγνεσθαι'. *Journal of Hellenic Studies* 123: 1–25.

Buttmann, P. 1821. *Scholia antiqua in Homeri Odysseam*. Berlin: in libraria Myliana.

Chandler, H. W. 1881. *A practical introduction to Greek accentuation*, 2nd edn. Oxford: Clarendon Press.

Chase, A. H. and Phillips, H., Jr. 1961. *A new introduction to Greek*, 3rd edn, revised and enlarged. Cambridge, MA: Harvard University Press.

Chvany, C. V. 1975. *On the syntax of be-sentences in Russian*. Cambridge, MA: Slavica Publishers.

Clarysse, W. 2010. 'Linguistic diversity in the archive of the engineers Kleon and Theodoros'. In T. V. Evans and D. D. Obbink (eds), *The language of the papyri*. Oxford: Oxford University Press, 35–50.

Cribiore, R. 2008. 'Menander the poet or Menander Rhetor? An encomium of Dioscoros again'. *Greek, Roman, and Byzantine Studies* 48: 95–109.

Crostini, B. 2019. 'A new manuscript of the *Iliad* from the Salento region: Ireland, Trinity College Dublin, MS 922'. *Νέα Ῥώμη: Rivista di ricerche bizantinistiche* 15: 137–65.

Cullhed, E. 2012. 'The autograph manuscripts containing Eustathius' commentary on the *Odyssey*'. *Mnemosyne* 65: 445–61.

Cunningham, I. C. 2003. *Synagoge: Συναγωγὴ λέξεων χρησίμων*. Berlin: de Gruyter.

Curio, V. 1522. *QVAE HOCCE LIBRO CONTENTA. LEXICON GRAECVM IAM SECUNDVM, PLVS trium millium dictionum auctario locupletatum, ad hoc multis ante parum latine redditis, elegantius ac magis apposite interpretatis. Ammonii de similibus et differentibus dictionibus ordine alphabetico. Vetus instructio militarium praefectorum, et eorundem denominationes. Orbicii de nominibus ordinum militarium. Cyrilli dictiones, quae pro literae uel accentus immutatione diuersa significant. Quàm multiplici sint significato τὸ ως καὶ τὸ η. Corinthi libellus de linguarum proprietatibus iam nouiter adpressus. De anomalis et inaequalibus uerbis ordine alphabetico. Herodiani et Cherobosci de encliticis et enclinomenis. Omina iam recens adiecta.* Printed by V. Curio in Basel.

Dalimier, C. 2001. *Apollonius Dyscole: Traité des conjonctions*. Paris: Vrin.

de Brocar, G. 1514. *Ερωτήματα τοῦ χρυσολωρᾶ. Περὶ σχηματισμοῦ τῶν χρόνων ἐκ τῶν χαλκονδύλου. Τὸ τέταρτον τοῦ γαζῆ περὶ συντάξεως. περὶ ἀνωμάλων ῥημάτων. περὶ ἐγκλιτικῶν. γνῶμαι μονόστιχοι ἐκ διαφόρων ποιητῶν. Erotemata chrysolorae. De formatione temporum ex libro chalcondylae. Quartus gazae de constructione. De anomalis uerbis. De encliticis. Sententiae monostichi ex uariis poetis.* Printed by Arnaldo Guillén de Brocar in Alcalá de Henares.

de Gourmont, G. 1523. *HABES TANDEM GRAECARVM LITERARVM ADMIRATOR, LEXIcon Graecum, coeteris omnibus aut in Italia, aut Gallia, Germaniave antehac excusis multo locupletius, vtpote supra ter mille additiones Basiliensi Lexico An.M.D.XXII. apud Curionem impresso adiectas, amplius quinque recentiorum additionum milibus auctum. Quibus ex receptissimo quoque scriptore seligendis, plurimum tibi desudarunt, Partim Gulielmus Mainus liberorum D. Budaei praeceptor vt doctissimus ita diligentissimus, Partim Ioannes Chaeradamus Hypocrates Matheseos et Grecae linguae professor non Poenitendus. Quae vero, quamque multa hoc Lexico contineantur, sequens Pagina Elencho te docebit luculentissimo.* Printed by G. de Gourmont in

Paris. Available at <www.deutsche-digitale-bibliothek.de/item/AK7EMWW57 LAUCMIGHMWEGPG67BRMEVGY>. Accessed 05/08/2022.

Demetrakopoulos, P. 1979. ῾Παλαιογραφικά και Μεταβυζαντινά᾽. Ἐπιστημονικὴ Ἐπετηρὶς τῆς Φιλοσοφικῆς Σχολῆς τοῦ Πανεπιστημίου Ἀθηνῶν 27: 192–229.

Demetrakopoulos, P. 2005. ῾Τα αυτόγραφα του Παχώμιου Ρουσάνου στην Ιβήρων. Ο επίσης αυτόγραφος κώδικας ΕΒΕ 1062᾽. In Παχώμιος Ρουσάνος 450 Χρόνια από την Κοίμησή του (†1553): πρακτικά Διεθνούς Επιστημονικού Συμποσίου (Αρχονταρίκι Νέας Πτέρυγας Ιεράς Μονής Στροφάδων και Αγίου Διονυσίου Ζάκυνθος 9–12 Οκτωβρίου 2003). Athens: Ιερά Μητρόπολις Ζακύνθου και Στροφάδων, 267–310.

Denniston, J. D. 1950. *The Greek particles*, 2nd edn. Oxford: Oxford University Press.

Devine, A. M. and Stephens, L. D. 1994. *The prosody of Greek speech*. New York: Oxford University Press.

Dickey, E. 2007. *Ancient Greek scholarship*. New York: Oxford University Press.

Dindorf, W. 1855. *Scholia græca in Homeri Odysseam*. Oxford: Typographeum Academicum.

Dobrynina, E. N. 2013. Сводный каталог греческих иллюминированных рукописей в российских хранилищах, i: Рукописи IX–X вв. в Государственном историческом музее, Часть 1/*Corpus of Greek illuminated manuscripts in Russian collections, i: Manuscripts of the 9th – 10th cc. at the State Historical Museum, Part 1*. Moscow: Skanrus.

Donnet, D. 1967. ῾La traité des particules enclitiques, attribué à Jean Tzètzès᾽. *Bulletin de l'Institut Historique Belge de Rome* 38: 11–48.

Dumarty, L. 2021. *Apollonius Dyscole: Traité des adverbes*. Paris: Vrin.

Dyck, A. R. 1983. *Epimerismi Homerici, pars prior, epimerismos continens qui ad Iliadis librum A pertinent*. Berlin: de Gruyter.

Erbse, H. 1950. *Untersuchungen zu den attizistischen Lexika* (Abhandlungen der deutschen Akademie der Wissenschaften zu Berlin, philosophisch-historische Klasse, Jahrgang 1949, Nr. 2). Berlin: Akademie-Verlag.

Erbse, H. 1960. *Beiträge zur Überlieferung der Iliasscholien*. Munich: Beck.

Erbse, H. 1969–88. *Scholia Graeca in Homeri Iliadem (scholia vetera)*. Berlin: de Gruyter.

Fontana, J. M. 1996. ῾Phonology and syntax in the interpretation of the Tobler-Mussafia Law᾽. In A. L. Halpern and A. M. Zwicky (eds), *Approaching second: second position clitics and related phenomena*. Stanford, CA: Center for the Study of Language and Information, 41–83.

Fraenkel, E. 1933. ῾Kolon und Satz: Beobachtungen zur Gliederung des antiken Satzes, II᾽. *Nachrichten von der Gesellschaft der Wissenschaften zu Göttingen, Philologisch-Historische Klasse* 1933: 319–54.

Fraenkel, E. 1964. ῾Nachträge zu "Kolon und Satz, II"᾽. In E. Fraenkel, *Kleine Beiträge zur klassischen Philologie*, i. Rome: Edizioni di storia e letteratura, 131–9.

Froben, J. 1524. *DICTIONARIVS GRAECVS, PRAEter omnes superiores accessiones, quarum nihil est omissum, ingenti uocabulorum numero locupletatus per utriusque literaturae non uulgariter peritum, IACOBVM CERATINVM. Ac ne libellorum quidem ac fragmentorum, quae superiores adiecerant, hic quicquam desiderabis*. Printed by J. Froben in Basel. Available at <https://books.google.co.uk/books?id=WjJZAAAAcAAJ>. Accessed 05/08/2022.

Gaisford, T. 1842. *Georgii Choerobosci dictata in Theodosii Canones, necnon Epimerismi in Psalmos*, i. Oxford: Typographeum Academicum.

Göttling, K. W. 1835. *Allgemeine Lehre vom Accent der griechischen Sprache*. Jena: Cröker.

Goldstein, D. 2016. *Classical Greek syntax: Wackernagel's law in Herodotus*. Leiden: Brill.

Goodwin, W. W. 1894. *A Greek grammar*, new edn. London: Macmillan.

Halpern, A. 1995. *On the placement and morphology of clitics*. Stanford, CA: Center for the Study of Language and Information.

Hammond, L. 2005. *Serbian: an essential grammar*. London: Routledge.

Hansen, H. and Quinn, G. M. 1992. *Greek: an intensive course*, 2nd revised edn. New York: Fordham University Press.

Harder, A. 2012. *Callimachus: Aetia*. Oxford: Oxford University Press.

Hawkesworth, C., with Ćalić, J. 2006. *Colloquial Serbian: the complete course for beginners*. London: Routledge.

Hermann, G. 1801. *De emendanda ratione Graecae grammaticae, pars prima. Accedunt Herodiani aliorumque libelli nunc primum editi*. Leipzig: Fleischer.

Hilgard, A. 1901. *Scholia in Dionysii Thracis Artem grammaticam* (Grammatici Graeci, I.iii). Leipzig: Teubner.

Humbert, J. 1960. *Syntaxe grecque*, 3rd edn, revised and augmented. Paris: Klincksieck.

Hunt, A. S. and Edgar, C. C. 1932. *Select Papyri*, i. Cambridge, MA: Harvard University Press.

Johnson, W. A. 2009. 'The ancient book'. In R. S. Bagnall (ed.), *The Oxford Handbook of Papyrology*. New York: Oxford University Press, 256–81.

Junta, P. 1515. *Ἐγχειρίδιον Γραμματικῆς εἰσαγωγῆς ἐκ διαφόρων συγγραφέων συλληφθέν. Ἐν τῷδε τῷ βιβλίῳ τάδε περιέχεται. Ἐρωτήματα τοῦ Χρυσολωρᾶ. Περὶ ἀνωμάλων ῥημάτων. Περὶ σχηματισμοῦ τῶν χρόνων ἐκ τοῦ χαλκονδύλου. Θεοδώρου γραμματικῆς εἰσαγωγῆς τῶν εἰς τέσσαρα τὸ τέταρτον, περὶ συντάξεως. Ἡρωδιανοῦ περὶ ἐγκλιτικῶν. Γνῶμαι μονόστιχοι ἐκ διαφόρων ποιητῶν. Κάτωνος Ῥωμαίου γνῶμαι παραινετικαὶ δίστιχοι ἃς μετήνεγκεν ἐκ τῆς Λατίνων φωνῆς εἰς τὴν ἑλληνίδα διάλεκτον Μάξιμος μοναχὸς ὁ Πλανούδιος*. Printed by P. Junta in Florence in 1515 (new style).

Kahn, C. H. 1973. *The verb 'be' in Ancient Greek*. (The verb 'be' and its synonyms: philosophical and grammatical studies, 6.) Dordrecht: Reidel.

Kahn, C. H. 1981. 'Some philosophical uses of "to be" in Plato'. *Phronesis* 26: 105–34. Repr. Kahn 2009*a*: 75–108.

Kahn, C. H. 2009*a*. *Essays on being*. Oxford: Oxford University Press.

Kahn, C. H. 2009*b*. 'A return to the theory of the verb *be* and the concept of being', in Kahn 2009*a*, 109–42.

Kaster, R. A. 1988. *Guardians of language: the grammarian and society in late antiquity*. Berkeley, CA: University of California Press.

Kenyon, F. G. 1897. *The poems of Bacchylides: from a papyrus in the British Museum*. London: British Museum.

Kühner, R. and Blass, F. 1890–2. *Ausführliche Grammatik der griechischen Sprache. Erster Teil: Elementar- und Formenlehre*, 3rd edn. Hanover: Hahn.

Lallot, J. 1997. *Apollonius Dyscole, De la construction (syntaxe)*. Paris: Vrin.

La Roche, J. 1866. *Die homerische Textkritik im Alterthum*. Leipzig: Teubner.

Lasserre, F. and Livadaras, N. 1976. *Etymologicum Magnum Genuinum : Symeonis Etymologicum una cum Magna Grammatica : Etymologicum Magnum Auctum*, i. Rome: Edizioni dell'Ateneo.

Laum, B. 1928. *Das alexandrinische Akzentuationssystem*. Paderborn: Schöningh.

Lehrs, K. 1837. *Quaestiones epicae*. Königsberg: Bornträger.

Lentz, A. 1867–70. *Herodiani technici reliquiae*. Leipzig: Teubner.

Lewis, G. C. 1832. 'Iliadis codex Ægyptiacus'. *Philological Museum* 1: 177–87.

Lipsius, K. H. A. 1863. *Grammatische Untersuchungen über die biblische Gräcität: Über die Lesezeichen*. Leipzig: J. C. Hinrichs'sche Buchhandlung.

Lord, A. B. 1956. *Beginning Serbocroatian*. The Hague: Mouton.

Luard, H. R. et al. 1861. *A catalogue of the manuscripts preserved in the library of the University of Cambridge*, iv. Cambridge: Cambridge University Press.

Ludwich, A. 1877. 'Die Scholien zur Ilias in Wilhelm Dindorfs Bearbeitung'. *Rheinisches Museum für Philologie*, neue Folge 32: 1–27, 160–210.

Luschnig, C. A. E. 2007. *An introduction to ancient Greek: a literary approach*, 2nd edn, revised by C. A. E. Luschnig and D. Mitchell. Indianapolis, IN: Hackett.

Maas, P. 1903. Review of Schneider 1902. *Wochenschrift für klassische Philologie* 20: 57–70.

Maas, P. 1907. 'Zu den Interpolationen im Text des Apollonios Dyskolos'. *Philologus* 66: 468–71.

Maas, P. 1911. *Apollonius Dyscolus: De pronominibus, pars generalis*. Bonn: A. Marcus und E. Weber's Verlag.

Maehler, H. 2003. *Bacchylides: carmina cum fragmentis*, 11th edn. Munich: Saur.

Mastronarde, D. J. 2013. *Introduction to Attic Greek*, 2nd edn. Berkeley, CA: University of California Press.

Matthaios, S. 1999. *Untersuchungen zur Grammatik Aristarchs: Texte und Interpretation zur Wortartenlehre*. Göttingen: Vandenhoeck & Ruprecht.

Mayser, E. 1934. *Grammatik der griechischen Papyri aus der Ptolemäerzeit*, ii. iii: *Satzlehre (synthetischer Teil)*. Berlin: de Gruyter.

Mazzucchi, C. M. 1979. 'Sul sistema di accentazione dei testi greci in età romana e bizantina'. *Aegyptus* 59: 145–67.

McKay, K. L. 1974. *Greek grammar for students*. Canberra: Department of Classics, Australian National University.

Miller, B. 2009. 'Existence'. In E. N. Zalta (ed.), *The Stanford Encyclopedia of Philosophy (Fall 2009 Edition)*, <http://plato.stanford.edu/archives/fall2009/entries/existence/>. Accessed 05/08/2022.

Miller, E. 1868. *Mélanges de littérature grecque*. Paris: L'Imprimerie Impériale.

Monro, D. B. and Allen, T. W. 1920. *Homeri opera*, i–ii, 3rd edn. Oxford: Clarendon Press.

Moore-Blunt, J. 1978. 'Problems of accentuation in Greek papyri'. *Quaderni Urbinati di cultura classica* 29: 137–63.

Morwood, J. 2001. *Oxford grammar of Classical Greek*. Oxford: Oxford University Press.

Moschonas, T. D. 1965. *Κατάλογοι τῆς Πατριαρχικῆς Βιβλιοθήκης*, i: *Χειρόγραφα*, 2nd edn. Salt Lake City, UT: University of Utah Press.

North, M. A. and Hillard, A. E. 1927. *Greek prose composition for schools*, 9th edn. London: Rivingtons.

Offord, D. 1993. *Modern Russian: an advanced grammar course*. London: Bristol Classical Press.

Pagani, L. 2015. 'Telephus'. In F. Montanari, F. Montana, and L. Pagani (eds), *Lexicon of Greek Grammarians of Antiquity*. First published online in 2015; consulted online on 19 December 2021. <http://dx.doi.org/10.1163/2451-9278_Telephus>.

Page, D. 1972. *Aeschyli septem quae supersunt tragoedias edidit Denys Page*. Oxford: Clarendon Press.

Pasor, G. 1646. *LIBELLUS De Graecis NOVI TESTAMENTI Accentibus*. Printed with separate pagination as part of *MANUALE Graecarum vocum NOVI TESTAMENTI, Cui accessit INDEX ANOMALORUM ET DIFFICILIORUM vocabulorum, item Tractatus de Graecis Novi Testamenti accentibus. Editio nova, prioribus auctior*. Herborn. Available at <www.google.co.uk/books/edition/Manuale_graecarum_vocum_novi_testamenti/W99JAAAAcAAJ>. Accessed 05/08/2022.

Pfeiffer, R. 1949–53. *Callimachus*. Oxford: Clarendon Press.

Pharr, C. 1959. *Homeric Greek: a book for beginners*, new edn. Norman, OK: University of Oklahoma Press.

Pontani, F. 2019. Review of Roussou (2018*a*). *Bryn Mawr Classical Review* 2019.05.26. <https://bmcr.brynmawr.edu/2019/2019.05.26>. Accessed 05/08/2022.

Prince, J. D. 1945. *Practical grammar of the Serbo-Croatian language*. New York: Stechert.

Probert, P. 2003. *A new short guide to the accentuation of ancient Greek*. London: Duckworth.

Probert, P. 2015. 'Ancient theory of prosody'. In F. Montanari, S. Matthaios, and A. Rengakos (eds), *Brill's Companion to ancient Greek scholarship*, ii. Leiden: Brill, 923–48.

Probert, P. 2019. *Latin grammarians on the Latin accent: the transformation of Greek grammatical thought*. Oxford: Oxford University Press.

Probert, P. In preparation. 'Open questions in Greek phonology: some new evidence from enclitics'. In J. de la Villa and A. Striano (eds), *Advances in Ancient Greek Linguistics*. Berlin: de Gruyter.

Reitzenstein, R. 1907. *Der Anfang des Lexikons des Photios*. Leipzig: Teubner.

Roussou, S. 2018*a*. *Pseudo-Arcadius' Epitome of Herodian's De prosodia catholica*. Oxford: Oxford University Press.

Roussou, S. 2018*b*. 'ὁμότονος: when did words have the same accent?'. *Mnemosyne* 71: 265–80.

Schironi, F. 2004. *I frammenti di Aristarco di Samotracia negli etimologici bizantini*. Göttingen: Vandenhoeck & Ruprecht.

Schironi, F. 2018. *The best of the grammarians: Aristarchus of Samothrace on the* Iliad. Ann Arbor, MI: University of Michigan Press.

Schmidt, M. 1860. Ἐπιτομὴ τῆς καθολικῆς προσῳδίας Ἡρῳδιανοῦ. Jena: Mauk.

Schneider, R. 1878. *Apollonii Dyscoli quae supersunt,* i, fasc. i: *Apollonii scripta minora* (*Grammatici Graeci*, II.i.i). Leipzig: Teubner.

Schneider, R. 1902. *Apollonii Dyscoli quae supersunt*, i, fasc. ii: *Commentarium criticum et exegeticum in Apollonii scripta minora* (*Grammatici Graeci*, II.i.ii). Leipzig: Teubner.

Schrader, H. 1879. 'Porphyrios bei Eustathios zur Βοιωτία'. *Hermes* 14: 231–52.

Semeonoff, A. H. 1958. *A new Russian grammar*, 12th edn. New York: Dutton.

Sessa, M. and de Ravanis, P. 1525. *DICTIONARIVM GRAECVM. Cyrilli collectio dictionum quae differunt significato. Dictiones latinae graecis expositae. Ammonii de similibus, & differentibus dictionibus. Vetus instructio, & denominationes praefectorum militum. Orbicii de nominibus ordinum militarium. Choerobosci de his in quibus attrahatur v. Significata* η *&* ως. *Io. Grammatici de dialectis cum interp. lat. De faemininis nominibus quae desinunt in* ω. *Eustathii de dialectis cum interp. lat. Corinthi de dialectis cum interp. lat. De figuris soloecis quae cuius sint dialecti. De anomalis uerbis cum interp. lat. Tryphonis de passionibus dictionum. Herodiani de numeris. Herodiani de encliticis. Io. Grammatici de encliticis. Choerobosci de encliticis. Theodori Gazae de mensibus. Thomae Magistri eclogae acticorum* (sic) *nominum, & uerborum. Phrynichi eclogae atticorum nominum, & uerborum. Epistolares styli*. Printed by M. Sessa and P. de Ravanis in Venice. Available at <https://archive.org/details/bub_gb_a6oWdETE_4QC/page/n483/mode/2up>.

Sicking, C. M. J. 1993. 'Devices for text articulation in Lysias I and XII'. In C. M. J. Sicking and J. M. van Ophuijsen (eds), *Two studies in Attic particle usage: Lysias and Plato*. Leiden: Brill, 1–66.

Skrzeczka, R. F. L. 1847. *Observationes in Apollonii Dyscoli librum de pronomine* (Einladungsschrift zur öffentlichen Prüfung im Kneiphöfischen Stadt-Gymnasium, 1–24). Königsberg: Gedruckt bei E. J. Dalkowski.

Sluiter, I. 2011. 'A champion of analogy: Herodian's *On lexical singularity*'. In S. Matthaios, F. Montanari, and A. Rengakos (eds), *Ancient scholarship and grammar: archetypes, concepts and contexts*. Berlin: de Gruyter, 291–310.

Smyth, H. W. 1922. *Aeschylus: with an English translation*, i. Cambridge, MA: Harvard University Press.

Sommerstein, A. H. 1983. *Aristophanes: Wasps.* Warminster: Aris & Phillips.

Swiggers, P. and Wouters, A. 2003. 'Réflexions à propos de (l'absence de?) la syntaxe dans la grammaire gréco-latine'. In P. Swiggers and A. Wouters (eds), *Syntax in antiquity* (Orbis Supplementa, 23). Louvain: Peeters, 25–41.

Taylor, A. 1990. 'Clitics and configurationality in ancient Greek'. PhD dissertation, University of Pennsylvania.

Taylor, A. 1996. 'A prosodic account of clitic position in ancient Greek'. In A. L. Halpern and A. M. Zwicky (eds), *Approaching second: second position clitics and related phenomena.* Stanford, CA: Center for the Study of Language and Information, 477–503.

Telesca, C. 2021. 'Il Περὶ ἐγκλιτικῶν dello Ps.-Arcadio nel. *Laur. Plut.* 58.24'. In R. Cantore, F. Montemurro, and C. Telesca (eds), *Mira varietas lectionum.* Potenza: Basilicata University Press, 21–49.

Theodoridis, C. 1982–. *Photii Patriarchae Lexicon.* Berlin: de Gruyter.

Thierfelder, A. 1935. *Beiträge zur Kritik und Erklärung des Apollonius Dyscolus.* (Abhandlungen der philologisch-historischen Klasse der Sächsischen Akademie der Wissenschaften, Band 43, Nr. 2.) Leipzig: Hirzel.

Thompson, E. M. and Warner, G. F. 1881. *Catalogue of ancient manuscripts in the British Museum, part I: Greek.* London: British Museum.

Toman, J. 1996. 'A note on clitics and prosody'. In A. L. Halpern and A. M. Zwicky (eds), *Approaching second: second position clitics and related phenomena.* Stanford, CA: Center for the Study of Language and Information, 505–10.

Turyn, A. 1972. *Dated Greek manuscripts of the thirteenth and fourteenth centuries in the libraries of Italy*, i: *Text.* Urbana, IL: University of Illinois Press.

van der Valk, M. 1963–4. *Researches on the text and scholia of the Iliad.* Leiden: Brill.

van der Valk, M. 1971–87. *Eustathii archiepiscopi Thessalonicensis commentarii ad Homeri Iliadem pertinentes.* Leiden: Brill.

van Emde Boas, E., Rijksbaron, A., Huitink, L., and de Bakker, M. 2019. *The Cambridge grammar of Classical Greek.* Cambridge: Cambridge University Press.

Vendryes, J. 1904. *Traité d'accentuation grecque.* Paris: Klincksieck.

Vuillemin-Diem, G. and Rashed, M. 1997. 'Burgundio de Pise et ses manuscrits grecs d'Aristote: Laur. 87.7 et Laur. 81.18'. *Recherches de théologie et philosophie médiévales* 64: 136–98.

Wackernagel, J. 1877. 'Der griechische Verbalaccent'. *Zeitschrift für vergleichende Sprachforschung* 23 = new series 3: 457–70. (Reprinted in Wackernagel 1955–79: ii. 1058–71.)

Wackernagel, J. 1893. *Beiträge zur Lehre vom griechischen Akzent*, Programm zur Rektoratsfeier der Universität Basel. Basel: Reinhardt. (Reprinted in Wackernagel 1955–79: ii. 1072–107.)

Wackernagel, J. 1955–79. *Kleine Schriften.* Göttingen: Vandenhoeck & Ruprecht.

Wade, T. 2020. *A comprehensive Russian grammar*, 4th edn, revised and updated by D. Gillespie, S. Gural, and M. Korneeva. Hoboken, NJ: Wiley-Blackwell.

Wentzel, G. 1895. 'Beiträge zur Geschichte der griechischen Lexikographen'. *Sitzungsberichte der königlich preussischen Akademie der Wissenschaften zu Berlin* 1895: 477–87.

West, M. L. 1966. *Hesiod: Theogony.* Oxford: Clarendon Press.

West, M. L. 1990. *Aeschyli tragoediae.* Stuttgart: Teubner.

West, M. L. 1998–2000. *Homeri Ilias.* Stuttgart: Teubner (vol. i)/Munich: Saur (vol. ii).

West, M. L. 2017. *Homerus: Odyssea*. Berlin: de Gruyter.

Wilson, N. G. 2007*a*. *Aristophanis Fabulae*. Oxford: Clarendon Press.

Wilson, N. G. 2007*b*. *Aristophanea: studies on the text of Aristophanes*. Oxford: Oxford University Press.

Wouters, A. and Swiggers, P. 2014. 'Word classes (*mérē toû lógou*), ancient theories of'. In G. K. Giannakis, V. Bubenik, E. Crespo, C. Golston, A. Lianeri, S. Luraghi, and S. Matthaios (eds), *Encyclopedia of Ancient Greek language and linguistics*, iii. Leiden: Brill, 516–21.

Zavakou, G. 2017. *Το ἔργο Οἰκουμένης Περιήγησις του Διονυσίου Περιηγητή στο χειρόγραφο 25 του Σπουδαστηρίου Βυζαντινῆς καὶ Νεοελληνικῆς Φιλολογίας του Εθνικού και Καποδιστριακού Πανεπιστημίου Αθηνών*. PhD dissertation, University of Athens.

Zec, D. and Inkelas, S. 1990. 'Prosodically constrained syntax'. In S. Inkelas and D. Zec (eds), *The phonology-syntax connection*. Chicago, IL: University of Chicago Press, 365–78.

Zoras, G. T. and Mpoumpoulidis, P. K. 1963–4. 'Κατάλογος χειρογράφων κωδίκων Σπουδαστηρίου Βυζαντινῆς καὶ Νεοελληνικῆς Φιλολογίας του Πανεπιστημίου Αθηνών: Α΄ Κώδικες Σπ. Λάμπρου (Συμπληρώσεις καὶ διορθώσεις εἰς τὴν καταγραφὴν Λάμπρου)'. Ἐπιστημονικὴ Ἐπετηρὶς τῆς Φιλοσοφικῆς Σχολῆς τοῦ Πανεπιστημίου Ἀθηνῶν 14: 205–65.

Zwart, C. J.-W. 1997. *Morphosyntax of verb movement: a Minimalist approach to the syntax of Dutch*. Dordrecht: Kluwer.

Concordances

On enclitics 1

Present edition, paragraph	Bekker (1821) page and line	Schmidt (1860) page and line	Roussou (2018a) page and line
a	1157.28–35	162.10–14	302.8–11
b	1157.35–37	162.14–16	302.11–13
c	1158.1–6	162.16–163.1	302.13–19
d	1158.7–18	163.1–13	302.19–303.10
e	1156.19–23	163.14–24	303.10–19
f	1156.23–31	164.1–14	303.20–304.8
g		164.15–18	304.8–11
h		164.18–165.13	304.11–305.2
i	1156.32–1157.2	165.14–165.23	305.3–10
j	1157.3–4	165.24–25	305.12–13
k		165.25–166.2	305.13–15
l	1157.5–6	166.2–19	305.15–306.4
m	1157.6–8	166.19–22	306.4–7
n	1157.8–10	166.23–167.6	306.7–13
o		167.7–10	306.14–16
p	1157.10–11	167.10–11	306.16–17
q	1157.11–15	167.12–16	306.18–21
r	1157.15–22	167.16–168.2	306.21–307.6
s		168.3–13	307.7–16
t	1157.22–24	168.14–21	307.17–307.22
u	1157.24–27	168.21–169.8	307.22–308.5

On enclitics 2

Present edition, paragraph	Bekker (1821) page and line
a	1142.10–15
b	1142.16–21
c	1142.22–29
d	1142.30–35
e	1142.36–1143.26
f	1143.27–30
g	1143.31–1144.8
h	1144.9–22
i	1144.23–34
j	1144.35–1145.17
k	1145.18–31
l	1145.32–1147.6
m	1147.7–23
n	1147.24–1148.12

On enclitics 3

Present edition, paragraph	Schmidt (1860) page and line	Roussou (2018*a*) page and line
a	159.4–18	299.11–21
b	160.1–5	299.22–25
c	160.5–17	299.25–300.9
d	160.17–161.6	300.9–301.9
e	161.7–21	301.10–20
f	161.22–162.9	301.21–302.7

Charax

Present edition, paragraph	Bekker (1821) page and line	Gaisford (1842) page and line
a	1149.7–13	19.12–19
b	1149.14–17	19.20–23
c	1149.17–19	19.23–25

Present edition, paragraph	Bekker (1821) page and line	Gaisford (1842) page and line
d	1149.19–21	19.25–28
e	1149.22–24	19.28–32
f	1149.24–27	19.32–20.2
g	1149.27–1150.2	20.3–14
h	1150.3–13	20.15–27
i	1150.13–27	20.27–21.8
j	1150.28–36	21.9–19
k	1150.37–1151.2	21.20–21
l	1151.3–17	
m	1151.18–1152.4	
n	1152.4–16	
o	1152.17–30	
p	1152.30–1153.20	
q	1153.21–31	
r	1153.31–1154.1	
s	1154.1–4	
t	1154.4–17	
u	1154.18–32	
v	1154.33–1155.7	
w	1155.8–31	

About ’ΕΣΤΙΝ

Present edition, paragraph	Bekker (1821) page and line	Schmidt (1860) page and line	Roussou (2018*a*) page and line
a	1148.13–20	169.9–12	308.6–8
b	1148.20–32	169.12–15	308.8–11
c	1148.32–1149.6	169.15–20	308.11–15

On enclitics 4

Present edition, paragraph	Bekker (1821) page and line	Hilgard (1901) page and line
a	1155.32–35	466.3–5
b	1155.35–1156.2	466.5–8
c	1156.3–6	466.8–12
d	1156.6–10	466.12–15
e	1156.10–13	466.15–17
f	1156.13–14	466.17–18
g	1156.14–17	466.19–21

Index locorum

Index verborum

Subject index

Parisinus Graecus 2654: 217 n. 46
Parisinus suppl. Gr. 58 (**Y**ᵦ): 164, 166
Parisinus suppl. Gr. 202 (**Ξ**ᵦ): 165, 166
Perugiensis G 11 (**Θ**): 101, 103–4, 213–14
Rome, Casanatensis 1710: 8, 9, 59, 83, 102,
148, 165
Turin, Taurinensis B VI 8 = Zuretti 10: 9, 83,
102, 165
Vaticanus Barberinianus Graecus 108:
102–3
Vaticanus Graecus 887 (**Vₐ**): 147, 149, 152–4
Vaticanus Graecus 1356 (**Gᵣ**): 9, 11, 82, 84
Vaticanus Graecus 1405 (**Gᵥ**): 8, 11, 82, 84
Vaticanus Graecus 1745 (**Yₑ**): 164, 166
Vaticanus Graecus 1751 (**Σ**): 59, 60, 102, 103–4,
147, 149, 152–4
Vaticanus Graecus 1818: 217 n. 47
Vaticanus Graecus 2226 (**Φ**): 58, 60, 100,
103–4, 147, 149, 152–4, 184, 213–14
Vaticanus Graecus 2246 (**Y_d**): 164, 166
Vaticanus Ottobonianus Graecus 384 (**Lᵥ**): 8,
101, 103–4, 213–14
Vaticanus Pal. Gr. 360 (**Ψ**): 147, 149, 152–4
Vaticanus Reginensis Graecus 104 (**Ω**): 59, 60,
147, 149, 152–4
Vaticanus Reginensis Graecus Pio II 54 (**Ξₑ**):
165, 166
Venetus Marcianus Graecus XI. 4 (coll. 1008)
(**Eₘ**): 82, 84
Venetus Marcianus Graecus XI. 26 (coll.
1322) (**P**): 60, 148
Venetus Marcianus Graecus Z. 453 (coll. 821)
('Venetus B'): 266 n. 62, 279 n. 76, 281,
282 n. 84, 294, 296, 299, 327–34
Venetus Marcianus Graecus Z. 454 (coll. 822)
('Venetus A'): 266 n. 62, 278–93, 299,
301–26
Venetus Marcianus Graecus Z. 512 (coll. 678)
(**Q**): 8, 101, 103–4
Venetus Marcianus Graecus Z. 530 (coll. 319):
217 n. 46
Wolfenbüttel, Guelferbytanus Gud. Gr. 20
(**Gᵥ**): 8, 11, 82, 84
metaphors for enclisis 114–17, 178–89, 203–6
morae 36–7, 48–9, 58, 70–1, 92–3, 120–1, 134–7,
172, 175, 193–4, 199
Musurus, Marcus 59, 148

'natural accent' 26–7, 28–9, 36–7, 98–9, 116–17,
134–5, 174, 175, 179–80, 182, 188, 191,
194–4, 197–9, 204, 247
nominal forms (ὀνόματα) 26–9, 72–3, 90–1,
114–15, 126–7, 132–3, 168–9, 179
nouns, *see* nominal forms (ὀνόματα)

ordered rules 37, 121
'oxytone', meaning 173
oxytone words in connected speech, *see* lulling
rule

papyri 223–5, 269–78, 299
P.Flor. 332: 226 n. 68
P.Flor. 367: 226 n. 68
P.Giss. i 17: 226 n. 68
P.Lond.Lit. 25 ('Harris Homer roll'): 269–70,
272–3
P.Lond.Lit. 28 ('Bankes Homer'): 266,
269–70, 273
P.Lond.Lit. 46 ('Bacchylides papyrus A'):
269–70, 274
P.Oxy. i 21: 271
P.Oxy. i 123: 226 n. 68
P.Oxy. ii 223: 271
P.Oxy. iii 448: 271
P.Oxy. v 841: 271
P.Oxy. vii 1065: 226 n. 68
P.Oxy. viii 1091: 271
P.Oxy. x 1231: 271
P.Oxy. xiii 1618: 271
P.Oxy. xvii 2091: 271
P.Oxy. xix 2211: 271
P.Oxy. xxi 2290: 272
P.Oxy. xxi 2299: 272
P.Oxy. xxiii 2362: 272
P.Oxy. xliv 3155: 272
P.Oxy. xlix 3441: 272
P.Oxy. xlix 3442: 270 n. 68
P.Oxy. lii 3663: 272
P.Oxy. lvi 3825: 272
P.Oxy. lxviii 4653: 272
P.Oxy. lxxxiv 5426: 272
P.Schub. 22: 272
P.Paris 47: 226 n. 68
P.Schub. 22: 272
Rev. Ég. 1919, p. 201: 226 n. 68
UPZ i, no. 70: 226 n. 68
'paroxytone', meaning 173–4
participles, never enclitic 26–7, 74–5
parts of speech 26–7, 90–1, 100, 114–15, 126–7,
168–9
Pausanias (Atticist) 220 n. 57
'perispomenon', meaning 173–4
Philoponus, John 124–5
poetic irregularities 40–1, 48–9, 138–9, 140–1
prepositions
never enclitic 26–7
pronouns after 40–1, 140–1
prepositives 98–9
proclitics 208, 221 n. 58, 275 n. 72